The Quran and the Secular M

In this engaging and innovative study Shabbir Akhtar argues that Islam is unique in its decision and capacity to confront, rather than accommodate, the challenges of secular belief. The author contends that Islam should not be classed with the modern Judaeo–Christian tradition since that tradition has effectively capitulated to secularism and is now a disguised form of liberal humanism. He insists that the Quran, the founding document and scripture of Islam, must be viewed in its own uniqueness and integrity rather than mined for alleged parallels and equivalents with biblical Semitic faiths.

The author encourages his Muslim co-religionists to assess central Quranic doctrine at the bar of contemporary secular reason. In doing so, he seeks to revive the tradition of Islamic philosophy, moribund since the work of the twelfth century Muslim thinker and commentator on Aristotle, Ibn Rushd (Averroës). Shabbir Akhtar's book argues that reason, in the aftermath of revelation, must be exercised critically rather than merely to extract and explicate Quranic dogma. In doing so, the author creates a revolutionary form of Quranic exegesis with vitally significant implications for the moral, intellectual, cultural and political future of this consciously universal faith called Islam, and indeed of other faiths and ideologies that must encounter it in the modern secular world.

Accessible in style and topical and provocative in content, this book is a major philosophical contribution to the study of the Quran. These features make it ideal reading for students and general readers of Islam and philosophy.

Shabbir Akhtar is Assistant Professor of Philosophy at Old Dominion University in Norfolk, Virginia, USA. He has taught in the International Islamic University in Malaysia and has published widely on Islam, Christianity and current affairs.

The Quran and the Secular Mind

A philosophy of Islam

Shabbir Akhtar

LONDON AND NEW YORK

First published 2008
by Routledge
2 Park Square, Milton Park, Abingdon, Oxon OX14 4RN

Simultaneously published in the USA and Canada
by Routledge
270 Madison Avenue, New York, NY 10016

Routledge is an imprint of the Taylor & Francis Group, an informa business

Typeset in Times New Roman by Keyword Group Ltd.
Printed and bound in Great Britain by Antony Rowe Ltd, Chippenham,
Wiltshire

British Library Cataloguing in Publication Data
A catalogue record for this book is available from the British Library

Library of Congress Cataloging in Publication Data
A catalog record for this book has been requested

ISBN 10: 0-415-43782-2 (hbk)
ISBN 10: 0-415-43783-0 (pbk)
ISBN 10: 0-203-93531-4 (ebk)

ISBN 13: 978-0-415-43782-0 (hbk)
ISBN 13: 978-0-415-43783-7 (pbk)
ISBN 13: 978-0-203-93531-6 (ebk)

To Nabeel and Foziea

Contents

A note on transliteration and abbreviations

I have followed the Library of Congress system for Arabic transliteration. I retain the final 'h' to indicate feminine nouns. Arabic has no upper case but I have capitalized proper nouns and the initial word in transliterated titles of Arabic works. Some words can occur with an upper case (*Al-Qur'ān*) and a lower case (*qur'ān*). This is explained in the text. Elision of vowels is not indicated.

Words such as 'Shi'ite' are now naturalized into English. In such words, the length of vowel, any diacritical dots, and glottal (') and guttural (') stops are not indicated. Other naturalized words include Islam, Quran, Ramadan, Muhammad, fatwa, jihad, and so on.

Abbreviations: References to the Quran are given in the text and are set apart by the use of a capital Q followed by the number of the chapter and verse. This is explained in Chapter 1, note 2. Other abbreviations used are standard.

Note on sexism

I have used inclusive language even at the expense of style. In a few cases, however, I could not avoid traditional language. For example, the Quran recognizes only men as prophets. It would be contrived to use gender-neutral language in such a discussion. Again, the Quran's discussion of human nature uses the male as a prototype.

Introduction

1

The aim of this book is to investigate the rationality and plausibility of traditional Muslim conviction, a conviction inspired by the Quran, the founding document and scripture of Islam. The context of our largely philosophical investigation is supplied by industrialized and secularized western and westernized societies. This ambitious task has not been attempted by any Muslim or non-Muslim analytical philosopher in our times. One book cannot fully address this problem but it can articulate the anxiety and thus create a framework for a dialogue between the interested parties. The vaguely felt Muslim sense of intellectual unease in the secular world is here reduced to the precise project of developing tools for assessing, somewhat obliquely at times, the rationality of Islamic conviction.

This essay is partly a philosophical contribution to the study of the Quran: a critical commentary on some controversial, that is, philosophically vulnerable, assumptions of the Muslim scripture. Although the Quran has stimulated an exegetical literature comparable in size and sophistication to New Testament exegesis and to rabbinic commentary on the Hebrew Bible, modern philosophers have not probed its central claims. Why should exegesis be an exclusively *theological* discipline rather than a form of reflective *philosophical* inquiry? In the aftermath of revelation, why should the role of human reason be drastically attenuated to being analogical (in legal contexts) and otherwise merely exegetical? For Muslims, post-revelation, why should all applied reasoning, all theology, and all philosophy collapse into hermeneutics?

Even Quranic hermeneutics should not be simply a close domestic attention to the text aimed solely at extracting what is useful to believers. The Quran is intended to be revelation addressed to humankind, not merely a fixed body of law and morals. I believe that Muslims should be alert to legitimate secular and inter-faith reservations about their scripture, ready to appreciate it in a way which supersedes the closed reverential commentary which continues to ambush the classical margins of the sacred text. The older static and nomological reading of scripture is no longer fully revelatory for it reveals nothing new about the essential state of modern humanity. Merely explicating a sacred text degrades and cramps its revelatory vigour.

An important intellectual deficit in the modern House of Islam is the lack of a living philosophical culture that could influence its narrowly religious outlook. Muslim society has been, internally, spared irreverent and abusive criticism but it has also forfeited an experience of the rigours of thoughtful secular probing which can extend the range of religious integrity and invigorate the intellectual and moral health of a civilization. For reasons explored in Chapter 2, many Muslims, including some men and women of genius, were siphoned off and wasted in the pursuit of mysticism and asceticism. These believers could have become philosophers. Islam's resulting lack of an extant philosophical tradition is examined and explained at the end of Chapter 2.

In this work, I counsel modern Muslims, as intelligent and reflective heirs of their faithful tradition, to establish a philosophy of Islam, in an analytical idiom. As there is no extant Muslim philosophical tradition, we must borrow terminology from analytical linguistic philosophy of religion developed primarily to reflect Jewish and Christian concerns. While natural (philosophical) theology is, as seen in Chapter 12, an endeavour common to these three faiths, many other Judaeo-Christian intellectual interests, in philosophy of religion and theology, find no parallel in Islamic thought. For instance, to take an example from the epistemology of doctrine, the Muslim interest in revelation, as we see in Part II, differs fundamentally, in crucial respects, from the modern Jewish and Christian interest. Indeed, some areas of theo-philosophical concern such as theodicy – the rational and moral justification of the ways of God, especially the justification of natural and moral evil in a God-governed world – do not exist in mainstream Islamic thought. This might partly explain the lack of a tradition of conscientious atheism in Islam, a theme of Chapter 3.

2

All thoughtful adult human beings are, in some measure, philosophers; all societies have a potentially philosophical component in their intellectual culture. While a society devoid of disciplined philosophical thinking has no practitioners who formally articulate philosophical problems, its members still entertain philosophical prejudices – as entertaining prejudice requires no training. Many fundamental opinions are absorbed from our heritage and environment and then taken for granted. These are philosophical presuppositions; and even anti-philosophical religious believers meticulously follow their philosophical prejudices. If a person can think systematically about truth, existence, knowledge and value (both moral and aesthetic), such a person is potentially a philosopher. If we add causation and the identity of persons and objects, we have the central themes of ancient and modern western philosophy.

Perhaps there is an intrinsic connection between philosophy and civilization. Once we develop beyond the level of customary thought, we must wonder about the right way to live and the role of reason. Do the constitution and structure of knowledge permit reason to perform the functions assigned to it? What is the metaphysical constitution of the natural universe which enables and supports our conceptions of knowledge and of goodness? The quest for wisdom implicit in such inquiries is sufficiently different in trajectory to distinguish it from the search for scientific knowledge. But if, let us say, a religion gives satisfactory answers to all these questions, this might abort the possibility of philosophy.

Philosophy, as the career of reason unfettered by the dogma and the constraints of institutional religion, perhaps even as an apology for (or defence of) truth, to sound rather pretentious, plays the role of saviour in one strand of Greek thought. (Revealingly, philosophy reaches its zenith in Athens at a time of decline in Greek power and prestige.) Some kinds of philosophy could still play a soteriological function today and thus save civilizations from falling victim to fanaticism; all ideologies, unless its practitioners are thoughtful, can leave their adherents' will defenceless against the onslaught of appealing but false ideas. In religion and politics, philosophy can save us from being dominated by special and partial interests – of a science isolated and insulated from morality and philosophy, of an absolute power of the kind so-called superpowers wield without accountability to any human or transcendent standard of political humility.

I am not arguing that philosopher-kings are needed. Rather, I am proposing a humbler function for philosophers within the power structures of society, as watch-dogs who provide an external check on the hubris of secular and of religious power when these wear the garb of power without accountability. Philosophy is, in its Socratic purity, a critic of powerful but unjust institutions; it plays an advisory role when it counsels the powerful to respect their profession of political humility. Regrettably, we witness a modern retreat of philosophy from public life: issues of moment are the sole province of the politician, the journalist, the novelist and the playwright. Philosophers have abandoned the battle-field and are now marching away from the sound of the guns.

In this essay, I have two different but related goals. I establish the discipline of a philosophy of Islam, a part of the philosophy of religions. It shares many themes with the philosophy of religion as normally understood – a philosophi-cal exploration of Christian themes with analogues in Judaism and Islam. This first aim is part of a second larger ambition, namely, to revive among Muslims the tradition of philosophy itself. Arab or Muslim philosophy was inspired by Islam's encounter with Greek philosophy and is therefore similar to much of western philosophy. Islamic philosophy is not part of the theological heritage of Islam; in this regard, it differs from eastern philosophical systems which were integral to those religions. Of the two ambitions, I engage in the first through much of this essay and I make a case for the second in Chapters 2 and 12.

3

What is the correct temperament for engaging with the urgent reality of religion? Unsympathetic western critics dismiss Islam as a self-evidently false religion with a uniquely dangerous political potential; Muslim apologists defend traditional

Islam root and branch. I seek to steer between polemical, abusively critical, perspectives and those of a wholly committed and zealous defensiveness. I subject Quranic claims to the bar of reason and analysis but without the prejudicial rigour to which Islamic claims are often subjected. We examine the challenges which modern scientific rationalism presents to all believers. Only an intellectually untested faith prefers the security of assumption and dogma to the rigours of intelligent exchange and the patience of the painstaking search for relevant evidence. We no longer live in an age of religious and moral innocence, an age terminated for all religions with the entry of the secular pretender. I deny, suspend and occasionally disown pietistic and apologetic motives in the larger interests of objectivity. This scholarly detachment, more at home in philosophy than theology, is part of a modern attempt to redress an ancient imbalance in Islamic reflection.

One would have to be consumed by philosophical zeal to say that 'Thou shalt think!' is now the first commandment. That presupposes a mistaken view of religion. We should be suspicious of any view of religion in which the intellectual dimension is prominent. To attribute seminal importance to thinkers, rather than martyrs, is a choice Islam has resisted, a decision which explains its virility in an age of secular indifference and relentless hedonism. In the hour of crisis, no religion has been preserved or saved by mental efforts alone. Sincerity of moral or religious commitment and the right kind of zeal are hardly something we associate with thinkers, let alone restrict it to them.

Nonetheless, as I argue in Chapter 3, Muslims must understand the complex history of the emergence of conscientious scepticism about religion. Respect for the authority of revealed scripture should not, I argue, blind us to the range and complexity of our modern inclinations, motivations and experiences. Muslims should not ignore the findings of that sophisticated body of theory about the personal and societal existence of human beings which is a signal achievement of secular intellectual culture.

The Quran must patiently tolerate disciplined secular interrogation. It is mistaken loyalty to Islam to think that its interests are best served by isolating its doctrines hermetically from the current of contemporary secular thought. If Muslim thought remains entrenched in the fortress of ancient doctrine, remains secure but provincial, the critic would rightly suspect that this faith needs a protective but patronizing lenience in order to survive the trials of contemporary rationalism. Equally, however, the Muslim has the right to critique the limitations, excesses and exaggerations of secular humanism, a neglected theme that receives its due at the end of Chapter 3.

I argue in Chapters 11 and 12 that Muslims must develop a religious rationalism with core doctrines responsive to religious needs and standards while they make appropriate, indeed unavoidable, concessions to modern thought. The result should be a rational religious outlook in which we defend only what is defensible and not the totality of the received tradition. In its full healthy development, such a religious rationalism aims to be a form of religious humanism. More modestly, it conscientiously refuses to cherish unempirical or otherwise questionable assumptions of the kind still innocently enjoyed by traditional believers, living in the immunity of isolation, untouched by the integrity of modern doubt.

4

What is the larger context of our inquiry? Much current non-Muslim writing on Islam, even among scholars, is restricted to an obsession with topical social and political themes such as the rights of women, minorities and apostates, the threat of politically motivated violence and conflict with the West, and the possibility of establishing democracy in Muslim lands. Reviews of books on Islam, even in academic journals, deteriorate rapidly into polemical tracts on all things Islamic with rarely any focus on the work in question. And everyone, other than the Muslims themselves, is now a reliable expert on Islam! In political and policy contexts, Islam is seen as a nuisance, a faith whose allegedly radical adherents need to be eradicated. It is not seen as a world faith with an enduring moral and spiritual legacy. These attitudes denature a faith whose integrity as a global civilization need not unduly interest any westerner.

We are dealing with the residue of an older problem. Many modern western scholars realize that today, unlike in the Christian Middle Ages, defiantly maintaining a shallow understanding of Islam is not a politically prudent strategy. In that sense, there has been progress. There are, even in the current toxic atmosphere, a few non-Muslim scholars who seek to contribute to our knowledge of Islam and Arab civilization. Indeed there have always been, in all ages, a small number of conscientious non-Muslim western scholars whose sincerity, imaginative sympathy and goodwill are indisputable.

Most Muslim writers, based in their homelands, reject all western critique of Islam as at best suburban and provincial, at worst propagandist and crudely abusive. Few, if any, Muslims anywhere have ever believed that what westerners say about Islam has any intellectual significance. One could argue that to worry about the partisan nature of western scholarship on Islam betrays an implied flattery of the West: it presupposes that the western scholar aims to speak the truth about Islam and merely fails. In other words, if Muslims acknowledge that western opinion about Islam matters, they do so solely because westerners are militarily powerful. And the way to rectify this situation is to oppose western imperial designs in the battle-field rather than waste time trying to refute western assessments of Islam by writing lengthy books, insightful newspaper articles or treatises in scholastic journals. This angry but partly justified Muslim attitude shows that, through a combination of ignorance and prejudice, western orientalism and its intellectual heirs have profoundly and permanently wounded Muslim sensibilities.

Muslims entertain the standard prejudices about the West: godless, unprincipled, too cowardly and self-doubting to defend its principles (as opposed to material interests), increasingly decadent and irredeemably morally corrupt. These are unpardonable prejudices. Fortunately, they are also harmless since few Muslims, before the age of the global internet, had any opportunity to voice their prejudices: virtually none of them edit a major western newspaper, decide broad-casting policy, own the big publishing houses, or occupy prestigious university posts. They do not operate the institutions which jointly create public opinion. Muslims shout loudly, protest frequently and demonstrate vociferously – all proofs of impotence. Powerful people never demonstrate on the streets; graffiti in the jail and the ghetto does not influence government policy. Some foolish Muslims rhetorically threaten the West with violence – chanting 'Death to America' – only to be then confronted by all too real western violence. Westerners have a virtual monopoly on power, not on prejudice.

5

Much has been said for secular humanism – and not only by secular humanists! In this book, I say much in favour of the secular uses of reason. I encourage, among Muslims, respect for agnosticism though there is no Quranic warrant for this essentially modern attitude. Secular humanism has evolved, like the world's major religions, into a sophisticated philosophy of human nature and a way of life. Only a facile religious apologetics would now declare, without argument, that atheism is a childish, immoral, and untenable confusion incapable of guiding modern lives. Since it is now intellectually dishonest to pretend that at root atheism is always an infantile, at most juvenile, denial of God, I recommend respect for agnostic and atheist options. Muslims must engage with secularism in all its currently hallowed dimensions. Confident of the ultimate lack of innate or revealed purpose in the universe, it is therefore responsive to empirical details, humanistic in its morality, utilitarian in its politics, and pragmatic in its philosophy of law.

This is a novel proposal which rejects the centrality of Christian–Muslim and Jewish–Muslim relations. Let me justify this redistribution of emphasis. There is little that is specifically Judaic or Christian about the objections, raised by Jewish and Christian students of Islam, about the contents of the Quran. The most profound objections about Islamic beliefs, raised by modern Jews and Christians, are in effect secular humanist objections to Islamic doctrine and policy. The concerns range from abstruse issues (such as the character of God) to moral questions (about the rights of women) to political anxieties (about attitudes towards apostates and religious minorities in an Islamic state).

Where Judaeo-Christian reservations are religious, as in the area of the com-parative authority of the Quran in a world that contains the rival biblical scripture, they are answered by Muslim apologists in debates with interminable and acrimo-nious twists and turns. These quarrels are no part of the philosophy of religion. We examine, however, one inter-faith debate in Chapter 4 because it has fundamental implications about the authority of every scripture in a secular age.

To understand my proposed re-distribution of emphasis, we must note that there are now few authentically religious Jews and Christians in the West even among the clergy and the rabbinate. All intellectually sophisticated Jews and Christians are secularized and, in their attitudes towards domestic issues, as opposed to foreign policy, are typically humane capitalists whose religious beliefs serve as a decorative veneer on their underlying secularized religious humanism. Conversely, however, all Muslim critiques of Judaism and Christianity remain religious. All charges are variations on the stock Muslim accusation, rooted in the Quran, that Jews and Christians have achieved a cosy accommodation with the world – or with modern secularism, in our day – at the cost of being unfaithful to their dogmatic traditions. Modern versions of Christianity and Judaism appear to be carefully disguised variants of secular humanism. Predictably, therefore, many Jews and Christians, unlike virtually all Muslims, live conscientiously and comfortably within the arrangements of the liberal secular humanist state. Islam is now unique in its existential decision, though not intellectual capacity, to confront rather than accommodate the secularist world-view. It is a faith whose adherents are sounding a lone note of courageous defiance in the battle against secularism while other trumpets are blowing retreat.

The larger issue here concerns the attitudes of entire civilizations. In Islamic culture, all issues, moral and political included, are still effortlessly conceived as religious. Muslims treat even secular and pragmatic issues as theological matters. Economic, foreign and political policy is often a surrogate for a theological position. For most westerners, however, 'religious' is often a euphemism for 'practically irrelevant'. When Muslims call a position 'religious', they intend to elevate it to a level where it is absolute and can no longer be negotiated or compromised.

This analysis could be questioned. The Cold War was interpreted by eastern European Catholic thinkers as a war to save Judaeo-Christian civilization from the clutches of Communism. This is, however, an instance of a pragmatic political matter being gratuitously interpreted in a religious light. Muslims sense that many westerners, especially Europeans, are insincerely opportunist in their profession of Christian belief: they become suddenly and proudly religious in the hour of armed conflict, especially with the Islamic world. The secularized West is clearly no longer enthusiastic about religion but its older Christian fanaticism and messianic zeal have been transformed and now re-appear as a ferocious commitment to secular causes such as the pursuit of absolute freedom and pleasure. It takes unlimited sophistry to argue that Christianity or Judaism, in their origins, also primarily aimed at these secular goals.

A final and conclusive reason for the proposed shift in emphasis is that western secularism is far more threatening to Islam than western Christianity, a faith everywhere on the defensive. We conclude this from the fact that while Christian missionary abuse of Islam was in the past intended to undermine Muslim self-confidence and hence persuade Muslims to become Christians, the same strategy is now used only to prevent Christians from embracing Islam. The older grossly abusive Christian caricatures of Muhammad and his faith, full of crude and fanciful detail pandering in fulsome obscenity to western prejudices, have given way to a more balanced assessment of a noble religious rival. Western secularism, however, is self-confident and vigorous; many secular humanists mock all religious values, especially Islamic ones, since western culture has sanctified and empowered its secularist ideology.

6

This book has a complex structure. There are three chapters in Part I. In Chapter 1, I explore the origins of Islam before locating contemporary Islam in a world of rival faiths and ideologies. These tasks are factual and historical but nonetheless interpretive; and all sustain broader conceptual and philosophical implications. I discuss the life and ideological achievements of Muhammad as he was inspired by the event of the Quran's revelation. Muhammad started his ideological career relatively late in life and he framed it entirely in terms of the descent of the Quran, that is, 610 CE to 632. The Arabic Quran inspired a unique religious achievement associated with a known historical figure.

Chapter 2 explores the office of secular reason, especially anxieties about its proper role in the appraisal of revealed religion. Chapter 3 examines the moral component in this tale of the emerging hostility between religions and the secular world, with special reference to Islam, a faith that has prevented the emergence of a tradition of conscientious atheism. I construct, as a by-product of this project, a framework for a dialogue between Muslims and atheists (and agnostics) of various leanings. This aim, self-consciously introduced in Chapter 3, remains a standing item on our agenda.

Parts II and III focus on the Islamic scripture. Until recently in the West, understood ideologically, not geographically, there was little serious scholarly interest in the Quran in its own right as the founding script of a major world civilization. There prevailed a special prejudice which prevented a western appreciation of the Quran: the persistent orientalist myth of 'primitive prophet, therefore primitive book'. In this philosophical essay, I examine the Islamic scripture in its phenomenological integrity rather than mine its contents for alleged biblical equivalents or, worse, Christianize and liberalize its doctrines and imperatives to make these (falsely) appear appealing to contemporary westerners.

This essay ranges over the whole of the Quran's vast religious and conceptual terrain. Quranic allusions and references to various themes may be unique, frequent or routine. I cite a representative selection for key claims so that the number and range of citations indicates the nature of the reference (isolated or occasional) and the quality of the emphasis (consistent, repeated, or terminative). Fairly well-known literary material recording the normative deportment of Muhammad is occasionally cited but only to supplement or reinforce an insight found in the Quran.

The four chapters of Part II explore the status and authority of the Arabic Quran against the backdrop of relevant secular (and some Judaeo-Christian) reservations. In Part III, four further chapters investigate Quranic themes that challenge the secular perspective: the alleged divine presence in nature and society, mediated through the 'signs of God'; religious faith and the varieties of rejection; the Quran's portrait of human nature; and the delicate task of making room for the partial autonomy of reason and morals in a world dominated by the decisive and ubiquitous greatness of God.

The concluding Part IV, consisting of one chapter, examines problems of religious knowledge in a sceptical age. We explore the terrain with Islam in mind. In effect, we investigate the problem of the defence and rationality of Islamic theism considered as a philosophical (rather than revealed or religious) position.

7

We can only now understand the complexity and scope of our undertaking. We shall survey the matter through four comments. First, some recurrent motifs are threaded into various chapters and examined in a series of contexts. Second, the distribution of philosophical versus religious emphasis within each chapter deserves comment. Third, two crucial areas of inquiry are omitted. And finally, we must note the larger political context of our project.

Five motifs receive attention in diverse contexts. The themes of external nature, human nature, the status and role of unaided reason, the similarities (and differences) between religion and philosophy and, finally, the history of the rise of western secularism, re-surface in several settings.

Thus, we explore empirical nature in the context of scientific method and the scope and authority of revelation, especially Quranic revelation, in Chapters 6 and 7; we discuss nature as the open book of God in Chapter 8 as part of an epistemological inquiry into the Quranic concept of signs of God. Finally, in Chapter 12, we run to earth the epistemological issue of nature's ambiguity by proposing a rational theology to disambiguate our modern experience. As for human nature, in Chapter 3, we explore the moral dimensions of our nature unaided by divine grace, all viewed through the prism of secularism; in Chapter 10, we analyse the Quranic portrait of humankind while being alert to secular and Christian reservations. In Chapter 11, we conclude by investigating Islam's response to the modern secularist's motto, 'Human beings are the measure of all things'.

Intellectually respectable and articulate objections to revealed religion are always presented as reason's bid for an independent stance – one that is virtually always against revelation. As early as Chapter 2, we examine the perennial conflict between human reason and transcendent faith. The conflict between empirical science and supernatural religion, explored in Chapter 8, is an aspect of this problem of faith versus reason. In the final chapter, we return to the proper role of unaided reason during our attempt to revive the tradition of Islamic philosophy in the context of natural theology.

The history of the secular revolt against God, to turn to the fourth theme, is the most complex of these strands. The modern period of European history lacks the simplicity and unity of the classical period and our tale is accordingly convoluted. It is further complicated when we seek to weave insights, gathered from the European setting, into the Islamic fabric. The history of Islam as a religion is wholly different from the history of both Judaism and Christianity. The concern with the emergence and relevance of the modern secular world preoccupies us throughout this essay, particularly in Chapters 1, 2, 3, 7, 8, and 12. Chapter 7 traces the sub-theme of the history of the secular revolt against allegedly revealed canons. Chapter 12 notes the role of philosophy in the emergence of the western sceptical tradition.

The final fifth strand is the similarity between philosophy and religion, two ancient concerns which along with language, art and scientific technology, comprise the handful of intellectual pillars of human civilization, antique and modern. We examine the similar role of inherited tradition in religion and in philosophy in Chapter 1, note several similarities between the two during a discussion of the work of Ibn Rushd (Averroës) in Chapter 2, and incidentally compare the scope of the two in Chapter 7. A few aspects of the comparison re-surface in the final chapter where we explore the scope of different epistemologies, religious and secular, prevalent today.

The second, more methodological, concern is the internal distribution of philosophical and religious reasoning in each chapter. For those accustomed to factual, historical and theological discussion, the philosophical material may appear as an intrusion. For the philosopher, however, the discussion of non-philosophical material is justified only as a preface to the argumentative philosophical climax. A danger in my eclectic approach is that while for the devout believer, it seems devoid of the certainty and conviction of faith, for the philosopher, it may appear to lack the rigour of bold philosophical reasoning undeterred by religious strictures. In each chapter, the discussion moves from the religious (sometimes factual or historical) towards the reflective (conceptual and philosophical) dimensions. The exceptions are Chapters 11 and 12: in the former the emphasis is religious but the chapter begins by recording philosophical concerns. In Chapter 12, the reverse is mainly true; the material is in any case mostly philosophical.

Third, since this scholarly probing focuses on the encounter between secularism and the Quranic mind, I omit two important themes covered in my other works on Islam. This essay contains no detailed study of Islam's political or theological relationship to Judaism and Christianity. Islam's rivalry with the 'deviant' monotheisms of Judaism and Christianity is, apart from brief comparative comments throughout the book, self-consciously addressed only in the early sections of Chapter 1. The second omission is faith and power, a serious omission in the case of a resolutely political religion in which qualified trust is placed in the efficacy of coercive power to achieve social righteousness. Islam was, as we note in Chapter 1, a twin birth of faith and empire. This essay seeks, however, to establish a new subject called the philosophy of Islam; our intellectual task is not primarily political even though it has political implications.

Finally, we must acknowledge our larger political context. Islam exists among rival faiths and ideologies. One can have a purely intellectual interest in religious and inter-religious matters or take a strategic interest in the political enterprise of harmonious relations between faiths. The academic discipline of comparative religious studies, a secularized and universalized form of ecumenical theology, often collapses into the political enterprise of maintaining good relations among the faiths. I do not deal with this latter issue. Nor am I a religious politician pressured by professional diplomacy.

Some readers might wish to discern the political implications of the positions adopted here. I am, however, simply a philosopher of religion investigating Islam's founding text in its confrontation with secular humanism. It would be naive to suppose that any writing on Islam can, in the current atmosphere, be viewed as politically neutral. In a context of fundamental hostility, suspicion and partisan loyalties, all work on Islam is political. For no authorship, no matter how private or merely academic in its conception is ever private, let alone irrelevant, in its consequences. No book on Islam is currently read solely for its academic merits or concern for truth. In any case, authorship is never a neutral vocation even in more innocent areas of inquiry, even in the most innocent of times.

Part I

Quranic Islam and the secular mind

1 Locating Islam in the modern world

1

We approach the question of the coherence and truth of Islam obliquely. We ask: Is it rational to entertain Islamic belief in the contemporary secularized world? We begin however with Islam's presence in the modern industrialized world rather than with the question of its rationality, coherence or truth. It is easy to criticize an existing and established religion; it is difficult to found a new one. (It is no different from art where there are few creative artists but countless professional critics.) The Islamic perspective still guides and inspires a major and growing constituency of the human race. It has informed all aspects of a world civilization for one and a half millennia. Terminologically, it corresponds to both Christianity, the religion, and to Christendom, a former empire based on it.

Secularism, the comprehensive alembic of modern civilization, is a visible and objective, not restrictedly academic or theoretical, social presence. It weighs down on us daily like the gravity of the natural environment: as social form, as science and technology, as an adjunct to a universal form of western capitalism, and as political organization and bureaucracy. We should not, therefore, scrutinize Islam's confrontation with secularist ideology solely through the filter of philosophical theology. The tribunal of secularism judges religious conviction in the market-place, the media, the university forum, and the shared world. No one can ignore the practical ubiquity of the secular western world. Facing the purely *intellectual* challenges posed by the secular vision of the world is, however, a matter of academic choice. Its larger implications are not narrowly intellectual. Away from the security of academia and the conference hall, remote from the acrimonious exchanges in the footnotes of academic journals, ordinary Muslims see themselves as fighting an urgent battle for the true image of humanity at a time of crisis in civilizations.

Intellectually, the community of Muhammad is poorly equipped to deal with the secular onslaught because, as we note in Chapter 2, Muslim civilization has no extant philosophical tradition. But while Islam faces special difficulties in its confrontation with secularism, it has unique strengths and resources including a unified (and reliable) scriptural canon and an honourable religious tradition that is, in terms of contributions to scholarship and civilization, among the glories of the human record. Unfortunately, in the case of Islam, any attempt to defend it, no matter how limited and modest, is dismissed as an apologetic gesture, as a form of triumphalism. This charge is a version of the older and cruder charge of fanaticism levelled more often at Muslims than at any other religious community. One can, however, state as facts what might be misinterpreted as boasts.

2

Islam is, for most westerners, a political nuisance, not a world faith of enduring spiritual fecundity. The world's headlines are crowded daily with messages about its motiveless malice and misanthropic political vengeance. Always marginalized in the Euro-Atlantic community, Muslims are now also criminalized, visible only as participants in an unmanageable politics of violence, at most symbols or victims or useful allies – but never equals. Such Islamophobia would decline if there were a single developed western white nation which was officially Muslim. Bosnia in eastern Europe, born after a holocaust in the former Yugoslavia, might eventually become one such nation.[1] Its existence would mean that Muslims, behaving as Muslims, could occasionally elicit sympathy from the West. Admittedly, westerners treated Afghan Muslims with respectful sympathy in their struggle against Soviet imperialism – but those Muslims were seen as anti-Communist fodder. By contrast, when Catholics behave as Catholics – in opposing abortion, for instance – they may be condemned as wrong but they are not dismissed as crazy outsiders with alien values.

Unlike other powerless western minorities such as black people – at least a respected cultural presence supplying famous names in sports, arts and music – the Muslim reputation is wholly negative. Therefore few western critics feel obliged to let mere facts disturb them in their increasingly simplistic prejudices against Islam. Muslims are not merely wrong, they are crazy. Such inflammatory prejudice sometimes passes for social commentary, even scholarship.

Islam is the only faith for which misunderstandings and even deliberate and systematic misrepresentations begin with its very name. The faith has been called 'Muhammadanism' as if Muslims worshipped Muhammad! One might, with much more justification, call Christianity 'Paulianity' since Paul was the chief proselytizer of Christianity. The mislabelling of Islam is ironic since it is by far the most fully and self-consciously defined faith at its source. The Quran itself calls believers 'Muslims' (Q:22:78)[2] and repeatedly names the faith chosen for them as Islam (Q:3:19, 85; 5:3; 6:125, 39:22). Islam, unlike Christianity or Buddhism, has no second or third founder or political patron.

One orientalist Arabist, the late H.A.R. Gibb, tried to justify the label 'Muhammadanism': 'In a less self-conscious age Muslims were proud to call their community *al-umma al-Muhammadiyya*.'[3] Muslims are still proud to be called 'the people of Muhammad' but they resent the implication that there is a generic relationship between Islam and Muhammad similar to that between Christ and Christianity or the Buddha and Buddhism. Muslims claim that their faith is universal and that the attitude of surrender (*islām*) is its correct designation.

Admittedly, some Muslims praise Muhammad as though he were more than a human guide commissioned to deliver a divine message, an adulation that has never, with impunity, spilled over into worship. ('Muḥammad' is an intensive form of a passive participle, and means 'the much praised one' though – another irony – he is the most maligned figure among founders of faiths.)

By asking for courtesy in naming the faith as its adherents do or by deploring these snide inaccuracies, which smack of colonialist arrogance and racism, one is not asking for a lowering of the standards of critical history. For the historian, Islam is centred in the personality of its founder. Only Muslims view Islam as the primordial faith inaugurated by God at the beginning of history, a view that, naturally, cannot be accepted by any historian who rejects the divine inspiration of the Quran. For the secular student, Islam begins in the early seventh century, as the faith of a certain Muhammad Ibn 'Abd Allah (570–632 CE). A faith founded by a particular man, however, need not take that man to be an object of worship. Surely, we can grant that level of courtesy even to Muslims.

Such terminological matters only appear verbal. They originate in underlying substantive concerns. In religious, as in political inquiry, the choice of nomenclature is crucial. The imposition of a term on one's opponent, the withholding of an approbative word from a scheme one dislikes, or the imposition of an arbitrary and unwarranted connotation in a given employment of a controversial word, are the crucial stake in debates that are inevitably part of a power struggle. These features of the situation are masked by an apparently innocuous intellectual context and the artificial civility of academic debate. The relevance of words in the case of a religion that has been the victim of a continuous terminological war for over a millennium needs no comment.

Words such as 'terrorist', 'moderate', 'fundamentalist', 'extremist', 'fanatical', 'radical' and so on, lack analytical import. These words remain, by and large, part of a western propagandist vocabulary that prevents the posing of deeper questions about the real causes of the age-old tension between Islam and the West. The adjective 'moderate' automatically means pro-West; 'radical' automatically means anti-West, independently of the merits of the stance. Deeper analyses are rarely tolerated, especially in the American context. No westerner speaks of innate western militancy and ruthlessness in the defence of material interests world-wide. Judging by western news coverage, one might think that Muslims have a monopoly on fanaticism and terrorism while westerners only occasionally intervene, benevolently, to remove a dictator. This ignores the occidental contribution to oriental despotism.[4]

3

In terms of extent of influence, depth and intensity of conviction and the quality of the allegiance given to its doctrines even in a hedonistic secular age, Islam can hold up its head in the best ideological company. It remains, unlike Marxism and other philosophies of social distress, a virile political movement, not merely a school of radical social criticism. A large section of humankind find fulfilment in living according to its dictates wherever it yields the sceptre of influence. Islam satisfies spiritual needs and stirs many to moral goodness and some to moral greatness. It remains in the tumultuous Middle East, Islam's land of origin and permanent presence, and endures there as the only constant variable, one that explains the Arabs' historic rise to permanent prominence long before the ambiguous blessings of oil.[5]

Who was Muhammad? Was he an ambitious and designing sheikh who used 'revelation' to have his way? Is Islam genuinely a religion? Or is it, as many who traduce it claim, an elaborate ideological disguise for political power? What is modern Islam's attitude towards its origins and early history? How do Muslims react to change, especially the drastically irreversible change that secularism fosters, challenging and threatening all religion as such? What are the practical consequences of addressing the modern situation of Muslims? Could a Muslim reasonably ignore or dismiss the secular rational challenge to traditional Islam? In this opening chapter, we address this apparently motley set of issues and identify connections between them. For example, the problem of change cannot be addressed without taking stock of the faith's formative self-image which, in virtue of operating at the origins, controls the range of subsequent development. Again, in matters of moment – in matters of religion – it is irresponsible to inquire theoretically without also addressing the practical consequences of those theoretical stances.

After exploring, in Sections 4 to 9, Islam's foundations and its tense and ambivalent connection to Judaism and Christianity, ancient and modern, I shall: trace the emergence of a European secularism which supplies the universal context in which the rationality of traditional Islam is assessed (Sections 10–11); assess the emergent and incipient secular presence in the Islamic world and the need to recognize, acknowledge and engage intelligently with it (Sections 11–12); explore the status of change and tradition in Islam against the background of its self-image as 'meta-religion' of intentionally comprehensive scope from the very day of its twin birth as faith and empire (Sections 13–19); record and assess the existing official Muslim response to the crisis precipitated by modern secular challenges to Islamic tradition (Sections 20–2); and evaluate the pragmatic significance, including some practical and institutional consequences, of engaging sympathetically with secularism (Section 23).

4

A pilgrim to Mecca, the sacred hub of Islam, would be surprised to note that there are no signposts on the path leading to the cave where Muhammad received his inaugural revelation. Instead one follows the Pepsi cans that litter its modern route. After a tiring journey in the heat, one is suddenly at the cave in a mountainside just outside Mecca. It is at first disappointing: one sees only the ungrammatical and profane graffiti of lovers who boast of having been there already. The cave at Mount Ḥirā', where Muhammad received his first revealed fragment (recorded as Q:96:1–5)[6], is never mentioned or alluded to in the Quran. It is a hint of the sacred volume's remarkable silences, omissions, and mysterious sense of priorities, a theme of Chapter 6.

The initial revelation occurred in 610 CE when Muhammad was 40 years old. The experience is affectionately described in the literary record of the Prophet's actions, speech, tacit consents and significant silences.[7] In Muhammad's case, 'life begins at forty'. By contrast, Jesus, like Alexander before him, is thought to have died in his early thirties; and the Hindu prince who was to become the Buddha started his spiritual quest at the watershed of about 30, the physical prime of life. The revelation of the Quran from 610 to 632 CE frames the career of 'Muhammad the messenger of God' (Q:48:29). This unique arrangement produced a book reliably associated with the enduring achievement of an identifiable figure of history.

Even an optimistic observer, situated in the large but marginal Arab peninsula in the early seventh century, would not have predicted a glorious future for the new faith or any substantial success for Muhammad, let alone the actual turn of events which led to the greatest ideological achievement to crown the efforts of a single known figure of history, religious or secular. The Arabs were an isolated and independent people. The Byzantine emperor Justinian died in 565 – five years before the birth of Muhammad.[8] Heraclius, a contemporary of Muhammad, and sometimes called the first Byzantine emperor (if we disregard Justinian) reigned from 610 to 641. In a rare notice of secular history, he is obliquely mentioned in a revelation, dated to 615 CE, which alludes to the recent defeat of the Roman Christians by the Persian Sassanids 'in a nearby land' (Q:30:2–5).

The mission of the Arabian iconoclast – the Greek word means image-breaker – remained immersed in a sea of troubles for over a decade. There were only a few converts: relatives of Muhammad, some poor and dispossessed slaves, and others on the margins of the corrupt urban Meccan environment. Meanwhile, pagan animus grew more rapidly. There was persecution, mild and severe. Those protected by clan affiliation, including Muhammad and his relatives, could avoid the worst. Unprotected individuals, especially slaves, suffered the full brunt of Meccan malice.[9]

'Umar Ibn Al-Khaṭṭāb, the second caliph, dated the Islamic (lunar) calendar not from the first Quranic revelation or the birth of Muhammad but from an event with far-reaching political significance: the mass exodus of Meccan Muslim refugees to the northerly city of Yathrib, mentioned uniquely by name at Q:33:13 and later renamed *madīnat al-nabī*, city of the Prophet. This exodus is the *Hijrah*, the migration. (The word literally means cutting off ties, including those of blood.) Why commemorate a time of defeat? By 622 CE, retrospectively dated as Islam's first year, the tide had turned. Some men offered Muhammad asylum in their city of Yathrib and asked him to judge disputes among their tribes. Muhammad accepted; after negotiating suitable terms of settlement for his few but devoted followers, he fled his native city some hours before an assassination attempt. His decision to move to Medina proved that tribal solidarity (*'aṣabiyyah*) could be subordinated to faith – a revolutionary decision.

The 13 years spent in Mecca did not go to the locust: Muhammad had been training a coterie of zealous neophytes and the Quran, like a file in a murder trial, had been haphazardly but steadily accumulating. Nor did the migration to Medina prove to be a move into obscurity and the fatal frustrations of exile. Muhammad skilfully used the new locale to serve his long-term mission. He implemented, with political power, what he had preached solely with the sanction of moral persuasion in the city which rejected him. Following scrupulously the Quran's guidelines, he challenged the power structure that had resisted his revolutionary proposals.

If a prophet is dangerous while he is in our midst, the pagans must have mused, he is doubly dangerous when he is in exile. The exiled Prophet and his pagan detractors reached stalemate. The Meccans were waiting and watching events; so were Muhammad and God (Q:6:135, 158; 10:20; 32:30; 39:39; 44:59). The pagans did not have to wait for long. The messenger's only duty was to deliver the message (*al-balāgh*) while judgement and vengeance (*al-ḥisāb*) belonged to the Lord (Q:13:40; see also Q:42:48; 50:45). The pagans did not, however, have to wait for God to do the reckoning in the old dramatic style associated with past sinners. Instead, Muhammad the apostle of God is made to mete out just punishment on behalf of his God: the messenger no longer bears the sword in vain.

About two years after the exodus to Medina, Muslims won the decisive battle of Badr (Q:3:123) waged between an infant Muslim community and the ancient flower of pagan aristocracy. The Muslims were defeated at the next engagement at Mt Uhud and learnt to fly their flag half-mast while the Quran explained the defeat in the face of pagan derision (Q:3:121–75). The causes of defeat included greed for booty by a group of archers (Q:3:152–3); and Satan was cited as actively involved in the affair (Q:3:155). God used the opportunity to purify the mixed intentions of believers (Q:3:140, 154), take martyrs for his cause (Q:3:140) and to test the mettle of the faithful as they faced worldly defeat and death (Q:3:142–3). Both failure and success are equally didactic in the life of faith. There is, naturally, no blame on God or his apostle. No pessimistic conclusion is drawn: a chilly hour in June is no more the end of the summer of success than a bright day in January is the end of the winter of discontent. The only cure for failure is success – which is promised (Q:3:139).

The climax of Muhammad's career was in 630 CE when he re-entered Mecca – in the least bloody revolution in history. There were barely a dozen casualties; Muhammad's enemies were forgiven wholesale. Only such a victory would be worthy of the man of God: it was the crown of godly endeavour, not an occasion for worldly exultation (Q:110:1–3).

The community in Muhammad's day was a voluntary civilian group attracted to and cohering around the shamanic charisma of God's messenger. It was not a state: it had no access to superior resources of coercion and violence that could destroy civil society. Muhammad relied on the persuasion of the word preached and the intelligent resourcefulness of his followers to implement the rules. There were no standing armies or bureaucracies or religious hierarchies, merely small bands of enthusiastic warriors all struggling equally in the way of God.

Through a combination of sheer will and skill, Muhammad succeeded *ex officio* as Prophet of God: he established an autonomous community that lived according to divine law, a successful theo-nomocracy which became the blueprint for later utopian ambitions. By the time of his death in 10 AH (*Anno Hegirae*), that is, 632 CE he was acknowledged as the ruler of a peninsula united under the banner of the new faith.[10] The Quran twice cites this unification of the Arab tribes as a miracle (Q:3:103; 8:63), hardly an exaggeration when we note how modern Arab tribes are divided: each party puts its petty goals and grudges first, and many are at each other's throats. A few insurrections, the so-called wars of apostasy, and a decisive battle to defeat a rival (false) prophet, tested the political stamina of Muhammad's first successor, Abu Bakr.[11] Some interpreted Muhammad's death to mean release from the duties of the social contracts and treaties he had signed. (Muslims have always obeyed the rulers, not the rules, a problematic attitude that survives to this day.) Mainly through the book he had brought, however, even from beyond the grave, Muhammad remained at the helm of Islam's political destiny for the next one and a half millennia. History knows of no other case of so decisive a posthumous literary influence.

Muhammad led a full life. As prophet, teacher, administrator, statesman, general, judge, husband, father and friend, he received, without reserve, inquiries from his community about everything, no matter how private, trivial or even sordid. *Bene vixit qui bene latuit* (He lives well who lives widely). This latitude in his life, combining the active with the contemplative, however, makes non-Muslims suspect his religious virtue. For Christians, his behaviour with women alone is enough to disqualify him, while Jews see political delinquencies in his treatment of Jews.

Tradition proudly calls him *al-nabī al-malḥama*, the warrior–prophet. Muhammad fought and was nearly killed at the battle of Uhud (Q:3:144). He was, unlike most other founders of faiths, willing to risk his reputation for holiness and to dirty his hands for the sake of his ideal city. He was no day-dreamer engaged in conventional speech-making. Islam rejects the ideas of absolute political evil or absolute virtue. We must participate in power and its legitimate violence for the sake of virtue. Power invariably limits virtue – but it need not destroy it. Accordingly, Muhammad did not merely fantasize about mending the world while avoiding the moral risks of direct action. He moved beyond the comfortable catharsis of merely moral outrage.

Repay good with what is better but repay evil with justice. That was Muhammad's practice, based on the Quran. It is impossible to assail this honourable position from any credible moral point of view. By rejecting the political life, one effectively froze at its source one of the springs of morally excellent social behaviour. Civil society is the chief nursery of the political virtues. But the political life of Islam is not autonomous: it is, in principle, under the aegis of the most radical form of political humility. In practice, Islamic rulers have been no less corrupt than other rulers, sometimes more so. Autocratic and feudal chiefs have always refused to abdicate power – without the additional inducement of assassination.[12]

Muhammad, as the model Muslim, did not think that being religious entailed exile from natural existence. The Quran dismisses the view that true believers are not of this world or not in this world. A true faith must have resources for easing the burden of healthy emotion, for finding a place for natural desires, including legitimate power and licit sexual gratification. Islam acknowledges the pressure of sex on our frame and seeks freedom only from the cares of the world but not from the world itself. We explore these issues in Chapter 11 and examine secular reservations about Islamic ideals.

As a unified enterprise of private faith and public practice, the Quran commends full 'appreciation of wholesome deeds' (*fi'l al-khayrāt*; Q:21:73) and actively invites a permanent struggle against the inhuman forces of wrong (*zulm*), a dual struggle the Quran calls *al-amr bi al-ma'ruf wa anhay 'an al-munkar* (ordering the good and forbidding the evil; Q:3:110). The *ma'ruf* (lit., known) and the *munkar* (lit., unknown) are two axiological categories in a simple universe where there is no tragedy. This noble principle, difficult to implement in a free society without causing civil friction, has been elevated by Muslim jurists into an article of faith.

The struggle must occur in the public square. The Quran rejects a religion which requires its votaries to retire from the real world (Q:57:27) of discordant advocacies, a few caring and innocent if increasingly fatigued, the rest irate, insincere, loud and propagandist. Islam's political aspirations, offensive to those who oppose any empowerment of a religious ideal, cannot be assailed from any reasonable angle: if our pursuit of power, like our desire for sex, is natural and instinctive, then the only question concerns its regulation. All ideologies and faiths, including those whose adherents ostensibly claim indifference to power, survive by courtesy of power: Muslims would argue that there is a fraud, if a pious one, in the claim that authentic religious ambition can even in principle, let alone in practice, disown 'the things of Caesar'.

Muhammad was a man of only one doctrine: *Allāhu akbar*. This confession of the greatness of God is the fulcrum of Islam as a vision of human destiny. Even an obscure and flickering recognition of the worth of this maxim dignifies a life lived in an industrial–commercial society that values only worthless ephemera and futile consumerism. This dogma, which needs rigorous argument to buttress it, is the basis of a distinctively Islamic humanism whose parameters we sketch in Chapter 11.

After the Quran, the major textual source of Islam is the record of the tradition of Muhammad whose life we have briefly sketched here. Believers zealously referred every concern, whether grand or sordid, to his authority and wisdom; after his death too, Muhammad's beliefs and decisions were considered normative for all Muslims in all ages. It is a measure of his decisive and enduring posthumous authority that all contemporary advocacies of Islamic movements, whether reformist or obscurantist, whether liberal or conservative, still have to pretend to wear his insignia. The classical sources portray him as simply an Arab prophet–chief. Modern Muslim writers represent him, variously, as a radical who fought for social justice, a socialist reformer ahead of Marx, an apostle of modern liberalism, a pioneer of gender equality, and even as a pacifist and reluctant mystic who accidentally made the mistake of founding an empire.

5

On the authority of the Quran and sayings of the Prophet, Muslim historians[13] stigmatized the pre-Islamic era as the Former Age of Ignorance (*al-jāhiliyyatu al-ūlā*; Q:33:33).[14] It was a time of corruption and bloodshed, marked by moral turpitude and social chaos: the rich oppressed the poor, infant females were buried alive at birth[15], women had few rights and slaves even fewer. Modern Muslim radicals condemn the modern age as one of ignorance judged by Quranic standards of justice and probity. The *jāhiliyyatu al-ūlā* was, they say, and as the expression literally means, only 'the first age of ignorance'.[16]

Muhammad famously conceded that the best among the Muslims were the best of those in the age of ignorance, a concession which implies that there were morally decent men and women in pre-Islamic Arabia; Islam made the good man better by 'opening his breast to Islam' (*yashraḥ ṣadra-hū li al-islām*; Q:6:122; 39:22). There was no extant Arabian version of monotheism. By Muhammad's day, the bygone presence of Abraham and his son Ishmael in Mecca (Q:2:125–9; 14:37) as well as the traces of pre-Islamic messengers (such as Shu'ayb, Salih and Hud) sent to the tribes of the region, were fragmented and contentious memories in the pagan mind. Pre-dating Islam, however, was the nascent monotheistic movement of the *ḥanīf,* a Quranic term for the rightly inclined religious seeker who sensed that institutional Christianity and Judaism were deviant forms of monotheism, errant in doctrine and morals. Such seekers hankered for a less institutionalized, more private and sincere, search for God. The Quran rejects the view that Abraham was a Jew or a Christian and calls him a *muslim* (submitter to God's will; Q:3:67) and *ḥanīf* (upright; Q:6:161; 16:120). We note a similar re-scripting of sacred history in the Pharisees' claim that Abraham was a Jew (John 8:33, 39) – though they had less justification for their claim than the Quran has for its.[17]

Muhammad preached that we must submit to the absolute holy will of the only God, *al-'ilāh* (the God), which contracts to *Allāh*, a proper name containing the definite article in it and thus making plurality grammatically senseless. Although grammatically the masculine pronoun (*huwa*) is used of God, he has no gender.[18] God is transcendent, therefore impossible to divide or dissect. He is simple, therefore not composed of parts or qualities.[19] God is unique (*al-waḥīd; waḥīdan*; acc., Q:2:163; 18:110; 38:5, 65); intrinsically and numerically he is one (*al-aḥad*; Q:112:1). These subtleties inspired the first rationalist Muslim theological school, examined in Chapter 2. God is *ṣamad* (lit., solid; Q:112:2).[20] Theologically, *ṣamad* means eternal and absolute, thus self-caused: without origin and therefore permanently independent of contingency. He is metaphysically indefectible, omniscient, omnipotent and beyond time and space: 'No vision can grasp him but he grasps all vision' (Q:6:103). As an incorporeal spirit, independent of the created world, he has no spatial location although he acts in space and time and guides us, through his messengers, to our final and true purpose. Separate from the world of his creation, God is not subject to its laws, moral or arguably logical.

The Arab pagan creed was polytheism with traces of animism. The pagans believed in monarchianism: one god, Allah, was elevated above others in a heavenly hierarchy in a way similar to Zeus (among the Greek gods) and Jupiter (among the Romans). The Quran did not preach monolatry (or henotheism) where worshippers devote their attention to one deity while recognizing that other gods genuinely exist.[21] It preached monotheism as a complete ideology on psychological, existential, religious and political levels.

God is the primal originator (*badī'*) of the heavens and the earth (Q:2:117; 6:101). He creates humankind and all things *ex nihilo* (Q:19:9): 'When he decrees some thing, he merely says to it, "Be!" And it is' (*kun fa-yakūn(u)*; Q:3:47).[22] This succinct maxim, too gnomic and sententious by analytical philosophical standards, is distributed into the entire Quran (Q:2:117; 3:47; 16:40; 40:68, etc.) This style of creation is supplemented by a *creatio continua* (Q:35:41) as God sustains existing creation and also continues to create novelties beyond human knowledge and competence (Q:55:29). He 'originates creation and then reproduces it' continually (Q:29:19, 20).

From dust, God created the first man, Adam, and his consort (Q:30:20; 35:11); from this pair originates the monogenetic human species (Q:4:1; 6:98; 49:13). Allah is the god of all peoples, not an Arab deity in a pagan pantheon. Independent of his human subjects' response to him, he is in himself all-powerful and self-sufficient. Intolerant of partners in his divinity and sovereignty, he has great expectations of his human subjects. While all creation – natural, supernatural, corporeal, incorporeal, animate, lifeless – proclaims the praise of God (Q:13:15; 16:48–50), often in ways we cannot recognize (Q:17:44), it does so through its very nature; only human beings and elemental beings known as the jinn, both considered rational creatures endowed with free will, voluntarily choose worship and show faith through righteous action that pleases God (Q:22:18).

God's intentions are known to us only insofar as he reveals them, hence the resignation in the devout aphorism: 'God alone knows his own intentions'. While his nature and intentions are inaccessible, he has clarified his will for us by choosing a series of inspired prophets, men of probity and patience. This divine initiative to teach humankind is virtually always rejected: every community plotted against its divinely commissioned warner (Q:23:44; 40:5). 'How many were the messengers we sent among the ancients. And whenever a prophet came to warn them, they mocked him' (Q:43:6–7).

The consequences of disbelief extend into eternity, a loss in and of both worlds (Q:22:11). No one can disobey God with impunity, prosper materially, or achieve purity without God's guiding grace (*faḍl Allāh*; Q:24:10, 14, 20). The active repudiation of God's will is the root cause of the colourful variety of vices that plague human societies: greed and niggardliness shown in the inordinate love of wealth (Q:100:8), the callous and hypocritical denial of the rights of slaves and widows, the refusal to feed 'the orphan kinsman on a day of great privation' (Q:90:14–5) and the rejection of even 'a small act of neighbourly kindness' (Q:107:7).

A supreme evil being called Iblīs (Satan)[23] encourages human beings to act treacherously towards their higher nature which was created to be submissive to God. Too proud to bow to Adam, he is a racist or 'speciesist' who argued that he was made of fire, a substance superior to the clay used to create Adam

(Q:7:11–3; see also Q:23:12). Evicted from paradise, Satan promised to seduce humankind from the straight path (Q:7:14–18). He continues to deceive them with false promises (Q:4:120) and tempts them away from 'the path made straight' (*al-ṣirāt al-mustaqīm*; Q:1:6); he makes it appear crooked (Q:14:3). While God creates and beautifies the world, Iblīs defaces creation (Q:4:119) and makes evil conduct look deceptively beautiful (Q:27:24). He is the persistent sceptic and rebel (Q:4:117) who questioned and disobeyed God when he ordered him to bow to Adam (Q:38:71–85), God's deputy or vicegerent (*khalīfah*) on earth (Q:2:30).[24] The slinking evil whisperer, as the Quran calls him in its final chapter famous for its onomatopoetic effect (Q:114:1–6), is hell-bent on misguiding humankind away from God (Q:4:117–21) and uses every nefarious strategy (Q:17:64) as he and his evil tribe spy on Adam's progeny (Q:7:27). He has misled 'a vast multitude' (*jibillan kathīran*; Q:36:62) of humankind. The foolish repudiation of the sovereignty of the compassionate God, at the instigation of this evil being, is the centrepiece of the Quran's account of human history.

Satan tempted Adam and his unnamed consort to eat the fruit of an unnamed tree in paradise. They both ate it simultaneously and became aware of their nudity, the great cultural discovery of our early history. God forgave Adam and then chose Adam and his companion and promised guidance for them both and for their offspring (Q:2:37–8):

> He said: 'Go down, both of you, from here with enmity among all of you. However, as it is certain, when my guidance reaches you, then whosoever follows my guidance shall not lose his way nor descend into misery. But whosoever turns away from my remembrance, for him is a restricted life. And we shall resurrect him on the day of resurrection – blind!'
>
> (Q: 20:123–4).

Although forbearing, God does not indefinitely tolerate perversity; he annihilates sinful societies. A typical scenario: a messenger counsels his community to eschew dead idols and pleads with his compatriots to turn in earnest to the living God. The leaders of the community, who live in sinful luxury, disregard the warning, mock the messenger's credentials and accuse him of being merely human, seeking superior social position and undeserved privilege (Q:21:3; 36:15). Suddenly, without further notice (Q:36:28), the community is destroyed dramatically (Q:91:14). The Prophet and those few who embraced his message are miraculously evacuated (Q:51:31–5). Ruins of the sinful society remain as a sign to warn a later generation of the divine retribution that awaits disobedient and decadent peoples (Q:29:33–5; 46:25). The pagans saw traces of divine anger etched in the ruins of bygone communities more powerful than the Meccans (Q:43:8), ancient peoples whose houses provided a welcome halt and hospitality for weary travellers along the caravan trade routes that threaded the northern and southern Arab peninsula (Q:34:18–19).

The heavens and the earth are both 'heavy with the burden of the hour' (Q:7:187); judgement has drawn near men and women while they play and frolic heedlessly

(Q:21:1; 22:1–2). These apocalyptic passages appeal to modern Muslims as they keenly sense an impending crisis, heightened by warnings from preachers who speak of an imminent judgement and the termination of history. Psychologically, the finality of the fourteenth century of Islam persists although the calendar has put an end to it; the fifteenth has already reached more than a quarter of its span.

At a time, known only to God, the hour will be established (Q:7:187; 31:34). The dead shall be informed in their graves that the last day has arrived (Q:36: 51–2). The sky will be split apart, the stars extinguished, and the earth convulsed and pulverized (Q:81:1–2; 82:1–2; 84:1–4; 99:1–2); the apparently stable mountains will be removed, from their roots, and scattered like dust by Muhammad's omnipotent Lord (Q:20:105–6; 27:88; 81:3; 101:5). Men and women will appear drunk though they are sober; the pregnant woman will suffer a premature deliverance of her burden (Q:22:2). Resurrected in bodily form, with even finger-tips restored (Q:75:4), everyone shall wait silently as the divine assizes commence on 'the day of anguished regret' (*al-yaum al-ḥasrah*; Q:19:39). Only those granted permission to speak will speak in God's presence and they shall say nothing but the truth (Q:78:38) since it is the day of truth (*al-yaum al-haqq*; Q:78:39). Human bonds are ruptured (Q:23:101). Everyone is friendless (Q:70:10) and has enough to worry about on the day when anxious anticipation and dread turn 'children senile and grey-headed' (Q:73:17). The sinner will offer his own children and other relatives to redeem himself from the punishment (Q:70:11–14). Muhammad's traditions add that all humankind will be naked on the day but terror and anxiety will prevent anyone from noticing it.

Several orthodox catechisms, including one compiled by the theologian–philosopher Al-Ghazālī, whom we meet in Chapter 2, claim that immediately after death, the soul is subjected to a preliminary interrogation. The questions are simple and the answers are known to the believer. 'Who is your Lord?' and 'What is your faith?' The devout believer, aware of the promise undertaken by the Children of Adam before history began (Q:7:172–3), answers correctly. The rejectors are trapped on account of shocked silence (atheists), hesitation and confusion (Jews, Christians and agnostics), unclear responses, incoherence and falsity (polytheists and all others). Those who pass the simple doctrinal part of the examination are subjected to a further test about their actions. Few expect to pass this portion of the examination. The sinners, according to some authorities, then request Muhammad to intercede for them. The appeal is presented to God. The final decision rests within the divine prerogative and is in no way subject to dispute.

Good and evil actions are weighed in the balance (Q:7:8–9; 23:102–3); a book, registering deeds itemized as good and bad, is prepared. Those receiving the book in their right hands have earned divine pleasure and shall enter paradise (Q:69:19–24; 84:7–9). Although the good pleasure of God's presence (*riḍwān Allāh*) is the supreme joy in paradise (Q:9:72), sensual delights are also described in lavish detail in many Medinan and Meccan passages (Q:13:35; 47:15; 52:17–24; 55:46–76; 56:12–38; 76:5–22; 71:41–4; 78:31–5; 83:22–9; 88:8–16). Those given the book in their left hands (or behind their backs) are people who, in their earthly lives, gave free rein to their whims and lusts (Q:69:25–37; 84:10–2). As they taste the torments of hell described with shocking directness in passages dispersed throughout the sacred volume (Q:4:56; 14:16–17, 49–50; 22:19–22; 25:11–14; 47:15; 56:41–55; 69:25–37; 74:26–31; 78:21–5; 88:1–7), they will wish they were dust and had never existed (Q:78:40). Martyrs for the cause of Islam, considered forever alive and in the presence of God (Q:3:169–71), do not receive the book of their deeds. According to traditions of the Prophet, without reckoning they enter paradise.[25]

6

In modern sympathetic western scholarship, Islam is invariably located by using the dual co-ordinates of Judaism and Christianity on the common axis of Abraham. The historical Abraham, about whom we know nothing from independent non-scriptural sources, transcends doctrinal classification and still inspires a trio of competitive pieties. Ironically, the Quran's reference to Abraham is made not in order to establish a link with Judaism but rather to establish Islam's disengagement from Judaism and Christianity (Q:2:135) – seen as errant monotheisms tainted with ethnic exclusivism and doctrinal error respectively. 'Abraham was neither a Jew nor a Christian' (Q:3:67; see also Q:2:140). The Quran claims that the community closest to Abraham, apart from his own people, is the community of Muhammadan Islam (Q:3:68). The covenant with Abraham does not extend to evil-doers (Q:2:124) which implies that Jews and Christians were disloyal to their professed traditions, an accusation made explicit elsewhere (Q:19:58–60). In particular Jews are faulted for failing to 'preserve the book of God' (Q:5:46) and Christians are accused of neglecting the pact they made with God (Q:5:14). The link with Abraham then does not make Islam part of the Abrahamic family. This family, if it exists, is, like most families, dysfunctional and artificial. Islam appeals to the pristine monotheism of Abraham precisely to establish that this alone was untainted by the later ethnic and dogmatic taints of Judaism and Christianity.

The Quran does call Islam 'the religion of your father Abraham' (*millat abīkum ibrāhīm*; Q:22:78). This is odd since Muhammadan Islam does not inherit any institution of 'Abrahamic Islam'. Praying, fasting, pilgrimage, and alms, are defining features of the Quranic conception of religion as such (*dīn*; Q:21:73) and are associated, without regard for historical development and evolution, with all prophets at least since Noah (Q:42:13). The *ḥajj* (pilgrimage) is the only ritual with a specified historical origin. It is associated with the Ka'ba (cube) in Mecca which was the site of the pilgrimage in pagan times. The Quran claims, surprisingly, that the original shrine was built by Abraham and Ishmael (Q:3:96–7); Abraham settled his offspring in an infertile valley near the sacred shrine he had built in Mecca (Q:14:35–7). The Quran calls this foundation 'the first house of worship erected for humankind' (Q:3:96) and honours it as 'the house of excellent pedigree' (*al-bayt al-'atīq*; Q:22:29, 33), a clear insult to the Meccans who thought their (pagan) ancestors had built it. A Quranic revelation made it the site of the Holy Mosque which marked the new prayer-direction (*qiblah*; Q:2:142–5; *shaṭr* at Q:2:150). The prayerful orientation – the word means to turn to the East – towards

Jerusalem, adopted by the earliest Muslims, was changed to the Meccan sanctuary (Q:2:150) after Muslims failed to convert the Jews. The break with the previous 'peoples of the book' was complete.

Muhammadan Islam then is not a departure from an existing institutional template that has survived inside history. Islam inherits nothing from the past in terms of ritual or institution; the grand idea of monotheism is the only and sufficient heritage. Islamic rituals are new and distinctive although the Quran, with uncharacteristic modesty, speaks of Quranic Islam as merely the *muṣaddiq* (confirmer) of its precedents (Q:3:3; 5:48). This is misleading since confirmation of the past might be taken to mean a lack of novelty in the present. Islam does not arise as a reform or revolutionary movement inside Abrahamic religion since that religion was not available as an institutionalized or organized faith in Muhammad's Arabia. The origins of Islam contrast with Christian origins where Jewish heretics, known as 'Christians', retained the Hebrew Bible (*Tanakh*) and mutated its arrangement, making the Prophets (*Nebi'īm*) end the canon. They re-interpreted the re-arranged canon, viewing it as a fulfilment of messianic prophecy. Muslims, unlike Christians, do not read the scriptures of a previous sister faith. While Christianity is rightly seen as a reform movement inside existing Second Temple post-Ezra sectarian Judaism, Islam does not arise as a moral reform movement inside a related existing faith.

The Quran only once mentions Ishmael and Abraham as ancestors of the Arabs (Q:2:128–9). A few references to Ishmael are parts of perfunctory lists of messengers (Q:2:136; 4:163). Two verses praise him for standard religious qualities (Q:6:86, 21:85) and he is once commended for keeping his family on a strict plane of religious duty (Q:19:54–5). The Quran nowhere mentions circumcision or the Abrahamic covenant of circumcision, despite containing references to many other covenants, including 'a covenant of the book' contracted with the Israelites (Q:7:169; see also Q:2:40), a covenant with all prophets (Q:3:81; 23:51–2; 33:7), with Adam and humankind (Q:7:172–3; 20:115), and with Muhammad and his community (Q:33:7, 23). Islam traces its origins not to Abraham but to Adam and Noah who are classed as 'Muslim' apostles (Q:3:33; 42:13).

Islam should not be seen as Christianity and Judaism combined, Arabicized and repackaged. It is neither a Christian nor a Jewish heresy. The case for a Judaeo-Christian approval of Islam as a family member need not be supported from such an untenable position. Islam is to be judged on the merits of its religious and moral principles, not on the basis of its alleged conformity with Jewish and Christian beliefs. Islam is not some unoriginal appendix to the Judaeo-Christian tradition. In this essay, Islam shall be treated as an original faith – insofar as any faith claiming to be a confirmation of the past can be original. A wealth of Quranic references will document the Quran's countless *sui generis* features and original theological claims.

7

God's latest choice has settled on a new people (Q:3:110). With the coming of Islam, the earlier people of the book are dismissed as a failed spiritual experiment

(Q:57:16–17). The Quran accuses the Jews of making a universally relevant faith into an ethnic family concern by concealing the scripture's comprehensively applicable regulations (Q:6:91). Muslims sharply reject any debt to Judaism as the prototype of western monotheism. Tracing intellectual indebtedness in this way presupposes a secular view of history. It is meaningless if one believes that God gave monotheism to the world – and did so much earlier than the Jews!

The Quran judges Jews and Christians, 'the people of the book' (*ahl al-kitāb*; Q:3:64, 65) or rather the people of 'a portion of the book' (*naṣīban min al-kitāb;* Q:3:23) since the Quran alone is the complete version of the heavenly book (Q:3:119) whose earlier fragments include the Torah, the Psalms (*Al-Zabūr*, lit. fragments; Q:17:55) and the Gospel (*Al-Injīl*). The Jewish and Christian scriptures were religiously all-sufficient for their time and place (Q:5:45–6, 49; 6:154) but the Quran alone is universally valid forever. The Quran dismisses the Hebrew Bible extant in Muhammad's time as 'some separate sheets for you to show' (*qarāṭīs tubdūna-hā*; Q:6:91), implying that its original unity and spirit were concealed or overlaid by miscellaneous later human additions.

Friendly and sympathetic generalized references to Jewish and Christian groups co-exist with censorious comments about unjust sub-groups in these communities (Q:5:51, 57–66). Jews were skilled in rhetoric and subtly mocked Muhammad through hint and humour (Q:2:104). The Quran reserves some mordant polemic for both Jews and Christians but mainly for Jews. Quranic rejoinders to Jewish claims, especially Jewish exclusivism and elitism, are not diluted by verbosity or detail. Pungent and concise dialectical exchanges punctuate the longer Medinan chapters (Q:2:111–2; 5:64). The sophisticated Medinan Jews were, like modern rabbis, learned, witty and talkative. When the Quran's replies did not silence them, the Quran reminded Jews that their own prophets had cursed them (Q:5:78–9). It accused Jews of being usurious merchants (Q:4:161; 5:41–3, 63) who defied the laws of God (Q:9:29). There were pitched battles. Some Jewish inhabitants of Medina were killed, others taken prisoner and dispossessed (Q:33:26–7); eventually the rest were deported into exile (Q:59:2–5).

The Quran claims to resolve Jewish anxieties about religion (Q:27:76) and directly addresses the Children of Israel (Q:2:40, 47, 122; 20:80). Jews are condemned for doctrinal errors (Q:9:30), for telling lies against God (Q:3:75; 4:49–50) and for moral misconduct including the taking of usury and consumption of unlawful things (*sukht*; lit., destructive or toxic; Q:5:42, 63; cf. Q:20:61). The rabbinate is condemned occasionally (Q:5:63) but also commended occasionally (Q:26:197; 46:10). A late Medinan passage, which abrogates earlier more lenient verdicts, excoriates the rabbinate by comparing that institution to a donkey laden with large books (Q:62:5–8).

The Quran confirms that God elected the Israelites for a special relationship (Q:7:140; 44:32) but it also attacks Jewish ethnic elitism and exclusivism (2:80–2, 94–5; 5:18).[26] In its accounts of the Moses–Pharaoh confrontation, Moses preaches pure monotheism to the Pharaoh and to the Egyptians; his mission is not restricted to the Israelites (Q:40:27). This contrasts with the biblical account. In a tradition unique to the Quran, the Pharaoh's wife converts (Q:66:11); an unnamed believer also converts and conceals his faith (Q:40:28). All Hebrew messengers, as we see in Joseph's speech to his fellow prisoners (Q:12:37–40), preach a universal message identical to Muhammad's message. All ethnic Jewish narratives are universalized; Jewish traditions of restrictive import are given in a modified comprehensive form. For example, after an account of the first murder (Q:5:27–31), the Quran comments that 'we ordained for the Children of Israel that anyone who killed a single person, except for murder or mischief in the land (i.e., just cause), were like someone who murdered the entire human race and, likewise, anyone who saved a single life were like someone who saved the whole of humankind' (Q:5:32). Jewish tradition knows this maxim in the restricted ethnic form: the murderer of a single Israelite has committed genocide, that is, unjustly killed all the seed of Israel.

Muslims accuse the Jews of a religious superiority complex. Ironically, many would convincingly accuse the Muslims of suffering from it: they mistake a psychological condition for a faith by frequently putting themselves forward as paragons for others to emulate. Provided they 'order right and prohibit wrong', the Quran itself calls Muslims 'the best community raised for the benefit of humanity' (Q:3:110), a view that is, in the contemporary world, restricted to Muslims. And it is an unwise self-image. Communities that insist on their own total uniqueness excite in others the desire for persecution. The next time there are gas chambers in Europe, we know who will be inside them.

The scripture condemns, to turn to the other people of the book, what it sees as egregious doctrinal errors in Christian dogma, errors that lift Christian belief from the realm of pardonable mistake to that of the unforgivable blunder of outright disbelief (*kufr*; Q:5:17, 72–73). But the Quran admires the moral character of Christian communities of the time, commending some Christians for their outstanding learning, piety, and humility (Q:5:82–5) and citing conspicuous compassion as a distinguishing mark of Christians but only insofar as they followed Jesus (Q:57:27). The Quran condemns, however, the misuse of public wealth by monks and priests (*aḥbār*) and anchorites (*ruhbān*; Q:9:34).

Sincere Christians are, condescendingly, seen as morally good but doctrinally confused. Many Christian missionaries think that the Quran pays tribute to Christian behaviour in order to win them over, a plausible enough claim: some Christian sects of the time were ripe for conversion to a simpler faith. The Christian to Muslim inter-faith conversion movement is historically the largest movement of its kind. Modern Muslims insist that colonialism is treasonable to the cause of Jesus and that these generous Quranic passages are to be read in the light of the caveat about following Jesus since most Christian nations today (as in the past) have been only nominally Christian, eager and ready to besmirch their Christian credentials.

The quality of the exchanges with Jews and Christians varies from authoritarian dismissal to searching and challenging engagements. One Medinan passage (Q:3:72) refers to a remarkable strategy by some Jews and Christians: 'A faction among the people of the book say, "Believe in the morning in the revelation sent to believers – but reject it by the end of the day. Perhaps the believers will turn back [to paganism]".' The Quran is unimpeachably alert to such plots and intrigues and unfailingly offers cutting rejoinders (Q:2:94–6; 5:18, 59–64). It is an enduring mystery of religious history, for non-Muslims, how Muhammad, living in a pagan culture, formulated a profound and unanswered critique of two established monotheisms, a critique that effectively punctured Christianity's hope of preaching the Gospel world-wide.

Muslims believe they have a revealed warrant for just relations with Jews and Christians. Imperial Islam has an excellent moral record during its lenient ascendancy in Europe. Some of the Quran's notices of Jews and Christians are hostile, others ambivalent (Q:3:75; 7:168; 113–5); a few notices of Jews (Q:7:159) and a lot more of Christians and people of the book as a generalized group are notably generous and charitable (Q:5:82; 28:52–5).

The Quran's revealed estimate of these rival faiths, one of which is a crusading faith with a competing colonial history, only appears to be a settled estimate of two historically diverse communities. Since the Quran is subject to interpretation and already contains a variety of claims about these communities, however, there is no scriptural ground for the operative veto on any empirical study of these rival faiths. Intellectually, Muslims have been lazy and arrogant in assuming that there is nothing worth studying. Many are irritatingly confident that there is a single true, monolithic Judaism and Christianity, contained in revealed Islam and known a priori. Unwittingly, they dispossess Jews and Christians of their intellectually rich heritage. In the days of Islamic ascendancy, some Muslim scholars attempted an empirical study of other faiths.[27] Intellectual adventurism, even scholarship, is perhaps a by-product of political power: powerful people are emotionally secure enough to indulge their intellectual curiosity and give charitable notices of their enemies and rivals.

8

We treat separately the encounter between Islam and Christianity, the global superpowers with competing colonial histories and rival missions in the modern world. Their mutual relations have been shaped by physical hostility accompanied by acrimonious polemical exchange for almost 1,400 years and punctuated by occasional sympathy and intelligent compromise. Islam claims to perfect Christianity and Judaism. It is a family affair, hence the bitterness. What is in common need not unite us; one need only think of sibling rivalry.

Islam offers an alternative account of the status and activity of Jesus, son of Mary, as the Quran calls him since it denies his divinity. The Quran claims to retrieve the truth about him by describing him as only a messenger steeped in piety. Steering between Jewish rejection and Christian deification, the Quran asserts that Jesus was a conspicuously pious prophet sent to reform impenitent Israelites, 'the lost sheep of the House of Israel'.[28] Christians entertain a blasphemous view of their spiritual leader. They indulge an over-developed sense of devotion to this honourable prophet who was only a model (*mathal*) of purity for the Children of Israel (Q:43:59). Jesus was a sign of God, not a (or the) son of God (Q:3:45–51, 59–62; 9:30; 23:50; 10:68–9; 19:21, 34–5). The Quran cautions Christians and Jews, the people of the book, against 'fanaticism in religion' (*ghuluww fī al-dīn*; Q:4:171).

The Quranic Jesus would have found blasphemous the views attributed to him by the Christian churches. He preached absolute submission to the will of God: *islām* in the generic, not historical, sense. While not a member of the historical community of Muhammadan Islam, he was a *muslim*. God empowered him to perform miracles, from the day of his birth (Q:3:45–6; 19:29–30). The Quran confirms the Virgin Birth three times (Q:3:47; 19:20–1; 66:12)[29] and rebukes the Jews for their 'calumny against Mary' (Q:4:156). Though born without a human father, Jesus is still fully human. He is not divine and he is not the Son of God. The Quran in effect accuses Christians of committing the fallacy of irrelevant conclusion: Christians regard Jesus as the Son of God because, they argue, he was born without a father. This conclusion is unwarranted since Adam, who was born without either parent would, if the Christian reasoning were sound, have a greater claim to divinity. But neither Adam nor Jesus was divine. 'The case of Jesus in the eyes of God is like that of Adam: He created him from earth and then said to him, "Be!" And he is.'(Q:3:59).

The Quran calls Jesus the Messiah (*Al-Masīḥ*; Q:3:45; Hebrew: *meshiākh*, anointed one; Greek: *Christos*) but is silent on the Jewish or Christian significance of the term.[30] While most Israelites rejected Jesus, a group also honoured him as a messenger of God (Q:61:14) and this latter group prevailed (Q:61:14). The rejectors intended to crucify Jesus. Presumably, these would be Sadducees and Pharisees but the Quran rarely condescends to mention historical groups or actors even in Muhammad's time, let alone those from an earlier epoch. The Jews were determined to crucify Jesus – there is no mention of the Romans – and Jesus was prepared, like other messengers carrying out their missions, to die in this manner, for God's sake. God intervened to rescue him from the cross. The Jews were misled by the substitution of another person; Jesus was not successfully crucified. 'They neither killed him nor crucified him' (Q:4:157). In compiling a full catalogue of the delinquencies of the Jews, the Quran includes their boast about killing Jesus (Q:4:154–7). Jesus was saved rather than killed on the cross 'but it was made to appear to them' (*wa lākin shubbiha lahum*; Q:4:157) as if he had been killed. Although many messengers had been allowed to be martyred, as we know from the Quran's condemnation of the Jews for killing the prophets (*qatl al-anbiyā'*; Q:2:61, 87; 3:183; 4:155; see also Matthew 23:29–32), God translated Jesus by removing him (Q:4:158), possibly without death, directly into paradise where he is among those closest to God (Q:3:45). God exercised his divine arbitrium since he is powerful enough to do as he wishes.

Muslim tradition, taking its cue from obscure Quranic allusions (Q:4:159; 43:57–61) and strange Prophetic sayings of varying authenticity, claims that Jesus will return near the time of the hour (of judgement), live as a Muslim, refute Christian interpretations of his mission by symbolically breaking crosses and prohibiting the consumption of pork and alcohol, and finally in an apocalyptic battle, subdue the Anti-Christ, identified with 'the great liar' (*Al-Dajjāl*). Jesus will then die, this time after completing his mission. A burial spot is reserved for him, next to Muhammad, in Medina.

Muslims honour Jesus as a true son of Israel, a prophet who upheld the rigorous monotheism of Abraham, Isaac, and Jacob (Israel). The gospel of Jesus, *Al-Injīl* (an Arabic rendering of the Greek *euanggelion*) was a revelation sent down on Jesus, presumably in Aramaic, not the name of the genre invented to capture the truth about him in four gospels composed by inspired human authors about a generation after his death. (The plural for *injīl* does not occur in the Quran.) Jesus attempted unsuccessfully to recall his people to the high standards of the Torah. God permitted Jesus to repeal some laws imposed on the Jews as a penalty for their sins (Q:3:50; 4:160; 6:146); indeed there were no dietary laws in the time of Jacob who self-imposed some restrictions (Q:3:93). Jesus did not intend to establish a new religion, his mission being to confirm the one faith of submission (*islām*), which God inaugurated, through his messengers, as early as Noah (Q:42:13) and, according to tradition, even earlier – with Adam, the first prophet.

The Quran accuses Jews and Christians of *taḥrīf* (lit., adding a letter or word), the sin of altering existing scripture in order to avoid acknowledgement of the truth of Islam and of the authenticity of Muhammad's prophetic status (Q:2:75; 5:13). Muslims claim, with no independent evidence, that there was a proto-gospel whose contents were compatible with the data revealed in the Quran. Malicious alteration (*taḥrīf*) of revealed scripture explains the present disparity between the canonical New Testament and the Quranic view of Jesus' life and ministry. This charge could mean negligence of crucial revealed doctrines, mispronunciation of words, wilful misinterpretation or deliberate concealment of key claims, even textual deletion or addition (Q:2:159–60, 174–5; 3:78, 187).

Ethnic pride and envy of Muslim good religious fortune are said to have motivated the concealment or wilful alteration of earlier scripture, thus obviating the need to acknowledge Muhammad's legitimate claim to be the final prophet. His advent, under the title of Aḥmad, a comparative form, meaning more praised, was allegedly predicted by Jesus (Q:61:6) (The word 'Aḥmad' is related to 'Muhammad'.) Jews and Christians, asserts the Quran, secretly recognize the truth of revelations sent to Muhammad as easily as they recognize their own sons (Q:2:146, 6:20).[31] The Quran reiterates that the Christian community speculates much but knows little about Jesus. The Christian view of the ministry and nature of Jesus is fallible conjecture (*zann*; Q:4:157). 'And certainly *zann* avails nothing against truth' (Q:10:36; 53:28). The Quran sternly warns Christians against uttering falsehoods about God: the Trinity and Incarnation are metaphysically untrue and morally unworthy of God (Q:4:171). The Quran claims to vindicate the reputation of Jesus against the calumnies of Jews (Q:4:156–7) and the opposed exaggerations of Christians (Q:4:171; 19:35). The whole truth about Jesus, Muslims conclude, is found only in the Quran (Q:3:59–62; 19:34).

9

We move away from sectarian and fruitlessly polemical inter-faith controversies and instead identify the most general Islamic ideals. The Quran rejects the Judaeo-Christian notion of sympathetic divine kinship: a God concerned for his people or for his faithful believers like a loving father for his children (Q:5:18). It repudiates the Christian doctrine of God as father. This is remarkable since the notion of paternity combined with divinity would have been especially welcome in the patriarchal culture of Arabia. Indeed it would have been easier for the pagan Arabs to accept Muhammad as 'the son of Allah' rather than as the messenger of Allah. In the event, Islam proposes a political model of absolute divine kingship: a benevolent ruler and his subjects. God is the sovereign whose laws are promulgated and enacted by his spokesmen, the prophets. Islam contains no call to an *imitatio Dei* since what is required is obedience to God's will by obedience to his apostles, not imitation of the divine nature or moral life (Q:4:59, 64, 69, 80–1; 24:51–2). Christians participate in the moral life of God by imitating Christ. Again, Jews observe the Sabbath and share by association in the divine holiness and joy of the seventh day of creation.

This sets Islam apart. Jews struggle with God convinced that they, as the original people of covenant, matter to him.[32] Christians seek a human partnership with the divine in the enterprise of incarnational Christology, an enterprise Muslims dismiss as blasphemous mythology. The Quranic God does not morally need humankind. It is a legal relationship tempered by mercy and love. Jews and Christians read this fact backwards into the character of the Quranic God and dismiss him as cold and indifferent. Such a God could not be great. Muslims retort that such 'indifference' is not a denial of his greatness but rather its true quality. The deadlock here is permanent.

After the age of revelation ends and prophecy ceases, the deputy (*khalīfah*), a human and fallible leader, rules righteously by following Quranic guidelines. The four caliphs who succeeded Muhammad were 'the rightly guided successors' (*al-khulafā' al-rāshidūn*). But, unlike Muhammad, they were not divinely guided. Tracing the trajectory of the divine will as it is inserted into politics explains why Islam's political institutions are, unlike those of Christianity, distinctively Islamic. This organic link between the faith and the polis derivative from it is alien to the western post-Enlightenment notion of religion. Neglect or denial of this organic connection creates the needlessly insoluble problem of explaining why the post-Enlightenment model of religion, as an apolitical form of privatized piety, is rejected by modern Muslims. It is coherent to privatize a religious creed; it is incoherent to privatize a law code.

Islam was born as a faith and an empire, a twin birth. Muslims created an empire while Christians inherited an empire. Admittedly, early Islam assimilated the cultural products of Byzantium and Persia, enthusiastically employing talented Jews and Christians to build the new cosmopolitan, multi-lingual and multi-legal Muslim civilization. This is true but irrelevant. In tracing the trajectory and dilemmas of modern Islam, we must remember that Islam was, from its birth, a compulsively political and indeed politically successful religion. To say that politics and religion – two interests segregated theoretically and often practically in the modern occident – have been wrongly joined in the Islamic imperium is to assume without evidence that the association of any religion with politics must always be a disguise for illegitimate political power. It is senseless to accuse a religion, conceived as political, to have become politicized – as if only adverse and hostile circumstances forced Islam to adopt what could only be an extrinsic, perhaps superficial, interest in secular polity.

Buried beneath the rubble of endless Christian–Muslim polemics is an intractable difference over the meaning of religion. We may define religion in Protestant Christian terms as private, individual and voluntary although it is unlikely that any religion exists thus abstracted from social and political reality. Islam is explicitly public, communal and politicized, that is, coercive if and whenever empowered. The unavoidably political nature of the Islamic vision, visibly and viably rooted in Muslim tradition, is fundamentally different from modern Judaism and Christianity. Muslim religion is, ideally, public and communal; the politically empowered household of faith is the right framework for private and public religion. All Islamic duties, even individual ones, have their personal and social aspect. Revealingly, communities will be judged as communities on the day of reckoning (Q:4:41–2; 45:28–9).

No one of good will and impartiality would deny the permanent significance of Islam's monotheism. Islam has produced many men and women of character, devoted to noble ideals, especially to the pursuit of personal and communal justice. But in our age, marked by secularity and moral relativism, Islam is seen as only one interpretation of the human condition. The Muslim believer finds 'interpretation' precariously subjective and too personal for a reality as public and objective as Islam. This word insinuates the modern predicament of religion as it is cut down to size and put in its proper place. We may now say only that the Islamic hypothesis is, for Muslims, supported by the demands of reason, the requirements of sanity and the realities of current experience.

Islamic ideals are not, by religious standards, austere. Unlike more ascetic faiths, Islamic principles are often secular and pragmatic, as seen in the faith's relatively open-minded attitude towards sex, a minor theme of Chapter 11. Although contemplative Muslim traditions, especially in heterodox Sufi forms, contain elements of a mystical asceticism – poverty, silence[33] and solitude – mainstream Islam has not required most believers to adhere to such ideals. While admiring such spiritually lofty aspirations, the mainstream tradition emphasizes a sane and balanced commitment to an objective orthodoxy, social justice and personal self-restraint, requiring only that we do not recoil from the rigours of traditional faithful practice. We must resist the temptation to relax a faithful conscience in the face of widespread modern laxity in conduct and belief.

10

Western secularists startled religious believers by asking the sceptical and sinful question: Why should we think there is an order, a being, to which, to whom, the human will is legitimately subject? Out of this rebellious inquiry flowed a new stream of theory about the social causality of individual lives, an innovative secular account of the moral and legal foundations of responsible communal and personal conduct, novel and autonomous cultural beliefs and practices finally freed of religious restraint and scruple. In Europe, emancipated secular ways of thinking about human nature and its true resources inspired the formation of new social and political organizations destined, courtesy of direct colonization and long-range empire-building, to have global influence. Once Europeans had developed an alternative and convincing way of understanding life's mysteries and pressures, the hold of the comprehensive religious vision inevitably weakened.

Since the revelation of the Quran, Muslim thought in all fields, especially law, has flowed smoothly along the deep-cut grooves of custom sifted and sanctified by appeals to revelation and the Prophet's tradition. This universe collided with European expansionism which aimed to make the entire world in the image of Europe. Muslims dismissed the modern world, thus constructed, as a hindrance and an intrusive nuisance, a creation wholly of the secularized post-Christian West, an ideological frontier which, for indigenous reasons, was implacably opposed to any religion empowered as statehood.

For Europeans, the process of secularization begins with the New Testament concession to Caesar. The Pharisees and Sadducees try to trap Jesus but he confounds them with this novel division of labour: to God what belongs to God and to Caesar his due (Matthew 22:17–21). (Would Muhammad have said the same if Mecca had been under Roman occupation in the early seventh century?) Features of primitive Christianity explain the emergence of secularism some 17 centuries later in lands with a Christian heritage. The politically consequential dichotomy of religious–secular is native to the outlook of original Christianity. It is no coincidence that it ripens and emerges fully and boldly in the later history of Christianity rather than of Islam. Only from a Christianity founded as a salvation religion, a faith minus its law, could the secular child be born. Secularism could grow only from a faith concerned solely with the things of God, not those of Caesar – a dispensation divested of the sacred social and legal dimension. For Christians, the law is worldly, secular and merely political; it stands opposed to the greater (religious) gifts of grace and truth (John 1:17).

Predictably, secularism is pre-eminently suited to Protestant Christianity, a religion based on other-worldly doctrine, not this-worldly law. Islam is secular, that is, world-affirming, as a religion. This is shown by its intention to regulate Muslim lives in their religious and secular dimensions and moreover by its imperial reach immediately after its birth. However, this circumscribed secularism is an organic part of Islam understood as a twin birth of faith and empire. It remains subordinate to the applied bifocal Islam conceived as a religious vision with an inherent secular perspective. The confrontation therefore between Islam and secularism is not over the question of the acknowledgement of the secular realm. That the secular realm is an integral part of Islam is already acknowledged by the Quran – for internal Islamic reasons. The confrontation is about secularism's bold bid to change from being subordinate to *any* religion to being autonomous of and from *all* religion.

Christianity has permitted that latter development, a development subversive of religion *as such*, not only of Christianity. Although secularism was born in the manger of Jesus, in the cultural context of Christianity, it is a threat to every religious kingdom. The crucible of Christendom is only the aboriginal context of the secular insurrection against all traditional religion. It is the birth-place of what has now become a secular condition whose burden is felt world-wide. The burden is not evenly distributed: it is still most influential in European lands historically associated with Christianity but the virus of aggressive secularism is contagious, carried by a western culture with global extension.

The Enlightenment was, both in effect and in intention, the beginning of a reconciliation of revealed religion with the secular world – on wholly secular terms. Islam, as a faith confident of its transcendent powers, has rejected such enlightenment. As a twin birth of faith and power, that reconciliation was effected in the womb of its parent: the Quran had settled the question of the relationship between religious truth and secular power when it declared that secular power may legitimately establish religious truth and then serve it. Muslims regard the Christian decision, in its origins and subsequent history, as evidence of misguided priorities. We return to this theme in Section 12.

11

To understand the emergence of modern secularism, we trace the history of the genesis of the secular revolt against Christianity. In the Christian Middle Ages, a static but certain knowledge about humankind co-existed with little knowledge about external nature. Now we know much about cosmic nature but experience paralyzing doubts about our own nature. The Greeks, the first Europeans to cultivate the sceptical mentality, saw human nature as shaped by the necessities of the ethical, political and rational life. It was an empirical view of humanity whose accompanying ethics referred to human merit, not divine grace. Medieval Christians, however, understood human destiny as decided legitimately only in the quest of the individual soul, embedded in the bosom of the church, for the pre-destined end of salvation and eternal life through the enabling but undeserved grace of God.

Both the classical and medieval centuries possess a view of human nature as agreed, certain and unified. European certainty about human nature began to decline from the fourteenth to the seventeenth centuries. This decline was accompanied and perhaps partly caused by a decline of belief in the objectivity of morals. No objective morals, no human essence; and vice versa. The Greeks were confident of the objectivity of morals and, accordingly, felt certain about the true essence of humankind; their speculative adventures and doubts were restricted to the physical cosmos. The European Renaissance started a process that reversed this situation. Since the Enlightenment, even most Jews and Christians have come to view the empirical realities of nature and human nature, rather than the revealed realities of God and the supernatural, as the core of our knowledge of the cosmos and the heart of the special disciplines. All knowledge became anthropocentric as religion was reduced to being a human response to the anguish about our human lot.

The challenges to religious authority came from every quarter. The medieval system, unified by Catholic Christianity, began to decay from the fifteenth century onwards as traditional feudal society was challenged by widespread peasant discontent and by the rise of the cities and universities which heralded the emergence of national secular culture. Meanwhile, the Lutheran Reformation questioned the role and plenary authority of the ancient church. Despite these revolutionary changes, medieval Christendom remained feudal, isolated, religiously homogeneous and authoritarian: its urge to persecute the interior heretic and the exterior infidel was deep and permanent. The culmination of this process of questioning the sanctity of authority is encapsulated in the revealing motto of the Royal Society, the oldest learned society in the world, established in 1663: *Nullius in verba*. Take nobody's word for it, to translate it colloquially. In matters of empirical knowledge, this effectively rejects the joint authority of citation of the ancients and concordance with divine revelation, the two foundations of medieval scholasticism. Understandably, Francis Bacon (1561–1626), a daring thinker we encounter again in Chapters 3 and 8, is often invoked as the guiding spirit behind the Royal Society.

The Age of Reason, dated from Europe's early seventeenth century, did not intend to deny the existence of God. Rather it aimed at purging religion of its superstitions and fantastic dogmas in the hope of finding a residue more worthy of belief. Thomas Paine's influential *The Age of Reason* (published in 1794–6) is a passionate defence of deism, a jejune version of theism. Paine's god is the *deus otiosus* (the redundant god) who reveals his rational will solely through nature, the open book of God, and via unaided human mind and conscience. Prophets, miracles, and scripture – the paraphernalia of established religion – are, for Paine and his anemic deity, dangerous superfluities.[34]

After the seventeenth century, the rapid growth of the natural sciences and the industrialization of all aspects of life eventually led to the industrial revolution, the systematic application of the methods and discoveries of empirical science to the ends of industrial production. The last 250 years witnessed the spread and impact of industrial technology, the continuing colonization of the non-western world abetted by occidental maritime power, the democratic revolt against aristocracy (especially among the French peasantry and middle classes), the spectacular increase of urban populations, increasing access to public education and the growth of literacy. The net result is a vigorous western civilization that arose out of the debris of medieval Christendom.

Over the past 200 years, Christianity has been gradually reduced to a source of cultural continuity and identity, and, owing to a mistaken view of its origins, a source of western racial pride, especially among evangelical and right wing Christians. The religious authority of Christianity, as measured by indices such as ecclesiastical sovereignty over beliefs, morals and institutions (especially marriage), has dramatically eroded in the ideologically western world and in the Catholic Americas. This irreversible decline has been accompanied by a spectacular increase in the power of the economic motive which originally actuated the industrial revolution of the nineteenth century. A rural life lived close to nature's harmonious cycles and soothing periodicities was desecrated and replaced by a harsh mechanical life in cities such as London, the first sizeable metropolis of the modern world. Time was, after the advent of railways and mechanical locomotion, measured in terms of the working hour rather than the natural cycles of the rising and setting sun. If the early industrial period is characterized by hard work and productivity, late capitalism is a byword for leisure and conspicuous consumption.

Militant humanism, forged by apocalyptic European thinkers such as Nietzsche and Marx, repudiated not only the Christian faith but also challenged the total religious picture of a universe created and sustained by a benevolent transcendent supervisor. The comforting notion of a morally responsible providence at work behind nature's morally indifferent façade is, argued these two doctors of modernity, a legend that must now be stripped of its fantastic elements. There are no benign moral intentions lurking in the vast empty spaces of the natural cosmos. The metaphysical instinct that lies at the root of all religion, they concluded, widening their thesis from ethics to ontology, is prey to tragically mistaken illusions that appear constructive and comforting. The desire to transcend the natural and human world, our only world, is not only doomed to fail, it ought to fail so that humankind might finally learn to live at peace in a godless universe deliberately drained of religiously imposed purpose.[35]

12

What is the parallel Islamic narrative here? Have Muslims reached the historical juncture where an intellectually open confrontation between traditional Islam and modern secularism is inevitable? Is secularism currently an artificial challenge for Muslims? Islam has survived into the modern world and must therefore, for that reason alone, the apologist glibly argues, be worthy of being in the modern world. More plausibly, historically, the integrity of secularism was first established in western lands. Does the western experience and subsequent repudiation of the Christian religion conceal a universal historical pattern? (Islamic history, as religious history, has virtually no parallel with Christian history.) Indeed, why not Islamize secular modernity rather than modernize Islam? A Muslim may justifiably wonder why the certainties of secular liberalism should remain forever unchanged while ancient religion is expected to evolve and, in the case of Islam, evolve quickly under concentrated western intellectual and political pressure.

As many have noted since Christmas 1978,[36] the distinction between religion and secularism and the related vocabulary generated by this distinction are both foreign to Islam. In classical Arabic, as in Islamic languages that derive their political and religious lexicons from it, there are no dualities corresponding to religious and secular, spiritual and temporal, ecclesiastical and lay. There is only *dīn* (faith) and *dawlah* (state) – and both are religious notions. Influenced by western colonialism in the nineteenth and twentieth centuries, Muslims began to find or create new words that express the secular experience, first in Turkish – Turkey being the first and only secular 'Muslim' state – and later in modern Arabic, Persian, Urdu, Malay, Swahili, and so on.

Partly owing to this linguistic restriction, almost all traditional Muslim thinkers and activists are indifferent to secular possibilities outside received religious doctrines. Khomeini, to take an example from the minority Shi'ite community, believed that western laicized thought should be ignored rather than engaged or refuted. The resurgence of Islam as a political force opposing western political designs has inspired a conservative scholarship which rejects issues such as secularism and religious pluralism as western issues and dismisses western criteria of rationality and plausibility as 'occidocentric'. The West, blinded by its own economic interests, is thought to be incapable of maintaining even a sympathetic, let alone a balanced or just, view of Islam.

Owing to the clarity and certainty of the Quran's message, new generations of Muslims remain convinced of the truth of Islam. Secularism is seen as a proof of our need for religion, not an objection to it. All Muslims, with the exception of those who have adopted western attitudes and views, often without sustained reflection, are indifferent to the secular sceptical verdict on religion. Even secularized Muslims are only ritually unobservant, not necessarily agnostic or atheist. Devout Muslims see the world of secular culture as a western colonial construct, a carefully crafted sinful chaos where divine norms are mocked as silly and infantile by godless European nations. Modern society is viewed as an environment created by Europeans with the express aim of violating God's laws.

Like Christians, Muslims proselytize; but Islam, unlike its rival, has not suffered a massive leakage from the vessel of faith. There is therefore no internal stimulus to develop a natural theology or theodicy or a principled response to secular challenges. Islam has no tradition of dogmatic theology; and its dialectical apologetic theology is largely an answer to the Judaeo-Christian attack on its bases. Few, if any, Muslims, have experienced the moral and metaphysical uncertainties characteristic of modern pluralist secularized culture in which doubt is virtually orthodoxy.

13

The public face of all ideologies and faiths is, however, a carefully crafted lie. Insight into the cunningly duplicitous behaviour of the Islamic chameleon is available only to the perceptive student, not to western liberal writers and journalists spending time with the natives in order to gather materials for their next book. A careful exploration confirms that the externally uniform religious discipline in traditional Muslim lands is internally disturbed by ferments provided by the internet, western permissive cultural forces, and the rapid transition into a world designed mainly by westerners. Only philosophy and its liberal influence are totally absent. We discern an unacknowledged fascination with foreign western exemplars (such as liberal democracy) even though Muslims are still madly in love with their glorious past. Their own present is inglorious – and they claim to be indifferent to the secular West's glorious present.

Unlike modern western Christianity and Reform Judaism, Islam has kept most of its followers on an exacting plane of religious, moral, and ritual obligation. The custodians of Islam have ensured that the contemplative and moral dimensions of faith are not substituted for, or elevated to being superior alternatives to, the regular performance of ritual duty. The result: all Islam is applied Islam. Until recently, the adjectives 'religious' and 'observant' were unnecessary in qualifying the noun 'Muslim'. The scrupulous external observance of the entire range of Islamic duties is now largely restricted to mosque personnel entrusted with the guardianship of Islam and charged with the transmission of its values to a new generation reared in the lap of western secularism with its promise of freedom, and, therefore, hedonism. The number of defiantly orthodox practising Muslims, however, even in the secularized West, is unaccountably and increasingly large. Insofar as modern Islamic reform movements seek to change the traditionally sanctioned priority of praxis, they must fail. Ritual duty, in the law-centred faith of Islam, cannot be attenuated into symbolic gestures or total negligence.[37]

Politically assertive revivalist Islam in the Muslim world co-exists with indigenous cultural forces which extol foreign exemplars, especially western liberal democracy. Muslim preachers from the Indian subcontinent now preach Islam not to Europeans but rather to Arab Muslims in the richer Gulf states where the antennae of new satellite dishes dotted on the sky-line compete with the older minarets. Leaders of revivalist movements call for a return to the pristine Islam of Muhammad and the early pious community (*al-salaf*).[38] Islamic history contains many recrudescences of this tenacious conservatism which seeks to restore the purity of the original faith by curing it of contamination by profane and miasmic foreign influences. A conscientious religious awareness of the world co-exists awkwardly with the anarchies of desire exported from the West and bearing the hallmarks of a free-ranging caprice alien to the regulated piety of Islam. In the 'theo-nomocratic' states of Saudi Arabia, Iran and Sudan, this orthodoxy is still largely enforced by a fervent and effortless belief in the reality of the threat of eschatological sanctions mentioned in the Quran and by the coercive power of paternalistic legislation in this world. Private religious virtue is enforced by public legislation that seeks to quell revolts against an ancient orthodoxy of intellect, taste and behaviour. However, this provincial orthodoxy is despised by some secularized Muslims since it stifles the human spirit as expressed in intellectual creativity, beauty and art.[39]

A theocracy is a society in command of its members' public and private moral and religious convictions. Islam contains a developed theocratic doctrine: every detail of life, including areas considered secular by post-Enlightenment westerners, is systematically subjected to religious jurisdiction. No area of human experience is, in principle, beyond the scope of the holy law.[40] Secular attitudes must therefore progress insidiously since no open acknowledgement of such tendencies is normally allowed. With the exception of Turkey, secularism is not explicit or pronounced in any Islamic nation. In Iran, the secular sub-culture is acknowledged and tolerated with condescension, a stance that contrasts with the western attitude of tolerating religious sub-cultures while letting secularism reign supreme in the public square.

An indication of the insidious presence of secular attitudes is the newly created ghetto for traditional religion in the midst of an otherwise markedly secular structure of thought and behaviour. The isolation and the subsequent attenuation of religion in this style are commonplace in the West. This natural next step has not been taken in the Islamic world where Islam permeates society and culture making such attenuation unthinkable.

Nevertheless, in countries such as Pakistan, Malaysia and Egypt, many social functions and television programmes, virtually wholly secular in content and ethos, are burdened by a religious preamble that is unrelated to, or in conflict with, the rest of the programme or broadcast. An obligatory prefatory recitation of the Quran conflicts with the bulk of the day's programmes which promote crass materialism and some sensuality though never in a way that might excite charges of blasphemy or travesty. This juxtaposition suggests that modern believers entertain a generally religious view of the aims of life but are in practice tempted by a secular view of life's potential. Islam is effectively relegated to the private sector of theoretical conviction while appearing to be in charge of the public sector of practical experience. The resulting schizophrenia is readily apparent to Muslims who have lived in secular or more honest cultures.

There is a larger politically charged dimension to this tense situation which must be briefly recorded though its implications are beyond the scope of this essay. Most Islamic regimes show plenty of rhetorical support for Islam while concealing their contempt. Kemal Ataturk of Turkey and the deposed Shah of Iran were exceptional in showing open contempt for Islamic symbolism in public life. Indeed Ataturk even Latinized the Arabic script of Turkish. The Iranian religious intelligentsia opposed the Latinization of the Farsi script and vetoed the proposed replacement of the Islamic calendar with the Persian imperial calendar. Islam would count the centuries.

14

Heraclitus of Ephesus (*c* 540–475 BCE), who sought a single unifying insight into reality, is credited with the aphorism *Panta rhē* (All things flow).[41] He might have meant that there are no permanent substances in nature, that only flux is real. But, in a more general sense, the transience of things impressed other ancient cultures too, especially the Arab poets as we see in Chapter 11. Everything changes over time; hence the necessity of tradition as an anchor.

The current ubiquity of dislocating change invites a discussion of the role of tradition, a strategic concept in religion, intimately linked to the anxiety about identifying and maintaining legitimate authority, especially the authority of the unalterable sacred word. The primacy of tradition is axiomatic in world religions, the most ancient of supra-national organizations. The issue of tradition, introduced here in a general way, is relevant to the rivalry between classical (traditional) and the liberal (contemporary) significances of the interpreted Quran discussed in Chapter 6, the dispute over the authority of the book debated in Chapter 7, and the maintenance of a continuous religious tradition threatened by reductionist capitulation to secularism, a theme of Chapters 11 and 12. Here I explore the crucial question of the status of tradition in a living religion undergoing seismic internal and external pressures for change and adaptation.

Islam has a complex and continuous history despite the trauma of colonialism which culminated in the symbolically significant wound inflicted on Islam's body politic with the abolition of the caliphate in Ottoman Turkey in 1924.[42] Muslims, in their legitimate desire to maintain continuity with their glorious past, have been reluctant to accept change and novelty in religious matters. This is an attitude with ambiguous potentialities. It is a mainspring of strength since Islam has not been plagued with a problem that potentially endangers every religion whose dogmatic credentials are part of its historical foundations. A historical religion cut adrift from its historical moorings must flounder for want of a doctrinal anchor in the present. The case of Protestant Christianity is a sufficient warning.

The liability is that a faith with too strong a sense of its tradition and history could easily become straitjacketed and irrelevant to our contemporary situation. A formative influence, in the case of a movement or ideology, no less than in the case of an individual, can be too decisive, even determinative. Moreover, Muhammad, unique among seminal religious figures of the past, is known to us intimately in the present. Perhaps we know too much of his normative praxis. This knowledge could act as an incubus on new reforming departures in the present. If Islam remains tethered to a partly outdated scheme of things Arabian, the explanation lies in the posthumous authority of a Muhammad known to history with excessive clarity and to Muslims with excessive authority. Such an Islam, unreformed and unresponsive to the present, paralyzed by its knowledge of its origins, may cease to be a relevant and live option for the intellectually sophisticated individual who has conscientious reservations about the truth of some its claims. Muslims will lose their faith only if, in a new age, their Islam creates more crises than it overcomes.

15

Before we probe normative Islam's attitudes towards change, we note the meta-religious dimension of Quranic self-consciousness. Islam represents the earliest historical attempt to take a perspective on religion as such, religion in its totality rather than as one religion among many. Some recent eclectic and syncretic religious movements, such as the Baha'i faith, seek to finalize, even transcend, all religion. Islam, however, remains at once the earliest meta-religion and the last largely successfully universal faith.

Normative Islam's self-estimate as climactic and ultimate (Q:45:6), a meta-religion revealed to correct and perfect all religion as such, dictates its attitudes towards change and towards rival faiths. The scripture is self-described as the final revelation (Q:7:185), a protector–guarantor (*al-muhaymin*)[43] of all revelation (Q:5:48) and a confirmation of previous revelations (Q:3:3), a finality that corresponds to Muhammad's status as the seal of all prophecy (Q:33:40).[44] Muhammad is ordered to avoid schismatic tendencies (Q:6:159) since there is only one religion before God and this religion is as old as Adam and Noah. By implication, the Quran authorizes Muslims to view Islam, once it has appeared on the historical plane, as complete, as the culmination of religion. No crucial new development is hidden in the womb of Islam's future.[45]

The Quran conceives of Islam not merely as another religion among religions but rather as the decisive religion, a meta-religion (*al-dīn*), a self-image that was bound to encourage universal expansion. The word *al-dīn* occurs only in the singular and with the definite article in the Quran since there is only one true religion. (The plural *adyān* never occurs.)

Islam, intentionally universal and universalizing, is conceived as a spiritual globalization project whose latitude is apparent in its self-naming as an attitude.[46] A religion is expected to be intimately linked with its founder especially in the case of Islam which, unusual if not unique among religions, was founded by the man considered to be its founder. 'Muhammadianity' or 'Arabianity' would have reflected a more generic link with the founder, the land of origin, and hence the ethnicity, location and reception of the aboriginal creed. But the faith is only attitudinally self-described.

Islam's self-image as meta-religion partly explains the Muslim decision to confront rather than accommodate secularism. Islam and secularism compete to be considered as the culmination of history, both entertaining a similar self-image: each assesses itself as the last rung on the historical ladder. Modern secularism, conceived as humanitarian liberalism, sees itself, not without reason, as the moral climax and end of history. Equally, from its own perspective, Islam, as meta-religion, represents authentic religion as such. Basically and subliminally, perhaps even intentionally, the secular tendency to single out Islam for attacks that betray prejudicial rigour, while shielding other – usually eastern – religions under a patronizing lenience, is motivated by the unconscious hostility between two competitive totalitarian visions of history's trajectory.[47]

This meta-religious Islamic self-image has profound but unexplored political implications. For example, Marxists often condemn what they perceive as Islam's antipathy to secular history interpreted as an inescapable force that conditions and tethers all cultures and religions. They abjure its ideologically motivated anti-historicism. Read correctly, however, the Islamic position is a commitment to the transcendence of history within history: Islam has already consummated all history, sacred and profane, through the success of its political utopia in Medina in the seventh century. Unlike Marxists, Muslims are not waiting for the historical process to patronize their cause. Any Quranic philosophy of history, inevitably providential, linear and universal, is also apocalyptic and climactic. Muslim activists taunt Marxist secularists that Islam has already succeeded in creating its utopia – in the past – while Marxists merely dream of one in the distant future.

16

Reflective modern believers cannot ignore the tension between the accumulated weight of tradition and the immediacy of the present moment. Many Muslims want to achieve co-existence with the secular world but they refuse to disown problematic parts of the Quran. Why do they hesitate to make this sacrifice at the altar of secularism when other religious believers, with equally proud and inflexible attitudes sustained by huge deposits of traditional faith, have gradually genuflected to the infant god of secularism? The main reason is that Muslims see themselves, from the earliest times, as alone in carrying the torch of pristine monotheism. They are proud to be custodians of the Quran in Arabic, a book revered by them as the world's only extant fully preserved scripture. In celebrating the book's undeniable freedom from textual corruption, they also laud it as the immutable word of God, equally applicable in all places and times. Muslims dismiss the Jewish and Christian accommodation with secularism as further evidence that these more relaxed freelance monotheists were always guilty of disloyalty to their revealed traditions (Q:2:44; 3:99; 5:59–60). Indeed, during Islam's lengthy and lenient ascendancy in Europe and the Middle East, Islamic law demanded that Jews and Christians be faithful to their own revelations and observe the laws revealed in the Torah and the Gospel (Q:5:66, 68).

The second reason is rooted in the traditional tendency to condemn all religious innovation *(biḍ'ah)* as heretical. The Quran interdicts hypothetical speculation and speculative curiosity in religious doctrine and practical religious conduct (Q:17:36; 49:12). The popular Algerian proverb, 'The conditional sentence opens the door to Satan', well captures this sentiment. The concept of *biḍ'ah* is used to oppose the notion of *sunnah*, the normative path trodden by Muhammad and the early community. A widely quoted tradition of the Prophet warns his people to avoid all novelties since these lead to error and hence to hell.

Islam's classical intelligentsia does not accept this tradition literally. An exception is the Hanbalite champion of orthodoxy, Taqī Al-Dīn Ibn Taymīya (d. 1328), intellectual father of modern Wahhabi literalism. He rejected all innovation as automatically heretical. The liberal opinion of Imam Al-Shafi'i, a founder of one of the four classical schools of law *(madhhab;* sing.; *madhāhib*, pl.), is universally respected. He distinguished between two types of novelties *(muḥdathāt)*. A novelty that contradicts the Quran or the Prophet's custom or a report *(āthār)* from the early community or the consensus *(ijmā')* of any current Muslim community is a reprehensible innovation *(biḍa'at ḍalalah)*. A novelty that is intrinsically good and does not contradict the above authorities is 'an unblameworthy innovation' *(biḍ'at ghayr madhmūmah)*. As Islam expanded into an empire, jurists were forced, by pragmatic considerations, to recognize further distinctions between forbidden, reprehensible, permissible (neutral) and indeed even recommended and obligatory innovations.[48] Innovation was considered reprehensible, however, in matters of faith: the Quran and the Prophet were jointly sufficient. No mosque councils met to hammer out dogma; and all philosophical adventurism that might have challenged orthodoxy's conservative certainties died in its infancy, as we shall see in Chapter 2.

The faith of Muhammad is a restoration of the pristine faith of Adam, Noah and Abraham (Q:42:13). This dogmatically motivated Quranic conquest of the past determines a special view of tradition. Chapter 46 (v. 9) instructs Muhammad: 'Say: "My case is no innovation *(biḍ'an)* among the messengers".' Muhammad does not bring a new message (Q:21:24–5; 41:43; 43:45); he claims no religious originality. (One wonders what would amount to originality in a historical religion claiming to be a confirmation of a precedent.[49]) 'A witness from the Children of Israel' has testified to the similarity between Islam and earlier revelations (Q:46:10).[50] All messengers belong to a single brotherhood (Q:23:51–3); all promised God that they would support fellow and previous messengers (Q:3:81; 33:7–8).

The motivation for the strong repudiation of innovation is connected to a feature of Muhammad's mission. The Apostle's sole divinely imposed duty is to convey a sacred message (*balāgh*) to an ignorant people (Q:13:40). (Martin Buber said that a prophet is a man of action who, unlike a thinker, has no ideas, only a message.[51]) The Quran warns Muhammad that he must convey the message exactly as he receives it, without addition or change (Q:69:44–7). A messenger commissioned to deliver a message cannot indulge in personal fancies, let alone take the high road to theological speculation and adventurism. This Quranic constriction of Muhammad's religious and literary role decisively influenced Islam's attitude towards theology, an enterprise suspect in the eyes of orthodoxy and often seen as irredeemably hypothetical and conjectural if not redundant or heretical.[52]

17

Defined neutrally as a system of belief rooted in the past, traditionalism is expectedly doctrinally unambitious: it cannot assign original dogmatic tasks to those who succeeded the first generation. The first generation itself has no original task since it receives the raw material from heaven – although it does actively witness it taking shape in the human world. The twofold duty of Muslims who succeeded the early community was to preserve this original pure Islam and then to transmit the faithful heritage to future generations, a duty that Muslims have discharged with dedication. The normative desire to bring the early Muslim vision within the range of every new generation implies that Islam, at a given point in its history, is authentic only insofar as it resembles the original faith. Therefore, doctrinal deviation, whether through addition, deletion, creative variation, or outright alteration, invariably earned censure and rebuke. Deviation was necessarily innovation – the unforgivable sin of doctrinal reform in a direction away from the original template. Muslims see themselves as either maintaining or debasing Islam, never as improving it. The perfect Islam could only be tarnished by later generations: religion in its history must always be a tale of the pilgrim's regress.

The potter's wheel continues to spin from its own momentum; the foot was released from the treadle some 1,425 years ago. It is lamented nowadays that no one has been able to stop the wheel from spinning in the same direction after the first push by the brave and energetic early Muslims. Islam, it is charged, has had no reformation or enlightenment. This is a standard but, for two reasons, incorrect reading of Muslim history. First, undeniably, Islam has had no reformation or enlightenment or an age of reason or liberal thought. But Islam was, in a sense, born already as a reformed faith. In principle, at least, it had no mediating and meddlesome clergy, little of the religious obscurantism of medieval Catholicism, and no iconography that could arouse a new iconoclasm. Original Islam was democratic and egalitarian: all believers had ready access to their scripture since there were no corrupt autocratic hierarchies and no official mediation between humankind and God.

Secondly, Islam has had several periods of reform but their impulse and direction was, with rare exceptions, conservative: each took the faith back to its pristine roots.[53] Islam has not had any reformation whose intention was to reform the faith in the direction of liberalism – a secular reform entailing greater respect for the autonomy of secular reason and for the agnostic option in religion. The only indigenous exceptions are the rationalist school of theologians, the Mu'tazlites, and the Islamic philosophers, neither of whom had any lasting influence on Muslims. We discuss both schools of thought in Chapter 2.

Western stimuli for reform of Islam were, as they still are, by virtue of externality, automatically suspect. Muslims suspect that the forces which masquerade as reformist movements are often aimed at the disintegration of Islam: they receive too enthusiastic a patronage from the Christian West for Muslims to believe that they are intended for their good. Only a major heretical movement internal to Islam could create a humanist renaissance that was theologically a credible response to the crises of secular modernism.

Granted that the Reformation, which led to the development of Protestant organizations in Europe, is a false parallel, the outsider still wonders how and when Islam will change theologically in the face of secular challenge. Martin Luther reformed Christianity some 1,500 years after its birth. Is not Islam about the same age now?

18

While tradition can act as an incubus, a weighty deposit inhibiting new doctrinal departures, equally it can be an organic part of the faith in every age, thus stimulating a healthy respect for the best of the past. We see this clearly if we examine the indispensability of inherited tradition in another ancient discipline: philosophy. Religion and philosophy are human endeavours of considerable pedigree and share much in common, as we explore in the next chapter. It is intriguing that the status of tradition in a self-consciously traditional religion such as Islam should resemble the (recommended) status of the received tradition in an ancient discipline such as philosophy.

As professors of western philosophy, we teach students to treat even past philosophers as though they were our intellectual contemporaries. We acknowledge that past masters worked under different historical conditions and few were trained to be professional academic philosophers sustained by university posts. Nonetheless, we expect each new generation of philosophers to think of, say, Plato as a fellow seeker after truth, someone whom we could imagine debating with us in our graduate colloquia. Most modern thinkers are as impressed by the arguments and analyses, though not by the scientific beliefs and theories, of Plato and Aristotle as they might be with the efforts of the best of their own strictly temporal contemporaries.[54]

To examine our proposed analogy, all extant intellectual disciplines, like all religions, have a history and a continuing tradition. But philosophy is unique in that its historical development is carried in the minds of its practitioners as part of their current intellectual equipment. This is not true of empirical science which has disowned its early rather crude historical efforts, such as those of alchemy and astrology, as mistaken in content and method. The tradition, judged as worth preserving, begins much earlier in philosophy than in other disciplines. Indeed the *whole* apparatus of philosophy is forwarded into each new epoch, as if there had been no progress. Admittedly, we do not transmit a tradition like a torch between runners in a relay race: we add and change before we transmit it further. A competent modern philosopher can therefore engage the seminal thinkers of our past, especially the Greek trio: we do not begin afresh in philosophy. In the case of Islam too, no one could, for example, ignore the past masters in exegesis or the early jurists. In Chapter 7, where we debate the continuing authority of scripture, we shall explore the link between the ongoing tradition of a faith and its earliest essence.

19

While neophobia is justified during times of rapid and global change, no religious tradition can avoid ossification or death if it is frozen or arrested in time. The House of Islam cannot be closed temporarily for repair or reform. Individual Muslims will change part of it, adapt it, perhaps transform it. There is no extra-historical Archimedean point from which believers could build a scaffold around their faith and try to amend it or alter it. It is a precarious undertaking within history; it must dirty and burn our hands.

No living religion can settle permanently into a supra-historical fixity of doctrine. If it does, it will be an ossified orthodoxy in danger of extinction. A mental lag in religious categories of thought, the secular suspicion that they are outdated, will make faith a superfluous and optional extra. Every historical religion is concerned both with the pedigree of inherited doctrine and its contemporaneous relevance. This necessitates periodic creative re-interpretations conditioned by the march of history. A revelation provides us with absolute immutability of dogma, sustained in a paralytic crescendo that continually transcends history – but at the level of interpretation, it remains relative and situational, reflecting and serving contemporaneous human needs. No faith can be understood or practised outside its actual tradition and doctrinal framework; equally, any faith which loses the capacity to transcend the loyalties of its existing adherents is inexorably destined for obsolescence.

Muslims must choose between an archaic conservatism that must surely perish and a flexible conservatism that knows the true value of tradition. Modern Muslims become instantly radical when they oppose the dehumanizing shibboleths of secularist individualism flourishing in late capitalism: the consumerism and alienation of an advanced industrialization that reduces all relationships to commodities. When Muslims, zealous for their faith, hold fast to anachronistic cultural and religious beliefs such as slavery and slave concubinage, they display not radicalism but an absurd obscurantism long refuted by the march of history. Traditionalism, in an approbative sense, is respect for the right traditions, not an uncritical adherence to all traditions. The latter stance trivializes the value of the past and denigrates the integrity of the present.

20

While a sacerdotal hierarchy still administers sacramental versions of Christianity, such ordained orders are, for Jews, largely vestigial as the relics of the *kohān'īm* (priests); in the case of the simpler monotheism of Islam, such delegated or mediated authority was never sanctioned.[55] Traditional Muslim scholars *('ālim,* sing. *'ulamā'* pl; Q:35:28) can and do, however, function as priests. Jurists and commentators on the Quran and the Prophetic traditions function as hierophants claiming privileged expertise and access to the true meaning of classical sacred texts. Their assets include a thorough absorption of the knowledge of their holy heritage; they are trained to appreciate its conscientious spirit and ethos. However, an excessive reverence for this sacred past, preserved as written text and appropriated through rote learning, helps Muslims to simply memorize rather than resourcefully master, their heritage. It accounts for a major liability: many traditional scholars are addicted to jejune and static criteria of assessment that prevent their core convictions from being purged of narrow inherited certainties.

Unlike the Christian and Jewish clergy, Muslim religious scholars survive on an imbalanced traditional diet of stale certainties – with little mainstream training in the general knowledge of the age. Recently, some Islamic seminaries (*madrasah*; *madāris*, pl.)[56] have started to update their curriculum to take account of the ubiquity of English as a strategically useful language of communication – though, naturally, not of identity, especially religious identity. Even today, some traditional Islamic scholars have difficulty forming even one complete declarative sentence in English, the language of the modern media. The obsolete educational curriculum of the traditional religious schools is the cause of the intellectual stupor and paralysis that has long gripped the Muslim world. All innovative thought is found outside the traditional guardianship of Islamic orthodoxy just as much of the current political activism has abandoned the quietist and apathetic strictures of a conservative piety indifferent to and insulated from the daily plight of vulnerable Muslim minorities world-wide.

Islam's traditional intelligentsia generally interprets the Quran and the Prophet's customary practice through the filter of legal canons established a few centuries later. By using the later (but nonetheless classical) legal parameters to monitor the degree of acceptable change, this procedure inhibits any truly innovative or creative interpretation of the two founding texts, the Quran and Muhammad's authentic traditions. This rigid definition of the parameters of traditional self-understanding ensures that Islam cannot now be discovered suddenly to be something essentially different from what it has been for some 1,400 years. The supremacy of initial conditions is as consequential in Islam as in big bang cosmology. Muslims proudly admit that Islam is not a progressive religion: its values and beliefs are immutably set down in a canonical book. This view is not implausible. A progressive religion, founded on change and doubt, the chief ingredients of progress, is unlikely to endure. The philosophical Protestantism, the deism of the eighteenth century, is a rare example of a progressive faith; it died a natural death.

Muslim literalists, unlike the traditionalists, claim to establish a direct link with the early community, an immediate charismatic connection with the authority of the word of God – by cutting through intervening history and by discarding the mediation of juridical schools. They claim to identify and follow a pristine Muhammadan exemplar where only the literal text of the Quran has coercive power: interpretation softens the keen-bladed existential impact of the sacred word, allowing casuistry and thus the devious escape from unwelcome divine demands.[57] These purists belittle orthodox Quranic interpretation and claim that so-called exegetes are merely translators – as if translation were not already a form of interpretation! Such literalist Muslims are hardly ready to substitute modern uncertainties and western platitudes of increasing generality for the comforting and trusted apodictic affirmations of the ancient Quran. In times of political crisis and irresistible social change, it is natural to desire infallibility and unequivocal certainty.

Literalists may adopt apolitical or political stances. Muslim activists, interested in empowering modern Islam, add (defensive) jihad to the other desiderata, in order to deal with external enemies of the faith. Management of internal dissent is considered irrelevant as it only arises in the absence of the caliph. Once appointed, he would be empowered to execute the will of God on earth – though he can only act after due consultation (*shūra*) with competent believers (Q:42:38).

In the case of the literalists, notwithstanding their lofty pretensions, all has been surrendered not to God but to a text which is gang-raped to yield whatever ephemeral slogan they need. The anointed ones speak the rhetoric of truth, goodness, and justice but they are gilding their hidden lust for power. Religious conviction is not something the *'ulamā'* possess; rather it possesses them. They are not readers of the book of God but rather slaves of the book since they mistake a closed canon for a revelation. A revelation must emancipate thought and reason rather than reduce the functions of reason to merely finding analogical parallels and mining exegetical treasures.

21

The changes taking place in the Islamic world for the past half a millennium have been caused mainly by contact with the colonizing West. Virtually all Muslim nations have been conquered or occupied by western powers. Ideologically, one goes West wherever one goes. There are also, however, owing to migration and settlement, sizeable Muslim communities inhabiting the geographical West which can no longer be seen as an amorphous and distant realm peopled by an abstract foe. Western Muslims deal with a democratic and lenient version of the West as embodied in institutions of elected government, voluntary charitable bodies, higher learning, art and culture. For the overwhelming majority of Muslims, however, the West with which they must contend is the powerful and militant West as it seeks to impose its economic, cultural, and political will on the Islamic world.

Only liberal, rationalist and reformist Muslim intellectuals, usually living in western lands, want a wholly new orientation towards antique text and tradition, one which would in effect elevate reason over revelation, and emphasize the primacy of the individual over the community. Typically, they are a product of western secularism imposed on Muslims during colonial times. Their motto is 'The West is the best'. Some are secretly atheists but not conscientious ones. Politically, they support laicism, political separation of mosque and state, the emancipation and enfranchisement of women and the promotion of the rights of protected religious minorities. They make an abject surrender to western criteria of judgement in all things and other Muslims therefore dismiss them as 'westoxicated'.

The term 'westoxication' (or 'westitis') translates the Persian word *gharbzadegi* coined in the 1960s by the Iranian social analyst Jalal Al-i Ahmad.[58] It described the suffocation felt by a world plagued by an all-encompassing western cultural and intellectual presence. Muslim, especially Iranian, intellectuals were West-smitten crypto-Marxists who flirted with and embraced wholesale western ideas and ideals at the expense of their indigenous and Islamic traditions of thought and scholarship. Many smuggled Marxism and political nationalism, suitably disguised as Islamic socialism or pan-Islamism, into the House of Islam. These intellectuals, some exiled from their nations, mistake their personal depression (over losing their homeland to the radicals) for objective political commentary. They are lucky enough to make a living out of their mistake since most are darlings of the western media. Muslims, however, do not recognize themselves in their lengthy tracts crowded with clichés – though they themselves imagine that they shall be heard and heeded for their many words.

The desire for a re-empowered Islam is a reaction against the excesses of colonialism which has made Muslims keenly aware of their political impotence. Muslims want to live with the West, not under it. A narrow and intolerant secularism has inspired a narrow and intolerant Islam. There are some Muslims and many Christians who now propose a powerless and depoliticized Islam as the best dialogue partner with modernism.[59] I believe the opposite: an appropriately empowered Islam will be a more confident and therefore more generous partner in the dialogue of civilizations. It will permit Muslims to make appropriate concessions to the modern world – by shedding outdated parts of their ancient heritage and burdensome tradition. If Muslims controlled their destiny and enjoyed the sanction of political power, this would limit the ability of powerful western nations to mock and demean, with total impunity, Muslim sanctities and sensibilities. Muslims would therefore feel respected by the community of nations. At the moment, most Muslims are powerless; and powerlessness corrupts. If the world does not care, there are ways of making it care. That is the callous reasoning behind the increasingly desperate strategy of indiscriminate political violence against innocent targets.

22

The current conflict in Islam is neither between reformers and conservatives, nor, as in modern Judaism and Christianity, between different reformers. The Muslim disagreement is between two types of conservatives: those who wish to conserve the received (revealed) tradition while making appropriate theological and political concessions to the modern cultured critics of Islam, on the one hand, and those who refuse to lift their heads above the dogmatic parapet, on the other, insisting that true Islam is a city besieged by the forces of western secularism, a city that must resist or die. The second group appeals to the raw simplicity of original Islam which never yielded to the pressures of recalcitrant historical experience or to the demands of pragmatism and professional diplomacy.

Muslims must admit that ancient Islam cannot manage the modern world in terms of the innocent categories of its classical tradition; therefore, Muslim civilization is in the throes of secularity. Strictly traditional Islam is being reduced to a legacy, a sign of decline. Western scholars study it and box it into multi-volume sets. No one cuts open the bark of a living tree to see if the sap runs: Muslims are not compiling encyclopedias of the secular western world.

An internal struggle between the intellectuals and the religious intelligentsia, both of whom wish to preserve the past, will pit religiously learned Muslim intellectuals, who recognizably belong to their faith, against the traditional intelligentsia who see themselves as God's anointed. This will be a religious battle, not merely a political squabble between radicals and moderns that leaves Islam theologically intact. Islam's unofficial clergy are jurists who pretend to sit in judgement on the possibility or impossibility of all knowledge, not only legal knowledge. Some jurists, given the pragmatic nature of law, are willing to compromise intelligently with modern society. The literalist exegetes among them, angered by the keen pace of history, want to turn Muslims into pure transparent vessels ready to receive a faith that grows out of nowhere, a historical vacancy. This fantasy of religious virginity is realizable only in small tribal communities. The rest of the world has moved on.

Muslims must face the fact that Islam originated as a revolutionary movement with the normal quota of bloodshed, compromise and hypocrisy. Apologists for every defeated civilization speak of a return to a pure past. Their idealism is forgivable as a factual error about a dead past; it is unforgivable as an error that leads to political tragedy in the living present. The past is paradise only because the present is hell. Muslim apologists often appeal to a mythical Islam of pure freedom, a utopian fantasy that collides with the facts of early Islamic history. There was, until recently, in the West, a similarly romantic view of the glory that was Greece and the grandeur that was Rome. Classical antiquity was, as western historians now realize, full of brutality and squalor.

This attempt to convince westerners that true Islam is perfect and that all true Muslims are, really, nice guys tormented by the immoral audacity of those few but omnipresent villains, the Muslim 'fundamentalists', is one of the recurrent fantasies of the moderate Muslim apologetic imagination. Though misguided, one can understand its appeal at a time of fundamental and universal hostility to Islam. But why should all Muslims be nice guys? There are no books by westerners arguing that all westerners, deep down, are rather splendid human beings. That any group of people be uniformly pleasant is an unacceptable moral demand.

Conservative Islamic forces now confront the opposed forces of a neoteric secular pragmatism. Religious tradition, expressed as convention, collides with the secularized individualism of a contemporary Islam which refuses to couch every novel proposal in traditional terms. The accumulated weight of custom and convention is thus occasionally simply ignored rather than assessed or countered. Only orthodox Muslims, nourished on staid theological repetition and utopian simplicities, still use the vocabulary of an innocent classical tradition.

Every reformer must, however, pay the obligatory lip-service to Muhammad's utopian vision. Every modern advocacy, no matter how secular in its guiding impulse, is strategically forced to claim the Prophet as one of its men. In different famous hands, he appears as anything ranging from a Sufi pacifist who spent all his time in his local mosque to a revolutionary keen to confront the Muslim version of the axis of evil (America, Israel and Britain), anything from a guarantor of gender equality to a confirmed misogynist. And this range does not include the more esoteric interpretations of Muslims who claim an elite mystical sophistication. One may admire the intellectual subtleties with which such theological adventurism is justified but one is religiously obliged to deplore its dishonesty. We return to these internal tensions in Chapter 11.

23

Until recently, people in virtually every culture spontaneously believed in fate and destiny rather than choice and freedom. They were convinced of pre-ordained courses of existence, of assigned roles and stations that were inherited, not created. Their social experience of and their negotiation with the external cosmos jointly confirmed and nourished this certainty. Moral and religious values were experienced as objectively located in a transcendent reality, a benevolent and universal providence that supervised and protected us. The instinctive tendency to envision the structural features of our condition in this way obscured the insight that questions and answers about the meaning and end of life are posed inside the framework of option and free reflective decision. Even if there is an objective purpose to life, an inherent meaning, only an intelligent being discerns the intended purpose and interprets the meaning. This existential truth about our predicament as choosers is prevalently recognized only in self-consciously pluralist cultures. Secular existentialism, after the two major European wars of the previous century, facilitated the recognition of humankind's undetermined and under-determined nature.

Our age is dominated by the model of the human being whose basic function is the exercise of rational choice, a form of intellectuality that accompanies industrialism, the vitality of a money economy, the migration of labour from the rural to the urban centres, and the growth of the middle classes. This is the secular dogma of choice as a sacrosanct category. Paradoxically, however, a life-style requiring conscious decisions might be *necessitated* by material changes and economic imperatives.

In traditional cultures, especially rural ones, people rarely chose anything since they were rarely confused and uncertain, despite the precarious dependence on nature for food and survival. The range of choice was narrowed down by religion which supplied certainties in areas which, if left to individual regulation, would defy simplification. Not only rites of passage (such as marriage) but all one's life was arranged, pre-arranged, and sometimes well-arranged. The same religious conviction which dictated life choices also consoled victims who had to suffer stoically for a whole life-time for choices wrongly made. Even tragedy and suffering here did not derive their character from the inherent uncertainty of choice but rather from the intensity of what one must suffer.

Life is complicated but religious conviction convincingly simplifies it. A guide, such as a pastor or sheikh, apparently has correct answers to the universal complications of life, identity and relationships and is therefore admired as an expert in the art of living well. Like sages and shamans, religious experts are thought to know the correct solution to every moral dilemma and they speak with seductive clarity and certainty. This was once the province of the philosopher. Modern secularized culture has lost faith in saints, sages and philosophers – though not in heroes, a type that pre-dates the rise of organized religion and outlives its demise.

'Wisdom' sounds pretentious to us; we replace it with psychologically prestigious words such as 'maturity' and 'healthy normality'. Many in secular society replace the authoritative guidance of the religious expert with the expertise of the fallible but learned doctor, the attorney, the car mechanic, the social worker and so on. But the delegation of responsibility and authority is present even in free secular cultures; the existentialists, particularly Søren Kierkegaard and Jean-Paul Sartre, were outraged by our modern preference for abdicating our freedom and the burden of responsibility it inevitably brings. They accused us of preferring to live in indolence and bourgeois prudence rather than in the intensity and heat of risky passion.

The range of unregulated, potentially free, conduct is much greater in modern western and western-influenced cultures than in Muslim cultures. The tradition-directed Muslim, unlike the inner-directed westerner, feels little need for making private decisions. For Muslims, sacred law (*sharīʿah*; Q:45:18) regulates in detail all behaviour. Revealingly, all schools of Islamic law are medieval canons formulated between the middle of the eighth Christian (second Islamic) to the middle of the ninth (Christian) centuries. While piecemeal changes were made in these closed legislative canons, no one updated them systematically to accommodate the cataclysmic changes caused by western colonization of the non-western world. Only family law remained, with one exception, unaltered by colonial penetration of the Islamic world.[60]

Through informal and undeclared social pressure and the explicit power of the law, traditional cultures dictate a blind conformity to inherited norms. This restricts freedom while reducing the amount of undue social awkwardness or confusion. Paternalistic legislation regulates conduct on the principle that the citizens are like children and know only their wishes, not their best interests. Both religious and secular ritual ensures that we have ready-made answers and postures for life's complexities, a socially healthy state of affairs since few people are poets capable of penning original lines of condolence or congratulation. So long as religious ritual does not deteriorate into a lifeless and hypocritically formal pose, it facilitates social intercourse.

If Muslims become free of religious strictures, what are they free to be or to do? From a religious perspective, there are liabilities in having freedom. For example, free inquiry need not lead eventually to the adoption of religious orthodoxy. Only foolishly optimistic religious professionals would patiently wait for the intellectually curious youth of their community to finally return to the fold after a subversive university education, not to mention the whip and lash of life's less intellectual changes of fortune. Modern liberal philosophy of education is founded on a respect for the autonomy and intrinsic worth of the unended intellectual quest rather than on a persistent defence of a dogmatic creed known beforehand with authoritative conviction. Dogma, concludes the liberal pedagogue, is a worse enemy of truth than mere falsehood.

In a free society with free inquiry, we cannot avoid apostasy from the faithful community. Some will reject the faith of their forefathers and convert to a rival and novel interpretation of life and its mysteries. After experiencing sceptical encounters, believers might sense a weakening in their religious commitment. If capable of thinking reflectively, they might become self-conscious of their faith and experience it as mere faith: a commitment that surpasses the limits of rationally established certainty and thus requires the supra-rational leap of faith. From here, it is a short step to total disbelief since certain liberties of thought tend inevitably towards agnosticism and atheism.

In the aftermath of freedoms of belief and action, we expect dissension in the household of faith. Modern secular societies enable us to study the world's faiths and ideologies; sincere seekers may therefore systematically scrutinize many options and decide to desert their communities of birth. A religiously free society must legalize desertion from the Islamic community too since some Muslims are Muslims only by chance, not by choice. Individual verses of the Quran, if we adopt a verso-centric and atomistic perspective on the book, support individual choice (Q:2:256). The Quran discourages this approach and accuses Muslims and earlier communities of being selective in their use of scripture (Q:2:85; 15:90–1). Islamic law, relying additionally on the Prophetic traditions, the learned community's collective opinion, and analogical reasoning, does not permit the conscience of the individual to over-ride the consensus of the community. Apostasy is punishable by death;[61] and the community is infallible. In a Prophetic report with a fairly strong chain of transmission, Muhammad said: 'God will not permit my community to agree on an error'.[62] The individual believer, however, is neither exempt nor secure from error.

2 Human reason and divine revelation

1

Philosophers of religion probe and assess the consistency, coherence, truth and plausibility of religious beliefs presented as truth-claims – but the value and function of such philosophical scrutiny of religion is not self-evident. I shall argue presently that it is both undesirable and impossible to immunize the Quran against the sceptical thrust of persistently rational examination. It is impossible because the aggressively secular condition of sizeable and influential segments of humankind is no passing phenomenon. Given the global reach of a western secularized culture that sets the mental fashion of virtually the entire world, all faiths must sooner or later endure trial by secular reason. It remains an open question, in the case of Islam, whether it will come out unscathed. The future of the hitherto determined Muslim resistance to secularization is one of the exciting uncertainties at the start of the third Christian millennium. Many western observers are convinced that Islam cannot win in the court of secular reason – though they think there might be some amusement in watching how it will lose.

The attempt to insulate the Quran against external probing is undesirable for it offends intellectual integrity: the unexamined scripture is not worthy of credence. If the Quran is found, after rational examination, to be irrelevant to our fundamental condition, we are free to ignore it. If a scripture is authentic in its doctrines and morals, it should be able to withstand hostile probing, in great measure and for an indefinite duration. If we come to judge scripture as false, we are spared the error of mistaking ancient falsehood for perennially relevant truth. A Muslim believer might retort that it is better for the negligible number of Muslim sceptics to ignore the Quran and leave it alone than to profane it through a critical inquiry that offends the faithful majority. We examine this sentiment now. The impasse between the faithfully committed and the rationally independent reading of scripture is elemental, causing anxiety among sophisticated reflective believers and simple believers alike in textual faiths with authoritative canons. In Chapters 6 and 7, we examine facets of this concern.

2

The word '*aql*, translated as reason or intellect, literally means, in its verbal form, to tie or tether something; perhaps the rational quest needs to be controlled and disciplined. The opposite of '*aql* is not faith but *naql*, meaning imitation, that is, the faithful transmission of a received tradition. The Islamic sciences are divided into '*aqliyy* and *naqliyy*, the rational and the imitative (or transmitted) sciences.

Al-Kindī, the father of Islamic philosophy, often contrasted '*aql* (as intellect or soul) with matter. He was impressed by Platonic views of the intellect (*nous*) as the essential or immortal aspect of the human personality. We discuss Al-Kindī and Islam's defunct philosophical tradition below. In the meantime, we define reason vaguely as any critical orientation. Theoretical reason is the faculty transcending unrefined common sense and providing a priori principles (of logical consistency) for guiding our understanding of experience. More broadly, reason, both theoretical and practical, is our accumulated and critically organized common sense and contains a normative kernel of widely accepted moral values and ultimate ideals. For the secularist, such a reason expresses itself abstractly as the intellectual self-sufficiency of human nature with a correspondingly optimistic assessment of unaided human rational potential. Expectedly, all cogent objections to revelation, including moral ones, have been presented as *rational* objections.

In a vignette in an early Meccan revelation, the prototypical disbeliever is portrayed as thinking and determining matters, weighing the issues, apparently reflecting long and hard and then, suddenly, frowning and scowling and, in his groundless pride, turning his back on guidance (Q:74:18–23). His perversity inspires him to concoct an intellectually specious critique of the word of God. Since both specious and cogent objections to revelation appear equally as reason's bid for an independent stance in the face of an allegedly compelling revelation, one urgent philosophical task is to distinguish the two. All objections to revelation, whether genuine or spurious, are presented as rational. Yet many objections to revealed imperatives, as opposed to metaphysical dogmas, need not be even intellectually viable, let alone wholly rational. Our passions and instincts are often strong enough to be the real motivation behind such rejection. We explore this in Chapter 10.

The Quran does not exalt reason as autonomous and disembodied – as an abstract faculty or capacity of the kind extolled in Cartesian rationalism where it is potent enough to discover truth by doubting all which can be doubted and then building a structure of deductive truths using the remaining indubitable axioms as a foundation. In the Islamic tradition, reason is intuitive and participatory, aware of its secondary role. Such reason partly overlaps with sound intuition. It can be analytical and discursive which coincides with its exegetical, legal, or analogical roles – all aimed at expounding and extracting new judgements from revered old texts. After the appearance of the revelation, the consensual reason of all competent believers guarantees infallibility in the understanding of the revelation. Collective, socially exercised, reason cannot be mistaken. This sociological theory of consensus is supported by the Prophet's famous remark that God will not permit Muhammad's community to agree on an error.

3

The religiously committed approach to the Quran may be incompatible with the rational philosophical approach. Believers suspect a mischievous sceptical intent in the proposed application of philosophical methods to religious faith. It is blasphemous for a philosopher to judge the word of God, favourably or otherwise. Is there not a concealed intellectual arrogance behind the practice of philosophizing about religion? The Protestant theologian Reinhold Niebuhr spoke on behalf of most believers when he wrote: '[T]he reason which asks the question whether the God of religious faith is plausible has already implied a negative answer to the question because it has made itself God and naturally cannot tolerate another'.[1] This view has affinities with fideism, the view that the intellect, devoid of enlightening grace, cannot judge faith while the intellect, blessed and enlightened by grace, can only judge it favourably.

Most believers admit that we must use reason in order to understand the contents of revelation. This is the place reserved for human reason – in the aftermath of revelation. The role of reason is attenuated to being exegetical: to understand and explain scripture. In Islam, theology insofar as it exists, collapses into hermeneutics. What could be a nobler role for reason than to serve revelation, muses the orthodox believer. Such a modest estimate of the capacity of reason is unacceptable only to those believers who think that the content of faith is intrinsically irrational and therefore requires supernatural grace to make it appear credible and rational to believers. Only some Christians of a 'revelationist fideist' outlook are tempted by this extreme irrationalist view.[2]

Most believers of all faiths would, however, reject the equally extreme rationalist view that having faith depends on having good secular reasons – conclusive and compelling evidence – for believing that one's faith is true. Understandably, believers would not allow secular reason a decisive role in the *validation* of revealed religious beliefs since such beliefs are thought to be known to be true on revealed grounds. The believers' argument is, as the quotation from Niebuhr implies, that if reason assesses the evidences and credentials of faith, then it is reason, not faith, that is supreme – hardly a religious view.

Intelligent believers reject only the final self-sufficiency of unaided human reason; they readily endorse the integrity of its reduced, exegetical role. Reason explains, develops and utilizes revealed ideas; it does not originate them. What is unknowable by reason is still believable by reason although one cannot believe what one cannot understand. Furthermore, for Muslims, reason in the aftermath of revelation is not the potentially anarchic reason of the private individual but rather the communal and consensual reason of the paradigmatic community, the community that, according to Muhammad, cannot agree on an error. This is the collective exercise of reason by the utopian society of faithful believers. In practice, it is the fallible opinion of a select constituency of jurists with political interests and human prejudices.[3]

The believer acknowledges the importance of reasoning: it supplies a procedure, a reliable method, for ascertaining truth, including revealed truth. If we reject reasoning in matters of faith, how could we in practice distinguish revealed truth from impressive-sounding falsehood? Moreover, if we reject rational assessment of faith – the need for rationally grounded criteria for judging the truth of religious claims – we risk leaving a believer's will vulnerable to the onslaught of false but emotionally appealing views. Few would commend a religion of fanatically intense conviction, with no resources for self-criticism. A faith deprived of independent critical checks administered by reason is liable to evoke fanaticism and sentimentality, thus falling easy prey to the secularist's charge that religious conviction is ideological in a pejorative sense. Reliance on reasoning is therefore legitimate. We would be guilty of Niebuhr's charge of idolizing our fallible intellects only if we endorsed the supremacy of reason *tout court,* allowing it to intentionally usurp the place of God and his word.

The faith–reason dichotomy, as absolute and confrontational, is largely absent from classical Islam and indeed from patristic Christian theology and later from the writings of St Thomas. Christian thinker–saints synthesized the two rivals since the whole truth was not likely to be found in one element, isolated or emphasized at the expense of the other. Both religious rationalism and its rival fideism are distortions. Each position makes totalitarian claims on behalf of one element – faith or reason – suitably isolated from the other and too exclusively emphasized at the expense of the other. For a phenomenon as complex as religion, the truth cannot be located in one element alone.

4

What is the Quran's stance on reason and its uses in the religious life? After answering this question, we shall return to the charge of the alleged impiety of rational methods. From cover to cover, the Quran uses verbs of reflection and consideration. The Quranic mandate ordering the use of the intellect is a central religious obligation. In Chapter 8 we shall note that the signs of God are pointers towards an infinite reality behind the finite phenomena of nature. The Quran condemns the disbeliever as unintelligent and irrational, a dumb animal who fails to reason and to ponder the signs of God. The devout believer engages in 'deep reflection' (*tadabbur*; hyperbolic form; to meditate earnestly; *yaddabbarū*; Q:38:29). Sinners in hell confess: 'If only we had listened [to the warning of prophets] and reasoned correctly (*na'qilu*), we should not now be among the companions of the blazing fire' (Q:67:10).

The Quran has a special reason for endorsing a pre-eminent role for reason in the life of faith. Muhammad's pagan compatriots noticed that Muhammad brought no miracles of the older dramatic type (Q:6:35, 37, 124; 13:7, 27; 21:5; 29:50) such as the ones given to Moses (Q:28:48). The Quran does not deny this but counters instead that those dramatic signs were also rejected in their time. Muhammad was distressed by these pagan taunts and desperately sought a divine sign (Q:6:35). Christian polemicists, especially Aquinas, argued that this lack indicated that Islam had no supernatural credentials and was therefore demonstrably inferior to Christianity.[4] Islam, it seems, had no probative miracles, no candidly performed marvels that might compel belief. The Quran records the miracles performed by Moses, Abraham, Jesus, John and other prophets and adds that the Arabic scripture Muhammad brings is a sufficient miracle of reason and speech (Q:29:50–1). Muslims add that it excels the sensory miracles of earlier messengers since those miracles, unlike the Quran, cannot be reproduced today.

Muhammad is asked to bring the dead back to life, to resurrect the pagans' forefathers (Q:44:36; 45:25), and to put the Quran to better use by using it to make the dead speak (Q:13:31). These are reasonable requests in an age when everyone expected marvellous and supernatural occurrences. The Prophet does not (or cannot) resurrect the dead. The Quran, like the New Testament, complains that such dramatic signs will be in any case dismissed by disbelievers as mere magic (Q:6:7), that only the wicked demand special signs and portents (Q:6:109–11; see also Matthew 12:38–9; Luke 16:19–31). If the dead generations, the pagan forefathers of Muhammad's contemporaries, are not to be resurrected, then there is an increased need to offer impressive *reasons* for the possibility of the resurrection transpiring in the future lives of the pagans. The objection to resurrection was made continually by Muhammad's enemies; the challenge remained unanswered on their terms. The Quran *argued* its case – albeit on its own terms.

One Quranic contention is the argument from analogy with the dead earth which is revived periodically by rainfall from the sky (Q:29:63; 30:24; 41:39; 43:11; 50:11). Again, the God who can create a human being from nothing (Q:19:9) or 'a base fluid emitted' (Q:86:6) can surely bring that human being back to life. Although Quranic retorts to the pagan sceptics are embellished with rhetoric and charm, there are only a few *substantial* responses to their reservations about the resurrection (Q:36:77–83; 75:1–6, 36–40).[5] The Quran does, however, counter the pagan demand with a counter-demand in a *tu quoque* rejoinder. The Meccan sceptics demand a resurrection of their dead forefathers while the Quran challenges the disbelievers to prevent the death of their existing tribesmen. The challenge comes elliptically at Q:56:83–7:

> Why do you not intervene when [the soul of a dying man] reaches his throat and at the time you are looking on [helplessly]; and we are nearer to him than you are but you cannot see this. So, then, if you are exempt from judgement, how is it that you cannot call back [the soul of the dying man], if you are right [in your claim to human autonomy]?

Part of the Quran's teaching is, like that of Jesus, in parabolic rather than syllogistic or argumentative form. There are scores of parables (sing. *mathal*; pl., *amthāl*). The Quran claims to have coined every type of parable to teach truth to the rebels (Q:18:54; 30:58). Indeed the pagans noted that many of the Quran's parables and verses even referred to insignificant creatures (Q:2:26) such as the fly (Q:22:73) and the spider (Q:29:41), to ants (Q:27:18) and bees (Q:16:68–9). The Quran responds that even a parable involving a gnat might guide someone (Q:2:26).

Unlike New Testament parables, there are few characters or development of plot. Among the best known are those of the fly, the spider, the slaves (Q:16:75–6), and the good and the evil word (Q:14:24–6). Lesser known parables describe this lower life and the futility of human endeavour when it is not aimed at attaining God's good pleasure (Q:14:18). One parable suggests that the scum that mounts up to the surface of a torrent (or when iron ore is purified) is like falsehood (*al-bāṭil*), a reference to false gods. The purified residues are like the truth (*al-ḥaqq*) that remains and abides, a symbol of the true God (Q:13:17). Some parables aim to show the correct attitude towards God as king by comparing and contrasting power relationships between human beings as equals, on the one hand, and unequal power distributions between slaves and masters, on the other (Q:30:28). There are three lengthy parables encouraging believers to spend their wealth for charitable causes and warning them against hypocrisy in charity (Q:2:261, 264–6). Finally, the parable of God's light (Q:24:35), popular among mystics, is so complex that one can barely comprehend it, let alone visualize it; perhaps its complexity is intentional.

5

Quranic commentaries contain a portion dealing with rational argument (*jadal*; Q:43:58).[6] Human beings are quarrelsome and fond of wrangling (*jadalan*; acc. Q:18:54); many dispute about God even while they witness the thunderbolts sent against them (Q:13:13). Man (*al-insān*), asserts the Quran, begins life as a mere sperm-drop (*nuṭfah*; Q:36:77) but he openly disputes about lofty matters, including God's creation (Q:16:4; 36:77–8). He is literally twisted or stretched out, the etymological sense of *ja/da/la*. There is a congenital torque in human nature, a bias towards evil (Q:12:53) which makes us accept anything and everything but faith in God (Q:17:89). Perhaps such disbelief and doubt is an inheritance one generation makes to another (Q:51:52–3)!

The Quran claims to refute the fallacious arguments and objections of disbelievers (Q:25:9, 23). To God belongs 'the conclusive argument' (*al-ḥujjat al-bālighah*; Q:6:149). Prophets are threatened by their communities once the sinners concede that their prophet's arguments are irrefutable. Disbelievers accuse Noah of bringing verbose and repetitive arguments (Q:11:32); the prophet Shu'ayb is told that he talks unintelligibly (Q:11:91). Muhammad's community is also contentious (*luddan*; Q:19:97), showing a quarrelsome contempt for such matters as the Quran's claims about some former prophets (Q:43:58) and about a future resurrection from the dead. That is why all disputation (*jidāl*) during the pilgrimage to Mecca is expressly forbidden (Q:2:197).[7]

The commonest fallacy is the appeal to the threat of force against a prophet and his disciples. The sinners, having lost the argument, are embarrassed and confounded (Q:2:258) and threaten to exterminate the warner and his group. Martyrdom is an occupational hazard of being a prophet. Messengers are threatened with death by stoning (Q:26:116; 36:18) while others, such as Lot and Muhammad are threatened with exile (Q:9:40; 14:13; 26:116, 167). Joseph is

imprisoned by the Egyptian authorities on the recommendation of his seduc-
tress (Q:12:32–5). The Pharaoh threatens to imprison or even execute Moses for
manslaughter (Q:26:14–20) especially if Moses continues to deny the divinity
of the Pharaoh – a scenario that evokes images of heroic Christian martyrs who
rejected the cult of the 'divine' Roman emperors.

The Quran sketches several vignettes of Abraham as a skilled polemicist and
iconoclast who provokes his people, mocks their idol-worship, and defeats them
in debate. The Quranic Abraham is a protean figure who is portrayed as both a
man of faith and as a sceptic who once requests God to show him how he gives
life to the dead (Q:2:260). Abraham is divinely aided in his arguments against his
pagan community (Q:6:83) but appears also as an empiricist natural philosopher
making independent inferences from observations of heavenly bodies and their
patterns of setting and rising. The Hebrew iconoclast watches events in nature,
noting finitude and limitation; he adores the temporary greatness of the rising sun.
But as the sun sets, he deduces, by elimination, the illimitable greatness of God
(Q:6:74–9). He argues with a sceptic about the divine cause behind the rising and
the setting of the sun (Q:2:258). Armed with an empirically grounded certainty of
faith, he argues with his people, the king, and the guardians of the temple where
idols are kept (Q:6:74–83; 2:258; 21:51–71; 37:85–98). Predictably, the pagans,
frustrated by his intellectual acumen, throw him into a raging fire – but God orders
the fire to be a cool refuge for the fiery prophet (Q:21:68–9; 29:24).

Moses, the most widely discussed prophet in the Quran, is self-conscious about
his lack of eloquence in argument (Q:20:25–31). The Pharaoh mocks him for his
inability to express himself clearly (Q:43:52). Moses asks God to make Aaron his
'helper in dialectic' (*rid'*; Q:28:34) since 'he is more eloquent than I am' (Q:28:34).

Muhammad's community also argues with him (Q:22:68). He replies by means
of a 'great jihad' (*jihādan kabīran*) whose weapon is the Quran (Q:25:52). The
scripture contains what logicians dismiss as an *argumentum ad baculum* (argument from force). The hell passages threaten the disbelievers by reminding them of
God's power to inflict everlasting punishment. This kind of reasoning is, if unsupported by other sound arguments, fallacious. Arguments from *arbitrary* authority
are invalid. But the Quran appeals to such divine ability to inflict pain in addition to
rational grounds. The Quran threatens us with God's power but couples the threat
with an appeal to meditate on the Quran's inimitability, a joint appeal to coercion
and reason: 'And if you doubt the revelations sent to our servant [Muhammad],
then bring a chapter similar to it. But if you cannot, and you certainly cannot,
then fear the fire whose fuel is humankind and stones, prepared for disbelievers'
(Q:2:23–4).

An argument for opting for faith is also placed in the mouth of an ordinary
believer, not a prophet, living in Pharaonic times, an unnamed man who kept his
faith hidden:

> And a believer, a man from among the people of Pharaoh, a man who con-
> cealed his faith, argued: 'Will you kill a man for saying "My Lord is God"
> while he confirms his case by coming with self-evident signs from your Lord?

If he is a liar, the sin of his lie is on his own head; however, if he is telling the truth, then some of the disaster he warns you about shall surely fall on you. Certainly, God does not guide liars and transgressors.'

(Q:40:28)

What vitiates this apparently impressive argument is a third possibility not mentioned by the believer: the prophetic warner could be self-deceived. This sceptical possibility is culturally unavailable to his audience, so the argument, given its presuppositions, is convincing. Death shall provide post-mortem verification for the religious protagonist's claims. But it will be too late: the Quran rejects avowals of faith made during the crisis of death or while actually facing divine punishment (Q:4:17–18; 40:85). If the prophets lied about a future life or were self-deceived, then those who rejected the divine dispatches will be vindicated – though neither party will be in a position to rejoice or mourn this realization. However, if the divine warners spoke the truth, then those who rejected their message shall have plenty of opportunity to regret the decision they made on earth.[8]

6

The Quran is self-described as an umpire in disputes among Muslims (Q:4:59; 24:51; 33:36; 49:9) and between the sincere Muslims and the hypocritical Arabs, and between Muslims and their Jewish and Christian opponents (Q:24:47–50; 27:76). The Quran is the criterion (*al-furqān*; Q:3:4; 25:1) that distinguishes truth from falsehood, guidance from error. Legal verdicts revealed in Medina are immediately and scrupulously implemented by Muhammad as the executor of God's will. 'Is not God the wisest of judges?'(Q:95:8). A believer cannot deny the wisdom of God's judgement. No proposition or judgement, once determined as divine in origin, can be dismissed as false. God's estimate of us is always more insightful than our estimate of ourselves or of God. 'God knows and you do not know' (Q:2:216; 24:19).

For us here, this is true but irrelevant. To use the methods of rational scrutiny for assessing the credibility and validity of God's (alleged) revelation is not to deny the primacy of such revelation. It is incoherent to deny the supremacy of a divine verdict once reason has established its identity, content and scope. To question the truth or reasonableness of the Quran is not to judge the word of God. To do that, a person must say of what is known and acknowledged to be an authentic revelation that it merely expresses God's opinions and that it remains an open question whether or not these opinions are worthy of credence until human reason has issued its verdict. While it is hubristic to reject God's judgement after it has been decisively determined to be divine, believers are not culpable if they employ their own reason merely to determine whether or not a particular judgement is or is not, in the first instance, genuinely divine.

Modern Muslims are acutely and subliminally anxious about the potentially subversive role of reason in matters of faith because the philosophical interrogation of divine claims and commands is reminiscent of the early sceptical rejections of God's word by Muhammad's arrogant contemporaries. It is emotionally difficult for modern believers to disengage from that hostile context, a religiously charged environment when the Prophet lived among his people (Q:3:101) and the faith was still struggling in its infancy. We today must, however, disengage from that ancient ethos in order to accept that the suspension of religious belief or its detached scrutiny, by reflective modern Muslims, is not a species of that ancient hubristic and perverse rejection of Islam. We are not like those who first heard Muhammad and disbelieved despite living in a zealous environment where the hand of God could virtually be seen in history.

7

The question of the intended scope of the Quran is explored in Chapter 6. Here we examine the religious argument that the Quran is addressed to believers seeking guidance and is not therefore a book whose credentials are open to non-Muslim scrutiny. The Quran seems to preach to the converted, the believers, rather than to disbelievers and philosophical sceptics. The Quran nowhere directly addresses disbelievers.[9] Indeed the revelation was originally vouchsafed to one believer. More restrictively but indefensibly, each passage could be interpreted to be relevant to only those handful of believers who first heard it from Muhammad's lips just as Paul's epistles were originally addressed to congregations of various sizes and read only to them – and only later read by all Christians.

The Quran is certainly a sermon for the faithful. 'This is the book, no doubt in it, guidance for the God-fearing' (Q:2:1). It is also self-described as 'a cure' (*shifā'*) for the human disease, as a guide and mercy for believers (Q:10:57). The address 'Believers!' is frequent; it dates from the time Muhammad founded a community in Medina. But many passages describe the book as a revelation to all humankind (Q:4:79, 170; 6:19; 7:158; 14:52; 21:107; 34:28; 38:87; 61:9; 81:27). Some verses describe it as 'a clear statement for all humanity' (*bayānun li al-nās*; Q:3:138) and simultaneously as 'a guide and admonition for the God-fearing' (*hudan wa maw'izatun li al-muttaqīn*; Q:3:138). Even passages about the credentials of the *Arabic* Quran are addressed to all human (and elemental listeners). The Quran is actually perused and assessed by varied readers: Muslims naturally but also idolaters and hesitant (or curious) readers intending to convert, hypocrites, errant monotheists, western and Arab policy-makers worried by the enduring power of Islam's political message, and so on.

Basing their view on Q:56:75–82, purist commentators believe that the Quran is too exalted to be touched by non-Muslims. By extension, sceptics are accused of intellectual desecration if they read and dissect the Quran like any other book. These verses could mean that the heavenly version of the book is inaccessible to impure human beings. Before reading or formally reciting the text, believers must perform ablutions to place themselves in a state of ritual physical purity, similar to that required for canonical prayer (Q:5:6). The Quran describes idolaters as impure (*najas*; Q:9:28), a term used by jurists to denote physical ritual impurity. If we see impurity as a metaphysical trait, however, then it is not removed merely with water. But such a view of impurity as occult and irremovable is dangerous: it implies a divisive verdict about other people's orthodoxy and level of faith and commitment. It leads to endless schism and dissension of the kind which has plagued Islamic and Christian history and continues to do so today.

8

The believer accuses us of being hyper-critical, of abusing valid methods of inquiry. We are accused of changing the status of exegesis from a theological (religious) discipline to a form of philosophical scrutiny of belief. A text written in the spirit of faith and requiring a response of faith is being read and interpreted in a spirit of philosophical disputation and detachment. Reason moves outside its proper domain if pressed in the service of doubt and subversion. Like other human faculties, it should be recruited in the service of faith rather than the destructive criticism of faith.

Perhaps virtue is its own reward, the religious apologist continues, but the reward of faith is entry into paradise, the eternal life with God. Therefore, our motivation in seeking to discern the will of God for us should be practical, sincere, and devotional rather than academic, professional or controversial. No doubt, in its first context, the Quran contains much that can be read for its polemical and controversial value since its guidance was offered to believers engaged in dialectical debate with pagan Arab detractors and with Christians and Jews resolutely hostile to its claims. The apologist's point, nonetheless, should not be despised.

I believe there is scope for detached reflection and reasoned speculation about one's religious beliefs and allegiances. In the cool hour, we should ascertain the objective validity of our faithful convictions. In ages of religious fervour, there was little room for such detachment but today we need perspective in our world of plural ideological offers. Life is short and our state desperate but, as the Quran admits, we have time, a few years perhaps, to make a considered critical judgement (Q:35:37). A fair-minded God would understand our reluctance to make a capricious choice, an urgent leap of faith in the dark.

I conclude this part of our inquiry by recording a version of this objection which has not been raised in the Islamic context. Some modern philosophers object to the rational detached study of any religion on the grounds that religious commitment requires an insider's (or participant's) understanding. We must play the religious language-game in order to understand religion. Converts often insist that religion is an experiential matter beyond the intellectual process. In religion, there are no detached observers. The German verb *durchleiden* captures this notion: knowing something through suffering, to suffer it through with one's whole being, not merely understand it through the mind. Submission to the will of God and to the authority of scripture includes *intellectual* submission. Can the rejector and the detached scholarly student of Islam understand the quality of such total submission? Is it not intellectual hubris to submit half-heartedly, hoping to keep the mind a free zone exempt from God's demands? The Quran certainly expects whole-hearted self-surrender of all faculties (Q:2:208).

The religious apologist constructs a dilemma to highlight the impossibility of entertaining a wholly theoretical or detached interest in Islam: either one genuinely understands it and then rejects it out of perversity – or else one fails to understand it. The first horn of the dilemma presupposes that to understand all here is to embrace all since God is a reality totally other (*totaliter aliter*) than any mundane reality: his reality secretes a prescriptive significance even for the allegedly detached student. The argument was anticipated by Søren Kierkegaard and espoused in a modified form by neo-orthodox theologians such as Karl Barth. We are never interested in religion – Christianity for both Kierkegaard and Barth – for its own sake. Neutrality is impossible and objectivity is undesirable. I have elsewhere argued against this position[10] and we return to it in Section 19 below. We record it here in order to make comprehensive contact with major objections to the use of reason in assessing revealed claims.

9

The self-admiring and cocky Roman Catholic apologist, G.K. Chesterton, wrote: 'It is very hard for a man to defend anything of which he is entirely convinced. It is comparatively easy when he is only partially convinced'.[11] This popular prejudice inspires the anti-intellectualism of much religious apologetics: rational theorizing about religion is due to want of faith. The thinker who produces a dozen proofs of the existence of God must have had at least a dozen doubts about the existence of God.

Chesterton's avuncular, complacently confident tone is unsuited to serious reflection but we shall move beyond his rhetoric. Who is here being accused of lack of faith? Although many motives actuate an interest in theology and philosophy of religion, it is mainly believers who study religion in depth. It is rare for an atheist to be interested in Christian theology or in the corresponding Islamic branches of learning, although some ex-Christian thinkers write incessantly against the legion they claim to have deserted. The group being targeted here by Chesterton must be the believing theologians and believing philosophers of religion rather than outright disbelievers. Believing theologians or, in the case of Islam, the jurists (*al-fuqahā'*) whose office includes and supervises that of theologians, would reject the charge of disbelief since they see themselves as professionally engaged in the exposition and defence of their faith.

Believing philosophers of religion may be suspected of lack of faith because their professional duty as philosophers requires a suspension of religious commitment. Their intellectual situation is unavoidably schizophrenic since they must entertain diametrically opposed views – though one of the two is a methodological pretence. The charge is that unless believing thinkers were assailed by doubts about their religious convictions, they would not need the props of academic or philosophical theology to support their faith through the dark hour of doubt: people of true faith know no doubt as they traverse the valley of doubt, singing hymns and knowing that sugar is sweet and their redeemer liveth. Those who need to produce evidence or intellectual justification for their convictions are not at heart believers.

Believing philosophers could reply, weakly, that their doubt here is merely professional, not sincere: we are only interested, not concerned. But there is also a fatal objection to the above arguments. The model of faith that inspires such religiously motivated anti-intellectualism is unsound. It is a stock piece of rhetoric thundered from the mouths of religious professionals and preachers that faith presupposes lack of proof, that psychological uncertainty is part of the mental state that precedes and accompanies faith. It is tempting to suppose that once the propositional content of faith is proved, that is, conclusively justified beyond reasonable doubt, then it can no longer be a candidate for the allegedly weaker psychological state of mere belief. Many a preacher has fallen victim to this temptation in the *khuṭba* (Islamic sermon)! Indeed even thinkers have assumed the validity of this ancient dichotomy between faith and knowledge.

One modern Christian philosopher has questioned this classical dichotomy which is found in the works of countless theologians, particularly Aquinas. Surely, faith and knowledge, certainty and uncertainty, often co-exist even in religious and secular life.[12] Do we not sometimes doubt what we know? Indeed, I would argue further that we also doubt what we 'know very well'. Knowing very well that *P* is true is, paradoxically, epistemologically weaker than simply knowing that *P* is true, especially when the former is a response to an accusation. Children may know very well that Pythagoras's theorem is true (or valid) and yet they require sustained effort and training in order to come to believe that it is true. One can, then, believe what one knows just as one can doubt what one knows. Faith and knowledge are compatible in secular and religious life.

Oddly enough, the view that posits a chasm between knowledge and mere faith is an *irreligious* view of faith. In the scriptures of the monotheistic trio, faith incorporates doubt with knowledge. Both the view that faith cannot co-exist with doubt and that faith cannot co-exist with the certainty of knowledge are mistaken and unscriptural. To explain this, I shall now construct a *sui generis* Islamic model of faith.

In the Joseph narrative (Q:12:3–101), God directly informs Jacob about the true circumstances of his son Joseph (Q:12:86, 96).[13] Jacob knows that sibling rivalry has motivated Joseph's brothers to harm him and knows this well before the story unfolds. Throughout the narration, he gives subtle clues of his knowledge of future events. As a prophet, he is blessed with clairvoyance and also senses human presence at a vast distance (Q:12:94–6). He has faith (*īmān*) – which literally means security (of conviction) – and also knowledge (*'ilm*). Faith is a confirmation (*taṣdīq*) of what is already known (*'ilm*). Even a prophet, who directly knows God, must still believe in him and have faith in his righteous purposes since these are recognized as righteous often only on the other side of experience – after prophets have been tested and purged of their unworthy doubts.

This is part of a larger debate about the scriptural notion of faith and unfaith. The Quranic claim that disbelief is perverse, not conscientious, presupposes the compatibility of faith and knowledge. Disbelievers conceal what they know to be true. They refuse to have faith in or believe in what they secretly know and acknowledge. Rejection could only be wilful if we could disbelieve in what we knew. Knowledge does not entail faith; but faith can entail and encompass knowledge. This explains why we meritoriously believe in God even though we *know* that he exists: it still requires faith to *believe* it and to act on it.[14]

We may conclude then that the religiously motivated opposition to a rational approach to faith, including its reasoned defence and proof, is due to a misunderstanding about the nature of faith. Faithful believers should produce proofs and systematic defences of religious claims in order to dispel the doubts and confusions of other believers who do not enjoy intensely certain religious convictions. Nor should we accuse believing thinkers of disbelief simply because they need to dispel their occasional misgivings in the hour of doubt. Faith requires firm decision and resolute commitment not only in the face of doubt and inconclusive evidence but even where certainty and conclusive evidence, even knowledge, are available. We may, in the interests of objectivity, allow believing thinkers to temporarily set aside their religious commitment to the book and the faith.

10

Before we examine the history of reason's clash with transcendent revelation in the Islamic case, I summarize the Quran's ahistorical position on the office of reason in matters of faith since this has always guided Muslim priorities. The Quran implies that God is in the first instance the revered object of faith, worship and enthusiastic obedience rather than of rational inquiry and discursive thought. Unaided reason is inferior to the gracious and undeserved gift of faith; reason is useful only insofar as it finds a use in the larger service and defence of faith. The Quran has a high estimate of the potential of the human intellect, a corollary of its optimistic view of human nature, as we explore in Chapter 10. Men and women are constantly invited to think and ponder in order that they may believe – but faith retains decisive priority over unaided human reason. Faith supervises and defines the functions, powers and limits of the intellect.

Muslim jurists have debated the true office of independent reason in sacred matters through the practical concern with *ijtihād,* the liberty and necessity to exercise the human mind beyond the limits of revelation – though not in opposition to it or in ways that might excite paradox and inconsistency. This effectively limits the role of independent reason in the assessment of revelation to an essentially hermeneutical one.

The subordination of faith to reason would, believers fear, make religion accountable to philosophy. Orthodox believers deny that revealed claims are properly subject to external philosophical reason or criteria secreted by natural science. Islamic fideism is, in its final character but not in its initial motivation, similar to its Christian counterpart with the proviso that Muslims do not view the reasoning faculty as irreparably damaged by the fall of humanity. Some Christian fideists even think that reason has no role to play in matters of faith; grace suffices to enlighten the believer. It follows that faith does not require rational or scientific or any external justification; indeed faith, based on revealed assurances, is the arbiter of reason and its pretensions in matters of faith.

In Islam, there is no extreme fideism of the kind popular among Protestant Christian sects such as Calvinists and Lutherans who celebrate paradox and congratulate themselves on the amount of irrationality in their religious beliefs. The primacy of faith, a feature of Islam and Christianity, is not, in Islam, achieved as a result of or at the expense of or after the resolution of tensions with reason. Rather, the supremacy of faith is ironically reflected in the fact that reason is at the service of faith! The Quran orders us to ponder the signs of God in the three loci of divine activity and sacred presence: external nature, human nature and society. These are places where we should be able to detect God's gracious association with us – but the divine reality is fully accessible only to faith. Such faith, and the purity that characterizes its possessor, are gifts of divine grace.

Is the content of faith intrinsically rational but merely appears irrational to those whom God has not guided? Tertullian asserted that the content of faith is in fact irrational – only this feature is welcome to believers (since they are influenced by grace) but unwelcome to disbelievers. Such paradoxes of faith do not rise in Islam but in both religions, faith remains, even if its content is rational, a supra-rational gift of undeserved grace. The leap of faith, however, as a desperate final and irrational step is foreign to Islam which sees itself as a rational faith. Kierkegaard's philosopher–knights make sense only in the case of a modern effete Christianity – although an anti-rationalist strain has persisted in Christian theology as early as (and partly owing to) Paul.

For orthodox monotheists, scripture seeks an affirmative verdict from its sinful human audience but it creates by grace the very verdict it seeks to elicit. It is a closed circle of faith. The Quran, many devout Muslims claim, yields its secrets only to those who radically trust its claims about the unseen realm while actively rejecting the promptings of secular reason. Scripture has the last word. It moulds the mind that receives its message and indeed God himself ensures that there are minds, under the influence of grace, who do receive it. Not all believers would accept the view that God's grace elects and rejects in a way that totally by-passes free and intelligent human involvement. But we should not forget, especially in Islam, this tenaciously conservative verdict. We shall note its implications when we consider the determined orthodox Muslim opposition to philosophy, a major theme of this chapter.

11

Granted that the rational scrutiny of faith is religiously permissible, is it religiously desirable? Does philosophy benefit faith? We shall see below that the Spanish–Arab philosopher Ibn Rushd (known as Averroës in the Latin West) held the questionable view that the Quran demands the study of philosophical wisdom, although admittedly only by an elite. The orthodox view, presented forcefully

by the devout philosopher–theologian Abū Ḥāmid Muhammad Al-Ghazālī
(d. 1111 CE) in his spiritual autobiography 'The Deliverer from Misguidance'
(*Al-Munqidh Min Al-Ḍalāl*), was that God wants a faithful response from us.[15]
Al-Ghazālī summarizes there his attack on Islamo-Hellenistic philosophy and
argues that God does not want us to indulge in philosophy and speculative metaphysics.[16] The kind of faith that pleases him is the effortless and child-like faith
of believers who said: 'We heard and we obeyed'(Q:2:285; 5:7; 24:51). In giving
us the truth, the Quran does not intend to satisfy our idle curiosity. Rather, God
shines his light directly into our hearts to liberate us from bondage to false gods
so that we may attain success in the life of faith. Following Al-Ghazālī's lead,
and fortifying an existing and already inveterate hostility to autonomous reason,
orthodoxy solidified into the view that the goal of the religious life is only to please
God and the sole purpose of revelation is to guide us towards heaven. There is
substantial Quranic support for these claims.

There is no extant rational theo-philosophical tradition in mainstream (Sunni)
Islam. The word for philosophy, *al-falsafa*, is borrowed from Greek. It does not
occur in the Quran though the scripture is self-described as wisdom (*al-ḥikmah*;
Q:2:269). Among its many honorific titles are *ḥikmah bālighah* (consummate wisdom; Q:54:5) and *al-kitāb al-ḥakīm* (the wise book; Q:10:1; 31:2; see also 36:2).
As part of its rejection of pagan ignorance and moral laxity (Q:48:26), the Quran
condemned many profane arts and crafts esteemed by the pagan Arabs, including
secular poetry, magic and astrological practices such as divination connected to
illusory divinities (Q:5:90). Would a 'Greek Quran', revealed in ancient Athens,
have condemned theorizing about the examined life?

The Arabic Quran has no occasion to outlaw Greek philosophy although some
of its verses, like some New Testament passages, are anti-philosophical, even
anti-intellectual.[17] As we noted earlier, the Quran often accuses human beings
of being the most contentious and quarrelsome of creatures (Q:18:54; 22:3, 8).
The Children of Adam are perverse doubters whose arrogant self-will makes them
resist surrender to the divine will. Some rebel openly; others are hypocritical,
pretending to have sincere reservations, arguing that they must probe religious
demands before submitting to them.

The Quran recounts an incident where the Israelites raise carping objections
to the divine commandment to sacrifice a yellow heifer (Q:2:67–71; cf. Numbers 19:1–10). Moses tells his community that God requires them to sacrifice a
particular cow. Including the initial request, Moses makes four separate trips to
his people as he mediates between them and God, each time giving them further
information about the animal. They finally sacrifice the intended cow but do so
reluctantly. One could discern here a lesson about the impiety of rational interrogation of imperatives secretly acknowledged to be binding. The philosophical
sceptic might be compared to the quarrelsome people of Moses. The story might
be read, allegorically, as a condemnation of a philosopher's desire to suspend
commitment. Ostensibly a reflective hesitation in the interests of objectivity and
the rigorous demands of intellectual integrity, it is actually a subtle defence of
wilful anarchy in thought and conduct.

12

I offer now a postcard summary of Islamic theology (*kalām*, lit. speech) and the emergence of the Mu'tazilah, the rationalist school which, as its name suggests, 'seceded' from Sunni orthodoxy. If we define theology as a religious discipline rooted in the Quran and the Prophet's sayings, subject to the supervision of *fiqh* (jurisprudence), its stimuli are indigenous and therefore the subject dates to Muhammad's life-time. *Dialectical* theology, however, was founded during the Abbasid revolution of the 750s which saw the emergence of Mu'tazilite rationalism whose origins are obscure but the movement took shape only after Greek writings, freshly translated into Arabic under Abbasid patronage, were made available. The heyday of the Mu'tazliah was from 833 to 848. It was the precursor of Islam's philosophical tradition.

In early Islam, an urgent question was how to judge the legal status of the grave sinner.[18] Must the reprobate sinner be excommunicated? The Khawārij, an ultra-conservative group, wanted to excommunicate or execute the grave sinners. The later, more moderate, Murji'ites argued that the judgement should be deferred (based on Q:9:106) until God judged the sinner, a view which had overtones of hope and divine lenience. It became Sunni orthodoxy. The earliest substantial Islamic creed, associated with the disciples of the theologian–jurist Abū Ḥanīfah (d. 767), the founder of the first school of Sunni jurisprudence, addresses this question and opts for a tolerant stance. It pre-dates the rise of the Mu'tazilite heresy. The Mu'tazilites argued that God's unity implies that his attributes (*ṣifāt*) coincide with his essence (*dhāt*). God was therefore obligated to live up to his attributes, especially the moral attributes of justice and mercy. He was morally obliged to deal justly with the sinner since God's actions reflected his nature, not only his reputation and will.

The Mu'tazilites argued that anthropomorphic assertions about God must be understood metaphorically since he had no body limited by space and time. Quranic expressions such as 'God's face' (*wajh Allāh*; Q:2:115; 6:52; 76:9) and 'God's hand'(*yad Allāh*; Q:5:64; 48:10) should be understood to mean God's essence (or presence or sake) and grace (or power) respectively. Divine attributes such as speaking and creating are not eternal but rather temporary attributes of actions and last only as long as the action is transpiring. The Quran was the created word of God, created as it was being sent down to Muhammad via Gabriel. From 833 to 848, during the life-time of the first Muslim philosopher Al-Kindī, there was a rationalist inquisition in Baghdad based on a test (*mihna*) of correct belief about the status of the Quran. It was instituted by the Mu'tazilites' patron, the caliph Abu Al-Abbas Al-Ma'mūn (r. 813–33) towards the end of his reign. It remained the official school of the Abbasid court until the accession of the conservative caliph Al-Mutawwakil (r. 847–61) who ended the inquisition only to restore an inflexible traditionalism which upheld that the Quran was the eternal word of God.

The theologian Abū Al-Ḥasan Al-Ash'arī (d. 935) deserted the Mu'tazilite school but used their dialectical methods to establish his own orthodox movement.

Al-Ash'arī, justly called Islam's Aquinas, was the first religious Muslim thinker to show that Greek philosophy was only a tool – and that as such it could be used to serve dogmatic orthodoxy. He co-opted Greek logical and dialectical methods and made the rest of philosophy redundant for believers. He anticipated the work of Al-Ghazālī who revered Al-Ash'arī as a significant predecessor in combating the harmful effects of irreligious rationalism.

Al-Ash'arī denied the Mu'tazilite identification of God's essence with his attributes. To deny that God sits upon a throne or speaks to humankind is to deny both the Quran and divine attributes. But to take it literally is to make God corporeal which amounts to *tashbih*, literal anthropomorphism. Both are incorrect. Quranic assertions about God, however, must be believed – but *bilā kayfā* (without asking how).[19] This last doctrine was originally developed by the orthodox theologian and traditionist–jurist Aḥmad Ibn Hanbal (d. 855), the founder of the last of the four Sunni schools of law. He was publicly flagellated in Baghdad and incarcerated for his views during the rationalist inquisition. But his traditional views were to triumph later to become not only an incubus but an operative veto on further inquiry into the metaphysical obscurities of the Quran.

13

We now turn to 'Islamic philosophy'. A preliminary consideration that must be recorded but not resolved: I am aware of the 'epistemicide' that racist and orientalist scholarship can commit by speaking of 'Islamic philosophy' or 'Arab philosophy' as if it were inferior to philosophy proper which is, of course, identified with western philosophy. 'Epistemicide' is a valuable term[20] which alerts us to the dangers inherent in the conjunction of knowledge with power, as we see when we discuss Francis Bacon in Chapter 8. It can be a way of reducing the pure search for wisdom into a mere ideology.

Muslim thinkers from the late ninth to early twelfth Christian centuries produced a philosophical tradition relatively free from religious domination. Individual philosophers such as Ibn Rushd (and possibly Al-Kindī) were mildly persecuted but no caliph behaved like the Byzantine emperor Justinian who, in 529, closed all schools of philosophy, including Plato's Academy. However, as in medieval Europe, some Muslim philosophers, particularly Ibn Rushd, probably concealed some of their real opinions and intentions. In Descartes' case, for example, to cite a fellow sufferer in a sister faith, the need for secrecy arose after the 1633 condemnation of Galileo's Copernicanism by the Roman Inquisition.[21]

Although the debate about a thinker's real ideas is often one that amuses only experts and lacks any other value, we note the pertinent principle that, in a traditional doctrinal scheme, it is necessary to conceal the novelty of an idea. The idea has to be presented and offered under the patronage of an older, usually revealed, text. Everything new has to be presented as a commentary on something old. Only in this way can doctrine evolve without exciting the charge of heresy. One could always claim that a new interpretation was truer or closer to the intention of the original. Islamic philosophical writings often appear as commentaries on ancient, including revealed, texts – and are the more likely to appear in this guise if the thought contained in them is original and heretical.

The attempt to synthesize the rational Greek elements and the revealed Quranic ones begins late in Islamic history, an indication that this impulse was external, not latent. There was no Arab philosophy under the first Muslim dynasty, the Umayyad caliphate (661–750), whose rulers were sometimes committed to ethnic rather than religious principles. The earliest philosophical efforts were made under the more religiously open-minded and politically universal rule of the Abbasids (750–1258) based in Baghdad. The father of Arab Islamic philosophy, Abu Yūsuf Ya'qūb Ibn Isḥāq Al-Kindī (d. *c.* 866–73; 252–60 AH), was the only important ethnically Arabian philosopher.[22] An aristocrat, he introduced philosophy to the Abbasid court at Baghdad, where he tutored the son of the caliph Al-Mu'taṣim. Like other Muslim philosophers, he did not have the privilege of knowing Greek but used translations made directly from Greek originals or via the Syriac translations executed by Hellenized Christians. He was probably secretly sympathetic to the intellectual tenor of the rationalist school of the Mu'tazilites.

Early in his treatise *Fī Al-Falsafa Al-Ūlā* (*Concerning the First Philosophy*), Al-Kindī establishes as religiously permissible a measure of cosmopolitanism in intellectual culture.[23] Al-Kindī is important today since respect for the achievements of alien cultures in scholarship is not found even now among some Muslims. He was ahead of his times and perhaps ahead of our times in being willing to seek truth in all places. In Chapter 12, we examine this issue when we discuss the Islamization of knowledge project associated with some twentieth-century Muslim apologists. This ambitious project seeks to dissolve the problem of the confrontation between Islam and secularism by Islamizing all knowledge claims and thus appropriating them as internal to Islamic civilization.

Al-Kindī is not an important philosopher of religion. He was indifferent to religious concerns and wrote on ontological and ethical rather than eschatological themes, re-directing from revealed faith to rational philosophy the metaphysical concerns of the earlier and contemporary Muslim rationalist theologians. His views are compatible with Islamic monotheism partly because he avoids religious themes. He defended standard tenets of orthodoxy: the existence and unity of God, the temporal creation of the universe by divine arbitrium, the human need for prophetic guidance, and the inimitability (*I'jāz*) of the Quran. He argued, radically, however, for the compatibility of Islam and philosophical reason. He defended the importance of a foreign science at a time when orthodoxy approved of only the transmitted sciences (*al-'ulūm al-naqliyyah*) which were considered fundamental to Islam.[24] The secondary rational sciences (*al-'ulūm al-'aqliyyah*) included orthodox theology (*kalām*) and some types of philosophy. But Al-Kindī's view that philosophers acquire knowledge through rational inquiry while prophets receive *the same knowledge* instantaneously through revelation was heretical.

While not important to us today as a philosopher of religion, his role was crucial in two ways: he introduced and defended, using arguments acceptable to Muslims, a measure of intellectual universalism, as noted earlier, and secondly he developed nomenclature that would enable Greek philosophical reflection to be expressed in Arabic. Al Kindī's work on definition (*Fī Ḥudūd Al-Ashyā'a wa Rusūmihā*; Concerning the Definitions and Descriptions of Things) takes concepts such as creation, the first cause and finitude, and re-defines them in Arab idiom. In this way, he prepared the way for later thinkers such as Ibn Sīnā (Avicenna; d. 1037) whose treatise *Kitāb Al-Ḥudūd* (Book of Definitions) had, by the eleventh century, replaced Al-Kindī's pioneering terminological endeavours.

The neo-Platonist thinker and musical theorist Abū Naṣr Al-Fārābī (d. 950) anticipated aspects of the thought of the last Muslim thinker, Ibn Rushd. Al-Fārābī was inspired by Plato's *Republic* and wrote a book modelled on it: 'The Opinions of the People of the Virtuous City'. In this utopian scheme, society realizes its full potential when governed by a philosopher–prophet. Al-Fārābī agreed with Al-Kindī that a prophet's intellect receives religious and philosophical truths as instantaneous intuition, without intermediate mental effort. He communicates only the religious truths to the masses since they cannot understand niceties such as Greek metaphysics. Although religion is an imitation of philosophy, the essential truth of philosophy and religion is the same. Al-Fārābī, like all the philosophers who came after him, insinuates that prophets, unlike thinkers, used rhetoric and affected their speech in order to make their point. Orthodox Muslims saw this view as derogatory since they revered prophets and, on Quranic authority, saw sincerity and truthfulness as the hallmarks of their speech and conduct (Q:19:54–6; 38:86). We shall examine this claim below in the context of Ibn Rushd's thought.

Finally, Ibn Sīnā, armed with a more precise ontology than Al-Kindī's, combined universal Islamic mysticism with an elitist Platonic idealism. He is the main target of the determined assault by the anti-philosophical but philosophically sophisticated theologian Al-Ghazālī. Ibn Sīnā is, as we shall see presently, unique among classical Muslim philosophers as his thinking survives the demise of Islam's mainstream philosophical tradition.

Al-Ghazālī was disturbed by the philosophers' eclectic and cosmopolitan approach to knowledge because, for him, every significant belief or project must find a basis in the Quran or at least in the mind and policy of the Prophet. If Islam is the best religion, how is it possible for God to have overlooked anything seminal – such as philosophy was claimed to be? Al-Ghazālī showed conservative thinkers the impiety of placing excessive confidence in the prowess of philosophical reason. He signed the death-warrant for philosophy in the Muslim Orient. But the subject was about to be revived on the western frontiers of the Islamic empire.[25]

14

The climax of Arabo-Islamic philosophy is reached in the work of the twelfth-century philosopher–jurist Abū Al-Walīd Muhammad Ibn Rushd, the greatest representative of radical Aristotelianism in Arab idiom.[26] He flourished in multi-cultural Muslim Spain and is the only western philosopher to have disturbed two orthodoxies: Islamic and medieval Christian. Some of his works were burned in

Spain, perhaps at the instigation of the Mālikī jurists who conducted a mild inquisition; an interpretation of his main epistemological ideas was twice anathematized at the University of Paris (in 1270 and 1277).

Ibn Rushd was born in Cordoba in 1126, about a millennium after the death, in that same city, of (Lucius Annaeus) Seneca (*c.* 3 BCE–65 CE), the Stoic philosopher who tutored the Emperor Nero. (The Jewish philosopher–halakhist and codifier Maimonides, another native of Cordoba, was born about a decade after Ibn Rushd.) Under lenient royal patronage, Ibn Rushd worked as a judge (*qāḍī*) and wrote philosophical commentaries and treatises. He launched methodical and trenchant attacks on Ibn Sīnā and on Al-Ghazālī.

Like the rationalist philosopher Leibniz (1646–1716), Ibn Rushd received extensive legal training.[27] His training, in the Mālikī school of jurisprudence, influenced his philosophical method. He remained sufficiently traditional to memorize the *Kitāb Al-Muwaṭṭā'* (The Book of the Beaten Track), the manual of law written by Imam Malik Ibn Anas (d. 795), the (informal) founder of that school. As the earliest collection of Islamic law, it reflects accurately the spirit of Muhammad's utopian society in Medina, the city where Malik lived. In two ways, Ibn Rushd, both as philosopher and jurist, was decisively influenced by his Mālikī background. First, Malik applauded the effort to deduce sound legal opinions by the exertion of independent personal reason, *ijtihād*, and emphasized it more than any of the later jurist–traditionists. Second, Mālikī jurists were guided in their independent intellectual effort by *istiṣlah*, the principle of discerning the intended good of the Quran's and the Prophet's injunctions only in relation to the empirical demands of human welfare (*maṣlaḥah*) rather than through an a priori attachment to revealed dogma.[28] The Mālikīs allowed this juridical principle to over-rule even a deduction from the Quran and Muhammad's custom (*sunnah*), sources which are in theory supremely authoritative.

Ibn Rushd's early biographers seem embarrassed to admit that he was also trained in Greek philosophy. They use euphemisms such as *'ulūm al-ḥikmiyya*, the sciences of wisdom. His chief Arab biographer Ibn Al-Abbār demurely mentions that Ibn Rushd inclined towards what Al-Abbār blandly describes as the sciences of the ancients (*'ulūm al-awwā'il*).[29]

It is necessary, argued Ibn Rushd, to inquire into the deposit of ancient learning provided that one has the intellectual capacity for it. He was commissioned by a liberal caliph to interpret Aristotle. He commented on the entire Aristotelian corpus except *Politics*.[30] Writing a commentary implies a measure of reverence for a human author and the genre was, among the devout, reserved for the Quran. Averroës wrote short commentaries or paraphrases (*dhawāmi'*) on some Aristotelian works;[31] the middle commentaries (*talkhīṣ*) were to follow.[32] Most of his original philosophical work, including the two short disquisitions we examine below, is sandwiched between these shorter commentaries and the long commentaries (*tafsīr*). The long treatises concede little to Islamic orthodoxy and were perhaps aimed mainly at his fellow philosophers. The medium and short commentaries, directed at the intelligentsia and ordinary believers respectively, are not intellectually daring. Ibn Rushd was shrewd enough to recognize the need to mislead obscurantists, a prudence that required the suppression of the nobler Socratic willingness to openly pursue philosophical truth even if one had to drink the hemlock for it.

During the last two years of his life, Ibn Rushd suffered a brief banishment and also had to tolerate some vulgar epigrams written by his critics. He regained the favour of the next prince, Ya'qūb Al-Manṣūr (r. 1184–99), but died soon afterwards at the end of 1198 in Marrakush (in modern Morocco). His body was buried in his native Cordoba. At once European, Arab, African and Muslim, Ibn Rushd was an intellectual bridge-builder whose life and work provides a unique symbol, native to Islam, of an approach to religion free of parochial limitations. Ibn Rushd took Al-Kindī's enlightened cosmopolitanism a step further. In Ibn Rushd's work, we see the Graeco-Islamic roots of western medieval and Renaissance philosophical thought which was eventually to flower into the Enlightenment. Sadly, most Muslims have refused to make amends even retrospectively for ignoring 'the Muslim Aristotle'.[33]

15

We examined earlier the impasse between faith and reason. Ibn Rushd uses a different terminology to explore this theme when he writes of the convergence between revealed law and philosophy. This is shown in the title of his short tract: *Faṣl Al-Maqāl wa Taqrīb ma bayn Al-Sharī'ah wa Al-Ḥikmah min Al-Ittiṣāl* (A decisive treatise and exposition concerning the harmony that obtains between the holy law and wisdom/philosophy). It is dated to 1179 (575 AH).[34] He cites the Quran often to show that the rational (philosophical) study of creation leads to knowledge of the creator. The rational method is therefore compatible with the teachings of revelation. He returns to a related theme in another short tract on the uses of reason in the examination of religious doctrines. This second treatise, *Kitāb Al-Kashf 'an Manāhij Al-Adilla* (Treatise on the Methods of Proof), also dated to 1179, mentions the *Faṣl Al-Maqāl*. At the beginning of this second treatise, he explores again the question of the accessibility of metaphysical truths to different levels of intelligence in varied classes of people.

Ibn Rushd recognizes the holy law, *Al-Sharī'ah,* as 'the milk sister of philosophy (*al-ḥikmah*)'. Both are valid disciplines; he wants to eliminate the pseudo-discipline of *kalām*, a meddlesome relative who creates needless problems, especially the false opposition between faith and reason. (Al-Ghazālī would concur with Ibn Rushd here but Al-Ghazālī condemned *kalām* as dangerous – but solely on religious grounds.) For Ibn Rushd, the pursuit of philosophy in the form of wisdom is not merely permitted but commanded by the *Sharī'ah* – but only for those of sufficient ability. The proviso is based on the Quranic maxim that God lays no burden too heavy for a person to bear (Q:2:286). Ibn Rushd marshals countless passages from scripture to support his view that the holy law commands the believer to think about the existence of beings and objects.

There are similarities between philosophy and revealed religion, if not between philosophy and religious law. Ibn Rushd was right to suspect some common ground between revealed religion and philosophy although one cannot reasonably cite the Quran in deriving these alleged similarities. It is nonetheless helpful to trace these similarities if only to lessen, indirectly, the tension between faith and reason.

First, theism is itself a philosophical position as we see in Chapter 12 when we discuss natural theology. Second, philosophy, like religion and ethics, is prescriptive, not descriptive. For example, to say that human beings are rational is not to say that we are actually rational – plainly untrue most of the time – but rather that we ought to be so and that we have the potential for it. We have 'normative ambiguity' here in the use of 'rational'.[35] The Greeks claimed that our rational capacity deservedly makes us distinctly and essentially human, distinguishing us from the animals. Apart from dolphins and some species of whales, reasoning is perhaps the only human trait that (potentially) distinguishes all of us from the lower orders of animals. Religion and philosophy both take a prescriptive interest in the essence of humankind; even their views of human essence are sometimes similar.

Let us explore some further similarities between religion and philosophy. Both are constructive in several ways. Philosophy, unlike religion, has no fixed body of doctrine but, like religion, it seeks answers to life's basic questions which relate to matters of moment. It is in that sense constructive. Religion begins in a diagnosis of sin or despair and moves towards salvation or religious success or enlightenment. Similarly, the philosopher who identifies the human predicament also shows us a way out. Even Wittgenstein, who refused to offer any philosophical doctrines, admits that we are trapped and enchanted by the tricks of language and that philosophy shows the fly the way out of the bottle. Religion and philosophy are both critical: religion as moral criticism since it critiques our individual and societal failings, philosophy as rational criticism.

The differences are in method and technique. Religion is more synoptic than analytical since it synthesizes materials to give a common vision that enables a culture or society. Religion changes the world while philosophy merely interprets it – although these two aims are not unrelated except in the creed of scholastic isolationism. The crucial difference is in the fallibilistic method of philosophy. The rational method of philosophy, like that of science, is in practice absolute and immutable but the results of its inquiries are acknowledged to be fallible and provisional, making for an open-ended and reflective quality often missing in religion. There are then, notwithstanding differences, also some genuine similarities between religion (faith) and philosophy (reason) – but this does not reduce the competition between them. What is in common need not unite here any more than it does in inter-faith encounter among related faiths.

16

Ibn Rushd addresses and resolves the problem of faith versus reason by effectively espousing a rather condescending view held also by al-Fārābī before him: the Quran, for most of its readers, appeals to emotion, not reason. Ibn Rushd endorsed an elitist Platonic view of intellectual classes according to which different people have different levels of understanding. He speculated that not all human beings give assent (*taṣdīq*) to proof by demonstrative syllogism (*burhān*). Theologians prefer dialectical discourses: (*al-aqāwil al-jadaliyyah*) and the masses prefer rhetorical speech (*khiṭabiyya*). Few accept proof by demonstration; many assent to dialectical discourse. The majority are convinced only by rhetoric. Therefore, Ibn Rushd concurs wth the Quran that we should 'invite all to the way of your Lord, with wisdom and through dignified admonition and argue with them in the best way' (Q:16:126).

For Ibn Rushd, only the intellectually gifted, the philosophers, can grasp truth in its abstract theoretical form; theologians can think rationally but only inside the limits set by revelation. The largest group, ordinary gullible people, possesses keen emotional awareness and can attain to truth only in its most material and unrefined form – in literal terms with the support of similes and metaphors that portray vividly what is by nature abstract. This view implies that, with respect to most of its listeners and readers, scripture does not convince rationally but rather merely persuades psychologically.

Nor is the elitism in this account the main problem. The Quran approves of elitism at the social, political and spiritual levels, often promoting it. It approves of social inequality and rank (*faḍīlah*, preference, from *faḍl*, grace; Q:24:20, 32) in this world, differentiating slaves from masters, men from women, and parents from children (Q:4:34; 24:22, 58; 43:32). Moreover, God raises the righteous, including the apostles, to different grades (*darajah,* sing; *darajāt,* pl.) in both worlds (Q:2:253; 4:96; 6:83, 132, 165; 17:21, 55; 43:32; 46:19; 57:10; 58:11). It tempers potential hubris among the pious and knowledgeable elite by reminding them that 'over every one who has knowledge, there is one who is all-knowing' (Q:12:76). Elitism is, in any event, inevitable where complex skills are to be acquired; and evidently it need not be objectionable if superiority and recognition are earned on the basis of excellence and expertise in a discipline.

Indeed, for the philosopher, as Plato would have argued, there are no final mysteries in the world: all is intelligible through organized and sustained reflection. Ibn Rushd believed that while the inner meaning of the Quran, its esoteric interpretation (*ta'wīl*; Q:3:7) was hidden from the masses, philosophers had access to its private and sophisticated significance. Like Al-Kindī and Al-Fārābī before him, Ibn Rushd proceeded as though faith merely seeks truth, revelation finds and expresses a part of it, while only philosophy fully possesses and expounds it. This is hardly a religiously acceptable epistemology. Even secular western philosophers have not accorded so immodest a role to philosophical reason! David Hume, for instance, assigned a strikingly circumscribed role to it.

A problem deeper than this elitism, indeed this intellectual apartheid, is Ibn Rushd's general outlook which implies that revealed religion is a simplified and popular form of philosophy, a diluted metaphysics for the masses. For him, religious truth is an allegorical form of a higher philosophical truth. Thus, the Quran and Aristotle are compatible and complementary. Ibn Rushd even seems to grant philosophy a degree above other valid routes to knowledge. He upholds the absolute sovereignty of reason; his inspiration is usually Aristotle rather than the Quran.

He tends to use the Muslim scripture to justify alien philosophical convictions found naturally in Greek thought. By contrast, for believers, including Ibn Rushd's predecessor Al-Ghazālī, the most resolute enemy of the content (as opposed to methods) of Greek philosophy, the Quran is directly the source of every significant true belief. We shall turn presently to this ultimate and perhaps irresolvable difference of perspective.

17

Arabo-Islamic philosophy was Aristotelian in its logic, physics, metaphysics and ethics; it was Platonist in its politics and neo-Platonist in its mysticism and theology. The tension between revealed Islamic claims and the rationally attained certainties of Greek philosophy was hardly felt in ethics. In epistemology, metaphysics and ontology, however, the ideas inspired by the encounter with the Greeks appeared to be a custom-made insult to Islam. In his *Tahāfut Al-Falāsifa* (The Inconsistency of the Philosophers), Al-Ghazālī lists 17 theses that imply heresy (*bid'ah*); three of them are tantamount to disbelief (*kufr*), a capital charge. Al-Ghazālī argued against Ibn Sīnā in particular but against all the 'Muslim' philosophers in general.[36]

The first heretical opinion, which plagued Islamic and Christian orthodoxies, was alien to both. Aristotle set one needlessly insoluble problem which exhausted the genius of medieval Christian thought: he pontificated that matter could not have had a beginning. The task of justifying divine creation against the Aristotelian dogma of the eternity of the world preoccupied Christians and Muslims. Abū Bakr Zakariyā Al-Rāzī (d. *c.* 926), a Platonist and free-thinker, even rejected the Quranic account of creation out of nothing in favour of Plato's view in the *Timaeus* that a demiurge imposed order on a chaos of primeval matter floating as atoms in an absolute void.[37]

The second heresy was that the resurrection was only in the spirit, not in the body, a problem that also agitated Paul in the Corinthian correspondence (1 Corinthians 15: 12–54). The Quran teaches a resurrection of the whole human personality with even the finger-tips restored (Q:75:4). The third unacceptable idea was that God's knowledge is restricted to universals (*katholou*) since his nature is too exalted and perfect to take an interest in trivialities such as particulars. The Quran teaches that God's knowledge extends to the most infinitesimal realities. Even a leaf does not fall without his knowledge (Q:6:59) and not even an atom's weight is hidden from him (Q:34:3).

A general point, which widens this debate, shall serve to end this part of our discussion: a revealing difference between Al-Ghazālī and the Muslim philosophers is the radically different roles they assign to God's agency in the material universe. Al-Ghazālī argues that believers are religiously obliged to deny the eternity of the world and the objectivity of causation. The origin and causation of events lies only contingently in this world since causation radically depends on God's direct volition. Al-Ghazālī even denied natural causality altogether: whenever God wills an act by a human 'agent', he creates both the act and its cause.

The Muslim philosophers admired Greek rationalism too much to subscribe to such a fanatically religious view of the world.

18

The battle for philosophy, which began with Al-Kindī, was won for religion by Al-Ghazālī who was distressed by the impiety of excessive confidence in the prowess of philosophical reason at the expense of revealed guidance and by the heretical conclusions that reason sometimes reached. Islamo-Hellenistic philosophy formally ended with Ibn Rushd; it was suffocated by the forces of orthodoxy. There is, especially in Iran, an extant Shi'ite tradition of reflection on mystical and devotional themes. It inherits Ibn Sīnā's mystical and existential theosophical speculation about the divine nature but it lacks the rigour and intellectual penetration of the Muslim scholastic theologians and also the logical precision and analytical depth of the mainstream Islamic philosophers. Most of the Shi'ite materials are mystifying rather than mystical: writers use exalted phrases of unclear meaning which enable them to shoot off into outer intellectual space where they feel free to adopt a very relaxed attitude towards the more mundane logical laws of consistency and contradiction.

Ever since his single-handed demolition of the Islamic philosophical edifice, ordinary Muslims have concurred with Al-Ghazālī that philosophy fathers unnecessary doubts and hesitations, raises questions about the duties of the faith and replaces revealed certainties with the ambiguities, confusions and conjectures of unaided reason. God has mercifully supplied believers with the knowledge required for success in the life-style he has chosen for them (Q:5:3). There is neither the time nor the necessity for philosophy in a world awaiting 'the hour' and blessed with the benefits of the most comprehensive and clear scripture given to humankind. For Al-Ghazālī, the implication of the view that philosophy is needed is that the Quran is deficient in guidance. Fortunately, God has supplied truths we could not have discovered alone – and moreover done so in a language accessible to the simple believer. No philosopher could improve on that arrangement.

Modern Muslims think that the philosophers were unfaithful to the spirit of Islam when they sought to replace its certainties with doubt and perplexity of foreign origin. Orthodox Muslims sensed the unsettling power of the independent rational mind and wanted to curb its freedoms. The rebellious philosophical mentality plagued the labours of orthodox Muslims who worked hard to provide detailed guidance for living the God-fearing life, an ambition cultivated from the Quran (see Q:3:104, 9:122). This ancient suspicion of Greek philosophy has, after the experience of western colonialism, widened out to include all modern western intellectual projects, especially orientalism.

Before I examine modern concerns, I summarize the historical issues by ranging over the terrain covered thus far but with a view to future developments. Theology, as a subject disciplined by the supervision of law (*fiqh*), relied on the exegetical use of reason in order to extract new opinions from sacred texts and thus to understand and explicate scripture. Theology was a form of hermeneutics and in that sense was systematically practised as early as Abū Ḥanīfah (d. 767) and Malik Ibn Anas (d. 795). The role of reason was neither ambitious nor subversive. Its stimuli were wholly internal and indigenous. Insofar as any discipline requires training and expertise, it was acknowledged that elitism was inevitable in theology too – but theologians entertained no condescending views which would require them to necessarily restrict their knowledge to a select group.

After Greek writings became available in Arabic, we encounter the first external and therefore potentially heretical stimulus: the methods of Greek reasoning, syllogism and other techniques of logic and some basic metaphysics and ontology. It led to the birth of a dialectical theology which reached controversial conclusions. Its aims, however, were internal to Islam since it sought to resolve anxieties inherent in scripture – worries about free will and responsibility and the justice of God. But any deep inquiry carries the risk of doubt. The Muʿtazilite rationalist school combined extra-Quranic methods of inquiry with a sincerely religious quest for finding truths embedded in a scripture which, for all its claims to clarity, contained much metaphysical obscurity.

Philosophy, however, emerged late: the impulse was not latent in Islam. Philosophy was not inspired by an internal struggle with the Quran's views on justice or during the attempt to solve the urgent practical question of excommunication (*takfīr*) of the reprobate sinner. It was born during a bid for the autonomy of secular reason – something bound to provoke orthodoxy. Thus, in its impulses, methods and priorities, philosophy contained the germ of a foreign and subversive idea. Predictably, it was aborted. Theology, however, survived as philosophical theology in the works of Al-Ashʿarī and Al-Ghazālī who borrowed Greek methods but did not treat the rational quest as an autonomous search for knowledge that may lead to an unpredictable destination. They remained believers.

19

We turn now to modern anxieties and plans for the future of philosophy, especially philosophy of religion, in the Muslim world. A preliminary observation: philosophy of religion in western academic departments is a philosophy of the Christian religion.[38] A few writers lump Judaism and Islam with Christianity and assume that the major problems of the philosophy of religion arise in all monotheisms. This is only partly true and we can gauge this from a fact in the sociology of philosophical debate: Islamic thought does not concede as fundamental the problem of evil (and the associated problem of the overwhelming amount of suffering it causes) in a universe created and ruled by a good and omnipotent God. No Muslim thinker or educated layman has identified theodicy as a project worthy of elaborate consideration. And yet, among western philosophers of religion, the problem of evil takes a place at least as prominent as the problem of proving God's very existence.[39]

We need three presuppositions – hypotheses we place temporarily beyond criticism – to establish the proposed discipline of 'philosophy of the Islamic religion'. As the minimal assumptions of an objective and detached study of Islam, these three assumptions, each controversial but defensible, underlie any philosophy of any monotheism.

First, religious belief comes under a subdivision of belief in general; as a category of conviction, it is not *sui generis*. It need not differ, epistemologically, from other beliefs such as historical or political or moral. The religious content of a belief does not endow it with a special quality called 'religious' which might make it automatically either true or false or implausible or plausible. Nor does any psychological certainty automatically accrue to a belief solely because it is religious. We entertain a religious belief in the same way, with the same attendant risks of error, as we entertain other types of beliefs. There is nothing special about religious belief except its object.

This is part of a larger concern. For some thinkers, notably Kierkegaard and the later Wittgenstein, the religious use of the verb 'to believe' is radically different from its use in non-religious, scientific and commonsensical contexts. This implies a total opposition of religious belief and all other kinds of belief. We must reject this dangerous dichotomy. Our stance has wider implications. The sceptic's demand for evidence in the ordinary sense of this word is justified and begs no question. Religious belief sets out to be rational; and it is a critic's right to convict it of irrationality if it violates a generally and sufficiently comprehensive and widely accepted standard of rationality.

Second, the object of religious belief, while special to the believer, must not be assumed to be so special that it is considered the cause of the belief itself arising in the believer's mind. The existence (or non-existence) of God is irrelevant to the possibility of holding the view that there is a God or of experiencing God. If there is a God, he would probably use the psychological need for him to be a basis for a belief in him. But the mere fact that men and women believe in God does not entail that the human mind is an arena for the direct activities of God (or his angelic agents). We could believe in God even if he does not exist; this is no different, in terms of the logic of the situation, from the way we could believe in fabulous entities of folk-lore.

The third assumption is partly related to the first but adds a new dimension to the notion of belief. Even if religious belief is a special gift of grace, it is at another level simultaneously a purely human conviction whose content is subject to ordinary rational appraisal and scrutiny. Religious belief is not autonomous;[40] a corollary of this assumption is that even if authentic revelation is the only source of fully true religious ideas, the thinker may still reasonably assess the truth and plausibility of revealed claims once these appear in the human world of reason. The element of grace does not add an extra dimension to the *content* of the belief. Admittedly, a religious belief may be held with far greater psychological certainty than most other beliefs, even to the point where the believer welcomes danger and death – although secular political beliefs are also held with marked intensity. In any case, nothing can immunize religious belief against secular scrutiny.

These three assumptions permit the possibility that a Muslim philosopher of religion can question and assess both the rationality and the truth of the Quran. The Muslim theologian, by contrast, expounds the faith and asks only to have the right to assess the rationality of the faith – and that only as part of the apologetic project of defending the faith against outsiders and heretics. Muslim theologians assume the truth of the Quran; this is a presupposition of their professional task. The Muslim philosopher, *qua* philosopher, can assume neither the rational plausibility nor the truth of the Quran's claims. The analytical philosophy of religion, narrowly conceived, analyses the logic of religious ideas, examines the religious uses of language, and elucidates the meaning of relevant concepts – but reserves judgement on the truth or falsity of the religious beliefs entertained. I understand it as aiming at conceptual analysis and logical rigour as means to an end, namely, the substantive inquiries that arrive finally at the truth of the matter.

A Muslim believer might object that, in making this trio of assumptions, I have begged the question against Islamic orthodoxy: these assumptions privilege the sceptical position by placing the burden of proof on the believer's shoulders. This is a valid but answerable objection. No method or project, whether sceptical or committed, can be free of presuppositions, even prejudices. The least controversial method is the one nourished by the least number of controversial assumptions. Crucial questions are begged inevitably no matter where one starts or terminates an inquiry. In a secular age, it is easier to argue persuasively for the modest position outlined above. If we start with only those three assumptions, we can still reach conclusions favourable to religious belief. The above view does beg the question against one robust orthodox position but it does not do so against every religious position. The believer might still retort that these assumptions are dictated by a secular view of revealed knowledge. We have reached a deadlock.

20

Can Muslims, tutored by the Quran, provisionally bracket the issue of the truth of Islam, and treat it as an open question? Can they reasonably combine an active fealty to Islamic beliefs with an endorsement of free inquiry about their true epistemological status? We have tried to answer these two questions. The Quran condemns the free-thinking rejector as 'an open disputant' who forgets his humble origins and even humbler future (Q:36:77). The believer is counselled to submit all his faculties to God (Q:2:208). The modern sceptic argues that our minds must submit to the authority of the reasonable and the factual and only derivatively, if at all, to the authority of revelation. We note here a conflict of basic loyalties. The believer must see doubt and suspended commitment as foreign to the religious requirement of sustained faithful commitment while the secularist seeks total exemption from the dogmatic pressures of religion. These are irreconcilably opposed attitudes. If philosophy is an autonomous branch of learning with reason as its only tool, then it cannot serve two masters. At best it might occasionally and indirectly serve religious ends.

Although the Quran does not explicitly ban free inquiry, we cannot convincingly extract from it a celebration of free inquiry in the modern sense of an unended quest that need not terminate in an already acknowledged creed or conviction. The Quran does not order Muslims to undertake a critical philosophical study of their core religious convictions; there are no specifically Quranic grounds for this distinctively secular ambition. Devout believers (of all faiths) see no value in free and sustained philosophical inquiry into religious claims since they think that revelation already and uncomplicatedly contains the whole truth.

It is indirect evidence of the intractability of the reason–faith dispute that we are obliged to deflect the debate onto a less philosophical plane – into a factual or soci-ological view of 'rationality', as opposed to reason, and as a corollary, onto a novel division of labour within the institutional pursuit of knowledge. We can secure a temporary truce between the free thinkers and the religiously inclined jurists and theologians by partitioning religious studies into three distinct categories. The first include the recently established descriptive (partly interpretive) academic disci-plines such as the comparative and historical study of religion. Their establishment and flourishing required healthy respect for the autonomy of secular reason and for the legitimacy of a private agnosticism about all robust religious schemes. The sec-ond group contains normative disciplines including dialectical theology, branches of Islamic law and jurisprudence, including *al-ʿaqīdah* (corresponding to dogmat-ics in Christian theology). These prescriptive branches of knowledge confessedly and legitimately rely on the authority of revelation and grew out of the historical and current practice of faiths as institutionalized and often empowered realities.

Third, in a class of its own, is the generic discipline called philosophy of reli-gion where we rationally examine competing religious claims, without deference to the authority of any revealed criterion of judgement. Philosophy of religion is parasitic on the existence of religion. Theology (or *kalām*) openly relies on the authority of revelation while the philosophy of revelations treats all types of reli-gious faith, scriptures and experience as its domain and employs only unaided reason to guide its endeavours. It does not presuppose the privileged position of any faith. It aims, through conceptual analysis and elucidation, at discovering what religious truths, if any, are implied by the findings of the established descriptive (or interpretive) disciplines of comparative religion and the psychology, anthro-pology, phenomenology, sociology, and the history of religion. The philosopher may also investigate the implications of the empirical findings of relatively new fields such as the psychobiography and psychopathology of religious genius and the biology of religious belief – including the study of neurological injuries which cause religious obsession and neuropsychiatric disorders which might affect the quality of religious conviction.

Theologies, unlike the philosophies of religions, start with the lived faiths of particular religious communities. Theologians expound and defend their chosen faith and cannot doubt its central tenets. If they seriously question whether a particular dogma is revealed and authoritative, they can do so only as philosophers of that religion.

If we accept as legitimate these distinctions and the related divisions of intel-lectual labour, then believing philosophers of religion will, as philosophers, seek exemption from any veto on independent assessment of the bases of their faith in relation to other faiths and secular humanism. Theologians will think inside the orbit of their faith. Institutionally, the faithful philosopher of religion may conscientiously teach the secular university syllabus while the theologian would appropriately teach in a *madrasah* (Islamic seminary).

Some Muslim thinkers might object to this arrangement because, in Islamic history, many jurists set themselves up as arbiters of all knowledge rather than of merely legal knowledge. The Quranic word *'ulamā'* means 'the learned ones' and refers to God's most devout and intelligent servants (Q:35:28). The term, like the word *al-'ālimūn* (those who know; Q:29:43), is vague. It can mean all religiously learned individuals and is used to denote both the rabbinate (Q:26:197) and the Muslim religious intelligentsia (*'ulamā'*). After Al-Ghazālī, and due mainly to his efforts, the word came to be used in a restricted sense to mean those trained in religious studies. This division is foreign to the Quran which uses *'ilm* to mean all knowledge. This bifurcation of knowledge led to a deleterious split between the secular and religious curricula. The split continues to exist in Islamic education with the damaging consequence that, unlike their modern Christian and Jewish counterparts, Muslim religious scholars are typically trained solely in religious studies.

21

There is a perennial friction between the demands of a rational scheme that cannot even in principle tolerate a curtailment of its autonomy by supernatural authority, on the one hand, and the equally rigid demands of a dogmatic orthodoxy which confidently sees itself as terminative and authoritative, on the other. We see this in the refusal of the Muslim philosophers to limit the powers of critical reason in the battle between the Quran and the Greeks. In this battle, the philosophers were, with much reason, suspected of being on the Greek side. For the believer, however, as we saw with Al-Ghazālī, the decisive thinker who signed the death-warrant for sceptical philosophy in the Sunni Muslim Orient, faith is an undeserved gift of divine grace, to be accepted on divine authority.

The most developed systems of faith were, ironically, reared in the bosom of rationalism. Islam's scholastic dialectical theology was developed in an age of intense faith. Indeed it is secular reason which is dogmatic and exclusivist. Ages of faith have nurtured great systems of reasoned conviction while, by contrast, the age of secular reason has, from its dawn, arrogantly rejected revelation without granting it a hearing. The most rigorously rationalistic systems of philosophy, such as medieval scholasticism and Thomism, matured in the bosom of faith. Absolute faith still allows an interface of faith and reason, an exchange between the two antagonists. But absolute reason is intolerant of the very possibility of revelation. It reasons in a circle: reason alone discovers truth and truth is that which reason discovers. The believer's methodology, which sanctions the use of reason only in the decipherment of the linguistic truth of the revelation, is as legitimate and as rational as any other. But does it adequately stretch the resources of reason? Should reason be restricted to such a modest exegetical role?

Islam and Latin Christendom, in their heyday, both cast a shell of faith over the adolescent mind of their respective communities. Within this shell, the scholastic philosophers of medieval Europe moved cautiously and narrowly from premises of revealed faith to conclusions of reasonable import – and back again. The syllogistic circuit of deductive reasoning was endlessly ingenious. We today see it as a baffling maze of unargued assumptions and religiously pre-ordained conclusions in which the greatest feat of logical legerdemain was to turn that inquisitive Greek – Aristotle – into a dogmatic Christian theologian! In the end, thanks to the continuing development of philosophy, the intellect of Europe burst out of that shell but, unfortunately, swung to the opposite extreme of scepticism and rejection of all supernatural truths. The Islamic shell is still intact; there is no philosopher who can scratch even its outer surface.

In the stalemate between faith and reason, the believer is also entitled to judge the truth of philosophy. Indeed a believer might argue that secularist defenders of reason are guilty of the intellectualist fallacy of reposing an unreasoning faith in the power of reason. What is the nature or ground of rational philosophical authority? The authority of our secular age is part of the contingency of history. The tenets of modernism include the universality of reason, the finality of scientific method and the primacy of history, all of which are rationally assailable. In the end, any encounter of reason and revelation produces a genuine impasse. There is no common foundational ground, no higher court of appeal, no accepted epistemological referee, and no recognized cognitive authority which could adjudicate such a fundamental dispute.

22

The conflict between faith and reason is rooted in variant epistemologies that dictate a different scope and rationale for curiosity. For Muslims, the problem of knowledge does not arise as a secular or autonomous matter but primarily as a religious one. Knowledge was not an end, only a means of attaining success in the religious life just as the feverish acquisition of knowledge today is driven by the need to control resources and exert power. The Quran addresses only the question: 'What should one believe and do in order to win the pleasure of God and thus enter paradise?' A direct and succinct reply is given at Q:61:10–2. This religious focus inevitably leads to a progressive limiting of individual reason and legitimate scope for speculation (Q:17:36). As a corollary of this restriction on speculation, we have a correspondingly greater dependence on authority. Could this explain the demise of the nascent philosophical enterprise among Muslims?

The Arabic Muslim philosophical tradition died in its infancy. There have been and continue to be signs of philosophical and original religious thought outside Islamic orthodoxy. But, as with the natural science that Muslims developed, there is no institutional transmission of these projects of pure inquiry, a transmission that would enable new generations to gain automatic access to it in places of higher learning. Science and philosophy were first culturally and institutionally embedded in western Europe soon after the rise of the medieval universities. Remarkably, these European traditions have continued unbroken to this day.

How do we explain the death (or dramatic decline) of Islamic philosophy? Perhaps the demise of philosophical methods of inquiry was part of the larger demise of a glorious Arabo-Islamic intellectual culture after the heyday of Muslim civilization in the thirteenth Christian century. Soon afterwards, Europe's colonial enterprise eclipsed the whole of the non-western world, including the Islamic Orient. This account fails to account for the fact that philosophy never took root firmly in the soil of Islam even in the intellectual heyday of Muslim civilization. This was a fertile soil watered by the Quran and Muhammad's example and it has up to this day yielded a religiously rich harvest. Was there something intrinsic to Islamic culture and heritage that blocked the philosophical outlet and siphoned off and sublimated latent energies elsewhere – into mysticism and theosophical obscurities?

To see why philosophy died a natural death among Muslims, making Al-Ghazāli's death-warrant unnecessary, we must ask what role Greek philosophy came to play in Judaism and Christianity, the other monotheisms that encountered the Hellenic philosophical enterprise as an independent force and engaged it. In the Jewish case, as we see in the work of Philo Judaeus of Alexandria (20 BCE–40 CE), the Greek philosophical component was used to temper the ethnic concern in Judaism.[41] The Greek philosophical pretension to rationality had universal appeal while Judaism never fully freed itself from the taint of being decidedly ethnic in its religiosity – despite its belief in a universal God. Philo found it natural to wed the ethnic Jewish dimension with the universal Greek dimension.

As for Christianity, Greek language and philosophy were both vital. It is no accident that the New Testament is in Greek, the language of scholarship and diplomacy since the rise of the Hellenic age. The whole development of Christian theology, especially Christology and dogmatics, is conceptually linked to the Greek language, to the philosophy of Plato and the metaphysical categories that Greek philosophy supplied to the Greek fathers of the church. It seems indefensible, to non-Christians, that Christian dogma formulated by the ecumenical councils of the fourth and fifth centuries and couched in Greek philosophical idioms, should be casually attributed to Jesus, a first century Aramaic-speaking rabbi. Placing Semitic texts in the hands of formerly pagan peoples with a penchant for speculation led to the Greek New Testament.

The Islamic case differs from the Jewish and Christian cases. The intellectual culture of pre-Islamic and early Islamic Arabia was not Greek, partly because, as we shall note in Chapter 4, Alexander had died barely weeks before a planned invasion of the Arabian peninsula. The Muslim thinkers had to mentally translate into Arabic, a language that belongs to the Semitic family, and is crucially different from Greek in its concepts of tense, mood, voice and so on. A thinker such as Al-Kindī was a pioneer mainly because he developed a requisite Arabic vocabulary that made Greek thinking expressible in the Arab idiom and thus accessible to Arab Muslims.

Second, Islam was born as an intentionally universal faith. There was therefore no need to introduce a universal component into it, via, let us say, Hellenic rationalism. Moreover, its beliefs were simple and transparent and did not require the convoluted and Byzantine categories of reflection that Christian dogma required as it went through several Christological councils. The inherent complexity of Christian dogma has remained a fertile recruiting ground for philosophy: many Christian theologians have been forced to become philosophers of religion in order to make sense of their faith. Paul Tillich (1886–1965), the Protestant theologian who left his native Germany for the United States, is an outstanding modern example of this trend.

The motives for engaging in Greek philosophy were absent in the Islamic case. Moreover, the faith was too fully developed at its origins to permit a philosophical variant to rise and flourish. Admittedly, the debate about the eternality versus createdness of the Arabic Quran was susceptible to philosophical sophistication. The details of this needless tussle were naturally largely restricted to an elite already suspected of placing too much faith in human reason. The Quran saw itself as climactic, perfected, final and finalized and therefore discouraged speculative curiosity. The Greek plant grew as an unnatural graft imposed on the tree of revealed Islam. Unsurprisingly, with one stroke of the axe, Al-Ghazālī, pruned the plant to leave behind only the original tree of revelation.

The Greek verb *skeptesthai* means to inquire closely into something. Literally, *skepsis* is both inquiry and doubt as though the two were connected. The sceptic (*skepticōs*) is usually a doubter. Certain liberties of thought lead towards doubt, hence the ambivalence about philosophy among all monotheists. As an accident of history, the three Semitic faiths encountered the Hellenic option and had to interweave it into their independent religious traditions. (In eastern faiths, especially Buddhism, philosophical reasoning is part of the faith.) The North African church father Tertullian laments: 'It is philosophy that supplies the heresies with their equipment'.[42] Philosophy is the discipline in which the Devil has perennially found many of his most zealous disciples. We shall return, in Chapter 12, to Islam's defunct philosophical tradition in the context of the continuous tradition of modern western philosophy. In the meantime, we explore the world-outlook of secular humanism, a product of the Greek faith in humankind's unaided reason.

3   The moral challenge of secular humanism

1

In this chapter, we examine the most astute and energetic contemporary antagonist of Islam. Unlike people living in ages when major religions were founded, we cannot dismiss atheism as an exemplary expression of the perverse and anarchic human will resisting surrender to God. Perhaps we are indeed alone in the universe although we can understand the wish to populate this barren immensity with supernatural beings. That puerile deception is, counsels the atheist, no longer for us: the three faiths of the Near East were a trio of oriental despotisms which delayed the birth of an empirical science and a rational political order. Theology is therapeutic mythology.

Post-Enlightenment, there is no credible religion that can make us good or reliably defend us against our own and other people's moral evil. What is the point of any religion any more? With secular humanism as our guide, the atheist continues, we are still defenceless against death – but we are no longer helplessly paralyzed awaiting external rescue on the road of life. Secular humanists proudly defend the intrinsic worth of life; they dismiss extrinsic divine validation which was traditionally expressed by the religious notion of the derivative sanctity of life.

Finally liberated from the ancient tyranny of belief in the supernatural, we may develop a naturalistic philosophy of our nature, external nature, history, society and culture. In the godless world, we will endow point to a pointless life by creating our own values – for we have become gods. Once upon a time, we thought, like the sages of Greece and the prophets of Israel and Arabia, that the purpose of life was to make a good death. The point of life, however, is to live well on earth, the only right place for truth, love, art, justice and happiness. We need no heavenly seal to guarantee the worth of our lives.

Although traditional Judaism and Christianity are no longer intellectually or morally fashionable in most of the advanced industrialized communities of the geographically western world and its satellites and colonies, a suitably revised version of the ethical dimension of both faiths is still considered laudable. It is thought to survive more or less intact the demise of the doctrinal component, an assumption we examine in due course. While many people have lost faith in God and the capacity of traditional religions to supply a purpose for life, they have not lost faith in the possibility of an independent secular meaning and purpose for life.

No modern Muslim thinker has asked whether such a rejection of God and divine purpose for us is intellectually defensible and morally worthy. By contrast, many Jews and Christians, in the scholarly, liberal and reform wings, have readily conceded that such an intelligent and considered rejection of God is sincere: it has grounds rather than motives for its refusal to locate a gracious providence behind the darkening saga of humanity. There are undeniably societies whose members apparently lack religious sentiments; the religious theoretician cannot dismiss the empirical presence of such successful 'godless' (though admittedly only semi-atheist) cultures in the West and in parts of Russia and China. Many people, it is concluded, sincerely find it difficult to believe in a supreme transcendent being who presides over a deferred future life in which the egregious errors in the moral government of this life are dramatically rectified.

Muslims have not conceded that atheism is a secure basis for responsible individual, let alone social, conduct. The cognitive falsity and moral inadequacy of atheism are considered self-evident and therefore not in need of independent support. In the Islamic lexicon, the word for atheism, *dahriyyah*, literally means temporalism. It is derived from *dahr*, meaning time; it is used, with the definite article, in the Quran and in the Prophet's traditions (*al-dahr*; Q:45:24; 76:1). Temporalism, the doctrine that everything that exists does so in time, is a form of materialism or metaphysical secularism. By its denial of transcendence, this secularism is, believers would argue, bound to collapse into the moral and cognitive abyss of nihilism. The word *dahriyy*, meaning temporalist, is a term of abuse although it is less emotionally charged than *kāfir*, the uniquely Quranic word for disbeliever. A rarer word, restricted to intellectual and philosophical circles, is the Persianized Arabic *zindik* (*zanādiqah*; pl.) meaning free-thinker, possibly a heretic or dualist. It occurs as a verb in the pithy anti-philosophical aphorism, *Man tamanṭaqa tazandaqa*: 'Whoever engages in (Greek) logic (*manṭiq*) commits infidelity', where logic symbolizes the philosophers' respect for independent reason.

As we begin to close Part I of our inquiry, we shall create a moral framework to enable Muslims to engage rather than dismiss the modern conscientious disbeliever. This is an unprecedented ambition in Muslim history. Nothing in the voluminous literature on the Quran, devotional and critical, engages with the problem of conscientious atheism, the phenomenon of the virtuous pagan who is conscientiously persuaded of the truth of atheism, the man or woman who heard and sincerely disbelieved rather than merely hypocritically disobeyed the word of God. Muslims were, from the beginning, pre-occupied with other matters such as the development and codification of the intricate and comprehensive legal canons of the *Sharī'ah*. This single practical anxiety and associated minor ancillaries exercised, to the point of exhaustion, the intellectual ingenuity of classical Muslim civilization. The relationship with Jews and Christians was also a potential source of practical problems but Muslims did not regard them as *conscientious* objectors to Islam's message. Politically and theologically, the Quran had settled the question of their place in the Muslim universe by categorizing them as deviant monotheists perversely rejecting the Quran's message but nonetheless deserving, on pragmatic grounds, protected and privileged minority status.

Islam, unlike its rival monotheisms, has successfully prevented the emergence of an internal tradition of conscientious (as opposed to merely fashionable or pretentious) atheism.[1] The western tendency towards a narrow, primarily moral, interpretation of religion accompanied by a related obsession with the problem of evil might jointly explain the emergence of a tradition of conscientious atheism in Christianity and Judaism. Indeed the dominant moralism of Christian piety has often led to a revolt against moral norms as such – as we see in the Nietzschean protest against both Christian ethical restraint and sometimes all ethical restraint.

We try to understand, with imaginative sympathy, the moral causes of modern conscientious atheism. We do so in two ways: first by tracing relevant aspects of European history, and second by examining the alleged autonomy of morals and the correct place of religion in the moral equation. We locate our inquiry in the context of the ancient Euthyphro dilemma. I relate its insights to the Islamic sceptical rationalism of Mu'tazilite scholasticism encountered in the previous chapter. We then explore the social and political dimension of ancient religious morality in modern societies. We conclude with a general survey of the secular humanist outlook – its moral appeal and its future – as it confronts, for the first time in about a century, sharp and incisive contemporary religious reservations about the discrepancy between its ambitious ideals and the depressing realities of the world it has created.

2

In the West, the causes of secularization are both social and intellectual. In Muslim lands, the causes are, insofar as secularization has created a dent in the armour of conservative Islam, entirely social and political. They are found in the processes of colonial conquest of the Islamic world, mentioned in Chapter 1, and also in the industrialization that is a global feature of our age. We shall remark briefly now on this second aspect.

In pre-industrial societies, most human beings were preoccupied with the provision of materials for their existence and survival in the face of scarcity and the vagaries of nature with its constant threats of famine and drought. A belief in the providence of God was a consolation. But this was unstable: countless prayers for food and prosperity arise from every mosque every day but, judging empirically, few seem to be answered. Perhaps the providence of God is not true as a dogma but rather only as a human project – when believers make it a reality. At any rate, in all agrarian cultures, material activities and anxieties are interwoven with ritual religious ceremonies which consciously link them with God, a dependable reality transcending the immediate vicissitudes of a precarious life. Prayers blend with gratitude for the good harvest; God demands 'his due on the day the harvest is gathered' (Q:6:141). As societies became industrialized, as rural populations were transferred to the cities and towns, people lost the older ceremonial way of honouring God for his gifts and bounties. The loss of the religious ritual did not automatically entail secular disbelief any more than it entailed a debacle of the associated morals. But it was the first step in the process of secularization, a process culminating in the loss of faith in nature and its harmonies and in the God who sustained them.

An intuitive awareness of the supernatural dimension saturated people's experience of the social and natural world in pre-industrial cultures. Life on earth was a temporary probation for testing the mettle of the God-fearing (Q:18:7; 21:35; 67:2; 76:2). Human life was like a cosmic drama composed by the master dramatist. It had a central theme, a rational plan, often tragic in the short-run, but ending with a morally satisfying denouement. The task of human reason in this scheme was, as we saw in Chapter 2, circumscribed: it demonstrated the truth of revealed knowledge by reconciling recalcitrant experience with the pre-ordained blue-print of the world vouchsafed by revelation. Rebellious truths, hard-won and protean human insights, were made to fit pre-ordained, revealed and rather innocent categories decreed by a simple faith in the mysteries of divine providence.

3

'Atheism' and 'secular humanism' are in one sense equisignificant: both doctrines claim the non-existence of the divine and the self-sufficiency of the human. Atheism is the core metaphysical doctrine of a secular and anti-religious creed. No supernatural (that is, disembodied and incorporeal) beings or spirits can exercise causal agency. Typically, atheists endorse a materialist metaphysics that reduces the mind to a physical reality. They also uphold the scientific method of inquiry – methodological naturalism buttressed by a materialist ontology – as the ideal way to establish claims to knowledge. Secularists appeal to consequences as the basis for judging moral issues: many endorse a utilitarian and pragmatic basis for assessing moral quandaries. All moral meaning and idealistic purpose is a human creation. Our lives are meaningful but also unavoidably tragic since we do not have much time to realize the lofty ideals of secular humanism, a generic name for the social, political and cultural projects inspired by the moral and metaphysical claims, attitudes and ideals, mentioned or implied above.[2]

The use of the qualifying adjective 'secular' in secular humanism suggests the parallel possibility of a *religious* (monotheistic) humanism. (The adjective 'secular' is redundant in 'secular atheism'.) Atheists might argue that this is a devious way of co-opting for religion the distinctive greatness of secular humanism so that all the best adjectives continue to describe religion since 'secular' means critical, rational, empirical, scientific and philosophical. We address this objection at the end of Chapter 11 when we define the parameters of a proposed Islamic humanism.

Three similar-sounding words – secularism, secularization, and secularity – shall be distinguished now although any specific way of making the proposed distinctions can be challenged: the distinctions cannot be defended in all their implications. Secularism is, philosophically, a theory of the proper limits of human knowledge and contains an attendant method. Sociologically, as secularization, it is a social process of history. Finally, as secularity, it is a state of culture, including intellectual culture, characterized by discernible and alterable features, sustained by determinable social and political currents.

Secularism was originally simply the rejection of ecclesiastical and sacerdotal authority and a corresponding assertion and empowerment of the private individual conscience at the expense of the former. This embryonic secularism enabled the birth of new sovereign European states. The Peace of Westphalia, a treaty signed in 1648, required European monarchs and rulers to adhere to the maxim, *Cuius regio, eius religio* (lit. whose territory, his religion), coined at an earlier treaty, the Peace of Augsburg (1555). The religion of a state was decided by the sovereign of that state, not by some catholic ecclesiastical authority. This compromise, inspired by Europe's endless confessional conflicts and violent deadlocks, effectively proposed geographical segregation of antagonistic Christian denominations as the sole solution to their political conflicts. It was a pragmatic and diplomatic 'solution' that shelved rather than solved the matter and, in effect, marked simultaneously the end of Christendom, the religion-based empire, and the re-birth of Christianity as private religion.[3]

This inchoate secularism was destined, after its marriage with liberal humanist ideals of social justice and equality, to evolve into a utopian model for political pluralism, an accompaniment and embodiment of secular democracy. Secularism also contains: a theory of our origins, a philosophy of history, and a social science according to which religious belief is a powerful illusion satisfying deep human wishes, not a simple intellectual error. Finally, secularism contains one epistemology of modern humanism according to which we may uphold an absolutism of scientific method while affirming the impossibility of achieving any final state of certain knowledge. All forms of secularism reject the authority of revelation while upholding the integrity and authority of unaided human reason. The eventual emancipation of public opinion from the antique shackles of religious mystery is, secular humanists conclude, the philosophical foundation of western democratic polities.

Both theism and atheism, thus understood, are compatible with most political opinions. Atheism cannot co-exist with theocracy (or more accurately 'theonomocracy') but all else is possible. Thus, Nietzsche's aristocratic radicalism was inspired by an anti-egalitarian outlook. Marx, like his countless followers who now teach in secular westernized universities, was a revolutionary. Unlike their master, however, many of these Third World Marxists (or Marxians) live in exile from their societies and plan a revolution from the safety of an apartment in London or Paris or from inside the security of the conference hall of academe. Atheists are generally liberal and radical but the ruling elite of Communist nations are, in practice, politically conservative, even reactionary, while officially espousing a radical socialist ideology. Conversely, religious sponsorship is theoretically available for the same range of political persuasions: liberal democracy, dictatorship, fascism, republican and monarchical patterns of government, even anarchy.

4

Historians of ideas trace the checkered development of European atheism from its origins in the Enlightenment to the dawn of the modern explicitly secular age that began with the appearance of Nietzsche and Marx.[4] The risks of persecution and prosecution for avowals of disbelief as late as the early twentieth century in Europe necessitated an esoteric tradition of liberal thought, ingeniously relying on hint, wit and irony to mask its real intent from the orthodox establishment while revealing it to select members of the free-thinking audience. The moment of frankness and truth came with the rupture of the traditional liaison between religion and morality, a break that eventually allayed partly the fear of atheism as morally subversive. It was only then possible to confess, with relative impunity, the atheistic creed.

Atheism inspired modern European humanism, secular and religious. The ambitions of this secular humanism evolved from disproving or ignoring the existence of God to the active pragmatic task of showing that our experience, including religious and especially moral experience, was properly understood in purely and proudly human terms. Once upon a time, a sinful Adam hid from God – but modern humankind answers to no one about anything.[5] A divine ruler is incompatible with a liberated and liberating intellectual, political and moral culture. Atheistic humanism creates a culture of freedom where we pursue happiness, where democratic participation among free and autonomous human beings helps to establish ideals with human and natural referents. We wasted our time and talents by constraining our will to suit the dictates of an allegedly higher morality, part of a life-denying religious idealism with its imaginary realm of benefits and burdens.

Almost 2,000 years into the Christian experiment, the imbalanced German genius Friedrich Nietzsche warned westerners that religion is a fetter on our wills, a monster of our own creation. He mocked Christians by asking: 'Is man only God's mistake? Or is God only man's mistake?'[6] He answered that moral and religious value is a creation of the human, not divine, will. Values are not immanent in the fabric of the world. 'God is dead'. The Nietzschean corpus is the long obituary for the God who died of being God. Few have followed Nietzsche in rejecting the moral constraints associated with Christianity. Nietzsche himself reasoned correctly and courageously that if we reject the creed, we should disown the moral code that grew organically from it. Therefore, he rejected Christian morality, the nursery of the European character for over a millennium, as a masked and perverted form of the will to power.

Nietzsche's secularist ideology is affirmative, not nihilistic; it is open to a world of dangerous possibilities, a world of tragic but Dionysian latitude for self-assertion. The Übermensch, the higher man, is whatever he chooses to be – and he is what he is out of strength rather than weakness. We no longer admire the strength to suffer but we do admire the strength to do daring things. Let us celebrate. 'Long live the Übermensch!' is the toast. Our cup is full too, boasts the Nietzschean humanist, but it is overflowing with wine, not suffering. We no longer belong to God's tribe. We became citizens of the godless new world by exorcising our past.

Just as the desert fathers withdrew into the wilderness to fight and expel their demons, we too need to kick religion in the teeth for the terrible things it has done to us.

If we soberly examine Nietzsche's megalomaniacal views written late in his mentally active life, we know that they are fit for the lunatic asylum. This is not to say that such views need no refutation because they are already nullified by the presage of his incipient insanity – but only that the eloquent passion and dramatic dogmatism of opinions, if their source is secular, does not automatically make them viable. Mainstream atheistic humanism, however, evolving from a Judaeo–Christian lineage, has made major contributions to the cause of humanitarian liberalism.

Western secular humanists contribute to our self-understanding as a species and initiate pragmatic if utopian political programmes for the amelioration of our plight. Many activists among them care for the natural environment – or what is left of it. They fight what they see as an ecocide and seek to halt further environmental degradation at the hands of commercial and corporate interests; many environmentalists seek to preserve animal, especially defenceless wild populations. Starting with Bertrand Russell, philosopher of mathematics and prophet of the liberal humanist society, many atheists campaign for nuclear disarmament. It is difficult to see how one can reasonably assail these noble ideals.

5

We shunt our train of thought onto a related rail to travel to a specific destination, namely, the autonomy of ethics. (We shall return to the larger terrain at the end of the chapter.) Humanists try to disengage ethics from metaphysics in general and from God's will in particular. Is morality independent of its traditional religious foundation? Unlike the conflict between faith and reason (and that between science and religion, which is a disguised variant of the same dispute), there was no initial conflict between morals and religion. On the contrary, so intimate was their liaison in the past that few could have predicted the divorce of the two happily married partners, especially since the moral partner's whole identity was submerged into the religious partner's identity: morality as separate category is foreign to the Quranic and biblical outlooks. The emergence of the moral as an autonomous category is of recent origin and is still largely restricted to western secularized cultures. Francis Bacon, that seminal Renaissance thinker, seems to be the first to distinguish a duty owed to God from a duty owed to the community. He terms the former 'purely religious' and the latter 'purely ethical'.[7]

In Islam, none of the canonical duties prescribed by the Quran were or are today perceived as straightforwardly moral. Fasting, prayer, payment of an alms-tax to support the poor, and pilgrimage to Mecca combine a believer's religious duties to God with moral duties to other human beings. The Quran, through such ritual obligations, instructs Muslims in their practical attempt to serve God and, via their moral dealings, each other. These are religious duties whose moral component is organically, not accidentally, linked to the religious framework. Let me put this in terms of intellectual history rather than ethical theory or theology: the moral duties of religion – duties such as charity to the poor – were divine commandments long before they were transformed into private moral imperatives or into public duties incumbent on politicians who see national compassion for the poor as morally necessary or politically prudential.

Atheists disown only the traditional attribution of the authorship of moral codes to God. We need not, they re-assure Jews and Christians, sacrifice all the moral rules contained in the biblical Decalogue. Only the ruler or law-giver is dispensable. Consider the Ten Commandments: four duties owed to God and six owed to our neighbour. A duty owed to God cannot survive the demise of God but the rest, suitably pruned of the rotten fruits of religious obscurantism, may not only survive but even flourish. In practice, this implies that if the moral teachings of religion require believers to behave in ways inconsistent with secular humanist ideals, the religious morals must be subverted by the enlightened universal principles of a rational philosophical morality approved by secular humanism.

Ancient believers could not discern, argues the humanist, that moral truths are only contingently acquired through religion and that their authority is independent of religious belief. Judaeo–Christian theism is the historical, not logical, basis of moral values such as comprehensive compassion, marital fidelity and the absolute sanctity of life. Theism was part of the long and painful but temporary teething process for morality started when we were, in moral terms, infants in the cradle of civilization. Morality is now finally perceived as autonomous after the religious encapsulation of morality had obscured this truth for millennia. Secular humanists rejoice that secularization has clarified a truth obfuscated by religion's long association with morality: the link between morals and religion was and is accidental. Owing to the secularization of learning in the past century, the argument continues, we now view religion instrumentally – as the long doctrinal ladder that should be kicked away since we have reached the high moral roof. Secular humanists, then, in their attempt to discredit the Judaeo–Christian heritage of western morality, need not jettison some of the nobler moral values associated with that outlook.

6

Plato's dialogues provide a place to begin our inquiry into the moral dimension of monotheism since these writings are, for the West, the earliest recorded testimony to the rational quest for knowledge of ultimate moral and metaphysical truths. In a short early dialogue, *The Euthyphro*, Socrates, the Greek controversialist who loved to talk people into the ground by exposing their ignorance and conceit, interrogates his friend Euthyphro who is bringing a law-suit against his own father; the charge is murder. Euthyphro is confident of his unexamined intuitions of piety, good, evil, and the complex linkages between them. Socrates shakes his confidence by asking him: Is an action holy because the gods love it? Or; alternatively, do the gods love it because it is holy? If we put it in modern terms and apply it to *mono*theism, the question is whether morality is autonomous, that is, independent of religion or merely an adjunct to it. Consider:

1   God says some acts are morally good because they are so.
2   Some acts are morally good because God says they are so.

Someone who is not particularly religious would argue that God wills mercy because mercy is good; it is not good because God wills it. God's good will can only reflect existing moral standards; it cannot constitute them. Why? If mercy were good solely because God wills it, then it is arbitrary that it is morally good at all. Either mercy is inherently good (in which case God need not will it to be so) or else it is only contingently good (in which case it is arbitrarily so whether God wills it or not). Unless there is a moral law independent of God's will, what is morally right is ultimately random since it is based on God's preferences which might be whims and moods.

A preliminary point: the dilemma is posed with regard to the *moral* law. Few doubt that logical laws, such as those of contradiction, are independent of God's will. Even God cannot do the logically impossible – such as make a square into a circle or make $2+2 = 5$. Even devout believers are not offended by these logically (or conceptually) necessary limitations on God.

Most religious believers belong to the 'divine command' school. They grasp the second horn of the Euthyphro dilemma since God created everything, including the moral law, by divine fiat. His will makes moral convictions absolute and objectively true since he is the originator and logical guarantor, not merely teacher or instructor, of morals. Abū Al-Ḥasan Al-Ashʿarī (d. 935), a seminal theologian who abandoned the rationalist (Muʿtazilite) school to establish an orthodox school, argued for God's absolute freedom to will and act as he chooses without being accountable or answerable to his creatures. He rejected the Muʿtazilite view that God was obligated to be just in view of an antecedent moral law. Thus, God is merciful solely because he wills to be merciful. He reserves every right to will otherwise; if he were to do so, his actions would remain right and good. Divinely imposed moral or religious obligation (*taklīf*; based on Q:2:286; 7:42; 65:7), a legal notion, is inapplicable to God. Good and evil are what they are, not intrinsically but solely because God decrees them to be so; their nature and scope are determined by divine legislation, not by human reason. Al-Ashʿarī argued that good and evil are, from God's perspective, neither moral nor rational but rather exclusively legal concepts. God has permitted human reason to discern good and evil but not to determine or legislate them, both of which are forever divine prerogatives.[8] There is some Quranic support for such audaciously absolutist views (Q:5:18; 21:23; 91:14–15).

The Quran is compatible with the meta-ethical claim that virtue and vice derive their character from their relationship to God's good pleasure (*riḍwān*; Q:9:21; 57:27; *riḍāʾ*; Q:58:22; 89:28; 98:8) or displeasure (*ghaḍb*; Q:2:90; *sakhṭ*; Q:5:80). Individuals and communities are rewarded or punished for obeying or disobeying God's messengers bearing God's orders, not primarily for the intrinsic rightness or wrongness of their actions. Thus adultery is an execrable offence primarily because it offends God, not merely because it injures human relationships or destroys trust. Why does it offend God? It involves deception, lies and exploitation; and no one, who is morally sane, wonders why these should offend God. The secular and religious bases for the moral condemnation of adultery may coincide; the secular person, however, considers only the intrinsic immorality of lying and deception, not the extrinsic fact that God disapproves of certain immoral attitudes.

Consider a more dramatic example: the binding of Isaac (*Akēdat Yitzḥāq*; Genesis 22:1–14; cf. Q:37:100–7). God orders Abraham to sacrifice his son to please God – which amounts to commanding murder. This divine commandment is abhorrent unless good and evil are at the mercy of God's whim. Do virtue and vice have an intrinsically moral (or religious) character? Strictly speaking, the Abraham case shows that God can command murder, in a particular instance, not that he can command that murder in general is morally right. Nonetheless, if what makes any given action good or evil is its conformity with the divine will, then the character or content of any given action is irrelevant in its own right. When God is the commander, only the *source*, not the *content*, of the commandment matters.

7

There are two ways of dealing with the Euthyphro dilemma. We could argue that the dilemma, especially when used by secularists to establish the autonomy of morals, is misleadingly posed.[9] It presents a false dichotomy since its horns are two mutually exclusive but not necessarily jointly exhaustive alternatives. There is a third alternative: a morally stable God of the kind found in scripture, a supreme being who would not arbitrarily change his mind about the goodness of compassion and the evil of sexual misconduct. Such a God always commands the good because his character and nature are good. The dilemma might re-surface, however, if this third proposed alternative collapses into the first: a stable moral law lodged inside the divine nature prevents God from doing wrong. If so, God is subject to the moral law; perhaps he even has a conscience.

The second strategy is to examine the two horns and demonstrate the incoherence of either or both. We begin by scrutinizing the second horn which assumes that an intelligent agent, including God, could hold something, merely by an act of will, to be good or holy without first valuing it, on some grounds, as good or holy. But, as Hume has argued, one cannot esteem anything as good unless one first values it on other independent grounds. Let us apply Hume's insight to this problem. In his discussion of the status of justice as a natural or artificial virtue, Hume makes three defensible claims:

1 'All virtuous actions derive their merit only from virtuous motives'.
2 'An action must be virtuous, before we can have regard to its virtue'.[10]
3 'No action can be virtuous, or morally good, unless there be in human nature some motive to produce it', other than the motive derived from a feeling of obligation or duty.[11]

The net implication of Hume's claims is that we cannot coherently value a thing simply by calling it good: in deciding to call it good we already express our appreciation of it. Hume makes his case by citing a case, more prevalent in his and in the Victorian age than in ours, of a parent who cares for his children solely out of a sense of duty and does not love them. We blame a father for neglecting his offspring because it betrays a lack of 'natural affection, which is the duty of every parent'.[12] Hume would not deny that there are parents whose affection is rooted mainly in duty; his point is presumably that this possibility presupposes that there is the more widespread case of parents who care for their children because they love them. Thus, no one can coherently value – ascribe virtue to – the care of children on the sole ground that it is a duty. In all virtuous action, we must suppose that there is a motive 'distinct from a sense of duty'[13] – because in acknowledging something to be our duty, we *simultaneously* show our readiness to value it.

Hume concludes that one's valuing of something as good, a primary consideration, cannot be the ground of it being good, 'a secondary consideration', a view which implies that the whole of morality, like duty in general, is a secondary end, not an end in itself.[14] Every system of morals focuses on something other than morality itself. The object may be family or human welfare or nation or God. It is never duty as such or the moral system itself to which we subscribe. We conclude that the second horn of the Euthyphro dilemma presents an incoherent alternative.

8

The first horn of the dilemma sounds more plausible: 'God says some acts are morally good because they are so'. Can we drop as redundant the prefatory 'God says?' If we remove God's will and authority, we can affirm the autonomy of morals. Morality would then be no longer logically parasitic on religion. Traditional believers would, however, object that being religious is a necessary condition of being virtuous.

Is it logically impossible to achieve virtue independently of religious belief? It seems not. The Quran claims that all human beings, believers and rejectors, possess the self-accusing soul (*al-nafs al-lawwāmah*; Q:75:2). The intensive form of *al-lawwāmah*, with its doubling of the middle radical to indicate explosive stress in pronunciation, indicates severe self-incrimination. It is the Quranic equivalent of conscience. (The modern Arabic word for conscience, *al-ḍamīr*, is not found in the scripture.) A part of man, asserts the Quran, is a hostile witness against his own self despite his disingenuous excuses (Q:75:14–15). This idea is found in the wisdom traditions of diverse ancient cultures. We have the Latin proverb: *Conscientia mille testes* (Conscience is a thousand witnesses). In Romans 2:14–15, Paul mentions an inward faculty of moral self-accusation and judgement, the upright conscience (*suneidēsis*), which is found even among Gentiles. Like an absolute internal tyrant, conscience controls all humankind.

If we concede that disbelievers are, in some measure, conscientious, we cannot then coherently claim that the capacity to discern the urgent demands implicit in moral consciousness is restricted to religious believers. From here, it is conceptually a short step to concede the possibility of virtue, even conspicuous virtue, among rejectors. However, the Quran, despite affirming the presence of the self-accusing spirit in each human being, does not authorize this step. The virtuous pagan is totally foreign to the Quran – though not to the Hebrew Bible.[15] Rejectors are described in the Quran, as we see in Chapter 9, in irredeemably accusatory language; their possession of a conscience is enough to justly convict them of moral blame in rejecting God. Their good works are unacceptable since they refused to believe in him (Q:17:19; 21:94; 40:40).

Orthodox Islamic scholasticism represented by Al-Ash'arī and his disciples held that religious obligation (*taklīf*; see Q:2:286) is known by revelation, not by reason. If a person were to attain knowledge of God by means of the natural light of reason and conscience, without the aid of revelation, he or she would be a 'believing monotheist' rather than a believer. Religiously neutral knowledge can be known by reason but knowledge of religious duty is known only through revelation. Someone who came to know God through reason alone would deserve no particular reward in the next life. However, since God does whatever he pleases and is not bound by human moral speculation, he might reward this person. That would be no different from his decision to reward any believer: both would be underserved and unaccountable acts of grace. Only the earlier (rationalist) school of the Mu'tazilites upheld the view, more compatible with our modern moral sentiments, that all human beings are capable of discriminating between good and evil, prior to and independently of revelation, and solely in virtue of their humanity. This has the morally attractive corollary that the reward or punishment is in proportion to one's just deserts since God is morally obliged to reward the virtuous and punish the guilty.[16]

The notion of a righteous pagan was not, culturally, a coherent possibility in Muhammad's day. Today, however, we find that many people's behaviour is, empirically assessed, ethically praiseworthy even though they refuse to believe in and honour God. Take the case of some secular philanthropist whose inherently elitist virtue – since it cannot be democratized – is nonetheless genuine. She performs benevolent actions, extends her generosity to strangers, evinces active compassion for the dispossessed and marginalized, refuses to condemn anyone unjustly and conducts her sexual life with care and scruple. Or, to take examples from the past, consider the moral excellence found in the life of the mind, of a polytheist such as Socrates, a martyr for the cause of philosophy, a thinker who chose to drink the hemlock so that his example might contribute to the world's stock of intellectual sincerity and sagacity. Again, the atheist Nietzsche's mental (rather than bodily) martyrdom at the age of 45, just before the presage of his incipient insanity, must be admired as a huge sacrifice for the sake of one's philosophy of life.

Virtue is evidently not an exclusively religious phenomenon as religion is understood by Jews, Christians and Muslims. The Buddha and Confucius were not religious in western religious terms, yet they were both outstandingly virtuous men. The Stoics developed a cosmopolitan and egalitarian ethical system suited to any citizen of the world, though they knew only the Graeco-Roman world.

Its foundations were secular and universal: each person had a spark of the universal reason which controlled the universe.

Do such secular human beings have moral integrity and excellence? Their ideals are godly even though the agents involved are godless! The argument that godly works are necessary and exclusive proof of godliness is compromised by the existence of the outstandingly virtuous atheist, a kind of secular saint. The argument that faith alone leads to virtue is challenged by the existence of the pious pagan in all ages. The burden of proof (or at least of plausibility) is on the shoulders of believers who reject as incoherent the notion of secular virtue: they must explain why the adjective 'virtuous' is superfluous in 'virtuous theist' and also why the same adjective logically cannot qualify 'atheist'.[17]

What distinguishes the virtuous believer from the virtuous atheist? The believer is agitated by fears and actuated by hopes of events beyond the grave. But is that cognitive – doctrinal or propositional – difference sufficient to deny the accolade of virtue to the disbeliever? A perplexing feature of our world, for the religious believer, is that good works can be performed by those who deny God. A person of no faith is capable of living accidentally or coincidentally in accordance with God's will and law.

9

It could be argued that religious belief hinders the achievement of virtue. Atheists often contend that an atheist is more virtuous than a believer since the believer's moral stance is corrupted by the fear of external transcendent sanctions and by selfish eschatological ambitions. This view is mistaken. A Muslim's hope of entering paradise is a valid motive for leading an ethically worthy life. It is fallacious to argue that since believers desire to enter paradise, they cannot really love God. The argument is that those who act morally in order to succeed in the religious life are not acting in a genuinely moral way since they treat morality as a means to a further end and thus attach no intrinsic value to their moral motives. Moreover, such agents intend to deceive God since their sole aim is to enter paradise! The reasoning is invalid since only some, not all, reasons for action are incompatible with morally praiseworthy action. If we act morally *solely* in order to serve our interests, we are not authentically moral. But it is absurd to think that if we act with *any* end in view, we are automatically disqualified from acting morally. Moreover, there are ends, certainly in religion, which can be achieved only where the means used to achieve them also have independent and intrinsic moral worth. Only a worthy life-style on earth is rewarded with the crowning glory of eternal life with God.

This type of fallacy is not committed only by atheists. Some Sufi mystics were seduced by it in their misguided desire to purge the religious life of all, as opposed to morally questionable or false, motives. Rābi'ah Al-'Adawiyyah (d. 801), a female ascetic, wanted to extinguish hell fire and set fire to paradise in her zeal for purity of interior motive. She rejected the fear (of hell) and the hope (of paradise) even though the Quran describes this attitude approvingly as *khawfan wa ṭama'an* (in fear and hope; Q:13:12; 30:24; 32:16) in the context of the thunder that symbolically glorifies God. She opted for the sole motive of the pure love of God, 'for the sake of his love' (*'alā ḥubbi-hī*; Q:2:177; 76:8).[18]

The wish to enter paradise provides a legitimate motive for a Muslim to love God. A natural corollary of one's love of God is that one desires to enter paradise. Islamic ethics, the instrument for achieving the Muslim's religious goal, is organically, not accidentally, tied to the hope of entering paradise. This outlook contrasts with the mistaken Kantian view of the role of motivation in moral action: behaviour cannot be moral if the primary motive is conditional on a goal. It must rather be freely chosen out of good will. The Kantian would object that those who pursue the reward of the religious life are pursuing their self-interest and are therefore not genuinely moral.

If we examine a secular parallel case, we can see the error in this view. If a woman befriends someone and desires the happiness that comes from true friendship, it is wrong to suspect that since she desires such happiness, her friendship is bogus. If the argument used to discredit the moral dimension of religious life were used in parallel secular cases, no human relationship would be legitimate since no such relationship, no matter how altruistic, lacks non-moral motivation. No one could be said to love their children or spouses since what one desired, while pretending to love one's family, was gratification of one's selfish desires. The argument is a *reductio ad absurdum*.

In the religious life, not only are there morally good and morally bad motives, the status of such motives is unstable over time. For example, the life of faith may be initially motivated solely by the fear of God, arguably a disreputable and merely prudential motive. Such initial fear may, however, change over time into the love of God. That fear is necessarily a bad initial motive is in any case denied by Muslims and Jews. It is upheld by those Christians who emphasize the exclusive role of love in the religious life. Admittedly, fear alone is a bad motive for being religious but it is not a bad motive if it evolves over time or if it is combined from the start with morally better motives.

We should give atheists no more than their due. Atheists cannot successfully impugn the sincerity of the interior motives or the moral legitimacy of the goals of the ethical life of religious believers. Atheists do, however, have the right to defend the integrity of secular virtue. Unbelief is not necessarily incompatible with morally good dispositions; revealed religion cannot claim a monopoly of moral sentiment. If we concede the empirically verifiable existence of moral virtue outside of all religious commitment, then we are forced to concede that belief in God is not the sole enabler of moral decencies.

I conclude our discussion of the Euthyphro dilemma by listing *four* defensible alternatives:

1 The view of the divine command school that ethical norms originate in God's will. Moral truths are ultimately arbitrary derivatives from the divine will and cannot be reliably distinguished from it.
2 An orthodox Islamic (Ash'arite) view similar to 1. God, as legislator, has ordained good and evil as a probation to test which of his creatures is best in

conduct (Q:21:35). God in fact acts for the sake of moral ends but does so purely by an act of will rather than through any moral compulsion. He need not do so and might some day not do so.

3   A religious view based on the Kantian view of moral autonomy as self-legislation. Religion is not the source but rather the enabler of moral truths. Kant made morality independent of religion and made religion subordinate to ethics. Kantian ethics is religious since it assumes the necessity of external religious sanctions for the moral life. To take seriously the moral demands which practical reason imposes on behaviour, we need the postulates of freedom of the will, immortality of the soul, and the existence of God. Only a future life, plus a God to guarantee it, can satisfy the rational demand that virtue and happiness must eventually coincide. The *summum bonum* (the highest good) is impossible without God. Religion is the recognition of all duties as divine commands: if there were no God, moral commands would be null and void.

4   Finally, an agnostic view that concedes that monotheism offers one distinctive and defensible version of human moral potential. Religion is an important interpreter of moral truths and the single most powerful source of the motivation to live the morally good life, especially though not only for uneducated people incapable of attaining to moral truths except through 'revelation'.

10

Even in a largely laicized West where popular, intellectual, and religious cultures have rapidly secularized over the past 50 years, there remains a powerful residue of prejudice against atheism. Many evangelical Christians in North America's Bible belt, for instance, to take an extreme example of bigotry, insist that atheists are automatically aligned on the side of immoral and lax conduct while religious believers always vote for decency and virtue.

The open-minded and reflective believer, by contrast, concedes that an atheist may be conscientiously faithful to the demands of moral awareness – but denies that an atheist is capable of fulfilling the higher and highest requirements of the moral life. The believer boasts that atheistic humanism cannot claim disciples who are as morally distinguished as the seminal figures of monotheism – its countless prophets, saints and martyrs. The atheist may deny the alleged greatness of men such as Moses, Jesus and Muhammad and dismiss their allegedly unrivalled piety as a stubbornly masochistic iconoclasm whose day is past. As we see in Chapter 7, the secularist may argue that, judged by modern moral sensibilities, the great heroes of theistic history were bad men who contributed to the world's stock of intolerant enthusiasm and violence in their own day and left enduring legacies of their bigotry and misogyny to this day. Revealed books have proved to be the earliest and most effective form of reactionary propaganda. Free artists themselves, such so-called great men were guilty of double standards: they impeded the free development of character in that vast crowd of yes-men politely called disciples.

The secular humanist adds that the relative infancy of the explicitly atheist tradition accounts for the paucity of secular saints. The recent origin of explicit atheism explains the lack of a generally accepted standard of merit and accusation used in judging the behaviour of an atheist. One does not say accusingly, 'You are not a true atheist' to someone in the same way (or as often as) one says to a Christian suspected of infidelity to the cause of Christ, 'You are not a true Christian'. A shared and widely respected standard is all that may be needed to stimulate the growth of conspicuous virtue among atheists.

Fair-minded atheists concede that many conscientious and virtuous people have been and still are religious but then point to the approach of a darker shadow: the common run of believers. The pretensions of believers are lofty but little evidence of lofty ideals is discerned in their lives which are rarely recognizably free of the selfishness and dishonesty that plague all human lives. Savour this penetratingly educational joke, popular in capitalist America: 'Christians pray for one another on Sundays and prey upon one another on weekdays'. Sceptics cite the gap between noble profession and base practice, a gap wide enough to be scandalous. Most religious people are a poor advert for the higher virtues of religion.

11

It would be premature and imbalanced to leave our discussion here without examining the causes of the persistence of theism as private belief, ideology and moral force. There are as many bad reasons for disbelieving in God as there are for believing in him. So far we have used too wide a mesh to catch the details. Let me narrow it down to one claim.

Religion, secularists often charge, is a dangerous distortion of reality, an illusion whose true character must be concealed even from the believer if the charm is to work. Many secular humanists virtually define religious belief as pre-rational or anti-rational delusion. Religion, they argue, consoles emotionally crippled people who are too weak to acknowledge their true condition. It is a soft option; it gives meaning to meaningless lives. Leaving aside the revealing conceit implicit in this – the laughable assumption that the lives of secular humanists are fulfilled and meaningful – even a cursory examination of the lives of the prophets and saints of western monotheism or of eastern holy men and women is enough to puncture the facile claim that courage, intellectual, moral and physical, is all that is required in order to abandon the self-deceptive consolations of religious enthusiasm.

We explore self-deception in Chapters 7 and 9. Here it suffices to say that if we scrutinize religious faith in its seminal instances, it vigorously rejects all consolations, false hopes and the comforting illusions supplied by self-deception. Genuine religious belief – and this is not a persuasive definition – is marked by its austerity. All solace of the flesh and of the spirit is spurned with painful rigour. Theism is an exacting option: the God of the Quran and the Bible, unlike the Roman or Hindu deities, expects moral excellence from us. The demands of theistic faith create much mental anguish – since we inevitably fail. Religious demands contribute to some kinds of fear; they challenge and destroy the comforts of secular self-sufficiency and warn us of a more thorough reckoning by an all-knowing judge after we die. We are always in the hands of the living God whom we cannot escape in earth or heaven. The affair altogether belongs to God (Q:4:78).

What are the consolations of this ideal? Is it not more comforting to believe that we may live as we please, within the increasingly relaxed moral constraints and increasingly comfortable facilities of the liberal state, and that the whole affair terminates on this side of the grave? Atheism is our best bet if we want consolation. Admittedly, faith offers us, as we see in Chapter 11, a career beyond the grave. The soothing prospect of immortality allays our natural fear of extinction and offers heavenly compensation for earthly misery and self-denial. But every belief-system or ideology offers a cure for our ailments. Like the Buddha, the wise therapist, every monotheistic prophet too diagnoses our condition after noting the symptoms – and offers us a prognosis and a prescription for future well-being. The atheist has to show that religious faith offers baseless hopes which cater simply to the human need for safety in a dangerous world. Only then can we lay the last wreath on the tomb of theism and return with new vigour to the task of living under an empty sky.

The atheist does not deny the massive purposive potential of religious faith: as purpose-laden myths go, religion is the best. But the celestial kingdom of deferred pleasures compensating for our earthly wretchedness is, the atheist scoffs, only a comforting illusion. The promise of liberation lies in active struggle, secular jihad, against human but intensely real tyrannies. As Marx, the inheritor of the western theistic tradition, has shown us, religion is not a cure for but a symptom of illness. The failure of the human condition is a breeding ground for transcendent illusion; we should transcend a perspective that requires transcendence. The religious believer answers that neurotic and wrongly motivated religious belief is discernibly different from healthy and emotionally balanced religious belief, a distinction available within religion. Faith has resources for making such distinctions and for effecting healthy self-criticism. It is unnecessary for believers to convert to Marxism to triumph over their own limitations.

12

To investigate the adequacy of religion as a foundation of individual and social life, we must disentangle the philosophical question of the viability of a secular ethics from the political question of the utility of religion for civil society.

Many believers think that religion alone can morally orientate us in our social role: revealed religion is indispensable for preserving the social integrity of communal life. Modern believers would admit that individuals can have personal integrity and self-restraint even if they see the world as godless. Dostoyevsky's sophistical atheist was wrong in claiming that in the godless universe all is permitted. That is the crass attitude of a sham human being who is, at heart, uncivilized: if the veneer of decency is so thin, then what it covers is also indecent, even if religion is the basis of it. Believers may add, however, that atheism disrupts the social and moral order. We cannot love and trust one another in our social and political relationships. Only eschatological sanctions could provide the restraint and motivation requisite for preserving a tolerable social life since 'man is to man a wolf'. Religious belief, then, enables human society today as in our past.

Perhaps philosophers and intellectuals can live moral lives without any religious convictions but uneducated, possibly obtuse, individuals cannot do so. In the past, religious faith gave everyone a purpose if not a reason for living. No one needs to die of despair merely for want of a purpose. Religious purpose could not be established on rational grounds alone. But that was a defeat for rationality, not for teleology. Nearly universal literacy and a high level of education in the humanities, the secularist argues, could today make even the masses into intellectuals capable of creating their own values. The techniques of mass education can perhaps achieve this in another 50 years. This would enable us to combine elevated moral ideals with an absence of religion. But 50 years is a long time in our volatile world: if nuclear, chemical and other taboo technologies are used in the near future, there may be no human race left to educate.

The secular humanist proudly concludes that belief in God – whether as a condition of individual moral sense or as a prerequisite of social cohesion and moral community – has been refuted in the modern world. An argument for the independence of ethics from religion can now be based on a verifiable soci-ological observation rather than on a logical or abstruse metaphysical basis: many individuals, even entire tribes, societies and cultures, live lives of mod-erate private and political virtue without believing in God. In the West, the gradual elimination of the supernatural warrant for morals has not, in general, undermined moral awareness at a social level. The overwhelming majority of humankind, however, especially in societies outside of the European West and the Communist world, continues to derive its moral guidance from explicitly religious sources.

Historically, most cultures flourished in virtue of their commitment to religious virtue; many modern western democracies, however, thrive as a result of their impiety. One example is the United Kingdom where the sea of faith has been receding for 150 years; the tide of Christian faith has now reached its lowest ebb. The question of the viability of a secular (or rational) ethic is only partly a conceptual quandary; its resolution also depends on an empirical verdict. The verifiable existence and operative sustainability of western secularized and eastern Communist societies undermines the religious claim about the morally subversive character of atheism. These 'godless' societies show no signs of imminent collapse; indeed they seem as morally viable as religious societies.

Secular humanism, with its defensible intellectual foundations, is potentially universal in its appeal. Some atheist humanists boast that the most successful cultures in the modern world – cultures with workable institutional structures – are atheist in all but name, while the most dysfunctional cultures are the religious autocracies and theocracies located in the Islamic belt from Indonesia to Morocco. Atheists may one day proselytize the non-western world on a large scale; indeed it is already happening indirectly as a result of the planetary spread of western secularist capitalism.

Could a totally secular ethic, grounded in atheism, undergird a morally healthy society? Yes – though there are few societies that are wholly religionless, at least in their history. The social structure of advanced industrial communities in the post-Christian West is not erected on exclusively atheistic foundations. Western culture survives on the capital of the Christian tradition accumulated over a thousand years. An agnostic or secular historian could argue, with some justification, that the moral trajectory of European nations, rightly admired for their singular achievements in the area of politics and human rights, was provoked by a reaction *against* Christian norms. This is an attractive thesis but it is a prejudice to discount radical Christianity's contributions to the triumph of just causes such as abolition, civil rights, and the amelioration of the plight of the urban poor.

Nonetheless, scientific industrialism and participatory democracy, rather than Christianity, should take the credit for spectacular European progress. Western civilization is secular, humane and capitalist. Christian moral principles count for little with the western elite, making one reluctant to use the adjective 'humane': the relentless attempt by westerners to impose their will on the non-western world through military force and the appointment of pliant but unrepresentative leaders is immoral and unchristian. The nobler versions of western atheistic humanism are, however, morally admirable.

13

The ease with which the modern West has macerated religion from morals should make us suspicious about the alleged infancy of its atheist tradition. Perhaps, for centuries, the process was progressing underground. With Islam, the traditional liaisons between religion and morals, and between ethics and law, remain firm. For Muslims, 'Muhammad is a good man' and 'Muhammad is a Muslim' are virtually indistinguishable. Modern Arabic and most Islamic languages, unlike modern European languages such as English and French, are still devotional languages. (Modern French, unlike modern English, does, however, retain its poetic and romantic resources.)

It is difficult to express cynicism about religion or religion-derived morals in any Islamic language. This differs from English where we face the opposite problem: we are unable to make claims such as 'He is a pious man' sound anything but mocking.[19] The moral language of Christianity is now decrepit and abused; only a poet-saint could renew the religious employment of English in order to invigorate the cultural project of rescuing words such as 'sin' and 'virtue' for their original and intended senses. Even the word 'Christianity' has unction about it as do 'righteous', 'Jesus', and 'salvation'. Religious life languishes in the West while intellectual life flourishes and reaches new heights. By contrast, even the most secularized Muslim would not use 'Muhammad' as an expletive in casual conversation. It would be an embarrassing attempt at blasphemy.

Significantly, after the advent of the Quran, in Muslim societies, no system of ethics was born outside the crucible of Islam. (Is this a cause or an effect of the lack of a philosophical tradition among Muslims?) In the West, by contrast, several comprehensive moral systems were produced by unaided human reflection, both before and after the event of Christianity. Indeed two of the most influential were developed by 'pagans' who took the basis of morality to be individual merit, not divine grace: Aristotle and the Stoics have left us enduring moral legacies.[20] Spinoza created an original ethical scheme and presented it in a geometric mode! Kant and (John Stuart) Mill constructed ethical systems, deontological and utilitarian respectively, with no or little regard for Christian moral values.[21] Marxist and Nietzschean ethical schemes, if we may call them that,[22] were self-consciously anti-Christian. Many systems of morality developed independently of religion not only in western nations. In China, there is Confucianism – which is not much more than a system of ethics and etiquette. Muslim civilization, however, has produced no moral system after the coming of Islam.[23] There could scarcely be a better proof of the strength of the liaison between Islamic religion and morality.

14

For the rest of this chapter, we investigate the broad theme of the religious vision versus the secular vision and do so in a way that reflects the urgency of the contemporary confrontation between religious and secular civilizations. We shall integrate our general observations here with the earlier, more academic themes.

The recent failure of the western experiment with religion has political consequences. God is dead but theology, morals and religion as civil forces are alive. Perhaps religion is kept alive artificially for its political utility. The distinction between the utility of religion and its truth is a modern one, unavailable in ages of sincere enthusiasm. In western culture, the truth of religion has not been a political issue since the Peace of Westphalia which bracketed the question as irrelevant. It was sufficient that religion should be useful in supplying good social morals. Moreover, one would have to be consumed by philosophical zeal or be fanatically attached to rationalism to deprive poor and uneducated people of the consolations and comforts of faith. Religion may also occasionally exercise a disciplinary power even over the callous rich and powerful. Many secularists would concur therefore that a certain type of religion is sometimes good for people: an inclusive and tolerant faith that avoids the unhealthy excesses of fanaticism and the over-literal interpretations of the unverifiable and untested claims of metaphysical faith.

There is, however, an apparent paradox of utility: religion is useful only if a sufficient number of people believe that it is true, not merely useful. This is only partly true: religion can be socially useful even if enough people are merely concerned to appear religious. In the enforcement of conformity, hypocrisy plays the crucial role of effective social cohesion as it helps maintain a conspiracy of silence in which no one admits that the emperor is naked. It is possible, as we see in the USA, for a sufficient number of people to be under the illusion that they believe in true religion when in fact their version of the faith is criminally secularized and tailored to the needs of capitalist imperatives of money and profit. Religion is easily exploited for commercial gain where a large number of people, at some level, inarticulately know this but feel no need to protest against this prostitution of a noble impulse. Only immigrants, misfits, and the few alienated but sincere members of American society see these truths clearly enough to feel moral indignation. The ruling elites recognize all too well the social utility of Christianity.

European cynicism is expectedly more profound. It treats the practical implications of sincerely held religious belief to be an acceptable kind of lunacy. Modern Europeans have merely inherited atheism, a notion many European thinkers were, until recently, vehemently denouncing as empty as the Gobi desert. For many people today, especially the intelligentsia, religion makes a graceful but hypocritical appearance at the tragic or significant events of birth, marriage and death. The culture of transition from faith to doubt to outright rejection of God begins with Cromwell, Locke and Paine, and ends with Nietzsche, Marx and Freud. European Christianity is now a benevolent sentiment rather than a theology: it is admired for its decorative aspect, a décor for the drab and bleak house of ancient religion. Liberal Christianity has preserved the incidentals of faith as an antidote against the essentials of faith, an issue we examine in Chapter 7 as part of the debate on the essence of a faith in the context of preserving its authority in a sceptical age.

In the United Kingdom, it is considered necessary and sufficient for the well-being of society that a small number of religious professionals believe what the rest of society has long rejected as false and pernicious. The internal secularization of the established Anglican church has made it hard to find even enough clergy who believe in the literal truth of Christian dogmas such as the incarnation and the resurrection. Ordinary people are outraged to learn that even bishops are now espousing demythologized versions of traditional dogmas. But it is unfair to demand that a quorum of people should believe fervently in the literal truth of dogmas that the bulk of lay society rejects as false. The principle of vicarious belief or action is not always wrong but, in matters of ultimate conviction, it is unconscionable to expect a person or group to entertain vicarious belief in what one oneself considers falsehood. Belief by proxy here is only possible and defensible if we assume that religion is correctly valued solely for its social utility, not for its truth.

Some atheists sense this residual role for religion. Hence the phenomenon of the atheist who struggles to wake up early and, unshaven and unkempt, takes his daughter to Sunday school. Religion is useful for one's children for it teaches them good manners. Even the idea that prayer on a Sunday (or a Saturday or Friday), at least, should amount to worship, rather than a socially prudent habit, is now seen as a ridiculous remnant.

15

At the beginning of the twenty-first Christian century, the secular age may be coming to an end in parts of the West as we enter a transitional era of ideological confusion and uncertainty. Secular notions of liberty and tolerance have triumphed locally; western liberals rarely extend such benefits world-wide. While no one argues for a return to the world of Latin Christianity with its medieval parochialism, there is a growing belief, especially in America, in the value of traditional notions of authority, family, and particularly in Europe, a new flirtation with fascist notions of ethnic purity. Western civilization is perhaps about to enter a new age that is religious in an obscurantist sense. Progress is not inevitable; the gains of secularism are not irreversible. Western nations, led by America, may soon become closed sovereignties suspicious of immigrants, hostile to the syn-cretic and eclectic political and moral values admired during their brief flirtation with that charming liberal temptress called multi-culturalism.

This is therefore the right time to assess the state of utopian Enlightenment sec-ularism, a product of the European Enlightenment. As early as the early eighteenth century, in the aftermath of religious wars, European thinkers were understandably reluctant to allow religious zealots to define the content of morality. What they did not anticipate was that in the aftermath of the rupture of the moral–religious and fact–value liaisons, there would be an inevitable break between ends and means. Weber saw into the future when he argued that the triumph of the Enlight-enment meant the triumph of instrumental or formal rationality which concerns itself solely with means. He realized that it could only happen with the death of the older substantive rationality – where one risked making judgements about both means and ends.

Secularized westerners are now living in an era of disillusioned maturity. Today, at the beginning of the twenty-first Christian century when many question Chris-tianity's universal right to count the centuries, we witness a widespread and growing dissatisfaction with the humanist vision that emerged out of the debris of western European Christianity. Muslims, the world's only articulate critics of the virtually omnipotent West, challenge secular humanists to explain how secu-larized European civilization has marched triumphantly, in a direct line, from the Enlightenment to several holocausts.[24]

The intellectual humility and scepticism of today's social scientists contrasts with the absurd confidence and naivete of those in the late nineteenth century. In the aftermath of Europe's worst century so far, utopian Enlightenment ideals no longer sustain the older and wilder chiliastic hopes. The spectacular amount of violence and cruelty (in concentration camps, gas chambers, in war and revolution) perpetrated mainly by European nations with distinguished cultural traditions, has emboldened scepticism about human nature – although the assessment is based on the dislocating experiences of only European humanity.

After observing the entrenchment of class privileges, the downward social mobility of many in the urban jungle, the triumph of crass commercialism, and the western elite's cynical exploitation of what remains of the traditional religious outlook, few can believe in the inevitability of social progress, in our unaided capacity for achieving moral goodness, let alone in the ultimate beneficence of the evolutionary process. The entrenchment of private depression about life's possi-bilities, the rise of organized violent crime and juvenile delinquency that make many a large western metropolis a haven of social anarchy by night, the recrudes-cence of European fascism and the continuing lure of totalitarianism world-wide, culminating in the general sense of a regress in the nobler cultural values, together shock us – and all the more so since it has happened in the face of almost universal education and literacy and a stable if not growing level of economic prosperity.

Some would add to the list here the undeclared civil war between the races and the genders, despite apparent commitments to pluralism, in most western nations, especially the USA. It has made us doubt industrialized humankind's potential for peace and reconciliation. There is finally the sinister turn towards universal holocaust that, in its nuclear version, casts an ever-darkening shadow on international affairs.

The wave of humanitarian sanguineness has run its course and the tide of humanist faith is receding. We are disabused of the Enlightenment's facile optimism about a human being's basic impulse to pursue goodness and opt for the altruistic alternative – even without the external sanction of religious conviction regulating the inner self. The optimistic humanist view had its roots in New Testament Christianity's exaltation of childhood and the ways of innocence.[25] Modern literature has convincingly questioned the innocence of childhood[26] and, armed with the priapic psychology of Freud, even questioned the sexual innocence of the child.

Although much of nineteenth and early twentieth-century English literature, particularly from the pens of Thomas Hardy and later D.H. Lawrence, prefigured modern sentiments about the sordidness of life without celestial support, it is only in late twentieth-century imaginative writings that their heretical and misanthropic sentiments have found full expression. The traditional literary convention which authorized only the use of soft and domesticated language, even in describing harsh and ugly realities, is now rejected. Modern misanthropes can use strong language, whether for effect or sincerity although they lose the refined intellectual pleasures of hint and ulteriority, quite apart from the vacuity of the gracelessly vulgar phrase when over-used.

The decline of Christian faith in a loving force sustaining nature and counteracting the human chaos has inspired a cynical view of life in which the self-centred pursuit of material possessions and pleasure dominate our efforts. The cynics of the school of Ecclesiastes said only that all is futile. But we now know that there are worse things than futility in the secular world: ignorance, prejudice, the casual brutality of war, the despair and hopelessness of many in the urban jungle as they sit down and weep by the modern and polluted rivers of Babylon, in corrupt urban environments where hope has gone permanently into the past tense. The most desolating kinds of cynicism might, ironically, be evidence of a sincere and trusting humanitarianism – but one frustrated by the immense forces that set us up for suffering and tragedy. It is a demoralized humanitarianism that cannot fulfil the ideals it intends. We are now fully disabused of the Enlightenment optimism about humankind's basic and impulsive altruism.

After the dismemberment of traditional values, we witness a dangerous if artistically creative experiment in cultural and moral insanity: we have the higher degenerate who is dissatisfied with life's pleasures and prospects, a person whose malaise is noted but not cured by the existentialist humanists who flatter themselves with the conceit that they will give, through freedom, salvation to modern humanity. An affirmative zest for life is the monopoly of religious civilizations and of pagan civilizations in their infancy – before the onset of disillusionment and maturity caused by passing through cultural rites of passage. People in the past believed in first love, first friendship, family, God, nation, truth; and this is an incomplete list.

In the place of those realities, we find a gratuitous sense of the futility of endeavour as we live and die tentatively, craving for certainty – in the midst of progress. There is, as one social critic concedes, no satisfying climax to modern lives.[27] The modern world has robbed us of the meaning of both life and death. We have endless mourning that never fully cauterizes the sadness. When we die, we are tired of life, not satisfied with it. We die in the midst of progress: the meaning of both our lives and deaths is provisional, never final. Unlike in a death voluntarily chosen or a death where one still believes in the eternal and the absolute, modern death conceals no climax of significance. The traditional dying patriarch, surrounded by his offspring, died at the zenith of his life and bequeathed a legacy. We simply leave the world, in a hurry, a world of progress without direction.

This is the modern nightmare in the urban jungle. The bold and daring take a temporary refuge in excessive self-absorption, motiveless acts of malicious violence, an increasingly sordid sexuality embittered by the loss of that natural eroticism found in such abundance in traditional cultures where the veil suffices to dignify and eroticize the male–female encounter. Humane anarchists find some meaning in their rebellion. The rest live and die in their conformities.

16

I shall soon put an end to what must seem more of a homily than a contribution to the philosophy of religion! Some secular humanists claim that what we now need is an utterly secularized life-style. The nineteenth-century materialists thought that once human beings were economically secure and understood the true basis of their alienated condition, they would look the dragon in the face – and we would make our way to a new heaven on earth. But we have not found the land of promise. Collective hope that historical advances will comprehensively improve the human lot confronts the frightening insight that each age finds itself beset with novel problems which are as, if not more, formidable than those recently solved. What is the future of secular humanism, the latest creed – with its offer of progress and salvation by science? It was, ironically, inspired by the Enlightenment's drive to seize the world, master the conditions of life, and thus emancipate us for our full human potential. Has it too, like Christianity, been defeated by our modern subversive emptiness?

Humanism was founded on three cardinal principles, all admired, like the ideals of the Renaissance, more in retrospect than in their own time: a faith in the elemental goodness of humankind, itself inspired by a reaction against the Protestant dogma of total human depravity; a belief in indefinite, almost inevitable, progress; and a trust in the power of unassisted human intellect and conscience, a view implied by deism, a halfway house between the robust Christian theism of the past and the aggressive atheism that then lay hidden in the womb of Europe's future. All three have been refuted by recent events. Humanism must accept some responsibility for the current victory of alienation, commercialism and sensuality, the bitter produce of irreligious cultures, just as institutional religion cannot avoid shouldering the blame for its past and present excesses.

The modern human situation is a signal defeat for those who initiated the Enlightenment project, confident of the didactic value of history, the inherent goodness of our species, and eager to inaugurate a political providence that would compensate for the failings of a divine providence that was at best a human and humane project, at worst a false dogma: many starve and die daily while praying to God in the face of callous and widespread human witness. After a century of vehement reaction against the absolutism of revealed religion, we find ourselves in a welter of urban and urbane hedonism, ruthless individualism not even tempered with the democratic conscience of modern life or the aristocratic honour and dignity of the past.

If someone wanted reassurance that doing good is not a waste of time, folly in a world that rarely rewards virtue, one place to find it is in the Quran. The Muslim scripture consistently, persistently, and confidently emphasizes the unbreakable link between morals – as the performance of good works – and faith as the certainty of success or salvation in the religious life (Q:19:76). Like Kant, the Christian Pietist, the Quran is confident of the perfect alignment of virtue with reward – in both worlds (Q:12:23; 39:10). Theism was not accidentally a form of humanism – some vague concern for human welfare that was an unintended by-product of a passionate concern for God. It was intended to be the noblest humanism in our history. By contrast, the modern consciousness of the world is an empty subjectivity facing the world only in a tragic mode of relation, at times despairing and melancholy, at others romantically exalting the absurd, sometimes mocking life and authority, often cynical about objective meaning and moral purpose, always in need of humour and irony to conceal its pain.

The source of the pain is the irrepressible insight that when we talk of grand realities such as humanity, we conceal the fact that our lives are no longer anchored in the tangible realities of the community – much as romantic writers with no one to call their own fantasize in their novels about successful human belongings. Where is the practical concern for mutuality, for our true capacity for community, in the secular humanist vision? This concern with an abstract humanity is reminiscent of ritualistic white liberals who sacrifice the human encounter with real blacks for the abstract liberal passion for social justice expressed in journal articles. Only the gesture matters; and they make sure that someone notices it. We need the courage to live among real people, the community of human suffering, in order to be disabused of the illusions of a theoretical philanthropy. Religion in its orthodox forms, for all its restriction of human sympathies, effortlessly enables community through its intuitive grasp of our psychologically ineradicable need for relationships that paradoxically both create and alleviate vulnerability. We need the traditional religiously grounded reality of the family and community, no matter how dysfunctional or fragmented, not the grand and perfectly whole myth of humanity, a humanity perfect in the abstract but harbinger of despair in practice.

Western monotheism aimed at putting humanity in its proper place in the cosmic scheme of things entire. Secular humanism was intended to aggrandize humanity but ironically, in a secular industrial society, no one needs to reduce the self to size since society does it for us – automatically, decisively and casually. As people jostle for places on an underground train or queue to receive unemployment benefit, they know they are nothing. No religion has negated the self, in all its pride, as effortlessly as modern mass society.

Who the hell are modern secular men and women? Are they truly modern now, larger and smarter than our simian ancestors, full of legitimate pride, finally deserving the appellation *Homo sapiens*? Do the new rational men and women have ideals that match the scale of their modern egos? Do they care solely for their bodies, their permanent homes – thinking each 'soul' can take care of itself? Are we moderns imprisoned, like frogs in a dry well, in a hell on earth, waiting desperately for ultimate liberation in a world on the edge of global war? Are modern human beings weak and lonely, everywhere in chains, dependent on Prozac and its derivatives, living alienated lives in a major city, battling against the bottle and indiscriminate offers of sex at night? Is the modern male a Luftmensch, a vulgarian happy in his frivolity or an Übermensch weighed down by his sincerity? Is the modern suburban home only 'a comfortable concentration camp?'[28] Is modern secularized humanity a dream or a nightmare, an ideal to emulate or a warning to heed? A time is coming soon when we will want the narrow dogmas of secular humanism to evolve gracefully into a more humane vision of the world – and then perhaps our disintegrating societies will welcome the call of enlightened religious duty as we finally learn to confess that modern secular human beings are no longer equal to the demands of their own history.

Part II

An Arabic Quran: Assessing its authority

4   The book sent down

Muslims see the Quran as a revelation directly *from* God (Q:27:6; 32:2; 39:1; 40:2; 41:2; 45:2, 46:2, etc.) but not a revelation *of* God. It reveals the divine will; God's nature is disclosed only insofar as it bears on his moral and legal purpose for humankind. The Quran implies that, in the Arabic original, it is the literal, direct and immutable speech of God (*kalām Allah;* Q:2:75; Q:9:6; 48:15; *kalimāt Allah*, word of God at Q:9:40) preserved in the book of God (*kitāb Allah*; Q:3:23). It is the *ipsissima verba Dei*: the facsimile of the divine words, not a paraphrastic inspiration diluted by human additions. The Quran is not a revelation of the divine nature but it points towards its revealer, God, the direct speaker through and throughout the sacred volume. The proper name Allah occurs some 2,500 times in over 6,000 verses.[1] God speaks through his human mouthpiece, Muhammad, who is often addressed by the masculine singular imperative '*Qul*' (Say! Q:2:97, 139, 189, 215, 217, 219, 220, 222; 109:1; 112:1; 113:1; 114: cf. masculine plural at Q:2:136). The Prophet, as vehicle of revelation, brings the divine speech into the human world.

The Quran is safeguarded on earth in Muslim memorization of its text; in heaven it resides in divine custody in the mother of the book (*umm al-kitāb*; Q:13:39; 43:4).[2] The expression 'with him [God] is the mother of the book'(Q:13:39) could mean that God alone has the correct interpretation of the scripture since he alone knows the essence of the divine law and will. The Quran was infallibly dictated to the illiterate Muhammad by the arch-angel Gabriel; when completed, it became the final and definitive expression of God's moral and spiritual purpose for all humankind for all time.[3]

In terms of its sacredness, the Quran is second only to God. Its majestic authority is expressed by its envisaged epiphany on a mountain: 'Had we sent down this recital (*qur'ān*) on a mountain, you would surely have seen it humbled, torn apart, out of the fear of God' (Q:59:21). The scripture is described as 'an unassailable book' (*kitābun 'azīzun*; Q:41:41) which repels falsehood (Q:41:42).

The Quran plays a capital role in the book-centred religion of Islam. Scripture – written revelation – is the fulcrum around which all else is organized. The Muslim must go by the book: 'And this is a book which we have revealed as a blessing, therefore follow it and be God-fearing so that you may receive mercy' (Q:6:155). With the exception of Orthodox Judaism with its Torah centrality, no book plays a comparable role in any other faith. Even in Protestant Christianity, a faith centred on canonical scripture as expressed in the Reformation slogan of *sola scriptura*, the authority of scripture is derivative, not intrinsic: scripture is a witness of (and to) a more primary revelation, namely, the dramatic self-disclosure of God in Christ, the *Christusereignis* (Christ-event).[4] Muslims see divine words, not historical events, as the primary medium of revelation.

In this Part, we assess Muslim self-understanding of scripture, its credentials and the authority these confer. In this chapter, we begin to explore the literary scriptural foundations of Islam by investigating the received Muslim account of the Quran as revelation and of Muhammad as its recipient. In Sections 1 to 5 below, we examine the factual and historical dimensions of the debate. The Islamic model of revelation is a religious model and, like the rest of Islam, defies secularization. In the rest of this chapter, we examine a challenge to this model. I argue that the Islamic model of revelation is *sui generis* and motivated by reasons that organically nourish the Islamic perspective on the authority of scripture.

The question of the authorship of the Quran is entangled with the question of the supposed bases of the authority of the revelation, especially the Quran's confident claim that its unrivalled literary genius is compelling evidence of its heavenly origin. We broach a few facets of this assignment here and defer the rest to the next chapter.

What is the extent of the intended relevance of the Quran today and in the past? Can we make it relevant and interesting to modern secularized inhabitants of a global westernized culture that is currently enduring a sterile materialistic phase, intoxicated on a euphoric technicism that accompanies a brash and adolescent science? In this culture, an indigenous Christianity is the despair of a narrow rationalism reared on a diet of confident doubt and mental independence. Anxieties about the basis and scope of revealed, especially Quranic, authority are carried forward into Chapters 6 and 7.

2

Arabs in Muhammad's day had political freedom, the precondition of linguistic integrity. Arabia was, unlike Palestine in Jesus' time, free of foreign domination. The Romans had dismissed central and northern Arabia as the barren *Arabia deserta*; they colonized only the *Arabia petraea* (stony Arabia), the northwestern portions of the peninsula. The emperor Augustus (r. 27 BCE–14 CE) sent an expedition, under Gaius Aelius Gallus, to the more fertile southern and southwestern *Arabia felix*, the 'happy' Arabia of (modern) Yemen. The mission failed. In an earlier age, the Greek adventurer Alexander had died days before a planned invasion of the Arabian peninsula.[5] The Sassanian Persians, one of the two superpowers of the day, dismissed the Arabs as barbarians not worth conquering. This 'island of the Arabs' (*jazīrat al-'Arab*) became therefore, for its size, the most geographically isolated piece of populated land in the world – which is especially remarkable when we note its strategic location even in the ancient world. This land and the illiterate Muhammad were both, Muslims claim, virginal containers for the final revelation.

If the Greeks, especially Athenians, produced great poets, dramatists and philosophers, the Arabs produced only great poets.[6] Pre-Islamic Arabia had some artistic and spiritual sophistication but it lacked the Hellenic philosophical environment of first-century Palestinian Judaism. Arabian pagan mythology in the seventh (Christian) century was neither as inveterate nor as powerful as the potent mythology of the Greeks which has decisively influenced the psychological development of western intellectual civilization. To compensate for their lack of a provocative and pregnant mythology, the Arabs had the art of oral poetry with its latent capacity for myth-making.

Having a poet in the family or clan was a matter for tribal boasting as shown by the *fakhr* (pride) portion which concluded the tripartite Islamic ode (*qaṣīda*).[7] Customarily, the wealthier urban households sent their children to sojourn with the nomadic Bedouins in the desert so that each new generation could learn the mother tongue in the undefiled form most apt for literary composition. The Arabs extolled the beauty of poetic and oracular speech. Like the ancient Greeks, they were (and remain) lovers of skill in oratory and rhetorical disputation. Some classical Arabic lexicons are still compiled on the basis of word endings, not beginnings or roots.

At the time of the Quran's revelation, the Arabs were experts in the art of recited poetry. Like the Greek Sophists, they believed that oratory was a means to acquire social and political influence in the tribe. According to Plato's dialogue called Gorgias[8], Socrates punctured the pretensions of rhetoric. During a dialectical exchange with the eponymous 'hero' of the work, Socrates showed that oratory was persuasion without knowledge and, worse, it was indifferent to the cardinal virtues of truth and justice. The Quran similarly dismisses pagan oratory as *zukhruf al-qaul ghurūran* (lit., gilded speech by way of deception; Q:6:112). For the pre-Islamic poets, however, poetry was a noble and effective art. Muhammad himself is credited with the remark that 'sometimes eloquence (*bayān*) is as effective as magic'.[9] In the Quran, Muhammad is once admonished mildly for being overly impressed by fine speech (Q:2:204).

Pre-Islamic poets wrote about life's transient pleasures and the inevitability of death. A sense of the dislocation, transience, and tragic nature of all things informed the sceptical wisdom of the itinerant Arab tribes and it inspired parts of their poetic canon. The Arab poets sang of the virtues of *muru'ah* (virility), a trait that enabled a solitary defiance of the arbitrary tyrannies of life in the desert. The manly virtues included generosity, reckless courage, lavish hospitality for friend and enemy alike, chivalry, and the constant desire to defend vigilantly one's own and one's tribe's honour. Pagan poetry could be playful and wistful, shallow and profound. It could be earthy and erotic but also crave for ideals that transcend our biological condition. The Quran proved to be the most merciless editor of pagan Arabian culture, especially its poetic canon.[10] Profane poetry was, like pre-Islamic mythology, only partly discarded. Its nobler impulses were, as we shall see in Chapter 11, rescued, Islamicized and recruited in the service of a new cause.

3

Muslim commentators claim that miracles reflected the age in which they were performed. Thus Moses preached in an age proud of magic; Jesus's healing miracles occurred in an age which boasted Greek medical expertise while Muhammad came in an era of eloquence (*zamān al-bayān*)[11], hence the miracle of the eloquent Quran. We should no longer rely, Muslim thinkers argue, on dramatic or sensory disclosures of the divine will. The only sign Muhammad brought was an intellectual miracle in which divine reason was expressed in fluent and majestic human speech. This marvel appealed to reason and therefore excelled the more palpable miracles of the Prophet's predecessors.

The Quran has always been admired for its restraint and grace of style, its eloquence and refinement. Its sapid prose and lapidary style are instantly recognized as ingredients of its sublime charm. Unlike Arabic poetry, which is ebullient and extravagant, the Quran is succinct to the point of ambiguity. It self-eulogizes its superlative literary taste (Q:12:2), its comprehensiveness as guidance (Q:39:27) and its own rectitude (Q:39:28). The scripture takes impressive oaths (Q:81:15–18) to support its self-description as 'a reminder for the worlds' (Q:81:27). The Quran describes its own status: God has revealed 'the most beautiful message in the form of a book internally consistent and reiterative' (Q:39:23).

Muslims regard the Quran, owing to the quality and purity of its diction, to be an unapproachably excellent literary production which could only be produced by God. The pagans believed that the jinn – elemental beings thought to inspire poets – composed the book. The Quran challenges humankind and the jinn together to produce something equivalent to it (Q:2:23; 17:88). The *taḥaddi* (daring) verses, that challenge humankind and the jinn, are scattered throughout the Quran. One Meccan verse challenges the listeners to produce 'ten chapters like it' (Q:11:13), subsequently reduced (in a Medinan revelation) to 'a single chapter like it' (Q:2:23; see also 10:38). Another Meccan revelation asks its audience to bring 'any discourse similar to it' (*ḥadīthin mithli-hī;* Q:52:34) which could mean even a single verse, a few Arabic syllables.

While Muslims believe in the matchlessness of the Quranic diction, some Arab Christians try to imitate and emulate it. Such parodies of the Quranic style, available on Christian evangelical websites, resemble the efforts of comedians who paraphrase and parody a biblical turn of phrase. These Christian Arab attempts are intended to mock Islam. Most sound as unconvincing as the attempts of cynical atheists to produce a biblical-sounding tract resembling the Hebrew Bible. Instead they produce pseudo-biblical tracts recognizably unworthy of the Bible, that unique mixture of poetry, politics and prophecy.

The Quran attributes no miracle to Muhammad except the all-sufficient miracle of the book (Q:29:48–51), a feature recognized in the doctrine of 'the inimitability of the Quran' (*i'jāz al-qur'ān*), the main subject of the next chapter. The Quran is

Muhammad's sole miracle and also, along with the example of his life, his only bequest. Later tradition claims many other miracles, perhaps to rival the many miracles of Jesus which are recorded in the Quran, without envy or rivalry, since all the credit belongs to God.[12]

4

Unlike the scriptures of other extant historical religions, the Quran is contemporaneous with the faith it established. The Hebrew Bible and the Christian New Testament, for instance, came to acquire belatedly the status of scripture within their communities. Groups of churchmen, in the case of the Greek New Testament, canonized a set of writings well over three centuries after the events those books and letters allegedly record.[13] The result is often seen, even by Jews and Christians, as a poorly edited anthology of religious literature. The Quran's status is different. It is self-described as revelation; and it single-handedly created the community that treated it authoritatively, not the converse.

No discipline among the sciences of the Quran (*'ulūm al-qur'ān*) corresponds to the critical historical concerns of critical biblical scholarship, a field covering textual criticism as well as form, source, redaction, literary, and historical criticism.[14] The Muslim reluctance to develop the discipline of critical Quranic scholarship is mistakenly thought to be connected to religious obscurantism. In fact, there are no materials and no need for such a discipline. The Quran, unlike the Bible, is not the heterogeneous work of many hands, in several genres, in a trio of languages, in varied geographical locales, stretching over millennia, surviving only in uncertain and fragmentary forms. It is a unified canon, 'revealed' in just over two decades, addressed to a man fully known to his contemporaries and to subsequent history, a man living in only two geographical locations in the same country. It was written in one language, the language of the recipient and of the first audience, a living language that is still widely spoken. The period between its oral revelation and final authoritative compilation is only about two decades. Apart from some variant readings that do not materially affect the sense, the text is invariant, defined and fixed. Textual emendation – editing the text to remove alleged corruptions and errors in copying – was never permitted. The text has retained perfect purity; a unique version has enjoyed universal currency during the entire history of Islam. I cannot see, barring motives of malice and envy (that should have no place in scholarship), any grounds for developing a critical textual scholarship of the Quran.

Textual criticism aims at recovering a lost original; in the case of the Quran, we have the original – in some sense. During Muhammad's prophetic career, the Quran was being gathered as it was being revealed. The Quran self-describes this process as a divine responsibility (Q:75:16–19). In an oral culture, this gathering of the sacred writ (*jam' al-qur'ān*) meant memorization. Many Muslims had faithfully memorized an oral prototype heard from Muhammad's lips. His companion, Ḥassan Ibn Thābit (d. 674), refers to the transcription of the revelation (*khaṭṭ al-waḥyī*). Efforts at collation, aimed at transmitting the text to future generations, were envisioned well before Muhammad's death in 632. During the reign of the first caliph Abu Bakr (d. 634), the Prophet's amanuensis and chief scribe, Zayd Ibn Thābit (d. 665), scrupulously collected the fragments of the text – especially after an external catastrophe provided a literary catalyst. In the battle of Yamamah in 633, many zealous neophytes with retentive memories – men who had memorized the whole Quran – were martyred. It was standardized under 'Umar (d. 644), the second caliph, and finalized and codified under 'Uthmān (d. 655), the third caliph who ordered the destruction of deviant copies.[15] The Quran's redaction and finalization were nominal since both were routine tasks requiring no creative judgement. Western Islamicists incorrectly call 'Uthmān's definitive copy a recension: there was no revision of the contents of an existing manuscript.

The Quran, like the original Hebrew Bible, was written in a *scripta defectiva* using lines and strokes. The original consonantal text was like shorthand although two important vowels (*waw* and *ya*), present in the bare consonantal text, functioned as both vowel and consonant. Meaning was partly unstable; and some errors in transcription cannot be ruled out absolutely. It was written in primitive 'Uthmanic orthography (*al-rasm al-'uthmānī*). The development of Arabic orthography was inspired by the need to write the Quran as a plenary text. Vowel marks (*tashkīl*) indicating vowels and their length are absent from the original text. Diacritical marks (*a'jam*) which differentiate between otherwise identical pairs or even trios of consonants are a later addition dating to the Umayyad Caliph 'Abd Al-Malik Al-Marwan (d. 705).

The Quranic text as we have it – fully vocalized, decorated, and written phonetically – dates to the mid-ninth century of the Christian era. It was continually amplified until it was festooned with dots, lines and bars that indicate variously diacritical marks, nominal case endings, vowels, lengths of vowels, the voice, mood and tense of verbs, and formal instructions to Quran reciters. This exhaustive vocalization and embellishment enables all readers, especially non-Arabs, who constitute the vast majority of Muslims, to recite the text correctly – but without understanding it!

The Quran was codified, not canonized. No time elapses between its composition and its canonization: the revelation is (internally) self-described as revelation. It took time only for the oral revelation to become a *scripture*. In deference to the maxim *scripta manent, verba volant* (what is written remains, the spoken word flies away), the Quran was given a tangible codex form within two decades of Muhammad's death.[16] This account of the meticulous preservation and collection of the Quran does not presuppose any a priori recognition of the Quran as the authentic word of God. This account, however, supports the Quran's claim about its own textual purity and preservation – expressed as the scripture's internal promise to guard the revelation against corruption (Q:15:9). With regard to the amalgamation of the Quran, the facts of history and the claims of orthodoxy coincide. Our account might be suspected of betraying the high standards of rigour appropriate to critical history. But that suspicion is inspired by envy among those who belong to sacred histories that cannot boast comparable strength in the area of canonization of scripture.

5

Who is the author of the Quran? We must avoid begging this question at the
outset, a mistake common to Muslim controversialists and their opponents. I use an
indefinite description, 'the author of the Quran', which may refer, depending on the
reader's convictions, either to Muhammad or to God. I shall argue below, against
a Christian critic of Islam, that these two possibilities are mutually exclusive: the
Quran should not be seen as a synthesis of the divine and the human.

Although the Quran is exceptional among the world's classical scriptures in
being reliably associated, in its origins, with a single historically known figure,
ironically Muhammad declined the privilege of authorship. He saw himself as 'the
unlettered messenger–prophet' (*al-rasūl al-nabī al-ummiyy*; Q:7:157) for whom
the Quran was a verbatim report. He was the passive recipient of verses that
God, via Gabriel, revealed '*alā mukthin* (at intervals; Q:17:106); like Jeremiah,
Muhammad finds that God has put words into his mouth.[17]

The Quran refers to the dictation (*imlā'*) model of revelation but does so, ironically, in the context of a pagan account of the origins of the revelation. The
disbelievers dismiss the new revelation as a forgery and speculate about the
human assistance Muhammad has received (Q:25:4). 'And they say: "Tales of
the ancients, which he has had written down for him; and these tales are dictated
to him (*tumlā alayhi*) morning and evening"'(Q:25:5).

The Quran claims that it is God who dictates his will to Muhammad and hence
to humankind – in accordance with the needs of the occasion. Muslims recognize
only the dictation model of revelation as being suitable for genuine scripture. The
Quran's revelation to Muhammad goes beyond dictation, an external act, into the
internal act of direct transcription into his soul (Q:87:6). Muslims therefore refuse
to attribute authorship to the Prophet even as a literary convention. They maintain
in a strict sense the exclusively divine authorship of the Quran. Thus no part of
the scripture is called 'The Book of Muhammad'. Jews and Christians call the
various books of the Bible by the names of their human authors even though the
whole work is considered a revelation or at least inspired, an attitude Muslims
rightly dismiss as incoherent. Unlike the classical writers of antiquity, including
the writers of the New Testament, Muhammad refused to share the privilege of
joint authorship with the inspiring agency, the Muse or the Holy Spirit.[18]

Muhammad's contemporaries were troubled by the event of the Quran: a book
of immense literary power, concocted by their untutored compatriot after his fortieth year, an age considered, in Semitic cultures, to be the beginning of the age of
religious maturity and wisdom (Q:10:16; 46:15). Muhammad's pagan detractors
were confused about the genre of the Quran and conjectured that it was perhaps
poetry, or oracular speech, or magic. Such variety in proposed genres is significant evidence of the book's power to dislocate and disturb native speakers of the
language.

The Quran answers diverse hostile questions about its nature and stature.[19]
Arabian sceptics suspected some human beings and some supernatural evil spirits
as being responsible for the melodious new composition which had a hypnotic

effect on the listener. The Meccan doubters, unlike Jewish and Christian detractors of the Prophet, thought that the elemental spirits, the jinn, who possessed poets and inspired incantations, had also composed the Quran. While some pagans dismissed Muhammad as a professional liar (*kadhdhāb*; Q:38:4), Muhammad's contemporaries did not in general see him as a finished master of the written word merely pretending to bring verses from another world. Given the mental fashion of a religious age, many surmised that their deluded compatriot was indeed being inspired. The damaging incident of 'the satanic verses', if indeed it occurred, suggested that the Devil could interfere with Muhammad's reception of the revelation.[20] The incident refers to the discarded ending of the pericope now recorded as Q:53:19–23. The Quran denies that the Quran is the word of 'an accursed satan' (Q:81:25; see also Q:26:210–12).

The pagans rejected Muhammad's claim to inspiration by the high god, Allah, who was viewed as too dignified and remote to contact human sinners. The rich and arrogant Qurayshi establishment wondered why God, if it were God who was responsible for the revelation, had not chosen as his mouthpiece an established poet or one of the Meccan magnates, 'some great man of the two towns' (Q:43:31).[21] Why should the divine choice settle on Muhammad? (Q:38:8). There was much envy; many desired to receive scripture (Q:54:25; 74:52). The confident Quraysh had noted the parvenu's progress: Muhammad belonged to the Hashim clan, a poorer branch of the aristocratic Quraysh and yet, through a judicious marriage to a wealthy widow, he had become an important man. Indeed, the Quran reminds Muhammad of his humble background as an impoverished orphan who had no one to shelter and guide him (Q:93:6–8).

6

We note points of nomenclature and summarize the received account of the Quran before assessing it. The Quranic word *wahy*, a verbal noun, refers to the prophetic experience of inspiration[22] while the noun *tanzīl*, from the verb *na/za/la*, refers to the sending down of verses. The hyperbolic form is *na/za/za/la*. The verb *anzalnā*, in the first person plural form, is causative and literally means 'We have caused to send down' (Q:12:2). The passive construction is also used as in 'what has been sent down to Muhammad' (*mā nuzzila 'alā muḥammadin*; Q:47:2).

The Quran is repeatedly self-described as revelation sent down. 'The sending down *(tanzīl)* of the book is from God, almighty and wise' (Q:39:1). The revelation is from God alone and excludes human and diabolic contribution. The Quran contains divine statements about God, humanity, and the divine will for humankind. There are quotations reporting human and angelic speech, and speech uttered by the jinn; it is all in Arabic composed by God. The revealed segments descend on a man who has no role to play in their production. Muhammad is a conduit who hears the word of God, receives it in his heart or mind, and repeats it verbatim to his amanuensis for recording. The Quran is not seen as co-authored. Each revealed verse passes through the mind of Muhammad much as a grain of corn will sometimes pass undigested through the body of a small bird.

Muhammad is warned that he is about to become an instrument of the divine will. 'We shall send down on you a weighty word (*qaulan thaqīlan*; Q:73:5). Again, 'We shall soon "quranize" you!' (*sa-nuqri'u-ka*; Q:87:6). An Arab man shall become the medium through which God's Arabic speech will reach us.[23] The sentences expressing the divine message, their arrangement, and the formation of thematic sequences are alike the work of the divine author. The tradition insists on this account because the message is too consequential to be left to fallible human designs concerning choice of language and structuring of themes. God's message for us, on the Prophet's lips, in God's Arabic style: that is the Quran in Muslim perspective. Muhammad is an instrument of God, his role analogous to that of the pen in the hand of the scribe where the scribe corresponds to God.

For Muslims, the Prophet is a passive recipient of the word of God, a literary instrument of his will. Taking their cue from the Quran (Q:53:3–5; 75:16–19), Muslim commentators see Muhammad as a mouthpiece, albeit sentient and intelligent. The Anglican Christian missionary scholar, Kenneth Cragg, has attacked this model of revelation as 'mechanistic', puzzling, unnecessary, contradictory, and misguided in its motivation. He claims that the implications of this traditional view of the revelation of the Quran for the exegesis of the Quran are desolating: creative interpretation tends to be restricted while readings promoting shallow surface meanings and literal readings with narrow theological significances flourish.

Cragg is amazed that even a distinguished poet such as Jalāl Al-Dīn Rūmī opts for this prosaic model. In endorsing the Quranic view of revelation, Rūmī offers us the image of a statue with water gushing from its mouth. The flow of water is controlled by clever engineers and craftsmen; the statue is merely a passage. A foolish spectator is misled by this arrangement and mistakes the conduit for the source. Similarly misleading, concludes Rūmī, is the *tanzīl* of the Quran: God is the hidden engineer and Muhammad, during periods of divine inspiration, is the lifeless statue.[24]

The Quran claims that the divine message descends on Muhammad's heart (Q:26:194). If Muhammad mediates between God and humankind only in the attenuated sense permitted by orthodoxy, then, argues Cragg, the message cannot descend on his heart. A descent on the heart, continues Cragg, must mean an active employment of the Prophet's will and intelligence, an arrangement that would contradict orthodoxy's insistence on the abeyance and total passivity of those faculties. For Cragg, a style of revelation that can only succeed by by-passing the prophetic 'yearnings of heart or processes of mind'[25] must be religiously defective. He concludes that only a misguided and unnecessary view of revelation would be content to make Muhammad into a robot. The mechanistic model is unnecessarily automatic and impersonal.

I note at the outset that the Islamic view of inspiration is not as strange, exotic or oriental, as Cragg implies. For one thing, the Jews held similar views about direct revelation; the holiest portion of the Tanakh, the Torah, was thought to be inspired verbatim. (It is a separate question whether the Torah we now possess is a verbatim report delivered to Moses at Mount Sinai.) The Christian view of inspiration is the odd man out in the Semitic trio. The Greeks too held a view similar to the Islamic one. Friedrich Nietzsche, to list a discrepant ally for a Muslim stance on the Quran, resurrects this Hellenic view in his intellectual autobiography written weeks before his mental debacle. Nietzsche claims that concepts and the appropriate language clothing them are both imposed from the outside on the person during the period of inspiration. The inspired person is reduced to being only an involuntary mouthpiece. During the period of trance, he concludes, all personal contribution is in abeyance.[26]

7

Cragg is not the only Arabist who believes that the traditional Islamic account of the nature and status of divine revelation is mistaken: misguided in its motivation, unaccountably rigid, and intellectually crude. In what follows, I shall assess only Cragg's critique of the ancient Muslim doctrine about the Quran as the literal word of God, that is, one undiluted by human linguistic and mental variables external to its allegedly divine origin. I shall argue that Cragg's worries – about Muhammad's experience of inspiration – are idle and that his proposed model of Quranic revelation is vitiated by a consequential confusion between the *genesis* of the scripture and the *interpretation* of its claims. I shall conclude by showing that his view of Quranic exegesis is erroneous and, moreover, guided by motives other than those professed.

We begin by noting Cragg's worries about the conscious components in inspired authorship. He ponders rather obscurely: 'How do words and their revealing relate to personality speaking by receiving?'[27] I interpret this to mean that we have a legitimate interest in asking about the relationship between revelation and its recipient. This question, Cragg believes, is vital to the understanding of Muhammad, the Quran and therefore Islam. Cragg contends, mysteriously, that a Christian assessment of Muhammad must centrally concern itself with his inner experience.[28] We shall presently discern the real, undeclared, reasons for this claim.

How should we interpret Cragg's anxiety? Even supposing, for the sake of argument, that Muhammad's or indeed anyone else's inner experience were accessible in any objective or straightforward sense, it is not clear why it is significant. Surely, the concern with the truth of the Quran's religious doctrines and claims is, in the final analysis, the much more, perhaps only, relevant question here, both for Muslims and for others interested in understanding Islam. For if the Quranic doctrines are judged authentic, why should we care about the nature of the prophetic experience? If the Quranic doctrines be judged false or unconvincing, the exploration of the psychology of prophetic inspiration can at best be a matter of wholly academic interest.

This is the more so if we accept Cragg's avowal that his intention is solely to comprehend, not discount or question, the authority of the Quran.[29] It is only because one sees the initiative in the revelation as genuinely divine that, he claims, one wishes to know whether or not the human recipient has a role. But Cragg's worry seems pointless and unmotivated once one accepts the authority of revelation as divine and its content as genuine.

Cragg confesses that he has a Christian ground for probing the matter. Does God seek partnerships, in literary enterprises, with us humans? It is a partisan theme concealing links with the Incarnation. The Islamic account of the human contribution to the divine project of revelation, jejune and barren as it appears to Cragg, raises a question about the nature and extent of the human–divine liaison. Cragg speculates that behind the Islamic picture of *waḥy* is the dogma, indeed prejudice, that 'the more an activity is divine, the less it is human'.[30] The more a thing is God's, the less it is ours. Cragg concludes that the Islamic view must be that 'proof of the divine stands in abeyance of the human',[31] a view he rejects as unnecessary and theologically unappealing.

Cragg wants to establish that anything that is, to begin with, authentically divine, can remain so subsequently even in partnership with the human. The divine quality of a text or action, he continues, can be secured by an appropriate change in the purely human faculty which serves as its medium. One might add that this procedure is surely acceptable to Christians and Muslims: God works in and through the natural and human world. His signs in nature and society, as we shall see in Chapter 8, are intimations of the transcendent mediated through tangible physical forms and media. Why could not these be also mediated in and through the human psyche of a chosen prophet? God takes the active human mind as his instrument, pacifies it through a kind of divinely assisted hypnosis, and then graces it with knowledge and wisdom. A human faculty is thus deepened and sanctified until it can be fully recruited for divine purposes.

8

Cragg overlooks the distinction between the genesis of scripture and the interpretation of scripture. Once we note this basic flaw in Cragg's argument, we can discern the true implications of the 'mechanistic' model of revelation, which Cragg rejects, and of the 'dynamic' one he endorses. This discussion has larger entailments about the alleged infallibility of the Quranic text and the authorial arrangement which secures such infallibility. We run these implications to ground in Chapter 7 but note them briefly towards the end of this chapter.

During the period of trance, the prophet's intelligence and volition are suspended so that there is no conscious participation in authorship, no active receiving of the revealed words. This is a doctrine solely about the genesis of scripture. It says nothing and implies nothing about the interpretation of scripture. The formative process of producing scripture must exclude non-divine, that is, human and diabolic contribution. After a revelation is produced, any human mind, including the Prophet's, can assess the truth or falsity of its claims. After the revelation is completed and the Prophet returns to his normal mental state, he is an Arab reader who can actively interpret the inspired utterances. His interpretation depends on his linguistic location as an Arab reader with particular beliefs, motives, intentions, values and perhaps biases. It would be absurd to pretend that Muhammad is no different from other readers of the Quran. He has privileged access to the intended meaning of the text in virtue of his office. He is the first interpreter of the Quran, the most authoritative commentator on the text and the founder of a vast exegetical tradition. But he is only an interpreter, not the author, of the Quran.[32]

It is only during the genesis of the text then that human contribution is excluded. The intellectual effort to interpret the Quran's meaning – the effort Cragg demands – comes after, not before, the production and delivery of the text. Conscious prophetic activity, the human component, has a decisive role to play in the interpretation of the final message, but no role to play in the prior events of production and delivery of the sacred diction. Cragg confuses the question of the undoubtedly indispensable role of the human faculties in the interpretation of the revelation once it has appeared in the created world with the logically different issue of the role of the human faculties in the production and delivery of the revealed materials during the period of inspiration.

Cragg observes that even scripture must unavoidably recruit existing linguistic facilities and that all preachers, including Muhammad, are obliged to make sense of revelation.[33] These claims are true, indeed truistic, but irrelevant: these are observations about the presuppositions of human interpretation, not about the unrelated prior process of producing revelation. Human faculties, pre-eminently reason, play a decisive role in the determination and assessment of the intelligibility and validity of revealed claims but such faculties have no role to play in the formation of those claims. This is the obverse of the equally true claim that even though human faculties, particularly reason, have no role to play in the genesis of revealed claims, such faculties can still play the more modest role of assessing the intelligibility and authenticity of revealed claims once these are presented to us in a (human) language. Human apprehension and interpretation of the Quran should not be conflated with its divine production and divinely aided delivery.

We noted in Section 6 that Cragg is puzzled by what he sees as the reductionism of the Muslim view of revelation: Muhammad is attenuated to a puppet, a pair of moving lips during the hour of *wahy*. Cragg mocks the suggestion that the Prophet, in a trance-like state, cannot even make sense of the Arabic sentences he utters. To claim, however, that Prophetic intelligence is virtually redundant during the production and delivery of the Quranic text is not to suggest that the language of the Quran is discontinuous with existing Arabic, still less that its message is unrelated to the thoughts and ideals of its listeners. Only a confusion of genesis of scripture with its necessarily subsequent interpretation could lead to any such absurd conclusions. Nor does the 'mechanistic' view of revelation as infallible divine dictation imply that the Quran cannot be properly subject to interpretation in relationship to different readers placed in various eras and milieux. The reason why such a restriction does not apply is that the 'mechanistic' view is intended to be a view about the supernatural genesis, not the human interpretation, of scripture.

Finally, we can now see why God's possession of the Quran does not, *contra* Cragg, make it less of a human possession. Divine possession is in the area of genesis; human possession is *vis-à-vis* interpretation. While human readers are free to interpret the Quran as they wish, the book itself is from God alone. This claim is not an unmotivated one: the attempt to make God the sole author is undertaken in order to make the text infallible in content. The very possibility of any fallible components creeping into the production of the text is removed by a radical decision to make its provenance entirely divine. This decision provides a bulwark against the erroneous contributions or distortions of a satanic or a human or even a human prophetic agent, all of whom are fallible. With respect to the genesis of its claims, the Quran, according to Muslim conviction, begins and ends within the territory of the divine intelligence.

9

The Quranic verses descend on the Prophet's heart and strengthen him in his resolve. Addressing Muhammad, the Quran comments that the revelation descends 'on your heart' (*'alā qalbik*; 26:194). Cragg mistakenly believes that this descent requires prophetic involvement in the genesis of the text. The heart, as seat of understanding, can be a passive recipient of revelation though admittedly it cannot be a passive interpreter of revelation. What is the role of the Prophet's mind? Muhammad retained only a minimal degree of understanding during the period of inspiration, insufficient to enable him to add a human element to the divine message by conscious or creative effort. One could compare the Prophet to a frightened pupil in a strict school. The pupil understands and then repeats what the teacher dictates; there need be only a minimal engagement of the pupil's faculties. Creative variation and addition are prohibited. Once the dictation has been completed, the pupil is free to read the dictated sequence and to interpret it.

Nor are we speaking here of the actively alert passivity of an engaged mind ready for creative endeavour, feeling fully the internal pressure of choice and editorial selection. No. The prophetic mind, according to Muslims, has all its creative, though not conscious, processes, switched off. The prophet's mind is inactive during the production of the Quranic segments so that Muhammad's psyche passively receives the sacred text. Passivity, however, is not unconsciousness. During the period of inspiration, the Prophet is aware that external thoughts and sentences are entering his mind, independently of his will. While he is in such a state of mind, however, he cannot resist, much less edit them to reflect his preferred interpretation.

If this sounds strained and artificial, remember that all *conscious* mental processes and volition are suspended routinely during deep sleep – although digestion and breathing continue as we remain *potentially* conscious of our state. The rupture in thought during the period of inspiration is not total: the Prophet's mind is not compartmentalized into the secular (uninspired) and religious (revealed) at the moment of descent of the revelation. The revealed and the human could co-exist in Muhammad's mind but only the revealed materials would be processed, as it were, during the period of *waḥy* – much as a man's urinary capacity is present but suspended temporarily during sexual intercourse.

The Prophet's mind, naturally, retains the minimal capacity required to receive and bear the burden of revelation: Muhammad must understand the words he hears. Once the revealed text has appeared, the Prophet's intellect is fully active again as it begins to discern, sift, and interpret the religious significance of the finished text.

This arrangement ensures that a revealed message that is, unavoidably, culture-laden and culture-relevant, and humanly received, remains nonetheless error-free. The presence of any human (or diabolic) contribution in the genesis of its contents could prevent the text from being wholly free from error.

We conclude that neglect of a single but strategic distinction undermines most dimensions of Cragg's analysis. This distinction is, once identified, plausible and obvious: it is not an abstruse sophistication. Cragg's 'dynamic' model, proposed as a model of the *genesis* of revelation, is acceptable only as a possible model for the *interpretation* of revelation. As a view about the genesis or origination of revelation, the dynamic model is, for Muslims, false, unnecessary and even dangerous for reasons we shall note in Section 11 below. As a view about interpretation, it is true and truistic. The divine quality of the text as God's word, writes Cragg, protesting against the Islamic model, 'is not by means of a human capacity deepened and tempered'.[34] A human capacity deepened is, however, a human capacity nonetheless and remains fallible. Cragg asks rhetorically: 'Can any of us go wrong if we begin and end with God?'[35] The answer is 'No'; and it applies, ironically, to the Muslim believer's verdict about the genesis of revelation.

10

I have argued that the Muhammadan psyche, even when enlightened by divine grace, remains human and therefore fallible. Orthodoxy rightly denies it an active role in the production and delivery of a cargo as precious as the word of God. The concession that there might be a Muhammadan, hence possibly fallible and certainly human, element in the Quran's divine genesis, the concession Cragg seeks, was made by one modern Muslim scholar, the late Fazlur Rahman (1919–88). He left Pakistan after his relatively relaxed attitude towards scriptural authority aroused hostility among orthodox Muslims. He taught at the Chicago Divinity School for two decades until his death. Rahman's view of the Quran is unrepresentative of Muslim scholarly opinion.[36]

My argument has its own liabilities. It makes Muhammad not only the recipient but also, controversially, an interpreter of the Quran, the first (and most authoritative) interpreter. Hence, it permits the unlikely possibility that even the Muhammadan interpretation of the Quran may be incorrect since Muhammad was only a man. I am here establishing the conditions for ensuring the infallible authority of only the Quran.

11

No revelation, according to Muslims, comes by Muhammad's commandment or desire even though all revelation has a human context. The science of *sha'n al-nuzūl* (lit., affairs of the descents), also called *asbāb al-nuzūl* (causes of the descents), deals with the context in which verses were revealed.[37] Revelation itself is, however, an *ex parte* (one-sided) decision. The Prophetic traditions corroborate that the experience of receiving revelation distressed Muhammad. The pagans asked Muhammad to change the Quran's contents; he is told to say to them that he is powerless to do so (Q:10:15). The message shall be indelibly written on his heart (Q:87:6). Muhammad will be hypnotized and mesmerized by God, programmed like a robot in respect of the revelation's appearance in this world – though not in its subsequent interpretation and practical implementation. The mechanistic view of the genesis of revelation sounds extreme and extravagant but we should note that Muhammad's overwhelming experience of the objective externality of the Quran is affirmed in the Quran (Q:15:87; 28:86; 75:16–19) and in countless Prophetic sayings.

Muslim exegetes claim that, at the moment of descent, prophetic capacities are mysteriously suspended by divine decree. This assertion is unverifiable. It is not, however, unmotivated as it guarantees that the received text is infallible. There can be no fallible elements in a work that is divine in conception, design and delivery. If we concede, as secularized and sophisticated Jews and Christians have done recently, that scripture is a synthesis of divine and human elements even in the genesis of its claims, we may legitimately ask: 'Are the human elements true?'[38] For a proposition X, human beings can believe it even if it is false. (They cannot know it if it is false – although they can know that it is false.) It is senseless to ask: 'Are the divine elements in the synthesis true?' These are true by definition. Whatever God believes automatically qualifies as knowledge. For God, and only for him, to believe X is to know X.

The Christian concession about the mixed composition of scripture makes conceptual room for undermining its authority. The resulting situation is intolerable for those seeking an authoritative canon that directs their lives and moral choices. A cynic might add that re-writing the commandments every decade is a necessary corollary as Christianity becomes everything by turns and nothing for long. Apart from the difficulty of deciding which elements are human and which divine, there is no reason a priori for the assumption that a book with false human elements – specific cultural and prevalent historical assumptions – is nonetheless infallible in its allegedly supernatural or supposedly inspired elements. If a work can be mistaken in its claims about, let us say, the origins of humankind and the empirical universe, there is nothing, except the self-confidence of faith, to prevent it from being mistaken about God and the transcendent universe. In Chapter 7, we address the problem of the authoritative integrity of a potentially or partly fallible scripture.

Why does Cragg insist that the orthodox Islamic mechanism should be replaced by the dynamic model of revelation? The question posed in the polemical context of Christian–Muslim rivalry invites an answer in terms of motives, which is one place where one finds it. If the Quran is even partly the product of Muhammad's mind, even if that mind is influenced and protected by divine grace, the possibility of error cannot be eliminated, since Muhammad was merely a man and therefore fallible. If Muslims relax the rigid but insightful orthodox view of *wahy*, they could be marking the beginning of the end of Quranic authority, because no one, as I shall argue in Chapter 7, can reasonably defend the authoritative integrity of a partly fallible scripture.

Muslims regard the Quran as the unadulterated word of God. The theoretical question of the exact mechanism of its revelation and reception is rarely discussed. Some Muslims and non-Muslims indulge a speculative curiosity about the mechanics of *waḥy* but, typically, such interest is motivated by scepticism or reserve about the authority and truth of the Quran. The question of the precise mechanics of the revelation normally engages someone who rejects its authority as divine – for unless the question of the genesis of the Quran, whether in the divine mind or the Muhammadan psyche, is an open one, there is little motivation for being seriously interested in the precise nature of the Prophet's experience.

Nor will it do to say, as Cragg does, that his concern is merely to enable the right kind of Quranic exegesis. That anxiety is, as I have shown, logically and psychologically unrelated to the manner of the Quran's appearance in the world.[39] The puzzle of the Prophet's experience normally interests us because of its perceived conceptual relation to the question of the possible presence of human, and hence fallible or potentially false, elements. The presence of these would contaminate the divine purity and thus undermine the infallibility of the sacred sequences. In view of this, it seems that Cragg has a partisan Christian manifesto behind his apparently unmotivated and innocuous probing of the ancient Muslim account. His questions are probably designed to induce scepticism about the authority of the Quran by introducing the possibility of a prophetic (human) component into the very genesis, as opposed to interpretation, of the text. If we permit the human, it is a short step to the fallible, even the false and dispensable. In no time we are struggling in the quicksand of modern Judaeo-Christian concerns about achieving a secure status for the authority of revealed scripture within the post-Enlightenment sceptical perspectives of secular modernity, the theme of Chapter 7.

The exclusively divine nature of the Quran is a corollary of the doctrine of Quranic inimitability (*I'jāz*) introduced in Section 3 above. If the text is partly human, then it cannot be fully inimitable since the human portion can be imitated. Therefore, the doctrine of *I'jāz* requires the mechanistic model of revelation developed by the earliest orthodoxy. If we concede that the text is partly human and fallible, we destroy the authoritative integrity of the whole Quran and also undermine the central credential of *I'jāz*. The two doctrines are aspects of a single and consistent view of the scripture's divine authority. In the next chapter we question and assess this doctrine of Quranic inimitability. In Chapter 7, we return to the problem of the Quran's authoritative integrity after determining, in Chapter 6, the scope and relevance of the Islamic scripture in a secular sceptical world determined to reject its audacious claims.

5   The book as 'the frustrater'

1

Muslims are reluctant to probe the source of the Quran's authority. Why are they unwilling to subject its alleged authority to a patient and disciplined investigation? To delve deeply is seen as evidence of a mischievous sceptical intent, a concealed lack of faith. The sympathetic non-Muslim often sincerely cannot believe that the Quran's verses emanate from a supernatural world. Are we humans incapable of producing such 'revelations'? Perhaps it is merely, as western orientalists pontificate, the product of an ambitious Arab imperialist's febrile solitude in the open desert, a setting devoid of the niceties of civilization. 'Primitive prophet, primitive book' was the dismissive verdict of an older brand of European orientalism which argued for a view, retrospectively seen as simplistic: the empty spaces of the harsh desert, where vulnerable human beings confront a terrifying nature away from the refinements and false comforts of urbanity, is the nursery of Semitic 'revelation'.[1] A modern pagan view, alert to the ecological crisis, condemns arid desert faiths as subtly harbouring imperialist and potentially totalitarian sentiments. This pagan view eulogizes as liberal and tolerant only polytheistic faiths – associated with fertile forests and concealing no colonialist ambitions.[2]

The Quran arises out of the desert, out of nowhere. That Muhammad's contemporaries denigrated him as a poet, a soothsayer, a diviner, an expert oath-monger, a lunatic possessed by demons, and a magician indicates that they could not fit the Quranic idiom into an existing category of speech. Since the Islamic scripture frustrates attempts at classification of its genre, one could reasonably call it *sui generis*. That would be, however, to shelve rather than address or resolve the question of its origins.

Unlike Jesus and the Hebrew prophets, Muhammad did not belong to a tradition of revealed wisdom or prophecy. Born and raised among pagans, there is little in his environment to explain the event of the Arabic Quran, let alone the intelligent critique of Jewish and Christian thought found in its verses. While biblical scholars have satisfactorily accounted for the two biblical testaments – that is, as the work of heterogeneous human (if inspired) minds over centuries (if not millennia) in different locales, in a trio of languages – the Quran's origins still defy adequate naturalistic (secular) explanation.

No one has found a known Arab or Persian contemporary of Muhammad who might be considered the real author of the Quran. Many western scholars therefore attribute the book's greatness to the genius of the Arabic language. This is a desperate explanation, the equivalent of arguing that the genius of the English language, by itself, explains the appearance of Shakespeare. Languages are not inert vehicles of literary capacity; they can hardly evolve dramatically without the creative labours of the pioneering writer. In the Quranic case, the writer is alleged to be a man unknown for his literary competence before the advent of his one and only book. Muslims, unlike westerners, are convinced that only divine authorship of the book could explain its otherwise unaccountable merits. They are therefore puzzled and offended by any reservations about the text's literary supremacy. We must now explore these two opposed attitudes towards the Quran.

Can we validly deduce divine authorship of a text from an impartial scrutiny of its literary qualities? Is the scripture's literary excellence, combined with the profundity of its content, intended to convince us of its heavenly origin? Should its literary genius alone persuade us? If so, which ingredient is crucial? Is it the dignity of style or the superiority of design, or choice of diction or profundity of content or all of these in some inimitable and unique combination?

2

The Latin adverb *frustra*, meaning 'in vain', is the origin of the English noun 'frustration' and related words. The import of the Latin adverb corresponds to the Arabic active participle '*mu'jizah*' which means 'frustrater'. The Muslim scripture is called, in the sciences of the Quran, though not in the Quran, the frustrater: it frustrates all attempts, including the combined efforts of human poets and elemental spirits, at an imitation of its linguistic style and contents (Q:17:88).[3] The Quran, Islam's only probative miracle, is an aesthetic literary challenge to writers and poets. It is remarkable that a religion which sees itself as the culmination of religion as such should found itself on such a precariously *intellectual* basis. Islam is indeed a religion of the book.

The Quran is, understood strictly, more than a miracle. Miracles, according to the Quran, are performed by prophets, always mere human beings, commissioned to perform them 'by permission of God' (*bi idhn Allāh*; Q:3:49). A *mu'jizah*, by contrast, requires not divine permission but rather direct divine agency: it is a special marvel that only God could exhibit. A formal recitation of any portion of the Quran, the world's most liturgically rehearsed and memorized scripture, is considered a *mu'jizah*. It does not require the agency of Muhammad, who is dead, but relies solely on God as performer using the power of any human voice, without the aid of music. In Muslim eyes and ears, it becomes the supreme miracle involving effective divine power rather than merely a divinely authorized suspension or rupture of natural law. Technically, the Quran alone is a *mu'jizah*, although the word admits of a plural (*mu'jizāt*). It is the unique and culminating miracle, 'the tremendous recital' (*al-qur'ān al-'azīm*; Q:15:87) which would have shattered a mountain (Q:59:21). This befits Muhammad as the seal of the prophets

(Q:33:40). His advent, supplemented by the Quran's finality, consummates the meta-religious and climactic self-consciousness of Islam noted in Chapter 1.

To confirm their mission, prophets bring miraculous signs often described as self-evidently probative (*āyah bayyinah*, sing. Q:29:35; *āyāt bayyināt*, pl. Q:17:101; 24:1; 29:49). These include eye-opening portents (*mubṣirah*, sing. Q:27:13; *baṣā'ir*, pl. Q:7:203; 17:102; 45:20; *mubṣiran*, acc. Q:27:86). Moses brought nine such signs to the Pharaoh and his community (Q:17:101; 27:12), each greater than its preceding sister sign (Q:43:48) – and all in vain. Jesus performed many significant miracles (Q:3:46, 49), most of which are also mentioned either in the canonical New Testament or its associated Apocrypha. Christians dismiss as apocryphal a few miracles recorded as canonical in the Quran (Q:3:49; 19:27–33) on the grounds that these are too fantastic. This is an especially weak argument in the case of a faith that is, even by religious standards, full of amazing and incredible events.

At a lower level, the *auliyā'* (allies) of God (Q:10:62), corresponding to Jewish and Christian saints, are granted the *karāmah* (*karāmāt*, pl.), a minor marvel of the kind Catholic theology stipulates for canonization. Many devout Muslims, especially Sufi saints considered as 'friends of God' by popular acclamation and reputation for piety and scholarship, claimed to be in different places at the same time, to multiply small amounts of food to feed their many disciples, and so on.[4] But Muslims single out the Quran as the only supreme *mu'jizah*, 'the challenger' that is divinely performed.[5]

3

Muslims claim that the Quran is a super-miracle of revealed but rational speech; they eulogize its classical language as the exclusive canon of literary taste. It is no repeatable literary achievement. Even to comprehend such hyperbolic claims requires some cross-cultural sensitivity. Westerners make no comparable claim on behalf of the Hebrew Bible or the Christian New Testament. The authority of the Bible is not grounded in the literary excellence of the Bible. Indeed a translation such as the Authorized King James version improves stylistically on the original, and is, for that reason, more influential than the original. These are unthinkable eventualities in the case of the Quran.[6]

From the opposite cultural angle, Muslims never view the Quran as literature or a saga that records the cultural history of Arabs. It is considered sublime revealed guidance which cannot condescend to the category of literature – that is, tragic drama, or divine comedy or poetry of great pathos. In the West, owing to a decline in orthodox religious belief and practice, many educated people see the Bible not as a revelation but rather as a religiously inspiring book, a form of self-help or spiritual hygiene not dissimilar to Buddhism. The scripture is highbrow literature that, despite deep recession in the serious publishing industry, continues to sell well.[7] Sophisticated Jews and Christians read the Bible from a literary and scholarly, rather than a religious or devotional, perspective. Even the most liberal Muslim rejects such a perspective on the Quran as secular and impious because of the justified suspicion that this liberty of thought undermines the right of scripture even to morally direct, let alone legislate for, modern lives. Literature is not revealed law, although literature, like other forms of art, as we note presently, influences the moral component of human life and effort.

All learned Muslims extol the Quran's literary virtues; Muslim experts in the technical and rigorous reading of the scripture expatiate on the book's superlative style. Such devout enthusiasm is informed and stimulated by an encyclopedic intimacy with the scripture's stylish nuances and intriguing contents. An outstanding example of this is the Egyptian martyr-exegete Sayyid Quṭb (1906–66) who was educated as a secular literary critic long before he fell in love with the Quran and died in his passion for what he called 'this amazing book'. The record of his love affair with the scripture's literary power and religious presence is preserved in a commentary, a massive work of scholarly industry, soothingly titled *Fī Ẓilāl Al-Qurān* (In the Shade of the Quran).[8]

Who could deny that the world's most widely read book, in its original language, must be an artistic masterpiece? Many Muslims deny it – for religious reasons we shall note presently. Western dismissal has involved motives. Of the world's literary masterpieces, the Arabic Quran is the one least accessible to western aesthetic appreciation, for reasons that relate mainly to political considerations and to rank prejudice against Islam, a former conqueror of parts of the European West. (Given the influence of Islam in the formation of modern Europe, classical Arabic is no less qualified to be a classical European language than Greek and Latin.) One must admit, however, that the Quran contains keenly negative assessments of Jewish and Christian doctrines. This alienates western readers.

4

While all Muslims regard the Quran as divinely revealed speech, as revelation undiluted by human additions, most would deny that it is a work of art. Is the Quran in part or at some level a work of art? If so, is it a type of literature? Is it poetry? The Quran denies that it is a literary production, a higher kind of poetry:

> We have not instructed him in poetry (*al-shi'r*) nor would it suit him.[9] This is nothing less than a message (*dhikr*) and a clear lecture (*qur'ānun mubīnun*) with the purpose of warning the living so that the word might prove true against disbelievers.
>
> (Q:36:69–70)

The Quran repeatedly denies that Muhammad is demon-possessed (*majnūn*; lit. jinn-possessed; Q:15:6; 52:29; 68:2, 51; 81:22), an accusation levelled earlier at Noah (Q:54:9). Nor is Muhammad an intellectually vain poet (*shā'ir*; Q:52:30; 69:41).The Prophet and the Quran despised the shamanic soothsayer (*kāhin*; Q:52:29; 69:42) and expert oath-monger (*ḥallāf*; Q:68:10) who fabricated shameless and predictable rhymes. The Greek word for poet (*poētēs*) means a maker or creator; the Arab equivalent means one who has keen perception (*shu'ūr*).

The Arabic for poet duplicates the sense of the Greek *aisthētēs* (perceiver). The Quran does not invent a derogatory neologism to denigrate the poet's calling. This is surprising: poets were revered in Arab culture as tribal spokesmen, as ideologues and sectarian propagandists who, despite being possessed by elemental spirits, could prove influential opponents of prophets.

The Quran contrasts the nobility of prophets with the vanity and hypocrisy of disbelieving poets (Q:69:40–1). The chapter named *The Poets* (although its main theme is the preaching of prophets) reads: 'As for the [disbelieving] poets, misguided evil-doers follow them. Have you not seen how they [the poets] wander aimlessly, distracted, in every valley? And they preach what they do not practise' (Q:26:224–6; see also v. 227). Allowing discrepancies between one's words and deeds characterizes hypocrites and infidel poets. Conspicuous integrity, exemplified by a symphony of word and deed, is the hallmark of God's servants (Q:19:54–6) – although ordinary believers rarely live up to such high standards (Q:61:2–3). The Quran has moral motives then for denying that Muhammad is a poet. Its condemnation of (secular) poetry is effectively a rejection of hypocrisy and insincerity in the life of faith.[10]

Muslims value the Quran solely as revelation, not as art. But why must we make this distinction? The motivation for making it and the justification for a particular distribution of emphasis are, given the assumptions that nourish the religious view, quite sound: the artistic merit of a text cannot be a primary or decisive consideration if it is intended to be an authoritative guide. Art can inspire and advise, thrill and encourage, but it cannot command obedience. A genuine revelation must seek to subordinate if not assimilate our aesthetic and moral impulses to the higher calling of ethical religion as commandment.

The Quran warns us of judgement, exhorts us to be good and threatens us with penalties if we wilfully reject the message (Q:14:1–2; 15:2–5; 16:44; 22:1; 23:1–11; 38:8; 39:25–8). While revelation has this purely educational and moral purpose, its message cannot reach its target – wayward human beings who habitually resist the divine will – unless it is impelled by rhetorical force, clarity and eloquence. Eloquence is therefore a strategic, not moral or religious, requirement: it makes moral exhortation appealing. However, it is unworthy of reverence, Muslims would argue, to conceive of God as a conscious artist committed to producing a carefully crafted literary design or performance. A non-Muslim, however, might justifiably view the Quran as didactic poetry with fertile and suggestive words patterned in a way that deepens the text's mnemonic potential and facilitates its reception among heedless human beings. The Quran itself notes these features of the text (Q:19:97; 44:58; 54:17, repeated as a refrain at 54:22, 32, 40). We examine these claims in Section 6.

5

Whether we classify the Quran as a work of art depends on our view of art. Art precedes not only religion, philosophy and science but also language understood naturalistically as strings of marks and noises used by organisms to negotiate with their world. We must first notice the world and interest ourselves in it before we can wonder about the causes of natural phenomena, the origin of our species, or the names of objects. Art is the pioneer of language, working ahead of it, minting for us, by exaggeration and hint, sensations for which we have as yet no name. These sensations are not biologically necessary for life. Poets often invent the right words for them.

Is art an imitation of the world? Should it portray things in their eternal essence, as they truly are, from the one right perspective? This Platonic view was popular with educated monotheists. Secular artists would interpret art as creative play, a form of leisure which gives pleasure and aesthetic fulfilment. Art has also been described as experience of the world, as empathy, and, especially in confessional poetry, as a public expression of an artist's internal and idiosyncratic state. For Nietzsche, art flows from a surging will that expresses states of ecstasy in the Greek sense of *ekstāsis*, a standing outside the self. Such art accentuates the positive forces of life and enriches reality. It is, unfortunately, opposed to the pursuit of truth. 'Truth is ugly. We possess *art* lest we *perish of the truth*'.[11] Nietzsche is being too generous to art since art can be as ugly as truth. It need not affirm life. In any case, truth is never enough, as we shall argue later in this chapter.

As for the purpose of art, most religiously inclined aestheticians claim that it should instill moral awareness while being directed towards the greater glory of God. Art should edify rather than entertain us – which is essentially the Victorian view of art as moral improvement. Many devout monotheists assign good art the function of transmitting a religious experience that unites human beings under one God, in a community, a religious fellowship. Their secular counterparts argue that its function is to 'reveal' alternatives to conventional ways of processing experience. (Many are thinking of poetry when arguing for this function of art.) Finally, some extremist aesthetes idolize art: it should exist and flourish for its own sake.

In a way, this discussion of the nature of art is irrelevant. For Muslims, the Quran is not art simply because it is not produced by human ingenuity. They treat it solely as revelation, not as great art, higher poetry, moving prose or imaginative literature. Believers would argue that all literary art, particularly poetry, is ultimately only an eloquent expression of our personal and communal fantasies about this or another world. Art as insight, where it attains depth, is confessional and therapeutic but it lacks the coercive power of revelation as commandment. No art can qualify as revelation since no art originates in a holy world. It is the instrumentality and origin, not the nature or aesthetic integrity, of art which decides whether revelation is simultaneously a form of art. Thus, the nature of God rather than the nature of art or of poetry might prevent the Quran from condescending to the level of art or, for that matter, of humour and pathos. If we decide to see the Quran as a work of *divine* art, then absolute artistic standards exist – just as the existence of God's holy will implies the existence of absolutely objective moral values. And we must also assume that God is an artist who maintains the aesthetic (and moral) integrity of his style.

6

To explore this further, we examine those uses of poetry which relate to religion. We divide the functions of poetry into experiential and linguistic and begin with the former. All visionary poetry, secular or religious, unifies our experience of reality, by alerting us to hidden connections on a grand scale, until the whole world appears as a cosmos. It aids us in intuiting reality at the level next to the interface between words and experience, almost beyond words, certainly beyond the perspective of natural science. Poetry may express what is analytically and passively presented to us by a metaphysician or ontologist or scientist. It goes beyond that, however, in enabling us to note that the mundane world remains forever, even after we understand it, mysterious, enchanted and magical. Again, poetry can connect us to nature which inspires us while remaining silent and secretive. A major poet, such as Thomas Hardy,[12] interrogates an indifferent and grand nature on behalf of a transient and volatile humanity's tragic struggles while a minor poet questions his lover, seeking only to 'flatter beauty's ignorant ear'.[13]

Poetry shapes a language by imparting unfamiliar connotations to familiar words. The Quran's Arabic is an outstanding example of this power to craft the religious contours of a language and hence a civilization. A great poet may name things and sensations that did not exist until they were thus named. Poetry, as a more potent and effective form of prose, can relate a story with greater emphasis on emotion and catharsis. It is natural to sing and chant poetry – a musical and lyrical version of prose. For the same reason, poetry has a mythopoetic function as it mythologizes, in a neutral or good sense, the human past and the present, giving us potent and eloquent words to describe social and natural realities beyond the reach of prose. Prose can express shrewd political insights of the kind we need to enable culture and society; only poetry can supply the myths that can explain the self-reflexive mystery of humankind to human beings. Poetry is, finally, the right vehicle for protest and therefore for the iconoclastic project of monotheistic religion.

Is the Quran revealed poetry? First class poetry, humanly produced, extends the range of our experience, perhaps only temporarily and only in some fugitive mood. Western writers admire it as 'revelatory', a term unavailable to Muslims since Arabic and other Islamic languages prohibit profane use of such religious words. Typically, poets express the personal traumas of life and vocation through the poetic use of language. If we say that the Quran records a personal trauma or a tentative attempt at communicating with other persons in the universe, then we imply that God himself is a poet, possibly an unstable one, searching for an identity. If the author were Muhammad, there would be sense if not merit in such a claim just as there is merit in admiring prophets such as Isaiah and Jeremiah as among the greatest poets of humankind. By claiming that the Quran is the literal word of *God*, we forfeit the right to classify it as poetry. Thus the denial that the Quran is poetry, even revealed poetry, is implicit in the view that its authorship is wholly divine. Pure revelation cannot be poetry.

We can read large tracts of the Hebrew Bible and the New Testament simply as reflective poetry about the human situation. In Europe, starting with Matthew Arnold, poetry and pathos became substitutes for biblical religion. Muslims suggest that this was readily possible only because the Bible already contains very little revelation: it is a collection of documents, written by inspired but fallible human beings, writings about the cultural and political history of the nations of the ancient Near East. Much of the material is secular and some of it, especially in the *Ketūb'īm* division, classed by Jews as the least holy (third) division of the tripartite *Tanakh* (Hebrew Bible), is openly subversive of ethical monotheism. It is harder to attenuate the Quran into poetry and cathartic pathos.

Granted that God is not a poet, is the Quran nonetheless poetry? All art transcends the intentions of its creator. The Quran is rhymed prose (*saj'*) usually without poetic rhythm (metre); it breaks the rules of rhymed poetry by repeating a rhyme or using false rhymes. Muslims dismiss this assessment as unfair since we are judging the Quran's poetic merit by using technical criteria when the book persistently denies its poetic status. The rationalist (Mu'tazilite) commentator Maḥmūd Al-Zamakhsharī denied that the Quran had metre and poetical rhyme (*muqaffā*). The themes (*ma'ānī*) of the Quran are, he continued, different from those that interest poets and, furthermore, Quranic structure or style (*naẓm*) does not resemble that of secular poetry. Al-Zamakhsharī concluded that the only thing shared by poetry and the Quran is that both are written in the Arabic language.[14]

7

The claim of *I'jāz* (inimitability) is not restricted to the Quran's literary qualities (economy of words or stylistic aptness) but includes the alleged profundity and wisdom of its contents. We examine the literary aspect before exploring the book's moral and religious profundity and truth; we obliquely investigate these latter features by pondering the incalculable influence and enduring impact of the scripture on individuals and societies.

Although the notion of *I'jāz* was formally part of Islam by the time of the jurist–traditionist Aḥmad Ibn Hanbal (d. 855), the last of the four eponymous founders of legal schools, its detailed defence is found later in the work of Abu Bakr Muhammad Ibn Al-Ṭayyib Al-Baqillānī (d. 1013).[15] His successor in this task, Abd Al-Qāhir Ibn Abd Al-Rahmān Al-Jurjānī (d. 1089/92), a pious adherent of the Shafi'ite school of law, rejected the rationalist theology of the Quran upheld by leading Mu'tazilite scholars such as Abd Al-Jabbār Ibn Aḥmad Al-Hamadhānī (d. 1033). Al-Jurjānī investigated Arabic linguistics in general, discussing poetic and prosaic rhetoric in his *Asrār Al-Balāghah* (Secrets of Eloquence). He examined Quranic style in his pioneering treatise *Dalā'il Al-I'Jāz* (Proofs of Quranic Incapacitation). Al-Baqillānī and Al-Jurjānī discussed the Quran's rhetorical effectiveness against the background of literary standards and assumptions prevalent in an age fascinated by the power and beauty of cultivated speech.

Orthodox opinion was not unanimous about the Quran's unqualified literary virtue which could allegedly disable all human attempts at imitation. Some contemporaries of Al-Jurjānī, such as Abu Al-Maʿāli Abd Al-Malik Al-Juwaynī (d. 1085), a teacher of the orthodox champion Abu Ḥamid Al-Ghazālī, entertained learned reservations about the aesthetic supremacy of the Quran.[16] My discussion below departs from these classical discussions and inhibitions and relates to modern secular literary criticism.

After Islam triumphed, fragments and residues of pre-Islamic poetry were systematically destroyed. Some non-Muslim scholars suggest, as a motive, the implied threat of rivalry with the Quran as unique literary achievement. Muslims think that the material was frivolous and undignified, its destruction part of the detoxification of the Hejaz. They do not look for literary rivals to the Quran because they assume that it is literarily in a class of its own. Believers claim that the Quran is more than a first class literary achievement since no imaginative literature could provide a comprehensive vision for billions. Before boarding a plane, most people quietly recite scripture, not poetry or wordly prose.

First, a logical quibble: the challenge of Quranic inimitability, taken literally, is senseless. An imitation of the Quran would produce something *quran-like*, not an identical copy of it. If it were identical with the Quran, it would not be a successful imitation but an exact replica. Logically and literally, there can be no perfect imitation of the Quran since nothing distinguishes two things, X and Y, as two distinct things if these resemble each other in all aspects.

Apart from the destruction of some poetic fragments, Muslims assassinated two pagan poets in Muhammad's day. Nadir Ibn Al-Ḥārith, who procured dancing girls to sing romantic Persian songs to distract people listening to Muhammad's latest revelations, is mentioned obliquely in the Quran (Q:31:6–7, 20; 22:3, 8–9). And Kaʿb Ibn Al-Ashraf was, like other poets in Arabia, a loquacious ideologue and polemicist in the days before mass media inherited the mantle of entertainment and indoctrination of the masses. Muslim historians and literary analysts claim that the verses produced by these poets were palpably inferior to the Quran; the two poets were executed instead for maligning Muhammad *ex officio* as God's messenger.[17] The murdered poets were being intellectually vain when they claimed to have produced verses equal to the Quran in literary merit and spiritual profundity. Labīd Ibn Rābiʿah, for example, by far the greatest poet among the Quraysh at the time of the revelation, was sufficiently overwhelmed by it to voluntarily abjure all poetry in his later years.

Can Muslims justify killing the two poets? It would be pointless to kill poets today, especially in western cultures, since poets exercise virtually no public influence. That poetry was practically and politically pointless was the famous and correct verdict of W.H. Auden. Poets write in a genre that is suffocated in mass liberal democratic cultures because there is, despite our freedoms, a prejudice against the inner life. Conformism requires similarity of tastes – which is only possible if all taste is externalized and homogenized. The television, the best friend of all lonely and alienated hearts, does it effortlessly for us. Modern culture lacks inwardness – as existentialist critics of society have noted but failed to cure.[18]

By contrast, poets in Muhammad's day were influential anarchists whose contemporaries wanted to hear about the sheer variety of inner, especially romantic and spiritual, lives of other human beings.

8

The Quran, the first text to become a book in Arabic, single-handedly formalized the nascent Arabic language.[19] The Quran's diction provides the standard of the Arabic tongue. It is considered the ideal form of the language and accepted as such even by those, such as Christian and Jewish Arabs, who reject its claim to supernatural origin. The scripture contains some aberrations from standard grammatical norms but these are seen either as acceptable deviations or as innovations that establish new grammatical rules.[20]

It is the unanimous verdict of critical, including hostile, Arabist opinion, that the Quran has been for 14 centuries the crowning achievement of a rich and varied Arabic literature. Even disbelieving Arabists eventually concede that the Quran's Arabic is outstandingly stylish: most of them reverse, after a whole lifetime of study and reflection, their own earlier dismissive judgements made in the active heat of juvenile 'scholarship' and missionary zeal. All competent authorities agree that while a translation could successfully convey the sense and the learned nuances of its fecund and mysterious vocabulary, it can never register the sheer range of its emotional effect. The unsettling impact of the recited scripture's sustained eloquence even on disbelievers is noted by western scholars who espouse a phenomenological approach to religion.[21]

I summarize and conclude this preliminary part of our investigation of the credentials of the Quran. It has a unique artistic temper best expressed by poetry: confident but meditative, assertive but searching for a voluntary response, unfailingly incisive and combative in its positive doctrines, unimpeachably alert to the subconscious human need for mnemonic and rhythm, and artistically creative yet subordinate, even captive, to the demanding ethical imperatives of the prophetic mandate.

In the Quran, conscious artistry is tactfully subdued in the service of truth. In the majestic original, the reader finds a mystique of spontaneity combined with a laconic authority, a combination that is the privilege of authentic poetry. Occasionally we are jolted by an anarchic expression of artistic prowess, suited more to poetry than to conventional prose: the strange opening of some chapters with unintelligible 'broken letters' of the Arabic alphabet constitute a fitting tribute to a sovereign deity exercising a *literary* prerogative that dismisses with impunity the creature's expectations of intelligibility. We forgive such unintelligibility only in poetry because poetry is existential, creating the whole world of mystery and imagination, the prerequisite of creativity. No admirer of the Quran could disagree with the Latin poets: *Carmina morte carent* (Poetry never dies).

A book can, however, be too decisive. The Quran, a religious anti-text to secular poetry, has acted as an incubus on any radical departures in Arabic literature. This can be explained. Literatures that begin with a masterpiece, as Greek and Arabic do, cannot concede the worth of later productions, especially if these are colloquial or demotic productions. Moreover, in Arabic, the pioneering masterpiece is not seen as humanly produced. This is bad for the development of Arabic literature; but if a book can inhibit the natural development of such a virile enterprise, that fact itself must be acknowledged and explained, not merely deplored.

9

A work which sets the criteria used in Arabic literary judgement cannot itself be assessed – without using some independent yardstick. For Muslims, the Quranic diction and its arrangement supply the ultimate standard of linguistic propriety and hence cannot be judged against any higher standard of excellence. Arab Muslims distinguish the eloquent classical (*fuṣ'ha*) Arabic of the Quran and classical works from the colloquial (*'āmiyyah*) dialects of the 22 Arabic-speaking nations. The latter are demotic dialects: corrupt regional variants of the classical language found in its full purity only in the Quran. We must therefore now consider four independent criteria for evaluating the literary quality of a piece of writing: intelligent choice of subject-matter; grace of expression combined with a sustained dignity of style; formal correctness of style (including high quality of diction); and superiority of design and structure.

A preliminary point: this debate about the Quran's literary excellence presupposes the privilege of knowing, preferably mastering, Arabic. Few non-Arab Muslims, let alone non-Arab non-Muslims, have had the time or inclination to master this rich language. Only a few scholars, whether they be Muslim, non-Muslim, Arab or non-Arab, are therefore qualified to judge the merits of the argument for or against the Quran's alleged supremacy of style and taste. Arabic is known, from studies of relative ease of acquisitions of languages, to be among the toughest to learn, let alone master. This is ironic seeing that it is a formal, scientifically accurate, language with strict rules and immutable and fecund trilateral roots. Its vocabulary is etymologically transparent, displaying its structure gratuitously to the intelligent student. It is also virtually fully phonetic – but uses, as we noted in Chapter 4, a 'defective' script.

The Quran's miraculous character could not, to turn to the first of our criteria, derive from its choice of theme; a work about God does not, for that reason alone, become a scripture. Some great works of world art, including poetry and fiction, have explored the theme of God but that alone cannot elevate them to scriptural status. Conversely, a book judged to be a scripture would not lose its sacredness solely because it dealt with profane, mundane or immoral themes – such as sexual perversion (Q:4:15–16; 29:28–30), concubinage (Q:4:3) and usury (Q:2:275–80; 30:39). Choice of theme is an external feature of a text; it reveals an author's interests but endows neither beauty nor authority on the writing. Even a vulgar or profane theme can be handled with reverence and tact. We must therefore examine the claims made, not merely the choice of subject-matter.

Does grace of expression and a sustained dignity of style, no matter how base a theme, indicate a sacred or miraculous status? This criterion is suspect on three grounds. First, a non-Muslim could sincerely question the grace and charm of the Quranic diction. A Muslim might reply that such a refusal to concede aesthetic merit was due to an undeveloped artistic taste just as some would say that the proletariat's inability to appreciate opera, the art Marxists dismiss as circus for the upper class, is due to an uncultivated aesthetic sensibility. Second, the allegedly revealed writings of all faiths could be seen, by their adherents, as supernaturally produced. This is admittedly a weak argument since, as we saw with the Bible, Jews and Christians do not even claim that supremacy of literary taste is the foundation of the Bible's claim to be the word of God.

Finally, someone could contend that certain works by human authors equal or excel the experienced beauty of the Muslim scripture. Perhaps the mystical poet Jalāl Al-Dīn Rūmī (1207–73) could claim divine inspiration for some of his better verses. Indeed, Rūmī's major work, *Mathnawi* (The Rhymed Couplets), was admired by the Sufi poet Nūr Al-Dīn Jāmi as 'the Quran in Persian'.[22] Again, Plato's dialogues are beautifully written although, unlike the Quran, they are not performed or chanted for their effect nor is it claimed that their credentials derive from an experienced effect of their public recitation. We conclude that style and grace, like dignity and charm, are inappropriately subjective.

Consider the third criterion: formal correctness of style and diction. Jewish and Christian polemicists, with a shaky command of classical Arabic, point to the Quran's glaring linguistic idiosyncrasies, including peculiarities of diction as reflected in syntax, vocabulary and grammatical accuracy. These have been meticulously examined by Al-Jurjānī and Al-Baqillānī in the context of the debate on Quranic incapacitation of the literary pretender; grammatical peculiarities were rigorously analysed by Maḥmud Al-Zamakhsharī, the Mu'tazilite commentator mentioned earlier.[23] To understand the full catalogue of the book's alleged syntactical and grammatical peculiarities would require technical expertise.[24]

Apart from countless neologisms,[25] some words are occasionally used with other than their usual or accepted meanings. As in daringly original poetry, the literal or lexical meaning of a word differs from its conventionally correct meaning. Important Quranic vocabulary has a literal (or lexical), that is, grammatical sense, and a juristic sense. For example, *zakah* means purity or purification and is occasionally used in that sense. For example, John, son of Zechariah, has been given purity (*zakah*; Q:19:13) as a divine gift. In its legal sense, as the alms-tax levied to purify wealth before it can be used, the word occurs often. Indeed, Chapter 19 uses it in both senses (see Q:19:13, 55). Important political words such as *fitnah* (treason), *ummah* (community) and *imām* (leader) have several different, often unrelated, senses. Despite claiming to be a clear book, the Arabic Quran contains many words of unclear,[26] foreign[27] or idiosyncratic import. (This is not unique to the Quran: about a quarter of biblical Hebrew words are virtually unintelligible.) Arabic dictionaries record idiosyncratic Quranic usages without offering any explanation for the way the scripture takes liberties with conventions.

Other odd textual features include ellipsis, a mark of most classical Arabic poetry and prose, but the Quran's elliptical compression is often severe enough to require editorial elaboration to make sense of its claims (see e.g. Q:39:9, 22, 24).

Again, a verse might open with a single word such as *dhālik*, meaning 'Such', translated as 'Such is the command' (Q:22: 30, 32). The scripture combines conventional ellipsis with unconventional modes of emphasis – such as the energetic mode not found elsewhere in classical literature.[28]

We explore examples of mysterious passages in Chapter 6 in the context of a contemporary appreciation of the Quran by secular readers; we merely mention this here in the context of the Quran's claim to literary perfection. Some mysterious claims lack context and, even when context is supplied, remain partly opaque and obscure. A few verses are unintelligible. We do not know enough of the context or intention to control or ascertain the meaning of some enigmatic Quranic claims. A related problem, partly common to scripture in general but conspicuous in the Quran, is created by the choice of deliberately vague claims elastic enough to cover the aspirations of many contending parties. The scripture's widespread use of indefinite descriptions nebulous enough to denote several different personalities contributes to this plasticity of meaning. Typically, a personality even in Muhammad's entourage is identified by indefinite description rather than by name; Muslims see this studied nebulosity as the hallmark of a comprehensive scripture that refuses to be tethered to its narrow historical origins.

Finally, consider the yardstick of superior design. Some discrepancies in crafting affect intelligibility of the whole passage though not the sense of the individual sentences. There are rarely prefatory explanations for historical events; important historical narratives begin in *medias res* and presuppose substantial background knowledge.[29] A few chapters begin or end abruptly and thus seem disjointed. For example, Q:4:176 concludes the long chapter on women. It should be placed after Q:4:12, not as the final verse. Again, the pair of verses that close Chapter 9 (Q:9:128–9) seem out of place. There are many awkward or abrupt transitions from one theme to another. Finally, the scripture, though only in translation, is repetitive – implying defective organization and lack of competent editing. The overall structure and design of the Quran has often been criticized; we scrutinize this charge separately in the next section.

10

The Quran contains genuine enigmas and idiosyncrasies that fascinate and outrage western Arabists while eliciting ardent Muslim defences.[30] Some orientalists mine the text for artificial difficulties, making vague charges of anachronism and error, suggesting that the Quran is an incompetent plagiarism of the Bible. Such an attitude is worthy of religious zeal, not objective scholarship. The issue of the scripture's repetitive nature and the question of the link between art and craft will be treated separately below. We begin with the charge of repetition, a stock orientalist accusation.

Jewish and Christian critics, far from disinterested parties to the debate, have popularized the view that the Quran is haphazardly repetitive. No Muslim reader perceives the Quran as repetitive, in the sense of dull and monotonous, partly because the original is splendidly adorned with literary embellishments. The Quran comments on its thematically repetitive (*mathānī*) nature but sees it as an asset (Q:15:87; 39:23). Cadence and rhythm require a generous amount of repetition. Such repetition aids fluency and serves as a mnemonic that assists oral recitation and memorization. The Quran is made to be 'fluent on your [Muhammad's] tongue' (Q:44:58). Again, 'We have certainly made the Quran easy to remember. But who remembers it?' (Q:54:17; refrain repeated at vv. 22, 32, 40).

For the rejector, the scripture's rhythms can intensify into repetition and obsession. Muslims would retort that the Quran addresses heedless men and women who need to be shocked out of their complacent inertia, hence the persistent appeals for us to recollect our true heritage (Q:38:1; 36:11; 41:41). Repetition, as the use of stereotypical phrases, effectively conveys and evenly distributes a core message and its associated emphases and motifs. The Quran was delivered as an oral homily in the context of Muhammad's mission in pagan Arabia making some degree of repetition inevitable. Muhammad was not a redactor of the text; he did not prune it in the cool detached hour. In translation, however, the written text cannot conceal the monotony of the monotheistic harangue – though stereotypical phrases and repetition are hardly unique to the Quran.

Take at random any subset of a dozen verses and the Quranic message is essentially the same. What is seen as repetition could also, more charitably, be viewed as the most radical comprehensiveness – since the important truths are never off the page. This is a 're-contexting' of the same truths rather than literal repetition. In Quranic narration, narrative parts are not related to one another episodically through the type of mechanical seriality we associate with normal prose. Instead, the beginning, the middle and the end are thematically related through measured repetition and capitulation. Chapter 12 of the Quran is a perfect example of this method.

The charge of repetition should be answered in its original inter-faith environment. Unlike the Bible, the Quran contains virtually no *verbatim* repetition. Both the Hebrew Bible and the Greek New Testament contain vast amounts of verbatim as opposed to thematic repetition. The books of 1 and 2 Chronicles are censored versions of Samuel and Kings; many long passages from the latter are openly plagiarized. In the New Testament, redaction and source critics isolate the striking similarities in two of the synoptic gospels and attribute this to a common source called Q (*Quelle*; German for source), used by Matthew and Luke. Biblical scholars see this as an issue of determining which text relies on another text rather than as an issue of repetition. Such textual reliance is assessed in order to determine priority of composition and hence fidelity to the most ancient witnesses. Christian scholars see repetition in the Quran, however, simply as repetition. Such are the ways of religious prejudice when it ignores its own double standards.

11

What is the link between art and craft, on the one hand, and intellectual innocence and artlessness, on the other? There are spontaneous and impassioned records whose (apparent) artlessness demonstrates their sincerity; equally the strategic use of language is often insincere and manipulative and may amount to propaganda. Craftsmanship can sometimes be dismissed as professional dexterity. If it succeeds in being persuasive, that counts against it. Poetry is distinguished from rhetoric and propaganda by poetry's self-directed (internal) faith in the veracity of its message. At the opposite extreme is a belief in one's own propaganda – the weakest kind of sincerity and found only among politicians.

The Latins were fond of saying *Ars est celare artem*! True art is to conceal art. Certainly, artists can be cunning. It is deceptive to conceal consciously the artistic nature of one's work, especially sources of inspiration. But if preoccupation with the immensity of the theme itself dwarfs the merely artistic dimension of the work, then we can defend the lack of art especially since conscious artistry may conceal insincerity of mood and intention. The artists are not fully absorbed or consumed by their art so long as they know or remember what they are doing. Unconscious artistry, paradoxically, produces the most authentic art. This was the Greek understanding of poetry where the poet was in ecstasy.

Indifference to craftsmanship could border on a denial of accepted technique or require a new use of existing resources. It could be a deliberate decision to avoid structure. None of this need entail lack of artistic achievement. Religious vigour and intellectual passion are often destroyed by a rigid environment of language and design. A vital theme thaws out language and makes it fluid by the power of the subject – without external control. It is no coincidence that the most influential books have been shapeless and unedited.[31]

A direct mood and a passionate tone mark the entire Quran. The earliest revelations, placed at the end in the final arrangement, are even more terse and elliptical than the rest of the book. The existing Arabic language is strained as its words try to contain the massive burden of Muhammad's actual and anticipated religious experience: 'We shall soon sent down on you a weighty word' (Q:73:5). Prosaic neologisms, daring poetic innovations and suggestive verse endings litter the text (see Q:69:19–29). The later longer (Medinan) revelations, dealing with the mundane details and caveats of law and ritual rather than solely with the greatness of God and the imminent nemesis of the final day, are equally simple, rigorous, and explicit. The sustained passion informing and determining the literary quality of the whole Quran is unaffected by Muhammad's move to Medina.

12

We examined the elusive orthodox claim about the Quran's heavenly origin being grounded in its alleged superiority and perfection of literary taste. Though apparently promising, it relies on subjective textual features such as grace of expression, the charm of the writing, correctness of diction, and superiority of design. Such features cannot make the content of a work authoritative, even supposing, for the sake of argument, that the Quran did possess these literary excellences. An analytical philosopher, trained in Euro-Atlantic schools, will say that the perceived beauty and impeccable style of Quranic verses does not guarantee their truth for the simple but sufficient reason that the truth of a written tract is not affected by our perception of its charm and beauty. Philosophers should search for truth, not beauty.

Beauty, in its relationship to truth, carries a different meaning and probative force in varied epochs and cultures. We today, unlike the classical world, distinguish beauty from truth and both from goodness. The triad no longer enjoys a close relationship. Nietzsche was incensed by the notion that anyone could identify these three especially since 'Truth is ugly'. By contrast, Plato defended the unity of value, truth and beauty although he did not argue for it systematically. In his *Enneads*, the neo-Platonist philosopher Plotinus (205–70 CE), defended the Platonic identification of the beautiful, the good, and the true. The position had distinguished advocates in the ancient world. The Islamic neo-Platonists also indirectly sympathized with Plato's view via the works of Plotinus and Porphyry.[32]

The Quran describes God as the reality (*al-ḥaqq*; Q:20:114; 22:6, 62) to distinguish him from the false deities which are collectively called the falsehood (*al-bāṭil*; 29:52; 31:30). God's goodness, mercy and holiness are mentioned through some of his 99 names most of which are in the Quran. As for beauty, 'all the most beautiful names belong to him' (Q:17:110; 20:8; 59:24). God is *dhū al-jalāl* (master of dignified beauty) in the Quran's majestic hymn to creation in Chapter 55 (Q:55:27, 78). After completing the seven heavens in two days, God adorned the lower heavens, our earth (Q:15:16); the Quran notes the cosmetic dimension of the cosmos (Q:41:12; 50:6; 67:5). God, a creative artist who appreciates beauty, comments on the aesthetic appeal of the human shape (Q:7:11; 40:64; 64:3). In Muhammad's traditions, God is often described as beautiful and said to delight in beauty, though these might be forged comments attributed to the Prophet in order to authorize or legalize the decorative arts cultivated in a later age.

Must our reason deny the importance of the aesthetic appeal of the doctrines for which faiths and ideologies demand ultimate loyalty and commitment? Even if we assume that truth is independent of beauty and of the emotions thus aroused, our access to important truths depends on the passionate side of our nature. This is not to claim – it would be untrue – that the appeal of a doctrine determines its truth. Beauty and truth are distinct. But are they not related, owing to entanglements entailed by the psychological needs of our nature as we seek objective truth?

The believer dismisses as imbalanced only a simplistic and aridly rational stance because it denies that the art and ritual inspired by the religious perspective has, like any other love affair, liberated emotion and embellished the world of sight and sound. Islamic calligraphy has sensuous curves that delight even the untrained eye. The recitation of the Arabic Quran constitutes the sole 'music' of the mosque. (Instrumental music is forbidden inside a mosque.) Recited revelation, like music, is a language of emotional association, not merely discursive meaning.

We have a legitimate emotional interest in the aesthetic dimension of truth: the ultimate truth about us and the world must satisfy this interest if it is to retain our complete allegiance long after the first flush of excitement. Truth needs to be beautified if it is to win allegiance among truth-seeking beings for they are not only rational and intelligent but also emotional and passionate. The beauty of a vision does not make it true but its beauty is nonetheless relevant to the psychological demands of plausibility and appeal. Most of us might adhere to truths we found irrational but few of us would adhere to truths we found aesthetically unappealing. It could be argued that beauty is seductive and glamorous and that its appeal is false and alluring. Plato, in the *Symposium*, argued that beauty is that aspect of ultimate goodness which first attracts us. Beauty is the gateway or entrance to moral truth. But beauty is often in the service of falsehood and propaganda too. Is it then irrelevant, even dangerous, to truth?

If beauty is solely a matter of taste, we must respect the maxim *De gustibus non est disputandum* (In matters of taste, there is no dispute). We can reasonably dispute only in matters of truth and putative fact. Where taste is concerned, we condemn or approve but it is senseless to call someone's taste true or false. There seem to be no empirical criteria for beauty. Most of our aesthetic judgements seem to suggest an objective and universal standard of taste but no empirical criteria are in fact universal. The most established and revered standards of excellence can be challenged and changed. As for beauty, the perception of physical beauty is, except in rare cases, immediate; it is not established by reasoning. One does not reason that a human face is beautiful. No amount of reasoning could make us alter our judgement that someone is beautiful if our senses had already established it and, conversely, we could not reason ourselves into perceiving someone as beautiful when the senses soberly tell us otherwise. One exception is a face at the interface of beauty and plainness – a versatile face, useful to an actor, a face with features ambiguous enough to be perceivable as neither ugly nor beautiful.

Many Muslims, including the former singer Cat Stevens, now known as Yusuf Islam, have noted and appealed to the peculiarly musical charm of the Quranic resonances, heard as beautiful and ennobling – and not only to Muslim ears. Our perception of beauty, however, is direct, immediate and subjective; it cannot bear the whole burden of the demand for probative evidence in support of the alleged truth of the vision it evokes and seeks to validate. The credentials of Quranic incapacitation are bound to be logically weak even if they are aesthetically strong.

The link between truth and beauty is not questioned solely by sceptics. Some Muslim apologists insist, for religious reasons, that the beauty of the Quran is irrelevant. They say that men and women do not live and die for the sake of literary beauty. Some Muslims, especially of the puritanical Wahhabi and Salafi schools dominant in Saudi Arabia, are suspicious of the art of *tajwīd* (lit., perfecting), the ornate recitation of the Quran, which sensationally exhibits the oral and aural beauty of its diction. They think that this art distracts from the moral message of the revelation since many non-Muslims, including Arab Jews and Christians, might admire instead the aesthetic appeal of the chanted scripture. The orthodox Muslim view that art is a distraction from duty resembles the Puritan suspicion of ornaments and visual embellishments.

We have examined the alleged link between the beauty of a book and the truth of its contents. In Chapter 7 we shall question the ancient connection between the moral trustworthiness of Muhammad and the alleged truth of the message he brings. The liaison between trust and authority has been ruptured in the secular age just as the bond between being religiously faithful and being morally virtuous, as we saw in Chapter 3, has been weakened, perhaps broken, in our sceptical age. The divorce of the two partners in the classical union of beauty and truth is the third major casualty in the war between ancient religion and modern secular modernism.

13

Traditionally, these issues were not investigated in the context of philosophical challenge since non-Muslims have rejected the Muslim contention as unworthy of sustained scrutiny while Muslims presented no arguments specifically for scrutiny by impartial students of the Quran. Therefore the claims discussed above have not been objectively formulated outside the opposed twin contexts of dogmatic devotion and dogmatic rejection.

Does the Quran's literary beauty make it true? Is its literary beauty an adjunct to its supernaturally guaranteed truth? The inimitability of the Quran, which ensures its credentials, does not distinguish between content and style but we have examined the Quran's linguistic merits and demerits in isolation. We now assess the apologetic claim that the Quran is a miraculous ideological achievement. Is it, to widen our discussion, reasonable to claim that the Quran frustrates any natural or historical explanation of its profound and enduring influence? If so, we have an indirect pragmatic argument for its claim to be the word of God. We examine two levels of Quranic influence: its transformation of individual lives and its impact on many cultures.

The Quran inspired new legislation, moving art, scholarly commentary, and stimulated the scientific enterprise – but it first influenced the individual through its recited and calligraphic aspects which are characteristic of its oral and liturgical centrality in Islam. It makes visual impact on the individual eye which traces the gorgeous calligraphy that adorns the borders of Islam's architectural glories such as the Dome of the Rock, a landmark that dwarfs every tourist postcard of Jerusalem. Some of the verses on the Dome of the Rock are, unfortunately, provocatively judgemental against Judaism and dismissive of Christian piety.

No matter where he opens the Quran, the intelligent reader is instantly engaged with a theme that dwarfs the mere beauty that conscious artistry produces. Some books, like some people, possess charisma. The Quran's passionate intensity of conviction makes it seductive. Its aura of directness and zealous sincerity has made it, notwithstanding its enigmas and subtleties, widely accessible and influential. Thomas Carlyle (1795–1881), the Calvinist who eventually lost his faith in God but admired human heroes, was the first European writer to note in the Quran a quality of direct appeal to the heart, which outweighed the book's allegedly haphazard and random contents.[33] The Quran is not pretentious in a literary sense but it pretends to substantive greatness, effortlessly creating a unique style to absorb massive content. Wholly self-styled, it is, like all masterpieces, inevitably 'pretentious' since it is *sui generis*.

The Islamic literature about Muhammad's life and views extols the externality and coercive power of the recited Quran in Muhammad's own experience. One can appreciate the scripture's aesthetic power in Muslim life by visiting an Islamic land in Ramadan, the month in which this lecture giving divine guidance 'descended', a time commemorated by intensified and purified devotion (Q:2:185; 97:1–3). Chanted in public gatherings in the ornate *tajwīd* style favoured by Indonesian and Egyptian reciters, such as the late Egyptian Sheikh Abd Al-Bāṣit Abd Al-Ṣamad, the audience listens to it with rapt attention.[34] The Quran advises on the ethics of attention to its recitation and reprimands the pagans for drowning out the sound of the chanted word (Q:41:26). During the silent rapture, believers possess the book and the book possesses them. No outsider can understand this although sympathetic westerners, committed to a phenomenological study of religions, concede that a spiritual force is unleashed when the scripture is rehearsed liturgically in famous holy precincts.[35]

The revelation was originally a running conversation with Muhammad. It recorded an internal tension which mounted from a brooding and ruminative inception to an active and soothing close as Islam was poised on the verge of becoming an empire. Today, we read the Quran as a written record which says everything at once: a book, unlike a coherent conversation, asserts all its claims simultaneously rather than in a sequence because one can read it anywhere at random. For public worship, Quranic recitation mimics the style of the original reception of the word. Recited on the principle of crescendo, a slow lethargic opening yields slowly to a powerful culmination, followed by a soothing close. Longer verses are recited with passion and gusto and the tension is built up and then carefully released towards the end. A verse with a sad or minatory content may be recited gently while a happier pericope, promising divine forgiveness or paradise, may be ardently recited. An experienced reciter can reduce a crowd to tears and loud pious exclamations; Muslims treat the recited scripture with a solemn reverence that surprises those who can no longer believe in their own scriptures with such dedicated sobriety. Could the Muslim confidence in the inimitability of the divine diction be vindicated perhaps by an experienced effect of the recited Quran?

14

Could the Quran's dramatic and enduring impact on the world be a ground for thinking its contents are inimitable, perhaps true? Let us first establish the nature and extent of this influence. The Quran is guaranteed to be an incalculably influential document since it is the world's most recited book in the original language of its incidence, a living language that is still known and widely spoken. Such influence is harder to appreciate in today's world where it is never the case that someone writes a book and governments fall. Such direct causation is an exaggerated estimate of the power of the written word. But Aquinas, a man of many books, was reputedly fond of the maxim, inspired perhaps by the case of Muhammad and the Quran: '*Timeo hominem unius libri*'.[36] 'I fear the man with one book'. Muhammad wrote one book, if we take a secular view of the matter, and many governments, indeed two empires, fell.

The question of whether the Quran is poetry is relevant here. Poets are secular mystics quarrelling with different states of their own disposition rather than fighting on behalf of some external, political, religious or ideological cause. W.B. Yeats once lamented, before the outbreak of the Second World War, that it takes 50 years for a poet's weapons to influence the issues. He offered an arbitrary and optimistic estimate though he has spared us the usual conceit about the pen being mightier than the sword, in any case a manifest falsehood. That the pen is useless without the sword is the tragic realization of all sincere reformers. It is intellectual vanity for poets to imagine that their work can produce a revolution or aid in the birth of a utopia.

It is not a disputed thesis that the Quran as political prose was uniquely influential in its own day. Neither of the two biblical testaments influenced contemporaneous events. The Quran, however, was revealed as a running commentary on Muhammad's nation-building. Its liturgical and legal provisions were immediately and scrupulously implemented and observed by the Medinan community and then by others inspired by that model. The Medinan *ummah* (community), the first and only full implementation of the Islamic vision, still provides the blueprint for the ideal political providence God intends for the human constituency. Muhammad, as Prophet of God, stood at the helm of that utopian republic until his death; in his life-time, he implemented in letter and spirit all Quranic edicts. Faith is as faith does. Muslims would mock, unfairly, the impracticality of Christian ideals which were rarely practised in any society and would note, unsympathetically, that the Torah's magnanimous provisions, especially the sabbatical (Exodus 23:10–11; Leviticus 25:2–7) and jubilee year (Leviticus 25:8–17), were never practised in any known Jewish society.

The Quran Islamized the Arabs irreversibly in a mere 23 years; no pagan recidivism undid Muhammad's efforts after his death although it took the sagacity of his successor Abu Bakr to enforce some treaties originally signed with the Prophet. Islam uprooted the ignorant pagan ways (*al-jāhiliyyah*; Q:33:33; 48:26) so thoroughly that it has prevented the growth of a conscientious atheism or paganism to this day, although Islam's critics would not see that as an achievement. Unlike western Christian civilization, Islam had no pagan re-awakenings. Western civilization is inspired not wholly by Christianity but often by a reaction against it. Many European cultural critics argue that some of Europe's greatest cultural achievements and its global industrial prominence were stimulated by a repudiation of Christian norms as politically juvenile and morally impracticable in favour of the older Graeco-Roman heritage. The first Hellenic re-assertion occurs as early as Julian the Apostate. A millennium later, the Renaissance erupted in the fourteenth century followed by the Reformation in the sixteenth and the Romantic Movement in the eighteenth – culminating a century later in the radical and militant secularism of Darwin, Marx, and Nietzsche.[37]

Unique among both secular manifestoes and scriptures, the Quran directly and successfully inspired a major world civilization. Founded on a religiously sanctioned respect for literacy and scholarship, it formalized Arabic (and later Hebrew) grammar, moving Arab cultures from oral to literate status in decades.

Concretely, it outlawed nuncupation – the oral declaration of testaments and wills – and insisted on fortifying such declarations with the testimony of witnesses (Q:5:108–10). (The Quran's recognition of female testimony was a revolutionary step which implied that women were legal persons, as we see in Chapter 11.) The scripture required important commercial transactions to be reduced to writing (Q:2:282), thus starting the process of creating cultures where written records in all departments of life eventually became commonplace. Its fluent text remains a material source of Islamic law. Admittedly, the Quran did not sanction free inquiry in our modern sense. But it did indirectly stimulate the project of science and hence the emergence of the modern world, a theme we investigate critically in Chapter 8. The Muslim scripture is a more proximate cause of the emergence of modern Europe than is the Bible.

15

We conclude by discussing a general question in the epistemology of religious doctrine. What is the relationship between passion and evidence in the religious life? 'Faith moves (the) mountains' is a proverb inspired by the New Testament. No one had enough faith to move mountains and Jesus accused even his disciples of lacking faith (Matthew 17:14–20). Faith these days needs to remove mountains, the mountains of modern doubt and hesitation. The sceptic mocks believers who cite this proverb and reminds them that every faith moves mountains. Different and incompatible doctrines alter our lives. Belief in Islam's Allah is no different in this respect from belief in Christ or belief in the transformative power of the Buddhist Eight-Fold Path or the Jew's Torah or the Marxist's historical process of dialectical materialism. We can verify that all such beliefs are powerful although it is harder to decide whether all such conviction is *equally* powerful, especially in today's secular and hedonistic age when Islam distinguishes itself for what its admirers call its determined resistance to the secular onslaught and its detractors view as misguided fanaticism. We could construct tables of comparative martyrdom rates for the world religions and ideologies but, as Shakespeare reminds us, blood is no argument.[38]

Belief in ideals inspired by secular realities such as reason and love are also efficacious although one rarely finds martyrs for the cause of pure reason. The most famous exceptions are Socrates and Boethius. The search for ultimate truth, the desire to know as Aristotle called it, is neither as instinctive nor as powerful a drive as philosophers like to think. Admittedly, Baruch Spinoza, Søren Kierkegaard, Friedrich Nietzsche and Ludwig Wittgenstein are four courageous modern thinkers who all led unhappy lives for the sake of their philosophies; each has been posthumously admired, especially Nietzsche whose mental martyrdom at the age of 45 must be saluted. Most modern academic philosophers, however, eagerly avoid drinking the hemlock for the cause of truth.

There are two issues here. First, can one believe, passionately believe, a false proposition? Certainly; it is perhaps widespread in the religious and the secular lives. (We turn to this question when we debate self-deception in Chapters 7 and 9.) The second concern is about the epistemological merits of thinking that the spectacularly powerful effects of belief in a given proposition are ever sufficient or necessary (or at least relevant) evidence of its truth. An aspect of this question traumatized the Christian existentialist thinker Søren Kierkegaard who, at times, inconsistently, believed that the integrity of the inward attitude we adopt towards anything, whether true or false, can make it authentic and hence 'true'. We examine this claim in Chapter 9 in the context of a debate on idolatry.

Passionate or dramatic impact is not a necessary concomitant of true belief: many true beliefs are entertained without ardour. The claim that water, under standard conditions, boils at 100 degrees Celsius, does not excite even a devoted chemist. A true belief or proposition need not have a dramatic impact since knowing a truth need not alter our outlook. Many people rhetorically acknowledge that truth is powerful but, in practice, even professional thinkers have seldom been interested in truth if an impressive-looking false substitute has sufficed. Revealingly, conventional wisdom does not contain the proverb 'Truth moves mountains' or more credibly 'Beauty moves mountains'. 'Love moves mountains', while not a proverb, is vague enough to qualify as wisdom.

No religion or secular ideology gains temporary assent, still less enduring and enthusiastic allegiance, unless it successfully evokes in its intended adherents a coercive sense of its own moment and finality. While the persuasive ardour of conviction, religious or secular, does not guarantee its truth, the capacity for generating ardour is germane to the question of its appeal. Self-certainty, like beauty, seduces. No faith was founded on self-doubt or ugliness. The Quran is self-described as 'a decisive word' (*qaulun faṣlun*; Q:86:13), the word that separates (good from evil), as 'news of great significance' (Q:38:67). 'It is', adds the quaint litotes, 'no pleasantry' (*mā huwa bi al-hazl*; Q:86:14). We today can acknowledge the Quran's colossal impact on modern world history without concluding that it is a comprehensive repository of truths about our condition. Neither the powerful, even hypnotic, effect of the Quranic rhythm, nor its disputed ability to frustrate the poets, can conclusively support the truth of its claims.

6   The scope of the book

1

In this chapter, I explore a strategic concern of scripture: the intended range of a revelation which determines and extends its relationship of legitimate authority to the wider disbelieving world. I examine the intended relevance and putative scope of 'an Arabic Quran' (*qurānan 'arabiyyan*: Q;12:2; 20:112; 39:28; 41:3; 42:7; 43:3). The book was revealed to one man and conveyed to a particular people at a given place in time. Can a book speak to the actual condition of one people while retaining the capacity to speak to the common human condition of all peoples? What was addressed to one temporary community of the past must be experienced as though it were addressed to a permanently ahistoric community located anywhere in subsequent history, so that the authority of the word transcends the (original) context of the word. This is an ambition of revelations which claim universal validity across generations. Is this attempt at transcendence of an original locale a coherent aspiration for any book, sacred or mundane?

A religion flourishes only in healthy relationship to the intellectual milieu that structures the daily routine lives of its adherents. This must not imply capitulation to the norms of that surrounding intellectual culture, still less an abject surrender. The opposite is the case: a religion cannot be a source of independent critical comment on the culture it has created or encounters if it accommodates itself wholly to external cultural requirements or borrows all its criteria of assessment from its surrounding setting. A refusal to accommodate or capitulate does not, however, mean a rejection of an intelligent and resourceful exchange with the surrounding recalcitrant realities. Such a refusal would eventually compartmentalize religious beliefs and isolate the scriptural understanding of the world from mainstream contemporary thought. This is an acute anxiety in a faith such as Islam which, as we noted in Chapter 1, defines itself as a comprehensive meta-religion. We also noted that the creation of a religious ghetto reduces or even eliminates the practical relevance of religious belief, leading believers to indulge in the schizophrenia that accompanies intellectual dishonesty. We defer to the final chapter a central desideratum for a meta-religion such as modern Islam: the need to assimilate contemporary knowledge (gathered by the special sciences) with the deposit of inherited Islamic teachings.

A virile living religious tradition ossifies as it isolates itself from the dominant influences which structure the lives of ordinary believers. The attempt to achieve relevance if not dramatic impact perennially tests the intellectual mettle of believers who seek to keep their faith appealing in all circumstances. In holding doctrines appropriate to our era, we must consider the correct degree of accommodation with the broader secular ambience. A simple doctrinal scheme that requires no adjustment and change is not guaranteed to be true. It may be simple, immutable, elegant, fixed in scope – and false. The medieval maxim *simplex sigillum veri* – 'the simple is the sign of the true' – is unproven. Equally, a doctrinal system that constantly needs re-interpretation and re-adjustment of scope in order to remain relevant is not always false. Achieving such relevance, without essential attenuation and crucial compromise, cannot follow a pattern fixed a priori.

2

The Islamic textual tradition begins with one book, a founding text that frames and guides Muhammad's religious career. The Quran, like the Bible, has been the only book that is read in oral cultures with limited literacy. It has often been the sole literary pillar of Arabo-Islamic civilization. Traditional believers think that the book contains all they need to know for success in this life and the next, a claim made by the Quran.

This ambitious claim about Quranic comprehensiveness has three scriptural versions. First: 'We have not neglected a single thing in the book' (Q:6:38). That everything is recorded in a book or register is a pictorial way of affirming divine omniscience (see Q:20:51–2; 22:70; 27:75; 35:11; 78:29). Second, the Quran is a perspicuous version of that comprehensive book: 'We have taken account of all things in a clear register'(*fī imāmin mubīnin*; Q:36:12).[1] The adjective *mubīn* (clear or perspicuous) sometimes qualifies the noun 'Quran' (Q:15:1; 36:69) and often qualifies 'a book' (Q:5:15; 27:1; 34:3) and, as *al-mubīn*, 'the book' (Q:12:1; 26:2; 28:2; 43:2; 44:2). The Quran identitfies itself with a clear book (Q:27:1) and the clear book (Q:43:2–3). Finally, the Quran itself is described as the book of comprehensive range: 'We have sent down to you [Muhammad] the book explaining all things (*al-kitāb tibyānan li kulli shay'in*), a guide, a mercy and good news for those who submit to God'(Q:16:89).

The adjective *mubīn* (also *al-mubīn*), meaning clear, applies variously to the book, the Quran, Muhammad as God's messenger (Q:44:13), and to other prophets (Q:43:29). In qualifying *balāgh* (message) as in 'the clear message' (*al-balāgh al-mubīn*; Q:29:18), it means that the Quranic message is unambiguous. It also implies that the scripture clarifies controversial matters (Q:2:213; 27:76). The adjective could mean that Islamic teachings are open, not esoteric, since Muhammad's preaching is addressed to all humankind, not only to a chosen or schismatic elite. The Quran accuses previous scriptured communities of sectarian parochialism and of hiding or forgetting the universal applicability of their scriptures (Q:2:75, 174; 5:13).

Can all truth be concentrated in one book, a compendium of all knowledge and wisdom? Has God successfully addressed humankind in the thought-categories of seventh-century Arabia? Secularists dismiss as pretentious, incredible and incoherent, the ambition of a single book to permanently record all significant truth relevant to every human being in any time or place. In many cultures, this totalitarian impulse appears in the related form of a desire to locate all ideals in a single personality, be it Christ or Confucius.[2] Whole cultures compulsively concentrate all that is worthy in a single figure of history much as academics lavish their affection on their one anointed thinker or writer. Many and varied are the biographies of men such as Abraham and the Buddha, Charlemagne and the Christ, as biographers smuggle their own preferred opinions and ideals into the stories of their subjects' lives – moulding history in accordance with the biographer's private wishes. Muslims link every modern advocacy, whether democracy or dictatorship, pacifism or militant radicalism, enslavement of women or their emancipation, to the mind and policy of Muhammad.

Secular reservations about grand claims on behalf of one holy book (or one historical figure) are justified. Equally, however, a tradition cannot be authoritative unless it limits the number of founding texts that determine its scope and direct its curiosity. Medieval Christendom was a unified religious and intellectual culture because it was founded on reverence for three canons: the two biblical testaments, naturally, supplemented by the Aristotelian corpus.[3] Knowledge was static while religious belief was held with total conviction; and all belief was essentially religious. In modern western culture there is no unified authority in religion, morals or culture, even for Christians, let alone for the rest of society. It is unclear how many founding texts are essential to the world-view of a modern sophisticated westerner? One cannot treat an indefinite number of books as authoritative without losing one's sense of final authority and orientation. If we may choose many books and see each as equally authoritative, no given book has ultimate authority.

3

The Quranic bid to be the repository of all knowledge is intellectually totalitarian. It conflicts with the intuitions of an equally confident liberal intellectual culture which accepts as final and authoritative the scientific method while conceding that knowledge thus acquired is tentative and provisional. As for 'revealed knowledge', the secular historicist temper reduces it to a human phenomenon that emerges in response to determinable cultural conditions and social pressures. Ancient religion, no less than modern science, is no more than a human response to the human problems of its own time. For the Muslim believer, however, revealed religion – the adjective is redundant in Islamic reflection – is an unveiling of eternal truths and principles, an unveiling that occurs inside history without making the revealed principles and ideals historically conditioned. Rather, these are vouchsafed to us, imposed on us, from a world beyond history and its limitations.

The Quran, like all revolutionary writing, is more critical than representative of its times. It partly transcends its moral and literary environment. The book is in its time but not of its time: hence it does not date. It still speaks to us only because it has successfully discounted its original parochial setting in an insulated corner of the world. Thematically, the Quran deals with recurrent, perhaps perennial, human concerns. Morally, the Quran is a revolutionary indictment of the pre-Islamic ways of ignorance. The pagan power structure had to be overthrown in the name of God; little of the original Arabian status quo was left after God and Muhammad had done with it. To call the Quranic onslaught on pagan Arabia 'revolutionary' is to use a decidedly lenient political vocabulary.

Yet despite impressive moral and political reforms, the Quran remains, as we shall argue later in this chapter, inevitably tied, in virtue of its language and metaphysics, to its location. Faced with the choice between situating the norms of a nascent Arabic grammar in the collective unconscious of the pre-Islamic linguistic community, on the one hand, and locating them in the Arabic of the literal revelation of God found in the Quran, on the other, Muslims chose the Quran. In this way, they achieved a literary transcendence of the pagan ethos of the language – but not a transcendence of the language itself.

If the Quran is revealed in a specific time and locale, should its directives enjoy a normative universality embracing all eras and places? One might argue that all places are, in a supra-historical essentialist sense, the same place – though places made contemporary by history need not be contemporary in ethos. Incidents occurring in the Quran's Arabia seem to transfer effortlessly outwards from one century indifferently to another, showing the timelessness of moral norm and human actions thus constrained. This assumption is not unique to revelation: it is called magical realism in modern fiction although admittedly, the strains on credibility, even intelligibility, are massive in both cases.

Is there any sense in which our essential condition is much the same in all places at all times? In one sense, all intelligible social and personal events transpiring in the world, in all places and at all times, are essentially the same since all the things we do, whether they unite us or divide us, inevitably unite us: all the important actors are human and even where there is rivalry in a game, the players are united because they play the same game. In the human game, there is perversity, weakness, failure, moral triumph and betrayal, whether the players be in the seventh-century metropolis of Mecca, defying God's ways, or in our century's corrupt urban environments confidently denying the need for the hypothesis of God to make sense of their world. The secularist will justifiably wonder whether it is even meaningful to explore, beyond a point, our modern predicament, in terms of seventh century settings. In Section 6 below, we examine this quandary with direct reference to the Quran's confident claim to normative universality.

4

We must deepen our historical understanding of the Arab dimension of Islam before we can explore the relationship between the ethnic Arabic character of the Quran's language and first context, on the one hand, and its intended universality of scope, on the other. During the century beginning with Muhammad's death in 632, Arab and other Muslims, fired with the enthusiasm of their faith, scored an unbroken series of spectacular military triumphs which humbled two empires – in history's fastest and largely permanent conquest. They imposed their faith and their language in the western expansion. In the other direction, the ancient and proud Persians were only nominally defeated by Islamic armies. In the past, Persia challenged Greece for centuries and later also injured Rome. Persians provided a buffer against the Hellenization of the East and were destined to provide another buffer during the Islamic conquests of the mid-seventh century. Indeed, as late as the nineteenth century, the presence of Shi'ite Iran was a bulwark against (Sunni) Ottoman expansion into India and thus into the Far Eastern frontier of Islam in Indonesia.[4]

In the early years of Islam, when Arabs were a ruling class, living in garrison cities in the lands they conquered, the local population of Persians, Egyptians, Palestinians and Iraqis, wanted to associate themselves with the rulers, often by changing their names to reflect an Arabic addition. This system of Arab aristocratic patronage permitted non-Arab converts, who had adopted the religion but could not, naturally, become Arabs, to Arabize themselves by association. They attached themselves as associates or clients to an Arabic tribal lineage and appropriated the Arab cultural ethos. These clients or relatives (*mawālī*, pl; sing. *mawlā*, lit., master or close relative; Q:33:5; see also Q:4:33; 19:5) hoped to assimilate both Arabic and Muslim ideals and become full converts.[5]

What does 'Arabian' mean? The word can intend a territory, a language, and an ethnic ideology. Arabs lived mainly in the Arabian peninsula (present day Saudi Arabia) and its outer fringes including Yemen and the northern regions towards the south of modern Jordan. Other 'Arab' lands, such as Syria, Egypt, Algeria and the rest of North Africa, were subdued by Muslim armies in the seventh century. (There are few racially pure Arabs today.) In their eastern expansion, however, Arabs failed to fully colonize the Persians, Indians and, at a later stage, the Malays, all of whom became passionately attached to Islam but retained their languages and some of their ancient customs.

If the Quran had appealed to, and been appealing to, solely its first audience, Islam would not have transcended its first context. It did so with marked success, making it the world's only *intentionally* universal faith yearning for comprehensive scope from the day of its establishment in the utopia of Muslim Medina. Judaism and Brahmanic-Vedic Hinduism gave birth to moral reform movements, Christianity and Buddhism, which gradually became, largely as accidents of history, universal faiths which found second founders and political patrons.[6] Judaism and Brahmanic Hinduism (Sanatana Dharma, the eternal religion), as parent faiths, contained latent universal impulses that were at a certain stage of their history no longer containable in the ancient vessel. Hence the birth of their associated universal faiths with enduring appeal, especially Christianity, the faith most widely distributed in the modern world. The situation is reversed with Islam: it begins as a universal, universalizing and intentionally comprehensive faith which, later in its history, inspires narrower ethnic movements.[7]

5

Even in its Meccan portions, the Quran offers a universal message (Q:6:19, 90; 7:158; 14:52; 21:107; 34:28; 38:87; 81:27) whose universality is confirmed later in Medinan passages that insinuate an imperialistic intention (Q:3:138; 4:79, 170; 61:9). It was, however, despite its potential for universality and expansion, originally addressed to Muhammad and his people (Q:43:44); its audience were, with few exceptions, Arabs only.[8] The Quran claims that the Arabs would never have embraced a divine revelation if it had been sent to non-Arabs charged with proUlytizing the Arabs (Q:26:198–9). Judging by the spectacular success of the Prophet's mission, the Quranic outlook must have appealed to many Arabs of the early seventh century. Admittedly, the Quranic address is invariably 'Believers!' rather than 'Arab believers!' or 'Arabs!' The Arab identity of the listeners is, however, presupposed by the context since revelation is always sent in the native language of the people to whom God's envoy is sent (Q:14:4).

No authentic Muslim of any distinction or credibility, Arab or non-Arab, argues for restricting Islam's message to the Arab Club although many argue for an organic link between Islam and the Arabs. The Palestinian–American stylist Ismail Raji Al-Faruqi, whom we encounter in Chapter 12, proudly defended Arab Islam in his at times rather totalitarian, even racist, obsession with the exclusively Arab genius and genesis of the faith. He argued in his *'Urubah and Religion: An Analysis of the Dominant ideas of Arabism and of Islam*[9] that the Arabs were a people especially suited to receive Islam. Al-Faruqi argued that Arabism was a divine vehicle of Islamic identity, integrity and unity: an Arab-centred Islamic brotherhood would once again redeem liberal western cultures from their chaos. This ethnic passion made him dismiss Arab Christianity, despise non-Arab Islam, and deny historical Islam's undeniable debt to Judaism. Ironically, he accused Jews of confusing race with religion while his own racist views were a libel on Islam if not a crime against humanity. I have elsewhere criticized these familiar fantasies of the ethnocentric imagination.[10]

Secular Arab nationalists, seeking to unite Muslims and Christians in Egypt and the Lebanon, often exalt the Arabs as a *Herrenvolk*, a master race of naturally superior ability. Some Arab socialists, impressed by Islam's astonishing potential for promoting social justice, annex the faith to their cause by celebrating 'the genius of Muhammad' (*'abqāriat Muḥammad*) – thus implying that the Quran is an ethnic Arab achievement.

No one denies the Arab origins of historical Islam or its Arab ambience, through its scripture, in all ages and varied locales. These are indisputable facts whose policy implications are more controversial. Arab linguistic imperialism is, for example, concealed behind the suggestion, made by some Arab nationalists who advocate the adoption of a single spoken tongue, namely Arabic, which would allegedly unite the world-wide Muslim community. About 25 Arab nations speak the same language without any signs of political unity. Iraq and Kuwait are not divided by a language barrier. A reading knowledge of classical Arabic is indeed indispensable for scholarly access to the Quran, the Prophetic traditions and the vast scholarship of Islamic scholasticism. Knowing modern (colloquial or demotic) Arabic is, however, not necessary to the religious identity or duty of a Muslim.

It is, ironically, difficult to erase the ethnic (Arabian) impress of Islam, the world's only intentionally and self-consciously universal faith and the last de facto universal faith. Islam is an Arabic word; Muhammad was an Arab messenger. Islam can be practised with too much ritual precision and reverence for its Arabic dimension. Many non-Arab Muslims revere Arabs as the white men of the East. The Quran is not theologically Arabian but it is, to some extent, ritually and behaviouristically Arabian. It promotes Arab interests by sanctifying the Arabic language – although it is only the liturgical use of the Quran's Arabic that is sacred and, moreover, the Quran sanctifies all human languages as among God's signs (Q:30:22). Nonetheless, the revelation consecrates aspects of Arab culture and effectively promotes an Arab-centred Islamic brotherhood through the annual Pilgrimage to Mecca. Some vague Quranic verses (such as Q:17:1) can be used to vigorously defend Arab Muslim political rights to the holy land. Given certain privileges granted by God, and supinely accepted by non-Arab Muslims, Arabs are unsurprisingly tempted to see themselves as patrons rather than as mere adherents of Islam.

6

The Quran not only records its Arabic nature, it proudly expatiates on it calling itself an Arabic Quran (Q:12:2; 20:113; 39:28; 41:3; 42:7; 43:3) and an Arabic judgement (*ḥukman 'arabiyyan*; Q:13:37). The Quran exalts its own quality of diction (Q:16:103). It also reveres the Arabic language (Q:26:192–5) – although it is unclear whether this is respect for the existing Arabic language or for Quranic Arabic or the Quran's use of Arabic.

The message is in the form of a lecture (*qur'ān*) in eloquent Arabic initially addressed to Arabs (Q:41:44). The Quran notes the ambivalent pagan Arab desire to become a society with its own scripture (Q:6:155–7; 28:47–8; 34:44–5; 37:167–70), an ambivalence caused by the knowledge that having a sacred book entails heavy moral demands. The pagans boast dishonestly that they, unlike previous communities, would be better guided and more devoted to a revelation if only they were lucky enough to receive it (Q:6:157). The Quran reprimands them since a book has arrived from God which the pagans vehemently reject: 'Will you make it your source of livelihood to deny it?'(Q:56:82).

The author of the Quran does not fear that an acknowledgment and emphasis on its Arabic linguistic identity might jeopardize its wider relevance or appeal. The scripture announces its universal relevance while extolling its Arabic status (Q:42:7–8) sensing no contradiction in elevating the specific language of an ethnic group while expecting and demanding universal acceptance of its message. The central argument for the Quran's divine origin is that its classical Arabic expression is the climax of the literary genius of Arabic. The Quran does not intend to erase the proud and enduring Arabic imprint on Islam.

The Quran acknowledges and sanctifies, as the signs of God, the diversity of human languages, the plurality of colours, cultures and religious rites (Q:22:34; 30:22; 35:28). Therefore, even when extolling its own Arabic character and quality, the Quran never addresses Arabs as an ethnic group. It never uses the direct address 'Arabs!' or 'Quraysh!' (The 106th chapter is called *Quraysh* but no chapter is named 'Arabs'.) Even when the Quran addresses the believers as Arabs and appeals to their overly cultivated sense of racial pride (for example at Q:21:10 and more conditionally at Q:3:110), it never uses an ethnic form of address. It uses expressions with a universal intent, typically addressing its readers as believers and humankind, and less frequently as Children of Adam. Muhammad addressed his fellow Arabs (*qua* Muslims) in a farewell oration, standing on the plain of Arafat, on the occasion of his only full pilgrimage to Mecca. He affirmed the moral and political solidarity of all Muslims rather than of all Arabs, adding that no human being is superior or inferior to another one, except on grounds of piety (see Q:49:13).

I conclude this part of our inquiry by making some broader practical and political observations. The struggle for the universality of Islam, a move away from its traditional Arabolatry, will mark Islam's fifteenth century. There is an instructive parallel in Christian origins. In two major authentic epistles, Romans and Galatians, Paul, at the beginning of Christianity, took the Jews to task for their self-image as people of an exclusive covenant. In doing so, he freed the nascent Christian movement from its Hebrew cultural background. Few today associate Christianity with Jews or with the Greeks. Islam, by contrast, is still too closely associated, almost identified, with Arab culture. To be fair, the Quranic vision was inherently comprehensive enough to create a multi-lingual and multi-cultural civilization in the heyday of imperial Islam. Moreover, jurists wisely permitted local custom (*'urf*) in conquered lands to become part of Islamic law thus accepting indigenous customs as valid unless they were morally repugnant to the Quran or Prophetic traditions, a criterion applied disinterestedly to Arab culture too in the merciless editing of the Arabian pagan past.

Even so, any close linkage between Islam and Arab culture, especially a literalist and puritanical Saudi-sponsored Wahhabism, must now be ruptured. It is beginning to happen – especially in Indonesia, the Far Eastern frontier of Islam, where scholars assimilate traditional Islam to national aspirations in the attempt to serve Muslim people rather than pay homage to an abstract and irrelevant political ideology. Many non-Arab Muslims are keenly aware of the limitations of a tribal Arab Islam that could act as an incubus on the development of an enlightened Islam finally free of the inveterate racism and sexism of many traditional Arab nations which pay lip-service to the Quranic vision of the world.

7

Although the Quran was initially revealed to Arabs, there were from the beginning Quranic grounds for casting the religious net into the wider ocean of humanity (Q:4:174) as, arguably, Arabia in Muhammad's day provided the blueprint for every kind of human community. Thus, in the Prophet's environment, which resembled the hostile environments of previous messengers whose religious careers were rehearsed in the Quran, we find the full range of human types: faithful and faithless men and women, perverse and rational, sincere and cynical, trusting and doubting, fanatical and pragmatic, kind and cruel, clever and stupid, every pattern indeed among our species. God therefore chose that society, it may be argued, to receive his final and consciously finalized revelation which is intended, eventually, for the benefit of all humankind. Chapter 2, verses 204–7, reads:

> And among mankind is the type of man whose speech about this life might dazzle you and he calls God to witness [to the truth of his speech] and yet he is the most contentious of enemies. When he turns his back [on guidance], his aim is to spread mischief and corruption throughout the earth and destroy crops and cattle. But God does not love mischief. When such a man is ordered to fear God, he is seduced by his arrogance to commit crime. Hell shall suffice such a man. And what an evil resting place that is! On the other hand, there is among humankind a type of man who sells his life to earn the good pleasure of God. And God is full of kindness to his devotees.

This kind of passage is characteristic of the Quran. The varieties of human nature, admittedly narrow in range, are unfailingly described in the most general way. Many men and women in Muhammad's entourage could fit the above descriptions although the occasion of this revelation is known to be specific. That every type of person existed in Muhammad's time and place is the implicit reasoning behind the exegetical principle that permits narrow and historically precise references in the Quran's 23 year incidence to possess simultaneously a general import transcending the original context. The Quranic indictment of humankind is intended to be universal in scope. In view of this implied Quranic intention, the Muslim may reasonably claim that the Quran was not revealed solely to reform the lives of its first Arab audience. No perversity or evil regnant today may claim the accolade of novelty since all the many ways of sin are time-honoured (Q:30:42; 39:25; 51:52–3). This timeless relevance alone befits scripture.[11]

An account of human diversity, in terms of moral and spiritual dimensions of varied cultures and peoples, can be anchored in the Quran, but it cannot be limited to it or by it. The Quran's encounter with humanity is limited in extent and variety in view of the wealth of anthropological and sociological data about different life-styles, political organizations, religions, pieties and ethnicities available to us today. There are no anarchists or Poles or Hindus or Mahayana Buddhists or Eskimo shamans in the Quranic world. It lacks the scope that modern life presupposes. The author of the Quran does not use too wide a mesh to catch the range and diversity that would concern that author's original readers but the diversity and anxiety of our experience make it difficult to contain everything within the categories of classical Islam.

The Muslim apologist might insist that the diversity the Quran captures is sufficient in terms of the range of human moral and religious types; the rest are merely details that need not affect our invariant and basic humanity. This essentialist claim is, however, questionable since no human being lays aside the particularities of culture and language to embrace a religion solely as a human being. No one is nothing in particular but merely something in general. Thus, for example, while moral self-mastery might be an aim shared by all faiths, the route to attaining it is culturally specific. What would be the contents of the Quran if, say, the Arabs had been indifferent to sexual pleasure but inordinately fond of alcohol? Indeed Islam encountered insurmountable problems in its attempt to convert some nations (for example, the Russians) who found its absolute ban on intoxicants to be unacceptable just as many polygynous Africans embraced Islam (rather than Christianity) often because Islam allowed them to maintain their existing ratio for wedded bliss.

The Quran upholds a monochromatic vision of human nature. In its myth of the primordial assembly of 'all souls Adamic' (Q:7:172), a theme of Chapter 9, we witness disembodied souls, before the start of history, acknowledging their accountability to God and their moral culpability in rejecting his sovereignty. If we accept this Quranic postulate, we must endorse the notion of an essential, eternally fixed, pre-linguistic and pre-historical human nature. Otherwise, the empirically known range of cultural and linguistic environments of different human societies, each with its own historically conditioned metaphysics of time and space, gender and race, and so on, poses an insurmountable obstacle for a faith that claims to be accessibly relevant to all humankind. How can any scripture, no matter how general or generalized in tone or content, successfully address its readers solely as human beings, as readers stripped of allegedly inessential features such as language and culture? Such an ambition seems incoherent, not merely pretentious.

8

In Chapter 4, we explored the orthodox account of the Quran's status as pure revelation but we omitted two relevant dimensions. First, simple orthodox Muslims assumed that the Quran's *Arabic* character was integral to the book's nature and message. The intrinsic suitability of Arabic as the vehicle of God's final message is assumed by many Quranic experts. Some non-Arab Muslims detect concealed Arab linguistic imperialism and racism in that claim and especially in its corollary, namely, that Quranic Arabic is the sole language of paradise. Most devout Muslims, including non-Arabs, however, believe that there is an organic link between Arabic and the final divine message: Arabic is the only language that could contain the massive fecundity of God's ultimate revelation. From God's perspective, however, the Quran's *Arabic* character must be contingent, not organic or necessary. Indeed the expression *qurānan a'jamiyyan* (a foreign or Persian Quran) occurs in the Quran (Q:41:44).

Second, as we saw during our survey of Islam's rational dialectical theology in Chapter 2, there is an entangled classical debate about whether or not the Quran was an uncreated reality that co-existed with God from eternity. The original

Quran was, according to the scripture, in the mother of the book preserved in heaven (Q:13:39). The speaking of language was, however, as the Mu'tazilite thinkers insisted, a human and mundane quality; it was improper anthropomorphism (*tashbih*) to believe that God speaks or reveals a message in Arabic, a human tongue. The Mu'tazilites believed that God had no attributes distinct from his essence. As for speaking and creating, these are not eternal but rather temporary attributes of *actions* and last as long as the action is occurring. The Mu'tazilite dogma of the Quran as the created word of God – created as it was being sent down to Muhammad via the archangel Gabriel – provoked orthodoxy into formulating an equally inflexible and unverifiable doctrine. The orthodox view, championed by Ibn Ḥanbal, was later canonized in official Ash'arite theology: the Quran was the speech of God, an eternal attribute, and hence uncreated in its sense but created in its sounds using the letters of the Arabic alphabet. To believe in a created Quran was anathema.[12]

Leaving aside such niceties, the language of the scripture is a human language, Arabic, albeit of outstanding luminosity. The Quran's *use* of Arabic is virtually discontinuous with earlier, poetic and rhetorical, employments of Arabic but the language itself, despite this allegedly divine employment, remains human and humanly accessible. A sacred language is a misnomer: no language is sacred. And yet all languages are sacred since any language can be recruited by God. Hence, Nietzsche's acid comment on the demotic (*koinē*) Greek of the New Testament: 'It was subtle of God to learn Greek when he wanted to become an author – and equally subtle of him not to learn it any better.'[13]

If a particular language is chosen as the medium of revealed expression, does that inevitably, that is, independently of authorial intention, restrict the range and relevance of the content of the message? Arabic has, like all languages, a tradition and a history of evolution in syntax, grammar, and vocabulary. In its classical and modern forms, it partly reflects but is also partly shaped by a metaphysical outlook on fundamental categories of time and space, existence and action, mind and matter, and gender and race.

Aristotle was the first to locate the categories (*katēgoria*), the most general concepts, the most abstract genera, of thought and linguistic expression. He found them in his native classical Greek by examining the empirical basis of language: substantives (linguistic devices for expressing existence), nouns, verbs, and adjectives. His ten basic categories are: substance (for example, man); relation (double); quantity (few); quality (black); time (today); place (here); action (expressed by the active voice of verbs); passivity (expressed by the passive voice); posture (expressed by verbs of state as in 'I am seated'); and possession (expressed by forms of the verb *to have*). We find these categories or their equivalents in Arabic and, presumably, in all languages; but their development and capacity for nuance are bound to vary. Every language determines and reflects a particular metaphysics; the Quran too is inevitably an Arabic document equipped with an Arabic set of such categories for linguistically interpreting the world. The stamp of the Arabic language on Islam, an Arabic word, is therefore irremovable.

9

The language-centred nature of the Quran's credentials creates problems that we are only now beginning to identify. A language not merely determines and fixes the form and individual features of an associated metaphysical system but, furthermore, provides the foundations for its construction. An influential school of philosophy, taking its cue from the labours of Ludwig Wittgenstein, has contended that language, far from being the humble servant of thought, as many in the past assumed, is its master. Language largely, if not wholly, determines our view of an allegedly independent reality. I shall lightly sketch this position before noting its implications for our exploration of the Quran's status and intended scope.

Language matters because it determines reality; there is no language-free standpoint from which we can survey the world. All reality is description-relative and culture-dependent. Nothing out there makes our beliefs true or false. Language does not represent the world since nothing extra-linguistic corresponds to our thoughts. Knowledge then is not a matter of getting reality right but rather a set of tools for coping with life in its complexity and convolution. The language of religion is no closer to reality than any other language, including that of science. Religion, no less than science, is only a fallible human response to our human anguish.

Is this view too extravagant? We should object that language enables thought, not existence. Experiences and objects can exist unnamed although naming them is a precondition of thinking about them in a public way. Notwithstanding Wittgenstein and his admirers, we do need a way of contrasting the world as it is with what it appears as – to us. Even if this empirical world may be all that we can know, why should it be all that there is? The world is not necessarily merely the world as we describe it although an investigation of our use of language is undeniably an investigation of the structure of the world as experienced by human beings.

We may reject as extravagant all robust versions of the anti-realism attributed to Wittgenstein. Such versions make a valid point and then exaggerate it to the point of absurdity. However, we cannot deny that, through choice of language as definitive of the Quran's essence and as probative of its credentials, the Arabic dimension becomes a part of Islam in a way that, for example, the subtleties of Greek are not constitutive of Christian credentials, only of aspects of Christian dogma. This is not to say that the Quran is in general, theologically or ritually or culturally Arabian. Few readers of the Quran's exordium (Q:1:1–7) could surmise that the Quran was historically addressed to Arabs. No moral ideal of Islam or the conception of its deity is peculiarly Arabian. Only the language and the metaphysics implicit in that language are, unavoidably, Arabic.

Muslims have a Quranic warrant for making their scripture relevant to people fatefully placed in different cultures and eras, nurtured in various linguistic environments, entertaining diverse outlooks on humanity and nature. 'It is he [God] who has sent his messenger with guidance and the religion of truth so that he may cause it to prevail over all religion (*al-dīn kulli-hī*) even though pagans resent it' (Q:61:9; see also Q:48:28).[14] If the Quran presents Islam as a universal faith, then

Muslim missionaries must incorporate into (or at least reconcile with) the Islamic vision the sometimes vastly discrepant outlooks of other cultures. Such disparity in outlook is represented and nourished by differences in the linguistic apparatus of diverse societies.

It is impossible to believe that the *metaphysical* outlook of the first custodians of Islam, displayed partly in the Arabic language, represents all world-outlooks among human beings in the past, today, and the future. We may argue, however, as we did earlier, that the variety in the *moral* attitudes of human nature in early seventh-century Arabia is representative of humankind in general – although even this can, within limits, be questioned. Would the moral imperatives of the Quran remain unchanged if, let us suppose, the Arabs had been indifferent to women but inordinately fond of strong drink?

10

In this and the next section, I shunt my train of thought onto a related rail before returning presently to the problem of establishing a universally valid body of religious knowledge. Empirical science has obliquely shaped the content of religious apology for over two centuries, a tribute to the success of science. Scriptures were compiled in the pre-scientific though not pre-historic age. How does scripture retain current relevance and credibility for contemporary scientifically literate moderns who find scriptural claims scientifically implausible? We examine now a contemporary reading that sees the Quran as prescient of modern science! It is an attempt to extend the scope and authority of the scripture to modern scientifically literate readers. There is an admirable aim behind such exegesis but the presuppositions nourishing it may be indicted as facile and false especially if modernist exegetes, in their obsession with the Quran's alleged prescience of scientific learning, ignore the scripture's religious resources.

The Quranic, like the biblical, world-view conflicts with the scientific perspective which assumes that the cosmos is a self-contained set of patterned empirical sequences intelligible to us in terms of natural causality; the spatio-temporal continuum is subject to discoverable lawful regularity. Recently, probability laws couched in statistical terms replaced the older laws of causality as physical indeterminacy complicated the picture at sub-atomic level. A metaphysic of events now supplants the older metaphysic of natural objects or substances uncomplicatedly locatable in three-dimensional space – but nature remains autonomous and self-sustaining. Islam posits an additional supernatural realm and denies the autonomy of nature (Q:35:41). Directly, actively, and continuously, God sustains the world after creating it; he prevents the lowest heaven, our sky, from collapsing on sinful humanity (Q:22:65), arranges the clouds, directs the winds that give rain and revive the dead earth (Q:35:9), holds the birds poised in mid-air (Q:67:19), and keeps the two seas separate (Q:25:53; 27:61).

The Quranic cosmology presupposes continuous interaction between the natural causal world and the supra-natural realm of occult causality. Supernatural agents routinely act within and interpenetrate the natural world of empirical causality.[15]

The jinn, elemental spirits found in the intricate nexus of Arabic poetry, possession and madness, are integral to the pre-Islamic outlook (Q:46:29–32; 72:1–19) and remain part of modern Islam. Indeed, Iblīs, the Devil, is a jinn (Q:18:50) created from fire (Q:15:27; 38:76); his arrogant free will led him to freely reject God's rule (Q:7:11–12; 38:73–7). He is an actively malicious agent in human history. God too is active: he shapes the embryo in the womb as he pleases (Q:3:6) and removes the souls of sleepers at night so that each day is a fresh resurrection as the souls of those destined to live are returned to life until an appointed hour (Q:6:60; 39:42). In the spiritual inter-action between the two worlds, human petition, prayer, piety, pure speech and good deeds ascend to the unseen world (Q:22:37; 34:2; 35:10).

This picture is incompatible with empirical science. Modern scientists feel obliged to reject on principle the possible existence of God, the Devil, indeed all spirits, including those of the departed dead, the jinn, demons, angels, and other immaterial or incorporeal entities lacking space–time co-ordinates. In an attempt to make the Quran relevant and interesting to modern readers, Muslim apologists argue that the Quran is an enigmatic manual of science. The scripture, it is claimed, miraculously achieves a prescience of the latest findings of natural science and anticipates, in startling detail, recent discoveries in fields as varied as nuclear physics, experimental physiology, theoretical biology and modern cosmology. One writer even suggests that the Quran is primarily a rich manual of scientific information with only an incidental interest in religious matters.[16] Thus, for example, a religiously powerful parable such as the parable of the fly (Q:22:73–4) is seen as artfully concealing scientific information from its earliest listeners. The parable ostensibly teaches that pseudo-deities are totally powerless to create even a fly or, should the fly snatch something from them, powerless to retrieve it. The scientifically minded commentator adds that modern biology has only recently discovered that the digestion of a fly is externally and immediately performed, making retrieval impossible! Again, we are told, the Quran asks its readers to consider the camels (Q:88:17) because these remarkable creatures internally manufacture metabolic water (H_2O) and store it for long-term use.

We read some embarrassingly crude and pseudo-scientific interpretations of the Quran. For example, 'We have the power to expand [things]' (Q:51:47) is interpreted to mean that the universe is expanding! Again, the whole universe was concentrated in one infinitely dense mass (*ratq*; Q:21:30), a singularity that exploded to become the universe, the strange process scientists call 'the big bang' – which hardly sounds any more sophisticated than the scriptural account. Commentators have extensively mined the Quran to unearth evidence of travel to the moon, the laser, microbes and the atom. The spiritual heart of faith re-appears as the organic heart studied by anatomists. The Quran mentions three layers or veils of darkness in which human beings are created in the womb (Q:39:6), an enigmatic verse which Sufi commentators interpret spiritually if rather speculatively. In the hands of a self-indulgent scientific ingenuity, however, it re-emerges as a reference to three types of biological tissue surrounding the embryo. This last argument is seductive since the Quran shows a pronounced interest in human reproduction (Q:22:5; 23:12–14; 36:77) and singles out the sexual capacity which enables us to perpetuate the human heritage as being among the most remarkable of the countless signs of God's grace and power (Q:30:21; 56:58–9).

The Quran is continually raped in order to yield the ephemeral findings of the latest scientific research.[17] The scripture's relevance to readers impressed by modern science is established by imposing self-indulgent and tortured interpretations on the ambiguous and malleable parts of the text. The Quranic vocabulary is forced to accommodate preferred scientific meanings which compete with the original or classical significances closer to the intention and the era of revelation. The modern meaning of the scripture can dwarf the original message which is primarily religious, spiritual and prescriptive. The text buckles under the pressure of detailed scientific meanings attached to vague and innocent expressions. The arguments offered for such meanings carry weight only with devotees. The Muslim apologist celebrates the undiscovered scientific potential of his book while the outsider is amused and puzzled by this facile and ingenuous handling of scripture.

Muslims are not alone in holding such views about their scripture; some Christians similarly mine the Bible. Nor is the tendency necessarily disreputable. If an allegedly revealed book unequivocally provided scientific knowledge in a pre-scientific age, this would strengthen the possibility that it had a superhuman author. If a scripture, produced before the advent of science, succeeded in attaining a broad and approximate compatibility with the picture secreted by current scientific learning, perhaps through a deliberate and studied ambiguity in its scientific claims, this would provide evidence in favour of its claim to be a divinely revealed book. But we do not have any indisputable scientific facts anticipated by the Quran. Given the general vagueness and elasticity of its sentences, the Quran sustains differing and incompatible interpretations. One enthusiastic apologist extracts one piece of scientific learning from a given pregnant passage while another extracts, with equal ease, a different, even rival, scientific claim from the same passage. We defer one aspect of this debate – about the implications of such exegesis for the authority of scripture in a scientific age – until the end of the next chapter.

11

We must distinguish the way the Quran is susceptible to interpretive treatment from the narrower issue of reading *scientific* significances into its verses. The Quran, far more than other scriptures, lends itself to a reading. Marked by a sustained and studied ambiguity in its choice of words and in its commentary on incidents, the author seems intentionally concerned to attain the greatest scope and relevance through maintaining the maximal level of generality compatible with precision. Geographical locations and events, both contemporaneous and ancient, are characterized by a vagueness and elasticity that permits different possibilities and satisfies the aspirations of several contenders.[18] Events in Muhammad's life and in the lives of those in his entourage are mentioned in a self-consciously generalized and didactic way rather than in a particular fashion that would limit their relevance. There is little familiar local Arab colour that might appeal to those looking for the exotic. For example, the serious slander against Muhammad's young wife 'Aisha is related in a detached way that makes it easy to recruit it for general moral and legal purposes (Q:24:11–26). The Prophet's wife, not mentioned by name, is the archetype of any chaste and virtuous but heedless Muslim woman whom licentious men and women might slander (Q:24:23). Only a few people in the Prophet's entourage are singled out by name (or epithet) for special comment.

This must be a deliberate feature of the Quranic narration of events. Jewish and Christian critics who claim that the Quran uses vague locutions because Muhammad had no clear knowledge of past sacred history have difficulty explaining why he apparently did not know the name of his own father-in-law, Abu Bakr, who is described in a circumlocution as a 'companion in a cave' where Muhammad hid during an assassination attempt (Q:9:40). Nor is this an isolated example. Abu Bakr is known to be the man described in another circumlocution at Q:24:22. The Quran avoids mentioning Abu Bakr by name as if such specificity would contaminate the supra-historical eternity of the moral imperatives implied in the verses inspired by his case.[19]

In the hands of discerning but self-indulgent commentators, potential ambiguities in words and phrases, mysterious and obscure idiomatic usages in need of a reading, and laconic hints can be easily recruited in the service of their own preferred views. The authority of God is then claimed on behalf of what is human and fallible. This is a liability of all interpretation; it is not restricted to Quranic exegesis. Although the original sacred text remains inviolate and unchanged, the Quran has become, in varied apologetic hands, a work of natural science, as we noted, but also a journal of social and political thought, an oblique commentary on modern secular culture, a manual of Sufi contemplation, not to mention more esoteric readings that presuppose even greater sophistication.

The text can sustain multiple layers of significance without necessarily distorting and denaturing the originally religious word. Quranic vocabulary conceals latent and patent meanings.[20] This is a tribute to the fecundity of Quranic vocabulary but there are dangers here. Revelation is like a well: as we gaze into it, we see our own image. One can find almost anything in a holy book! All that counts is the authority and prestige of the exegete since the text is often a pretext for finding something that the technical reader, the exegete, already wants to find. Exegesis becomes *eisegesis* as we read our own preferences into the text. Although the context might, in principle, restrain us, the ingenuity of the exegete can overcome that limitation too. Owing to the plasticity and instability of textual meaning, scripture is pliable to human desire.

The very word 'hermeneutics' should give us cause for suspicion. It comes from the word Hermes, the herald of the Greek gods who was no trustworthy messenger: he was a perjurer, a liar, and a fable-maker who took false oaths. Mischievously, he reversed signs to mislead the recipients of his messages. Many were tempted to shoot this messenger. Hermes was a false prophet and we should therefore be suspicious of all hermeneutics. Perhaps the chronic subtleties of scriptural exegesis, as of ancient philosophical masterpieces, are really our own ingenious opinions smuggled back into opaque texts – and attributed to others whose names have greater authority.

12

The Quran is not only self-described as comprehensive revelation, it also eulogizes itself as the most inclusive manual of revealed moral guidance (Q:2:1; 14:1; 16:89; 17:9, 41; 30:58; 39:27). It is guidance (*hudā*) and good news (*bushrā*; Q:27:2), a healing mercy (*shifā'*; Q:41:44), a reminder (*dhikr*; Q:65:10; *dhikrā*; Q:11:114; 29:51; 50:8), the reminder, *al-dhikr* (Q:15:9), a universal reminder (Q:68:52) full of clear signs of wisdom (Q:10:1; 31:2–3; 36:2; 38:1), 'an explanation of all things' (Q:16:89; 17:12; 18:54), 'a convincing proof' (*burhān*; Q:4:174), a scripture full of 'eye-opening evidences' (*al-baṣā'ir*; Q:45:20). 'And in this lecture we have struck every type of similitude [parable]; perhaps human beings will reflect. An Arabic lecture without a trace of crookedness; perhaps humankind will fear God' (Q:39:27–8). The contents of the book are free from confusion, inconsistency and error (Q:4:82; 41:42). God's teachings cover all human concerns in a single recital (*qur'ān*) that guides us to all that is 'most upright' (*aqwam*; Q:17:9).

The Quran claims to present clearly all that we need to know and do in order to enter paradise. However, we are permitted merely to know what we need to know, not to know everything we wish to know. The Children of Adam are unnecessarily contentious (Q:18:54), perversely resisting surrender even when faced with conclusive arguments. Many passages condemn the inveterate human perversity that rejects and challenges God (Q:16:4; 36:77–8; 80:17).

Speculative curiosity is condemned; we must not seek knowledge beyond the limits of reasonable concern (Q:17:36).[21] The paternalistic emphasis on guarding these self-protective limits to curiosity is a part of prudential piety (*taqwā*) and is therefore central to the Quran's message. God warns believers not to ask their messenger unnecessary questions in case these return a disturbing answer from God (Q:2:108). However all questions will be answered if asked during the event of the Quran's revelation. The discouraging hint is added that previous peoples had probed certain matters, presumably metaphysical, only to lose faith after hearing the divine responses (Q:5:103–5).

If such provincialism appears unique to Islam, note a similar sentiment in some sayings attributed to Jesus and to the Buddha. To be pointlessly inquisitive is perhaps sinful. 'Blessed are those who believe without knowing', adds Jesus, speaking in a post-resurrection appearance, after dispelling the doubts of Thomas, the sceptical disciple (John 20: 24–9). The Buddha told Malunkya Putta, an inquisitive disciple, 'the parable of the poisoned arrow' in which a fatally injured victim dies of his wounds because he wishes to interrogate those who wish to help him rather than immediately receive their assistance. Ignoring the emergency situation, he continues to ask pointless questions until he dies – in his ignorance.

13

Before we can assess the Quran's claim to be an inclusive scripture, we note relevant features of the age of Muhammad and compare it to our sceptical era.

The Quran was initially addressed to people whose collective temperament and perspective, belief and prejudices, differed fundamentally from those prevalent in today's industrialized and secularized cultures. The first audience was innocent of the secular and sceptical tendencies associated with the rise of critical history and its canons for assessing the reliability of historical events. The audience was, moreover, inured to hyperbole and exaggeration. Today we want facts, including historical facts, to be isolated from our sentiments and ideals. But such notions of historical accuracy and value-free fact are anachronistic for pre-modern thought. In Europe, such awareness is culturally available only after the Enlightenment or arguably after the Renaissance.

Some assumptions at the bedrock of contemporary intellectual culture must, if we are to avoid talking at cross-purposes, be accepted by all parties to this debate. Revealed claims should cohere with other revealed claims; internal contradictions are unacceptable. There are rarely any contradictions in the Quran; a few are partly mitigated by the doctrine of abrogation. The gradual revelation of edicts on alcohol consumption, inheritance laws and warfare with pagans and with Jews and Christians enables us to remove earlier passages that conflict with later ones. For example, the period of maintenance for a widow out of the estate of a dead husband stipulated in one passage (Q:2:34) contradicts the provisions made in a passage six verses later (Q:2:40). If we assume that the chronological order is reliable, then the later one over-rides the earlier one.[22]

All scriptural claims must be consonant with the basic canons of unaided secular reason, critical history and ordinary experience. A revealed claim may question the received wisdom but such questioning must proceed by accepting other norms of common sense. Common sense is a problematic criterion since common sense need not be common! The French wisely call it '*le bon sens*' (the good sense), implying a critical version of common sense which need not be widely distributed. A degree of internal consistency in combination with measured respect for the verdicts and findings of secular reason, critical history, ordinary experience and critical common sense[23] is what we must demand of scripture – unless we abandon worldly criteria and, in the company of early church fathers such as the anti-rationalist Tertullian, or modern existentialists such as Kierkegaard in some moods, celebrate apparent falsehood, paradox and inconsistency as the hallmarks of ultimate truth.

14

How do modern non-Muslims – atheists, agnostics, and secularized Jewish or Christian readers – react to the tone of the Quran? The sacred author sounds like an aristocrat who asserts and commands rather than argues or pleads. The Quran never stops midstream in a narrative to probe its self-confidence. In this regard, it differs markedly from parts of the Bible. A Muslim would argue that if the author is God, there are no grounds for diffidence. The massive Hebrew Bible contains the anguished record of prophetic self-doubt and questioning in conscious proximity to the majestic and self-assured voice of the Lord God Yahweh. The Quran, however, is no amalgam of the secular fallible voice and the infallible voice from the whirlwind.

The Quran contains passages of reasoning; dialectical exchanges between prophets and their hostile communities litter its punishment narratives. But these are not open-ended reflective deliberations that would appeal to inquiring sceptics. The Quran is revelation: the superior profundity and wisdom of the author are not in doubt. Readers are invited to reflect and ponder the contents of the holy volume but this is an invitation to submit practically to its revealed imperatives. It is a call to obey the good will of God after due reflection, a command to acknowledge the whole authority of the divine word. It cannot be interpreted as a request for human contribution to the content of the revelation, still less a request to impose on believers a human assessment of the unimpeachable a priori credentials of the book. Even Muhammad is admonished to observe the requisite etiquette while listening to the word. His zeal to receive the divine word is mildly criticized (Q:20:114). Another revelation is blunt: 'Do not move your tongue to hasten the revelation; it is our [divine] duty to collect it and to recite it. Once we have recited it, follow the recital. It is our duty to explain it too' (Q:75:16–19). God reveals and explains while Muhammad listens in reverent silence. If that is the protocol for the Prophet, it is even more so for the rest of us. All listeners are advised to hear the Quran in silent awe (Q:7:204), an attitude unsuited to sustained reflection concerning controversial matters.

The Quran is, as we saw in Chapter 4, self-consciously composed as purely divine revelation. We created a space for a human contribution to it by noting the distinction between infallible divine genesis and fallible human interpretation of the text. This amount of space for a human margin satisfies only the devout believer. The secular repudiator remains dismayed by the audacious and magisterial tone of the sacred writ, particularly the exordia of most chapters (see Q:2:1; 10:1; 12:1–3; 25:1; 41:1–4; 57:1–3; 64:1). Laconic in its authority, the Quran is written with the urgency of a telegram.

One must not expect pedantic precision or scrupulous detail from this genre of writing. Serious problems arise when the Quran's lapidary style, admired for its unique combination of dignity, authority and concision, becomes elliptical to the point of obscurity and unintelligibility. Ellipsis is a feature of all classical Arabic prose. Not all such prose is, however, didactic in its moral or legal intentions, whereas the Quran is the manual of education and guidance for a whole civilization. Important themes are discussed piecemeal and desultorily, scattered in several places. Admittedly, the motivation for securing precision and comprehensiveness in discussing a theme, present in academic and scholarly endeavour, is alien to poetry, journalism and scripture, forms of writing that speak to vast numbers of people of varying ability. Erudite academic precision is incompatible with the expansive and muscular originality of the kind found in a self-styled scripture such as the Quran. One may only wonder about its contents if it were revealed to sceptics and philosophers. It would be a book more congenial to our modern anxieties but the actual Quran is scripture, not systematic theology or academic philosophy or neo-romantic existentialism.

15

Muslims want to widen the appeal of the Quran so that a spiritually sterile and increasingly materialistic culture will see something worthwhile in it. The Quran claims religious all-sufficiency, the doctrinal analogue to the juridical principle of radical comprehensiveness *(al-shumūliyyah*; lit., inclusivity) reflected in the extensive scope of the holy law. What hinders a modern secular appreciation of this universalist and inclusivist aspect of the Quran? Sceptics in Muhammad's day would not have raised the following objections to the Quran's claim to be a perfect and comprehensive manual of tuition for humankind:

- the book's selective silences and omission of matters we consider important;
- the scripture's professed refusal to comment on some matters;
- its vagueness about certain practical duties of the faith;
- its ambivalence and ambiguity, unintentional or studied, on crucial religious issues;
- its mysterious and unintelligible verses;
- its inclusion of material now seen as trivial or too localized, outdated and irrelevant.

A few of the scripture's silences surprise us. Circumcision, a universal practice among Muslim males, is not mentioned. The problem of Muhammad's own circumcision *(khitān)* was embarrassing to orthodoxy. He is vaguely said to have been 'born already circumcised' *(wulida makhtūnan)*. Abraham's circumcision, central to the symbolism of the covenant made with him (Genesis:17:10–14) is nowhere in the Quran. Again, the book has nothing to say about the appointment of Muhammad's political successor. The Shi'ite–Sunni split originally occurred over the theology of political leadership. Shi'ites reject the first three caliphs and the first dynasty (of the Umayyads) as usurpers and believe that Islam is a family affair; Ali, a member of Muhammad's family, should have been the first caliph. A Quranic revelation, sent just before Muhammad's death, could perhaps have settled this matter – though human perversity can persist even in the face of a clear revelation. In the event, the Shi'ite schism, as old as Islam itself, has permanently fractured the community of Islam.

Second, despite the radical increase in our knowledge as a result of the Quran's revelation, it cautions us that our knowledge of spiritual matters and the next world remains limited and conjectural (Q:17:85; 27:66; 30:7; 34:53); the outer limit *(mablagh*; Q:53:30) of our knowledge cannot touch the knowledge of things divine. Fair enough; but then the Quran declines to clarify certain matters of mundane interest. At the end of the first of the two long verses that form the basis of the intricate laws of inheritance, the Quran casually adds, after carefully detailing the portions allotted to various relatives: 'You never know whether your parents or your children are closer *(aqrabu)* to you in terms of benefit' (Q:4:11). We do not know whether our biological family of origin or the family we create through marriage is the one which gives us greater benefit, intimacy, and emotional satisfaction. Our ignorance in this vital area is recorded, not resolved.

Third, the Quran gives vague information about some practical duties. It does not prescribe the five canonical daily prayers whose performance is a ritual requirement, legally enforced in some countries. Details of formal ablutions that precede canonical prayers (and recitation of the Quran) are given, with provision made for symbolic ablutions with sand in case of water shortages (Q:4:43; 5:6). Despite mentioning prayer often and insisting that it is 'a timed ordinance' (*kitāban mauqūtan*; Q:4:103) which cannot be forgone or delayed even in battle (where it can be shortened out of fear; Q:4:101–2), the Quran only vaguely mentions different times of prayer (Q:18:28; 20:130; 30:17–18). A verse which orders prayers at 'the two ends of the day and at the approaches of the night' is perhaps a reference to the five canonical prayers (Q:11:114). It was Muhammad who established the number, movements, and precise timing of the prayers. The obligatory alms-tax is mentioned often in the Quran but the amount is not fixed. The annual pilgrimage to Mecca, including the mini-pilgrimage (*'umra*), is the only pillar of Islam ordained in relative detail (Q:2:158, 196–200; 3:97; 22:26–37).

The Quran is ambivalent about conflicts such as free will versus predestination, a theme that tested the intellectual mettle of classical Muslim theologians. The earliest debate on the freedom of the human will is linked to the problem of the reprobate sinner, a problem latent in the Quran. It erupts at a time of disagreement over the legitimacy of the Umayyad dynasty. Later heresiographers gave the appellation 'qadarites' to those who, ironically, denied divine decree (*qadar*) and upheld free will! (The name qadarite came to mean anyone who was not orthodox: Shi'ites, Mu'tazilites, philosophers, and other 'heretics'). The opponents of the qadarites were labelled 'jabarites' since they defended compulsion (*jabr*), that is, pre-determinism understood as the unilateral divine initiative to control and manage all events. The jabarites represent official Sunni orthodoxy although both opinions find adequate Quranic support since the scripture contains vague maxims elastic enough to cover the aspirations of both groups.

Most Muslims believe that answers to these types of question are within the province of the mysterious or unseen (*al-ghayb*) and are rightly placed beyond human knowledge. The Quran contains clear guidance on all that matters, more than sufficient for anyone who wishes to live a God-fearing life. Inquiries inspired by an idle speculative curiosity are condemned as dangerous and misleading (Q:17:36; 18:22). Muhammad also discouraged believers from asking metaphysical questions, especially questions about the intricacies of predestination and fate.

The silence and vagueness of the revelation, on significant matters, is interpreted by Muslims, following Muhammad's lead, as good for believers. Divine silence automatically makes room for free human option and choice. The individual's choice may need communal endorsement if its adoption affects others; otherwise, it may be exercised as a prerogative of the private individual. The existence of such option indicates divine compassion rather than indifference to humankind, let alone neglect or oversight. The devout believer does not misuse freedom in areas where divine law leaves a degree of latitude for the human will. In this way, the believer acknowledges the generalized rule of God and reveres it even on occasions where the divine legislator forgoes his right to dictate human destiny in detail.

Fifth, the Quran, despite lauding its own clarity, contains verses which are mysterious to the point of unintelligibility even with the aid of commentary and knowledge of historical context. Consider for example: 'Do they not see that we gradually reduce the land from its outlying borders?' (Q:13:41). The context is the Meccans' plot against Muhammad's life and mission. Another peculiar passage claims that God had considered giving disbelievers silver and gold ornaments as an automatic reward for disbelief (Q:43:33–5), insinuating that such embellishments are worthless in the divine estimation. But God decided not to do this since 'all humankind would then have become a single community' (Q:43:33). This means that wordly temptations are already severe enough for the righteous: in the strange possible world envisaged, there would have been only one community, consisting of disbelievers only, since no believer could have resisted such severe temptation.

Such odd Quranic claims alienate the secularized reader while evoking in believers a sense of the book's mystery. The enigmatic Gog (*Ya'jūj*) and Magog (*Ma'jūj*; Q:18:94; 21:96) tribes are mentioned in the context of the travels of the mysterious character *dhū al-qarnayn* (Q:18:83–98), literally, the one with a pair of horns or lord of two epochs (since *qarn* can mean horn or epoch or generation). Popular opinion identifies this figure with the adventurer Alexander. Commentators prefer a Persian king or pre-historic Yemeni potentate. The Quran says nothing about his identity. Other bizarre claims include the reference to 'a beast from the earth who shall talk to them' (*da'bah min al-arḍ tukullimuhum*; Q:27:82) presumably on the day of judgement. In a variant reading, the beast will wound (*taklimihum*) those who rejected the signs of God. Such claims excite much speculative commentary. As the devout formula has it, 'God knows best'.[24]

The final problem is God's priorities. The Quran occasionally discusses matters that we today find trivial or too localized to deserve inclusion in a book of eternal principles. Critics charge that some incidents, particular and anecdotal (Q:80:1–12) or concerned with the Prophet's strained domestic life (Q:66:1–6), should have been omitted. Some of the Quran's 33rd chapter deals with grievances specific to Muhammad's domestic life, including the ban on re-naming adopted children (to disguise their biological parentage) and the permission to marry the divorced wives of adopted sons (Q:33:4, 37). The latter problem was a personal one for Muhammad, critics complain, and yet it entailed a divinely sanctioned re-writing of the laws of incest. Again, the etiquette for attending a meal at the Prophet's home is of restricted relevance – although the widely practised principle of *imitatio Muhammadi* could be invoked in defence. Finally, the Quran elevates into permanent significance a random petition from an aggrieved party embroiled in a pagan prelude to a divorce – although again it uses the occasion to enact legislation and to make moral observations (Q:58:1–4).

What is the religious response to these objections? It is not for us mortals to dictate the terms on which God is to involve himself with humankind. The economy of divine revelation, its casual attitude towards matters that agitate us today, its scandalous silences and its mysterious priorities, are indeed disturbing. They disturb our complacent attitudes and set new standards. The mystery of divine action will always leave us with a blank page to fill because the God of the prophets is not the transparently intelligible deity created by philosophers. The Quran is the criterion (*al-furqān*; Q:25:1) which judges and discerns. We must submit, in body and mind, to the wise God. The motto is *Allāhu akbar* (Greater is God) in all departments of life.

16

Reading the Quran requires much modern patience. From the many mysterious and unique Quranic claims, I choose two that interest us in the pluralist world: first, the assertion that humankind was originally one community whose religion was ethical monotheism (see Q:2:213; 10:19); and second, a surprising and uniquely Quranic claim about the universal reach of revealed guidance. After the expulsion of Adam and Eve from paradise, prophets appeared among all human tribes, up to the time of Muhammad's appearance in seventh century Arabia.

The Quran claims that 'humankind was a single community; then God sent messengers with good news and as warners; with them he sent the book in truth to judge among humankind in controversial matters' (Q:2:213). This implies that primitive humanity, in the earliest stages of the world's existence, endorsed monotheism. This view, common to the Quran and the Hebrew Bible, that a monolithic monotheism prevailed, seems unempirical and unhistorical. Perhaps all primitive human beings, apart from pagans, in the then inhabited world, worshipped a supreme deity resembling the Quranic God. Polytheism, however, must have seemed equally plausible to them. Gods and goddesses controlled different departments of life and nature: a god of war, a goddess of love.

This conception of the origins of humanity, namely, a unified group with one normative outlook battling a frequent recrudescence of a stereotypical idolatry, offends criteria of critical and historical objectivity. Moreover, this stereotypical account of the origins of revealed monotheism narrowly directs and unduly restricts the evidence of empirical observation and of philosophical and religious reflection and speculation. The procedures for investigating such religious claims differ from those of a purely empirical inquiry into the procedures, let us say, for determining whether cannibalism was 'the universal primitive form of disposal of vanquished enemies'.[25] The second type of claim is uncontroversially anthropological: there would be, except among modern educated cannibals concerned with political correctness, little emotional investment in either outcome. Religious claims of the kind found in the Quran, however, are always maximally controversial: while not wholly unverifiable by empirical means, the claims involve appeal to evidence that is extracted from controversial interpretations of already complex and keenly disputed social and historical data.

Religion is a pervasive phenomenon; it is not entirely absent from any society. But this demonstrates the ubiquity of religion, not of monotheism. Despite the efforts of modern scholars, our knowledge of preliterate cultures is, unavoidably, limited but we know that our most remote ancestors probably entertained religious sentiments. For example, Neanderthals flourishing between 100,000 and 25,000 years ago buried their dead, a practice that suggests a possible regard for an after-life, a major emphasis of the Quran. The Cro-Magnons, European successors to the Neanderthals, living in late Paleolithic times have left some cave drawings which insinuate an artistically articulate religious awareness. They buried food and provisions with the dead, evidence of belief in a bodily resurrection, a belief found in the trio of Semitic monotheisms. Archaeological findings imply the ubiquity of religious sentiment and support the existence of belief in its twin corollaries of resurrection and life beyond the grave.

We are investigating the content of religious conviction rather than the question of whether or not we are, in an amorphous sense, religious beings who wish to live beyond the grave. Today we cannot ignore the opposed secular understanding of the evolution of religion as a wholly human phenomenon. In the beginning, there were animist and polytheistic intuitions which were refined as they passed through henotheistic and ethnic religious conceptions before arriving gradually at the rigorous and pure ethical monotheism we find in Islam. Ancient Hebrew religion, which the Quran mentions without regard to its historical development, probably evolved from a kathenotheistic origin: the Hebrews worshipped one god at a time and while worshipping that one god of the tribe, they did not deny the existence of other gods. In a henotheistic variant, they acknowledged, for example, the existence (and divinity) of Dagon, the Philistine god, but preferred the mighty Yahweh. A religious view which universalized a tribal deity's powers evolved and matured into Judaic monotheism.

Can we date the transition from primitive superstition to rational sophisticated religion? We know that ideographic and hieroglyphic images, especially of ani-mals, stimulated idolatry. We mark the transition from superstition to rational religion from the moment we move from such images to the alphabet – an abstract symbolic reality that is a coded and condensed form of expression, including theological expression. Only with the development of the alphabet could ancient humankind think abstractly and thus formulate monotheism and its accompany-ing theology. Were pre-literate men and women, then, for conceptual reasons, inevitably idolaters? If so, the suggestion that the ancients were destined to become monotheists can be tied to considerations of literacy and the acquisition of abstract thought via language. This plausible account, however, contradicts the Quranic assertion of an aboriginal monotheism, a view that buttresses the scripture's a priori monochromatic view of religious awareness.

17

The second provocative Quranic claim is that all communities were warned by an ethnic messenger about the consequences of faith and disbelief. In Judaism and Christianity, claims about the universality of guidance arise as a moral concern for conscientious believers and are part of theology and theodicy; they are no part of the Bible, except inexplicitly.[26] In the Quran, these moral concerns are explicit in the revelation. Moreover, controversial moral themes that exercise Jewish and Christian theologians are often in the Islamic scripture but not in Islamic theology. A biblical analogue to the Quranic claim of didactic universality, incidentally, is the view that after the Flood, all humankind spoke one language (Genesis 11:1), a claim not made in the Quran. This symbolic human solidarity through a community united by speech is as unhistorical as the Quranic claim about the universality of revealed guidance.

Although God favoured some individuals and communities such as 'Adam, Noah, the family of Abraham and the House of Imran' (Q:3:33–4),[27] revealed guidance was vouchsafed to all communities at one time or another (Q:10:47; 13:7; 35:24). 'For every community, there is a guide' (Q:13:7). Again, 'there was never a community (*ummatin*) but a warner (*nadhīr*) has passed among them (Q:35:24). A messenger was sent to each community (*ummatin*; Q:10:47) but not to every generation of every community. Thus, Abraham's father had no guidance (Q:19:43); Muhammad's people were not warned and received no scripture until Muhammad came with the Quran (Q:28:46; 32:3; 34:44; 36:6; 43:21). Unique among the nations, the Children of Israel received many special favours: the privilege of revelation and prophethood in the family line (Q:29:27; 45:16; 57:26), the gift of monarchy (Q:5:21) in addition to the common grace of divine guidance.

The content of the universalist Quranic claim is morally attractive. But what is the motive behind it? The Quran mentions that a witness shall be brought against every nation while Muhammad witnesses against his community (Q:4:41; 16:89). Is this a way of indicting all human beings and ensuring their culpability? If so, the morally attractive claim about universal guidance is in the service of a morally less attractive motive, namely, the desire to convict humankind, albeit justly, a desire explicit in some comprehensive and inclusivist passages (e.g., Q:4:165; 6:155–7; 7:172–3; 33:7–8, 72–3). The factual claim then is made for moral reasons: it is needed to increase the range of just divine chastisement. The reasoning is that universal culpability would be morally wrong without universal guidance; hence there must be universal guidance. Therefore there is universal guidance.

Leaving aside this moral syllogism, the factual claim seems unempirical, unhistorical and perhaps false. It is defensible only if it is made in conjunction with the earlier claim about the unity of all humankind at some primitive stage of history when it was a single large community, diversified by a few smaller tribes, settled in a narrow geographical region comprising of the Mediterranean basin and the Levant.

Classical Islamic tradition cites an arbitrarily sizeable number to indicate an indefinitely large group of inspired messengers, based on the Quranic comment, 'How many were the messengers we have sent among the ancients!' (Q:43:6). (By contrast, the Quran does not claim an indefinite number of revealed scriptures: it specifies the few sacred books that Muslims must revere.) The scripture comments on the careers of a handful of apostles and adds that not all messengers are mentioned in the Quran (Q:4:164; 6:34; 40:78). Muslims must believe in all divinely inspired messengers (Q:2:136; 4:150–2), named or otherwise, whether fortified by a scripture and law or sent with only a moral message. God has exalted some messengers above others (Q:2:253; 17:55) but the ranking is not given. Perhaps only the most exalted messengers are mentioned by name; perhaps only those relevant to the Arab mission are recalled.

Some messengers such as Zechariah, Job and Ishmael receive only honorary mention (*dhikr*; Q:19:2; 38:41, 48). The Quranic list is indicative, not exhaustive. Nor does it distinguish between types of prophet. The *Nebi'īm* (Prophets) division of the Hebrew Bible mentions different kinds of prophets: the suffering servants of the word (such as Jeremiah and Hosea), the literary prophets (such as Isaiah, Micah, and Amos) and false prophets such as Hananiah who opposed Jeremiah (Jeremiah 28). The Quran does not recognize these categories. As for the concept of a false messenger, that is total anathema, an intolerable interrogation of the Quran's axiomatic liaison between truth and apostleship.

The Quran's choice of messengers for mention or discussion is at most representative, not comprehensive: not all messengers are mentioned even by allusion. And the list is representative only of messengers sent to communities in the Near East, the Levant and the Near Mediterranean. The Quran discusses the religious careers of Noah, Abraham, Jacob, Joseph, Moses, David, Solomon, Jonah, Jesus, John the Baptist, Zechariah, Mary, and, in less detail, those of Isaac and Ishmael, and a few others. It concedes that there was a great 'break in the apostolic succession' (*fatratin min al-rusul*; Q:5:20) between Jesus and the advent of Muhammad (see also Q:5:48). We estimate that there were no messengers sent to any people for over half a millennium, itself a puzzling fact.

The Quran contains extensive detail about the preaching of three probably Arabian prophets, Shu'ayb (possibly Jethro, Moses' father-in-law), Hūd, and Ṣāliḥ, sent to wayward tribes in pre-Islamic times in regions that were, judging by clues in the Quran, close to locales and haunts frequented by Muhammad's contemporaries (Q:20:128; 37:136–8). Sabā', the Arabicized name of the biblical Queen of Sheba, receives extensive mention in a story of rare charm (Q:27:22–44; 34:15). There is a Quranic chapter named in honour of the sage Luqmān (Q:31:12–19) who is never mentioned outside his chapter or in the company of other divine messengers. Luqmān, famed for his wisdom and known to Arabs in pre-Islamic times, is often identified with the African slave-fabulist Aesop. The Quran portrays him as a prophet.

The Quran is concerned solely with the *religious* mission of the messengers it mentions. It cares little for cultural variations in the geographical locale of individual messengers – all of whom, whether sent to small or large tribes, whether major or minor figures, preach a virtually identical monotheism. Occasionally, there is local or specialized flavour such as the rare demographic detail about the population of the city to which Jonah was sent (Q:37:147). Neither the context nor the content of the message of the prophets is ever wholly stereotypical: a supporting narrative uses a rich and varied vocabulary which alleviates what must seem, in translation, the monotony of the monotheistic harangue.[28]

The Quran says nothing about messengers sent to warn communities settled in regions considered (by the Arabs) to be remote from Arabia – lands such as

China and India, significant contemporaneous civilizations known, if vaguely, to Muhammad and his compatriots. Indeed Muhammad is credited with the remark: 'Go even as far as China to acquire knowledge'. It is irrelevant to object that this tradition might be forged: that it could have been plausibly attributed to the Prophet implied that the Arabs knew about China – as the limit of the world. (The Arabs conquered parts of India and China within about a century of Muhammad's death.) Although the Arabs were not a maritime people when Islam was born, Muslim refugees, fleeing Meccan persecution, sailed to East Africa. Even Muhammad's contemporaries could have reasonably asked: Were divinely guided messengers sent to any generation of Chinese, Indians and Africans? This is still relatively local and leaves unaccounted and unwarned large tracts of the civilized world. We would ask also about the Far East, the two Americas, Scandinavia, and the two cold extremities of the earth. Europe is covered – albeit, in Muslim eyes, inadequately since, as the Quran claims, the Christian dispensation was corrupted, hence the need for a new faith (Q:30:41).

If we patiently sift the empirical evidence by discipline of scientific method, it does not support the Quran's bold claims which, though morally attractive, are factually questionable. Muslims are proud of the Quranic stress on the universality of revelation and divine instruction because they sense its moral appeal. But is it historically true? This claim about universal revealed tuition is different from other controversial, more or less supernatural, claims in the Quran – such as the denial of Jesus' crucifixion and hence resurrection (Q:4:157–8). God acts within history to frustrate the attempted crucifixion and then translates Jesus, assertions which are only partly verifiable. Some Quranic verses are, evidently, irreducibly mystical and can only be allegorically rather than literally or historically true (see Q:7: 172; 11:44; 16:48; 24:35; 33:72; 41:11; 84:1–5; 99:1–5). The claim about the universality of divine guidance is, however, an empirical claim subject to falsification. It can therefore be rationally supported and verified using the canons of critical history.

18

We saw earlier how those who uphold the biblical or Quranic 'theory' of the origins and prevalence of monotheistic religion cannot reconcile their sacred beliefs with some recent findings in archaeology, ethnography, palaeography and anthropology. Although the evidence by itself decisively supports neither the religious nor the secular view, such evidential inconclusiveness is plausibly interpreted, in a laicized age, as a presumption in favour of the secular conclusion.

Did human religious awareness pass through animist and polytheist forms to arrive gradually at a refined version of monotheism? The rival scriptural view of a pristine Adamic monotheism degenerating into polytheism and animism, punctuated by occasional irruptions of the primordial monotheism – as God's messengers came and preached the message only to meet a temporary success – needs independent support. Muslims have not lifted this precarious assumption beyond the level of dogmatic presupposition. Religious apologists can distill undefiled monotheism out of the dark and colourful mixture of ancient cultic superstitions but only by taking some religiously sanctioned liberties with the anthropological, sociological and ethnographic data.

A secularist might claim that the earliest form of religion was the earliest philosophy of nature: belief in an indefinitely diffused power or influence. Later it was localized and perhaps coagulated into animistic and totemistic rituals. At the tribal stage of culture, there was belief in and worship of many spirits (polydaemonism), including those of natural objects and of the dead. This was the precursor of polytheism which required additionally the naming of spirits and assignment of personalities. As polydaemonism evolved into polytheism, tribal life changed into national life. Accompanying all stages of religious evolution was mythology, a primitive form of theology, an interpretation of first order religious practice, conduct and intuition.

A Muslim believer, alarmed by the direction of these doubts, might object that this style of inquiry is inspired by the wrong kind of curiosity. We are talking about religion, not empirical social science. But, surely, we are entitled to know whether or not, on the basis of material discussions of various messengers, this significant Quranic claim about original monotheism and the alleged universality of guidance can reasonably be made to bear a *stricto sensu* interpretation. Why is it wrong to take the Quran at its word? The scripture often invites world-wide travel, suggesting that this will supply empirical proof for its claims about the rise and fall of nations and the universal prevalence of warning and nemesis (see Q:3:137; 30:41–2).

Muslims might object that we have misunderstood the Quran. Form criticism in biblical studies can be applied to the Quran to enable us to identify the literary form used in a given passage. This dictates appropriate expectations; we judge what we may reasonably learn from a given literary form. Thus, for example, parables are not intended to be read as history; and mythologized history yields absurdities if we read it as though it were modern critical history. If the Quran's accounts of the origins of humankind, early humanity's religious belief, and the universality of guidance are read as mythologized history, the problems we identified cannot even arise. Only if we treat it as literal historical truth do we encounter the problems raised by modern scientific history with its strict canons of evidence. We return to this theme in Chapter 7 where we finally run it to earth.

19

Three comments will suffice to conclude this chapter and introduce the next. First, despite the Quran's intention to radically extend its scope, it is indifferent to secular details in its narrations, declining on principle to discuss matters that lack a religious or moral import. The Muslim scripture never, for instance, gives detailed genealogies of the type found in Genesis and the books of Chronicles in the Hebrew Bible and again in the New Testament in the Gospels of Matthew and Luke. The Quran contains virtually no secular history, not even of the kind that would have interested Muhammad's listeners. The book is silent on current events – except for one notice of contemporaneous external history (Q:30:2–6). Occasionally, the Quran condescends to supply secular or historical details in order to resolve an inter-faith dispute (Q:3:93–8; 6:146–7; 27:76). Sometimes the details are requested by Muhammad's detractors seeking to embarrass him or to question the authenticity of his calling. For example, the Jewish rabbis of Medina challenged him to apply to God for esoteric information about the itinerary of the mysterious traveller *dhū al-qarnayn* (the man of two epochs; Q:18:83–98), mentioned above in Section 15. The Quranic verses, sent in response to this request, weave religious motifs into a narrative that can be read solely for its geographical and historical interest.

Second, an emphasis on the secular, especially scientific, resources of the holy volume loses focus of its essential resources as a guiding scripture, as a primarily religious and moral, as opposed to historical or scientific, document. While modernist exegetes correctly attempt to make the Quran relevant and applicable to our modern problems, their exegesis is unacceptable once it neglects the religious meaning of the book, a meaning partly but significantly determined by examining the views of believers in the formative period of the faith. The attempt to decode the Muslim revelation, in order to locate scientific meanings that might interest modern readers, is misguided sensationalism. We return to further ramifications of this issue at the end of Chapter 7.

Finally, this chapter on the determination of Quranic scope supplies the background to the attempt to 'update' Islam through a modernist exegesis. Modern readings of this ancient authoritative text enlist the old dicta in the service of new moral exigencies and thus bring the regulation of modern lives within the ambit of the scripture. Muslims are, however, surprisingly reluctant to concede that, owing to changed circumstances, the authority of some dicta might have altogether lapsed. It is this concern that we must now examine.

7   The authority of the book

1

Like the Hebrew *Ḥummash*[1] (Torah), the Quran is a highly internalized scripture: memorized and cherished in a legal, moral, ritual, and artistic possession bordering on possessiveness. Virtually all Muslims hold in defensive reserve the question of its authority: it is beyond reasonable doubt or discussion. Non-Muslims complain that the *amour propre* (self-respect) of even secularized Muslims is outraged when anyone broaches this theme. We shall now assess the attempt to establish the authority of scripture in a sceptical world. Can we secure a safe haven for revelation in an age intellectually hospitable to reason and experience but not to mystery and metaphysical speculation?

In evaluating the status of revealed authority in the modern world, we are investigating another dimension of the problem of faith versus reason. The case for absolute respect for authority must fail in an age that is sceptical, democratic, and therefore angry at any unaccountable and mysterious authority which emanates directly, or via prophetic mediation, from a supernatural source. Only the authority of the rational and the factual, especially in the shape of empirical science, is now treated as absolute. As we saw in Chapter 6, some believers try to borrow the kudos that attaches to this modern shibboleth by claiming that their revelation anticipates it! At the end of this chapter, we assess the dangers of using science to buttress the authority of scripture.

All believers, whether simple or sophisticated, observant or lapsed, are to varying degrees unsettled, even traumatized, by secular questioning of the authority of their scripture. They are offended by the suggestion that part of the canon is now dispensable, rendered redundant by progress in science, critical history and moral reflection. In higher education, religiously active undergraduates, of all monotheistic persuasions, are unduly distressed by the detached or sceptical reading of a book they revere as sacred. Even devout students, however, are untroubled by the charge that there is an incompatibility, at an unspecified abstract level, between science and religion or between faith and reason: indeed the most devout students often study science, mathematics and technology.

Secular humanists are disturbed by the continuing authority of scripture. Polemical atheists argue that scriptures have been the most ancient and effective form of propaganda. They note extrinsic and intrinsic problems with alleged revelations, problems that make these texts inaccessible to modern appreciation and acceptance. There is one major extrinsic problem: the 'revealed' books of the Near Eastern monotheisms date from a pre-scientific, largely pre-literate, and pre-technological era. How much of the world-view of the first recipients of the Quran, for example, do modern Muslims need to entertain in order to believe that the scripture remains a revealed authority with the right to direct rebellious modern lives? And there are, as we shall note presently, several intrinsic difficulties rooted in the invariant and unalterable text of a scripture such as the Quran.

Modernist exegesis seeks to soften and liberalize Quranic claims and imperatives but it cannot ignore the text's immutability and sacrosanct authority. The Quran is now a closed canon, a legislative heritage; while it was still being revealed, believers could expect legislative innovation inside it (see Q:4:15; 65:1). Now only the interpretation is fluid. As we shall see in Chapter 11, during a discussion of women's rights, some modern commentators maximize existing scriptural resources by emphasizing the charity, tolerance and compassionate legislation already there. Secular readers condemn the scripture's supine acceptance of slavery and of slave concubinage – euphemistically called 'possession of the right hand' (*milk al-yamīn*; Q:4:3). And the Quran, regrettably, explicitly endorses limited polygyny. Fortunately, however, Islam merely inherits slavery, concubinage and unlimited polygyny from its Semitic heritage. None are institutions introduced by the Quran; we may therefore advocate their formal abolition today. Additionally, western strategists worry about the political consequences of both defensive and expansionist jihad; the former is a Quranic innovation and the latter was, until the easily predictable collapse of the Ottoman empire in the early twentieth century, the religious basis of the Islamic imperial tradition. Finally, even some Muslims regret the clarity of the Draconian imperatives contained in the law of retaliation and in the penal code for extreme (*ḥudūd*) offences. All these ordinances derive from the unalterable Quranic text.[2]

As Muslims have not asked certain philosophical questions about the status and nature of Quranic authority, we can locate the relevant issues only by exploring the Judaeo–Christian encounter with secular doubt concerning revealed authority. This chapter investigates possible and instructive parallels with Judaeo–Christian views about maintaining scriptural authority in a sceptical age. It is sometimes less focused on the Quran than the three previous chapters; it raises philosophical questions about all revelation, including the Quran.

2

Most Meccans initially rejected Muhammad's unwavering claim to be an inspired messenger of God. They thought that the supreme God was too exalted to condescend to an interaction with sinners. Although Arab pagans did not possess the equivalent of the suggestive mythology that the Greeks gave Europe, a mythology that has rivalled Christianity in its appeal to Europeans, they did believe in an other-worldly realm populated by gods, invisible elementals such as jinn, and the female progeny of the high god Allah whose three daughters are mentioned by name in the Quran (Q:53:19–23). Many thought Muhammad was tutored (*mu'allam*) by someone and possessed by the jinn (*majnūn*; Q:44:14). Impressed by the magical and incantatory power of Quranic verses, some pagans speculated that Muhammad had learnt sorcery.[3] Muhammad retorted that the only God, despite his majesty, was not a remote and otiose deity; periodically, he communicated his good will to humankind.

The Quran records many objections to Muhammad's claim to heavenly inspiration. We encountered in Chapter 4 some Meccan doubts about the book's supernatural origins. The pagans rejected Muhammad's claim to have privileged access to God and proffered their own criteria for an authentic divine communication. A sacred book, the pagans objected, should descend as a single volume, not piecemeal over decades. The Quran replied that the gradual descent of relevant portions of the message was intended to console Muhammad's heart in his daily struggle against the pagans (Q:25:32). The Quran adds that some people would not believe even if a parchment from heaven descended on them and they touched it with their own hands (Q:6:7). Jewish rejectors expected a true prophet to produce a sacrifice consumed by fire sent from heaven. The Quran retorted that previous prophets, including those who had brought that very miracle, were nonetheless rejected and some were killed (Q:3:183).[4]

Historical detail is inappropriate in a primarily philosophical exploration; we investigate one controversy between Muhammad and his pagan enemies which exposes fundamental differences between the character of ancient scepticism about religious truth and revealed authority and the character of modern doubt based on more radical reservations. Before his call to prophethood at the age of 40, the Meccans, having recognized Muhammad's exemplary character, awarded him the title *Al-Amīn*, the trustworthy man, a title he shared with the archangel Gabriel (Q:26:193). By the age of 25, as a result of his scrupulous honesty and sobriety, he had won the heart of Khadījah Bint Al-Khuwaylid, his employer, who later married him. The Quran affirms that Muhammad received God's immense grace (Q:4:113; 17:87; 33:21, 46, 56) and had 'an exalted moral character' (*khuluq 'azīm*; 68:4). Presupposed by this repeated appeal to Muhammad's exemplary character, which is used to establish the credentials of the book he brings, are two controversial, that is, epistemologically assailable, assumptions prevalent in Muhammad's day: a man is as good as his word and, to reverse the maxim, the word is as good as the man who brings it. A good man is bound to bring a true divine message; an evil man, a false message. We explore this liaison presently.

When Muhammad, having lived 'a whole life-time' (*'umur*) among his compatriots (Q:10:16), declared that he received heavenly messages, the Meccans rejected his claim but did not accuse him of being a selfish imposter who had invented the message. He was known to be illiterate. The Quran affirms it: 'You could not read any book before this revelation; nor were you able to transcribe this book with your right hand. In that case, the charlatans would have had grounds for doubt' (Q:29:48).

Muhammad was a sober and trustworthy Meccan; even his enemies acknowledged that he scrupulously discharged his trusts. When he appealed to this acknowledged trait, the Meccans were confounded. During the frustrating early years of his call, Muhammad once shouted to his people from the top of a local hill. He asked the gathered multitude whether or not they would believe him if he told them there was a hostile army in battle array on the unseen side of the hill. The crowd answered with one voice that they would do so without hesitation since no one had ever heard him utter a lie. So, he continued, hoping to press his advantage: 'I warn you of a day of judgement and of God's wrath'. The crowd, unimpressed by the analogy, dispersed.

3

What are the Quranic criteria for judging the character of the messenger who brings us an allegedly revealed scripture? After exploring the scripture's perspective on messengers, we examine its criteria for assessing the contents of a revealed message. We begin a philosophical analysis of these issues in Section 4.

Prophets are men (*al-rijāl*; Q:12:109) chosen by God.[5] No one can claim to be a prophet by personal decision (Q:22:75; 27:59; 74:52–3).[6] God chooses men (and angels) to convey his messages and revelations to humankind (Q:35:32) although some special women, including Muhammad's wives, receive revelations too (Q:33:30, 32–4). Prophets preach in the language of their people (Q:14:4; 41:44)[7] and teach only their own community; uniquely, Muhammad's mission is universal and finalizes all revelation (Q:4:79, 170; 7:185; 34:28; 61:9). Some messengers are only warners while others bring a new dispensation – a law – or a book.[8] Prophets invite their communities to reflect, making no unreasonable claims or demands (Q:6:50; 34:46). Prophets are harbingers of religious good fortune but they are also warners who threaten punishment (Q:2:213; 6:48). They bring some good news (*bushrā*; Q:27:2) and, for the disbelievers, some very bad news (Q:6:49).[9]

Prophets are mortal men (Q:21:7–8) aware of their mortality; a true prophet would never preach idolatry by setting himself up as a god or by recommending worship of any being or reality except God (Q:3:79–80). The Arabs and other communities before them, judging by the Quran, expected divinely guided prophets to be more than human (Q:21:3; 36:15; 54:24). The sinners refused divine guidance since the (human) messengers who brought it were not accompanied by angels testifying to the truth of their claims (Q:6:8–10; 15:7; 23:24; 25:7), a pagan request the Quran dismisses as mockery (Q:15:8–15). After Muhammad's death, Abu Bakr quoted the Quran (Q:3:144) to prove Muhammad's mortality.[10] The Quran affirms the absolute humanity and unqualified mortality of

Muhammad and of his prophetic predecessors, especially Jesus and his mother.[11] All prophets are created mortal (*bashar*; Q:14:11; 17:93; 41:6) and constrained by a fixed life-span (Q:21:8; 25:7). All have bodies that need food for survival (Q:5:77; 21:8; 25:7, 20). Prophets had wives and children and led normal lives (Q:13:38; 25:7).

Prophets are obedient servants of God and cannot and do not distort the divine message or refuse to deliver it to the people (Q:39:13). Exceptionally, Jonah initially refuses but repents soon afterwards (37:139–44). Muhammad is threatened with immediate death if he refuses to deliver the message or tries to alter or fabricate it to suit his own fancies (Q:6:15; 69:44–7). Equally, prophets must be obeyed by the community to which they are sent (Q:4:64). To obey the prophet of God is to obey God (Q:4:80; 48:10).[12]

While mortal and fallible, prophets were, as God's spokesmen, infallible expert witnesses to divine truth. We must therefore trust their verdicts about the unseen world. The prophets' credibility is based on their honesty, wisdom and good-ness. These selfless men lived modestly and moderately, not seeking personal benefits or domination over others (Q:23:24); they were radicals, however, in their patient determination to fight and die for social justice and the promotion of goodness and virtue, all in the name of the holy one (Q:6:34, 162). Despite per-sonal risk, prophets delivered God's verdict on sinners, no matter how unpopular the verdict. The great honour of martyrdom in the way of God was an occupa-tional hazard and a privilege of the prophetic vocation. The prophets' devotion to the cause of God was absolute, sometimes requiring painful ruptures of personal relationships (Q:19:41–9; 60:4). Prophets did not pray even for the salvation of relatives after it became clear that they were going to die as unrepentant pagans (Q:9:113–14; 60:4).

The man of God is a man of his word (Q:19:54–6). Never false to his trust in worldly matters, he is also, by extension, faithful to the divine trust he has under-taken in 'the covenant of the prophets' (Q:3:81). The messenger bears the higher trust of God's word and assists other prophets in discharging their commission. Relatedly, in an earthy military context, after the Muslims are defeated at the bat-tle of Uhud, the Quran rejects the accusation that any messenger of God would commit the crime of deceiving others (*ghul*), a charge that reduces *in situ* to the misappropriation of war booty (Q:3:161).

Prophets expect rewards directly from God; no prophet demands payment for his commission (Q:10:72; 11:29, 51; 26:109, 127, 145, 164, 180). Muhammad is ordered to tell the pagans: 'Say: "I ask no reward (*'ajr*) from you; it is all in your own interests. My reward is due only from God; and he is a witness to all things"' (Q:34:47; see also Q:42:23). As Paul boasts, those doing the Lord's work are not paid workers (1 Thessalonians 2:9; 2 Thessalonians 3:8). A true prophet not only charges nothing for the guidance he brings, he is, moreover, himself rightly guided (Q:36:20–1).

Finally, a martial criterion of prophethood: 'It is not fitting for any prophet to take prisoners of war [for ransom] until he has first thoroughly subdued (*yus-khina*) the land. You have your eyes on the perishable goods of this lower life; God intends [for you] the hereafter' (Q:8:67). The present tense of the quoted verb (conjugated absolutely as *yus-khinu*) means 'he massacres'. The Quranic chapter called 'Muhammad', originally called *Al-Qitāl* (The Fighting), confirms and commends this ruthless policy as part of Muhammad's war effort (Q:47:4). The Quran elsewhere too explicitly (Q:33:26–7) or implicitly (Q:59:2) confirms such harsh measures. We have, to be fair to Muhammad, the Torah to hand for a more atrocious decree called the *herem* (Hebrew for ban or curse). During wars conducted by Moses, all booty was cursed, therefore, indiscriminately destroyed; unauthorized seizure of spoils was punished by collective execution of the culprit and his family.[13]

We add a criterion found only in the prophetic literature, a criterion that completes the moral portrait of prophetic character. Unlike ordinary men and women, a prophet cannot be inherited by his relatives. On his death, Muhammad's remaining possessions were given away in charity. Muhammad left behind virtually nothing having already spent everything in charity, especially during his last Ramadan on earth. His sole bequest, apart from his noble example of life, was the Quran.

Finally, are there any criteria for false prophets? In Muhammad's day, there arose a rival Arab prophet called Maslama Bin Habib who wrote a letter to Muhammad offering to share with him the title of Messenger of God. Muhammad responded by giving him the nickname Musaylimah, a derogatory diminutive of his name, and dubbed him 'Musaylimah, the little liar'. This incident is not in the Quran. Unlike the Bible, the Quran rejects the category of 'false prophet'. Even the expression never occurs in the Quran: the juxtaposition would be an intolerable interrogation of the Muslim scripture's confident but unspoken alignment of 'prophet' and 'true'.[14]

As for content, no divine revelation could recommend indecency and evil or promote idolatry (Q:7:28). Satan cannot inspire or insinuate divine revelation although he can successfully intercept it (Q:17:52–3) once a messenger allows his personal wishes (*'umniyyah*) to cloud his divine commission (Q:22:52). God eventually annuls the satanic contribution and establishes the divine signs (Q:22:52).

A true revelation must be consistent with all previous revelations in their pristine form (Q:12:111); the Quran cites its compatibility with earlier scriptures as proof of its divine source (Q:10:37). The content of scripture must be internally consistent and free of error and contradiction (Q:4:82). In the context of its condemnation of nocturnal conspiracies by the Medinan hypocrites, the scripture claims to be free of internal discrepancy and therefore confidently invites the hypocrites to deliberate on its divine provenance rather than on their evil clandestine plans to undermine its message (Q:4:81; 47:24).

As a postscript, we note the mode of delivery of a revealed message: 'It befits no mortal that God should speak to him or her except by inspiration or from behind a veil, or by the dispatch of a messenger to reveal, by God's permission, what God wills' (Q:42:51). Inspiration could come as divine suggestion, insinuated into the heart or mind of a messenger, or as verbal (or literal) inspiration enabling divine speech to be conveyed in a human language. The veil is not a material separation but rather the numinous presence of God's face (*wajh Allāh*; Q:2:115) understood as spiritual light (based on Q:24:35). The messenger can be an angel or an archangel (such as Gabriel who brought the Quran).

4

In the age of revelation, the moral character of the messenger and the truth of the message he brought were organically related. In a secular age, we reject the liaison: even a morally good man need not bring a revealed message. The Meccans' confused ambivalence about the Prophet's claims, noted in Section 2 above, itself arises out of confusion. They reasoned that either he is as honest about the revelations from God as he is about mundane matters or else he is honest about his worldly affairs but not his religious claims. But this dichotomy is false since it omits a third possibility we readily notice in a psychologically literate age, an age that gave us psychoanalysis, the systematic exploration of self-deception and its complex motivations. Even honest and great human beings can be mistaken, and sincerely so, an eventuality plausibly explained by the secular psycho-biography of religious genius. Just as the Quran cannot, as we saw in Chapter 3, recognize even in principle, the pagan who conscientiously rejects the word of God but remains nonetheless virtuous, the Meccans could not say to Muhammad: 'We admit you are not lying but we fear you are mistaken, sincerely mistaken'. The distinctions presupposed by such judgements were logically possible in Muhammad's day but culturally unavailable.

We shall note some dichotomies that occur in the Quran to assess the ethos of the time. In one medium-sized Meccan chapter alone, we encounter three dichotomies, the first put into the mouth of the pagans, the remaining two proposed by God and put into the mouth of Muhammad. In each case, we can imagine a third or fourth missing alternative:

> [The disbelievers wonder]: 'Has he [Muhammad] invented a falsehood against God, or is he a lunatic?' On the contrary, it is those who disbelieve in the next life who are [living] in chastisement and in the greatest error.
>
> (Q:34:8)

> Say [to the disbelievers]: 'Who gives you sustenance from the heavens and the earth?' Answer: 'It is God; and one thing is for certain: it is either we or you who are guided or in plain error'.
>
> (Q:34:24)

> Say [to the disbelievers]: 'If I am astray, I stray only to my own loss; if I receive guidance, it is only owing to the inspiration my Lord sends me – for he hears everything and he is close enough to answer the calls [of his devotees]'.
>
> (Q:34:50)

5

Men and women who are otherwise great might nonetheless be unable to safeguard themselves against the insidious power of a false self-image. They might have insufficient self-knowledge to know their own limitations. Why should we expect artists to understand the nature and status of their own creativity? Self-knowledge depends on intellectual as well as moral and spiritual honesty. One may wonder, for example, whether Jesus was self-deluded and therefore shocked by the actual turn of events as the Jewish establishment, which probably sensed that he was scripting his life to fit that of the Messiah promised in the Hebrew scriptures, decided to nail him to a cross, where he was finally disabused of his pretensions. Equally, Paul exaggerated the imminence of the *Parousia* (the return of Christ). These are consequential errors; and greatness is always partial in those who misjudge themselves.

Similarly, the greatness of Muhammad's character, a disputed thesis, and his stupendous achievements as a reformer, which is an indisputable thesis, cannot even jointly supply a bulwark against the illusions caused by self-deception. It is as possible for individuals to live in the cocoon of a fantasy all their lives as it is for them to live in the active heat of a single authentic emotion all their lives. What complicates the secular dismissal of Muhammad's case is that nothing happened in his life to persuade him that he had built his life on insecure foundations. On the contrary, much confirmed him in his self-estimate as a messenger of God: towards the end of his life, his mission in Medina flowered into the consummate success (Q:110:1–3)[15] which the Quran had confidently predicted during the hour of unpromising beginnings in Mecca (Q:93:4–8; 94:1–4).

In all areas of our lives, we may be the victims of self-deception, a form of self-persuasive rationalization that inhibits our ability to take account of our less conscious hopes, expectations and desires. The knowledge that we claim to have of a world external to our thoughts, intentions, feelings and wishes, has to be achieved in a way that can withstand critical challenge and scrutiny, if it is to count as knowledge rather than opinion. The only partial exception to this is our alleged knowledge of our own mental states; here are we considered authorities, albeit still fallible. The Meccan sceptics asked Muhammad: 'Are you sure?' Today, we would ask him: 'How do you know?' The subject is generally in the best position to judge the authenticity of his or her perceptual experience as the Quran rightly implies in its question: 'Will you [pagans] dispute with him [Muhammad] concerning what he saw?'(Q:53:11–12). Even here we cannot preclude the possibility of error. As for our own mental states, we are authorities on such intentional states, being in part the author of those states, but we remain fallible authorities. Thus, for example, our thought of the object we fear or adore determines in part and usually, but not wholly or always, what we objectively fear or adore.

Muhammad had self-doubt, as the Quran testifies (Q:93:3). After the inaugural revelation (Q:96:1–5), he took refuge in his wife's company and asked her to confirm that the voice was divine. She re-assured him on the grounds that God would not permit the Devil to seduce a good human being; there followed what

Christian theologians call a discernment of spirits to make sure that some evil being was not the cause of the inspiration. A brief initial period of doubt and hesitation, familiar to mystics and prophets, was followed by a barren silence which was broken perhaps by the revelation of portions of Chapters 73, 74, and 93. After that, however, Muhammad found his experience to be regular and self-authenticating. Nonetheless, he had periodic doubts about his mission judging from the regular Quranic reassurances to him about the truth of the message he receives (Q:2:147, 211; 10:94–5; 11:17; 32:23). Instead of doubting, he is told to seek Jewish and Christian approval and confirmation of the Islamic message (Q:2:211; 16:43; 21:7).

Before we conclude with comments on Muhammad's sincerity, we record some nuances in the Quran's epistemology. The scripture condemns doubt and excoriates the sceptic (*murtāb*; Q:40:34); true believers do not, after graduating to the level of faith, ever doubt the truth of Islam (Q:49:15). (As noted above, even Muhammad is warned against doubting the revelations.) Intellectual doubt is called *shakk* (Q:14:9; 27:66; 38:8); *rayb* is used for moral or emotional disquiet, a suspicion of fraud or deception (Q:2:2; 32:2; 45:26) and its victim is called *murīb* (Q:14:9; 50:25). Both types of doubt are opposed to certainty (*yaqīn*), the psychological state suited to knowledge (*'ilm*).

There are three states or levels of certainty. The lowest is certainty by reasoning and inference (*'ilm al-yaqīn*; Q:102:5): we deduce corollaries from known truths. We appraise evidence and use our judgement to arrive at conclusions that are probable or certain. With sense-perception, error is possible and hence an intermediate level of certainty attaches to it. This is the certainty of sight (*'ayn al-yaqīn*; Q:102:7), gained by personal inspection, as expressed in the questionable motto 'Seeing is believing'. A self-authenticating visual experience with this degree of certitude is the vision of hell – one of the Quran's predictable illustrative examples (Q:102:7). The highest level is the absolute certainty of assured divine truth (*ḥaqq al-yaqīn*; Q:69:51), a truth revealed and protected against the possibility of error. It is this last certainty that Muhammad has in virtue of his office.

Was Muhammad then sincere but mistaken or insincere and mistaken? A deliberately insincere, consciously dishonest, and misguided Muhammad might have been lured by the love of power, fame and glory, temptations that are hardly exceptional in the hierarchies of the religious life.[16] Dismissing Muhammad as an insincere imposter was never a convincing account of the origins of a major world faith. Many *engagé* (morally committed) Jews and Christians still feel religiously obliged to believe the worst about him. The dismissal of the Arabian iconoclast as consciously dishonest is a polemical accusation that moves beyond all impartial and defensible, let alone convincing, historical judgement. A sincere but misguided Muhammad is the most charitable modern explanation. Muhammad acted in good faith – but no amount of sincerity can change error into truth.

6

The Quran focuses on the sincerity of the messenger and on the truth and urgency of the message he brings. A modern verdict about the validity of claims to revealed insight is based only partly on moral considerations about the content of the message or the character of the messenger. Our modern concerns are more fundamental and preliminary: the coherence and intelligibility of the message and the precarious contingency of its historical setting as this bears on the question of its allegedly eternal truth and universal scope. The assessment of a prophet's character in a psychologically aware age is an equally demanding task partly because the problem of truth is more 'medicalized'. Competent modern judges, intending to give a truthful verdict, must consider psychological capacities and possibilities of self-delusion, neurosis, even psychosis, and other less severe personality disorders. They must assess the intricacy of religious motivation. As secular students of hagiography and the psycho-biography of religious genius warn us, such motivation is not uniformly noble. More broadly still, we must weigh in the balance the ready availability of alternative and sometimes persuasive secular humanist explanations of what really took place. We should at least record the dangers in our susceptibility to the glamour of the supernatural explanation in preference to the humdrum offers of secular natural and social science.

Although doubt and rejection were common in the Prophet's time, their character and scope have drastically changed since the beginning of the Age of Reason. We now live in an aggressively secular culture which denies the plausibility, sometimes even the intelligibility of the religious outlook; the coherence, intelligibility, and truth of transcendent theism have all been meticulously interrogated. A modern school of philosophy, no longer fashionable, has held that we cannot even grasp the meaning of the religious outlook, let alone accept it as valid. The ancient anxiety about whether to grant priority to revealed faith over unaided reason[17] has been replaced by the modern realization that the two antagonists cannot coherently be ranked: the sense, the cognitive significance, of the claims made by the religious believer is in doubt. This worry is, as we see in Chapter 9, unique to our age: few experienced it in ages of revelation and enthusiasm where sinners guiltily but rarely sincerely or conscientiously rejected God.

Today we offer a psychological explanation for the continuing appeal of the prophets and couple it with an explanation of their behavioural motivation too. Let me explore these twin issues in the rest of this section and in the next. People detest doubt and crave for certainty. That is the human temptation: we lust for certain truths. Probable and plausible truths do not appeal to us though that is all we are ever capable of attaining. Moreover, personal freedom is often a burden; we prefer divine guidance. A seductive charisma surrounds those who profess absolute religious creeds. A disciple thinks: 'I cannot understand this man but somehow he knows. So, let him decide for me: I don't want to make my own mistakes'.

Prophets disdain experimental proof for their hyperbolic claims; their certainty is based on a 'revelation' vouchsafed to a single, usually isolated and lonely individual, as a consolation for an earlier period of trauma. If this sounds like a reductionist medicalization of the problem of religious knowledge, remember that the implications for the religious position are not always negative: the wounded soldier sometimes has the best view of the battle.

Depression of psychotic intensity is followed by a euphoric commitment to a utopian vision. A prophet mistakes a solution to a purely personal problem for universal esoteric wisdom. In fact, the content of his so-called revelation is a subjective confession, not a new branch of knowledge. The prophet, however, seeks to make the whole world in his own image: he offers himself to the rest of us (who are actually his equals), as a model of superior perfection. And many believe.

The revelation is seen as a gift of grace, beyond all rational criticism. A prophet may revise his own ideas but only as a result of new insights he himself experiences. He has privileged access to truth and the right to amend his opinions. All independent critics are enemies; all doubt is from the Devil who seduces us with his plausible-sounding arguments which are nothing but spiritual pornography.

A prophet's hyperbolic confidence, however, does not preclude doubt. The master has 'feet of clay'.[18] The infantile desire and need for external validation persists – as though truth were the privilege of the elect only in theory, not in practice or experience. The external validation is achieved through the unquestioning faith of many disciples and fans, never through the balanced intellectual support of friends, equals, or intelligent critics.

7

If a bearded man wearing a white sheet and sandals claims to have received a sudden revelation, our judgement about the validity of this claim cannot be sudden or instantaneous. We must patiently evaluate his routine moral deportment pre-dating the declaration of such abnormal claims, scrutinize the content of the message he brings, and examine the alleged truth of the factual, especially prognostic, supporting claims. No one either today or at the time of the 'prophet' can assess, in advance of such considerations, the status of his pretensions.

In assessing the genuineness of the man and his message, we find some criteria are shared by modern and ancient appraisals. The application of any selected criterion, however, may differ and occupy a different status in our considerations. For example, we today examine the moral credentials of a prophet in order to assess the validity of the religious message he brings because we, like his contemporaries, believe that no man is worthy of the mantle of prophethood unless he is virtuous and pure. But what counts as morally upright by today's standards sometimes radically differs from ancient judgements.

The appeal to the conspicuous moral goodness of the divine mouthpiece can be questioned. Are prophets morally outstanding by modern standards? Every ancient prophet seems fanatically attached to his spiritual ego, monomaniacal, dedicated to one cause only. Secularized modern believers do not always discern in him the virtues of honesty, sincerity and courage, let alone moral perfection. We cannot reasonably ignore the cultural chasm that separates us from societies in which the seminal figures of 'ethical' monotheism lived. Do we today find the personalities of Abraham, Moses, Saul, David, Solomon, Jesus and Muhammad morally attractive?

Modern educated (therefore partly secularized) theists would condemn the violent, megalomaniacal, and intolerant tendencies in their personalities and convictions. Men who tried to shrink their physical selves in the service of God have indulged a degree of self-praise that would be called pride if it were found in ordinary people.[19] Humility and hubris – I wish a milder word would do – took turns to kindle the flame of piety. The Quran vindicates some prophets (such as Lot and David) from the outrageous sexual accusations found in the Bible but there are scandals in the Quran too. It confirms and tacitly approves of some sanguinary details of the Torah. Moses orders the Levites to massacre sinful fellow Israelites (Q:2:54) to please Yahweh. In the Quranic version of the binding (*Akeidah*), Abraham is far too ready to lift his hand against his innocent boy.[20] Again, Muhammad's military activities are recorded, without apology, in the Quran (Q:8:67; 47:4) and in the Prophetic traditions.

In Muhammad's case, it could be said in mitigation of these charges of political and moral delinquency that it is unfair to expect the Muslim Prophet to be morally outstanding or politically tolerant (judged by modern standards) in an age in which no one else was so. But this argument overlooks the moral rule that any one, like Muhammad, who claims *ex officio* to be in advance of his times, should be judged by a standard higher than the prevalent one. For otherwise, Muslims would be unfairly allowed to light their candle at both ends: to be admired for introducing an ideal of morality in a largely immoral and barbaric age and yet excused for their immoralities on the grounds that these are merely a reflection of the times. We rightly expect divinely guided moral reformers to be ahead of their times and moreover to be considered morally excellent in all subsequent times.

8

The conventional religious appeal to the moral excellence, even perfection, of God's spokesman is, according to modern secularism, epistemologically irrelevant: the morally good man can be mistaken in his doctrinal and metaphysical claims. A believer would argue against the secular dismissal of this linkage and insist that a man's argument is as good as his character. Only an impeccably conscientious and morally trustworthy person, he contends, can guarantee a faithful transmission of the divine message. This moral impeccability is a proclamation and guarantee of the authenticity of the revelation. We must scrutinize the moral probity of the transmitters of truth as much as examining the alleged truth itself. The arbiter of cognitive soundness is the piety and sincerity of a human personality rather than any abstract and impersonal method; believers trust good men, not valid syllogisms. Authority, the believer concludes, widening his thesis considerably, is the basis of both religious and secular epistemology.[21] The Muslim believer trusts the human perfection of the Prophet; the philosopher trusts the infallibility of abstract reason. Neither stance is negotiable in the face of external critique.

We see the linkage between personal probity and objective truth in the prophetic (*ḥadīth*) literature. A sub-genre called *'ilm al-rijāl* (knowledge of the men) consists of a critical compilation of the biographies of those who transmitted the Prophetic traditions. It was assumed that, among other things, a morally good man or woman (of sound mind and reliable memory and so on) always conveyed a true *ḥadīth* report. This is a method for establishing the strength of the transmission, not the veracity of the content of the report. But for the believer the two coalesced: if it could be traced to Muhammad, then it was automatically thought to be substantively true. Modern sceptics question the truth of the content of Muhammad's claims too since only in some disciplines, such as mathematics, what is procedurally valid coincides, albeit by convention or definition, with what is true.

God's ways may encompass moral choices considered outrageous by human standards or at least beyond our understanding – though this is more of a biblical concern than a Quranic one. The Quran upholds a morally conventional and intellectually intelligible deity unlike the biblical God who, as seen in much of the Torah and in some of the paradoxical teachings of the New Testament, sometimes makes or endorses morally outrageous decisions. The Quran frequently boasts that God does whatsoever he wills (Q:11:107) but, in practice, a great deal of what he does, as recorded in the Quran, makes good sense, morally and doctrinally. Nonetheless, it is possible for the Quranic God, as sovereign, to make moral choices that disturb our moral scheme (see Q:91:14–15). One may, however, for all intents and purposes, assume that God, a morally perfect being, reveals himself only to those men and women who are either virginal containers for his holy message or become exceptionally virtuous as a result of receiving the message and the divine grace that accompanies it.

9

What is the relationship between the truth of the message and the integrity of the message? If it is true, must it be *wholly* true? Can a partly fallible scripture be authoritative? Perhaps we can legitimately create 'a canon within a canon', so that we retain only those parts of scripture that are still valid and true as assessed by modern secularized standards. Are we being intellectually dishonest when we selectively retrieve from our sacred scriptural heritage only those doctrines which we consider to be defensible in the present?

Consider this argument, popular among secularized Jews and Christians: prophetic religious teaching was only understood by the first audience because it was embodied in the historical and scientific presuppositions prevalent in a given prophet's era and culture. These presuppositions, it is conceded, have been abrogated by the progress of human knowledge. To assess the contents of a scripture, we must appreciate the original setting of the revelation: a pre-scientific, pre-literate, pre-technological culture at a late stage of religious evolution pre-dating the rise of critical history. We must, the argument continues, sternly distinguish between the religious import of scriptural claims and the largely false trappings needed to convey the message to a scientifically and historically illiterate people. Since a genuine religious message must be encapsulated in the false historical and scientific beliefs current in that age, the contention concludes, we today need to excise the false non-religious trappings and retain the residual scriptural message.[22]

In practice, the attempt to draw this distinction – to separate the true religious kernel from its false concomitant cultural husk – may beg the crucial question at stake since the distinctions between the true and false in scripture are not neat and obliging. How does one distinguish the religious message, presumed true and eternally valid, on the one hand, from a culturally specific incarnation judged to be temporary and false, unless we already know, on independent grounds, which are the true and which are the false elements in the scriptural amalgam? We are giving secular cynics a chance to tell one of their best jokes: distinctions between religious truth and secular error must have been providentially designed to coincide exactly with the wishes of religious apology in an age of reason!

Consider this cluster of criteria for verifying the truth of a revealed message:

- Revealed claims made by a prophet must not be evidently false for the modern reader or for the first audience.
- A factual teaching or prophetic prediction must not be proven false during a prophet's life-time.
- Those revealed portions of the prophetic teaching which can be humanly verified to be true must be found to be true.[23]

The application of these criteria, however, is ineffective if we simultaneously claim that a true religious message may need to be wrapped in false historical or scientific presuppositions. Let us suppose a factual claim made by a true prophet turns out to be demonstrably untrue either in his life-time or since. Why should the falsity of a factual claim made by an inspired prophet be regarded as detrimental to his religious credentials if true religious messages sometimes need to have false embodiments?

If we expurgate the religiously irrelevant falsehoods while retaining the religious truths, we are assuming that the authenticity of the religious substance can be judged independently of any decision about the truth of the surrounding non-religious paraphernalia. But is the kernel of revealed truth in a scripture so easily separated, indeed even separable, from the outer layer of falsehood? The sceptic reminds us that if a putative revelation can contain errors of astronomy and biology, there is no reason a priori why it could not contain errors of religious doctrine. If its factual claims are obsolete and untrue, why are its religious claims spared that fate?

It is uncontroversial that no reasonable decision concerning the truth of a religious message can be made without examining the surrounding non-religious context, particularly the truth of the non-religious claims being made. It is controversial, however, to decide whether the presence of *non-religious errors* in a scripture has *religious* consequences, that is, affects the religious integrity of the message. There are different types of errors in scripture and not all are equally important. We return to this anxiety in Section 12 below. We conclude here by noting that the seductively appealing distinction between a religious message and its contemporaneous non-religious presuppositions is merely theoretically tenable. In practice, drawing such a distinction presupposes the truth of the revealed message. We can salvage the truth of a revealed message but only because we assumed, from the beginning, that we knew which parts were true and which false – hardly a respectable procedure.[24]

10

In the face of an aggressive wholesale rejection of revelation as a form of knowledge, theologians in the Christian West tried to solve the problem by securing an enclave, a safe ghetto, for revelation. I will critically assess this exclusively modern theological ambition before seeing how much of it applies to Islam's uncharted encounter with the expanding estate of an aggressive secularism. As a preface to this part of the debate, we briefly trace, in this and the next section, the history of European secularism as it sought to challenge the authority of the Christian revelation.

Even before the onset of the critical nineteenth century, some Protestant exegetes exhibited marked misological tendencies: they hated a rational faculty that was perceived as too totalitarian in its ambitions. The capacity for deliberation and critical judgement, in fallen humankind, was corrupted and irreparably damaged. We see a climactic theological expression of this disaster in Karl Barth's work which expresses the early twentieth century's most anti-secular neo-orthodox dogmatic manifesto. It is epitomized in a few mottoes in his two volumes on *The Doctrine of the Word of God*. The first is *Peccator non capax verbi divini* (sinful man is incapable of the divine word); its twin is *finitum non capax infiniti* (the finite is unworthy of the infinite).[25] Sinners cannot attain revealed knowledge, let alone judge its contents; rather revelation judges us. Barth's position was a hasty and irrational reaction to positivism and the associated rise of science as the sole culturally esteemed method of acquiring knowledge.

Although it was the Enlightenment that first placed the heavy burden of rational defence of religion on the shoulders of apologists, it was the nineteenth century, the first age of serious doubt co-existing with the relics of ancient Christianity, which supplied the secular straw that broke the backbone of religious orthodoxy in the West. After Darwin, Nietzsche and Marx, the three prophets of modern secularism, entered the battle-field, the forces of tradition began to blow their trumpets of slow retreat. Few Christian writers now remember that the controversy over the precise epistemological status of problematic parts of the Bible, especially the pre-historical materials found in Chapters 1 to 11 of the first book of the Pentateuch, is both novel and fairly recent in the history of Christian exegesis. Towards the late nineteenth century in western Europe, intellectual observers, including the religious intelligentsia, were eagerly watching a straight duel between Darwinian evolution and the biblical story of creation. It is painless for clergymen to admit now that the nascent biological and zoological establishment, represented by Darwin and his supporters, won. At the time, however, the scale and the perceived future implications of this defeat traumatized conscientious Christians.

Most devout Christian thinkers sensed that their faith had suffered a heavy blow from the Darwin affair on home ground even though Christianity became almost universal in the nineteenth century, its best century, as it witnessed a fulfilment of the great evangelical commission (Matthew 28:18–20) – in the global missionary expansion of the Gospel, courtesy of European colonialism. But it was also the century of tribulation: there was Darwin and there were Nietzsche, Marx and Freud too. As the historical sense took deeper root, many knew that the search for a permanent essence of Christianity, an absolute core or foundation, was the only way to deal with the vicissitudes of an uncertain history and uncertain future. We explore this suggestion, with respect to any faith, especially Christianity and Islam, in Section 14.

In the 1950s, about a century after the hey-day of Darwinian ideas, a new era dawned in Christian thought when it became fashionable for Christians to celebrate uncritically all things modern: positive *theological* appraisals of secularization became commonplace as Christian thinkers competed with secularists to extol the virtues of the secularized outlook. The older demythologization programme was replaced by the speedy laicization of traditional Christian doctrines and moral imperatives. Many Christians argued that the victory of science over religion, won in the previous century, was empty.

This re-interpretation of what was originally a defeat was only possible in the context of a debate about the true essence of Christianity, a context that permitted the illusion that the victory of the scientific establishment over religion was not only empty but also a divine blessing in disguise. Secular critique did not damage the religious core of the ageless biblical revelation. Instead, unintentionally, it alerted modern Christians to the need for distinguishing the false cultural husk from the true kernel in which revelation was contained; one peeled away the false outer layers to find intact the true substance.

Not all Christians applaud the service performed, albeit inadvertently, by the secular critique of religious faith. Fundamentalist and neo-orthodox theologians, especially in America, insist all the more vigorously in the face of secular, sometimes mocking, scrutiny that the Bible is a corpus of factually inerrant propositions about us, God, sacred history and human salvation from the clutches of sin. In this view, scripture has, by divine fiat, an intrinsic authority independent of the inevitably hostile verdicts of secular rational scrutiny. Simple believers must simply appropriate the salvifically vital biblical truth from the verses they read; there is no need for any fallible human interpretation or selective canonization of portions of the text in the face of profane challenges.

11

Although the intellectual climate of the nineteenth century was inclement, it took the Darwin affair to clinch the case for the secular opposition. The revolutionary ideas of natural selection, mutation, and the simian origins of the human race were a direct affront to biblical views confirming the instantaneous original perfection and subsequent fixity of our species, not to mention the scriptural claim that we have no precursors in the natural world – except Adam and Eve. Humankind, the crown of divine creation, was reduced to being merely a part of nature. This implied that our mental, moral and spiritual constitution was as explicable as our physical constitution and biological needs – and all in terms of natural scientific laws or something analogous.

Charles Lyell (1797–1875), Darwin's predecessor, participated in the 1820s in the debates about reconciling the biblical account of the flood with geological findings. His seminal work on the antiquity of the earth and the uniform forces moulding it, *The Principles of Geology* (published in 3 volumes, 1830–3) influenced Darwin. Many believers of the time desperately argued that God had planted fossils in order to deliberately mislead us about the true age of our planet, reckoned to be no more than a few thousand years, according to Bishop James Usher's chronology of the creation which dates it to 4004 BCE.[26]

Darwin's doctrine endowed the concept of nature with a depth, consistency and, eventually, an autonomous application which was to be the death-warrant for the purposive interpretation of nature favoured by pre-Darwinian Christian teleologists such as William Paley. Inquiry into purposes came to be seen as futile for the prediction and control of events in nature. To predict an eclipse, it is sufficient to know its causes. Its purpose, if it has any, is irrelevant to science. Matter is governed not by purpose but by natural law.

Movements of secular thought vary in their impact on religious belief but the dramatic increase in the authority, scope and cultural esteem enjoyed by the sciences of nature and society, during the last two centuries, has directly and decisively influenced the development of both western Judaism and Christianity. In principle, it also challenges Muslims and invites them to distil an Islamic essence which alone might survive in the asphyxiating atmosphere of an aggressively confident secularism which has been canonized in the aftermath of the failure of western Christianity to control the subversive movements in the culture it has historically spawned.

The sceptical rationalism of the eighteenth century, to revert to the Christian saga, failed to damage radically the traditional Christian views of human nature and God's revelation, especially the unique dignity of humankind and the authenticity of the Bible. That larger catastrophe was reserved for the succeeding century in which the historical mentality took deeper root as thinkers supplied it with a secular metaphysical foundation. The historical study of the scriptures assumed new importance; ancient religious documents were subjected to unfettered rational inquiry with its strict canons of critical history and literary criticism. Traditional ideas concerning the authoritative integrity of scripture, belief in a pre-scientific cosmology, along with belief in miracles and divine inspiration – the entire underlying thrust of literalist exegesis – were declared untenable.

The concession that the Quran may contain some false claims has been, as we saw in Chapter 4, resolutely resisted up to this day by Muslim interpreters. Among Christian apologists, until relatively recently, we note a similar reluctance to concede that the Bible may contain errors. For Christian thinkers in the

nineteenth century, the hey-day of the debate between the ancient church and a
nascent scientific establishment, the admission of factual error in the biblical canon
was feared to be a liberty of thought that would eventually lead to the total collapse
of the authority of the Bible.

In this anxiety, they proved to be prophets. Today, from a safe distance, we
can dismiss the controversies of the nineteenth century as all sound and fury
signifying little. We can condescendingly disparage those Christian apologists as
sincere but misguided apologists who could not distinguish between the poetry of
scripture and the prose of scientific discourse, between the sublime creativity of
God and the pedestrian geology of Genesis. Given the dramatic rise of atheism in
Europe, however, one wonders whether those Christians, no less than Nietzsche,
anticipated the modern landscape which is littered with the casualties of the war
between religious tradition and supernatural faith. They showed a sound intuition in
opposing some characteristically modern ideas such as the apparently innocuous
notion of evolution defined as the ascent from inorganic physical simplicity to
animate organic complexity.[27]

12

Any believer, who endorses the autonomy and authority of secular reason, must
concede that some statements of cosmogony in the Bible and the Quran are,
empirically assessed, apparently false. More broadly, judged by secular criteria, both scriptures contain some demonstrably false or unempirical claims, a few
anachronisms and historical improbabilities, and perhaps some arguably immoral
imperatives. We explored a few of these problematic features of the Quran towards
the end of Chapter 6. Does the religious core remain intact despite such a concession about a given scripture's secular claims – that is, claims peripheral to doctrine?
Can we distil a residue of pure religious truth, purged of factually false accretions?
These accretions may be no more than culturally conditioned falsehoods unrelated
to religiously essential revealed doctrine.

Even a revealed text, written in a human language, is inevitably culture-laden.
No book, whether secular or divine in authorship, whether wholly true or partly
false, is ever culture-free. But why should culture-dependence imply fallibility and
error, especially in a revealed text? Could not a truly revealed text escape being
error-laden despite being culturally relative to its original audience?

A believer might undercut this discussion and try to dissolve the problem by
arguing that God would not want to give us a wholly true, perfectly error-free scripture in case this forces a faithful response from his otherwise free human subjects.
There is, however, no danger of this happening given the perversity of human
nature; and this move has one unintended disastrous consequence. All monotheistic scriptures teach that perverse sinners reject scriptural truth even though they
secretly recognize and acknowledge it. To be able to repudiate God's revelation is
a privilege implicit in being free and sinful. And there is no shortage of those who
have exploited this facility in every age. The defensive stratagem proposed above
can be reversed: if an error-free scripture would not necessarily compel faith or

destroy the freedom to disbelieve – since sin and perversity are the real causes of our rejection of God's truth – then what prevents God from sending a wholly true revelation? It is an unwise move that creates a greater difficulty than the one it was intended to solve. It invites speculation about the hidden motives and intentions of an inscrutable deity – which is, even by theological standards, a fruitless inquiry.

How do we deal with the problem of apparently false claims in a scripture, to turn directly to the Quran, which claims to be comprehensively true? A believer might plausibly contend that God is the kind of being who is primarily concerned with the spiritual efficacy of his revealed word, not with the factual accuracy of peripheral claims made in the attempt to convey the spiritual message. For the sake of argument, let us grant that the distinctive power of scripture does not lie in its putatively factual dimension. Perhaps it is insensitive to ask some factual questions in a religious context; it might betray a misunderstanding of the nature and scope of religion. We must not indulge the wrong kind of curiosity. We may, however, with reason, and without malice, ask whether we should tolerate all types or only some types of factual untruth in a revelation. Are some factually inaccurate claims merely harmless pious frauds perhaps similar to lies for the sake of the public good, the kind of falsehood we condone in politics?

An extreme solution, applicable more to the Bible than to the Quran, is the view of St Augustine and other patristic saint–thinkers, promulgated by Pope Pius XII in 1943 in his encyclical *Divino Afflante Spiritu* (Inspired by the Divine Spirit), a papal directive to promote critical biblical scholarship among Catholic thinkers. In a desperate attempt to account for scandalous passages in the Bible, passages not found in the much shorter Quran, the pontiff recommended St Augustine's speculation that God deliberately inserted into the Bible some claims to puzzle believers. The presence of apparent errors and discrepancies was intentional: forced to study the word of God with greater care and application, believing readers would collide with the limits of their sinful and limited understanding. This would produce, argues the Pope, a measure of intellectual humility as the readers would 'be exercised in due submission of mind'.[28] This is partly analogous to the Kierkegaardian claim that the paradox and absurdity of Christian faith encourage humility by reminding us that the certainties sought in faith are not attainable through the exercise of human faculties alone.

Although this notion of a deliberate divine contamination of scripture sounds crassly apologetic and moreover implies that God is an imposter, the proposal is not *ad hoc*. For one thing, knowledge is not, according to the priorities of traditional monotheism, considered more important than religious success or salvation. Knowledge is merely a means to an end – the eternal life with God. Moreover, one biblical passage (Psalms 7:9) implies that God tests our hearts and our minds, a passage that finds no unequivocal Quranic analogue although there are hints of it in 'We certainly put [humankind] to the test' (Q:23:30), repeated in a variety of ways (Q:2:155, 214; 7:163; 29:2–3; 33:11; 38:24, 34). Errors deliberately woven into the fabric of the revelation could be seen as a trial to test the *intellectual* mettle of the (Christian) believer. This drastic solution is not required in the milder Quranic case and could not, in any case, be defended on Islamic grounds since the Quran claims to be a rational scripture which requires neither a suspension of critical faculties nor a crucifixion of the intellect.

Someone desperate to save scriptural authority might argue that scripture should avoid, if possible, recording any facts: the aim of God's revelation is exclusively practical and morally functional. It is to show us the way to heaven rather than to satisfy our idle curiosity. Secular life has room for speculative curiosity, this contention continues, but the religious life should be focused on the attainment of salvation or religious success. A scripture would not become inauthentic if it remained silent on matters unrelated to the religious dimension of human life and destiny. In this way, it could avoid recording any facts and thus in turn necessarily avoid any subsequent falsification.

The details of this position can be worked out on the principle that scripture could attain prescience of secular scholarship in all ages by maintaining a studied, wholly deliberate, ambiguity in every non-religious claim made in it. Take an example from the problems of cosmology and the origins of life on our planet. The Bible and the Quran need not have committed themselves to any putatively factual or precise cosmological or creation details, not even in poetic form. All allusions could have been so nebulous that no subsequent science would have had any occasion to discredit the contents of either scripture.[29]

Factual errors in a putatively revealed text intensify our anxieties about the integrity of scripture. Why does God not wish to correct culturally prevalent errors of fact while he is passionately concerned to rectify the moral and spiritual deficiencies in our behaviour? It is true that revelation does not introduce new factual errors into the world-view of those who first hear it. However, even to accommodate itself to existing error, of any kind, seems wrong. Is it right to allow human beings to remain in error concerning matters of astronomy and biology, including the vital question of their origins, while meticulously correcting all moral and religious errors entertained by them? If God can send a revelation that enlightens us radically on matters of morals and spirituality, why not send a similar revelation to teach us the truths of physics and biology? A religious apologist might answer that in the face of the momentous realities of human salvation or success in the religious life, such a juvenile concern with mere facts, whether scientific or otherwise, betrays religious immaturity. Or perhaps, it might be argued, the lack of scientific sophistication on the part of the audience (both ancient and modern) makes it difficult even for God to convey certain facts and truths.

13

Sophisticated Christian, Jewish and Muslim believers acknowledge that the Enlightenment was enlightening. They concede that the advance of rational and moral thought, allied with the spectacular increase in the scope and authority of the sciences of human and external nature, have together exposed as embarrassingly fantastic, perhaps false, even incoherent, some of the traditional accoutrements of antique faith. But, they add, we can save the authentically religious core of the revelation once we note that the traditional apologetic understanding of the epistemological status of the scriptural record is defective. The geology of Genesis, like the Quranic narrative of creation (Q:2:22; 10:3; 25:59; 32:4; 41:9–12; 57:4; 67:3), is, if the scientific picture is even remotely true, a masterpiece of inaccuracy. The believer might concede that the creation stories are merely 'poetic' though such a concession is, as we saw in Chapters 4 and 5, never made by Muslims since they are, for reasons explored earlier, religiously obliged to reject the Quran as poetry.

A way to solve this difficulty is by using the scholarly technique of form criticism to differentiate rhetorical poetry from scientific or factually precise prose. The form critic tells us that scripture contains many genres, including parables, aphorisms, narratives of miracles, history and legend, myth and poetry, and so on. Mistaking poetry for prose is an error of the same order of magnitude as mistaking a parable for a piece of history. The account of creation in the Bible or the Quran was not intended to convey factual scientific information. The point of these narratives is to teach us the most fundamental religious truth: all finite things depend totally on the continuous creative activity of an infinitely powerful and wise God. If we try to extract historical or geological information by imposing a literal interpretation, we do so by ignoring the true resources of a (primarily) religious document.

A radical solution, which dissolves rather than solves the problem of arguably false claims in scripture, is found by conceding that revealed claims cannot be reconciled with a limited human understanding and its mundane logic. Revelation supersedes our rational strictures and our logic; it is not subject to potentially blasphemous human assessment. Hostile sceptical probing should be ignored. This response is reasonable so long as one accepts the religious assumptions that nourish it. We however, as early as Chapter 2, rejected these assumptions as obscurantist. Our project in this book would not get off the ground if we accepted such orthodox strictures.

Simple Muslim believers, sensing the unwelcome sceptical direction of this inquiry, quote with guilty haste and terminative emphasis some verses from the Quran in support of their certainties. The liberal influence of scientific and philosophical reflection and the challenges proposed by sceptical reason invariably place faith on the defensive. Unsurprisingly, all revealed religions discourage inappropriate kinds of curiosity. Orthodoxy encourages 'safe thoughts', the virtue known as *sophrosūnē* in Greek thought. Islamic history, for example, gives ample evidence that Muslims refuse to countenance any intellectual or emotional subtlety that could undermine Islam. This deliberately cultivated self-protective innocence safeguards faith in an age of mental adventurism. But one pays a price for that protection.

14

A more appealing way to deal with the crisis of authority in scripture is to shift the debate onto the question of the essence of a faith. This crucial concern of post-Enlightenment Christian thought was externally inspired by the findings of radical historical criticism and by secular challenges to religion. In the aftermath of such doubt, Christians began to distinguish between the quintessence of Christian belief and its supposedly incidental, historically and culturally specific, features. This was not an *ad hoc* move. In religion, other dualities include the literal and the figurative in scripture. There is also the intention versus the application of the religious law: we distinguish the spirit from the letter of the law in order to separate its intention (removal of sin, purification of the heart) from its achievement (often merely the identification of sin). Similarly, perhaps we should distinguish the permanent from the transitory in revealed doctrine.

The distinction between the essential, and hence true, religious message as opposed to its false social and cultural expression, seems deceptively simple but it is beset with complications we shall note presently. How is the distinction to be made and on what grounds? What are the presuppositions of the view that the distinction is worth making?

To begin with, the distinction between the essential and the peripheral in religion relies on a questionable interpretation of the scope of religion. Unlike, for example, science and history, religion is, like philosophy, more ambitious: it deals, in some sense, with everything. In this respect, it is unlike science (which is restricted to whatever is subject to lawful regularity) and unlike history (which deals with whatever is judged significant in the human past). The proposed distinction, to be tenable, presupposes that the cultural embodiment of a religion is in autonomous terms and forms, perhaps outside the scope and authoritative jurisdiction of religion. A religious core is wrapped in layers of independent secular material supplied by its cultural setting. This assumption begs the question about the comprehensiveness of religion for it implies that some things, such as its attendant covering and accompaniment, are outside its scope of interest and range of commandment.

Islam, as meta-religion, refuses to distinguish between the religious and the secular. It rejects the division of 'the things of God' and 'the things of Caesar', a distinction found only in religions which were, for historical reasons, Muslims would argue, forced to curb their ambitions and scope. Christianity was born in political weakness and had to canonize such a doctrine. Modern Christians make a virtue out of a weakness when they elevate a contingent quality to the status of intrinsic necessity of all genuine religion. Indeed, even in Christianity, it is applicable only to a distinctively modern conception of that religion dating to the failure of the 'Radical Reformation' (the left wing of that sixteenth-century movement) in whose aftermath the newly Reformed Churches were, like the parent Catholic Church, forced to relinquish their totalitarian hold on some aspects of life and culture, especially their supervision of nascent scientific endeavour. They had to concede essential areas of the public interest to secular rulers and civil authorities. The Enlightenment continued and completed the process when it privatized religion and permitted only an emasculated and apolitical Christianity to participate in the public life of European nation-states. Therefore, this distinction presupposes the authenticity of a post-Enlightenment model of religion.

We are not yet at the bottom of this barrel. We examine two objections to my claim that the required contrast between religious and secular can only be meaningfully formulated if religion is circumscribed in its scope and permits the autonomy of the secular.

First, someone could concede that religion is comprehensive in its range of concerns but object that the correct analogy with history and science is not supplied by religion but by theology. And theology need not be comprehensive in its scope. Let me address this objection. Religion tends towards comprehensiveness since it necessarily aims at a degree of social cohesion, an ambition that reflects the meaning of the word from its Latin origin. Religion is a communal participation in ritual (worship and prayer) even when it is centred on a form of experience that involves a personal confrontation with a divine being or holy things. Theology is an intellectual matter: an articulated, potentially rational attempt at understanding the first-order data of religion, including its rituals, practices and experiences in the light of their relation to other parts of human experience, all in terms of hypotheses and convictions about the nature of things entire. I believe that a religion does not need an accompanying theology; and Islam is an example of a religion that thrives precisely because of its freedom from an elaborate theology. But that aside, if a religion has a de facto theology, as all religions in practice do, there is no reason a priori why it should not aspire to be a supervisor of other disciplines. In that sense, nothing is outside its scope and, structurally, in terms of being an epistemological arbiter of all knowledge, theology typically has the same totalitarian intellectual ambitions as the religion it serves.

Second, modern sophisticated Christians might rejoice in making such a distinction and argue that this way of drawing the distinction between the sacred and the secular is useful – for religion. Islam and pre-Enlightenment Christianity cannot deal with secular modernism precisely because these faiths refuse to honour this division. Things are, however, not as easy as they appear for Christian believers who propose this view. How precisely, if we accept their proposal, should we delineate the ever-dwindling estate of the sacred and the ever-growing domain of the secular? How much of revelation is religiously necessary and how much of it is extra-religious and thus dispensable without loss of faithful integrity? Judaeo–Christian jettisoning of problematic scriptural claims is indefensible if not outright arbitrary and *ad hoc*. In the next three sections, we explore the entailments, for the future of religious authority, of such disavowal of scriptural claims.

15

As traditional claims in scripture are exposed as false or fantastic, the sophisticated believer is obliged to disown parts of the revelation considered suspect on rational grounds. This procedure, however, can only be respectable if the believer offers a generalized and systematic account, in advance, which explains why certain revealed claims are no longer valid. I admit there is something reactionary and conservative in my account of the authoritative integrity of revelation according to which all scripture is, necessarily, a holistic collection of doctrine and dicta, all equally true or significant; such a view implies that no part of scripture can be rejected as false or unworthy. In practice, all modern believers select their favourite canon within the canon as they sift scripture and choose to emphasize or ignore different strands. This is especially true of a long and heterogeneous scripture, such as the Bible, which has evolved as a result of changes in dicta and creeds over millennia. The Quran is a shorter, remarkably homogeneous and, barring the abrogation of a few of its verses by others, highly consistent scripture. It is therefore, even today, easier to accept it in its entirety. Indeed the earliest Muslim community wholly accepted it – and fully implemented it.

Arguably, we have an obliquely relevant and partial precedent for disowning parts of the scripture in the Quranic doctrine of abrogation (*naskh*) according to which some verses internally cancel out others (Q:2:106; 13:39; 16:101). All remain part of the final fixed canon since the words of God cannot be altered or deleted (Q:10:64). Commentators must prioritize the conflicting verses, especially legal verses about the gradual ban on intoxicants, the permissibility of gambling and other games of chance. For example, Q:5:90–1 abrogates the more permissive interim ruling at Q:2:219. Commentators use the divine authority of the whole text to annul the divine authority of part of the text.[30]

Can we find a scriptural verse which would allow us to disown parts of the revelation? This procedure would combine the Quranic doctrine of abrogation with an application of the Reformation's hermeneutical principle 'Scripture interprets itself' (*scriptura suae ipsius interpres*). This is an involved issue at the interface of Quranic hermeneutics and Islamic jurisprudence[31] but the simpler point here is that only a principled account of the limits of this sacrifice at the altar of secularism can help mitigate what is otherwise not a method but merely a mood. Jews and Christians are so inured to making frequent sacrifices at the altar of secularism that such a claim must smack of pre-Enlightenment obscurantism. Islam's confrontation with secular modernism is, however, precisely centred on this decision to refuse all sacrifices to the jealous god of secularism who cannot tolerate half-hearted concessions. If we jettison whatever offends against current secular moral, emotional or aesthetic standards, we are, from a religious point of view, guilty of seeking first the secular kingdom – and one that is forever expanding.

We need grounds, not merely motives, for establishing a co-incidence between the alleged essence of a faith and just exactly those scandals to the intellect which today's secularized and 'cultured critics'[32] will tolerate. If today we disown what we see as factually erroneous, tomorrow we will reject moral anachronisms, including scriptural claims which exalt patriarchy or condemn 'deviant' sexual behaviour. From here, it is a short step to the rejection of morally or metaphysically questionable doctrines about the nature and activity of God. It is no coincidence that, in the Christian and Jewish cases, such liberties of thought have eventually led to outright rejection of the authority of scripture.

16

Faced with the difficulties outlined above, there are no fixed a priori expectations about the correct course of action for a sophisticated theist. The discovery and reluctant acknowledgement of scientific and historical errors, contradictions, anachronisms[33] and morally questionable or outdated claims in an alleged revelation, creates an epistemological predicament with serious religious consequences. Notwithstanding the views of the sophisticated Christian Club, one has no right to assume that the only correct (or a correct) solution is found by retaining the religious core, in the pious hope that it is true, while abandoning the secular husk.

There are other possibilities. If the object of our devotion is God, not our beliefs about God, a believer should examine impartially any rival scriptures to see if these contain truly revealed doctrine. Everyone, especially the religious believer, has an irrational interest in being right all the time – but we need instead to cultivate the desire to take a rational interest in knowing the truth, wherever that might be found. A Muslim might scrutinize the Bible in favour of the Quran – though it is unlikely as the Bible contains greater puzzles and more factual errors than the Islamic scripture. The predicament itself indicates no correct solution. Because the object of our devotion is truth, even if that turns out to be atheism, we may have to abandon the very notion of revelation and thus radically remove any grounds for the puzzlement that sophisticated believers experience when studying their holy book in the light of reason, the very bright 'light' of the 'Enlightenment'.

Here is another option. If a book is accepted as the word of God, believers can always find some reason or other for the presence of occasional 'errors' in it. Theologians maintain that if there is a God, it is to be expected, a priori, that we should be puzzled in regard to some of his alleged activity in the world. He is the arcane God of faith, not the transparently intelligible deity of the thinkers. We should not then expect believers to solve every conundrum in a revealed text. The secularist dismisses this strategy as taking refuge in a convenient *exit in mysterium*, a move into mystery that demonstrates religious evasion in the face of secular critique. The charge of evasion is, however, problematic. To accuse theologians of evasion on the ground that they cannot resolve all such problems immediately is illegitimate and uncharitable. Perhaps we are smuggling standards of competence and performance suitable to wholly secular areas of inquiry where reality is merely indefinitely complex, not irreducibly mysterious.

Many believers will be tempted to abandon the sophisticated stance in favour of a simple fundamentalist handling of scripture. To avoid the pejorative connotations of this word, I define fundamentalism to be the view, whatever else the position might imply, that scripture is an authoritative and fundamental source of divinely revealed and therefore wholly correct beliefs and morals. Such a view is normally the sole prerogative of orthodoxy, neo-orthodoxy and fundamentalist options in religion. But, at least in matters of scriptural authority and exegesis, a religious modernist can also be a fundamentalist. The contrast is, in this respect, wrongly drawn.

The view that revelation is wholly correct is unfashionable among educated believers who normally seek to soften and domesticate the stark and demanding imperatives of faith. The absolutist implications of the fundamentalist position disturb sophisticated believers; they therefore hastily deride fundamentalism as a religious cul-de-sac without pausing to consider that the fundamentalist, or more accurately integralist, position which sees all scripture as wholly revealed and correct might conceal the only defensible attitude towards the *authority* of the *whole* word of God. Can we defensibly and conscientiously endorse the authority of a partly fallible and false scripture? It will not do to retort that only the inessential, that is, non-religious materials are false and therefore dispensable. If the non-religious elements in an allegedly sacred book are, under secular pressure and scrutiny, acknowledged to be false or fallible, what, apart from the self-authenticating self-confidence of faith, prevents the religious doctrines from being false too?

I have contended directly in Chapter 4 and indirectly here that the only correct attitude towards what one takes to be the word of God is that it is from God *alone*. There is a liability in this ambitious claim. Since even a prophetic contribution could in principle endanger the possibility of a totally true text, that prophetic contribution must be excluded by fiat. The Muslim exegete will resist root and branch any suggestion that the Quran is some wholesome amalgam of the divine and the human prophetic elements in synthesis. The opposed, exclusively modern, view is that the truth of a religion such as Christianity depends solely on the truth of its alleged essence and is wholly independent of the truth of any given doctrine among its constitutive doctrines. This view is, as I have shown above, open to devastating criticism.

17

Some Christian writers avoid these criticisms by appealing to a different, uniquely Christian, model of revelation. This proposed solution is not, as things stand, available to a Muslim, since, as we saw in Chapter 4, Muslims hold a strictly literal view of the Quran as the *ipsissima vox Dei* (facsimile of the divine voice). But the Islamic model of revelation could be mistaken. In any event, we should explore the proposed Christian option to see if it can in principle provide an instructive paradigm for other faiths, including Islam, seeking to secure an enclave for revelation in a secular age.

Many Christians contend that revelation is not primarily informational. Biblical verses are not, by contrast with the Muslim view of Quranic verses, God's direct formulations of divine beliefs. We should reject as juvenile the notion of God revealing himself or his will by dictating his eternally valid beliefs and commands in the unavoidably imperfect and mutable medium of human language. God discloses himself in gracious relationship with his creatures, especially his chosen people of covenant. Scripture is a written record, as the word literally means, of human encounter with God and it consists of our fallible impressions of our dealings with this infallible reality. This record is revelatory in a secondary and attenuated sense. The experience of relationship with the personality of God, the relationship with the living reality of Christ, is primarily revelatory, a view reminiscent of Friedrich Schleiermacher's theology. For Jews and Muslims, then, divine revelation assumes the form of a written document in a sacred language; for Christians it is through a self-disclosure of the personality of God as the Christ. Thus, one can be in a genuinely revelatory relationship with God even though the content of a written record of this experience – sacred scripture – is unclear and even erroneous. What matters is the messenger, not the message.

Now, even if God reveals himself in this way, we must still theorize about what it is that has thus been revealed to us: the record of what Christians have, rightly or erroneously, interpreted to be their encounter with God has to be assessed for authenticity. While the distinction between revelation *qua* self-disclosure and revelation *qua* written record of divine beliefs is tenable, it does not help to establish the authenticity of the religious experience. It is a correct but irrelevant distinction. Moreover, it is *ad hoc* and motivated by considerations other than those professed. Could there be an apologetic motive concealed in this stratagem? Only in modern times is revelation as acquaintance with the divine personality considered more fundamental than revelation as written transcript of such an alleged acquaintance. It is not a coincidence that the proposal has gained currency and popularity in the wake of two other circumstances: unwelcome discoveries in critical biblical scholarship, particularly, textual criticism, and, secondly, the unsettling findings of comparative religion, especially hostile scrutiny by a powerful rival such as Islam.

18

To end this chapter and hence Part II, we touch on a larger issue: 'What would be an honest exegesis of the Quran in the modern world, an exegesis that respects both the integrity of the revealed text and the integrity of the modern experience of the world?' Much modern Muslim reading of the Quran seeks to impress Anglo-American audiences by arguing that the scripture is not a text manacled to the past but rather one set into free motion and therefore fully abreast of contemporary developments, including 'the best of the West'.[34] A version of that attitude is seen in the notion that modern empirical science, the great symbol of western achievement, is anticipated by the Quran. We shall see it again in the 'Islamization of knowledge' programme, a theme of Chapter 12.

Before we re-examine the scientific exegesis of the Quran, we note a more general point. The frequency of Muslim attempts to find an Islam that is abreast of the highest cultural and political achievements of western civilization implies idolization of the West. Trendy Muslim exegetes are all in favour of something called western civilization even when their own acquaintance with the western shibboleths of Voltaire, opera and liberal democracy is evidently slight. Modernist exegetes seek to attach to Islam the prestige associated with current western theories and practices. They respond to liberal accusation by offering adventurous interpretations of the Quran which reject polygyny and theocracy while endorsing liberalism and democratic polity. The West becomes the measure of all things – hardly a defensible Islamic exegetical axiom.

We examined in Chapter 6 one appropriation of modern science according to which the Islamic scripture not only stimulated curiosity about nature, it advanced actual scientific claims well before the age of science. Classical commentators believed, as we saw in Chapter 5, that the Quran frustrates anyone trying to imitate its style and content. This conception of the incapacitation (*I'jāz*) of the book has recently been, informally, extended by Muslims who detect in the Quran a prescience of recently discovered scientific learning. They argue that the scripture has subtly concealed for centuries scientific claims that must now be decoded.

Such a view, through its topical and fashionable obsession with a triumphant science, denigrates the religious and spiritual resources and capacities of revelation; it prostitutes revelation. This way of establishing the authority of scripture relies, ironically, on an appeal to the authority of science which is in turn a disguised appeal to the authority of secular reason. Secular humanists rightly dismiss this as an apologetic move to keep religion, wounded but defiant, in the battlefield at a time when a youthful scientific establishment has vanquished a rather senile religious interpretation of the world.

Believers do not consistently appeal to the criterion of compatibility with current scientific knowledge. The appeal is not principled but *ad hoc* and desultory. If the Quranic claims seem to tally with modern scientific views, religious believers are ecstatic since their faith receives a boost from the most prestigious and culturally esteemed contemporary intellectual enterprise. If there is a discrepancy between the two, it is argued that the hypotheses and theories currently prevalent in the scientific community are, as it happens, erroneous. On occasion, it is also admitted that secular scientific truths, like other rationally discovered truths, are irrelevant to judgements about the veracity of revealed claims. The variety of such reactions betrays confused and dishonest attitudes towards the authority of scripture as well as a shallow and opportunistic view of science.

At a basic but subconscious level, believers sense that a *consistent* application of this criterion amounts to an exacting demand upon revelation: the Quran's authority becomes necessarily and always dependent upon its ability to achieve conformity with current scientific scholarship. The stringency of this requirement inhibits believers who wish to recruit scientific findings for religious ends. If believers celebrate the authority of the word of God whenever science corroborates the scientific findings concealed and implicit in the Quran, then it is science rather than revelation that is the measure of all things. Science becomes the measurer of all reality, including religious reality. Supernatural religion is defeated once the eternal authority of a revealed canon depends on the mutable cultural superiority of empirical science, an enterprise that replaces a dying Christianity and, along with liberal democracy, provides a new foundation for western society.

Part III

A Quranic Lebenswelt
in a secular age

8   A sign is enough – for the wise

1

The Quran contains magnificent praise of God, edificatory and monitory accounts of sacred history, systematic critiques of the 'deviant' monotheisms of Judaism and Christianity, and legal provisions written in sapid prose.[1] Part of its literary prowess is, however, focused in passages that speak of an artfully concealed divine providence, permeating nature and human nature, mysteriously undergirding the fragile human enterprise. The Quran repeatedly mentions 'signs' (*āyah*; sing.; *āyāt*; pl.) of God as manifestations of the divine presence in the world but transcending it. A universal system of such signs, runic tokens symbolizing divine generosity and mercy, encompasses us in external nature, history and society and, inwardly, in our nature and humanity (Q:2:164; 14:32–4; 16:10–16, 66–7, 79–81; 40:13; 45:3–5, 12–13). Constant and continuous intimations of the transcendent are conveyed evasively to us through the 'open books' of nature and history in addition to God's explicit revelation of his will in the privileged form of language, especially in the finality of the Arabic Quran.

Nature's flawless harmonies and the delights and liabilities of our human environment, with its diverse and delicate relationships, are invested with religious significance (Q:30:20–5, 46). Created nature is a cryptogram of a reality which transcends it: nature is a text to be deciphered. Evidences accumulating in the material and social worlds and in the horizons of history jointly point to a hidden immaterial order. The Meccan Quran uses the particle *wa* (by) to take oaths in the name of a range of natural and social phenomena including the compelling realities of transience and human moral self-awareness, all seen as divine signs (Q:51:1–5; 56:75; 74:32–5; 75:2; 77:1–7; 79:1–5; 84:16–18; 85:1–3; 86:1; 89:1–5; 91:1–10; 92:1–4; 93:1–3; 95:1–4; 103:1). The Quran locates the signs on two major axes: in the cyclical phases and periodicities of nature (Q:36:37–40) and in the linear continuity and progress of sacred history from Adam to Muhammad. Divine hints and clues embedded in the world enable us to discern God's transcendent presence and dynamic power in external and in human nature, society, history, and the inner self (Q:51:20–1; 88:17–20). So prevalent are the signs that Muslim mystics visualize the entire universe as a mosque (lit., a place of prostration; *masjid*; sing., *masājid*, pl.; used often, e.g. at Q:7:31, 9:17), and nature as its main entrance.

In this chapter, we assess the Quranic demand that human beings must comprehend the sacred significance of their curiosity about their location in this subtly concealed but comprehensive social and natural network of divine mercy and providential provision. It will introduce a dimension of the Quranic mind relevant to the persistent ambiguities and ambivalences of our current secular situation characterized by chronic uncertainty about a divine presence in the world. This is also the proper context for examining the relationship between Islamic monotheism and the emergence of modern secular science. We conclude with observations on the consequences of a perceived ambiguity in nature, including the need for a natural (rational) theology which could dispel some doubts about the existence and activity of God, a project carried forward into Part IV.

2

The complete descent of the Quran by 632 CE marks the end of the age of revelation (Q:5:3; 33:40) and the beginning of the age of realization. The religious evolution of our species is complete and humankind has reached the age of spiritual majority. (It is a refined irony that the same claim is made by modern atheists who suggest that, in view of our maturity, we no longer need God.) The verses of the Quran consummate and terminate revelation (Q:7:185; 77:50); God has spoken clearly, decisively, comprehensively, and, therefore, finally. Muhammad, as the seal of the prophets, warns of the final judgement and brings the good news of divine mercy. His appearance closes the penultimate chapter in history. God will no longer speak as revealer through his spokesmen. One day, he will speak again, as judge, and requite us for our good or evil.

There are two orders of revelation. The Quran, written revelation preserved as *al-kitāb masṭūr* (the inscribed book; Q:17:58; an inscribed book; Q:52:2; cf. Q:33:6), supplements the unfolded (or open) scroll (*raqq manshūr*; Q:52:3), the disclosure of divine power and mercy through the created natural order. One reads the signs from the index of nature, the open book of God, as the deists call it. But the signs are not parables. A parable (*mathal*; sing; *amthāl*, pl.) is a literary device, a narrative, not an event.[2] Nonetheless, the word *āyah* refers both to the verses of the Quran, a literary reality, and to those natural and significant social events and realities which mediate the divine signs. The Quran prefers the neologism *āyah* to the normal word *'ajībah* (*'ajā'ib*; pl.) which means strange or extraordinary realities; its verbal root (*'a/ja/ba*) is conjugated and its derived adjective declined in the Quran. In secular literature, *'ajībah* refers to the natural and humanly crafted marvels and novelties found in nature, architecture, and society.[3] Muslims consider it blasphemous to use *āyah* to refer to works of human ingenuity.

Only thoughtful human beings discern the clue encoded in the tangible material signal. Created nature and the social environment have an intrinsically religious character that is easily discerned but also easily ignored. The intelligent believer, however, detects the encompassing presence of a compassionate providence that counteracts the arrogant impiety and folly of the majority of humankind

(Q:36:33–46; 40:13). Some signs are exclusively for believers (Q:15:77; 48:20) but most are catholic in their relevance. A few signs are directed at the Quraysh, Muhammad's tribe, reminding them of the divinely preserved Meccan sanctuary whose safety enables trade and prosperity in all seasons (Q:28:57; 29:67; 106:1–4).

Nature is properly perceived and deciphered only by the power of reason guided by faith. Believers must therefore educate their religious instincts in order to recognize the intended significance of these signs. Sustained reflection on these signs, unlike scientific curiosity or philosophical speculation about natural events, should be continuous with practice, informing and deepening the practical life of faith. Natural regularities can be detected without scientific training or disciplined observation: pre-scientific, pre-technological, humanity noted the rising of the sun and the change of seasons. The Quran implies that not only is there enough concealed evidence to persuade scientists who professionally probe and decode the mysteries of the material natural environment but rather that the existence, wisdom and power of the creator are manifest to all sincere seekers who use their sight and reason (Q:67:3–4).[4] The scripture alerts us to the constantly miraculous divine presence concealed in *routine* natural events and phenomena in a divinely created and organized universe (Q:2:164; 3:190–1; 6:97–9). The pedestrian reality of the diurnal and nocturnal are 'a pair of signs' (*āyatayn*; acc. dual; Q:17:12). For the Quranic mind, it is only the irrational eye that looks intently at the world without any clue or perspective to guide it.

Remarkably, 'Read the signs!' does not occur as a complete imperatival sentence in the Quran. Perhaps it would be too blatant since a sign is already enough – but only for the wise, obedient and penitent believer who responds with admiration knowing that God did not create the heavens and earth 'without purpose' (*bāṭilan*; Q:38:27). A sign is sufficient for 'those who understand by tokens and hints' (*al-mutawassimīn*; Q:15:75).

God establishes his signs despite human neglect and satanic hostility to their proper appreciation by human beings (Q:22:52–3). Most people wantonly misread and despise these easily discerned and dependable tokens of God's kindness and goodness (Q:6:95–100; 34:15–19). Few people are appreciative and attentive when observing the regularities of nature; most are heedless, callous and ignorant. Even the sagacious and educated may be illiterate with respect to the divine signs (Q:29:38). The obtuse mistook them for sorcery (Q:7:132); most of the ancients were deluded by a paganism which seduced them with its false gods and the unreliable technique of magic.

In the face of pagan hostility or for their own satisfaction, prophets sometimes request such signs (Q:2:260; 3:41; 19:10). Occasionally, God authorizes a prophet to perform a miracle – a divinely planned and prophetically executed spectacular derogation of natural law. The declared aim is to weaken and discountenance the hesitation to believe, to soften the hearts of perverse disbelievers who habitually overlook the unique God's ubiquitous presence mediated through a reliable sustaining providence. In Chapter 9, we see how those who persistently contemn the comprehensive variety of divine signs, whether routine or miraculous, become in due time justly the victims of divine wrath (Q:25:37).

3

We record the range of Quranic uses of *āyah*. A finite and familiar nature is saturated with indications and intimations of the infinite and mysterious divine presence. The signs can be divine favours and blessings or natural phenomena which facilitate human life, ranging from the providential arrangements of family and social life to the refinements, comforts and luxuries of both settled and nomadic existence (Q:16:10–1, 14, 66–9, 72, 80–1; 30:20–3; 36:33–7). Facilities such as vessels of transport, including ships and beasts of burden in a natural order made subservient to us, provide the staples of the divine signs (Q:14:32–4; 16:5–8; 17:70; 30:46; 36:41–2, 71–3; 40:79–81; 42:32–4). The Quran lists human sperm and the farmer's seed, metonymies for germination in society and nature, along with water and fire, as phenomena outside human control, realities that should elicit wonder and gratitude (Q:56:58–73).[5] Water, considered essential to all life (Q:21:30; 25:54), also regenerates a dead earth (Q:43:11). That the same water should irrigate all crops while the yield and the taste of the fruits differ is cited as a sign (Q:13:4).

The signs can also be exemplary miraculous punishments intended to teach humility to sinners and to warn believers of the ever-present possibility of divine anger (Q:2:66; 17:59). The empty and ruined houses of dead sinners are, like Noah's ark carrying a remnant of humanity (Q:36:41), an instructive sign (Q:27:52; 29:15). The Quran refers summarily to plagues that afflicted Pharaoanic Egypt as 'the self-explanatory signs' (*āyāt mufaṣṣalāt*; Q:7:133). The signs can be punitive hints or gracious reminders; both point equally to the underlying transcendent framework of nature and daily life.

The word *āyah* denotes a vast range of events and situations. Like God, the signs of God are omnipresent, varying from self-evident to subtle events in nature and culture. The range shows a poetic sensitivity to nature in its seasons and many moods. The Quran notes the tempers of natural forces, the winds that fecundate the flowers (Q:15:22), the luxuriant orchards (Q:27:60; 36:34) and gardens with trees bowed down with fresh fruit (Q:6:99, 121; 50:7; 78:16), even the ripening of fruit on the day of the harvest (Q:6:99). All are God's signs and favours. Although the Arabs were not then a maritime nation, the Quran frequently refers to ships sailing through the sea and appearing 'as lofty as mountains' (Q:42:32; 55:24). The wind that enables the motion of the ships, a natural force with its ambiguous potential to bring a storm or bring the travellers to a safe haven, is a staple of the signs related to travel (Q:42:32–4) despite the fact that this experience was not part of the audience's life. The only events omitted are those that were absent from the experience of any human being at the time; a Quran revealed today would perhaps invite our awe in the face of the pregnant silence of the empty spaces between the galaxies.[6]

We tend to think that a miracle qualifies as a token of the transcendent since it ruptures the normal order of mechanical causation. On the contrary, the course of nature, in the form of regular, predictable, dependable, and thus routine sequences is also miraculous. The day turns into night, the sun rises in the East and sets in the West, the clouds collect moisture and then release rain thereby reviving the dead earth (Q:2:164; 41:39). These natural events are also divine portents, not reducible to natural occurrences. Mundane realities bespeak a divine presence: the apparent death of the soul in sleep (Q:39:42), the inclination to like a member of the opposite sex (Q:30:21), and a human personality seen as an index to higher truths.[7]

4

A trio of considerations will enrich this discussion: the definition of nature, the range of Quranic vocabulary connected with the notions of sign and signal, and a comparison with the Christian notion of sacrament.

If we define nature as external reality, as the sum of phenomena, including their causes and the capacities within these causes to produce other phenomena, it would include animals, plants, and landscapes. We can also define nature as everything that occurs without the voluntary agency of human beings. This corresponds to the distinction between 'natural' and 'artificial', art being the transformation of the spontaneous course and order of nature under the influence of human volition and action.[8] The Quran has no single word to denote nature in either of these senses. The scripture refers to 'whatever is in the heavens and the earth and all that is between them and all that is underneath the soil' (Q:20:6). The root *qa/da/ra*, conjugated as a verb and declined as a noun (Q:15:21; 27:57; 42:9; 43:11; 77:22–3), creates words associated with fate, measured power, measured capacity and nature. The word *taqdīr* (decree or ordinance) describes the perfect balance of power in nature as shown, for example, in the heavenly bodies held firmly to their ordained orbits (Q:6:96; 36:38; 41:12). The derived word *qudrā*, not in the Quran, is used, in Islamic languages which derive their vocabulary from Arabic, to refer to material and measurable external nature. *Taqdīr* and *qudrā* imply equilibrium of physical power and moral value. Muslim philosophers used *al-kawn* for the universe and natural growth; the modern word for the natural universe is *kaynāt* related to *kaynūnah* (existence), both derived from the auxiliary verb *ka/wa/na* ('to be').

Second, only an *āyah* is a sign in a semiotic and symbolic sense. The word has a uniquely religious significance. In one idiosyncratic usage, it means a monument or other outstanding human achievement (Q:26:128), a usage that resembles the secular sense of the marvelous captured by *'ajībah*, already mentioned. The Quran uses almost a dozen other words to capture different nuances:

- Sign-posts or marks (*'alāmāt*; pl. Q:16:16) in the context of measurement.
- Gestures that signal intention. As Zechariah stood outside the sanctuary, he used sign language to convey his meaning (*awḥā ilayhim*; lit., he inspired them; Q:19:11).
- Clarification of intentions 'by use of gestures' (*ramzan*; acc., Q:3:41).
- The ostensive gesture (*ishārah*) of Mary pointing to the infant Jesus (*ishārat ilayhi*; 'she pointed towards him'; Q:19:29).

- *Sha'ā'ir Allāh* denotes signs or symbolic rites of God in connection with pilgrimage rituals (also called *manāsik al-ḥajj*; Q:22:32, 36; see also Q:2:198; 5:2).
- *Āthār*: traces, remnants or relics (*āthārah*; sing. at Q:46:4; *āthār*, pl. at Q:30:9; 40:21, 82; *āthārāt*; pl. of pl. at Q:30:50).
- *'Ibrah* (Q:12:111; 16:66), meaning an instructive lesson, a sense close to that of a parable. This word partly replicates the religious meaning of *āyah*.
- *Dhikr* (lit., mention, remembrance or symbolic allusion; Q:19:2) can mean in effect an *āyah* (e.g., at Q:39:21); the related words *tadhkirah* (memorial; Q:69:12, 48; 73:19) and *dhikrā* (reminder; Q:11:114; 50:8) can also mean a warrant or an *āyah*.
- *Tabṣirah* (insight; Q:50:8) is related to the sense of *āyah*.
- Modern standard Arabic uses additional words.[9]

Third, belief in sacraments along with the symbolic realism of Roman Catholic and Eastern Orthodox Christianities is foreign to Islam. In the Eucharist, for instance, one thing represents something which is not that thing but for which it stands. The material element participates in the power and reality of the holy reality that is represented; a sacrament is symbolic and representative, an outward sign of an inward spiritual grace. The word *sacramentum* originally referred to the act of joining oneself by oath to a contract, an agreement that involved divine participation. A sacrament is therefore more than a human oath: it is an effective sign of divine power. Signs of God (*vestigia Dei*), however, in Islamic and Christian theology, are not symbolic or revelatory of God's *nature*; typically they are representative of God's power or mercy.

In Islam, the above limitation is absolute: a sign of God can be participatory of his power and goodness but it can never be a disclosure of his essential nature or moral nature. This limitation is imposed in order to avoid the misguided deification of nature which the Quran castigates as idolatry or *shirk*, the Quranic word for the wrong kind of association of God with creation. While dissimilar from a sacrament, the Quranic sign of God resembles the biblical notion of theophany where an aspect of the divine inhabits a natural site and transforms it. We return to this dimension of the debate in the next section when we examine the link between the signs of God and pagan animism.

This theme of sign–sacrament is connected to Islam's broader and ultimate conceptualization of the universe. Islamic consciousness is, in theology as in art, critical and iconoclastic, hence largely asymbolic, aniconic and deconstructionist: it insists that no symbol can apprehend the ultimate reality of God, the truth of his essential nature.

5

The Quran encourages us to read off from nature the spiritual meanings inherent in creation. In what follows I employ sign and symbol interchangeably although some theologians try, unsuccessfully, to neatly distinguish the two. A sign in logical, mathematical and scientific contexts is fixed in intention, and stable and transparent in meaning and significance; equivocation in the use of a sign in such contexts is prohibited. Signs can function as symbols in religious contexts: a primary meaning, the letter, grounds or tethers a more controversial secondary meaning, the spirit, which arises out of the primary meaning. Symbols are inevitably equivocal, meaning different things to different interpreters[10] since their meaning and significance are not fixed unilaterally by their user. The amount of meaning they convey varies with the interpreter. They can also be misunderstood. Signs are symbols with conventionally fixed meanings; equally, symbols are signs with conventionally fixed meanings. The debate is purely verbal.[11]

Reading and interpreting signs is a distinctively human activity; we learn to discern meaning in our environment as we interpret ourselves to ourselves and to each other. Reading signs and symbols is antecedent to our capacity to acquire and use language. We are interpreters of the hint. Perhaps what differentiates us from the lower orders of animals is not speech – parrots and monkeys talk and chatter in some sense – but rather our tendency to discern symbolic significance in material events and realities. Dogs and cats show evidence of ingenuity and intelligence; many animals, no less than human infants, can communicate their needs by making noise (such as braying and neighing) and by making gestures. But none can use symbols to conceptualize realities not immediately present to the senses.

The idea that X stands as a sign of Y is a tenacious intuition in human beings as they negotiate with their environment, in its physical, social, and natural complexity. We attend to signs – signs of rain, certainly, but also signs of happiness or anger or, most abstractly, signs of the times. We read the morning newspaper, a letter from a friend, a recipe on a cereal box. We attend to practical or coercive signs which guide conduct: traffic signals, flashing neon lights, signs indicating proximate danger and forbidden zones in public places, indicators on the car panel warning of temperature, oil, speed, and other relevant changes and indices. We give signs and signals to indicate intentions that affect others. The immensity of this range is revealing of our nature as meaning-seeking creatures: a cloudy sky (indicating a rainy afternoon), a firm handshake (signifying the promise of friendship), a footprint or broken twigs in a forest (alerting us to the proximity of humans and animals), the thunderous roar of an approaching vehicle (making one anticipate a truck around a corner), a cry of pain (suggesting danger and sentient suffering), the price markers at an expensive fashion store (as concrete evidence of inflation), and so on.[12]

We encounter confusion and ambivalence when the signs lack universally or conventionally accepted meaning. The setting of the sun might be an occasion for giving glory to God but it is not an uncontroversial symbol or sign of that glory. Events in nature are complex and ambiguous signs which contain many layers of significance, being no less fertile and suggestive than words with multiple connotations: the moon in its varied appearances can be studied as part of natural science, pagan folk-lore, and of the psychology of poetic and artistic inspiration. Simpler signs do not contain such a range of significances. A red traffic signal might be ambiguous and thus fail to guide us but its primary meaning is settled entirely by convention though not necessarily an arbitrary one since there are, in choosing the colour red, some considerations about the psychological capacity for immediate recognition of clear and present danger.

A sign of God is a particular manifestation, in the material, natural or social world, of a reality that transcends that order of reality, that world. It is, paradoxically, immanent at one level and, on another level, transcendent. This appears contradictory but the contradiction dissolves when we note that a thing X transcends another thing Y when X goes beyond Y, not when it is wholly distinct from it. This is, using Platonic terminology, analogous to the idea of a universal form transcending a particular instance of it in the world: particular blue objects partake of the concept of blueness without being either wholly identical with or wholly distinct from the entity called blueness. The form of blueness is grasped through a particular finite number of instances of blue but cannot be identified with them.

For Muslims, nature does not resemble God. To detect God's wisdom and power or image in what is not God, indeed in what is unlike God, requires the intelligence of a human being, the only creature made to be fully capable of such discernment. Finite realities can display traces of the infinite God, traces which do not resemble his nature but can nonetheless signal his presence. They direct us towards a God whom they could never represent in his essence – just as the ciphers and figures in mathematics and the words in language bear no direct resemblance to the realities to which they refer. Nor are the signs sacramental: the signalling event does not participate, whatever that means, in the divine nature.

The Quranic view of nature as the locus of the divine signs is not intended to give vitality to an animist interpretation of the external world. If the earliest philosophy of nature entertained by our ancestors was a belief in an indefinitely diffused and amorphous power or influence, the second stage was perhaps localization and dispersal of this single mysterious power so that nature was viewed as being filled with innumerable spirits, thus making all of nature alive and animate. Arabian paganism is compatible with this perspective according to which all natural phenomena had, so to speak, a soul. Thus, trees, streams, sand-dunes, oases, hills, and other natural features of the landscape were thought to be the dwelling places of spirits. These were the jinn, important elemental beings (Q:72:1–19) who remained part of the Quranic cosmology albeit as subordinate to the supreme God. The presence of these elemental spirits and the now discarded animism of Arabian paganism are, however, both unrelated to the much subtler intellectual invitation to penetrate nature's appearances in order to discern a transcendent divine presence and activity – the challenge of the signs.

The category of sign of God stands at the interface of direct and indirect divine communication because the sign, as divine portent and sign-post, has a transcendent reference while being rooted in the earthy reality of the material environment. The signs resemble good works as both are like 'the good tree whose root is firmly fixed on earth while its branches reach heaven' (Q:14:24). The revelatory reality or event *qua* sign of God indicates a meaning that surpasses its finite form as an individual or sequential thing or event but it cannot represent the divine content with clarity, let alone exhaust its meaning. The signs are directive and suggestive, never compelling or coercive. This will prove problematic in an age of secular doubt, as we shall see presently.

6

Since classical monotheism emerged in cultures without empirical science, no distinction was drawn between the laws of physical nature and the normative signs of God, just as no culture inspired by monotheism has, until the advent of secularism, distinguished the moral from the religious (or spiritual) aspect of life. (We noted the rupture of the ethical–religious liaison in Chapter 3.) What was once called a divine ordinance would now be seen as a lawful natural regularity (or perhaps natural persistence or recurrence). The movement of the clouds and the setting of the sun are now studied in meteorology, not theology. For the ancient believer, the constitution of nature was experienced as a synthesis of the natural and normative. The very fabric of the observable world was both religious and moral and hence grounded the objectivity of religious and moral values. Natural laws were not discontinuous with God's purposes and intentions expressed in nature – even if natural law and divine purpose were not identical.

The fact–value distinction, like the antagonistic dichotomy of humankind versus nature, emerged in the mid-seventeenth century in Europe.[13] The fact–value dichotomy enabled the growth of modern observational science but it also undermined religious belief because it implied that religious (along with moral, aesthetic and other) values were not immanent in the external environment. Values became problematic and merely subjective while facts remained objective and determined reality. The elimination of purposes, goals and forces allegedly operating inherently in the observable and measurable realm was the crucial step towards the achievement of autonomy for nature. The world became an autonomous reality; its character was morally and metaphysically neutral, thus value-free. There was no need to assume that there was a sustaining agency behind nature: the cosmos was functionally independent of God, even if he existed and acted.

Modern empirical science has taken the final step in the desacralization of nature for two reasons. First, it has avowedly eliminated God because there is no need for such a hypothesis; second, subconsciously, it has removed God because a transcendent being acting in the spatio-temporal continuum might, through miraculous interventions, especially surreptitious ones, complicate and hinder the scientific task of discerning the normal regularities in the natural world.[14]

7

The Quranic notion of the signs of God, as reliable indices of the divine craft, implies an optimistic epistemology: the truth is veiled but potentially manifest since it reveals itself to the devout and intelligent observer and seeker. While God himself is mysterious, his will for us is evident. As the inaugural revelation declares, humankind has been blessed with the power to discern truth and acquire knowledge (Q:96:3–5).

This is a suitable context in which to ask: What is the relationship between the emergence of empirical science and the seventh century Islamic revelation which stimulated an intense interest in the signs of God understood as the discernible patterns and sequences of external nature? In Chapter 6, we rejected as puerile the notion that the revelation of the Quran was intending even in part to supply detailed scientific learning, and that enigmatically, to a generation placed one and a half millennia later in the stream of history. However, the Quran did inspire curiosity about nature's workings and unintentionally facilitated the modern achievement of autonomy for nature, an autonomy presupposed by the secular scientific method. It is a justified Muslim boast that Islam gave a major impetus to the development of modern observational science.

How did Quranic monotheism inspire and promote the nascent scientific establishment of the Arab Muslims and the talented peoples they conquered? Did the Quran intend to arouse reflective and deliberative consideration of nature? To answer these questions, it is pertinent to relate another aspect of the Quranic narrative about the appointment of Adam as God's deputy on earth. Adam is taught the essences (*asmā'*; lit., names) of things, an indication of the human capacity for naming and hence the ostensive use of language (Q:2:31–3; cf. Genesis 2:19–20). This Quranic passage is perhaps referring to the uniquely human gift for scientific classification of material objects: the angels, when asked, by God, to name the same (unspecified) objects, predictably admit their ignorance (Q:2:31–2).

The biblical and Quranic revelations reassure us that nature is purposively created and hence intelligible, thus making science possible and the works of technology accountable. The rational perception of the orderliness of nature is possible because nature has an antecedent structure. By contrast, a metaphysic such as Taoist pantheistic naturalism disables science by stipulating that the real causes of natural patterns, though present in them, are occult and unknowable. Additionally, science could only arise in a world-view that did not treat the world as an illusion. India, the birth-place of several faiths seeking release from this illusory material world, has produced no scientific tradition.

Apart from providing this metaphysical backdrop of an intelligible and authentic reality, monotheism enabled science in three ways, one unique to Islamic monotheism and two common to western monotheism. We gauge the specifically Islamic contribution by discerning the motives behind the Quran's emphatic condemnation of pagan polytheism and the magical techniques associated with it. Magic and necromancy are outlawed in Islamic law derived from Prophetic traditions; the Quran also denigrates sorcery (Q:2:102; 20:69). Presumably, magic is castigated because it is a misguided method inspired by false religion. Magic fails to compensate for the pagans' ignorance of the ways of nature. It is moreover a pseudo-technique; therefore, one cannot improve it or recruit it in order to construct a reliable technology.

Second, a negative point: paganism cannot achieve satisfactory knowledge of the world since it is the battleground of capricious rivalries between opposed deities. Polytheism, asserts the Quran, results in chaos in the heavens and the earth (Q:21:22). If there had been many gods, each god would have taken away his share of creation and a hierarchy of divine beings would have inevitably emerged (Q:23:91). Polytheism is then inherently disorderly and unstable; it patronizes a disorder that frustrates rational intelligibility. Only a single creator liberates us from the irrational and unpredictable whimsicalities of the fragmented pagan chaos.[15]

Third, a positive point: an awareness of God's unique sovereignty in nature enabled the unification of the experienced cosmos and gave an objective basis to the sense of perceived regularity on which science rests. The believer can confidently, as worshipper and inquirer, rationally and systematically seek to understand an order that is intelligently supervised. Our grasp of natural reality presupposes a stable regularity of perception which is in turn grounded in the assumption that reality is a rational structure which is in principle accessible to human reason. Monotheism grounds this assumption in the creative and partly knowable will of God.

Though not unscientific or anti-scientific, the Quranic cosmology is nonetheless pre-scientific. If it were opposed to science, we would not be able to explain the historical fact that Islamic civilization is the cradle of mature empirical science. The Quran inspired Muslims to investigate nature's secrets; this eventually led to the establishment of the institutions of modern experimental science. Part of this achievement was inspired by the Muslim transmission of classical Greek learning to the Latin West.[16] Some inchoate tension persisted between the orthodox custodians of official Islam and the talented Muslim polymaths who were at once thinkers, poets and empirical scientists. In particular, orthodoxy banned surgery on human persons and the exhumation of corpses. Religious law outlawed the mutilation of bodies for medical research; the integrity of the corpse was required for a proper burial as the dead person awaited the physical resurrection.

Official Islam was never as implacably opposed to the rise of science as the medieval Church. There was no Muslim equivalent of a scientist such as Galileo – who was reassured by the Church that science was its legitimate daughter but one who must not rebel against her long-suffering father. Nonetheless, there was suspicion among orthodox Muslims about an enterprise which was perceived to be inspired by forces outside the Quran. For devout believers, the Quran is directly the source of every significant true belief and worthy enterprise. While the development of religious law and the establishment of the caliphate found some Quranic warrant, it required much sophistry to argue that enterprises such as philosophy and science were expressly sanctioned by revelation.

To summarize our thesis thus far: a rudimentary science of nature's secrets equipped the believer with the means to understand, control and exploit nature, within certain moral limits, and to develop a reliable if primitive technology. Science does what magic merely intends and pretends to do. Unlike magic and sorcery, the religio-scientific attitude towards nature enabled a more active management of experience – a management based on trust in the consistency of nature.

8

Nature is the most ancient locus of mystery in religious and pagan cultures. The Quran claims that nature contains mysterious (but not magical) hints about a hidden order of reality and meaning. Nature can today be seen either as a machine or as a place of moral and teleological value. If it is the locus of the signs that mediate God's presence and greatness, our relationship to it cannot be wholly defined as subject to object (as it is in empirical science) but rather essentially as subject to subject since the personality and power of God are mediated through it.

This subject-subject perspective explains why a relatively developed Islamic science remained free of the undercurrent of scepticism and value-freedom that marked western science even in its infancy. European science eliminated the purposive interpretation of nature as a necessary prerequisite of the scientific enterprise. A scientifically minded madman, armed with Occam's razor, cut out of the fabric of the world all intrinsic and ultimate values, imperatives, teleologies, qualities, immaterial entities, beings superior to humanity, and transcendent minds. The more intelligible the universe became, the less meaningful it became in human and evaluative terms, reflecting an inverse relationship between intelligibility and meaning. By contrast, Islamic science wanted to preserve the link between intelligibility and significance: the Quran ensured that the more intelligible the universe became, the greater the perception of purpose within it. In this way, the Quran patronized the new scientific impulse founded on secular curiosity but also harnessed it towards the discernment of divinely ordained value in nature, an arrangement that prevented science from becoming value-free and ultimately nihilistic.

Max Weber (1864–1920) noted that the modern supremacy of institutionalized science, natural and social, has eliminated objective meaning by reversing the relationship between philosophical reason and sociological rationality, between substantive and formal (instrumental) rationalities. Calculations of efficiency are no longer controlled or limited by over-riding moral values. Rather, substantive moral norms are judged by instrumental reasoning. A technical and value-free assessment is given without regard to the human or moral cost. Modern secular reason offers procedural guidance without commenting on the morality of the ends or of the means employed to achieve them.

We conclude this part of our inquiry with one general observation. While religion can outlive individual scientific discoveries, including inimical ones – being flexible enough to absorb novelty – it cannot accommodate the scientific assertion that there are no values or causes immanent in the universe. I shall explain. The medieval age of faith ended and the modern age of doubt began when seventeenth-century scientists rejected 'formal and final causes'. Aristotle distinguished four causes in the development of a thing: material cause (its matter); formal cause (its form); efficient cause (cause in our modern sense); and final cause (its intended purpose or end).[17] The final cause of a thing (or event) was its intended cosmic purpose in a grand scheme while the formal cause was the idea in the mind of a creator. Aristotle and Plato believed in final and formal causes and the whole medieval Christian world enthusiastically espoused this Greek idea. The Muslims, who transmitted Greek science and Indian mathematics to the West, found Quranic affirmation for it: 'Our Lord is the one who gave to each created thing its form (*khalqa-hū*) and guided it [to its intended purpose]' (Q:20:50; see also 32:7; 87:2–3). As for formal cause: 'If we will the existence of an object, we merely say to it: "Be!" And it is' (Q:16:40).

9

Much of the scientific study of religion presupposes that religion is an inherently irrational and rudimentary attempt to control and placate nature. But religion persists despite the triumph of the superior rational and experimental techniques of science. Was Islam then merely part of the teething process of modern empirical science or is there an enduring institutional bond between monotheism and science? Modern scientists assume that there exists an objective physical reality, intelligible and orderly;[18] they cannot endorse the other monotheistic assumptions, especially the teleology that accompanied it and, in the Islamic case, motivated the project. The world is now viewed as a self-sufficient deterministic system where scientists no longer need the hypothesis of God.

The answer to our question above depends on the meaning of science. If science is defined as the pursuit of wholly naturalistic explanations for events and phenomena, then it is incompatible with theism since its premise is atheistic. If, however, science is any systematic exploration of nature, involving examination of evidence for or against a proposed theory, then the enterprise is compatible with theism and was originally stimulated by it. For science liberally defined, it is an open question whether the evidence we extract from nature, by studying its causal sequences, supports theism or atheism as this liberal conception of science does not assume that the universe is unplanned.

Scientists who examine recalcitrant natural events search indefinitely for causal explanations couched in naturalistic terms: nothing is allowed to count as evidence of an operative supernatural agency in external nature. In the human sciences too, where human nature, sound or disturbed, is the theme, the human personality has mysterious inner motivations. But no scientist would countenance the possibility of, let us say, some demon influencing the behaviour of a serial killer. For social theorists, inner human motivation is explicable in terms of the behaviour of secular entities postulated by psychological theories. Hypotheses that require visitors from a contra-natural realm are dismissed.

The Quranic onslaught on magic, to return to our tale, succeeded only to make science the champion. For modern science regards both magic and religion as inferior precursors to science. And while magic produced an inferior auxiliary technology, science has generated a monster in the shape of modern technology. The rupture of the traditional liaison between morals and religion might not have damaged either, as we saw in Chapter 3 but the break between science and religion has damaged science. Science and technology freed from reference and responsibility to transcendent values will cause irreversible damage even while aiming to confer immeasurable benefits. For our generation, which lives desperately under the shadow of a global nuclear holocaust and the threat of taboo technologies of chemical warfare, this fear is not baseless.

What has triumphed in the modern world is not the Quranic vision of science but rather the ideology of the Renaissance's most daring intellectual reformer and philosopher of natural science, Francis Bacon (1561–1626), who ruthlessly equated knowledge with power. He envisioned humankind assuming an 'empire over nature' by recognizing nature as 'second scripture', the open book of divine works. He was impressed by the truthfulness of nature (*veracitas naturae*): if we read it with a pure mind, we could not misread it.[19] Modern science reads nature carefully in order to conquer and control it – as part of civilization's war on nature. Since Bacon, western science has been motivated by the perceived serviceability of nature: scientists have unmasked the workings of this vast natural machine in order to alter its course and extract some benefit. For Muslims, this exploitation, using scientific technique, is a misunderstanding of nature's true and intended purpose. To reject nature's discernible religious teleology is to reject the signs of God. The explorer refuses to move on to the more dignified station of the worshipper.

If nature could tell its own story, it would need no revealed commentary. In a secular age, it has no creditable sacred commentators. Art and science are now its two exclusive and exclusively secular interpreters. Nature is currently seen through the prism and prison of empirical scientific and aesthetic experience. It has no accepted moral or religious patronage. Religion has retreated in the face of these secular commentators, one ancient, the other a new pretender. Bacon insisted that we must ask nature and then force nature to answer. Science has an ideological interest in nature, a part of the larger scientific programme for making the world serviceable. Environmentalists, scientists, naturalists, poets, painters and engineers are all engaged with nature. But only the worshipper, suggests the Quran, takes nature's true measure as a place providing the material matrix of a unique transcendent agency whose actions are intelligible to a devout human mind.

10

Only in childhood, secularized westerners experience the world as enchanted and inhabited by supernatural beings, an experience later privatized into diffidence, discussed apologetically in public once the supernatural character of the world ceases to be experienced. By youth, everyone becomes like Mr Thomas Gradgrind, the philistine schoolmaster in Charles Dickens' *Hard Times* (published in 1854): a utilitarian pragmatist who banishes all but the unadorned facts. When secularized moderns look up into the night sky, they know that it stretches for trillions of miles. They see the stars and the constellations since these are palpable to the senses despite their titanic distance – but the ancient vision of the glory of God completely eludes them. It was not always so. Barely a century ago, European settlers in America and other lands world-wide were still reared in the lap of divine providence: their art was obsessed with the images of a gracious eschatology – of an idyllic prosperity in a land flowing with milk and honey. The religious dimension of nature informed their consciousness of the world. The divine presence in nature was intuited and sensed. It has now been attenuated to the inferred intellectual demand of a desperate theology struggling against a secularism canonized by science.

The beauty of nature, experienced as neutral, not religiously assertive, is acknowledged by many atheists and agnostics. Poets vividly describe nature in its subtle moods, and yet refuse to assign religious significance to this knowledge and experience of natural beauty. The believer, no less than the poet, is arrested by the dignified beauty and variety of the natural world. Only believers, however, experience a humbling gravitas as they marvel at the order behind and beyond nature, exhibiting power, justice and mercy sustained in perfect equilibrium. In a secluded spot in a wilderness untouched by human touch or technology, many moderns still experience a quasi-religious sense of sanctuary. Only those who have lost all sympathy with the supernatural dimension of life would fail to feel even this sense of enveloping safety.

Intellectually, the religious interpretation of nature is now optional. Thus, for example, the epiphany of the burning bush, an enduring symbol of the human quest for the transcendent, can be explained away as an optical illusion: light falls on a desert plant that retains moisture and water in its surface layer. In our religious past, all natural phenomena were signs pointing to God as the Quran hints in its account of Moses' encounter with the burning bush. Moses notices merely a simple natural phenomenon, namely a fire, but, intriguingly, speculates that he might find guidance at the fire (Q:20:9–10; 27:7).[20]

Did the ancients 'see' the glory of God when they gazed into the night sky? The heavens declare the glory of God to the penitent worshipper. It is not a publicly verifiable declaration since one must educate one's instincts in order to recognize the signs of God. The Quran schools the believer to interpret nature as a carefully crafted system of signs. But if this perception of nature were psychologically com-pelling, a part of common sense perception, scripture would not need to *cultivate* the art of recognizing the signs.

Even if the universe is a concealed testament of praise, evident to the believer and opaque to the rejector, its *observable* sequences need not support a divine teleology. Modern scientists do not sense any purposive 'ulteriority' in nature. Our perception of the divine signs latent in nature differs from our immediate perception of, for example, the odour of the leaves of a tree on a summer's day or the deserted aspect of a winding path at the close of an autumn evening. The subtlety of nature's appearances, smells and sounds, no doubt eludes the untrained eye. But even a poet with a developed sensibility is not compelled to concede the religious, as opposed to aesthetic, significance of nature's moods and aspects.

Natural scientists probe the expanding universe up to its observable limits while modern poets, when freed from the petty seductions of autobiographical and con-fessional obsession, are irresistibly attracted to the charms of nature. They extol its ability to humble the observer who now usually observes it from the perspective of a shared sentimentality called love rather than a solitary fear of the awesome presence of the deity. We see the natural world in its majesty but the spirit and glory of the divine being eludes us. Is that a defeat for faith or for reason – a reason blinded by hubris? Is the religious versus secular explanation of nature a matter of attitude and temperament or of truth and fact? If nature has been divinely intended to elicit a specifically religious response from the attentive observer, why is that response so rare today?

11

The sceptic concludes that nature is what it is; it does not, because it need not, transcend itself. The sceptic admits that nature arouses curiosity and provides a beautiful décor for the drab house of life but denies that it is a subtly concealed invitation to discover an underlying order in which transcendent mercy and goodness reign. That is a religious fantasy, the genetic fallacy, of reading our own wishes into the external world.

Modern secular scientists assign autonomy to nature and relegate to the psychology of wonder the problem of incredulity in the face of the undeniable aesthetic power of nature. In its enduring grandeur and marvelous detail, nature simply happens to exist and persist without an originating or sustaining transcendent supporter. Wonder and amazement, stimulants of philosophical curiosity and inquiry, cannot support or justify a *logical* demand for explanation. No argument can be based solely on an emotional appeal to our sense of awe and wonder. Wonder has stimulated fascinating ventures including philosophy – but wonder itself requires no explanation. Our wonder at the world no more implies the existence of God than the pursuit of philosophy automatically implies the attainment of wisdom. Our awe in the face of the amazing cosmos psychologically suggests a theistic explanation – but it does not logically require it. In any case, what was once awe and wonder is now anxiety, a secular sentiment less in need of explanation.

Most contemporary philosophical views opposed to theism do not attempt to give any rational explanation of the world. The universe, the totality of all that exists, is, secularists claim, an inexplicably brute fact or datum neither susceptible of nor requiring explanation. How Olympian the serenity with which the modern scientist views the mysteries of nature! The religious apologist retorts that secularism lacks a metaphysic of ultimate realities. It is intellectually more satisfying, the defender of religious faith argues, to prefer some rational explanation (for the totality of things) to none. We obtain such a rational explanation if we discern the course of the world as being determined by value and purpose. Thus, if we adopt the heuristic principle, often used in science, of seeking to develop a coherent rational system, of accepting that hypothesis which makes the natural universe more of a rational totality, then theism emerges as a pre-eminently reasonable choice. The atheistic alternative claiming that there is no rational explanation for the world violates the deepest intuitions of both believers and sceptics alike in some moods. Should we not seek to do justice to the depth of our pre-rational hunches concerning such crucial matters?

Resistance to the notion that ultimate meaning resides directly in the nature of things is inveterate in modern intellectual culture. It is difficult to locate uncontroversial purposes in nature. But to stipulate a priori that questions about final purposes and the search for supra-naturalistic explanations is misguided, even incoherent, is unpardonably dogmatic. 'What is the ultimate purpose of nature?' is declared a senseless question. Believers retort that the question makes good sense and that the fundamental groundwork of the real – the natural, the essential structure of reality as such – is spiritual (or mental or transcendent) rather than material (or physical). This is a philosophical claim with controversial (and currently unfashionable) metaphysical and epistemological presuppositions. There is, however, insufficient reason to dismiss it as false.

12

In Sections 10 and 11 above, we delineated the outlines of large issues in the hinterland of natural (rational) theology. The argument from the signs of God to God's existence is a Quranic version of the teleological argument. It was popular among Muslim thinkers impressed by the frequency of Quranic allusions to nature as a vast network of indirect divine presences. Ibn Rushd favoured it above other contentions. Jews and Christians find it hidden behind the superb poetry of the Book of Job (Job 38–41). We examine classical natural theology in Chapter 12.[21] Here we explicate and assess only the design argument.

If the cosmological argument appeals to one empirical fact – the existence of a contingent universe – the teleological argument appeals to many empirical facts about our particular world. There are two forms of the argument from design but in Islamic scholasticism both are called the argument from providence (*dalīl al-'ināyah*). There is a deductive form of the teleological argument, identical to Aquinas' fifth way, according to which a sentient intelligent being directs the growth of an insentient object, such as a seed or grain, along the correct or intended path which is not known to the inanimate object itself. Aquinas considered it analogous to the arrow being directed by an archer where God is the master-archer. This form of the argument is in the Quran (Q:20:50; 27:60; 52:35–6; 56:58–9, 63–4, 68–9, 71–2) and in one Pauline epistle (1 Corinthians 15:37–8).

An inductive form based on analogy is also found in the Quran, as we shall see below. The observable world significantly resembles objects known to be the products of intelligent design within that world. The pre-Darwinian Christian teleologists were fond of citing the example of the human eye as a divinely designed camera. It is absurd, they argued, to suggest either that the eye was not consciously designed for the purpose of seeing or, what is even more ridiculous, that it might fortuitously be serving that function.

The teleological argument is meant to appeal both to people of faith and of unaided reason. The natural order is allegedly dominated by a purposeful harmony that is evidence of the activity of a benevolent intellect. The epistemic notion of the signs of God as probatively evidential underlies the Quranic version of this argument. When rational human beings observe nature, they can deduce from this index the existence and goodness of the creator.

The Quran rarely accumulates evidence for God's existence and activity on the basis that there is a world but rather on the ground that the world assumes a specific character. It appeals often to the flawless harmonies of nature (Q:36:39–40; 50:6–8). The observable world is created perfect (Q:67:3–4) and 'in truth' (*bi al-ḥaqq*; Q:14:19; 15:85; 16:3; 29:44; 39:5; 45:22; 46:3), the opposite of a 'pointless' (*bāṭilan;* Q:3:191; 38:27) creation. God is the supremely skilful creator (*al-khallāq al-'alīm*; Q:15:86; 36:81) whose artistry (*ṣun'a Allāh*; Q:27:88) is consummate as 'he made all things in perfect order' (*atqana kulla shay'in;* Q:27:88) and in the best way (Q:32:7).

There is a nuanced version of this simple Quranic argument: only the existence and activity of God could explain the presence of finely tuned conditions that must obtain in the universe to enable intelligent life to emerge on it. Contemporary scientific researchers admit that the problem of the emergence of life is far more complex than earlier scientists had imagined it to be. The modern version of the old argument therefore appeals to the improbability of the universe producing intelligent life without the intervention of divine design. Chance and natural law are insufficient to explain the world's existence and actual character. Although the incredibly high improbability of the universe as we know it being created by chance does not by itself prove that the universe must have been designed, the combination of this truth (about high improbability levels) combined with the emergence of a particular pattern constitutes a presumption in favour of the teleological argument. The Christian philosopher William Lane Craig gives a compelling example to buttress this thesis. Imagine that Bob was born on August 8, 1948 and he receives a car for his birthday. The licence plate reads: BOB 8848. Would it be rationally justified for him to attribute this plate number to chance on the grounds that one combination of letters and numbers is as probable as any other?[22] The combination of a given pattern *and* high improbability together make the chance hypothesis more unreasonable than the design hypothesis.

Many philosophers of religion inspired by Hume, the first western philosopher to divorce religion from philosophy, argue that the character of the world as we know it is incompatible with the existence of a metaphysically and morally perfect creator. They concede that the world provides evidence of the existence of some kind of deity – but not of the unique deity of mature monotheism. An atheist might argue that the observable and measurable world is not the work of a single author. In his *Dialogues Concerning Natural Religion*, Hume argues that we know that ships, houses and other products of human creativity are produced with the co-operation of many intelligent human beings who, moreover, seek to improve their performance over time. Arguing almost a century before Darwin's theory of evolution, Hume makes a sceptical character mock the analogical reasoning of religious teleologists: the experienced cosmos could be the work of a committee of gods, of an old and incompetent god, of a dependent deity or perhaps of 'some infant deity who afterwards abandoned it, ashamed of his lame performance'.[23]

13

The Quran often speaks of the divine will; it uses 'he intends' (*yurīdu*; Q:4:27–8; 5:1; 22:14, 16) and 'we intended' (*aradnā*; Q:16:40) and 'he wills' and 'he willed' (*yashā'u*; Q:9:27; *shā'a*; Q:9:28) to express such intention and volition. The Quran has no distinctive words for purpose, meaning, or function, whether secular or religious. It uses the adverb *muta'ammidan* (intentionally) and a related verbal conjugation to denote the deliberative component in human intention (Q:4:93; 33:5). Modern Arabic uses the non-Quranic word *maqṣid* to denote purpose.[24] The word *'ināyah*, used above, which refers to divine providence or purpose, is not Quranic.

In human contexts, what we do *on* purpose, we do *for* a purpose. If that is true of God when he deliberately made nature, then nature has a purpose, independently of our recognition. But this view requires that we think of God as a purposive agent, the author of nature. If we observe nature as a *fait accompli*, however, we need not conclude thus.

Purpose need not inhere in the natural world even if God made it. We need to assume further that he acted purposively when he made it. When God acts in and through nature, the performance of a function is exhibited in the natural product and an intention is also fulfilled. (This might be achieved by a type of causality similar to human agency.) We have *ex hypothesi* no access to God's motives and intentions – if our only data is nature rather than the additional data of divine self-avowal (revelation). Without revelation, we are assuming that he did it on purpose for each item he created. If we see a twig in a forest we wonder: What is the purpose of this twig? This question could mean: Can we decide to give it a purpose? But there is another interpretation too: What is its purpose independently of our decision to give it one? Merely by looking at a twig, we cannot decide that it has a natural purpose *endowed by God acting purposively*.

If X has a purpose Y, then it has a maker Z. The syllogism is: If anything has a purpose, it has a maker; objects/events in external nature have a purpose; therefore, these objects/events have a maker/designer.[25] The first premise is analytically true if we mean a purpose that is imposed rather than a natural purpose inhering in objects generated without conscious agency. It is difficult to prove the truth of the second premise. We cannot discern the purposeful character of natural objects unless we already believe in a supernatural purpose-giver. Judging from appearances alone, we cannot discern the difference between the purposive and the erratic behaviour of a given agent unless we have access to the agent's avowals and motives. We have no access to divine motives except through controversial interpretations of disputed revelations allegedly from him.

The claim that 'Event X (or item X) serves a purpose Y' is compatible with any and all sense experience unless one already believes that there exists a purposive agent who could cause X and was, moreover, acting purposively when causing X. The design argument is based on the claim 'Event X serves purpose Y as intended by an agent Z'. But to prove, even discern, purpose in nature, one has to presuppose, not discover, the existence of a purposive agent. When believers discern natural purpose, they already believe in God, as a purposive agent, on independent, allegedly revealed, grounds.

14

The Quran, unlike the New Testament, does not contain any professedly paradoxical teaching. But there is an apparent paradox in the signs of God being immanent and transcendent. The hidden God approaches us, in a concealed manner, through the open book of nature. He whispers to those who turn a deaf ear.

Nature is, for Muslims, a subtle index to the divine presence in nature. To use the Sufi metaphor of the woman's veil, God is veiled in nature, a hint of the potential for abuse and misuse of nature. We can study and subdue nature through the crass supremacy of technical manipulation. That was Bacon's dream as he speculated that nature could be put 'under constraint and vexed ... forced out of her natural course, and squeezed and moulded'.[26]

Nature contains, moreover, imperfect and ambiguous messages. Natural events are not as uniformly benevolent as believers claim. Natural operations are a mixed blessing providing material for gratitude and trust but also for disbelief and cynicism. Natural mercies and bounties are mixed with natural disasters and cruelties. It is an ambiguous stimulus to gratitude. The sun that warms us also grills a traveller to death in the lonely desert; and the hurricane is a force for pure destruction.[27]

There is a larger context to this debate. Events occurring in the natural world (shared by believers and sceptics) are inherently ambiguous, open to rival and incompatible interpretations. Theism and atheism as total systems of thought contain mechanisms for explaining the existence and contents of the rival. Take the example of the signs of God. The believer accuses the atheist of perversity while the disbeliever accuses believers of wishful thinking. Each interpretive scheme can subsume its rival by absorbing apparent counter-evidence, thus deflecting the opponent's criticisms. While each side can explain away the rival position, neither can accuse the other of irrationality without appealing to a controversial standard of rationality. It is impossible therefore to proffer neutral reasons for preferring a secular world-view to a theistic one.

In this secularized age, nature can indefinitely and with equal plausibility sustain naturalistic and theistic outlooks. The signs no longer compel recognition since theism now over-determines, rather than simply determines, the shape of our experience: the atheist is ready with an adequate secular explanation for any event in nature that stimulates the admiration of the believer. The religious interpretation of nature is not necessarily false but it is an optional extra, an inferior alternative that can be plausibly dismissed as a remnant of a religious past in which gullible men and women adored and feared nature.

What follows from the moral and metaphysical ambiguity, perhaps neutrality, in nature? To put it in Quranic language, nature as a whole is a sign. It is, in the Quran's own hermeneutical terminology, a *mutashābihāt*[28] (ambivalent or analogous) sign, not *muḥkamāt* (lit., decisive, hence, legal) sign (Q:3:7). It does not compel belief or conduct. The sign is suggestive, not coercive. It hints but does not state. The Quran implicitly recognizes the need for the disambiguation of nature when it acknowledges that God constantly dispatched messengers to warn human beings, a concession which implies that the divine signs and our consciences did not jointly suffice to guide us. Since nature is now an ambiguous sign, we today need natural (rational) theology to disambiguate our modern condition, a theme of the final chapter. In the meantime, unprejudiced observation can sincerely, it appears, fail to detect the hand of God behind the impressive but ambiguous marvels of nature and human life.

9   Faith and the varieties of rejection

1

To identify the actors in sacred history, the Quran uses ethnic, religious, and ideological labels, some frequently, some rarely or once. It refers to groups with distinct beliefs and rituals, including Arabs, Bedouins, Jews, the Children of Israel, the Children of Adam, Christians, the Byzantine Greek Christians (Q:30:2), Persians (Q:16:103; 26:198; 41:44), people of the book, people of the gospel (Q:5:49), the Magians (*al-Majūs;* Q:22:17), the Sabians (*Al-Ṣābi'ūn;* Q:2:62; 5:71; 22:17), and several others.[1] By contrast with the variety of such labels, the religious typology is simple: the faithful, the submitters, the disbelievers, the idolaters and the hypocrites. The complexity now derives from the subtlety and nuance of the Quranic nomenclature. The scripture elucidates and appraises the life of faith and rejection by describing generic attitudes held by various groups, coining fertile new words and investing old words with new spiritualized meanings.

Faith (*īmān*, lit., security, presumably from doubt) is the most meritorious attitude towards God; it is the means whereby believers who seek guidance are guided (Q:10:9) and, once guided, receive more guidance (Q:19:76) which culminates in the gifts of piety (*taqwā*; Q:47:17), rectitude (*rushd*; Q:21:51) and righteous conduct (*khayr*; lit., goodness; Q:6:158). The Quran distinguishes faith from the mere profession of submission (*islām*) to God's will, a political act of surrender, required equally of all adherents, nominal or sincere (Q:49:14). The faithful (*al-mu'minūn*) are distinguished from the submitters (*al-muslimūn*) as only after due effort and the indispensable grace of God does a Muslim matriculate into the community of 'the purified faith' (*al-dīn al-khāliṣ*; Q:39:3) and thus become a man of faith (*mu'min*) or a woman of faith (*mu'minah*).

One can reject God by neglecting his will for humankind, persecuting his messengers or by being ungrateful for his favours. This attitude is *kufr* (lit., concealment, presumably of truth). Denial of God can also take the form of idolatry which corresponds to what the Quran calls *shirk* – which literally means ascribing or associating. It is the sin of associating partners with God's unique divinity. These two guilty groups are the *kāfirūn* and the *mushrikūn* respectively. As religious terms, *kufr* and *shirk* are fecund Quranic neologisms. The Quran, like the New Testament and the Hebrew Bible, intends to generate sincerity in the inner life of believers, hence its concern with hypocrisy (*nifāq*), a type of disbelief rooted in dissimulation. The hypocrites (*munāfiqūn*) sow dissension among the ranks of the faithful, especially in times of social distress.

Three attitudes towards God found in the Quran – *īmān, kufr, nifāq* – are still relevant to the situation of modern believers. The Quranic concept of *shirk*, however, might be anachronistic, as I shall explain presently. I lightly sketch the factual and historical contours of the Quranic terrain in Sections 2 to 6 below. There follow, in Sections 7 and 8 respectively, interludes on the political and practical dimensions of the scripture's interest in the faith–rejection dichotomy. The Quran's practical interest in the question of God's existence, discussed in Section 8, is located in an isthmus that broadens out and reaches into the outer borders of the modern radical and theoretical neglect and denial of God. In Sections 9 to 12, we assess the assumption that human beings are naturally disposed towards monotheism; this provides a context, in Sections 13 to 18, for a detailed examination of the revolutionary change in the status of the charge of idolatry as directed against ancient pagans, on the one hand, and modern secularized humankind, on the other.

After examining idolatry, a scriptural notion whose relevance has sharply declined in a secularized age, I argue in Section 19 that the concept of *shirk* should be extrapolated, perhaps replaced, to reflect the spiritual needs of our times. I propose the notion of *istibdāl* which I translate as 'substitutionary replacement' or surrogacy. In the final section, in a postscript to the discussion of idolatry, we examine a mistaken view of idolatry, associated with the existentialist thinker Søren Kierkegaard. If adopted, this stance would dissolve the problem of idolatry by identifying sincerity or insincerity of motive as the sole relevant consideration – thus reducing idolatry, in any age, to a form of hypocrisy.

2

Unlike Marxist materialism, the Quran reveals a primordial human condition outside and antecedent to history and empirical nature. It portrays an assembly of the souls of the Children of Adam, convened before the commencement of their earthly sojourn. This pre-historical vision of humankind supplies supernatural foundations for our moral accountability to God. It is unique to the Quran. All human beings, as disembodied souls, are located here in their true original, pre-temporal, position awaiting embodiment and the start of history:

> Recall the time when your Lord extracted from their loins (lit. backs) all the descendants of the Children of Adam and made them testify against themselves saying: 'Am I not your Lord?' They replied: 'Yes, we do testify'. And this was done in case you should say on the Day of Judgment: 'We know nothing of this!' Or in case you say: 'Only our forefathers worshipped false gods before us but we were merely their descendants. Will you destroy us for the actions of those who followed such falsehood?'
>
> (Q:7:172–3; see also Q:20:115)

Before we assumed this corporeal form, we confessed the eternal truth about God's sole lordship, a truth supplemented by a confession of the apostleship of different messengers in actualized history. This is the background to the first pillar of Islam, the public act of witness known as *al-shahādah* (lit. the evident; Q:59:22; opposite of *al-ghayb*, the hidden; Q:59:22). The believer publicly confesses the final and original religion of all humankind: 'There is no god except the true God; Muhammad is the messenger of God'. But disbelievers, in the hurly-burly of this lower life, forget their promise to God and therefore witness against their souls: 'It is not fitting that idolaters (*mushrikīn*), who witness to infidelity (*al-kufr*) against their own souls, should maintain the mosques of God. The works of such idolaters bear no fruit. In the fire they shall abide' (Q:9:17). Believers, mindful of the original assembly, witness to their fidelity to their primordial selves and hence to God. Infidelity to one's soul has political consequences. Disbelief is an act of rebellion against God, high spiritual treason against the king of kings, 'the master of the kingdom' (*mālik al-mulk*, Q:3:26; see also Q:67:1).

The postulates of divine unity and of human accountability to the divine are inscribed in human nature (Q:7:172–3). The Quran eulogizes Islam as the manifestly right and straight religion (*al-dīn al-qayyim*, Q:12:40; 30:30; *dīn al-qayyimah*; Q:98:5), the religion of our original and pure human nature. Denial of God's sole sovereignty is intentional perfidy to the higher believing and submissive (*muslim*) aspect of our nature. This is the central practical truth that should guide conduct. No sane person is invincibly or congenitally ignorant of either the existence of God or of his (innately acknowledged) moral claim on us. A well-attested tradition of the Prophet claims that every child is born submissive to God's will (that is, a *muslim*) but Jews and Christians and others pervert the child into other faiths.[2] The child's nature is made *muslim* by divine fiat (Q:30:30), whatever nurture may do with it. An atheist would retort that we are all born atheists and then subverted into theism through religious indoctrination at an early age, a subtle kind of child abuse.

3

The Quranic model of faith was delineated in Chapter 2; our discussion here is factual and exegetical rather than analytical or critical. Although faith, like rejection, varies in intensity and quality, it is always marked by an effortless trust (*tawakkul*; noun; verb conjugated at Q:5:25; 9:129; 13:30; 14:12; 27:79; 29:59; 67:29, etc.) placed in God's plan and providence, a trust inspired and sustained by active enthusiasm. A continuum stretches from the casual neglect of God's will by those who pay lip-service to their faith, merely claiming to obey God (Q:2:8–10), to those believers who actively seek his good pleasure and lay down their lives in that pursuit (Q:2:207; 33:23). Between these two types are believers of weak faith who serve God 'on the verge' (Q:22:11), opportunists who are content to be believers so long as it costs them nothing. As soon as they are persecuted for the sake of their faith, they lose their faith – incurring losses in both worlds. These believers, whose faith endures as long as there is no persecution for the sake of

God, are reminded that no one can enter paradise without persecution and testing on earth (Q:29:2–3). But the persecution sinners inflict on the righteous is nothing compared to the chastisement God will inflict on those who refuse to struggle in his path (Q:29:10).

In distress, a believer prays 'lying down on his sides, or sitting, or standing' (Q:10:12) and becomes *dhū duʿāʾin ʿarīd*, 'the man of prolonged prayers' (Q:41:51). In a crisis, we effortlessly believe in the one true God and purge our faith of association with false deities. Being on the open sea in the face of an imminent storm is a surprisingly frequent Quranic scenario (Q:10:22–3; 29:65–6) given that the Arabs of the Arab peninsula were not a maritime people at the time of the Quran's revelation. On dry land, however, most revert to impure idolatrous worship (Q:29:65–6). Times of danger and anxious anticipation elicit fervent and sincere but short-lived faith. During the course of a pregnancy, for instance, the worried parents pray fervently for a male child. Their prayer is granted; after delivery, the parents revert to paganism (Q:7:189–92). How ungrateful is humankind! (Q:80:17).

The opposite of faith is rejection (*kufr*). One insidious version of it is hypocrisy, condemned as 'the lesser *kufr*'. Insistence on the sincerity of interior motivation is common to all faiths. The Quran, like Jesus and the Israelite prophets, condemns hypocrisy as a form of insidious disbelief. In the Medinan chapters, it is a social sin associated with political intrigues to crush the infant faith by exterior Jewish dissidents working with fellow hypocritical Arab conspirators within; the Arab Muslims were only nominal believers who secretly sympathized with Jewish tribes settled in the city long before Muhammad was invited there as an arbiter of disputes. The Arab pagans are described as disaffected malcontents who are lazy and distracted in their prayers (Q:4:142–3). Their disobedience, caused by an actively rebellious will, is the social crime of *fisq* (see e.g. Q:5:26, 47, 49), the legal precursor of apostasy (*irtidād*; *riddah*; see e.g. Q: 5:54), a form of treason against the Islamic state. More generally, hypocrisy is identified with any tepid, politically expedient, or deviously external allegiance to the cause of God and his eventually triumphant messenger (Q:8:49; 9:66–8, 73–87, 63:1–8).

Unlike the Jewish and Christian scriptures, the Quran's discussion of hypocrisy, like its discussions of the other attitudes, is in a political, not solely theological or devotional context although meditative meanings colour the political references. During times of civil friction, the hypocrites weaken the Muslim community by sowing seeds of dissension and sectarianism (Q:9:47). The Quran condemns conspiratorial assemblies (Q:58:8–10). One late Medinan chapter (Q:9:42–110) and portions of earlier Medinan chapters (especially Q:8:49–62, 33:12–20, 59–61, 63:1–8) instruct Muhammad to eradicate the menace of duplicity in the midst of a faithful community struggling to survive.

The Quranic references to hypocrisy are frequent and spiritually profound. We read some telling parables against the hypocrites (Q:2:17–20), especially their moral exhibitionism, their desire to 'be seen of men' (*riʾā al-nās*; Q:8:47; cf. Matthew 6:1–18). In times of war they act insolently and boastfully (*baṭaran*; Q:8:47). They fund the cause of evil and rebellion to God and his Prophet and refuse to spend in the way of God (Q:9:67, 75–6). God has therefore 'put hypocrisy into their hearts' (Q:9:77). It is a spiritual sickness, a malady (*marad*) which flourishes in hypocritical hearts (8:49; 9:125; 33:12; 47:29) and God aggravates it (Q:2:10; 9:125).

Muhammad knows the hypocrites by 'the tone of their speech' (Q:47:30). They come running to him for judgement – but only when they suspect they will get a favourable verdict (Q:24:47–50). Their cowardly melodrama and paranoia deceive them since 'they think every cry is against them' (Q:63:4). Divided among themselves, they pretend to be brave fighters united for a cause – only while securely behind a fortified city (Q:59:14). Since they fear Muhammad more than they fear God, they are 'a people lacking sense' (Q:59:13). They are hollow and weak, 'like pieces of wood propped up' (Q:64:4), a description reminiscent of the New Testament writers' moral use of *hupokritēs*, the word for the Greek stage-actors who relied on theatrical prop and stentorian voice to mask their true faces and intentions. Hypocrites are afraid of a revelation that might expose their duplicity (Q:9:64) and God tests them once or twice every year in case any wish to repent (Q:9:126).

4

There are two conceptions of denial (or rejection) of the divine. One derives from the verb *ka/dha/ba* (*takdhīb*; noun) which is used with the prepositions *bi* and *'alā* meaning 'with' and 'upon' respectively. It means dismissing as false a claim or the person making the claim. Its religious meaning ranges from denial of God's messengers and of his signs in nature and history, to a graceless rejection of divine favours and bounties enjoyed by all humankind, culminating in a scornful dismissal of the momentous reality of resurrection and final judgement (Q:95:7–8). 'And woe, that day, to the rejectors' (*al-mukadhdhibīn*) is a refrain (Q:77:15; repeated nine times at vv. 19, 24, 28, 34, 37, 40, 45, 47, 49). The tension is built up, using the refrain at carefully spaced intervals, so that a slow and meditative opening suddenly collapses into an unbearably tremendous close. For extra rhetorical effect, *ka/dha/dha/ba* is used in its intensive form as indicated by the doubled middle radical.

The second, more innovative word derives from *ka/fa/ra*, a fertile triliteral root meaning 'He concealed'. The noun *kufr* means 'concealment' and, in Islamic theology, it means 'perverse concealment of the truth of Islam'. *Kāfir* (one who conceals) is a Quranic neologism for disbeliever. (It is a masculine singular noun in Arabic.) In a unique usage in Q:57:20 (*kuffār*; acc. pl.), we glimpse the word's original meaning: farmers, tillers or husbandmen who cultivate the soil. Some commentators add that the farmer sows and conceals the seed under the soil just as the disbeliever conceals the seed of truth. This etymology is speculative but the figurative associations of the word are suited to its Quranic usage.[3]

The Quran condemns the *kāfir* for his improbity and intransigence and accuses him of being stupid, ignorant, and superstitious (Q:27:47; 36:18–19). The disbeliever ought to know better: he has disfigured his noble heritage as a son of Adam, the first man to receive revelation, and ignored the warnings delivered by God's subsequent messengers. The *kāfir* is perverse and proud (Q:16:22; 27:14), preferring his own blindness and error to divine insight and guidance (Q:9:23; 41:17). He is hard-hearted and disobedient, 'a partisan (*ẓahīr*) against God' (Q:25:55). The rejector is ungrateful, another meaning of *kāfir*. When he actively disobeys God's will, he is virtually insane, 'driven mad by the touch of Satan' (Q:2:275). Disbelievers, killed en masse by God, are called scum (*ghuthā'*; Q:23:41).

The *kāfir* is portrayed as luxuriating in his wealth and possessions (Q:90:6; 100:8; 104:1–3), greedy and covetous, openly refractory (*'anīd*; Q:74:16) to the divine signs. He dismisses the Quran as magic brought by a man (Q:74:24–5) and impatiently demands immediate heavenly punishment if Muhammad's threats are true (Q:27:71). The Quran sometimes descends into righteous indignation that borders on personal insult: the disbeliever is of illegitimate birth (Q:68:10–13). He is more misguided than an animal (Q:7:179; 25:44); only faith could retrieve his humanity:

> Do not be like those who say, 'We hear' but do not actually listen. The worst of beasts in the sight of God are certainly the deaf and the dumb, those who lack all understanding. If God had found in them any good, he would surely have made them listen. But if he had made them listen, they would still have turned back and declined [faith].
>
> (Q:8:21–3; repeated at 8:55; see also Q:2:18)

5

The inhabitants of sinful cities exult in their life-style of luxury and casual neglect of God with apparent impunity (Q:21:11–15; 28:58). Only one community repented in time to avert divinely threatened disaster (Q:10:98). In one punishment narrative, God's messengers find a single household of believers in a populous community of sinners (Q:51:36). Most human beings are ungrateful to God (Q:12:38). Addressing the House of David and ordering gratitude, God notes: 'Few indeed of my servants are grateful' (Q:34:13); in the same narrative, David laments the paucity of just men in the world (Q:38:24). The Devil (Iblīs) is satisfied with this situation: 'Certainly, Iblis found true his opinion (*ẓann*) of them so they all followed him – except for a party of believers' (Q:34:20).

God is merciful and forbearing but not long-suffering. *Al-ṣabūr* (the extremely patient one) is the last of his 99 'most beautiful names' (*al-asmā al-ḥusnā*; Q:20:8, 59:24) culled mainly from the Quran. This name is not in the Quran.[4] God does not indefinitely tolerate obduracy and repeated disobedience. He warns through the prophets but the sinners remain heedless and persistently indifferent. A city rejects two messengers; God sends a third as reinforcement (Q:36:13–14), all to no avail. The warners and the warned are deadlocked. The divine judgement falls suddenly but after due warning. The sinners are often heedless, enjoying the ease of the afternoon siesta (Q:7:4); punishment also comes at night so that morning finds an entire people lying prostate in their houses – a posture marking defeat by death, not the voluntary submission of the limbs in worship.[5]

The Quran paints a lugubrious portrait of incorrigible sinners, addicted to disbelief and ingratitude, refusing to repent until their cup is full (Q:22:45). Muhammad's contemporaries walk, carefree and unrepentant, in the very ruins where more powerful communities had flourished (Q:14:45; 20:128; 32:26; 37:137–8), possibly in recent memory. The Quran's philosophy of history is constantly reiterated: God sends messengers along with adversity so that the nations may suffer and thus repent in humility. Instead, perversely, their hearts harden and they reject the divine message and the messenger. The Devil notes an opportunity to intervene and lures them to his path and 'beautifies their evil actions in their own eyes' (Q:27:24; 29:38). Strategically, God then increases the amount of luxury in the lives of sinners, dramatically increasing the good things of this life. Then, suddenly, divine punishment seizes the rejectors in the midst of their new enjoyments; and the community is eradicated (Q:6:42–5; 7:94–5; 17:16; 25:18; 34:34–5).

The Quran recommends travelling through the earth as a religious duty and as a source of empirical proof of this pattern of history: 'Travel through the land' and note the end of those who rejected God in the past (Q:6:11; 27:69; 30:42). Many were more powerful, in the traces (*āthār*) they left behind, than the pagans who reject Muhammad (Q:30:9; 40:21, 82). The Meccans have not received even a tenth (*mi'shār*; Q:34:45) of the power and glitter of former nations annihilated for their sins (Q:6:6; 19:73–5, 98; 40:21; 46:26; 50:36). Men and women reject the didactic and hortatory significance of history and archaeology while God must judge societies which patronize oppression and evil. 'Surely, the evil-doers shall never prosper' (Q:6:21; 12:23). The modern believer would add that today's earth, aided by the pill of archaeology, still vomits out the remains of its ancient inhabitants. But how few moderns take heed!

Sinners rarely sense the subtle but decisive approach of divine judgement from unknown quarters. They are bound to note its destructive aftermath (Q:7:182; 39:5; 68:44–5). 'God took their structures from the foundations and the roof collapsed on them from above and the divine wrath seized them from unexpected directions' (Q:16:26). Whether this refers to the debacle of an ambitious building project in a nearby land or to a symbolic collapse of the plots of all oppressors, the message is that doom approaches gradually and suddenly, often in unanticipated ways.

The prevalent and casual rejection of God puzzles and grieves believers. The Quran notes but does not fully explain this perplexity. God sympathizes with Muhammad: 'Perhaps, you may even grieve yourself to death, chasing after them, since they do not believe in this discourse' (Q:18:6; see also Q:5:41; 6:33; 10:65; 15:97; 26:3; 27:70). Unlike God, Muhammad is wounded by the rejection of God's latest message (Q:6:33). God rebukes him gently for his solicitous and zealous nature: 'No matter how eager you are, the majority of humankind will never believe' (Q:12:103). Perhaps it was naive of Muhammad to expect the Jews and Christians, with established religious traditions, to believe in the new message[6] although he was not alone in his innocence: Paul agonized over his fellow Jews' refusal to accept Jesus as the risen Messiah (Romans 9:30–11:32). Muhammad's prophetic predecessors were similarly traumatized by the arrogant rejection of God. God consoles Moses as he faces the rebellious Children of Israel who persecute him (Q:5:26; 61:5). Noah, the prophet of 'the laden ark' (Q:36:41) over-reacts in his indignation, condemns his persistently disbelieving community and prays for their annihilation in a divinely sanctioned global genocide (Q:71:26–7).

Our denial of God does not emotionally affect God.[7] Denial debases and devalues the Children of Adam. Nor does our foolish rejection of God tragically dislocate creation. Rejection of God unilaterally affects the human creature but there is a rare divine lament: 'Ah! Alas for the servants! There never comes to them a messenger but they mock him' (Q:36:30). The expression 'the servants' creates remoteness; the pathos is restrained. Elsewhere the Quran uses 'my servants', sometimes in the vocative case (Q:29:56; 43:68), to add warmth to the encounter (Q:2:186; 14:31; 15:49; 21:105; 39:10, 53).

The poetic language used in describing this foolish human rejection of God is marked by pathos but the sense of tragedy remains latent: 'How many a population of evil-doers we have destroyed! Roofs tumbled down, wells lying idle and neglected, and lofty castles too' (Q:22:45). A special kind of pathos pervades things that reach ruin through neglect and the passage of time rather than through war and violence. We are warned that this God-governed world is burdened with a decisive but postponed nemesis (Q:21:1; 22:1). Human beings, however, continue to mutiny against God, deny the reality of the future resurrection, and disbelieve in the 'meeting with their Lord' (Q:30:8).

6

Disbelief (*kufr*) is often caused by heedlessness (*ghaflah*; verb: *gha/fa/la*), an attitude that borders on indifference. We tend to forget God owing to an arrogant self-absorption and unconcern sometimes caused by wanton and luxurious living (Q:25:18). We forget a truth we secretly acknowledge in our reflective moods. Our situation resembles what psychiatrists call anosognosia, the habitual lack of awareness of one's own true condition. The Quran's parables and edifying punishment narratives seek to rectify *ghaflah* by appealing to reason and religious sentiment in order to erode our casual negligence of the divine demand on us. The choice of such techniques suggests that *ghaflah* is a compound of a self-imposed limit of imagination, resistance of will, and sinful motives. All three are mentioned throughout the Quran in countless deliberative contexts. Asking us to reflect is the scripture's insistent demand (Q:3:190–1; 34:46; 35:28).

Rejection as *kufr* is, in the Quran, not caused by incredulity or ignorance. These are dominant causes today since credulity is in short supply in the face of religious claims and many cultures actively resist the knowledge of monotheism. In the Quran, disbelievers are always *perverse* rejectors of truth, seeking release from acknowledged but unpleasant divinely imposed duties (Q:40:56).

The rejectors are well aware of what they do. Divine initiative in setting a seal on the hearts of disbelievers is, therefore, seen as a more credible explanation than the possibility that sinners could sincerely turn away their faces from the gift of guidance.

The causes of rejection of God and an after-life include complacency rooted in an optimistic assessment of human potential (*istighnā*, lit., freedom from need), an accusation found in the earliest revelations (Q:80:5; 92:8; 96:7). Obstinacy, abetted by perversity and spiritual myopia, explains the case of famous disbelievers such as the Pharaoh. Groundless pride called *takabbur*, the Quranic equivalent of hubris, led to the downfall of Satan. Seconded further by perverse self-wronging, the *kāfir* prefers human folly to divine wisdom and guidance, chooses misguided ancestral custom over the latest divine offer (Q:2:170; 43:22–4). Intellectual self-deceit, the Quran implies, insidiously leads disbelievers to concoct specious defences of an indefensible and destructive position. Culpable prevarication is disguised as detached rationality. Rejectors have only a fixed lease on physical life in this world and yet they sacrifice the next world for it, an attitude extensively excoriated in the Quran.

Rejection is incomprehensibly asinine (Q:2:130; 2:171). God seals the hearts of sinners and covers their eyes and ears but only after they freely reject divine grace (Q:61:5). A sinner can deliberately and literally 'darken his remembrance of the merciful God' (*ya'shu 'an zikr al-raḥmān*; Q:43:36) and thus earn diabolic companionship and misguidance (Q:43:36–7).[8] God permanently debars us from receiving his grace only after repeated rejections (Q:4:137; 7:100–1; 10:74). Once that threshold is reached, a sinner's disbelief is an intended result of divine fiat (Q:2:7).

This account is generally true but the Quranic Pharaoh's case is exceptional. Moses complains to God about the Pharaoh's fabulous wealth in the material life while the believing Israelites endure abject poverty (Q:10:88; 43:51–3). Out of rather vindictive motives, Moses requests that the Pharaoh's heart be hardened so that he is bound to meet a harsh divine judgement. This unwise request is from Moses, a prophet but nonetheless a human being (Q:10:88). God merely assents to it (Q:10:89).[9]

7

This debate has an ineradicable political dimension. In Medina, Muhammad built a community of able and devout believers committed to an intensely shared vision; anyone could join it by declaring, in public, the one-sentence creed of Islam. We have an accurate portrait of this community whose vision still inspires Muslims. It was a society which excluded the disbeliever. Past communities have been based on religious allegiance rather than secular notions of ethnicity and citizenship. Nation-states, with secular ideals of citizenship independent of religious allegiance, are recent. European national sovereignties, for example, date to the Peace of Westphalia (1648) although the notion is contained in an embryonic form in an earlier treaty, the Peace of Augsburg (1555). Westphalia eventually led to the disintegration of the historical *corpus Christianum* – thus completing the debacle of Latin Christendom, an empire founded on Christian ideals of polity.

An implacable hostility between faith and disbelief is evident in the Quran which ordains that these are absolutely dichotomous stances. Believers must not keep the company of disbelievers in preference to believers (Q:3:28, 118; 4:144) especially if disbelievers mock Islamic values (Q:4:140; 6:68). The disbeliever is not fit company for the believer whose daily life displays constant repentance (*taubah*) and constant gratitude (*shukr*), qualities incompatible with the rejector's ingratitude rooted in disbelief, two attitudes captured in the word *kufr*. Believers sleep little at night and abandon their beds at dawn to seek divine forgiveness (Q:32:16; 51:17–18); disbelievers are busy, day and night, in their frivolous games and diversions (Q:15:2–3), eating, drinking and living like animals, even worse. 'Not equal are the people of the fire to the people of the garden' (Q:59:20) is an unduly restrained comment.

While the free social inter-mixing of the sexes is expressly prohibited in many Islamic lands, a greater gap than gender is the faith–rejection dichotomy which is not a divide but an unbridgeable chasm. The believer is contaminated by the idolater's presence (Q:9:28). Marriages between believers and idolaters are forbidden (Q:2:221). Existing marriages between pagans and Muslims are dissolved (Q:60:10–11), a provision reminiscent of Ezra's harsh policies, after the Babylonian exile, though his concerns were both racial and religious. In the sixth year after the exodus to Medina, Muhammad had to arrange for divorces for men with disbelieving wives and vice versa, in fulfilment of the terms of the Treaty of Ḥudaybiya. The Quran calls the required rupture 'a divine judgement' (*ḥukm Allāh;* Q:60:10) as it provides the painful instructions (Q:60:10–11)[10] which the Prophet scrupulously followed. The *Sharī'ah* today, based on this practice, provides for an apostate to be automatically relieved of his or her believing spouse without legal proceedings or notice, in virtue of 'separation by reason of apostasy'. While Paul, in his personal opinion, permits unions between pagans and Christians so that Christian grace can sanctify the profane vessel and thus the children of the union (1 Corinthians 7:12–16), the Quran absolutely prohibits marriages with idolaters (Q:2:221). The Muslim scripture throbs with the tempo of this total and irreversible dichotomy.

Although the absolute disjunction between faith and rejection is in the Quran, it was jurists who created the *political* bifurcation between the house of peace (*dār al-salām*; Q:10:25) and the house of war (*dār al-ḥarb*). The latter is not a Quranic expression. The Quran's distinction is, however, both descriptive and prescriptive. Moreover, Muhammad said: 'Disbelief is a single system' (*Al-kufr ummatun wāḥidah*), a view implicit in the Quran (Q:6:129; 9:67; 45:19) along with the collateral and explicit Quranic injunction ordering all Muslims to form one community (Q:9:71; 49:9–10). Muslims later came to accept an intermediate house of covenant (*dār al-ṣulḥ*) where treaty obligations prevail with friendly non-Muslim states, a compromise restricted to the Shafi'i school of law but based on Muhammad's own practice as enshrined in the Treaty of Ḥudaybiya whose judiciously compromising terms were commended by the Quran (Q:48:1–10).[11]

8

Faith, disbelief and hypocrisy are approved or disapproved within an active faith community throbbing with the tempo of the choice for or against God. The concerns are practical matters of life, death and eternity. A revolutionary theoretical atheism which disputes the existence of a transcendent being or questions the coherence of the concept of such a strange being is alien to the age of revelation. The Quran, like the Bible, does not speculate about the existence of God. Both scriptures treat the question of the reality of God as a matter for practical resolution, not for purely theoretical interest or intellectual certitude. If so, do the author of the Quran and the modern sceptic have any common ground? Or are they talking at cross-purposes?

The Quran makes practical demands, expressed as moral and legal imperatives, as it alerts believers to the difficulties they may encounter, including the problem of sustaining faith in the face of Satan's avowed enmity to humankind (Q:43:62).[12] The promulgation, not analysis, of faith is the Quran's primary concern. Worship of God, not intellectual assent to the proposition that there is a God, is the focus of religious faith. Admittedly, the Quran, like the New Testament (Hebrews 11:6; James 2:19), asserts the existence of God.[13] It does so in the twofold confession of faith whose halves occur separately in the Quran (Q:3:2; 20:14; 48:29). God's *metaphysical* existence is asserted through the claim of his uniqueness: even the pagans believed that there was a deity called Allah but they rejected his uniqueness. To convince them of the uniqueness and majesty of this God, regarded by the pagans as one member of a pantheon, was the burden of Muhammad's preaching.

Kufr is not metaphysical disbelief in the reality of a divine power; it is practical neglect of divine imperatives informing daily life and its priorities. The existence of God and *a fortiori* the coherence of the concept were thought too obvious to need proof; the modern 'folly' of speculative radical atheism was not a live option. Arguably, those who lived in the zealous environment of Muhammad's Medina had no good reason to reject Islam. When the mighty hand of God could almost be seen in history, rejection was sinful, presumptuous and unreasonable. To the extent that modern rejection is based on honest doubt and sincere disbelief, it cannot be classed in the same category as the kind of hubristic, self-deceived and perverse rejection prevalent in ages of faith. Many intelligent modern human beings articulate complex worries about the coherence and sense of the theistic world-view. Others grant that it is a possible outlook but question its viability and plausibility in an age dominated by the successes of empirical science, technology, and an increasing awareness of the religiously and politically plural context of modern life.

9

Knowledge of God is part of our natural endowment and makes us human. It is a religious analogue to the secular Greek dogma that our rationality makes us essentially human. We explored the moral dimension of this theme in Chapter 3 and we now examine this issue in the context of the Quranic ambience of faith and rejection. We examine arguments proffered from both camps. A preliminary observation: those who dismiss as irrelevant or trivial the issue of God's existence are usually the dogmatists – in both camps. Dogmatic believers find it self-evident that there is a God; dogmatic atheists think the opposite is equally self-evident. The aggressive disbelief of most secular humanist organizations parallels the unreflective dismissal of secular humanism by narrow-minded believers professing adherence to an organized religion.

Although every human being is said to know implicitly about God, this does not amount to faith and need not lead to submission; but it is knowledge. Therefore, God can justifiably hold us culpable if we reject him. The Quran, like Paul (Romans 1:18–23), pontificates that all human beings are naturally inclined to believe in one God, a view for which the empirical data has formerly been inconclusive and ambivalent, and is, in the modern world, inadequate. The claim that all human beings, in all ages, potentially confess the existence and greatness of God and acknowledge the moral claim of his revealed law is, in this secularized age, an unsupported assertion in need of elaborate defence and justification.

Since we have all professed the unity of God, the Quran is only a reminder to heedless human beings. We deduce from this Quranic claim that belief in God is aroused naturally: being indigenous, it arises spontaneously and effortlessly in our minds. It takes effort of will to suspend, not endorse, belief in God. Thus, belief in God is not artificially or culturally crafted: it is as intrinsic to our nature as love and hate. Belief in God is also natural in the sense that it is universal and invariant, perhaps permanently present in our minds, hence unforgettable. This empirical claim is harder to justify in a secular age in which many see it as controversial and unempirical, that is, going beyond or against the evidence, and possibly outright false. Perhaps all human beings secretly or tacitly acknowledge the existence of God, denying it only out of pride or perversity – but to deduce such a conclusion from the observed evidence alone is unwarranted. It is, moreover, unstable: the evidence is fragmentary and future accumulation of evidence might overturn the current verdict. All in all, it seems unreasonable: it violates the canons of (secular) reason and probability.

If we proceed without Quranic preconceptions, then the notion of a monolithic religious inclination for our species is unempirical. As we saw in Chapter 6, empirical evidence indicates a vast range of religious conviction. Inside monotheism, the existence and nature of God have both been keenly disputed while healthy sceptical traditions have accompanied all faiths in their origins and subsequent histories. The religious theoretician is forcing an artificial unity on the empirical data in claiming that all the varied and recalcitrant data, the vagaries and vicissitudes of the religious record, eventually distil into a single form of religious conviction – and that a stereotypical monotheism.

The Quranic 'myth' of a pre-historical assembly of souls (Q:7:172–3) ensures that no one radically lacks the faculty appropriate to belief. Sinners deliberately suppress the will to acquire it and are, therefore, legitimately charged with moral blame. Belief arises naturally in all sane human minds but it is actively suppressed by pride and arrogance. Even the Pharaoh, who claims to be a god and mocks the notion of another divinity and a day of universal reckoning (Q:28:38), secretly believes, no less than the defeated magicians, in 'the Lord of Moses and Aaron', perhaps the most modest divine self-description in the Quran (Q:26:48; 26:34–52; cf. Q:53:49). The Pharaoh finally acknowledged God as the waters engulfed him and he entered the fire (Q:10:90–2).

10

While belief in God remains natural and normal for most people even today, it is mysteriously difficult and unnatural for some, usually intelligent, people. Many of our contemporaries, in alienated and atomized urban cultures, earnestly want to be and humanly need to be religious. They need religious belief as the psychological foundation of sanity in a world of futile consumerism and empty ephemera. But many of them are, apparently sincerely, unable to believe. In modern literature, we read about characters who find it hard to sustain religious faith. Think here, for example, of Graham Greene's Catholic characters – although their doubts are often mild and contrived. A better example is the sincere disbelief we encounter in the New Testament where Jesus berates many for their little faith. Since faith is the precondition of healing, the father of a demoniac boy appeals to Jesus: 'I have faith (*pisteuō*). Help my lack of faith (*apistia*)!'(Mark 9:24).

There is the will to believe, and politically there is the right to believe. But where is the capacity to believe in an age of incredulity? Many sincere atheists cannot successfully discern a beneficent supernatural force behind the pervasive cruelty and inhumanity of our species. How does one help the atheist's unbelief? There are techniques for inducing belief in God, including living in religiously fervent environments in deference to the maxim 'Faith is caught, not taught'. Modern atheists who desperately wish to believe could also cultivate habits of *intended* worship: stand reverently outside the walls of mosques, churches and synagogues and pray fervently to God, behaving as if he exists, and asking him to quell their sincere doubts.

God guides whomsoever he wills and no one comes to faith without his guidance (Q:28:56; 81:27–9). Some verses mitigate this divine control by suggesting a human role in the process (Q:73:19; 80:11–12). The Quran encourages believers to seek 'means of closeness' (*wasīlah*; Q:5:35) to God and to strive in his way, and thus kindle the light of faith into a flame. It mentions two kinds of people whose lack of faith or newly found faith needs active nurture. First, a group 'whose hearts were [only recently] reconciled' (*al-mu'allafati qulūbuhum;* Q:9:60) to the truth of Islam. The Quran lists these individuals – usually repentant enemies of the newly established community – among the main recipients of state charity. Second, it encourages Muhammad to grant asylum (*ma'manah*; lit. place of security or faith; Q:9:6) to pagans who express an interest in conversion so that, placed in a protected and pious atmosphere, they can hear, unmolested, the word of God. The Prophet granted this facility in a time of active military conflict.

If faith is natural, why is it difficult to attain it and even more difficult to sustain it? It should be effortless – but it is an ordeal. Believers introduce grace here with its irresolvable paradoxes and add, as explanatory causes, our perversity and self-deception abetted by the wiles of the Evil One. This rarely convinces those who are not already religious. I believe that the religious view does not imply that religious conviction appeals equally – that is, is roughly equally natural to all human beings in all contexts. Rather it suggests only that the ability to cognize God is widely and equally distributed, not necessarily equally developed, in all of us. Thus, what is natural to all is effortless only to some.

Religious belief is allegedly natural while atheism is unnatural – yet commitment to both involves responsible choice. How does one choose to believe something that is unnatural? How do we choose to disbelieve in God if the belief in him arises naturally in the (sane) human mind? It is either impossible or redundant. Believers would say that we should consciously choose to believe rather than disbelieve. The idea, however, that holding a belief is wholly a matter of our volition seems incoherent.

The Quran contains many imperatives: it orders us to read (scripture), submit (to God), believe (in him), fear and worship (him), and be just to each other (Q:96:1; 2:131; 4:47; 5:2; 4:36; 5:8 respectively). The command to believe is problematic. Can we deliberately choose to believe in something – the existence of an entity – or believe a (true) proposition? The Quran adds the complicating caveat that none shall believe without God's permission (Q:81:27–9). Muslims hold that the freedom of human agents, to the extent that they are held responsible for their acts, is not contravened by the omnipotence and predestination of the God portrayed in the Quran and the Prophetic traditions.[14]

11

The Quran supports the view that disbelievers choose to ignore and suppress religious truth. They are self-deceived. Such self-deception is abetted by Satan, an actively malicious agent in human affairs, enjoying a warrant for partially autonomous action until the day of judgement (Q:7:11–18; 38:79–83). The Quran calls self-deception self-seduction as in the passive phrase 'your souls have seduced you' (*sawwalat lakum anfusukum*; Q:12:18, 83). It also conjugates the verb *fa/ta/na* (to tempt or try), in the active voice, as in 'you tempted your souls' (*fatantum anfusakum*; Q:57:14). Such self-reflexive temptation and trial is analogous to the central Quranic notion of self-wronging (*zulm al-nafs*) which we shall discuss in the next chapter.

Now, self-deception misleads us in many areas of our emotional lives. For example, a man deceives himself into thinking, despite counter-evidence, that his friends or children or wife are loyal and faithful to him. A jingoist blinds herself to the virtues of other nations. Self-deception and self-persuasion are prevalent, perhaps routine in the secular life. Why should their presence be considered remarkable in the religious life? Few human beings, including professional thinkers, zealously search for the truth about their own nature, let alone believe in it when they attain it. Even perceptive professional students of human nature are often deluded about themselves while 'doing therapy' on others. In Chapter 7, we noted the dangers of self-deception and self-persuasion even in the prophetic mind.

Self-deception may be widespread. But is it immoral? As a cognitive component of sinful attitudes, self-deception is only culpable if it is, after due effort, avoidable. Presumably, it involves voluntary judgement even if it is stimulated by an external agent such as the Devil. We could be provoked or enticed into judging, sincerely and rationally, that some sceptical proposition (such as the claim that there is no God) is true. The result is an act of persuasion (or self-persuasion) and simultaneously self-deception.

We need not believe what we have been persuaded to know, as we saw in Chapter 2 when we analysed faith. Our deepest behaviour-influencing states are rarely states of knowledge. We may know that there is a God without necessarily believing it just as many alcoholics who are convinced by the irresistible logic of arguments against drinking still drink. Self-deception is possible since we can, paradoxically, refuse to believe what we know. Weakness of will (*akrasia*) is a supplementary explanation since a will can act autonomously in making us act intentionally against our own intellectually better judgement. Paradoxically, then, to know something is not necessarily to believe it, let alone to desire to act on it.

The religious believer indicts, for intentionally religious reasons, disbelief in God as a moral failure to live up to a religious demand. Disbelief is thus both a responsible and a guilty choice. Although this assessment of disbelief is plausible in religiously charged environments, it is implausible in a secular culture where the traces of God are overlaid by a surfeit of culturally sanctioned scepticism and mockery of religious faith. The burden rests on the shoulders of believers: they must show that modern rejection is an actively perverse, fully responsible, intellectually avoidable, and hence guilty preference.

12

I conclude this philosophical exploration with two related empirical observations in the sociology of religious commitment. It should give a flavour of the full dish. First, belief in God does not depend on individual temperament, intelligence or personal circumstances. People of different dispositions can believe in God – which is, significantly, indirect evidence for the Quranic-biblical claim about the potential universality of such belief. Moreover, an easy life need not lead to faith; a difficult life need not encourage rejection. Living in luxury is not always allied with atheism any more than living in abject poverty is always coupled with rejection of God and his providence. This is partly because genuine believers, at least in modern times, never treat religious belief as an experimental matter.[15] It was perhaps treated thus in the past as we see in patriarchal attempts to make a prudent bargain with God, parochially conceived, in the earliest parts of the Torah (Genesis 28:20–1).[16] In our times, experience of tragedy, such as the loss of a child, leads some people towards, even closer towards, faith while the same tragedy leads others altogether away from faith.

Second, intelligence as the exercise of reason is, like the experiences of tragedy, hardship and luxury, neutral in respect of faith and rejection. Some intelligent people have been devoutly religious believers: Blaise Pascal was unashamedly desperate for religious certainty while accepting tentative hypotheses in the world of experimental science.[17] Devout Jews, Christians and Muslims have sometimes been outstanding philosophers. From Islam, it is incomparably that mercurial genius Abū Ḥāmid Al-Ghazālī; from Judaism, the philosopher–halakhist Maimonides. Three saints, Augustine, Anselm and Aquinas, in that order, defined the intellectual heritage of the medieval millennium (fourth to fourteenth century) of Latin Christendom. On the other side of the divide, many seminal thinkers have sometimes, admittedly without reflection, rejected religious faith as puerile. Nietzsche boasted that he never believed in God even as a child because he 'was never childish enough for it'.[18] Sartre lost his faith all of a sudden at the tender age of 12 and in circumstances that are nothing short of laughable; yet he never once thought about the question for some 60 years.[19]

13

We now analyse the third type of rejection in the Quran by probing the pivotal accusation of idolatry (*shirk*), the uniquely unforgivable heresy of associating partners with God. It is Islam's only irremissible sin (Q:4:48, 116); God forgives other sins absolutely and 'wholly' (*jamī'an;* Q:39:53). The Quran condemns Arab pagans and some Jews and Christians as idolaters. Human beings associate false deities with the true God whom they acknowledge as the only deity worthy of worship; this partial recognition of the divine grandeur does not affect their practical conduct. When the intellectual error of associating partners with God contaminates our volition, our conduct is sinful. We must re-assess the relevance of this charge to modern Muslims and non-Muslims: the content and character of scepticism about revealed religion has changed dramatically since the days when Muhammad preached in the market-place only to find men and women distracted by the sight of newly arrived spice and silk caravans from Syria (see Q:62:11).

The accusation of idolatry is found in the writings of Jewish, Christian and Muslim apologists. The new idolatry, the charge reads, is subtler than the ancient varieties: today's pagans, fed an imbalanced sceptical diet of science and reason, do not lose sight of God's sole dominion in a plethora of colourful idols carved out of wood and stone. Instead they are intoxicated by the proud but illusory claim of self-sufficiency as rational beings exercising supremacy over nature and their destinies. Modern pagans supplant the mysterious and intangible God with a tangible but human fabrication – thus making a fetish of what is only human. Modern humankind is guilty of self-deification.

Before we examine the character of modern idolatry, we explore the Quranic noun *shirk* which means 'share' (Q:34:22; 46:4). The root triliteral verb *sha/ra/ka* means 'he shared'; verbal derivatives and nominal inflections have mundane meanings in modern (standard) Arabic. For example, *shirkah* and *sharikah* both mean a trading company. Now, 'Allah' is a contraction of *al-'ilāh* meaning 'the God'; the definite article is contained in the proper name of God (Allah), making plurality grammatically senseless and theologically impossible. But sinners can nonetheless *associate* false partners with the true God.

The idolater delights in associating the uniquely true God with false gods (Q:12:106; 39:45); most people have been idolaters (Q:30:42). The *mushrik* (idolater; pl., *mushrikūn*) compromises God's uniqueness by associating a partner (*sharīk*; Q:6:163; 17:111; 25:2) with God's exclusive divinity or sovereignty. The worship of false auxiliary gods hinders but does not fully replace the worship of the true God (Q:27:43). In distress, we purify our faith and call only on one God, never on his so-called partners (Q:6:40–1); once delivered from distress, we revert to pagan associationism (Q:7:189–92; 30:33).

Shirk is the most religiously distinctive and most frequently used word.[20] The Quran also uses the neutral word *juz'* (share) (Q:43:15). The disbelievers hold God 'justly equal' (*ya'dilūna*; from '*a/da/la*; Q:6:1; 27:60) with his partners. Other expressions of idolatry include a phrase used by sinners addressing the false partners: 'We did hold you as equals to the Lord of the universe' (*nusawwikum bi rabb al-'ālamīn*; Q:26:98). Other gods are called rivals (*nid'*; sing); only the plural occurs (*andād*; Q:2:22, 165; 7:138; 14:30; 34:33; 39:8; 41:9). The complex derived verb *ishtaraka* refers to the act of sharing in mundane things such as different sinners sharing punishment in hell (*mushtarikūna*; Q:37:33; 43:39).[21]

The Quran condemns *shirk* as an unjustified transgression. It is not as though the false gods created part of the universe thus confusing human beings who are now unsure whether to worship God or his co-creators and auxiliary gods (Q:13:16). In dialogue with his son, the sage Luqman condemns *shirk* as 'the supreme injustice' (Q:31:13) before he lists the vices that flow from it. As a capital offence against the dignity of God, it is generically 'injustice' (*zulmin*, lit., a wrong; Q:6:82). The phrase *min dūni Allāh* (to the exclusion of or in derogation of God) occurs often (Q:27:24, 43; 29:17, 22, 25, 41; 43:86; 45:10; 46:4, 5, 28; 71:25). Idolaters dilute their commitment to the only God and under-estimate his uniqueness and hence unique greatness (Q:29:61, 63). God in his glory is immune from false human ascriptions and far exalted above the partners associated with him (Q:27:63; 39:67; 40:15; 43:82).

Muhammad saw himself as an iconoclast who, like Abraham, risked his life to attack his people's idol-worship (Q:21:51–70; 37:83–98). Iconoclasm, like charity, begins at home: the Quranic Abraham condemns his father, named as Āzar (Q:6:74). Commentators add that he earned his livelihood by selling idols. In Muhammad's time, the merchant Quraysh's prosperity depended on their guardianship of the Meccan sanctuary which housed many idols (Q:106:3–4; see also Q:28:57). Ironically, this sanctuary was, the Quran claims, originally built by Abraham the iconoclast and his son Ishmael (Q:2:127). The Quran opposes the worship of idols, not necessarily the manufacture of images. Solomon orders the jinn to make harmless decorative images (*tamāthīl*, pl., Q:34:13).

We now return to the question of modern idolatry. The ancient pagan alienation from God was expressed in a crudely material and literal attachment to idols (Q:37:95). By contrast, the mechanics of modern idolatry are invisible and complex. Human beings temporarily suppress but cannot eradicate their innate knowledge of God; secular propaganda cannot brainwash the idea of God from our minds and consciences. When we reject God, we invent a substitute deity to replace him. We temporarily allow mundane realities – human reason or love or power – to exhaust an allegiance properly owed to the divine ruler. Teenagers make gods of musical performers; virtually all academics indulge in a cult of personality by idolizing their one chosen thinker or artist.

We cannot then, it seems, avoid worshipping God in some guise or other, usually under an innocuous description. Our ineradicable awareness of and attraction to God is exhibited, it is concluded, by the prevalence of religious language and metaphor even in secular life; 'implicit religion' survives the demise of formal religion in secularized cultures. Even the frantic search for the one perfect lover or partner is perhaps a secularized and perverted form of the original and innate quest for God.

When we dethrone God, we create a void we are desperate to fill. Wine, women and song make idolaters of most of us since we are pleasure-seeking and self-centred sinners. The three young men in the Persian court, mentioned in the apocryphal book of 1 Esdras, the Greek Ezra, defend the three strongest idols as wine, the King, and women. The strongest reality, according to the third contender (who initially pretended to defend women as the most powerful idol), is the truth grounded in God's reality (1 Esdras 3:1–5:6). More subtly, mystics and religious poets identify the egocentric predicament as the final locus of inveterate idolatry. We seek the kingdom of sin, of self, of the world, but all are in fact displaced desires for the kingdom of God.

Idolatry persists then as long as God stands second in the queue. Apart from the trite and formulaic temptations of wine, women and song, there are other illusions, fantasies and deceptions that plague everyone: the lust for power, fame, glory, youth and wealth and its undeserved privileges; the misplaced trust in unaided human reason and its intellectual products (such as empirical science and technology); the seductive and nearly universal quest for the illusory and transient charms of a romantic love that sets us up for suffering as it culminates inevitably in the crushing burdens of marriage, mortgage and children; a trust in the political sagacity of a perverse jingoism boasting 'My country, right or wrong, left or right'; racial pride and loyalty to family and tribe; and the misplaced trust in power as panacea for social ills, a trust culminating in the utilitarian myth of a dependable political providence, a providence marked by perpetual progress without direction.

14

The religious apologist concludes: although false absolutes can temporarily become ersatz replacements for the true divine absolute, the divine imprint on human nature, mind and conscience cannot be eradicated. We are addicted to God. He remains and reigns supreme: God is greater (*Allāhu akbar*).

Can we accuse the modern rejector of being an idolater? Is modern *shirk* conceptually continuous with the Quranic notion of *shirk*? I suggest that the category of *shirk* was originally unavoidable but provisional: it provided for the need to accuse the pagans in terms they could understand. But the category was of temporary relevance. The argument for this will be made in the next few sections. I begin by exploring a few further facets of *shirk* in its original setting. Then I examine the reasons that might make this charge problematic in a modern culture whose intellectual presuppositions are intentionally naturalistic. I shall conclude that we need a new vocabulary for condemning modern humankind's rejection of the existence and authority of an only God.

God has no partner (*sharīk*) in his divinity; and 'he has no partner in his kingdom' (*lam yakun la hū sharīkun fī al-mulk*; Q:25:2), a stock phrase introducing Islamic sermons. He needs no helper (*zahīr*) from the false gods (Q:34:22) who cannot give life or death or resurrect the dead (Q:25:3). The idea of a son of God is also repudiated as a form of associating partners with God's divinity (Q:18:4–5).

Idolaters are associationists, not merely polytheists; typically they are both. Someone who believed only in false gods but rejected the existence and divinity of the genuine God would not qualify as an idolater. Thus, Hindus are apparently not idolaters (*mushrikūn*) because, unlike their pagan Arab counterparts, the Hindu polytheists do not believe in Allah. The Quran rejects this possibility: human beings, in virtue of being human, instinctively believe in one God. Hindus suppress belief in the true God with a surfeit of false deities whose existence enters the range of their conscious awareness. Therefore, all polytheistic disbelievers are automatically, if subliminally, *mushrikūn*.

Jews and Christians are accused of idolatry, even disbelief, but the presuppositions that make this charge coherent and meaningful, arguably true, are available. Both religious groups claim to be monotheists. But, charges the Quran, Christians associate Christ, as Son of God, with God, which amounts to both idolatry and outright disbelief. Jews are frequently accused of moral and doctrinal errors; in one passage they are accused of committing blatant idolatry by associating 'Uzair with God, where 'Uzair might refer to the post-exilic priest-scribe Ezra:

> And the Jews say: "Uzair is a son of God' and the Christians say: 'The Messiah is a son of God'. This is merely a word out of their mouths. They are imitating the speech of disbelievers from the past. May God fight them! How perverted! They have taken their religious scholars and monks as lords (*arbāb*; *rabb*, sing.) besides the true God while the Messiah, son of Mary, never ordered them to do anything except worship one God; there is no God beside him. Glory be to him! He is above all that they associate (*yushrikūna*) with him'.
>
> (Q:9:30–1)[22]

15

A necessary condition for committing idolatry is belief – whether firm, intermittent or casual – in the existence of the only God, a condition unfulfilled for many today. We commit the sin of *shirk* if and only if we believe in the true God, in some moods, and dilute our monotheistic belief by affirming one or more gods that we could be persuaded to reject as illusory. Explicit atheism, as the denial of the existence of all supernatural realities, is a recent development. The doctrines of radical rejection were, as we saw in Chapters 1 and 3, forged in western Europe during the nineteenth and twentieth centuries. The other world was rejected as a figment of the religious imagination of primitive and frightened human beings in need of security and consolation in this one.

The Quran assumes the reality of a supernatural realm. It does not invent the name 'Allāh', a familiar name for the high and remote god. Muhammad's pagan father was called '*Abd Allāh* (servant of Allah). The pagans already believed in him (Q:43:9, 87) but their unforgivable sin was setting up 'another god besides God' (Q:50:26). Some held the elemental spirits, the jinn, to be equal to God (Q:6:100). The goddess Al-Lāt (lit., the only goddess) was worshipped in Mecca (Q:53:19). Muhammad's pagan listeners inhabit the same world as Muhammad but have different priorities in the ranking of deities. The Quran aims to redirect their fervour by expatiating on the supreme being's uniqueness and robust majesty and thus investing the name 'Allāh' with exclusive religious significance.

Muhammad warns the pagan Arabs and the Jews and Christians that Allah, a jealous God, tolerates no divine partners. The iconoclastic refrain is consistent: 'There is no god – except God'. The Quran does not merely tell the pagans that they shall 'have no other gods besides me', to use the biblical phrase, but rather that there are no other gods besides God, denying the very existence of all pseudo-deities (Q:34:27; 28:62 repeated verbatim at v.74). Some passages challenge the pagans to name or point to the false gods (Q:13:33; 34:27). The Quran rarely condescends to name the idols housed in the Meccan shrine – except for one reference to the three so-called daughters of Allāh (Q:53:19–20) and an unclear allusion to two idols, *al-Jibt* (symbolizing magic) and *al-ṭāghūt* (lit., rebel; symbolizing the Devil), apparently worshipped by some Jews and Christians in Arabia (Q:4:51; 39:17). Five idols worshipped by Noah's community are also named (Q:71:23); these might have become, judging by their Arabic-sounding names, part of the Arab pagan pantheon by Muhammad's time.

The false gods must exist at least in a literary sense. Perhaps for rhetorical effect, the Quran claims that God shall raise the false partners (*al-shurakā'*) for questioning on the day of judgement (Q:10:28–9). The resurrected idols will speak out (Q:25:17–18) and will be hostile to their devotees, rejecting their adoration (Q:19:82; 29:5; 46:5–6) just as Satan also rejects the pagan tendency to associate him with God (Q:14:22). The idols will fail to intercede on behalf of pagans (Q:6:94). Indeed the idols themselves seek to be close to the only real God (Q:17:57) and are enslaved to him (Q:7:194).

The Quran's dismissal of lesser gods traumatized pagan Arabs because they were, like all ancient peoples, emotionally pagan: religious to the point of being superstitious, anxious to placate nature and the gods responsible for their welfare, keen to honour all supernatural or superhuman beings, including Allāh (Q:43:9, 87) and his three daughters (Q:53:19–23). Expectedly, the polytheistic pagans have a religious instinct since all human beings instinctively acknowledge the true God. It is a shame that the pagans made a wrong choice which God, via Muhammad, seeks to alter so that all knees may finally bow to God alone.

The Quran has a larger concern in insisting on the authenticity of the sole God. It warns us against entertaining an irreverent or frivolous attitude towards the regions of mystery inaccessible to our intelligence: the unseen (*al-ghayb*; Q:2:3; 27:65) or the realm of secrets (*ghayb*; sing; *ghuyūb*, pl; Q:2:33; *ghayābah* at Q:12:15). We might today call it the supernatural although the distinction between the natural and the supernatural is in substance a modern one. The Quran does not need to argue for the existence of the supernatural since the experienced reality and the pervasive presence of that realm were self-evident to both Muhammad and his detractors. The point of contention was the attitude towards that realm. The idolater, as anti-prophetic magician or demon-possessed poet, develops a profane relationship with the supernatural, manipulating the sacred for profane ends, thus earning divine wrath. The prophets, by contrast, show us how to cultivate a reverent connection and association with nature and the holy dimension in it.[23]

Our problem is that modern godless humanity is not temperamentally pagan; many moderns do not believe in any supernatural being. The profundity of modern doubt forces believers to demonstrate even the *coherence* of the concept of a (supreme) supernatural being. There are no gods, angels or demons and there never could be such beings. The atheist's ontology radically rules out the possibility of accepting the second half of the Islamic creed. The atheist accepts only the opening claim that literally reads, 'No god'. Its revolutionary continuation no longer requires, as it did in our pagan past, a dethronement of false divinities. It requires us to endorse a concept which atheists, in the West and in (the formerly) Communist countries, have for over a century denounced as empty, false, and senseless.

Ancient disbelievers were *mis*believers who worshipped things which they recognized to be unworthy of unconditional respect and honour. They also ignored and devalued, wilfully or through weakness of the will, realities that they recognized, in their more reflective moods, to be worthy of allegiance. Modern disbelievers are not *mushrikūn* since the presupposition that once made that a viable charge is now unavailable. When ancient *mushrikūn* associated other gods with God, they denied not the reality (existence) but the divinity of 'God the exalted and tremendous' (*Allāh al-'aẓīm*; Q:69:33). Today's 'idolaters' deny the reality and *a fortiori* the divinity of God. If the modern denial and denigration of the transcendent are justified, the accusation of *shirk* is incoherent.

There are necessary and sufficient conditions for being an idolater. Potentially conscious belief in God is a necessary prerequisite. It is both necessary and sufficient that one believes in the one true God while also believing or worshipping one or more false gods. The ancient disbeliever associated false gods with the true god and also lived in practical neglect of the will of the true God. The ancient pagan was therefore an idolater (*mushrik*) and a disbeliever (*kāfir*); the modern disbeliever is at most only a *kāfir*.

16

At this stage in the dialectic, Muslims would re-affirm that the contemporary rejection of God is essentially no different from ancient paganism. The irreligious ideals which usurp the *de jure* sovereignty of God are, they would argue, the new gods which should be condemned as illusory. We human beings need ultimate ideals, whether religious or secular, to retain our allegiance. We are by nature worshippers; if we do not worship truth, we shall certainly worship falsehood.

Much argumentative apologetics includes this stock argument: the uneasy and agitated hankering of our hearts and minds for *any* ideal is prima facie evidence of a universal foundation for the desire to seek God. Some would argue, in a more secular form of this contention, that we become religious beings simply because we interact thoughtfully with the mysterious cosmos – which automatically makes every reflective person a religious believer. Paul Tillich called religion 'an ultimate concern'. A.N. Whitehead famously remarked that religion was whatever a man does with his solitariness.

This popular contention, in all these related versions, is unconvincing. Genuine believers never define religious belief in terms of psychological attitude rather than theological content. If any and every ultimate concern is religious, then, trivially, we are all religious by definition. As for Whitehead's definition, suppose that stamp collecting or indulgence in sexual fantasy fills a man's leisurely solitariness. Is that then his religion? [24]

We should avoid labelling as 'religious' any purely humanistic or naturalistic belief-systems such as Marxist humanism. Why? Not every ideal can defensibly be described as 'religious' because some ideals, such as secular political nationalism and applied Marxism, are explicitly and intentionally proposed by their adherents as irreligious, even anti-religious. Such ideals have mundane referents. Moreover, the religious ideal presupposes the possibility of espousing irreligious and anti-religious ideals. If no ideal could be genuinely irreligious, the contrast between the sacred and the profane, essential to defining the sacred, could neither be drawn nor, therefore, transcended. The proposal that any and every ultimate norm for human allegiance is inescapably religious implies the trivialization if not the impossibility of a contrast fundamental to the religious perspective on the world. It remains impressively plausible, even for believers, to argue for a restriction of 'religious' to ideals that intentionally have or presuppose a transcendent reference.

The religious apologist retorts that the claim has been misunderstood. The claim is not that some ideals are not irreligious in content – they plainly are – but rather that the decision to espouse any ideal, whether religious or irreligious in content, is a religious decision in terms of its motivation, whether that motivation is conscious or unintentional. The decision-maker's attitude, not the ideal espoused, is inescapably religious. But this claim needs independent support as, by itself, it openly begs the very question at stake. (Begging questions persuasively and surreptitiously is a more pardonable offence in philosophy.) The apologist's argument would succeed only if human nature were agreed to be irreducibly religious. If we are religious beings, then espousing any ideal, independently of its content, is necessarily a religious (or irreligious) act since the actor is religious. But this assumption, axiomatic to Islam, is controversial, that is, epistemologically assailable.

17

The apologist's argument above inadvertently hints at why we are failing to rehabilitate the concept of idolatry in the modern world. It invites the question: If we are idolaters, are we *intentional* idolaters? The more removed we are from the age of revelation, the more unintentional our idolatry. Muslim thinkers distinguish between *al-shirk al-jallī* (manifest or explicit idolatry) and *al-shirk al-khafiyy* (concealed or implicit idolatry); the latter category ensures that modern hubris is within the ambit of iconoclastic accusation. This distinction is extra-Quranic and appears in commentaries. The very need for it implies that the Quranic net does not catch all the miscreants. Intentional (or manifest) idolatry was, it might be argued, as prevalent in the past as unintentional (or hidden) idolatry has been in ages since, including our times. In the Quran, the idolatrous pagan entertains an intentional, not accidental, preference for disbelief. I shall explain.

A crucial preliminary point about *shirk* in the Quran: it is often discussed in the context of divine warnings against Satan (Q:24:21), our 'open enemy' (Q:12:5; 12:42; 18:63; 35:6; 43:62), that traitor (Q:25:29), that evil companion (Q:22:13) and arch-deceiver (*al-ghurūr*; Q:35:5; 57:14). The Quran presupposes the existence of both God and of his supreme opponent, *Al-Shaytān*, who is hell-bent on misleading the Children of Adam (Q:7:11–18; 37:74–85). The idolater prefers guidance from diabolic rather than divine sources (Q:36:60; 43:36–7). Describing Abraham's confrontation with his father (Q:19:41–5), the Quran links idolatry with the worship of the Devil (Q:19:44).

We are now able to examine cases of intentional idolatry. The Pharaoh proclaims himself a god and his people take him to be one despite knowing, as a result of Moses' preaching, about the existence of the one true God (Q:28:38; 79:24). Like the later Arab pagans, they are true idolaters. Sheba (Saba') is a sun-worshipper (Q:27:24) before her conversion (Q:27:44). The Quran warns us against idolizing the sun and the moon (Q:41:37). Again, Abraham, while searching for God, commits intentional idolatry by saying of the rising sun: 'This is my Lord; this is greater!' (*hāzā rabbī, hāzā akbar*; Q:6:78). His words remind one of Islam's iconoclastic 'God is greater!' (*Allāhu akbar*).

Nearer our times, Goethe's epic *Faust (Faustus)* is inspired by a German legend about a learned man who, in his quest for forbidden advanced knowledge of material realities, summons the Devil – in the guise of the evil spirit Mephistopheles. The spirit offers to serve him for a time on condition that Faust sells his soul to him. Faust was willing to barter his soul so that he could fulfil this longing. Jesus had expressly condemned this type of bargain: 'What does it profit a man to gain the whole world and lose his soul?' (Mark 8:36). Similarly, Shakespeare makes two lovers commit intentional idolatry when Juliet requests Romeo to 'Swear by thy gracious self /which is the god of my idolatry'. [25]

Again, Sir Walter Raleigh (*c.* 1554–1618), formally a Christian, began to idolize Death during his incarceration in the Tower of London. Imprisonment has often been a great spur to scholarship and sincere reflection. Raleigh began to reflect on Death's omnipotent reach as he awaited execution on charges of treason against King James I. In a moving correspondence with the sovereign, he shows hints of virtually worshipping Death as the forceful god who reduces life's greatest achievements to a handful of churchyard dust and shoves it under our eyes under the motto *Hic jacet* (here lies!).[26]

These are cases of intentional idolatry: one replaces the avowedly superior reality of God with something acknowledged, at least occasionally, as inferior. Although this type of idolatry is paradigmatic and representative, it is rarely committed in ages subsequent to the ages of faith. In Islamic literature, we find only one case – and that is part of romantic folk-lore! The tragedy of the woman Leila and her lover Majnūn, the Romeo and Juliet of the Muslim Orient, enjoys a prodigiously massive reputation among Persian-speaking and Indian sub-continental Muslims. It is inspired by a true story but its details are legendary. In his passion, Majnūn took Leila, not God, to be the referent of the Muslim prayer. This ritual is punctuated by the phrase 'God is greater' (*Allāhu akbar*), Islam's versatile prayer movement marker which doubles as a battle-cry. By going through the postures of prayer while addressing his beloved, Majnūn insinuated that God is not greater! Since actions speak louder than words, he committed the capital sin of 'association in worship' (*shirk al-'ibādah*).[27] 'Leila is greater' was his unexpressed thought. He was called Majnūn, meaning lunatic (lit., demon-possessed), an epithet Muhammad also received from the pagans. When rebuked by devout elders, Majnūn retorted that he worshipped Leila, not God. He was spared on account of the madness of love.

Such a clear case of idolatry is a far cry from the unintentional idolatry of the weak-willed or worldly man whose body is at prayer in the mosque while his mind is elsewhere, perhaps dwelling on the deplorable state of his bank balance or regretting his addiction to wine, women and song. Many people effectively enthrone a lesser reality on the pedestal of allegiance but they do not, by that act alone, deliberately intend to dethrone a higher one. At a mosque, synagogue or church, practically no one is like Faust or Majnūn or a modern Satanist intentionally making a deliberately irreligious choice – that is, recognizing and acknowledging the existence of God but refusing to worship him and instead preferring to worship a lesser reality. The closest we get to intentional idolatry in the modern world is the widespread and literal worship of artists, stars and cult leaders by some mentally deranged teenagers and desperately bored housewives.

18

In terms of ontology and motivation, our secular alienation from God differs from the ancient pagans' alienation. S*hirk* is a misguided deification of the natural and human world resulting from the attempt to reduce God to the level of creation when in fact he is exalted above what pagans associate with him. But given our cultural and religious distance from the world of Arab paganism, can we legitimately use *shirk* for any *revolutionary* religious accusation of modern secularism? Perhaps idolatry is an outdated accusation. To be fair, the Quran occasionally targets our modern type of 'idolatry' when it claims that human beings sometimes identify – as opposed to merely associate – their whims and desires with ultimate truth or value:

> Have you considered the man who took his fancy (*hawā-hū*) to be his god (*'ilāh-hū*) and God led him astray despite his knowledge and God sealed his hearing and his heart and placed a covering over his eyes; so who then, after this, could guide him? Will you not be admonished? And they said: 'There is nothing but this our life of this lower world; we die and we live and nothing except Time (*al-dahr*) destroys us.' But they have no firm knowledge of this matter; they are conjecturing. And when our self-evident signs are rehearsed for them, their sole argument is their [old] claim: 'Bring back to life our forefathers if you are truthful in your claims!'
>
> (Q:45:23–5; see also Q:25:43, 28:50)

In this passage, we note a pagan analogue of modern secular humanism. In the pre-Islamic world, this orally transmitted view inspired pagan poetry. We live and die inside the rigid parameters and 'the indifferent ravages of time and fate' (*rayb al-manūn*; Q:53:30). The pagans received the proposals of resurrection and eternal life with persistent disbelief and scorn (Q:6:29; 17:49–51; 27:67–8; 32:10–11; 34:7–8; 50:3–4; 79:10–12). It is a measure of the Quran's frustration with the intransigence of disbelievers on this point that it even calls the denial of the resurrection 'the supreme sin' (*al-ḥins al-'azīm*; Q:56:46–7), making it compete with the unique enormity of *shirk*.

Is the Arab pagan decision to attach finality to death and an associated futility to life roughly equivalent to our modern self-satisfied creed of secular humanism, itself only a polite word for paganism? If so, the Quran might have cast its net wide enough to catch our characteristically modern brand of idolatry. A similarly partial awareness of modern idolatry is also evident in the New Testament where the moral vices of sexual desire and greed are explicitly equated with the worship of a false god (Colossians 3:5; Ephesians 5:5). Perhaps the ages of revelation were more aware of the conceptual reach of idolatry than I have suggested. If so, this might be a starting-point for believers seeking to update the notion for modern use. But they must still re-interpret and extrapolate the concept of *shirk*, the characteristic form of rejection in the Quranic world, in order to link it with the current debate on faith and rejection – which revolves around speculative atheism, the denial of the existence, not merely unique divinity, of God.

19

Today we rarely appreciate the literalism of the iconoclastic mind confronting paganism; the concern with idolatry has inevitably therefore dwindled into metaphor. Modern culture is irreligious – but not pagan in the sense of believing in the wrong supernatural powers. Modern secularists are modern pagans who believe in nothing beyond nature.

Some *practical* concerns connected to idolatrous conduct have long been anachronistic for Muslims, Jews and Christians. Thus, the Quran's prohibition on the consumption of meat ritually dedicated to idols or slaughtered in the name of a false god (Q:5:3; 6:121, 145) is hardly a pressing concern among modern Muslims. Similarly, Paul's agonized discussion of whether Christians should eat meat offered to idols (1 Corinthians 10:14–32) has lapsed permanently into a matter of academic interest. But our concern is with the *conceptual* question of the modern applicability of the religious accusation of idolatry.

Muslims are attached to the accusatory connotations of *shirk* but the intellectual content of the idea must now be re-assessed. Modern men and women are no longer fruitfully seen as intentional associationists. They might be unintentional idolaters but that accusation begs the question, as I have shown, against the secular opponent. I propose therefore that we see the modern rejector or disbeliever as a 'substitutionist' who seeks to replace God with a secular surrogate reality that he or she (mistakenly) regards as the highest god or good. The modern disbeliever is guilty of what I call *istibdāl* which I define as a desire for replacement of one reality with another that is (mistakenly) perceived to have parity with it. If we construct a model of *istibdāl* consonant with though not implied by the Quran, it would signify the intentional replacement of God with something considered equally worthy of unconditional worship. For the believer, the replacement would be misguided since the substituted reality is sham and inadequate.

The verb *istabdala* (to seek to change or replace) is derived from the root *ba/da/la* (to change) by adding an augment. It occurs a few times in the Quran. It refers once to a man intending to substitute one wife for another to maintain the permitted quota of four in a serial polygyny (Q:4:20). It is also used in the frequent divine threat that God could easily replace the disobedient (Arab) Muslims with a new people who would be more eager to serve him (Q:9:39; 47:38).[28]

Our modern alienation from God differs from the ancient alienation of the pagan just as our style of scepticism about the supernatural is alien to the biblical and Quranic worlds. Idolatry is an organically religious term. Today we may employ it as a tool of accusation – but only by a massive, perhaps illegitimate, extension of meaning, combined with a deracination from its original context. If it is understood vaguely as the misguided deification of the natural and human world, it retains value today but it cannot retain its intended original significance.[29] Idolatry has lost its primary meaning since modern disbelievers are culturally and religiously no longer pagans. Indeed, strictly speaking, in terms of the *logic* of concepts, *shirk* lost its original sense even for the second generation of believers, born to Muslim parents, after the advent of Islam. But this fact could still be ignored in ages that were religious but not pagan. By contrast, we are now living in an aggressively secular era which is neither pagan nor religious. The oddity, perhaps incoherence, of the charge of idolatry can no longer be concealed.

Should we discard *shirk* in its traditional sense? Islam's confession of faith effectively declares: 'Do not associate any partners with God'. Such iconoclasm, central to the Islamic lexicon, can be re-formulated without recourse to the concept of *shirk*. Let me explain.

The original concern with *shirk* was not religious in a narrow sense; it was also ideological and political – if we understand these terms without pejorative modern connotations. The creed warned against placing a disproportionate trust in the power of profane political power in individual or communal life. To say *Lā 'ilāha illā Allāh* (there is no god but God) is to impose an operative embargo on oneself from conceding ultimate reality or power to forces that enslave individuals and societies. For any human reality or facility, be it power without accountability, pleasure without restraint, wealth unlawfully gained, progeny as dearer than God, reason as absolute guide, anything or anyone seeking to usurp the top place, the iconoclastic conscience shouts: '*Lā*'(No!) (We shall explore this dimension of Islam in Chapter 11.) Politically, the creed is better formulated if we interpret it as forbidding *substitution* of a lesser reality for the supreme reality of God – which is, in effect, what modern idolaters do. The modern ideologue, unlike the ancient idolater, is not associating God with a lesser reality but rather denying God outright by, unintentionally or intentionally, replacing him with some reality judged inferior by Quranic criteria. The conversion process today, unlike that of pagans in our religious past, begins when atheists see that they formerly *replaced* God with something unworthy of ultimate allegiance rather than *associated* him with false gods.

The wisely chosen word *tauḥīd*, translated as monotheism, denotes the Islamic creed. Literally, it means the act of unifying things. It is idiomatically translated not as unity or monotheism but rather as unification – with its welcome overtones of actively making the gods into one God. The Meccans accused Muhammad of uniting the gods (Q:38:5). But how do we today make the gods one – when there are no gods?[30]

20

I have assumed a realist (objectivist) position on faith and idolatry: the idolater worships objects or realities independently known to exist but unworthy of worship.[31] I now assess and refute a view of idolatry in which the integrity (or authenticity) of our inward attitude towards whatever we take to be our object of worship in itself decides the status of that object. The sincerity of intention is alleged to be the decisive, even sole, factor. If this view were true, the problem of idolatry must be re-formulated as idolatry could be committed in any age, secular or religious, because the only requirement would be insincerity of intention, hardly something ever in short supply. We would then have anonymous idolaters. It is a view found in the voluminous writings of Søren Kierkegaard who apparently believed that all worshippers can become idolaters if they dishonour God, an infinite being, by directing their adoration towards a finite object.

Kierkegaard mentions two worshippers one of whom lives in the heart of Christendom, attending the house of the true God and entertaining a correct conception of this God – but praying in a false spirit. The other worshipper is an idolater living among idolaters but praying with 'the entire passion of the infinite' although he prays to an idol. Kierkegaard asks us to judge which of the two worshippers is a true worshipper. He answers: 'The one prays in truth to God though he worships an idol; the other prays falsely to the true God, and hence worships in fact an idol'.[32]

Before applying this to the Muslim case, we note a relevant internal inconsistency in this account. Kierkegaard believed, as we know from his other writings including the *Concluding Unscientific Postscript* from which we quoted above, that faith cannot be conceived in non-Christian terms: it cannot be directed towards any reality except the Christian deity. But he also argued, inconsistently, that through any sincere act of existential commitment, 'the individual is in the truth even if he should happen to be thus related to what is not true'.[33] Kierkegaard's emphasis *seems* to fall on the integrity of the inward attitude we take towards whatever is the object of our worship; and yet he still speaks of a 'true conception of God'. However, if truth and faith are defined as 'personal subjectivity', one cannot consistently speak of a 'true conception of God' available independently of the subjectivity of the passionate believer. We conclude therefore that faith, for Kierkegaard, is not a subjective expression of a believer's wishes or of what the believer imagines is true: it is rather a form of knowledge. The object towards which true faith is directed is not the product of an individual's will or intellect; it is an objective reality. If so, Kierkegaard's proposal reduces to a concealed counsel of perfection: he is encouraging hypocritical Christians, who are Christians nonetheless (and not idolaters), to be perfectly sincere in their devotions. Believers should be authentic; they must not believe in the truth in a false spirit. This presupposes, however, that there is an accessible truth independent of what the believer's will or imagination or intellect creates.

Imagine now a Muslim believer praying in a false spirit and a *mushrik* praying in a true spirit. Does the sincere and passionate *mushrik* become a monotheist while the hypocritical and lukewarm Muslim becomes, anonymously, a *mushrik*? No. Both might be idolaters. Integrity and sincerity have no intrinsic worth; the inward attitudes they engender cannot be religiously sound if the worship is directed towards what is independently judged to be an idol or illusion. To take a parallel case, morally evil persons cannot attain religious integrity, no matter how sincerely they profess their religious convictions, since such integrity is impossible where moral rectitude is missing. Similarly, idolaters cannot become believers solely in virtue of their sincerity. A sincere idolater can be sincerely mistaken and remains a true idolater since sincerity cannot alter falsehood into truth – provided we accept the realist view that there exist, objectively, falsehood and truth.

Insincere believers fail to qualify as true believers; they are usually hypocrites. The availability of this vocabulary suffices to make the requisite distinctions.

The notions of sincere and insincere worship are available in the Quran and the Bible. Both scriptures aim to eradicate hypocrisy from the interior life of genuine faith. Luke's parable of the self-righteous Pharisee and the self-effacing tax collector together in the same temple (Luke 18:9–14) well illustrates this gulf between sincerity and insincerity in the life of faith.

10 Human nature and the Quran

1

During the inter-wars years in Europe, particularly in Germany and France, away from the fury of fascist politics, an intense interest in the problem of human nature was brewing. The strenuously assertive secular philosophy that emerged out of that maelstrom came to be associated with Jean-Paul Sartre. It is an anti-religious version of existentialism. The movement, in its aboriginal form, is found in the writings of the Christian philosopher Søren Kierkegaard. As its name suggests, it deals with the experience of our existence, an internal reckoning with the fact of our being. Human beings, unlike objects, have no assigned essence and are therefore radically free to decide their own nature. Existence precedes essence: we exist before we behave in a given way.[1] In Sartre's version, we must remove the props of religion and the consolations of another life which could support or distract us; we must bear the burden of freedom on earth. 'Nothing can save a man from himself, not even a valid proof of the existence of God', pontificates Sartre, the Pope of existentialism.[2]

We shall now assess the view that human essence is externally fixed by examining the unique philosophical anthropology embedded in the Quran. We shall assess the Islamic scripture's theo-metaphysical contribution to the problem of understanding, defining, and refining human nature. In Sections 2 to 9, we examine the Quranic portrait of human nature and note the reservations of modern readers. We also note and explore – though not deplore – the failure of individuals and societies to conform to divine demands, a theme which received extended treatment in the previous chapter. In Sections 10 to 16, we enter the deeper end of the pool and wade through the causes and implications of such failure. Why do we, particularly today, fail to live according to divine dictates? Can we be justly blamed for our failure? Can we resolve the discrepancy between the exacting demands of Quranic piety, on the one hand, and the capacities and possibilities of unaided human nature in our quest for moral and spiritual excellence and perfection, on the other?

In the last section, we broaden the debate by assessing the ancient insistence on transcending our natural humanity in the context of the modern tendency to reduce it to an unalloyed animality. We conclude by noting the exclusively modern question of the status of the natural body, its plasticity and the implied radical indeterminacy of human nature – as the very notion of a biologically stable human nature becomes controversial.

In Sections 10 to 16, we address three questions:

1   If human nature is created to be submissive to God's good will, as the Quran claims, why is human nature recalcitrant to virtue and guidance?

2   Given the constitutional limitations of human nature, acknowledged in the Quran, how is the required degree of religious enthusiasm achieved by any believer in any age?

3   If we acknowledge divinely sanctioned weakness in our nature, is it legitimate to expect enthusiastic commitment from all believers today?

A point of method: a believer troubled by the sceptical tone of our inquiry, could complain that the puzzles identified above arise only when we turn mysteries into mere problems, as if we were doing social science. Human beings should not be treated as objects among other objects. We have free will; and furthermore, in religion, the intentions of a mysterious deity are a factor. Deliberately creating human beings to be weak involves a divine decision that is, by definition, part of an undiscoverable motive.

No doubt, believers can at best offer only a partial explanation for the phenomena of human failure and weakness. 'Why are human beings created weak?' is a mystery because it asks about the motives of a deity whose nature and intentions are defined as irreducibly mysterious. The believer is being asked to resolve a problem which refers to the radically inaccessible motives and intentions of an arcane deity. In such cases, the mystery of God's choices and actions can be mitigated only by recourse to further or alternative, perhaps more comforting, mystery. One should not therefore expect any wholly naturalistic answer to be fully satisfactory. Part of the believer's point about the nature of our limitations in this inquiry is granted.

2

Human beings are, in Islamic reflection inspired by the Quran, the apex of God's creation. All things have been subjugated to *al-insān*, the Quranic word for man (as masculine singular) and for humankind. Nature, including the aquatic and animal kingdom, has been made serviceable and subservient to us (Q:14:32–3; 43:12–13; 45:4, 12–13; 67:15).

Humanity is praised in Islamic doctrine as *al-ashraf al-makhluqāt* (the crown of creation), a description reminiscent of the Psalmist: 'You made him [man] lord of the works of your hands, put all things under his feet' (Psalms 8:6).[3] This description of human beings as the zenith of creation is not Quranic but the scripture does say: 'Surely we have created humankind (*al-insān*) in the best of moulds' (*aḥsani taqwīm*; Q:95:4). Some passages temper this exaltation of our species: the creation of humanity is a marvel but the creation of the heavens and the earth is a greater one (Q:40:57; 79:27). We humans are, however, appointed as imperialists with dominion over nature – but only on condition that we serve God. On the way home from the laboratory, we must stop by at the mosque.

An exalted view of humankind is implicit in the divine assertion that 'I have breathed into him [Adam] of my spirit (*ruhī*; Q:15:29; 32:9; 38:72). One passage uniquely claims that God has strengthened the 'party of God' (*hizb Allāh*) 'by a spirit from himself' (*bi ruhin min hū;* Q:58:22). Jesus is fortified by 'a holy spirit' from God (*ruh al-qudus*; Q:2:87, 253), a reference to the archangel Gabriel. The anthropomorphic image of God blowing his spirit into the human frame is mysterious; perhaps it means that something divine affects and partly determines our supernatural endowment.

If we closely read sacred texts and speculate on their deeper meanings, we could extract an entire transcendental anthropology from a few desultory Quranic remarks. Muslim jurists would veto any unduly conjectural interest in human nature fearing that the results might be subversive of orthopraxy: believers might adopt a relaxed attitude towards the revealed law and justify their laxity on the grounds that their nature is already partly divine and hence, reasoning fallaciously, exempt from complete conformity to the law. Such softening of Islam's legal religious demands offends orthodoxy; devout Muslims emphasize that Islam has one short creed but four associated practical duties, a ratio of theory to practice that is no accident. We attend to the implications of this stress on practicality towards the end of the chapter.

Orthodox Muslims reject the Hebraic–Christian claim that human beings were made in the *tzelem Elohīm* (image of God; Genesis 1:27) since traffic with images, even abstract ones, is deemed idolatrous.[4] But this resourceful metaphor helps to distinguish the Greek notion of human dignity as intrinsic from the monotheistic notion that human worth is derivative. Greek idealism identified the human essence with *nous* (theoretical reason) which survived death. Human beings are essentially rational and moral, not religious. This debate is vital to a correct understanding of *religious* humanism, a view which appears, to secular humanists, inauthentic, incoherent and degrading, as it derives the dignity and sanctity of human life from an extrinsic reality, namely, our relationship to God. Monotheism does stress that it is not our nature but rather our special relationship to God that distinguishes us from the rest of creation.

An image, like a shadow, has no intrinsic reality; it derives its existence wholly and its character partly from the reality of which it is the image. Our humanity is constituted by our potential for relationship to God: our status as *species humana* is intended in our relation to our divine creator although neither the Quran nor the Bible commits itself to a view concerning the precise respects in which human beings reflect the image of their creator. For the Greeks, human dignity inhered in us by virtue of our remarkable capacities and qualities; for monotheists, human dignity derived from a derivative relationship. Although our relationship to God is part of our essence, this does not mean that we have no nature of our own. While our distinctive capacities and qualities depend on our relationship to God, they also exist in their own right and belong equally to our essence. An image is parasitic on the reality that casts it but it still exists apart from that original reality once it has been cast. It is, unlike an optical illusion, real.

For Muslims, asserting the affinity of the human to the divine is sustainable if conjectural but, strictly, blasphemous: 'There is nothing like him [God]' (Q:42:11), no one is worthy of the same name as God (Q:19:65) and 'nothing could attain parity (*kufuww*) with him' (Q:112:4). But to say that nothing wholly resembles God is not to say that nothing resembles him in any respect. God, as unique, may share some qualities, in limited measure, with his human and angelic creatures. Which qualities and to what extent – these questions are evaded under the pretext of *bilā kayfā* (without knowing/asking how), the anti-intellectual scholastic slogan we encountered in Chapter 2. Are the norms of reason, goodness and justice applicable to us, also applicable, fully or partly, to God? The answer is: 'Yes – but we are religiously obliged to abjure precision.' It is safe to add that the Quran rejects any robust divinity immanent in our humanity.[5]

God has made plans for us and entertains great expectations. 'We do put [humankind] to the test' (Q:23:30), an ambitious claim about human potential. Individual prophets and entire communities are tried and tested (Q:2:155, 214; 7:163; 29:2–3; 33:11; 38:24, 34). Some moderns may resent this moral burden. Many today reject such a God as too demanding, needy and noisy, always wanting us to prove ourselves to him. Perhaps he made us in his image because he needs an image! Atheist existentialists dismiss God as irrelevant: we are answerable to no one. Muslims, however, are flattered to read about the divine decision to ask the angels to bow to the first man. God has honoured humankind by elevating the human race above the angels who did eventually prostrate to Adam to acknowledge his superiority (Q:15:30–1; 17:70; 38:73–4).[6]

The *moral* seriousness of creation is a Quranic emphasis (Q:6:70, 7:51; 21:16–17; 38:27; 44:38–9; 45:22; 67:2). Human beings are obligated to God – who created them for two purposes only: to worship him (Q:51:56–7), a view popular with apolitical and quietist Islamic sects, and secondly to show God, while worshipping him, 'which among them is the best in conduct' (Q:18:7). We are put to the test to try our moral mettle (Q:21:35; 67:2; 76:2). Against pagans, the Quran denies that the creation was pointless or done for amusement (Q:21:16–17; 44:38). The world was not made 'without [moral] purpose' (*bāṭilan*; Q:3:191; 38:27) or 'frivolously' (*'abathan*; Q:23:115). Most Muslims accept this emphasis but some Muslim mystics, who probably find the moral stress too solemn, mitigate it by arguing that God made the world for aesthetic purposes, a notion reminiscent of the Hindu concept of divine play, known as *līlā* in Sanskrit. The mystics cite as evidence a Prophetic saying that is revealed but not part of the Quran: 'I was a hidden treasure, and I desired to be known; therefore I created the creation that I might be known'.[7] Even if this saying were authentic, it could not over-ride the scripture.

Despite humankind's significance in creation and the divinely guaranteed integrity of the moral foundations of life in this lower world in which we are on probation (Q:21:35), the Quran nowhere concedes that human beings, even good believers, matter to God. Those who believe and do good are 'the best of created beings' (Q:98:7). But the Quranic God does not volunteer to suffer for the sake of his people let alone condescend to come down to earth to take upon himself the sins of the world.

3

A nebulous and elastic Quranic comment about the travail of being human reads: 'We have surely created humankind into toil and struggle' (*fī kabad;* Q:90:4). The preceding verse – an oath, 'by the father and what he produces' – is an oblique reference to the nexus of sex, procreation and birth. If the consonants are vocalized differently – as '*fī kabid*' – the verse means 'into the liver'. In Arabic poetry, the liver is a seat of emotion and travail, hence the anguished poet's exclamation, 'O my liver!' (*yā kabadī*), not 'O my heart!' (One suspects alcohol abuse by Arab poets, hence their concern for the liver!) The associated verb *ka/ba/da* in modern Arabic, formed by lengthening the first radical, means 'to suffer, to endure'. The Quranic phrase, fertile and suggestive as it is, sustains vigorous connotations of endurance in the face of adversity and trial.

We were created in a state of physical weakness (*ḍu'f*), followed by the strength of youth which terminates in the infirmity of old age (Q:30:54). Moral weakness is also essential to our nature: God wants to lighten our difficulties 'for humanity was created weak' (*wa khuliqa al-insānu ḍa'īfan* Q:4:28). This was deliberate as the use of the theological (past) passive (*khuliqa*) indicates: the creation of humankind is according to the decree of God, the unstated subject. The Quran also uses the active voice, with emphasis, as in the earlier quotation: *laqad khalaqnā* (we have surely created; Q:90:4).

God has intentionally created humankind with a limited capacity for self-mastery. This limitation is partly caused by an unspecified weakness in the human frame, just mentioned, and by an innate capacity for (and proclivity to) evil. In the story of Joseph, recounted in a mixture of continuous narrative and dramatic dialogue interrupted by many spiritually pregnant hiatuses, we learn that our natural structure conceals 'the soul that strongly urges [us] to do evil' (*al-nafs al-ammārah bi al-sū*; Q:12:53). Mentioned uniquely here, the intensive form of *a/ma/ra* (to command) is used to convey the force of this evil impulse. God decrees the evil impulse; it is no unintended tragic by-product of human recalcitrance. Part of the divine design, this inclination towards injustice is integral to our God-given nature. Obedience to the evil soul distorts and fragments our originally unified higher nature (*al-fiṭrā'*; lit., the creation; Q:30:30). We possess the constructive force of the self-accusing soul (*al-nafs al-lawwāmah*; Q:75:2) which counter-acts the evil soul's destructive power in the human personality. The intensive form *la/wa/wa/ma* indicates severe self-incrimination by this innate, rather tyrannical, inner disposition.[8]

A human being is 'made of haste' (*khuliqa min ajal*; Q:21:37). The context is the Arab pagans' repeated demand for details of the time and hour of judgement (Q:34:29); many request that the judgement be hastened on (Q:29:53–4) and some request an immediate and complete display of the signs of God. Even in prayer, human beings are impatient: 'Man prays for evil as fervently as he prays for good – for man is given to haste' (*'ajūlā*; hyperbolic form; Q:17:11). Haste is a characteristic rather than a constitutional liability.

We are foolish and short-sighted and therefore quickly despair of divine mercy; we are impetuous and weak-willed, thus incapable of constancy (Q:30:36). God's experiment with Adam, the father and prototype of the human race, failed: 'And we had already taken the covenant from Adam but he forgot; and we never found firm resolve in him' (Q:20:115). As we saw in Chapter 9, this refers to the pre-existential covenant taken generically from the Children of Adam before history commenced (Q:7:172–3). What is true of Adam is true *a fortiori* of most if not all his descendants (Q:7:102).

The Quran uses three words to sketch a portrait of human nature as impatient, anxious, and mean. Our natures conceal a permanent emotional imbalance redressed only in the remembrance of God: 'Man was certainly created (*khuliqa*) extremely impatient (*halū'an*); when misfortune befalls him, he is fretful (*jazū'an*); when prosperity is his lot, he is niggardly (*manū'an*)' (Q:70:19–21). These qualities are not permanent: the next verse exempts 'the worshippers' (Q:70:22). Through pious effort aided by the grace of God, the believer overcomes these negative traits which include dispositions such as being prematurely despairing (Q:41:49) and grossly ungrateful (*kanūd*; Q:100:6). These are dispositions, not irresistible impulses. Such negative proclivities are inertial – and persist if there is no religiously motivated and sustained attempt to transcend or re-direct them. The Quran implies, as we saw in Chapter 9, that most human beings remain uncorrected.

Intrinsic deficiencies in human nature differ from merely typical human limitations found in some contexts. For example, in a strained military situation, the Quran notes a temporary weak spot (*d'af*; Q:8:66) among the Muslims. Muhammad was urged to fight the disbelievers and assured that 100 patient believers will defeat 1,000 rejectors (Q:8:65). The next verse revises this ten to one ratio to a two to one ratio: God notes a temporary weakness and lowers his expectations. Such a weakness is not intrinsic.

Whatever is not remediable, through unassisted effort of will coupled with a change of circumstance, is constitutional. What is primary or innate to our constitution is identified with those features of our nature that are part of the divine design. The rest are secondary qualities that are prevalent but not innate. The tendency to *ghaflah* (forgetfulness), despite its prevalence, is a secondary attribute. The Quran nowhere states that human beings were created in a state of *ghaflah*. This remediable defect is, however, traceable back to Adam, the proto-typical man who habitually forgot his covenant with God (Q:20:115).

Despite these innate and temporary limitations, God enables us to please him by achieving 'the wholesome peace of submission' (*salām al-islām*), the fruit of active and continuous submission to his will. The Quran approves of 'the tranquil soul' (*al-nafs al-mutma'innah*: Q:89:27–30), our final end, achieved after a life-long struggle between the evil-commanding and self-accusing souls.[9] It is, after a long journey, a return to our original home, our original nature; it is how we become what we are.

4

The Quran notes the liabilities and weaknesses of human nature. Accordingly, God is, despite human ingratitude, gracious and magnanimous towards humankind (Q:27:73): he has 'imposed on himself the rule of mercy' (Q:6:12, 54; 7:156). He is master of immense mercy (Q:6:147; 18:58), 'the Lord of forgiveness' (*ahl al-maghfirah*; Q:74:56). All but one Quranic chapter open with a declaration of self-imposed divine mercy.[10] God is especially kind towards his believing servants. The scripture uses a devotional plural of servant (*'abd*; sing., Q:50:8; *'ābidīn*; pl; Q:21:84) to indicate divine kindness. It uses two neutrally descriptive plurals to indicate ordinary plurality: *'ibād* (Q:21:105; 24:32; 50:11), applicable both to human slaves belonging to other human beings (Q:24:32) and to God's servants, and *'abīd* (Q:50:29) which refers to all creation in servitude to God.

God must show his mercy often since we are often unfaithful to our higher nature; our actions are treasonable to the cause of piety. Heedless and obstinate, we refuse to discipline the God-given faculties and facilities of hearing, sight and the heart (Q:23:78; 67:23). We use them instead to casually translate wicked intention into wicked conduct (Q:42:20). On the day of judgement, a seal shall be set on the mouths of sinners while their limbs (and skin), which were used as instruments to extend the range of sin, will bear verbal witness to such misuse (Q:24:24; Q:36:65–7; Q:42:21–3).

In Quranic pleas for the remembrance of God, the mechanism of treachery towards him is linked with infidelity towards our own selves. The Quran advises believers to fear and remember God. If they forget him, he will cause them to forget themselves (Q:59:18–20). The generic human defect is *zulm al-nafs* (injustice to one's own soul), mentioned often. For example, Sheba, when she converts to monotheism in Solomon's court, confesses that, as a sun worshipper, she had wronged only her own soul (Q:27:44), not God. The verb *za/la/ma*, used with the preposition *min* (from), neutrally indicates a deficiency in what is expected of something or someone, a failure to realize an intended purpose or *telos*. In the parable of the garden (Q:18:32–44), two men, one humble and penitent, the other proud and boastful, engage in a didactic dialogue. The proud man is tested with the gift of two gardens producing luxuriant growth and 'not failing in any respect' (*lam tazlim min hū shay'an*; Q:18:33). The verb *za/la/ma* is conjugated as *tazlim* to agree with the feminine singular subject, *al-jannah* (lit., the garden).[11] It is here used neutrally and descriptively, not in accusation. Two verses later, the passage reverts to the standard moral usage contained in *zulm al-nafs* (Q:18:35).

This self-wronging is committed through treachery to our higher nature. We forget God when we commit the intellectual error of associating false deities with the one true deity – the unforgivable sin of idolatry (*shirk*, lit., partnering), discussed in the previous chapter. Once the mental crime of *shirk* is placed on the level of volition, the practical result is conduct treasonable to our higher nature.

Acknowledging our capacity for such perfidy deepens and darkens what is other-wise an idealistic portrait of humanity. The darker side of human nature is implicit in the Quran and often eludes commentators and casual readers. While the darkness deepens the account intellectually and morally, the Quran, unlike the biblical tes-taments, never suggests or implies any irreversible tragedy in the divine decision to create humankind.

The innate knowledge of God that we possess acts as a heavenly counter-poise to our God-ordained potential for waywardness. When we acknowledge the sovereignty of God by recognizing his signs, we allow the celestial side of our nature to dominate. We yearn for the higher world and God takes up our case and makes us rise above the angels. However, when we wantonly deny the divine portents and prefer our folly to divine wisdom, we become like the man 'to whom we [God] sent our signs but he let them pass him by until the Devil took up his case and thus he became one of the misguided people' (Q:7:175). God could have elevated him through his signs but the fool 'gravitated heavily towards the ground (*akhlada ilā al-arḍ*) and followed his vain desires' (Q:7:176).

Not all moral evil is intrinsic to human nature or caused by mortal weakness. The Devil, known variously as Iblīs, Al-Shayṭān, and Al-Ṭāghūt (the rebel),[12] has sworn, by the majesty of God, that he will mislead Adam and his progeny and seduce them away from the remembrance and worship of God. Armed with a limited warrant for autonomous action until the day of judgement, he seconds and abets the self-destructive tendencies in our nature (Q:7:11–28). The Quran warns us about this arch-deceiver (Q:34:5) and advises us that he is an enemy, 'therefore treat him like an enemy'(Q:34:6).

Humankind is stretched like two outposts of an empire; one is godly, the other is a sub-human, possibly diabolical, frontier – and the intervening territory is human. This Quranic portrait is shrewdly ambivalent, nuanced and fruitfully tense. It concedes to the secular dimension of our humanity by granting some demands of our nature while emphasizing equally our transcendent endowment. It permits optimism: men and women are inclined to accept self-surrender to God (*islām*). The Muslim faith is the *al-dīn al-fiṭrā'* (Q:30:30), the religion of divinely created human nature, a faith to which the repentant sinner reverts rather than converts. This Quranic optimism is reminiscent of the Mahayana Buddhist confidence, nourished by different assumptions, that our original nature is Buddha: once we are self-awakened, we will spontaneously avoid all evil and pursue all good.

5

The Quranic picture of humankind is sanguine. It contains a high estimate of our capacity for submission to God and it implies that the attainment of virtue is highly probable as the opposing forces of good and evil are regulated in the spacious and tense theatre of human dispositions. Moreover, it is compatible with an optimistic theory of knowledge.

Let me address this last point first. In our natural (*fiṭriyy*) or pure state, we possess knowledge of God (Q:7:172; 30:30); the innocent eye and pure heart precede our entry into the world of error, contingency and temptation. As we saw in Chapters 8 and 9, this optimistic religious epistemology assumes that all truth, known on and grounded in divine authority, has been pre-programmed in us. We must re-discover it by removing the veils of heedlessness and pride.

Regarding the moral life, the Quran tempers its optimistic confidence by emphasizing that the attainment of a virtuous life-style requires relentless patience and constant struggle (*jihād*) against our lower nature. Only the steadfast shall receive God's reward (*thawāb Allāh*; Q:28:80). We shall reap what we sow; the last harvest will be gathered in a supernatural field. Our baser nature – an alliance of natural desires and constitutional weaknesses and liabilities – bars us from religious success. We do not welcome the steep moral climb (*al-'aqabah*; Q:90:11). The path straightened out (*al-ṣirāt al-mustaqīm*; Q:1:5; cf. *ṣirātin mustaqīmin*; a path straightened out; Q:6:39, 87)[13] for us is straightforward only in that we must turn right and go straight – to paradise!

We can lead God-fearing lives but we prefer the easier option of disobeying God's law. The rotten fruits of this propensity are gathered every season in the decaying ruins of 'the overturned ones' (*al-mu'tafikāt*: Q:53:53; 69:9), the Quran's euphemism for the cities mown down by the hand of God (Q:21:15). Our ability to oppose the divinely endorsed cause of justice and purity is evident in the Quran's numerous rejection narratives which portray the unheeded prophets, men without honour in their native lands. This innate capacity to resist the divine law and to thwart, temporarily, God's purposes is the central truth of sacred history.

We possess and are possessed by dual opposed capacities; these make us crave earnestly for ideals of piety which lie dormant in our nature. In the heat of life's struggles, however, we also wish to disown those very ideals. This arrangement generates religious success and failure. Few people achieve conspicuous virtue although many achieve some degree of moral excellence and self-restraint. Most of us are spiritually and morally mediocre. Mysteriously, God permits us to resist his will, to our final detriment. By setting high moral and spiritual standards, God endorses religious elitism: a whole generation is often netting only a few saints although, remarkably, Islam in its heyday made morally excellent self-restraint commonplace and moral laxity rare.

The Quran's optimism about the faculties of reason and conscience (which essentially constitute human nature) impressed Muslims who laid the moral and philosophical foundations of the central discipline of jurisprudence. Muslim jurists confidently claimed that applied Islam, based on Quranic doctrine about human nature and its resources, provides practical and spiritual knowledge that satisfies the canons of reason, a reason unaffected by our capacity for sin. The sacred law (*sharī'ah*; lit., a path; Q:45:18; also *shir'ah* at Q:5:48) derived from the Quran and the Prophet's exemplar[14] specifies in meticulous detail the correct exercise of the will in our imperfect attempt to attain purity of heart and intention. The holy law, rationally justifiable and comprehensive, covers ritual obligation, moral regulation and extends to etiquette. This *shumūliyyah* (radical comprehensiveness) of the law is seen as evidence both of historical Islam's relevance to all times and places and of the universal mercy of a God who guides believers to the paths of peace (*subul islām*; Q:5:16) and enlightenment (Q:14:1; 57:12) in every age.

The holy law, as the comprehensive enactment of the sovereign divine will for humankind, was a command of secular but divinely endowed human reason (*'aql*). Being revealed, it is indeed antecedent to society and creates society – just as divine revelation predates the faithful community it engenders. The sacred law teaches us to attain the felicity of faith while, as practical reason, it aims at achieving both our individual happiness (*sa'dah*) and the common good (*al-maṣlaḥah*). We are innately, that is, outside of any social context, equipped to attain the highest good by acting rationally for the sake of the good.

This account is saved from naive optimism by a Quranic acknowledgment of the need for law which itself presupposes that we need more than mere knowledge of the truth through recollection. Paternalistic Islamic legislation further presupposes continuous re-enforcement of the law, another indication that we are not naturally virtuous or law-abiding. The recalcitrance of human nature often has the last word and explains the widespread failure of societies to fulfil God's laws. Only on the day of resurrection, an event beyond history, shall we witness a resolution of the ambivalence that makes our nature vacillate between doing right and doing wrong, a problem beyond the reach of law. The anxious sinner on that day will be asked to read the book of his actions – as sufficient judgement against himself (Q:17:14).[15]

6

We sketch the Christian portrait of human nature to assist us in refining the largely opposed Islamic one. For Christians, the human situation is tainted by sin and alienation from God; for Muslims, human beings merely forget the truth about God's sovereignty over them, hence the constant fear of a stark encounter with the master when the servant's only clothing is 'the garment of piety' (*libās al-taqwā*) which the Quran recommends as the best form of covering (Q:7:26).

The exacting demands of Islamic law emerge out of the Quran's optimistic account of human spiritual potential – part of its theology of original righteous-ness. The essential element in human nature is an intellect (*'aql*) that can acquire knowledge and appropriate a revealed truth which informs practical religious con-duct. For Christians, the human will and intellect are defiled and, especially for Protestants, disabled by sin. Human nature is corrupted by the fall, a contingent event with ineluctable consequences. Being fallen into sin separates us from God. Therefore, the intellect, no longer enlightened by divine truth, holds false opinions; the will, no longer guided by divine love, makes evil choices. The fall, according to most Christian theologians, was a unique disaster which fully determined and denatured the total nature of humankind.

Adam's lapse from grace disfigured his original nature and, hence, that of his descendants: human beings are fallen creatures with corrupted wills and irreparably damaged reasoning faculties. Catholic theologians have softened this view by adding that some traces of the *semen religionis* (seed of religion) survive the fall and therefore all men and women, unless they are congenitally or invincibly ignorant of God's existence, retain the *sensus divinitatis* (sense of divinity) that is their birthright. Against this background, Christian thinkers isolate the crisis of sin as the deepest crisis in the human personality. We are being sucked in by the quicksand of sin and cannot save ourselves; only someone standing on firm ground can offer us the hand of help. Men and women know themselves only as sin-infected creatures; we do not know human nature in its integrity. Only God can save us and redeem us from our own evil nature (John:3:16). In fear and trembling, Paul worked out the details of this offer of salvation (1 Corinthians 2:1–5).

Unlike Christians, Muslims reject any permanent crisis in the human personality caused by a single act of sinful disobedience to the divine will. The incident in paradise is a consequential but contained act of disobedience to God's will, a transgression with no larger implications for human nature or even Adam's nature. The sinful act was jointly caused by the extrinsic factors of ignorance and weakness of will. If men and women are determined to follow divine tuition, they can still rise above the angels. The expulsion from heaven is an opportunity to dispel the satanic scepticism about human nature.

Adam asked God for forgiveness and God forgave him because God is most forgiving and merciful, as the Quran repeats from cover to cover. Why did God forgive him? Answer: God does whatsoever he pleases or wills. It is not in vain that he is God. Muslims, insofar as they indulge in theology[16] would say that God is God precisely because he is not answerable to external critiques. In any case, as the Quran comments with pointed sarcasm, God dispenses his grace as he wishes and is not bound by the requirements of Jewish or Christian theology (Q:57:29).

If the Christian assessment of human nature is true, we need salvation, not guidance, a saviour, not a mere teacher. An ethics of law (as duty) must be replaced by an ethics of virtue (enabled by grace). As Paul argued, the Law of Moses frustrates its internal intentions because it identifies the scope of sin without enabling us to escape from its consequences (Romans 2:12–7:25). Someone must rescue us from our folly, not simply educate us about the failings of our corrupt nature, something we already know and know all the more for being incapable of eliminating. We are sinners who crave redemption from our sins followed by reconciliation with a holy God. We need therefore grace to transform us, not only revelation to guide us: what we are by nature can only be rectified by what we may become by grace. This view of human beings, as creatures victimized by sin and lust and trapped in a self-centred concupiscence, was transmitted via Augustine and Aquinas to medieval Europe and has survived, albeit in a diluted form, among Christians to this day.

The Islamic position is morally and doctrinally opposed to this proposed external rescue from the plight of sin. We are not innately deviant or crooked or unsound although we are easily misled into temptation. Divine education therefore suffices. We need mentors who can guide us out of our heedlessness. Muhammad is not a saviour or our advocate (*wakīl*; Q:10:108; 17:54; 39:41). We must manage our own affairs: if we do well, we do well for ourselves and if we do evil, we do it only to our own detriment (Q:17:7). One isolated passage mitigates this strict view of personal responsibility by implying that the Prophet can, through the revelations he brings, ease if not carry the burdens of sinners (Q:7:157). Some Muslims believe he will intercede on their behalf during the final reckoning, a view which lacks clear Quranic sanction. The scripture preaches that we are on our own: 'No soul already laden bears the burden of another' is repeated at regular intervals (Q:17:15; 53:38, etc.)[17] in case its moral earnestness fails to register.

7

And [recall the time] when your Lord said to the angels, 'I will appoint in the earth a viceroy (*khalīfah*)',[18] and they retorted: 'Are you going to place in the earth one who will create disorder in it and shed blood while we celebrate your praises and glorify your holiness?' God replied: 'I know things of which you have no knowledge' (Q:2:30).

Once translated into the earthy reality of history, the honorary appointment of Adam as God's deputy carries the risks of high office. Our political destiny is reflected in what shall turn out to be a mandate to shoulder the colossal social responsibility of building a just order on earth. The activist ramifications constitute Islam's nature as the most sincerely political of all faiths, frankly placing its trust in the social efficacy of power exercised on behalf of righteousness.

The normally obedient angels initially doubt the wisdom of this divine intention. Human beings, they blurt out, will shed blood and cause corruption in the world. Since the empirical history of our species is in the womb of the future, the angels have no empirical evidence to support this insight. They must have reasoned: 'How can an imperfect and weak-willed creature be a trustee on behalf of a perfect and infinitely strong creator? The world should not be entrusted, for responsible stewardship, to such a weak and unstable creature'. Or perhaps the angels share God's perspective and see all *sub species transcendentia* (in the perspective of transcendence). Human beings, located in history and living *sub species saeculi* (in the secular perspective) can sympathize with the angelic reserve. The Quran itself raises doubts elsewhere when, in one mystical verse, it claims that God offered 'the trust' (*al-amānah*) of power and moral responsibility to the heavens and the earth and the mountains but they all refused to undertake it and were afraid of it. 'But man undertook it; he is extremely unjust and foolish' (*ẓalūman, jahūlan*. Q:33:72; hyperbolic forms of *ẓālim* and *jāhil*).

The context of this passage is the intrigues of hypocrites and secret agitators in Medina as Muhammad struggles to create an ideal theocracy. Here it seems that it is our decision to be vicegerents of God; we voluntarily and stupidly undertook the trust, the stewardship of the earth and the commitment to serve God and thus refute the satanic scepticism about our potential for godliness. Human beings are morally ambitious but also foolhardy. This passage seems to contradict the standard narrative of the election of Adam (Q:2:30). Muslims resolve this apparent textual discrepancy by affirming the standard election narrative as canonical, thus allowing it abrogate a sceptical passage that contradicts it.

The 'religious' doctrines of the Quran have social and political entailments. Compared to the Christian estimate of *homo politicus*, the Quran harbours an optimistic anthropology which presupposes the political perfectibility of human nature, an assumption that explains the scripture's repeated insistence on the struggle to establish a just and righteous order on earth. Muslims see Islam as providing a habitat for the cultivation of what were known to the Greeks as the political virtues. The excellences of civic life were to be developed and nurtured during participation in the political life whose demands enlarged the sphere of religious duty, thus providing another arena for the service of God. The sea of faith should have a specifically political estuary.

Thus, despite fearing the awesome day of resurrection, Muhammad calmly and systematically built a civil community in Medina and remained at the helm of its political destiny until death removed him. Zeal for a better world yet to come did not prevent him from founding the heavenly city in this imperfect world. This attitude sounds unremarkable in a secular age where large-scale planning for the future is commonplace. Consider, however, the feverish apocalyptic anticipation of the end of the world and the imminence of judgement both in first century Palestinian sectarian Judaism and in the earliest authentic Pauline epistle (1 Thessalonians) addressed to the community at Thessalonike in roughly 50 CE. Both Paul's and Jesus' religious enthusiasm precluded the possibility of founding an enduring socio-political order. The New Testament contains only an interim politics and ethics as Christians await the end of history. Some Christian thinkers have entertained optimistic views of human nature, including our political potential. But these are not canonical New Testament convictions. Among Christian philosophers, for example, John Locke's view of human nature is similar to the Quranic view: human beings are decent, rational and capable of self-imposed discipline, a view that decisively influenced the republican experiment called America. Hobbes's more pessimistic estimate of human nature is closer to the Pauline view with its stress on sinful depravity.[19]

The Quran rejects the resigned and tragic view that human beings are radically incorrigible. Muslim historians have therefore reasoned that, given Muhammad's success in establishing a virtuous city in Medina, we can also create a God-centred culture in any time and place. We shall critically examine this claim in due course.

8

Many human beings worship God despite distractions in a world that has many opportunities for neglecting the divine will. Defying the tribulations and temptations of 'the lower world', countless human beings remember God in formal daily prayer and in informal petition and supplication (Q:22:18). Unlike angelic worship, however, human devotion is, inevitably, imperfect and infrequent. Angels ceaselessly worship God, as they remind him when he decides to create humankind (Q:2:30); they do so, however, in the evil-free environment of paradise.[20] In a moral condescension for the heedless rebel man, the angels ask God's forgiveness for believers and for all those on earth (Q:40:7; 42:5). But then man was created weak; and Adam was always heedless and neglected God.

Despite this, countless human beings struggle against their lower passions, subdue their undignified impulses and wanton whims and desires, and seek to please their creator. Moreover, they do so while contending with the avowed enmity of the Devil, the malicious being dedicated to their ruin. Despite our sinful desires, we cultivate virtue, even conspicuous virtue. Some human beings, the 'friends of God' (*auliyā' Allāh*; Q:10:62), the saints of Islam, successfully live their lives in the active heat of pious emotion. The Quran proudly informs Muhammad that believers love God with greater intensity than the idolaters love their idols (Q:2:165). Many men and women respond enthusiastically to the divine summons; the lord-devoted ones (*al-ribbiyyūn*; Q:3:146) worship God in times of persecution and, despite being outnumbered, ceaselessly battle against their disbelieving oppressors. The Quran startles us with its laconic mention of 'the power prophets' (*ulū al-'azm min al-rusul*; Q:46:35), so-called on account of their outstanding patience.[21] Over the men and women of God, the Devil has no authority (Q:16:98–9). God's judgement about true believers is found to be and bound to be true.

The occasional worship of the free and rational human creature must surely be morally superior to the ceaseless devotion of any angel made precisely for obedient worship. When acts of supererogatory virtue and self-restraint reach heaven, presumably the angels apologize to God for their initial doubts about the human creature's potential for righteousness and moral excellence.

9

How did the Quran generate an enthusiastic embrace of the divine will? How does it inspire modern Muslims to align their wills with the divine will, to trust in the divine plan for them? Beyond worship and self-restraint, only those who 'strive in the way of God' (*jahadū fī sabīl Allāh*; Q:9:20) attain humanity. Enthusiasm is demanded of all believers with the exception of the disabled and infirm (Q:9:90–1; 48:17). Zeal is assessed by the willingness to spend in the way of God and to fight for the cause of Islam. The early Muslims did not want to fight even in self-defence; the Quran erodes their inertia and reluctance by reminding them that God is the best judge of what is good or bad for them (Q:2:216; 4:77).

The ninth Quranic chapter, a late Medinan revelation, is one of the two *al-jihādān* surahs, 'the Jihad duo'[22] whose unifying theme is divinely sanctioned violent struggle against militant pagan opposition. Much of this chapter deals with a military expedition. The Quran offers no current political or geographical background; it concentrates on spiritual aspects of warfare (Q:9:38–99). Muhammad's biography records that he heard rumours of an imminent attack by the Christian (Roman) Byzantines settled in the province of Syria (which then included Israel–Palestine). Byzantine forces were probably gathering near Tabuk, at the northern frontier of the *Jazīrat Al-'Arab* (the Arabian peninsula) near present-day Jordan, and intended to annihilate the infant religion. In AH 9 (October 630 CE), about two years before his death at 63, Muhammad began to enlist volunteers for this vital expedition. He meticulously planned this campaign, traditionally called 'the army of hardship' (*jaysh al-ʿusrah*), an expedition which pioneered Islam's elephantine military triumphs after the Prophet's death in June 632.[23] Islam remained confined to Arabia during his own life-time, however, and during that of his successor, Abu Bakr, whose caliphate lasted about two years.

While Muhammad and his devout companions were treading the hot and dusty desert paths to please their Lord (Q:9:120), the commitment of others was tepid by ironic contrast with the heat of the late summer in the Hijaz region of central and north-western Arabia where a drought that year had made it stiflingly oppressive. 'The sitting ones' (*al-qāʿidūn*; Q:4:95) is the Quran's contemptuous description of believers who prefer to stay home rather than struggle in God's path. The eleventh Islamic lunar month of *zū al-qaʿdah,* one of the four months in which war is prohibited, literally means the sitting one. *Al-qāʿidūn* are effeminate and weak men who enjoy the company of their wives as they gather early autumn fruits.[24] They prefer to 'stay behind (*yatakhalafūna*)' the Messenger of God because they prefer their own lives to his, opting for the safety and comfort of their persons rather than striving like the holy warriors (*mujāhidūn*), particularly the ageing but indefatigable Prophet (Q:9:120).

The Quran creates enthusiasm for the faithful cause (Q:9:38–41) even though the materials with which the Prophet works are unpromising: recently retrieved from paganism, ignorant, hypocritical, and only human. The men are unwilling to go far from home and complain vaguely: 'Among them is also one who says: "Give me leave [to stay behind] and don't tempt me"'(Q:9:49). The temptation in the distant land is thought to be the outstanding beauty of its women. The Quran warns that such a man has already fallen into temptation, presumably the temptation to put one's fear of temptation above the service of God. Islamic jurists, however, would sympathize with this man's complaint since the Quran commands Muslims to avoid, not merely resist, temptation (Q:17:32, 36) – unless, as during jihad, one cannot avoid the environment of temptation and must therefore enter it, determined to resist temptation.

'Do not go out into the heat!' This was the advice of lukewarm hypocritical Muslims who worried about their physical health and comfort rather than the welfare of their souls. 'Say: "The Fire of Hell is hotter still, if only you knew!"' (Q:9:81). The worldly attitudes of the hypocrites and other time-serving elements added to Muhammad's headaches during the Tabuk campaign. He returned from the expedition only to find that his troubles were not over: during his absence, a hypocritical rival party had, 'by way of mischief and infidelity' (Q9:107), established an alternative mosque, the only house of worship which Muhammad felt obliged to destroy.

10

What is the rational motivation for religious enthusiasm? What motivates the fervour required for the attainment of continuously enthusiastic obedience to

God's commandments which, as divinely sanctioned duties, constitute the good life? We address this question before we turn, in Section 12 below, to the more general problem of our limited resources in our quest for religious excellence.

Western and Islamic philosophers have alike extolled the importance of reason, the intellectual faculty, in achieving the good life. From Socrates, Plato and Aristotle to Spinoza and John Dewey, from Al-Kindī to Ibn Rushd, all have maintained that intelligence and virtue are organically linked: only those who know what they are doing are likely to do what is right. Moreover, what is good for us is known by knowing who we truly are – linking ethics with ontology and self-mastery with self-knowledge. This philosophical consensus, inspired by too sanguine an estimate of reason, must face the fact that the overwhelming majority of morally good people have not been particularly learned or intelligent or self-consciously aware of their own nature and limitations. Certainly, the intelligent have no monopoly on virtue. Kant (1724–1804), the true father of modern philosophy,[25] was the first to note the importance of the will rather than the intellect in the good life. Our awareness of the compulsion of the moral ideal is the cornerstone of the Kantian ethical system, a compulsion that, unlike the intense life of the mind, is experienced universally by human beings. Kant wisely emphasized the role of the good will, not the refined intellect, as being central to the ethical life.

Even for a rationally inclined person, the principal motive for religious enthusiasm is, to focus on our theme, not knowledge. In religious as in secular life, knowledge of important goals, especially short-term ones, can partly motivate some rational persons. But knowledge alone never actuates religious zeal even in circumscribed or short-term goals. In goals whose pursuit essentially requires enthusiasm, both in the religious and the secular lives, we are primarily actuated by desire and the will to experience it. The will and desire can jointly motivate us where the intellect fails to induce action.

Enthusiasm requires, as the Quran recognizes implicitly, more than an active awareness of the existence or desirability of the goal. Its remoteness or accessibility is also relevant (Q:9:42). In religious as in secular life, even a lazy or unmotivated person is moved to action when that person perceives imminent danger. Equally seductive is the imminent prospect of extreme pleasure. Entertaining the prospect of pleasure, an intellectual act, coupled with an active desire for such pleasure, can arouse the will and stimulate it into action, thus generating enthusiasm. Aquinas correctly noted that a motive can be sufficient to persuade the will without being sufficient to persuade the intellect.[26]

The function of the intellect here is to co-ordinate diverse desires into a united and harmonious will rather than to motivate it into action. The boundary between impulse and action, absent in children, is heavily guarded in adults. It is prior desire that probably conditions the will. There are no pure, that is, desire-less, acts of will – except in God's mental life. Our will is driven not by our intellects or even talents but rather by the innate *impulsion* of our passions and instincts that are often strong enough to be autonomous. The instinctive desire to avoid pain and obtain pleasure, to be specific, supplies more powerful motives for action than knowledge alone does. This explains the Quranic emphasis on the terrors of hell (Q:4:56; 14:16–17, 49–50; 22:19–22; 25:11–14; 47:15; 56:41–55; 69:25–37; 74:26–31; 78:21–5; 88:1–7) and the delights of paradise (Q:13:35; 47:15; 52:17–24; 55:46–76; 56:12–38; 76:5–22; 71:41–4; 78:31–5; 83:22–9; 88:8–16).[27]

11

By and large, religion offers rational motivation, not rational evidence, for living the religious life. As we saw in Chapter 2, however, the Quran also argues its case. It offers an argument for forgoing the pleasures of this world in order to seek the pleasures of the permanent next world, including God's everlasting good pleasure. Rhetorically, the argument has two *ad hominem* versions, reflecting different opponents, but logically the grounds of both are identical. The first version is given in the context of pagan mockery of the Quran's threats. The Meccans request that their portion of the punishment be forwarded and fall on them immediately. The Quran answers: 'Consider! If we let them enjoy [this life] for [a few] years; then there comes to them at length the promised [punishment], the pleasures they enjoyed shall not [then] benefit them' (Q:26:205–7).

This Quranic claim defensibly presupposes that pleasure, unlike goods such as knowledge or virtue, is not cumulative. (In Ecclesiastes, the biblical book of sceptical wisdom, a similar observation about this feature of pleasure is embedded in Chapters 2 and 6 *passim*, with much depressing supporting detail.)[28] Pleasure is enjoyed and then it is no more, except as a memory. The memory of a pleasure enjoyed can be either a source of further pleasure or alternatively of pain in the realization that it is no more. In any case, no matter how much pleasure we have experienced in the past, none of it can mitigate the pain of the moment of chastisement when that arrives in the present. Even sexual pleasure, held to be the most powerful passion known to us, is however, notwithstanding its intensity, disappointingly brief, repetitive, and, like all pleasure, it fails to be cumulative.

A version of the argument is also advanced against the Jews of Medina who are accused of hiding parts of the scripture and telling lies against God. The Quran mocks the view that the Jews are a chosen people who are especially or exclusively destined for an after-life.[29] Untroubled by the Quran's threats and not frightened by the prospect of going to hell (Q:2:175), some rabbis tell Muhammad that the fire shall 'touch us only for a limited number of days' (Q:2:80; 3:24). The Quran replies:

> Say: If the final abode, in God's presence, is exclusively for you and for no others from among humankind, then wish for [immediate] death, if you are sincere. But they will never wish for death: they know well what their own hands have sent on before them [i.e., evil deeds]. And God knows well those who do wrong. You will find them, of all people, even more than idolaters, greedier for any kind of life (*aḥraṣa ...'alā ḥayātin*).[30] Each of them wishes

he could be granted a life of a thousand years but the grant of such longevity would not save him from [due] punishment. For God sees well their actions.
(Q:2:94–6)

12

We examine human weakness now in the context of less demanding, more routine, Quranic requirements, especially fasting and prayer, duties that require sustained observance rather than difficult single acts of enthusiasm. This is another dimension of the problem of maintaining a high degree of religious enthusiasm.

The duty of ritual prayer is the most relaxed form of the Quranic regimen, its difficulty lying in the frequency and constancy of its performance rather than its severity. The Quran recommends regular prayer as a way of combating lust and indecent desires (Q:11:114; 29:45). We must, mainly through prayer, maintain an awareness of God virtually all the time, every day of our lives. Apart from the five obligatory prayers of the conventional framework for remembering God, prophets and mystics add supererogatory prayers at night; the Quran orders Muhammad to pray in the deepest reaches of the night (Q:11:114) and to recite 'the revelation at dawn' (*qurān al-fajr;* Q:17:78–9). Muhammad prayed for forgiveness some 70 times a day despite the assurance that his past and future sins had been forgiven (Q:48:2) and despite his release from burdensome oaths which, if broken, could be a source of sin (Q:66:1–2). He took to heart the Quranic order: 'Believers! Enter whole-heartedly into Islam (*al-silm*)[31] and do not follow the foot-steps of Satan. He is your avowed enemy' (Q:2:208). The half-hearted attempt at aligning one's sinful will with God's good will is excoriated as satanic.

In the traditional collections about Muhammad's actions and speeches, we read candid complaints from his companions bashfully and guiltily admitting to him that they find it difficult to retain and sustain an awareness of God – after they leave the mosque to return to their wives and children. Some found the obligations of family life irksome and spiritually distracting to such an extent that the Quran orders believers to live with their wives 'on a footing of kindness and equity: if you dislike them, it could be that you dislike something through which God brings about much good' (Q:4:19). Such a revelation would be unnecessary if the spiritual and other benefits of married life were self-evident. Despite its high estimate of marriage and offspring, as shown by its many verses on the subject and as exemplified in the life of Muhammad, the Quran criticizes family life where it interferes with the service and remembrance of God. It warns believers that 'among your wives and your children, some are your enemies' (Q:64:14). Indeed, 'your wealth and your children are only a trial (*fitnah*); with God is the greatest reward' (Q:64:15).

A religiously charged milieu facilitates the remembrance of God's omnipresent and stringent demands on believers. God has, however, made human beings crave naturally and forcefully for the immediate, natural and human satisfactions and consolations enjoyed in the company of their offspring and spouses. Yet God is intolerant of disloyalty to him. A natural disposition is, admittedly, not an irresistible impulse – but it can occasionally be strong enough to be virtually autonomous. We shall presently start to consider the implications of this intricate puzzle.

Consider first, however, Islam's canonical fast, an ordeal of self-denial that many modern Muslims still endure every year in Ramadan, the ninth lunar month. Nutritionists classify it as a 'true fast' since no food or beverage, not even medicine, may enter the body for a sustained period of time. It was initially ritualized at Medina during this humid and sultry month, to mark retrospectively the Quran's first descent onto the earth (Q:2:183–5). Unlike the modern lenient version of the fast, the original lasted from the evening meal of one day until the evening meal of the next, one day and night.[32] Such complete abstinence from food and drink entails physical hardship in the dust and heat of the desert; moreover, sexual intercourse was prohibited during Ramadan nights.

Under this severe regime, some men fainted and a few nearly died. The Quran relaxed the requirement (Q:2:187) by reducing the duration of the fast: it lasted only from sunrise to sunset, the lenient form of self-denial practised ever since. Sexual gratification during Ramadan nights was also permitted. Many believers had already secretly broken the ban on sex and therefore 'committed treachery against their own souls' (Q:2:187). The Quran recommended a period of retreat into celibacy (*i'tikāf*, lit. adherence), during Ramadan, a seclusion inside the mosque compound (see Q:2:187; *'ākifūna*, you are adhering – to God). Muhammad withdrew thus for the last ten days of Ramadan and some believers still imitate him. A burdensome but optional prayer, in which large portions of the Quran are sandwiched, is attached to the final (late evening) prayer in the holy month. Initially optional, it was made virtually obligatory under the second caliph 'Umar Ibn Al-Khaṭṭāb. Although it remains legally supererogatory, it is virtually canonical in practice.

The final verse of the Quran's longest chapter reads: 'Our Lord, do not burden us with what we do not have the strength (*ṭāqah*) to bear' (Q:2:286). The word *ṭāqah* denotes strength that might fail. It is never used of the divine strength, *qadr*, which is strength combined with a correct awareness of the value or worth of the situation encountered. God is competently powerful (*qadīr*; Q:2:20), not merely powerful.

A moral quandary here is about the resources of human nature in Islamic anthropology. This question was never debated theoretically but the Muslim jurists who constructed the holy law were mindful of the Quran's morally unassailable maxim: 'God does not charge a soul beyond its capacity' (Q:2:286). Exemptions and exceptions were accordingly codified in the legal codes derived from the Quran and from the Prophet's customary practice. The holy law exempts travellers, ill and elderly individuals who are 'barely able' (*yuṭīqūna*; Q:2:184) to fast, pregnant and lactating women, warriors engaged in active military conflict, and children who have not reached puberty.[33] But even these categories of persons (except for children) had to make up for the fasts missed or else expiate for their sin through feeding indigent people during the holy month (Q:2:184).

13

We investigate further now the joint problems of engendering religious enthusiasm and of maintaining a consistently high degree of routine religious awareness. Both are aspects of the religiously conceived challenge of self-mastery.

Why do virtually all human beings resist the life of virtuous self-restraint? The pre-Muhammadan Arab prophet Ṣāliḥ, whose name means righteous, stands up alone against his sinful tribe, the nomadic Thamūd, and asks a searching question in an idiom suited to his age: 'My people, why do you prefer (*tast'ajilūna bi*; lit., hasten on) evil to good?' (Q:27:46; see also Q:13:6). He risks his life in posing the question (Q:27:48–52). He is, like Muhammad in the early days of his prophetic career, protected by a system of clan affiliation so that his life and property are sacrosanct. But a gang of nine men in the community is contemplating assassinating Ṣāliḥ and avoiding the vengeance of his heir (Q:27:48–9). Until he began to vex his people with tough moral questions, he was admired as one of the group, 'a centre of [our] hopes' (*marjuwwan*; Q:11:62). He loses his popularity and is accused of dividing his people (Q:27:45).

I shall offer three answers to Ṣāliḥ's ancient question, bearing in mind our modern context. First, the life of impiety is easier, more appealing and glamorous, at least in the short-term. To attain even a modest degree of righteous self-restraint requires sustained moral labour, as the Quran reminds us although we scarcely needed the reminder. God's moral demands constantly call for unwelcome privations and uncomfortable sacrifices. The Quran acknowledges the force of our natural desire to defy our higher nature (Q:12:53). It notes, without regret, our prevalent natural proclivity to seek the easier option (Q:8:7; 9:42). Faced with the choice between engaging in physical combat an armed caravan and an unarmed one, even the ardent believers preferred 'the one unarmed' (*ghayra dhāti shawkati*; lit., 'the one without the sting'; Q:8:7).

The Quran acknowledges the urgent presence of human desires and agitating passions. Its list of desires in the lower world (*shahawāt al-dunyā*; Q:3:14) opens with women, a metonymy for sexual desire. The sexual pressure on the human frame is profound but the Quran's list would have been different if the Arabs had been indifferent to women and inordinately fond of strong drink, an item not listed at all. More generally, we humans are self-centred; we seek power and unfair privilege. Niggardliness is virtually in our nature (Q:17:100): salvation is repeatedly linked to spending charitably in the way of God (Q:59:9). Pride (*takabbur*), the primordial sin committed by the Devil, completes the list. The angels complain about the human penchant for bloodshed, a tendency linked to pride in John Calvin's insightful verdict: 'Pride therefore is the mother of all violence' (*Ergo superbia omnis violentiae mater*).[34]

Second, the inclination for piety, even when attained, is difficult to sustain. Few people can live continuously on the spiritual or religious heights although many have, in a fugitive mood, lived briefly on that higher plane. Few Muslims feel every day what they feel temporarily in a mosque on a Friday afternoon; even fewer could live throughout the year the way they live for one month in Ramadan, the month of intensified devotion. This discontinuity in religious experience is now evident: Friday afternoon has become the hour of the modern Muslim conscience. The motivation for *tawbah* (penitence; lit., turning around; Q:9:104), unlike the impulsive and continuous determination to seek and enjoy pleasure and power, has little more than its hour or at most its month. Once the penitent hour is past, the mood for self-incrimination and for conscientious self-examination (*muḥāsabah*),[35] constantly required in ethical theism, needs an outlet and relief – often in the form of compulsive desire for indulgence and pleasure, without moral inhibition. The instinct for goodness and piety must patiently lie fallow for a season before it can be replenished for more virtue. Sometimes, the season might last almost a life-time since no one, except the saint, cultivates virtue in youth, the universal season of pleasure.

Apart from saints, who now wears the seamless garment of virtue? No doubt, even a selfish and depraved individual may occasionally experience exalted sentiments. But it is capricious and infrequent. A noble feeling of great intensity rarely endures. How do we increase the duration of a religious emotion – lengthening and deepening it into a mood, perhaps even a disposition? In the religious life, as hagiography testifies, it is more the longevity rather than the quality or character of devout sentiments and intentions that makes some human beings saintly while most remain spiritually mediocre.

We can all be temporarily inspired to aim at conspicuous virtue especially when we see exemplary purity in the conduct of others who are otherwise no different from us. We may, at a funeral, be chilled by the thought of the impermanence of our passage through the material world and form a short-lived resolution to do nothing but good for the rest of our days. It is wrong and pointless, we privately think, to contribute to the world's stock of sorrows since most people are already miserable enough. All of us occasionally achieve the noble state Buddhists call *muditā* (empathetic or sympathetic joy): we take pleasure in someone else's freedom from suffering. Even those who indulge in *Schadenfreude* (lit., harm-joy), the malicious vicarious enjoyment of another's misfortunes, sometimes wish for the happiness of their enemies. Such exalted sentiments, however, last no longer than a New Year's resolution: the cold season of sin sets in and the moral temperature drops.

Third, closer to our world, far from Ṣāliḥ's era, knowledge of long-term realities and goals such as death or final judgement has no existential impact on our daily behaviour and decision-making. The final inevitability of death rarely alters our priorities in life for we still have a few hours before the lid is closed on the coffin. In the past, however, devout men and women lived in constant fear of divine wrath. Modern religious believers do not keenly perceive the other world and do not live in fear and trembling day and night. In religiously charged environments or in apocalyptic ages where the clock of sacred history was constantly positioned at one minute to the midnight hour, many visualized in vivid colours the constant threat of death and nemesis. In fervent environments – seventh-century Medina under Muhammad or sixteenth-century Geneva under John Calvin – many people practised godly self-restraint.

Religious enthusiasm is now restricted to a few small religious communities in conservative lands.[36]

Most people today, including believers, live as if they were destined to live forever. The inevitability and constant possibility of death carry no weight – except with the saintly or the terminally ill or with travellers on a flight that runs into turbulence. The religious goal is remote in an age which makes plausible promises of proximate freedoms and pleasures. The terrors of hell, distant and remote, rarely motivate even committed religious people. Our most powerful natural impulses are toxic and morally bankrupt, custom-made to reduce and humiliate our higher humanity. Our only antidotes are, the modern believer sadly concludes, the low voice of conscience and the unclear voice of revelation.

14

The broader question here is the control of the body in the pursuit of the higher pleasures of self-mastery, a modern question with ancient roots. Asceticism is the conquest of one's own body – and other people's, especially women's, bodies. It has few modern admirers. Now we are told to be relaxed about the body although some of us frantically seek the elixir of life to make youth a permanent state. Faced with the choice between downgrading the body for God's pleasure and kicking religion in the teeth for teaching us to despise the body, many today choose the latter.

In our past, especially though not only the Christian past, asceticism took the form of abstinence from pleasure in order to attain spiritual hygiene and salvation. Christian ascetics enthusiastically added flagellation and other self-torments while Muslim ascetics became famous for weeping constantly (inspired by Q:53:60–1). The Church Fathers and some anchorites retired into the desert to fight against the self and, literally, their demons. These men not only suffered in the body, they suffered the body. If the psycho-somatic sexual pressure on the body and the spirit proved insufferable, even castration was welcome (based on Matthew 19:12). Blessed are those who neither reap nor sow.

Paul encouraged an internal discipline to replace the external rituals of his inherited Judaism. The Apostle commends training (*askēsis*) for righteousness. The ascetic is like an athlete, as Paul tells the Roman governor Felix who is judging his case; but the ascetic exercises the soul, not the body. 'I exercise (*askō*; Acts 24:16) my conscience', he confesses in the governor's presence. Paul compares himself to an athlete determined to win the race and the prize (Philippians 3:12–14). The Apostle is concerned only about his soul; presumably, the body can take care of itself. To the modern secularist, this appears as one-sided salvation and we moderns would reverse the maxim.

Although religious styles of self-denial are unpopular today, there are, especially in the post-Christian West, several secular forms of it. Not all the articulate motivations for self-denial are religious. Trying to earn a doctorate, for instance, is effectively a secular training in intellectual asceticism and patience; few doctoral theses advance our knowledge. Serious writing is a secular form of penance since it rarely earns financial reward. Being on a diet is the commonest form of self-denial, a worldly version of fasting. Many people today are still committed to self-restraint but often for wholly secular reasons.[37]

15

Unlike the New Testament, the Quran seems to contain no counsels of perfection, only counsels of prudence. A few of Jesus's injunctions set a standard of perfection for the spiritually elect (based on Matthew 19:21); these were supererogatory requirements that went beyond the commandments.[38] The Quran, however, asks us to do the best we can, to fear God as much as possible (Q:64:16). God burdens no soul with more than it can bear (Q:2:286; 7:42; 65:7). As a practical and practicable revelation, the Quran draws on the resources of human nature: 'It will be good for whoever obeys (*taṭawwaʿa*) his own impulse to goodness' (Q:2:184; see also Q:2:158). We can do otherwise: a son of Adam chose to obey (*ṭawwaʿat*) his soul's impulse to evil and murdered his brother (Q:5:32).

We note a discrepancy between what scripture demands and the reality: widespread human failure. A strict application of Quranic justice would not 'leave a single soul unpunished on earth' (Q:16:62; 35:45). Saints admit that the achievement of virtue transcends human resources. Given the variety and power of the corruptions and temptations to which the human will, devoid of grace, is prone, the achievement of complete self-surrender (*islām*) remains elusive. Parts of the Quran, read today, are a counsel of perfection. How few today walk on the 'the straightened path' of those whom God has blessed (Q:1:6–7)! Can we still harness the resources of our consciences and wills to attain the religious goal?

I am not arguing that religious demands should be easy to fulfil. Every faith, rightly, gives its adherents ideals that require sustained commitment for at least one average life-time. Buddhism assigns us many life-times to attain nirvana. It would be spiritually disastrous if we could easily attain our religious goals – only to find that our lives are then empty. It would be like the case of a hedonist who succeeds in finding every material comfort and pleasure only to be then jaded and bored with life's prospects. However, while the divine demands should be heavy so that failure is commoner than success, they must not be so heavy that failure becomes inevitable and success virtually impossible. Moral rules that are impossible to obey are as pointless as those which are impossible to disobey.

A practicable religion must command us to make only those righteous choices that we have the strength to make. For our strength, unlike the divine strength, is of the kind that may fail us. The magnitude of the natural impulse to good should match the quality of piety demanded. Muslims would re-iterate that the Quran promulgates realistic and practicable ideals that make allowances for the divinely created weakness in our nature: 'God does not burden a soul with more than it can bear' (Q:2:286).

Can unaided human nature obey fully the divine commands? To answer here that divine grace enables us to fulfil the stringent requirements of faith evades the question of whether or not human nature is intrinsically capable of fully obeying God.

Does divine grace enable or only facilitate complete obedience? With regard to our capacity for virtue, what is the *intrinsic* endowment of human nature?

There is no precise moral calculus. Aristotle correctly argued that in ethics, unlike in mathematics, we cannot expect clear proofs or precise and absolute rules.[39] The degree of rigour is relative to the subject matter – which is true *a fortiori* of religious ethics since these involve moreover God's mysterious intentions. With due respect to Baruch Spinoza, we cannot construct an ethical algorithm *modo geometrico*! But we may assert that in the absence of a natural (secular) impulse to good, commensurate with revealed demands, no religious ethics can be convincingly relevant to the practical moral life.

We judge religions by their professed ideals rather than by the practice of those ideals by their adherents. But the practicability of an ideal is relevant to the question of its worth and nobility. For what is the point of an ideal that is impossible to follow, one that is an embarrassing reminder of our duties, duties we acknowledge all the more for being unable to fulfil? To be practicable, a religious ideal must correspond to the potential moral and spiritual resources of human nature; the required ideal must be proportionate with the potential resources of its adherents.

The problem of human failure should not be assessed a priori but rather against the background of the resources of human nature. The maxim, 'Where there is a will, there is a way' is too generous in its estimate of the unaided will. The believer modifies it: 'Where there is a will and the operative grace of God, there is certainly a way.' Certainly so; but then it is not solely a human achievement since God has decisively enabled it. (Pagan and secular ethical systems, including those of Aristotle and the Stoics, by-pass this difficulty by appealing only to merit, never to grace.) Without God to facilitate the human will, we can only say that where there is a will, there may be a way, a cautious comment that hardly qualifies as an unforgettable maxim – not to mention its loss of the encouraging spirit found in the original.

The Muslim apologist retorts that the Quran contains rules of practical reason: intelligible, capable of being followed by all according to their capacity, rules that are neither causes fully determining conduct nor merely platitudes that completely fail to guide it. Global in scope, but not uniform, these are flexible guidelines with room for exceptions, for judgement and creative variation. The Quran, however, the apologist continues, rightly condemns sentimentality, the bane of the modern liberal age, as an enemy of practical reason (Q:11:42–7).[40] Emotion immobilizes practical reason and blurs the distinction between wrong conduct and right conduct where the latter amounts to obedience to God. That is why, the apologist concludes, Islam also prohibits tragedy – where the concepts of right and wrong both drop out as equally inapplicable.

The Quran expects total and enthusiastic commitment from every believer. Yet few human beings, even in ages of enthusiasm, have placed God at the forefront of their personal loyalties. Why have most human beings in all ages cared more for their wives and children than for God? Few religious believers would be willing to do what Abraham was prepared to do in the binding of Isaac, an event regarded by Muslims and orthodox Jews and Christians as historical but treated by secularized

Jews and Christians as an audacious moral fable. A trial of that magnitude is peculiar to Abraham although one cannot imagine Muhammad or Jesus failing the same test. Abraham the iconoclast of the Quran, and Muhammad's predecessor in that role, is not typical of seminal religious figures, let alone representative of the ordinary run of believers. Leaving one's family behind to go to holy struggle for God's cause is one thing; to sacrifice one's child is quite another. The Quran has good reason to call Abraham a friend of God (*khalīl Allāh*; Q:4:125; see also Q:26:77–80).

The secular critic of religion watches the religious rope being tightened around everyone's neck. Here, in vivid colours, the atheist shouts, is the concealed anti-humanism of this monstrous but seductive thing called religion. This disastrous life-style where one degrades the human element is eulogized as the ideal life-style for all human beings. Judged by the strict normative codes of ethical religion, the majority of us have fallen morally – and yet the demands remain totalitarian and universal, unresponsive to the empirical realities of widespread failure.

16

Muhammad predicted that the requirements of Islam would be harder to fulfil in ages increasingly removed from the age of the Quran's incidence. The Quran itself hints at it (Q:56:12–14). The perfect community of Muhammad and his companions has been steadily declining morally and spiritually, through successive generations, in proportion to their distance from that original group, as we noted in Chapter 1, during a debate on Islam's self-image as religion perfected. The Prophet is reported to have conceded that while those in his era might be doomed for disobeying one tenth of the law, others in future ages need perform only one tenth to be saved from the fire of hell.[41] Was he suggesting that the yoke of the *Shari'ah* might become too heavy for people living in our century?

Islam, like Judaism, is a law-centred religion rooted in correct practice rather than solely in right belief. Faith is as faith does. Christians believe, however, that Christ delivered humankind from the tyranny of a law whose demands no one, except Jesus in his divine capacity, could fulfil. The Mosaic law was repealed by the grace of Christ. The new law of love (*agapē*), the new covenant, binds us to God without the coercive bonds of legality although there is ambivalence about this since Paul's radical antinomian claims (Romans 10:4; Galatians 3:23–8) contradict Jesus's more conservative sayings (Matthew 5:17–18).

Progressive Muslims might conclude that the original Quranic ideal is, in this age of indifference to self-restraint, unrealistic and impractical. It is an embarrassing reminder of virtues impossible to attain – and all the more embarrassing since we are self-consciously aware of our limitations. This explains, the contention concludes, the radical discontinuity in the modern life of faith. No wonder that the Friday afternoon is now merely a painful reminder to believers who cannot maintain such piety through the rest of the week.

A traditional Muslim retorts: 'There is nothing wrong with the ideal. Blame yourselves! You live in a soft age that prefers the luxurious life-style of sin to the hard climb of the straight path. Life's edges are no rougher today than in the Prophet's day.' There is force in this reply. God demanded more of earlier communities (as Q:2:286 implies) and he makes prejudicially rigorous demands on his chosen servants – though grace compensates in their case. The requirements of Quranic piety (*taqwā*), adds the Muslim jurist, already contain a sufficient and appropriate concession to our frail natures. To say that we should relax the standards further to reflect our modern predicament is a disguised plea for self-indulgence to suit an age of libertinism in which the egoism of the will to serve one's own pleasures has supplanted the humility of the will to serve God.

Theists recognize and even applaud human limitations. The Quran rejects optimistic estimates of the unaided human potential for self-perfectibility through obedience to revealed rules. Theism endorses a permanent discrepancy between the stringent demands of piety, on the one hand, and the ambiguous resources of human nature as created by God, on the other. Our divinely designed human nature is intrinsically incapable of being fully malleable to the divine will: human recalcitrance is not accidental. The capacity for frustrating our higher nature is a divinely intended and therefore irremovable feature of human nature. We shall therefore always need divine grace to become fully submissive to God. And, accordingly, our ability to sustain enthusiasm shall remain partly mysterious, owing to the operation of such grace, and therefore only partly meritorious.

17

I end this chapter by recording a modern reductionist view of our human nature in the hinterland of a debate about the meaning and biological stability of our humanity. This should concern Muslims who seek to maintain the integrity of the Quranic image of humankind in a rapidly changing secular world.

Like the other, lower, orders of animals, we have bodily needs, drives, and instincts. If we have nothing spiritual in our nature, religious believers fear, we are forever tethered to our biological condition. Without God, we are merely the most complex biological organisms. The Quran reminds us of our contemptible origins in 'a base fluid' (Q:32:8; 77:20). Without the dignity that divine election confers on us, we are no more than ephemeral biological realities.

Are we merely social animals? Much distinguishes us from the animal kingdom, though not necessarily to our advantage. It is a staple of reflection that no animal can reach the minimum threshold to attain the capacity for linguistic communication. We also have the capacity for reflective suicide that comes with our self-awareness; our laughter and cooking compensate. The faculties of reason and conscience are, argues the secular humanist, useful social conventions rather than gifts of the gods. These human faculties, capacities and qualities – including reason, conscience and the impulse to limited altruism – are rooted in human needs. The entire human condition is only the conventional veneer on a higher animal condition.

Is human nature a biological reality in danger of being reduced to the animal level rather than an ordained religious reality that seeks to transcend the merely human? Is our physical survival no longer a preparation for a higher religious end? For the humanist, our physical survival is an end in itself – though human nature is fully realized only in goals that transcend mere survival, ends such as the pursuit of art and truth. The humanist dismisses the divine warrant for human dignity as an external fiction that has for too long humiliated the deepest urges of the purely human condition, a condition that arduously achieves authenticity, in the socialist version of humanism for example, only in the hinterland of a securely classless economic order.

If we ask for the ideals and loyalties that might help us achieve our humanity, the humanist begins by cautioning us against the excesses of the past, chief among which was that hubristic picture of humankind as the apex of creation, made in the image of God. Modern imaginative literature and social theory concur that the human condition is a version of an animal condition to which we are chained. This condition is made bearable by being graced with a few uniquely human delusions, including the irrepressible desire for a perfect future world, a desire not limited to religious visions of the world. After slaying the ancient gods, secularism is now placing the last wreath on the tomb of humanity. The believer, by contrast, rejects the view that we humans are the ultimate reality in the universe and instead argues for a humanism which fulfils our humanity – but only if we willingly acknowledge the divine.

Acknowledging God's signs elevates us to our true nature; a denial of God and his mediated presence in the external world and our souls humiliates human nature to an animal level. The Quran's professed aim is to free us from domination by our material and animal biological desires and needs. Our material and biological nature is not identical with the original, therefore ultimate, form of our humanity – informed and shaped, according to all monotheists, by an elusive divine or quasi-divine component.

Second, I locate the larger hinterland of our modern anxiety about our species. Given current advances in technology, can we maintain the *biological* stability of human nature? The recently engineered biological instability of modern human nature undermines both ancient religious and more modern ideological projects – all of which relied on the assumption that while human nature was morally and politically malleable and plastic in the face of beneficial influence, there was a fixed biological reality called human nature.

In some way, our nature seems empty or plastic, arguably indeterminate, possibly reactive. That is why we can change it, sometimes radically. Law and morals control and nurture it in secular schemata; divine grace can radically transform it. But what could 'it' refer to in the previous sentence unless there is an unchangeable biological human nature which religions and ideologies can change through grace or human effort?

Secular humanism, informed by modern evolutionary biology, provides a flexible new self-image by replacing the a priori religiously motivated exaltation of humankind with a sober biological estimate of us as socio-physical beings with an unflattering lineage in the animal kingdom. We are species of living organisms that have over time gradually evolved from other lower species through a process of natural selection and mutation. Once thought to be the epitome of creation, made in the image of God, humans are now considered no more than one order of animal among others. We are 'social animals', biologically higher if morally degenerate ones, aware of our unalloyed and untamed nature, motivated by earthy instincts and needs, and dominated by our relentless biological drives.

Modern science, aided by singular advances in the technology of biological engineering, might take a further step in the reduction of humankind. It could enable us to transcend our current biological nature altogether: contemporary scientists talk glibly of stem cells, cloning, sleep-deprived humans, deliberate amnesia for traumatized patients, altering brain chemistry, taboo technologies that alter human potential, and a radical and escapist evolutionary eugenics which parallels the cosmic escapism of earlier decades where we fantasized about colonizing other planets after wantonly destroying this one. Until now the sole concern of our history has been the ideologically driven, as opposed to the physically or biologically driven, transcendence of human nature. The Buddhist ideal, the Nietzschean notion of the Übermench, political ideologies such as democracy and capitalism, and so on, have all assumed the biological stability of human nature. A biologically (as opposed to philosophically or ideologically) stable human nature has provided a subject for our inquiries and our utopian schemes. This datum is now suddenly controversial. In slaying the ancient gods, modern science has not spared humankind either. Perhaps we should lay the last wreath on the tomb of humankind and then re-learn to look up toward heaven.

11 'Greater is God!'

1

The Quran uses a potent vocabulary to spurn the worldly life calling it *al-dunyā* (the near or low one) when it is embraced at the expense of *al-ākhirah* (the later or last one), the hereafter. *Al-dunyā* is easy to attain; low shades and fruits within close reach, in paradise and on earth, are described by an adjective derived from the same root (*dānin*; Q:55:54; *dāniyah* at Q:6:99; 69:23; 76:14). Condemning a generation of Israelites who neglected the Torah, the Quran accuses them of 'grasping the vanities of this lower world' (*ya'khuzūna 'araḍa hāzā al-adnā;* Q:7:169; cf. *adnā* at Q:33:59) where *al-adnā*, a comparative of *al-dunyā*, intensifies the contempt. Sinners unwisely prefer this life to the next (Q:79:37–9).

The Quran loses no opportunity to degrade this life as transient and deceptive (Q:6:130; 13:26; 42:36); it denigrates it as 'the fleeting one' (*al-'ājilah*; Q:17:18; 75:20; 76:27) while exalting the enduring next life. Parables about the impermanence of this life (Q:10:24) conclude with the divine invitation to the eternal 'home of peace' (*dār al-salām*; Q: 6:127; 10:25), 'the abode of stability' (*dār al-qarār*; Q:40:39). Many passages condemn the material life as frivolous and falsely glamorous (Q:3:185; 6:32; 20:131; 28:60; 57:20). 'The life of this world is nothing but amusement and play and mutual rivalry in wealth and children' (Q:34:37; 102:1–2). 'But certainly, the abode of the hereafter, ah, that is life indeed (*al-ḥayawān*) if only they knew!' (Q:29:64; see also Q:47:36).[1]

The supremacy of 'the latter world' (*al-ākhirah*) over 'the former world' (*al-ūlā*; Q:53:25; 93:4) and the greatness of God are twin Quranic emphases. We noted in Chapter 1 that the Quran established the magnificence and uniqueness of God through revealing his metaphysical attributes: he is self-subsisting and eternal (*al-ḥayy, al-qayyūm*; Q:2:255; 3:2; 20:111; 40:65) and also eternal–absolute (*al-ṣamad*; lit., solid; Q:112:2), a perfection which combines infinity and aseity. Aseity (Latin: *a se*, in himself) denotes that which God is, his self-sufficiency. The ground for the possibility of God's nature being revealed lies in the nature of God, that is, in him, in his aseity: the divine attributes and perfections endure eternally although the creatures who comprehend them do so imperfectly and temporarily. God also has moral perfections which include absolute forms of wisdom, knowledge, power, goodness, mercy and so on. We explore the greatness of God in terms of his moral and legal purpose for us, a revealed relatedness that depends on a suitably humble human acknowledgement of divine perfections.

This divine sovereignty is *de jure* and absolute: divine mercy does not mitigate divine power or reduce its scope. No design to domesticate this divinity can soften it to suit secular humanism. Islam, as an absolutely rigorous and unqualified monotheism, views the voluntary rational submission to God as providing the yardstick of human worth. *Allāhu akbar* is no empty slogan. But what could the priority and greatness of God mean when the human state is the necessary starting-point of religious reflection? We answer this by exploring the Quranic life-style, demanded of believers who recognize the divine greatness, against the backdrop of the contemporary acknowledgement of the autonomy of morals, a theme introduced in Chapter 3. Here we establish the possibility of humanizing theism by sketching lightly the shape of a critical Islamic humanism that takes the measure of both the inherited religious tradition and the current secular reservations about traditionally religious ideals.

Our religious exploration, tinctured with a philosophical streak, traces the outline of the broad contours of problems inherent in the shift towards a humanized version of religion in general and Islam in particular. We survey general features of this terrain in order to map out the contours of an Islamic humanism responsive to the pressures of secularism. It is charged that Islam cannot enter the modern world and make appropriate concessions to the secular challenger. The charge often settles on two issues. First, an axiom of modern secularist rejection of Islam: the faith is inherently sexist and therefore incompatible with the emancipation of women, roughly half the human race. The case for an Islamic humanism cannot succeed without including women as equal members of the faith community. Second, Islamic enthusiasm, inspired by a passionate belief in an after-life, is alleged to have unmanageably anarchic political consequences. This significant charge is not wholly within the scope of this essay but we do explore the more preliminary reality of the centrality of martyrdom in the Quranic mind.

2

God has retreated from community and nature but we can sense his totalitarian omnipresence in architectural works; believers call it a sense of sanctuary as they relax in the cool shade of a mosque or cathedral towering above the turbulence of a modern city and would resent any suggestion of dictatorial subservience. Many grand mosques in Cairo, Cordoba and Istanbul celebrate the supremacy and visible glory of God. Everything in the heavens and the earth glorifies God and declares his majestic grandeur (Q:45:36; 57:1; 59:1, 24; 61:1; 62:1; 64:1). All creation, including the shadows of objects, bows to God (Q:13:15; 16:48) though such worship is unlike the voluntary, rational and loving worship of human choice. The perceptible divine dignity is described as *jadd* (Q:72:3; see also *majīd*, glorified; Q:11:73), *kibriyā'* (overwhelming greatness; Q:45:37), *subhān* (glory; Q:17:1), *jalāl* (dignified beauty; Q:55: 27, 58), *ikrām* (honour; Q: 55:27, 78) and *waqār* (gravitas; Q:71:13). The Quran often expatiates on God's omnipotence, omniscience and transcendent majesty (Q:2:255; 59:22–4).

We decipher on mosque walls and columns God's greatness and power: He is the first and the last, the evident and the hidden (Q:57:3). *Huwa al-Qāhir*: He is the conqueror (Q:6:18, 61)[2] or, in an intensive form, *al-Qahhār*, the irresistibly dominant (Q:12:39; 13:16; 14:48; 39:4; 40:16). 'And God dominates in his purposes' (Q:12:21; 65:3); his word is exalted (Q:9:40). He himself is great: *Allāhu akbar* (lit., Greater is God!). *Huwa al-Ghaniyy*: he is the all-sufficient, free of needs (Q:14:8; 27:40; 29:6; 31:12; 57:24; 64:6). Each divine self-description reveals the Quran's axioms and priorities. Finally, he simply is God. The sentence, *Huwa Allāh* (lit., He *the* God; Q:59:22, 23) needs no copula, making the sentence compact, its words paired and sitting juxtaposed. Aided by the elision of the two vowels, the words merge into each other as *Huwallāh*. The calligraphic expression of this dogma even looks weighty and dense.

A literal translation of *Allāhu akbar* is 'God greater'. The popular idiomatic translation 'God is great' is misleading since the original contains a comparative adjective (*akbar*). 'God is great' could be rendered by *Allahu kabīr*, which lacks the force of a comparative phrase. It is as though the comparator (*min*, than) is implicit: *Allāhu akbar* is shorthand for *Allāhu akbar min kulli shay'in* (God is greater than everything). The strict translation that highlights this comparative feature (namely, God is greater or God is a greater one) is equally misleading since it appears as if the sentence is incomplete – awaiting mention of the object than which it is greater. Greater is God, by reversing word order, gets the sense theologically correct although the word order, in English, sounds inappropriate to prose. But then the Quran is not prose; and Muslims even deny it is poetry!

The Quran never says, in the subjunctive or optative mood, 'Let him/May he be great'. That reflects the Christian temperament: 'Your Kingdom come, your will be done'. Literally, 'Let it come (*elthatō*) the kingdom of you, let it come about (*genēthētō*) the will of you.' Matthew 6:10 uses imperatives (in the aorist active third person singular and passive respectively) but the theological ethos is more suited to the grammatical subjunctive. It sounds like a precariously expressed and indecisive form of the sentiment implicit in the indicative phrase '*Allāhu akbar*'. The Christian expression is not inappropriate: the unpredictable and mysterious will of our rebellious humanity is involved. Both are ways of privileging the will of God above our recalcitrant volition but the theologies antecedent to these pithy expressions are diametrically opposed. The Quranic intention is factual and declarative, rarely optative or subjunctive or even imperative issued in a human voice. The twin expressions *tabāraka* (blessed be; Q:7:54; 23:14; 25:1,10, 61; 40:64; 43:85; 67:1) and *ta'ālā* (exalted be; Q:16:1, 3; 17:43), used of God, are optative in intention though Arabic lacks a specially constructed grammatical mood for it. The formula of praise contained in *subḥān Allāh* (Glory be to God; Q:27:8; 28:68; 59:23) is equivalent to both in mood and content.

The order to magnify God (lit., make him great) is characteristically Quranic and occurs in the intensive (*kabbir-hū*; Q:17:111) where it is a divine imperative, not a human suggestion or wish. It occurs in a softer form too as 'that you might magnify

God' (*li tukabbirū Allāh*; Q:22:37). Typically, however, the mood is indicative if not imperative: 'The remembrance of God is greater' (*zikr Allāh akbar*; Q:29:45) because it is the only source of spiritual satisfaction (*iṭminān*; conjugated. at Q:13:28). The intelligent believer therefore is, paradoxically, actively resigned to the good will of this magnificent God.

A better comparison is with Judaism where the divine imperative *shemā' Yisra'ēl* (Hear, O Israel), 'the Lord our God, the Lord is one', is a part of 'the acceptance of the yoke of heaven' (*kabbalat ol malkhut shamay'im*).[3] The surrender of our faculty of audition corresponds to the greatness of God. In the struggle between the infinite and omnipotent creator and his finite, free but weak creature, the creator dominates in his purposes (Q:12:21; 65:3); no one can outwit him (Q:70:41).

3

'The revelation of the book is from God, exalted and wise, who forgives sins, accepts repentance, is severe in retribution, has far-reaching power; there is no God except him; towards him is the final goal' (Q:40:2–3). He alone is the dominant, exclaims the devout believer, awed by the majestic reach (*al-ṭaul*; Q:40:3) of this kingdom. The exclusive divine greatness emerges as an index to the Quranic message at every level, especially the existential and the moral.

Existentially, enthusiastic believers want God to dwarf his creation. While Muslims, as worshipful servants, love God, mystics aim at an absolute union with God where only God continues to exist; the attributes of the mystic lover are annihilated in the divine attributes. In the state of *fanā'*, God speaks and acts through the apparent agency of the mystic, his instrument. Such a Sufi pantheism, a view that persuasively claims partial scriptural support, sees God as the only being who truly exists. He exists by essence, in Christian Scholastic terminology; in his case, uniquely, his essence is his existence. One ontological implication of this view has substantial Quranic support. God is the only genuine agent: he is able to command anything according to his will (Q:5:1; 3:154), do all things he intends (Q:11:107) and directly cause events in nature (Q:25:45). Indeed he alone is able to do anything since human agency is over-ridden by divine actions (Q:8:17; 85:16), especially in the exercise of the divine prerogatives of bestowing life and death and of giving life to the dead (Q:3:156; 15:23; 42:9; 44:8; 50:43; 53:44; 57:2). The scripture repeatedly explicates God's inalienable rights over humankind and creation.

The ninth-century mystic Bayazīd Bistāmī (d. 874), who represents the ecstatic Sufism of the mystic lover aiming at absolute union and hence total annihilation in God, is famous for an instructive witticism. When a novice remarked that once upon a time, there was nothing but God, Sheikh Bistāmī added: 'There is still nothing but God'. Bayazīd Bistāmī, aware of his genius, teased a humourless orthodoxy as he enjoyed the controversy generated by such megalomaniacal comments as 'Glory be to me, how great is my majesty'. It was not long before an outraged orthodoxy arrived at his home to interrogate him about his true identity.

These shock tactics disturbed both the uninitiated and the official scholars – but Bayazīd was known to be a scholarly and observant Muslim[4] who led a rather schizophrenic life: while antinomian during his intoxicated mystical utterances, he otherwise scrupulously and soberly observed the holy law.[5]

If critically probed, such elite mysticism introduces intolerable complications. Its extravagant monism – the view that there is nothing but God – contradicts the Quran, on a plain reading innocent of private or esoteric refinement. It effectively denies freedom of the human will while exalting the freedom of the divine will, thus making a mockery of the moral struggle between good and evil in the life of the believer. Although it appears to be concerned to praise and exalt God as much as possible, in practice, ironically, it could be subversive of orthopraxy. Many of the intoxicated Sufis were accused of a mystical anarchy that led to laxity in conduct and belief.[6] Their views also implied that Muhammad, the bearer of the Quran, was, like the Sufis, an illusory being who deserved no independent existence. The difference was of course that these mystics, unlike the Prophet Muhammad, were eager to obliterate the distinction between themselves and God.[7]

4

The Quranic God has the last word in the moral life. But is he himself above and beyond reproach? Is his conduct exempt from moral assessment? This controversy, inspired by moral rather than doctrinal concerns, exercised the mettle of classical Muslim theologians, the Mu'tazilite rationalists. God's behaviour and nature occasionally appear callous and indifferent, immune from human moral appraisal (Q:5:18; 21:23; 27:51; 91:14–15). Does he, however, have the last or the sole word in the moral affair? Is there any human variable in the moral equation?

Describing the fate of sinners who have been drowned or annihilated by divine anger, the Quran apportions blame: 'We did not wrong them; rather, they wronged themselves' (Q:9:70; 10:44; 29:40; 43:76). No community is ever destroyed without a widely broadcast warning (Q:28:58–9). God intends no injustice to any part of creation (Q:3:108; 4:40; 40:31). Again, God is not in the least unjust to his servants (Q:22:10; 41:46; 50:29) where an intensive (zallām) is used to underline immaculate divine behaviour. Nor is God unjust to his prophetic spokesmen: the rebellious prophet Dhū Al-Nūn,[8] after disobeying and defying God, repents in a self-reproach cherished by popular piety (Q:21:87).

While God is independent of creation, all creation depends on him and is answerable to him. He is our king, owner, and master. We are his servants, citizens in his kingdom. God is not accountable to his creatures – though he has voluntarily enjoined mercy on his nature and conduct (Q:6:12). As 'their rightful master' (mawlā-hum al-ḥaqq; Q:6:62), he has inalienable sovereignty over human lives (Q:1:2). As obedient servant ('abd Allāh), the wise man seeks security against divine anger (Q:1:4). God is independent not only of his creatures, he is also unaffected by their response to his summons (Q:2:57; 39:7). Humankind is dispensable, even disposable (Q:35:15–17). Whether human beings respond in penitent obedience or impenitent rejection, it makes no difference to God. However, God has honoured men and women by his gracious decision to reveal his will for them (Q:17:70; 76:3). Though the initiative here is divine, it is we who need God (Q:14:8).

It is prudent to be aware of the God to whom we are accountable (Q:1:4; 21:23; 43:44), a prudence extolled as 'a bargain' (*tijārah*; Q:61:10). God warns us that we must be cautious of him (Q:3:28, 30). Hell's terrors are described in Meccan and Medinan passages whose tone is unfailingly direct, literal, sincere, and peremptory; it is unconvincing to eviscerate their content into metaphor or allegory. These violent threats indelibly impressed the Prophet, his companions and thereafter every generation of Muslims.[9]

The mysterious God does not permit the presumption of human expectation and understanding of his unaccountable ways which are inexplicable and morally absolved of the need for explanation (Q:21:23). God is merciful to whom he wishes and gives wisdom and guidance to whomsoever he pleases (Q:2:269). He forgives whom he wishes and punishes whom he pleases (Q:5:18, 42; 42:8; 48:14; 76:31) though in context the claims are made *ad hominem* against the arrogant pagans and against Jews and Christians claiming exemption from divine judgement (Q:5:18). A dominant scriptural strand is free from apology and self-justification; dismissive-sounding claims are made emphatically and repeatedly. This is no incidental emphasis diluted later by a retrospective regret over the vehemence of the original idiom. It is consistent and terminative, not haphazard or provisional. The Quran seems, in the total quality of its conviction, an amoral scripture, beyond our categories of good and evil.

5

The tone of the Arabic original, though aristocratic, can nonetheless nourish tentative and nuanced moods. The scripture absorbs many emphases and strains without losing its essential and easily noticed but indefinable ethos. The Quran was fecund enough to inspire a mystical stream of contemplative piety that has trickled into the lives of believers of all levels of education and wealth. A meditative moral undercurrent runs close to the surface of the scripture. Heart-searchingly reflective passages thread a diffident mutuality and tenderness into a tale that is terrifying in the intensity of its unilateral conviction. The God of the fiery furnace is also self-described as merciful, appreciative, forbearing and just, always rich in pardon for a corrupt humanity (Q:13:6); if men and women believe and act virtuously, he is eager to reward them generously (Q:2:62). While irresistibly powerful, God tempers his just judgement with mercy and generosity but never with pity for humankind; all mawkishness remains foreign.[10]

We can assess the Quranic God's moral character by exploring the scripture's concern with the sanctity of the word pledged. There are two dimensions of this issue. First, the Quran orders the fulfilment of covenants and pledges (Q:5:1; 17:34); God is the guarantor (*kafīl*; Q:16:91) of the contracts the righteous make (see also Q:12:66; 28:28). A promise made to God, with conscious intent, is not to be taken lightly (Q:2:225; 5:89; 17:34; 33:15) and may require expiation if it is annulled or reneged upon (Q:58:3–4). Second and equally, God never fails in his pledges (Q:3:9; 4:87, 122; 9:111; 21:104; 39:20). The Quran contains many morally dependable but qualified pledges ratified by God (Q:29:69; 47:7). Embedded in the climax to several Medinan pericopes are conditional assurances of success for the patient believers who struggle in God's way (Q:8:20–9). 'If anyone has faith in God, he guides his heart' (Q:64:11). If anyone fears God, God finds a loophole for him (Q:12:76)[11] and provides for him from unimaginable sources (Q:65:2–3). Again, if anyone reveres God, he facilitates his path in life, blots out his sins and enlarges his reward (Q:65:4–5). Sadly, human beings rarely honour their side of the bargain (Q:7:102).

The Quran contains sensitive applications for a considered spiritual reaction from the reader. God appreciates our moral efforts and cares about our destiny. Good and evil are not alike and shall not be treated alike (Q:38:28; 45:21; 68:35–6). God is *al-shakūr*, the appreciative one, one of his beautiful names which occurs with moderate frequency (Q:35:30, 34; see also Q:76:22). Lists of divine blessings and favours are followed by the tentative comment: 'And perhaps (*la'alla*) you might show gratitude' (Q:28:73; 45:12). The particle *la'alla* conjoined with various subject persons (usually the second person masculine plural *la'alla-kum*) occurs often with emphatic verbs of deliberation and assessment. Perhaps you shall receive admonition (*yatazakkarūna*; Q:39:27); perhaps you may reflect (*yatafakkarūna*; Q:7:176; 16:44); perhaps you might reason (*ta'qilūna*; Q:12:2; 43:3; 57:17); perhaps you might learn self-restraint (*tattaqūna*; Q:2:183). These are stock phrases. The Quran is at times more direct: 'Humankind! What seduces you away from your gracious Lord, who creates you, then perfects you, and proportions you with a just balance; in whatever shape and form he wills, he creates you' (Q:82:6–8).

Is there a moral relationship between humankind and God? We require reciprocity between parties to a moral relationship; a friendship or a sexual liaison presupposes mutuality. Most moral relationships presuppose commonly held ethical rules which enable some moral reciprocity. Exceptionally, between adults and children (especially infants), between adults and mentally handicapped people, and between human beings and animals, the moral relationship is partial and unilateral. For example, a cow has no moral obligation towards a farmer while the farmer, as a full moral agent, has the duty to care for the cow. Our human moral relationship to God fits in somewhere on this continuum – but it would be insulting to us if our relationship to God turned out to be as unilateral or incomplete as the one between adults and dependent life, let alone between adults and animals.

The Quran summons humankind but not as slaves or chattels or mere servants of an arbitrary and ruthless dictator. Two parables confirm the dignified moral status of believers as responsible agents:

> God expounds the parable of a powerless slave–servant (*'abdan mamlūkan*) and of [another] man on whom we have bestowed favours and provision out of which he spends privately and publicly. Are these two equal? All praise

is for God but most of them have no knowledge. And God expounds another parable of two men, one of whom is dumb and powerless, indeed a useless burden to his master; whichever way he directs him, the man brings him no good. Is such a man equal to the [other] man who commands justice and is moreover on the straight path?

(Q:16:75–6)

The Quran is neither uniformly gentle nor predictably harsh despite some planned rhetorical repetition in its appeals to humankind. Some passages sharply puncture any conceit that we can annex or domesticate God. 'God singles out for his mercy whomsoever he pleases' (Q:2:105), guides whom he pleases and leads astray whom he pleases (Q:6:39) and punishes whom he wishes and forgives whom he wishes (Q:2:284; 5:42; 29:21; 48:14). Such scornful indifference to human choice and conscience is usually tempered by an accompanying reassurance of divine mercy, justice and love which jointly make God accessible and compassionately immanent in creation. The hyperbolic passages remind us that he is 'God in heaven and God on the earth' (Q:6:3; 43:84), not some tame deity we can fashion in our own image.

Quranic passages suggesting that human creatures are slaves with no rights must not be read literally. Passages extolling an exaltation of the arbitrary prowess of God were intended to anger the self-satisfied and powerful Qurayshi establishment whose tenacious conservatism was blind to the power of greater forces. Such passages are intended to dislodge complacency. This Quranic message addressed to the Quraysh is intended for all unjust powers and sovereignties in all times and places.

It is instructive to compare here the biblical book of Job which seems to portray Yahweh as an arbitrary tyrant (Job 42). A righteous Job, defiant even during the whirlwind encounter, interrogates God. Job has some of the best lines, some marked by sarcasm; the whole encounter is subtly subversive of ethical monotheism even though this book is canonical. The Quran portrays a just God who ensures a perfect alignment of virtue and reward, of moral goodness and material prosperity – though admittedly only in an after-life which suggests that the alignment is imperfect on earth and must wait for postponed rectification. In our world, there are too many corrupt people who are prosperous and too many virtuous people who are destitute for us to think that either alignment is entirely fortuitous or that the divine promise is true. The account of Job (Ayyūb) in the Quran, which confirms the alignment of divine reward with patient virtue (Q:6:84; 21:83–4; 38:41–4), in effect opposes the biblical account of Job as faithless.

In one respect, however, the Quranic God is also dictatorial. The hell threats, intentionally graphic, even hyperbolic, are no incidental feature of the revelation. But perhaps they are, as the Quran occasionally admits (Q:39:16), intended merely to counteract heedlessness and complacent negligence. The signs of God (āyāt Allāh) are intended to cause fear, to serve as exemplary punishments (Q:17:59). The Quran is a deterrent (*muzdajar*; Q:54:4). Again: 'We have sent it down thus: as an Arabic Quran; and we included in it a few threats (*min al-wa 'īd*) so that perhaps they might fear God or at least remember him' (Q:20:113). Threats alternate with mild pleas as the scripture moves from direct and upbraiding messages to coaxing and gentle admonitions. The root word for promise (*wa/'a/da*) is ambiguous, meaning both to promise and to threaten – to promise good or ill.

The Quran is moral revelation for creatures who are encouraged to have expectations of a God whose power is absolute but not dictatorial or tyrannical. 'What can God gain by punishing you if are grateful and believe? No, God is appreciative of good (*shākir*) and knows all things' (Q:4:147). God will, for example, reward those believers who migrate in his way and are then killed or die naturally in exile (Q:2:218; 3:195; 4:100; 16:41; 22:58). One passage states that it becomes 'incumbent upon God to reward such a person' (Q:4:100). God voluntarily binds himself by his holy promises and categorical pledges (Q:9:111; 13:31; 14:47; 25:16; 39:20; 45:32; 46:17). Such passages confirm that the operation of moral law establishes a standard of accusation and vindication applicable to the creator.

In the context of the classical debate on freedom and predestination, the extreme rationalists (Mu'tazilites) brazenly contended that God's creatures have absolute free-will even if this entailed a limitation in God's power to will and act as he wishes! The extreme Ash'arites, the orthodox theologians, were reacting to these Mu'tazilite excesses when they opted for God's absolute freedom at the expense of human liberty – arguing that humanity is predestined to whatever God decreed, the view of orthodox Islam in subsequent ages. The Quran, on balance, favours the orthodox view which gives the power of choice to God, not humankind (Q:4:78; 6:111, 134; 28:68; 53:24–5; 57:22–3; 68:38–9; 74:55–6; 81:28–9). A few verses suggest absolute human freedom to choose guidance or error (Q:73:19; 80:11–12). Muslim theologians such as Al-Ash'arī, as we saw in Chapters 2 and 3, abandoned the rationalist school and claimed that divine actions must not be assessed by using moral rules ordained for the human world. The distinction between good and evil is not intrinsic; it is attained and maintained by divine fiat. Among the Mu'tazilites, however, the central doctrine of 'the promise and the threat' (*al-wa'd wa al-wa'īd*) was precisely the insistence on the absolutely dependable divine promises about hell and heaven based on categorical Quranic pledges (see Q:19:61).

We should take sides in this classical debate: the God of orthodox theology (*kalām*) is unworthy of our modern reverence. His amoral prowess repels us. If God need not respect moral rules that he has ordained for the moral government of the created world, then the conflict of good versus evil is an inauthentic duality for humankind and God. Good does not matter; evil does not matter. The conflict was spurious since the forces of good and evil only appear to be opposed. We should therefore view the historic struggle between good and evil with a mocking and amused detachment.

This stance is itself a moral one and has moral consequences. If good and evil are illusory for God – which entails that they are simply illusory – then the drama of human history is a lie composed by an imposter. But good and evil are not illusions; on the contrary, these are the most profound categories in creation. Men and women were created with moral awareness and given the gift of guidance

(Q:76:2–3); each soul innately knows its piety (*taqwā*) and its evil (*fujūr*; Q:91:8). God speaks the truth (Q:4:87; 122; 33:4, 22) while his arch-opponent is a deceiver (Q:17:64). Truth and falsehood frame this conflict; and these are primarily ethical rather than legal or aesthetic categories. God orders justice (Q:4:135; 5:8; 16:90; 57:25) and dislikes corruption, ingratitude, disbelief and injustice in his human subjects (Q:5:64; 39:7). He promises to requite good with generous reward and evil with stern justice (Q:40:40). God is pleased with human gratitude (Q:39:7) and rewards those who are truthful, charitable, devout and just (Q:3:76; 12:88; 49:9). On those who believe and do good works, 'The Merciful will bestow love' (*wud'*; Q:19:96) since he is loving (*wadūd*; Q:85:14) and kind and gracious (Q:6:12, 54, 42:19; 57:9). He will befriend the righteous (Q:6:127). Does this sound like the description of an arbitrary tyrant indifferent to human moral yearnings?

If God loves just and good actions and loves those who do such acts, he himself must be a just and good being. For a being unaware of or indifferent to such moral qualities could not admire goodness and justice in others. The decree of moral regulation therefore makes the divine art, exhibited in creation, ultimately moral as opposed to neutral or merely aesthetic. This moral view is implicit in the Quran (Q:3:191; 21:16–17; 23:115; 38:27; 44:38). We conclude that any morally appropriate portrait of God presupposes moral reciprocity which in turn implies that both creature and creator are indifferently under the yoke of moral dictates.

6

Before we turn to the question of Islamic humanism, we must identify the presuppositions of the religious life-style suited to the traditional recognition of the sovereign majesty of God. Appreciation of this practical religious vision safeguards the modern believer against facile capitulation to reductionism or to excessive compromise under the pressure of contemporary challenges. It will also help us to understand how, and if, a continuity with that original life-style can be a viable contemporary aim.

God is greater (*Allāhu akbar*), a refrain punctuating the Muslim prayer-cycle, is an index to the scripture's active promotion of the service of God. Only through constant and sincere struggle in God's path (*al-jihād fi sabīl Allāh*: Q:9:20; 60:1) can we learn to place him above our desires and natural inclinations (Q:3:14–15; 9:24). Placed under the iconoclastic axe are all our varied temptations and desires: lavish wealth, business interests and property (Q:9:24), gold, silver, horses of pedigree, cattle and fertile lands (Q:3:14), the distractions of material possessions, family, spouse, and progeny, especially sons (Q:58:22; 63:9; 64:14–15; 74:12–13), illicit sexual pleasure, sensual comfort and the anarchic wish for a total freedom from external restraint (Q:9:24; 75:36; 96:6–8).

The human bonds of lineage and matrimony, created by God (Q:25:54), are temporary. God intervenes between a man (*al-mar'*) and his innermost self (Q:8:24; 50:16). No kinship, whether of family or tribe or matrimony, should obstruct the course of righteousness. All human bonds will dissolve in the face of the final divine judgement (Q:23:101; 80:33–7) as we finally realize the futility of human connections. The day of judgement is called 'the day of mutual disillusionment' (*al-yaum al-taghābun*; Q:64:9). Apart from the righteous few, even close friends shall become enemies (Q:43:67).

'No bearer of burdens can bear the burden of another' (Q:6:164; 17:15; 39:7; 53:38). This strict view of personal responsibility is mitigated by Quranic references to collective judgement of nations (Q:4:41; 17:71; 45:28–9). We do, of course, bear each others' burdens in this life since we are members of families and groups. But the Quran rejects the Torah's notion of inter-generational justice where God visits on the children the sins of the fathers up to several generations. However, the actions of the righteous person can outlive them and their offspring might enjoy the benefits of their parents' piety. God can visit on the children the virtues of the fathers (Q:18:82). The Quranic maxim of individual burden-bearing is a moral stance in its own right but is simultaneously directed against the Christian doctrine of vicarious atonement.

What is our basic condition, stripped of the artificialities of status, the vagaries of birth and biography, the contingencies of relationship and occupation, and the remaining paraphernalia of social setting? A man boasts of his wealth and sons (Q:19:77–80), the chief hiding-places in this ephemeral life. But God shall inherit all that he mentions and he shall appear before him 'bare and alone' (*fardan*; Q:19:80; *furādā* pl. at Q:6:94). Every person belongs to God (Q:10:66) and all things likewise (Q:10:55). Both claims are interpreted literally: Islamic property law treats land as a trust.[12] This is our unadorned condition: alone and divested of the particularities of sociality and filiation, aware that we are dust of the earth and to it we shall return (Q:7:24–5; 71:17–18). The Quran, as practical scripture, aware of our spiritual myopia and weakness, orders us to bring our eyes and ears close to the texture of our mortality so that we may register the brevity of our tenure on this good earth (Q:59:18). 'Every soul shall taste death' (Q:3:185; 29:57).

God is omnipresent in society (Q:57:4; 58:7), close to each person (Q:50:16); accordingly, the Quran orders us to cultivate piety (*taqwā*) to enable us to live in awareness of our duty to the divine king (Q:3:102; 4:1; 22:1; 57:28; 59:18). *Taqwā*, prudence in religious form, is a scrupulous concern to avoid stepping on the 'limits set by God' (*ḥudūd Allāh*; Q:2:187; 4:13–14; 65:1). Lest believers become complacently self-righteous, they are warned of 'trials which do not afflict solely the evildoers among you' (Q:8:25) and of 'sin that can accrue without [our] knowledge' (*muʿarratun bi ghayri ʿilm*; Q:48:25). The heart and mind can conspire to think thoughts and do actions that render our works null in the divine estimation; we might earn punishment while we do not realize it (Q:24:63; 49:2). The context of the two verses just mentioned is raising one's voice above the voice of Muhammad *ex officio*, thus betraying disrespect for God's Apostle. A vigilant divine compassion pursues and catches all human wrongdoing and disobedience in its corner. 'Eschew all sin – open or secret', warns one Meccan revelation in the context of dietary regulations (Q:6:120). The heart, the most secure citadel of the self, is no hiding-place; it is only a small chunk of secrecy, privacy and solitude – and it is not our own. 'God knows the treachery of the eyes and what the breasts conceal' (Q:40:19). He besieges the fortress of the heart until its surrender.

Repentance and patience are the joint pillars of the life of *taqwā* (piety). Repentance functions as a religious analogue of secular self-awareness and self-examination, attitudes related to the virtues of selflessness and unselfishness. The believer recognizes and thanks God amid the contingencies and vicissitudes of an uncertain life. 'All is from God', says Chapter 4 (v. 78) when, in the aftermath of a military reverse, some people speculate that the good in human fortunes comes from God while the evil comes from his Prophet. The next verse clarifies that all good is from God but we have only ourselves to blame for the evil (Q:4:79). Believers harness every faculty, knowing that no area of their thought, experience, volition or imagination is excused or exempted from divine supervision. The fabric of life is dyed with 'the dye of God' (*sibghat Allāh*; Q:2:138), an Islamic equivalent of baptism. From the moment of conception – some Muslim sages count from conception, not birth – to the moment of death, and beyond, the human being's life is lived inside parameters set by a wise, observant and powerful God. 'And your Lord is not unaware of the things you do' is a quaint Quranic litotes (Q:11:123; 27:93; see also Q:6:132).

Only the patient and righteous shall inherit the reward of the next world (Q:12:90; 28:80); they are indeed people of good fortune (Q:41:35). Patience (*sabr*) is a virtue actively exercised as part of an intelligent and strategic acquiescence with vicissitude and misfortune, a temporary state for the believer awaiting external but deserved and guaranteed vindication at the hands of God. The verb *sa/ba/ra* is used often in the imperative form and in the active voice. In Arabic, it is transitive only: the imperative is not to be patient but to actively practise patience. The Quran also uses the intensive form of the verb where the middle radical is doubled to achieve intensity of meaning and explosive stress in pronunciation. Thus, the scripture exhorts believers to persevere in the reasonable hope of God's mercy, to continue to excel habitually in patience (Q:3:200) and to mutually recommend patience among themselves (Q:103:3).

7

The confession of God's greatness translates into practice; religious conviction leavens the whole of life. The Quran aroused the curiosity of polymaths who were at once scientists, mathematicians, theologians, and sometimes philosophers. Its practical legal consequences, however, extracted by jurists, became the foundations of Muslim civilization. Reflection and scholarship had their place: among Muslims, as among Jews, religious scholarship is a form of virtue. The Quran added, however, that sustained reflection about God and the world, unlike mere speculative curiosity, must be co-extensive with religious practice.

Following Muhammad's example, which we noted in Chapter 1, there are two areas of life where acknowledgment of the overwhelming greatness of God dictates practical conduct: sexual activity, including relationships between the genders, and secondly, in discerning the type and degree of zeal commensurate with a sincere profession of the greatness of God. We address here the issue of women's place in the Islamic community and defer to the next section an investigation of Islamic enthusiasm for an after-life.

In constructing the framework for an Islamic humanism alert to modernity, we must investigate the question of gender equality, an issue crucial to the development of such humanism. Virtually all westerners see Islam's perspective on women to be a decisive proof of its inferior and alien nature. We look at the Quran's reforms against the background of Islam as a form of egalitarian theo-nomocracy. After exploring the scripture's view of the sexual instinct and its institutional consequences, we examine one strategic reform which established the legal and moral personality of womankind. We then explore contemporary issues of rights, duties and inequalities in the hinterland of the Quran's view of the sexual dimension of human nature and its charter for a sexually healthy society. We conclude with observations about the limits of a liberal exegesis of the Quran. Our aim in this brief survey of a vast terrain is to understand the social and religious conditions for the emergence of an Islamic humanism.

The opening verse of the chapter called 'The Women' succinctly establishes the framework for sexual relationships:

> Mankind! Revere your Lord who created you from a single person (*nafsin wāḥidatin*) and created from it its companion of similar nature and from the pair of them scattered abroad countless men and women. Therefore, fear God in whose name you demand your mutual rights and also revere the wombs [of your mothers]. Certainly, God is constantly watching over you.
>
> (Q:4:1)

The very first Quranic revelation alludes to the elemental mystery of our birth. 'Recite! In the name of your Lord who created, created humankind from a blood-clot (*'alaq*)' (Q:96:1–2). The Quran invites us to ponder our capacity for sex and the vulnerabilities and bonds based on it (Q:22:5; 23:14; 30:21; 56:58–9). It treats the matter as worthy of tenderness, not merely scientific curiosity. Men and women are like a garment (*libās*) for each other (Q:2:187), the Quran's metaphor for the mutual love, compassion and attraction that mysteriously reside in the gender division (Q:30:21). The only human beings who note these subtleties are those given to intensive reflection (*tadabbur*, noun; *yatadabbarūna*; they reflect deeply; Q:4:82). The sexual and the sacred are often discussed together (Q:2:223). Sex is next to godliness – as though it were sacramental! The human fruit of sex, in the shape of progeny, is a divine marvel (Q:16:72).

The awareness of God, which comes from recognizing his greatness, is the best background to sexual activity. Sexual pleasure, considered instinctively private in pre-modern cultures, is, however, not beyond divine supervision. Believers invoke God when they intend to conceive their children: the faithful are aware of the gift of sex as the capacity which, by the grace and power of God rather than merely through a biological mechanism, perpetuates humanity's heritage (Q:2:223) and shows our continuing and justified trust in life.

The Quran's view of women and particularly of motherhood (Q:31:14; 46:15), as of sexuality more generally, is generous, liberal and charitable, whatever the shameful realities of parts of the Muslim world. While the Hebrew Bible, on a Christian interpretation, convicts women as original sinners (Genesis 2:4–3:24), the Quran reverses the biblical narrative and blames Adam alone (Q:20:120–2) or both Adam and Eve equally (Q:2:35–6; 7:19–23), but never Eve alone. The Devil approaches them both (Q:7:20) or Adam alone (Q:20:120).

Only one general, non-legal, passage, neither widely known nor often quoted, is sexist by modern standards. The context is the Arab pagan claim that God has daughters while the pagans have sons. The Quran, commenting on the oddity of this allotment, claims that women are naturally ostentatious and have a genius for finery and embellishment – not necessarily a pejorative observation. But the Quran then links this to an alleged lack of rational and dialectical ability: women cannot make their point clear in an argument (Q:43:16-18). This is a strange claim: women rarely seem to have difficulty getting across their point of view in an argument, as any married man will readily testify. To be fair to the Quran, part of this exchange is *ad hominem*, merely reflecting existing pagan Arab prejudices against women. But the Quran acquiesces in the prevailing attitude. A scripture, as I argued in Chapter 7, must confront rather than accommodate existing social biases. Its aim is to reform ugly social reality, not merely to record it.

More generally, the Quran is kind to women but in a patronizing way. They are seen as the fair or gentle sex in need of male protection. Mainstream Muslim culture sees women as emotional, deficient in rational ability, a view not restricted to Islamic cultures and, in Muslim societies, not based on the Quran. Indeed the Quranic God addresses select female believers. The scripture uses exclusively feminine plural imperatives in the revelations sent to Muhammad's spouses (Q:33:33-4); one revelation directly instructs them to fear God (*itaqīn Allāh*; Q:33:55). The Quran, through Muhammad, contains formative canonical revelations that address women believers. This suggests a spiritual equality for women and men in their relationship to God, especially as one who rewards good, a view explicitly affirmed elsewhere (Q:3:195; 9:71–2; 33:35; 40:40).

The Quran established a charter for a sexually just society by treating women as legal persons, a revolutionary innovation. Pagan society ruled that anyone who could not participate in war was not an autonomous or legally recognized person. Since women were barred from physical combat, they were not legal persons and could not inherit property. Indeed, as in most ancient cultures, women were themselves movable property or chattels that could be inherited or possessed by relatives or by the victor in war. The Quran outlawed the forced inheritance of women as property (Q:4:19). In pagan Arabia, a step-son or brother could inherit a dead man's widow (or widows) along with his goods and chattels and marry the widow against her will, customs outlawed by the Quran (Q:4:22).

By recognizing women as capable of giving independent testimony (as opposed to joint testimony with the male spouse), the Quran enabled women to be considered full legal persons, something which was formally achieved in the Christian West only as a result of the triumph of secularism. The Quran regards the female witness as equivalent of half of the male witness in commercial transaction (Q:2:282) but it equates it in cases of marital accusation. Where a man brings a charge of infidelity but cannot produce four witnesses, the accused woman's counter-testimony, in the form of unsupported assertion of her innocence, in effect outweighs the man's testimony given in the form of an accusation without independent support: the woman can escape punishment on the strength of her word (Q:24:6–9). This improves on the barbaric provisions of the Torah (Deuteronomy 21:13–21). The Quran, however, is still patriarchical: it does not envisage a situation where the woman, without producing evidence, accuses the man of sexual irregularity.

The Quran's reforms seem minor by modern standards. But one should recall that Roman law, the basis of modern western law, restricted testimony to males. The word testimony, derived from the Latin *testis* (singular of testes) meant witness to masculinity; the verb *testificari* (to testify) is from the same root. Jewish law, except in areas such as marital contracts and in divorces based on unexplained disappearance of the husband for an indefinite duration, rejects all female testimony as invalid. In the New Testament, Jesus appeared to Mary after the resurrection but her witness was dismissed as worthless by the male disciples (John 20:17-18; Matthew 28:5-10) since women were regarded as incurable liars by mainstream Jewish culture and especially by apocalyptic first-century schismatic–ascetic groups such as the Essenes.

Muslim women as legal persons can sign a marital contract. The Quran does not absolutely command marriage although it recommends it occasionally (Q:2:25; 24:32). Marriage is only normative since, as the Islamic marriage ceremony states, it reflects Muhammad's life-style. While devout Christians, following Paul, have seen even monogamy as a concession to human weakness rather than as a divine commandment or intention, Islam sees monogamy as normal while the polygynous form of polygamy is perhaps partly a concession to aggressive male desire.

Islamic law derived from the Quran and Prophetic traditions treats marriage as simply a solemn and binding legal contract with conditions and consequences (Q:4:20–1). It differs from the Christian ideal of monogamous sacramental marriage, an ideal dismissed as unrealistic by Muslims who wonder how often any spouse tears the veil of individual personality to attain complete intimacy. Christians and Muslims agree that we cannot legislate for harmony, fellowship and love in a relationship, virtues probably unattainable in this life. There is, according to tradition, no marriage in paradise. Al-Ghazālī is, however, popularly accredited with the remark that 'a good marriage is a foretaste of paradise'.

In the rest of this survey, we examine issues of inequity, male regulation of female conduct, the empowerment of women and the autonomy of their sexual lives. The question of the equality of the sexes is central to any secular interrogation of traditional faith. Female activists fear that 'God is greater' translates into patriarchy: men are dominant over women. It is further feared, incorrectly, that the scripture itself is either complicit or acquiescent in the abuse of women. The masculine *interpretation* of the Quran certainly seeks to maximize masculine privileges and minimize feminine rights. Biology can be destiny; being a woman often means being marginalized. Historically, this was untrue. Women in early and medieval Islam participated in politics and commerce. In intellectual and spiritual circles, some looked for and found a measure of equality. For example, the mystic Rabi'ah Al-'Adawiyyah, whom we discussed in Chapter 3, was respected as a great saint by male Sufis. Many learnt from her and some wanted to marry her. She declined. 'Aisha, the Prophet's only virgin wife, played a decisive role in the transmission of prophetic traditions and religious learning, especially on domestic matters. Individually, many women, depending on their class status, negotiated a modestly influential and respected if not powerful social standing for themselves.

We begin with polygyny. Is the type of polygyny permitted by Islam a social evil? It is not clear that polygyny discriminates against women as a class. It discriminates primarily against poor men and undesirable women: a rich man can marry four of the most eligible women, leaving behind only the least desirable ones. Second, the argument against polygyny, based on liberal grounds, is weak. If commitment is the only requirement, then polygynous marriages are morally no more indefensible than homosexual marriages or no marriages at all. Working out a fair contract is the only issue – and we can leave that to the parties concerned. 'Parties' implies unnecessary confrontation only if one sees marriage, somewhat sentimentally, in terms of sacrament and harmonious fellowship rather than hierarchy and law. The Quran, incidentally, permits divorce (*al-ṭalāq*; Q:2:227–34; 65:1–2, 4–7) but only the husband can initiate it; jurists follow Muhammad in permitting it as a reprehensible last resort.

The Quran permits a man to have more than one wife but only if he treats them all equally well (Q:4:3) but cautions that absolute equality of treatment is beyond male competence (Q:4:129). The man uses his discretion to decide whether or not he can, without injustice, marry four wives. It is, therefore, unfortunately, a unilateral male decision: a man can defend his right to marry more than one wife and he is the sole judge of whether or not he is justly treating his multiple spouses. It would be better to have an independent legal mechanism to judge the merits of candidates for polygyny. Conservative male interpretation of the scripture uniformly minimizes female rights in order to secure this type of privilege associated with patriarchy.

I turn now to the broader question of the regulation of the sex drive and thus broach the issue of the supervision of sexuality and the question of social leadership. No society is indifferent to sexuality; it must be regulated and monitored. The Quran intends to create a genuinely erotic and properly sensual society. It endorses scrupulous and puritanical strictures against any abuse of the sexual drive. It is axiomatic that men in Islamic culture are struck by desire easily, anywhere, anytime. Sex is seen as a powerful drive capable of causing social chaos. 'When a man and woman are together', reinforces one of Muhammad's most famous traditions, 'the third party is the Devil'. It is primarily a woman's duty, however, to avoid being the cause of temptation. Admittedly, the Quran orders both sexes to cultivate modesty. The rarely quoted short verse requiring modesty in male deportment (Q:24:30) immediately precedes the verse, about five times in length,

requiring female modesty (Q:24:31). The Quran restricts young women's movements to certain groups of males, mainly relatives, children incapable of desire,
and slaves. It appoints men, on grounds of physical strength and economic power,
as supervisors of women's lives, including sexual lives (Q:4:34).

The weaker party is the woman in the Quran's patriarchal context. The Arabic
word *'awrah* means woman in some Islamic languages; it literally means vulnerability. Frailty, thy name is woman! Legally, the word refers to parts of the
body that are vulnerable and defenceless and must be covered during prayer; the
Quran uses the word only once – to describe houses left exposed and vulnerable
to attack (Q:33:13). According to militant puritans, such as the Taliban, all of a
woman, even the accessories of voice, scent and natural beauty, needs protection
and concealment. The Quran itself is suitably vague (Q:24:31).

The Quran decrees that 'men manage (*qawwāmūna*) the affairs of women'. The
verse translates literally as: 'The men are standing upon the women' (*al-rijālu
qawwāmūna 'alā al-nisā'*; Q:4:34). The associated noun *qawwām* means one who
vigilantly protects someone's interests in a business context. The verb *qawwamūna*
used with the preposition *'alā* indicates obligation of the second party in the phrase,
women in this context, to the first party, the men. If the verb were used with the
preposition *ilā*, it would mean that men stand up *for* women, implying chivalry
and hence extra protective duties imposed on the men. The quoted verse (Q:4:34)
also gives the husband the unilateral right, as a last resort, to beat a recalcitrant
wife guilty of *nushūz* (lit., insurrection; see also Q:4:128; 58:11). A husband can
also be guilty of *nushūz*; the word then means cruelty (Q:4:128).

The Quran's conservative rulings rather than its egalitarian spirit and compassion, have, in most cases, influenced Islamic cultures and made them a byword
for repressive conservatism. Muslim women often depend completely on their
men, whether as fathers, brothers, husbands or sons; a woman's life can be
a waiting period for marriage. Some Muslim men readily resort to violence if
they perceive or suspect that their honour is impugned by a flirtatious sister or
wife or daughter. The newspapers report some so-called crimes of honour among
conservative communities in countries such as Jordan and Pakistan. All Islamic
nations officially denounce such crimes as brazen outrages against defenceless
women.

We need to be cautious with the above assessment. The public face of Islam, like
that of all political ideologies and religions, is a carefully crafted lie. The actual
balance of domestic power varies from family to family, culture to culture, class
to class; there is no shortage of domineering Muslim women. Many non-Muslims
think that, given such legal inequalities sanctioned by scripture, feminine self-
esteem is necessarily impossible in Islam. But legal privileges for Muslim men
are often merely formal rather than real. Muslim women are incorrectly seen as
invisible victims, muffled up and out of sight, passive victims of polygyny and its
evils. The veil is not always a form of self-suppression; often it is an alternative,
more modest, style of beauty, even a symbol of seduction rather than seclusion.
Ordinary female adventurism, especially in countries such as Iran and Pakistan,
can easily outwit the ingenuity of the male religious elite.

Some Muslims, such as the Taliban, have gone to fanatical extremes and treated even the shadow and the voice of a woman as erotic accessories. While in the West, only genital contact constitutes sexuality, in traditional Islam, even the second glance is reprehensible. This is absurd and unwieldy in a world where all one needs is a decent environment for men and women to work in and inter-act honourably. The puritan North African theologian Ibn Al-Ḥajj Al-Abdāri (d. 1336 CE), ideologically a precursor of the modern Taliban, developed a science of the exits (*adāb al-khurūj*): a woman should leave her home only on the day of her marriage, the day of her parents' death, and on the day of her own death. This entombment of living women is a shameful masculine excess, not the law of a just God. Ibn Al-Ḥajj was not only incensed by the freedom of Egyptian women, he also disapproved of the study of logic and philosophy during his stay in Alexandria (Egypt). Ibn Al-Ḥajj, named to reflect his passion for performing the pilgrimage to Mecca, would accuse modern Muslims of laxity; he is, however, contradicted by an earlier authority called Muhammad whose tender sayings such as 'Women, prayer, and perfume are worldly things made dear to me' are irreconcilable with such brazen misogyny.

Muslims differ about the correct standards of modesty and sexual propriety but all are exercised by the question: How does one limit the opportunities for temptation in order to control sexual appetite and adventurism while still securing an erotic society with a genuine respect for the family? Normative Islam advocates sexual apartheid. But this can be misinterpreted and abused; unhealthy excesses in either the conservative or the permissive direction are equally toxic. The prostitution of sex, as seen in commercial, especially abnormal, pornography is an inevitable, not contingent, consequence of the rupture of the traditional liaison between the sexual and the religious, itself part of the larger connection between faith and morality. No secular society can avoid sexual permissiveness. Since sex is an energetic instinct, the sexual demand can degenerate into a humiliation of the higher aspect of human nature. Perhaps only the genius of a modern Muhammad could teach us about the erotic value of sexual restraint symbolized by the veil of separation (*ḥijāb*; Q:19:17).

There are some irreducible legal inequalities between men and women as reflected in inheritance, the ratio of men to women in polygyny, and in the reduced status of female testimony. These co-exist with a strong scriptural strand advocating moral and spiritual equality for the sexes. A charitable interpretation of the Quran is not an imposition requiring torture of the text. The Quran has extensive intrinsic resources for encouraging compassion and equality. One cannot, however, always impose on the Quran interpretations favourable to modern secular thinking. Some Muslim and non-Muslim writers maximize the 'secular feminist' resources of the Quran and Prophetic traditions – perhaps in subconscious deference to the maxim, 'The West is the best'. Such an attitude has been denigrated as 'colonial feminism'. The predominantly male interpretation is certainly biased; and female interpreters are rare in the history of Quranic exegesis. The scripture does not, however, outlaw polygyny as an absolute evil. Some of its norms governing the lives of women (Q:4:34) must therefore appear irreducibly sexist in the eyes of modern enlightened secularism.

The main obstacle to equality is the political one. The Quran envisages a society under male leadership although it makes no adverse comment on female sovereigns (Q:27:22–44). The *khalīfah* (successor or caliph) must be male since only Adam is appointed as God's deputy in the Quranic narrative (Q:2:30–4). The noun *khalīfah* has no feminine form although lexically the word already appears to be feminine. Like the Salic law of dynastic succession, the *Sharī'ah* prohibits a female *khalīfah*. Most jurists do not even recognize a female prayer leader. The imam (lit. one placed in front) is virtually always male. Indeed *imām* has no feminine form; the feminine noun *imāmah*, in Sunni theology, refers to the institution of prayer-leadership, not to a female prayer leader.

If believers identify in the Quran a divine intention which conflicts with their own unaided human insight, must they still accept in good faith the scripture's verdict? Yes. Men and women might regret what divine authority has enjoined but since God is above human conscience, he has the last word. An inequality endorsed by scripture cannot be dismissed or removed by believers although its presence may be acknowledged as theologically puzzling, certainly a matter for regret. Believers are religiously obliged to contend with their doubts if they accept that 'God is greater'.

Muslims cannot uncritically accept the ideals of western emancipation and feminist empowerment. An Islamic feminism, no less than an Islamic humanism, must respect the qualifying adjective. The western feminist movements have failed to create a suitable sexual culture: instead we have the nightmare of societies self-reflexively embittered by their loss of that age-old natural eroticism between the sexes. The destruction of the family unit and the continuing undeclared civil (or uncivil) war between the sexes are merely toxic by-products of a feminist ideology gone wrong. Western feminine 'emancipation' has now, in any case, been fully recruited into the service of capitalist exploitation.[13]

8

Only the lucky reach an age when they can look back at life. One cannot engage in a meditative survey of one's biography at 18. If life begins at 40, then the age for retrospective regret over one's errors begins correspondingly late too. The notion of some 'stable state' located in the unpredictable future, marking an age at which we are finally settled in life, secure against error, could be the origin of an idea which perhaps later metamorphosed into a desire for immortality. For this grand ideal is otherwise unaccountable; there is, apart from reports of disputed paranormal and near-death experiences, little if any uncontroversial empirical evidence for it.

A contributor to a volume on secular transcendence writes: 'I have believed for as long as I can remember in an afterlife within my own life – a calm, stable state to be reached after a time of troubles'.[14] The author mentions that, as a child, he fantasized about his adolescence, the projected state of being grown up. He saw the threat of change – constant, irreversible, and intense change – as the great enemy of his peace of mind. A secular social scientist might locate in this feeling of insecurity and the constancy of change the psychological foundations of the notion of a stable after-life to be enjoyed after we leave the earthly scene. Secularists would no doubt dismiss this as an infantile desire for the perfect but illusory final and eternal condition.

The desire for immortal life is a unique but ubiquitous feature of our species. In Cro-Magnon culture, for example, we find fallen hunters buried in fetal position, surrounded with hunting weapons and cooking utensils, as though they might be raised to life in another world. Mature classical monotheism supplies a distinctively rational ground for this belief in the possibility of experiencing another life. Through its faith in the immortality of the soul and the physical resurrection of the body, theism offers hopes and ambitions beyond the grave.

Philosophers of mind who investigate personal identity have been troubled by conceptual difficulties with belief in such survival, both disembodied and corporeal. They wonder about the precise mechanism for maintaining the continuity of mental states such as memories against the physical background supplied by bodily discontinuity. But if we assume here, for the sake of our case, that the notion of survival beyond death is not flatly incoherent, we may extol the moral value of this conviction which has made life bearable for countless millions. It has supplied, for many men and women who would otherwise have led pointless lives, one general purpose to the whole of their lives, as opposed to merely several short-term purposes within their life-spans. Arab pagans, for example, believed in a religious aim within life; Islam purged, crystallized, institutionalized and radically expanded the content of this intuition.

Additionally, religious purpose, expressed as an active belief in an after-life, provided life-long moral motivation for some of those who are considered to be among the most morally active if not among the intellectually best of our species. Such consequential religious belief must not be despised. The Quran claims that God chose some men such as Abraham, Isaac and Jacob for the noble purpose of teaching humankind about the permanent abode in the after-life (Q:38:45–6).

The Quran contains rich descriptions of an after-life where contrasted fates await good and bad human beings. Pre-Islamic pagan poetry expressed a muscular and wistful tribal longing for a transcendence of the human and natural order. But the Quran is, for Arabs, the first writing to discern a religious significance in the keenly noted facts of impermanence and mortality, features of the nomadic Arab condition which inspired pathos and sentimentality. The pre-Islamic poets were traumatized by the transience of love; the second portion of the tripartite Islamic ode (*qaṣīda*) contains a tragic portion where the poet addresses the dead stones near the ashes of the departed (female) beloved's empty and cold camp-site and receives no answer to his anguished inquiries. Pagan poets never linked this tragic transience with some majestic reality that knows no change.

In meditative pericopes where the Quran is skirting the tragic outlook, translation destroys the plangent beauty of the original. In some passages (Q:22:45–6; 44:25–9), pathos and compassion mingle to create a romanticism and sadness that are profound precisely because they must never ripen into sentimentalism, let alone tragedy. The Quran, unlike the Bible, contains no elegiac passages of lamentations or jeremiads of inconsolable grief; it teaches instead that while the world is transient, God is permanently real (Q:19:40; 55:26). 'Everything is in decay (*fānin*), except the countenance of your Lord' (Q:55:26–7; 28:88).[15] The Quran frustrated the will to tragedy by positing an after-life that would satisfy the desire for a conclusive triumph over the limitations of physical extinction.

We saw in Chapter 9 that the pagan Arabs gave a robust sceptical verdict against resurrection. They found it incredible and therefore endlessly mocked it. How did the Quran make them believe in it so quickly and so irreversibly? Muhammad did not live in a society that was already monotheistic. Far from believing in a resurrection, the Arabs did not even worship dead ancestors (necrolatry). Indeed, there is no evidence of any necromancy – the prediction of the future by supposed communication with the dead. The pagan Arabs consistently rejected an after-life and mocked the suggestion of a bodily survival after death. This is not true of other Semitic cultures where such belief culturally persisted despite a religious ban on necromancy (Leviticus 19:31) and despite the lack of revealed sanction for belief in a resurrection of the dead. For example, Saul visits the witch of En-Dor after failing to obtain information about the future from Yahweh through the normal channels of dream, divination and prophetic rebuke and counsel. He asks the witch to conjure up the ghost of the prophet Samuel so that Saul can inquire into the mystery of the future (1 Samuel 28:3–25).

Islam found the pagan mood of recklessness and insouciance tinged with despair and took it and sublimated it; it retrieved this mood and rehabilitated it. The Quran spurned the martial ethos of internecine tribal violence and the indiscriminate blood-feud. It sanctioned the law of retaliation but limited the reach of the vendetta: by encouraging unilateral forgiveness and letting vengeance belong to God, it cut the entail of endless cycles of bloodshed. But its notion of virtue was a notion of prudence, the literal meaning of *taqwā* (translated as piety). The traditions of virility (*al-muru'ah*), not a Quranic term, were ingrained in the Arab mind but rejected by the Quran as part of the uncouth and immoral days of ignorance. Central to Arab manliness and chivalry was the single great gesture of a life-time, a dramatic act of magnanimity or spectacular generosity in which one squandered the accumulated wealth of a life-time or even one's life. It was not dissimilar to the existentialist's fantasy of enacting one great act of gratuitous freedom. In that famous act of greatness, one had to be caught and seen by the multitude; and the pagan poets, armed with their pens, were ready to eulogize it. The third part of the Islamic ode was a eulogy (*fakhr*, lit., pride or boast) to the tribe and any members who had done such acts. Inevitably, such high drama was more likely where one was doing something reckless rather than prudent. And this took courage; but courage, unlike honesty or justice, is a morally neutral virtue since it can be exercised equally in the cause of good or of evil.

The Quran often changed the old into the new while maintaining the link with the old. For example, it retrieved, from the clutches of paganism, the ceremony of the pilgrimage to Mecca and restored it to its original Abrahamic purpose of honouring God.[16] And analogously, it transformed the pagan protest against death, transitoriness and the brevity of our tenure on this good earth by recruiting the old recklessness for the new faithful cause. The old virtue of *muru'ah* was put to a new and more dignified use.[17] Martyrdom became an egress for latent violent pagan energies as the old recklessness was re-baptized as the supreme virtue of divinely sanctioned courage for the sake of God's religion. The future of the nascent cause was completely ensured.

Islamic history overflows with episodes of sacrifice of life for the cause of faith. By standing robust witness to an after-life that transcends this petty and ephemeral life, the Quran inspired an impressive record of courageous zeal in the holy struggle against militant evil. Islamic martyrdom was usually situated in physical struggle in the battlefield rather than in the Christian locale of passive resistance to evil as witness to the spiritual power of a physically powerless Christ:

> God has certainly purchased from the believers their persons and possessions in exchange for the garden [of paradise]. They fight in his cause; they kill and are killed. The promise [of paradise for martyrs] is binding on God, in truth, and runs through the Torah to the Gospel and the Quran. And who is more faithful to his covenant than God? Therefore rejoice in the bargain you have made. And that is the supreme achievement.
>
> (Q:9:111)[18]

According to the Prophet, martyrdom was the best way to enter this higher world of *al-ākhirah*. A recognition of the greatness of God required dramatic actions from the human creature who is, after all, created solely to serve God (Q:51:56). There are unspectacular ways of pleasing God; Muhammad preached that all acts, including domestic duties and the simplest acts of charity earn merit.[19] Even the pursuit of legitimate pleasure is meritorious – indeed an act of worship – on the grounds that the pursuit of illicit pleasure is censorious and blameworthy. But martyrdom is the most glamorous way to please God. Islamic tradition maintains that martyrs for the cause of Islam are the only exceptions to the rule of strict reckoning on the day of judgement.[20]

The Quran forbids believers from thinking of martyrs as dead, claiming that they are living, satisfied in the presence of God, enjoying his grace and favour. They feel secure in the knowledge that God's promise is true: he does not deny the reward of those who do good deeds. Moreover, as the martyrs rejoice in their new state, they look forward to an increase in their number as others join them (Q:2:154; 3:169–71). Such a vigorous doctrine cannot be eviscerated into a reductionist sentimentalism which allows the dead to live in the memories of the living, conceding only that good and evil actions leave a permanent heritage while the agents responsible have departed from the human scene. There will be a firm limit to the secularization of such a central Quranic motif.[21]

Death is at least a biological fact. Beyond that, there is controversy. Is it a tragedy or a triumph? Francis Bacon casually dismissed it while Walter Raleigh idolized it. Marx and his followers see it as part of an ideology, a capitalist trick which, like birth, is actually only a contingent natural fact with no political significance.

Paul claims that a resurrected Christ has defeated it (1 Corinthians 15:54–7). Søren Kierkegaard argued that death is not a theme we can tackle objectively or with detachment or neutrality since it involves our whole being and destiny: we have too much emotional investment in it to be dispassionate. For secular existentialists, death is an external and therefore humiliating and irrelevant limit on freedom. Reason cannot defeat it, laments the secular humanist. A humane anarchist therefore wants to make this finality called death painless, rational and casual: suicide, as euthanasia, is a wise and empowering option to combat this arbitrary tyrant who would otherwise choose the hour and the place.

The Quran orders believers to see death as God-ordained and hence no longer a mystery, only a part of the mysterious divine will. If this is still inside the arena of mystery, it is a comforting mystery which mitigates what would otherwise be arbitrary and thus saves us from the presumptuous finality of understanding it all. Islam, like all viable belief systems, asks us to reckon existentially with the fact of our own death while recognizing the divine prerogative: God gives life and death, gives life to the dead, directly and to whomsoever he pleases (Q:3:156; 15:23; 42:9; 44:8; 50:43; 53:44; 57:2). Death is, for the Muslim believer, neither a mystery nor a tragedy. Theism would not be an improvement on Greek tragedy if the believer did not know how to dismiss the finality of death.

9

The divine omnipresence was once experienced directly and irresistibly but today it is often a dogmatic obligation easily flouted. Those who built the mosques from Cairo to Cordoba were hypnotized by the visible majesty of the invisible God. The grandeur of the grand mosques, especially in Ottoman Turkey, re-enforce subconsciously now, but intentionally in the past, totalitarian sentiments about the domination by God, Master of the Kingdom (*al-mālik al-mulk*; Q:3:26).[22] This sentiment, useful to rulers in a feudal culture, correlated with submission to the will of a very human autocrat, the caliph, who ruled in the name of God. The totalitarian implications are unwelcome to us today since we want the Kingdom of God to become a republic to suit our modern estate.

We do not care here about the cynicism of politics where we must deal with human nature at its worst; rather we explore the views of those simple and sincere believers, enchanted with the religious vision, who had not tasted the forbidden fruit of doubt. The Quran, as they read it, was replete with certainty. No faith was founded on doubt; only certainty seduces. Human beings were pilgrims with a fixed lease on physical life living on an earth adorned in bright colours, especially the green symbolizing the earth's resurrection from the dead (Q:22:63). All earthly things and beings moved inexorably towards decay and oblivion while God remained as their sole inheritor (Q:19:40; 28:88; 55:26). Perhaps the land looked as though it had suffered on behalf of its dwellers, as some landscapes do, capturing the pathos of our inevitable transience. We are in love with what vanishes. That makes for tragedy – as all the best poets from Homer to Yeats, the last great poet of the romantic era, knew and lamented.

Modern Muslim believers, aware of the emancipatory potential of secularism, might feel suffocated rather than moved by Quranic inscriptions extolling the overwhelming greatness of God on the mosque wall and column. Rejecting the claustrophobia of the sublime setting, they might wonder whether humankind too is dominant in some sphere of life. The secular mind rebels at the moral suffocation at the hands of religion in the old style. Today, we accept the primacy of the human and natural just as ancient believers, addicted to the primacy of another and better world, greeted revelation with docility and unqualified obedience.

While the devout hope is that we will willingly allow God to be the dominant force in our lives, the humanist objects that the externality of this ideal automatically makes it unacceptable. The blue-print is imposed, thus choking our human birth-right to prescribe our aspirations and duties in an autonomous secular naturalistic ethics or in a pattern of government where sovereignty belongs to the people, not God. If the human order is an imposed datum, even one imposed from a superior world, we cannot expect our human natures to flourish. Theism is, unavoidably, an external perception of human destiny. But no exterior force can endow us with our moral and political destiny since that can only be engendered internally through human choice.

To break this deadlock, the believer must show that transcendent religion, far from humiliating our nature, enables us to realize our full potential. The theist must convince the atheist not merely that that there is a God – the spiritually sterile project of natural theology – but rather that there is a viable religious humanism which cherishes ideals of value derived from a supernatural point of reference. Our current attempt at self-realization can be inspired by faithful theism or by atheistic rejection. Humanists cannot reasonably reject God once they realize that religious faith can perpetuate the noblest humanism.

10

Today many people value transcendent religion because it enables a dignified humanism. This appears as misguided priorities to the believer who thinks that the central quarrel involves the nature, will, and dignity of God, not the nature and value of humankind. But today, to use Alexander Pope's famous line, the proper study of man is man. The human and the natural take priority over the supernatural and the divine: this world is the locus and focus of the religious quest, though not its destination.

It is not solely the secular content of modern intellectual culture that prevents the revival of the religious vision. A more formidable obstacle is the paradigmatic shift in focus and direction of contemporary thought, reflected in the anthropocentric emphasis of theology, which has multiple if predictable entailments. For example, the student of comparative religion interprets the Crescent and the Cross as lengthy and continuing battles over the true image of humankind and only derivatively as quarrels over the will and nature of God. No Crusader or his Muslim opponent in the Christian Middle Ages interpreted the roots of Christian–Muslim rivalry in this way. Again, modern historians, depressed by the dark shadow cast over us by the continuing catalogue of universal conflict and bloodshed, discouraged by most people's callous indifference to injustice and by the focused brutality of many in the modern world, gradually lose their faith in God. They conclude that the universe contains only us: angry, cruel and self-alienated beings trapped in the narrow passage of life that leads to eternal death.

In this setting, secular humanists offer their version of a dignified humanism. We should build safe and politically secure societies where poverty can be tackled through the compassion of a welfare state, while death and disease are sanitized and privatized if not conquered. In time, there will be little reason for people to ponder the few remaining reminders of human vulnerability. Only death shall remain unconquered.

Before we examine further the question of humanizing theism, I locate the broad parameters of this stalemate. Contemporary secularized humankind is the measure of all things. The Quran teaches, however, that the divine is inescapable; human adroitness and skill cannot outwit the death and divine judgement that indifferently await everyone (Q:21:35). The correct attitude therefore is a constant consciousness of God, an attitude fundamental to the human and humane consciousness of the world. It alone endows us with a purpose that corresponds to the divine design of our human nature. We must confess the reality of God as the first step towards becoming human; complete submission to the divine will shall make us fully human. Otherwise, much remains mere potentiality. As we are lulled into secular comfort and complacency, our freedoms, without God, seem temporarily greater. Our final destiny, however, is doom.

11

We begin with our humanity; we do not end there. Theism was never a doctrine about affirming human autonomy. In Islam, the secular dimension, the things of Caesar, is acknowledged: we have a legitimate interest in the world but our actions require regulation through the sacred law. As we noted in Chapter 1, the secular–temporal realm must be, according to the Quran, subordinate to the spiritual–religious world. God has the decisive, not the sole, word in the human affair. He is the dominant agent in the universe; we cannot outwit him (Q:29:4, 39) or frustrate his purposes (Q:29:22).

If we argue that theism should be humanized in order to win the allegiance of modern humanity, this implies that traditional theism is not already sufficiently concerned with human welfare and values. The more legitimate ambition is to relate the demands of faith to the realities of current life, a concern of the Islamic legal codes. These codes remain closed medieval canons with no serious recent attempt at a comprehensive updating. Such indifference to the current plight of Muslims, including their intellectual conscience, is a brazen rejection of the integrity of the contemporaneous moment. It privileges the past over the present in the interests of a dead tradition; it dehumanizes and devalues the sufferings of the modern community of faith. It smacks of obscurantism and a bloody-minded indifference to even the best of the modern experience.

Modern, perhaps secularized, Muslims need not reject the tradition of Islam. They often wish merely to negotiate a more empowered place in it. This attitude resembles the attitude of Muslim women who embrace the nobler aspects of Islamic tradition but resent the way in which male commentators, eager to maximize patriarchal masculine privileges, ambush the human margins of scripture. The secularized Muslim believer, like the female commentator, would read the Quran differently; and God is the party with whom we must all, male and female, negotiate.

Another sense of humanizing religion is the proposal to reduce it to its human origins since religion is a purely human invention. No believer can endorse this view. Genuine theism must refer integrally to a unique supernatural reality that secretes a moral significance for human life on earth. This supernatural reality will ensure the objectivity of our otherwise contestable, perhaps ultimately subjective, moral values and conscience. Theism cannot be reduced to being solely an instrument for revising our self-understanding or only a useful tool for effecting radical anthropological criticism. Transcendent religion cannot be a source of merely enlightened comment on human nature. God must enter the scene – and dominate it. Greater is God.

12

Protestant Christianity, especially though not only in the liberal scholarly tradition, has not ignored modern secularism. In an extreme strategy, some Christians transformed theistic metaphysics into a moral policy. Virtue was declared to be its own reward. But this view is mistaken: while virtue may be its own reward, faith is not. We may be moral for the sake of morality; we ought to be so. Moral conviction is purified by shedding some kinds of external backing, including some supernatural and some human legal sanctions and rewards. A religion, however, as understood in the Judaeo–Christian and Islamic traditions, ceases to be a religion once it is divorced from its supernatural context of attendant benefits and burdens. We cannot be religious for the sake of being so. Faith, if it is to succeed in being directed towards an objective reality rather than a self-contained subjective fantasy with no external referent, essentially requires a transcendent component in its definition and its reference. The goal of the religious life is neither virtue for its own sake nor truth for truth's sake: it is the Kingdom of God – for God's sake.

In a related strategy, Kantian in complexion, theism is not the source but rather the enabler of moral truths. Once we take seriously the moral demands which practical reason imposes on behaviour, we must accept the postulates of freedom of the human will, immortality of the human soul, and the existence of God. Only a future life, plus a God to guarantee it, can satisfy the rational demand that virtue and happiness should eventually coincide. But if theism is thus defined as essentially ethical and universal, what is religious about it? God and another world are not merely postulates of morality, *contra* Kant, but rather these realities determine the meaning and content of ethical concepts and values.

To see religion in human perspective is not, then, to reduce it to a purely human reality or a moral policy or a quasi-religious doctrine in the service of morality. Rather, it is to concede and salute afresh the existentialist point first made self-consciously by Søren Kierkegaard: faith and rejection are both human choices. The motivation for embrace and rejection is the same, namely, to make sense of this whole nasty human affair we politely call life. The quarrel is over the correct interpretation of human nature, the right characterization of our plight. Is humankind radically independent of external parameters? Or is human nature necessarily subject to the scrutiny and supervision of a transcendent intelligence? 'Does man (*al-insān*) think that he is to be left purposeless and uncontrolled?' (*sudā*; Q:75:36). It is a modern question. The word *sudā*, used uniquely here, describes the state of a camel broken loose and thus astray. It captures the modern secular anarchy of total freedom that borders on licence. The Quran wants to tether modern men and women by the firm rope of the sacred law. If the yoke is not placed firmly on the neck of these rebels, it is reasoned, there is little chance of it staying on at all. The religious thinker must acknowledge a new moral urgency about the creaturely significance of our humanity. Even so, if the human ethos matters, it matters derivatively, not intrinsically. No verdict could be authentically theistic if it held otherwise.

13

I must wade through another tributary to this stream. Muslims find no existing model of a religious humanism that is religious on its own terms. Secularized western Christianity is seen as a disguised and truncated form of secular human-ism; secularized Christians pride themselves more on the adjective than on the noun. Muslims dismiss such Christians as uncritical celebrants of modernity, as inauthentic believers who permit the excesses of secular reason and godless scien-tific technique to remain unchallenged. Christianity and Judaism are both seen as virtually adjuncts to western secular civilization, retained for their political utility rather than their dogmatic truth. Christianity serves a conservative political func-tion in an agnostic age: if westerners were to be denied this bogus spiritual outlet, they might seek refuge in utopian politics, the greatest fear of the capitalist ruling elite.

Secularism occupies commanding cultural heights in Europe and America only because historical Christianity has abandoned the fortress. Despite posting its privileged tribes at prestigious universities world-wide, Christianity has failed to save the faith while Islam, with no thinkers in its realm, is still toppling the dynasties.

This is partly an unfair indictment. Protestant Christianity has conscientiously faced the cold gaze of aggressive secularism more self-consciously and for longer than any extant faith. This does not mean that the Christian reaction to secular mod-ernism is wholly commendable. Excessive and incautious capitulation to secularity is self-defeating, as many Thomists and evangelicals lament. Christians in the lib-eral scholarly wing have, perhaps unwittingly, sold their faith down the river.

The result is a capitulation, not a response, to the jealous god of secularism. Admittedly, an admirable religious tolerance has been achieved – but at the expense of Christianity as it has withdrawn further into the private sector. If Christianity had succeeded in controlling the subversive developments in its own culture, Europeans would still be practising Christians and their disputes would still be religiously conceived as they were in the Middle Ages.

Many men and women have failed to measure up to the Christian ideal; today many question the validity of the ideal. Educated modern Christians often concede the loss of intellectual innocence, a loss which has inaugurated an irreversible trend towards greater uncertainty in morality and dogma. The comforting belief in providence is now replaced by a new practical and pragmatic concern with the mechanics of providing secular welfare and making people happy on this side of the grave. Some Christians celebrate this secular trend as heralding our emancipation from the bondage of illusory and superstitious religion and marking the emergence of a purified and godly religiosity. Others mourn this radical doubt as a lapse from grace, a second fall.

Muslims, however, see Christians as welcoming wholesale the social, political, cultural and economic forms of secular modernism, giving not just two but three cheers for secularism.[23] They are unwittingly committing the apostasy of secular humanism. A Christian would reply that parochial dogmatic theology (for example Karl Barth's) has been replaced by the apologetic theology (of theologians such as Rudolf Bultmann, Paul Tillich, Hans Kung, and Wolfhart Pannenberg) which does engage Christianity's worldly and cultured critics. Such self-justification, through a dialectical apologetic theology, re-interprets the Christian kerygma to the secular world and fruitfully enmeshes the church with its circumambient culture, a sterile materialism which dismisses Christianity as a form of foolishness, merely a means of oppressing artists.

The lack of Muslim sympathy for the Christian predicament is rooted in the uniqueness of the Muslim historical narrative. Islam's formative self-image motivates it to confront secularism. The quest for spiritual fulfilment is, as we saw in Chapter 1, linked to political aspirations. One denatures Islam by removing its public, communal dimension since its private religious duties require a community and its social duties require an empowered community, the state. Only a community enables the discharge of even private obligations since Islamic duties are typically simultaneously individual and communal.

The only way to confront secularism, the Muslim critic of Christianity would conclude, is to remain a contender in the public arena. Protestant Christianity has preserved the faith against external attack by claiming a private status, a subjective truth that is not open to public assessment or critique. By a constant change in emphasis and profile, some Christians have immunized historical Christianity against new or revolutionary advances in rational and philosophical thought, as we saw in Chapter 7 during a debate on the essence of a faith in relationship to scriptural authority in a secular age. This way of defending a faith is self-defeating for it is a disguised surrender to the forces of secularism.

14

De facto the measure of many things, modern secularized humankind wishes to wield the sceptre of all knowledge. That was the fanatical ambition of one school of twentieth-century western philosophy which proposed that philosophy should become empirical by issuing a death warrant for metaphysics and revealed 'knowledge'. Logical positivism, run with the passion of a political project, has died. In Chapter 12, we shall examine its demise in the context of rational theology and the possibility of reviving a theo-philosophical tradition inspired by Islamic humanism.

The natural, the mundane, and the human are the contemporary threads but the fabric must remain religious – with divine revelation the dominant strand. Secularists strenuously insist that our life cannot have a meaning that is externally imposed on us, a meaning independent of the sense we make of life by using our unaided human reason. They dismiss the religious view as obscurantist and exploitative: if we are made for something, then that degrades us into inferior commodities. An anti-humanist proclivity is therefore irremovable from monotheism; religion delimits and thus denatures human nature. We can never reconcile humanism with religious faith.

The meaning of life externally imposed seems humiliating. Yet, an inner force that imposes its will on us is no less humiliating simply because it is internal to our nature. In some artists, for example, the aesthetic drive is a form of bondage, a mysterious force whose power is not attenuated just because it is internal. Is it not degrading that a man, in the grip of an aesthetic vision, should desert his family and friends to go and paint in a distant land? If we need outer freedom from constraints and inner freedom from forces within our personalities, then it is untrue that the religious law is any more humiliating to human nature than our natural passions which are often strong enough to be autonomous.

15

Western Muslims will, in the next 25 years, construct a religious humanism that is responsive to the cultural imperatives of societies which assume as proven the primacy of the human. This should supplement Islam's confident classical portrait of men and women as servants of God. Morally, the implications of this portrait have been explored earlier in this chapter. Politically, it will imply a charter of human rights grounded in an Islamic metaphysics of humanity, a metaphysics we explained in Chapter 10.

The project of being human and humane must be constrained by a meta-human point of reference if it is to be an *Islamic* theo-anthropology. We must, however, begin with humankind on earth, not God in heaven. Every religion, in every age, begins with men and women in their actual condition. We need not be Marxists to believe that religion begins in the human ambience. The traditional thinker, however, gave priority to revelation, seeing the world under the impregnable shield provided by a supernatural vision. But today's thinker, whether religious or secular, interprets the human condition and experience knowing that their primacy must be taken for granted.

Modern educated believers think that men and women must be autonomously valued in some aspect of their being in the world. This is also the wish of the sceptic, the modern rebel who is angry at a God who leaves no room for humanity. The anxiety here is whether modern believers should create an arena of dominance at the expense of divine hegemony or instead locate in their scripture a warrant for an area of exemption. Roughly corresponding to this are two types of rebellion: that of secular rebels, such as Nietzsche or Sartre, who reject God even if there were a God because they 'do not even like the guy', on the one hand, and the religious rebels who do not reject the old religious solutions to life's problems but rather the old authoritarian manner of posing the issues.

The Quran protests that rejectors do not make 'a just estimate of God' (*haqqa qadarihī*; Q:6:91; 22:74; 39:67). In context, the protest refers both to ignorant Arab pagans and also to Jews and Christians, classed as errant theists, who ought to know better. The thought is intended to be universal in scope although we must re-interpret it today to make it intelligible and accessible to the modern disbeliever. We must translate and transvalue the phrase: men and women, in spurning God their creator, misjudge and denature themselves. In repudiating the sovereignty of God, secular humanists do not make a just estimate of themselves.

Muslims must construct a viable framework for giving humanity its just due while being mindful of the dangers of excessive capitulation to secularism, on the one hand, and equally, on the other hand, of an arrogant indifference to the intellectual and moral consciences of other men and women with valid objections to Islamic beliefs and practices. Some contemporary unbelief is inspired by distaste for religious behaviour that is narrow-hearted, provincial, and readily capable of obscuring one's humanity. Some concessions to the modern notion of our dignity are irresistible in this secular hour but no humanism which maintains ideals of value wholly immanent in this world is acceptable to an Islam true to the Quran. Reductionism will forever be anathema to the faith of Muhammad.

From the opposite angle, the term 'Islamic humanism' will be resisted and rejected by secularists as an illegitimate attempt to co-opt the credibility and moral attractiveness of secular humanism by using the veneer of humanist ideals over an essentially religious and hence anti-humanist substance. Equally, however, Muslims should argue that an Islamic humanism is an antidote to the conceits of a modern secular humanism that has degraded men and women while intending to aggrandize some abstract thing called humanity. That was the burden of the argument at the end of Chapter 3.

If we argue for the 'humanity' and justice of a God worthy of worship, perhaps on the basis of the divine names in the Quran, we may establish the basis for a modern and noble humanism. But reductionism constantly poses a threat. It is tempting, for example, to say that religion is nothing but good morals. In the western context of agnosticism and atheism, only some decent men and women any longer endorse Christian metaphysics but virtually all decent men and women endorse some version of a morality that bears a family resemblance to Christian ethics.

The temptation is to offer the code without the creed and thus increase the size of the group. But we are merely warming up yesterday's stew; we gather a congregation of the confused. Modern western culture has been overly and mistakenly impressed by the power of the moral impulse in humankind. All one needs, it is naively asserted, is the dignity of the private moral conscience – as if that were a strong enough force to curb our tendency to do wrong. Indeed, for some modern Christian thinkers, any engagement with moral value is a disguised form of theism, a view implicit in some extreme versions of theological reductionism.

The Quran, in its origins, was not solely a call for social justice or human amelioration. It was a complete amalgam of metaphysics, ethics and ontology. A few writers from Islamic backgrounds have, under Christian and liberal influence, read their Quran as no more than a plea for social justice and reform. It reflects a growing trend in contemporary Anglo–American Islam. One such 'progressive' writer has re-interpreted the Quran as a purely moral guide whose author is indifferent to the distinction between faith and disbelief, two attitudes dismissed as merely human labels that carry no weight in the eyes of God, a transcendent arbiter of human worth. We worship a God, he concludes, who attaches no moral value to labels such as faith and disbelief.[24] No orthodox believer has read the Quran in this way. Evidently, the Quran was not originally intended as merely a call for social reform. It was, as I argued in Chapter 7, a demand for an enthusiastic response to the *whole* authority of the word of a God who is greater than us and our human morality.

The supernatural emphasis is integral to applied Islam, a historical faith which exists in a human community whose human components remain tributary and derivative. Humanity has its due but no more. God is still God – independent of our recognition or acceptance of his divinity. Even if God's truth, after being broadcast by his servants, is rejected by human beings, it remains truth nonetheless. At the end of the chapter, it is human creatures who are debased if they spurn God; our denial debases and devalues, disfigures and denatures, only us. We attain human stature via faith in God while God does not attain his divinity through human acknowledgement of it. We must therefore submit to the divine will, not the other way round. Greater is God.

Part IV
Conclusions

12 Preface to a philosophy of Islam

1

The past two centuries have, notwithstanding religious revivals world-wide, witnessed the largest eclipse, for size and intensity, in the religious consciousness of humankind in recorded history. Christianity, especially in its Protestant version, has been engulfed in its darkest reaches. The crisis of historical Christianity in its dogmatic detail has been acute and dramatic: many Christians are anxious about the future of its western incarnation. (The largest Christian communities today are outside the geographic West – in Africa and South America.) Though its epicentre remains in the Christian heartland of Europe, the secular condition is widespread. In this essay, we obliquely investigated the rationality of Islam, Christianity's most ancient and formidable rival. Islamic belief has been judged by criteria alien to Islamic culture, history and civilization. The ubiquity of the West's secular heritage ensures that all faiths face the tribunal of western secular reason emancipated from Christian-influenced strictures. We can only understand the *Muslim* confrontation with the modern world by understanding the consequences of the *Christian* capitulation to secularism, a concession that made western Christianity rhetorically religious but operationally secular.

The European attempt to harmonize religious belief with modern needs and intellectual habits, the attempt to adapt it to current trends and fashions, is not recommended as a model for emulation. We explored the reasons for our preferred stance in the previous chapter. Christian theology has responded to modern challenges after enduring the external stimuli of criticism from Marxism and radical secular and militant atheism. Marxism, as an independent political force, forced Christians to justify their dogmatic claims. Marxism itself was, however, essentially a truncated secularized form of Christianity – with an identical messianic and eschatological fervour but stimulated by the hope of a historical rather than supra-historical utopia and a secular version of salvation.

The long season of torment continued with the internal development of historical and biblical criticism as intellectually honest Christian thinkers critiqued even their own cherished convictions. This development refuted the authority of the Judaeo-Christian scriptures; revisionist Christians then turned the full fury of critical biblical scholarship on Christian dogmatics. The scholarly weapons of modern critical history were the product of a scepticism that was secular, almost heretical. Christian thinkers ignored the internal religious veto on self-criticism of the bases of revealed theology. The historical traditions of the faith, its scripture, and its notoriously complex dogmatics, were indifferently subjected to searching criticism. These developments preceded the intelligent encounter with rival faiths, particularly Islam. The story extends over half a millennium and reaches a climax in the moral, aesthetic, and intellectual pluralism of the secular age in the West.

2

The modern intellectual context in which religions receive a hearing is hostile to all faculties other than reason. For the scholastic and medieval Christian, Jewish and Muslim thinkers, reason, along with revelation, intuition, sensation, and mystical experience, alike provided grounds of equally genuine kinds of knowledge. Today, given the insidiously widespread influence of some forms of positivism, caused by an increase in the scope and authority of the sciences of nature, many intellectuals regard the scientific method as the most rational if not the only appropriate basis for understanding the world. They contend that we have the right method for acquiring knowledge although we do not have the content of final knowledge. An absolutism of method is, therefore, wedded to a fallible view of the world: we believe only what is warranted by the evidence and abdicate any claim to absolute or final knowledge. The human sciences, and theology and metaphysics, are accordingly relegated to pseudo-factual disciplines. We live under an epistemological apartheid: the genesis of an idea in the different faculties of reason, revelation or experience, privileges or debases it, without regard for its intrinsic merit or content.

The classical frameworks clothed religion in categories derived from speculative metaphysics; most modern proposed frameworks for expressing religious insight are anti-metaphysical. Religious claims are now interpreted non-cognitively as, for example, moral poetry or a special way of seeing the empirical world. No traditional believer can endorse these reductionist frameworks which assume that religious beliefs lack authentic ontological status, implying that there corresponds to religious beliefs nothing except the self-created reality of the religious life. The other world is a fabrication of alienated human beings seeking to do something worthwhile with their solitude.

Countless moderns are sceptical of (allegedly) revealed knowledge. They find the persistence of religious belief to be miraculous – as we see in the work of one of Hume's admirers, the late J.L. Mackie, who captured his exasperation by mockingly titling his last book *The Miracle of Theism*.[1] The religious apologist today cannot satisfy the sceptical bent of mind with its persistent demand for empirical evidence. Before we can establish the possibility of a modern natural theology, an ambition of this chapter, we must acknowledge the problem of the very possibility of revealed knowledge.

Atheists remind believers of the remarkable variety and range of opinion about the nature and existence of God. It ranges from militant atheism, through agnosticism and indifference, to theistic conviction. And theistic belief is hardly monolithic: it covers fundamentally opposed interpretations of God conveniently labelled as Jewish, Christian, Muslim and Sikh. These ethical monotheisms are internally divided by passionate sectarian differences almost as substantive as those between the major households of faith. And this range of religious conviction does not even include the competing spirituality in the non-theistic universe of Hinduism, Buddhism, Confucianism, animism and so on.

In assessing religious claims, we cannot appeal to uncontroversial or even widely accepted criteria which might provide a decision-procedure. This is not so with most scientific claims where there are crucial experiments and falsification procedures that, indirectly, confirm the truth of a hypothesis. Religious assertions, if we may call them that, are not publicly testable. There persists keen controversy, both inter-religious and intra-religious. Nor is there much progress in religion. Unsurprisingly, some sceptics conclude that the content of theological propositions must fail to be factual, even putatively factual. Indeed, some philosophical extremists, usually devout logical positivists, dismiss claims about God and the transcendent as, in the last analysis, incoherent: religious claims cannot even attain to falsity, a privilege of the proposition that has enough meaning to be false.

In the rest of this chapter, we address a cluster of related problems about religious knowledge. In closing this essay, I offer some excursive remarks on some fundamental concerns. Given the size and nature of our concerns, the argument here is unavoidably inconclusive. In Sections 2 to 6 below, we examine further the broadest features of the modern age and the general intellectual challenges posed. In Section 7, we focus on one problem with reference to modern Islam: the 'integration' of secular and religious knowledge. The bulk of the remainder of the chapter, Sections 8 to 14, explores the possibility of rational (natural) theology, a task common to the three major monotheisms. There are special reasons for developing natural theology: as philosophical theology, it is already a part of the philosophy of religion, a discipline that might provide a starting-point for the proposed revival and development of all branches of philosophy in the Islamic world. We conclude in sections 15 and 16 with general remarks about the nature of modern western philosophy and its future in the context of speculation about the revival of philosophy in the House of Islam.

3

The late Salvador Dali (1904-89), the Spanish artist whose tortured torrent of fantasy is kindly called surrealist painting, wrote in his autobiography: 'Don't bother about being modern. Unfortunately it is the one thing that, whatever you do, you cannot avoid'.[2] Dali assessed the burden of the modern condition in his pictorial survey of the confused contents of the suppressed subconscious mind overloaded with bizarre and irrational juxtapositions of images. Modern life is inescapably schizophrenic: the old and new, the sacred and the profane are its twin hallmarks, inescapable even in holy cities such as Mecca, Benares, Rome and Jerusalem. The official spaces of faith, once zealously guarded against the common and profane, are now permeated world-wide by the aggressively secular imagery of commercialism. The taboos and parameters set by fervent faiths are casually dismissed by doubt, indifference, and the pursuit of immediate gratification, the unofficial orthodoxies of modern culture.

The triumph of western secular civilization – western materialistic universalism sustained by a global capitalism and mercantilism – ensures that one goes West wherever one goes. The global secularized and industrialized world is the common context for every tolerably well-informed life-journey undertaken today. We are cultivating a cultural and linguistic uniformity in the midst of unyielding and ever-deepening political differences. The reliable hope lies in the opposite direction: a political unity based on social justice, sustained by respect for international legal standards and implemented by force, providing an atmosphere in which cultural and linguistic differences can safely flourish. That is, however, a theme, a hope and an ideal, for another occasion.

Modern religious thinkers must begin with men and women leading urban lives under a polluted sky populated with moving metal objects. Technologies of steel now pierce through the clouds where once believers looked for angels bearing signs from heaven. This shift of emphasis is dislocating to Muslims since for them everything still begins and ends with the supremacy of God. The ancient sky was never empty: God regularly intervened in the world he had created by launching an intrigue and revealing a mystery, by comforting his messengers and destroying a tyrant, by effectively entangling the course of nature and human lives. With the retreat of visible divine forces from the external world, the modern sky is emptied of mystery. Nature, seen by many today as the last remaining divine preserve, is still marvellous although our modern ingenuity in the form of technology competes with it and even tries rudely to rape its unassertive beauty.

In this intellectual situation, we cannot uncritically begin with God and the simple, though not, as we saw in Chapter 3, necessarily comforting, certainties of revelation. Rather we must begin with the confused and confusing condition of an irate, alienated and bored humanity. Gone are the halcyon days of faith when everyone knew the drama and script of life. All the characters in it, even the worst actors, had memorized their lines. God was the master dramatist and the story he wrote concluded with a satisfying denouement as good triumphed over evil. In an age of cynicism, maturity and realization, few believe that wisdom, as revelation, was vouchsafed to anyone in the past. Owing to this decisive turn towards the new self in its doubt, privacy and subjectivity, we must re-locate the starting-point of theological reflection so that the religious subject becomes primary while the object of religious experience, if there is one, becomes secondary.

4

The direction of modern religious thought is from the mundane to the celestial, a cataclysmic shift that motivates the still ongoing transition to the secular modern world. The Christian schoolmen of the Middle Ages and their Jewish and Muslim counterparts saw God's alleged revelation as the starting-point for reflection about human nature and God. A blue-print, vouchsafed by revelation, provided a priori the categories required for understanding the world. In the secularized western and western-influenced world, however, a sceptical world-pattern, inspired by belief in a godless cosmic geography, determines the direction and character of thought.

Take, for example, contemporary reflection about God's relation to nature. Nature was once thought to be rationally intelligible to the scientist who professionally probes its mysteries because God was conceptualized as an architect, an intelligent artist morally committed to maintaining the integrity of his creative style. The direction was downwards from the deity to empirical nature. The reasoning was sound and convincing if, as was the case, one already believed in God. Today, religious apologists reverse the direction of thought: a hidden sustaining intelligence, namely God, must exist because nature is rationally intelligible. This argument is, as we saw in Chapter 8, unconvincing, since nature's intelligibility to us need not require a transcendent agent acting purposively inside nature.

The existence of God remains interesting in the modern West solely because it supplies the metaphysical and ideological hinterland to the battle for the true image of humanity. This humanization of theology is the successor to the demythologization of the earlier part of the twentieth century. Such humanization seeks to appease secular humanism at the expense of religion just as demythologization was a capitulation to the power of empirical science at the expense of revealed scripture.

What is the context of a modern religious awakening? Many westerners have snapped the already tenuous traditional linkage with the supernatural while others wish to travel light doctrinally, carrying with them only the central tenets of Christian faith, its essence. Secular reason, recently emancipated from theistic strictures, promises total self-sufficiency: it aims to satisfy our curiosity about the origins of the cosmic process, our residual need for morally conscientious steering in a receding sea of metaphysical faith, and the intuitive wish for finding an ideal or purpose that can supply the whole meaning of life. We no longer need God.

5

Is secularized contemporary humankind, scientifically literate and free of religious restraint, in practice the measure of all things? Are we modern humans the measurers of everything? The axiom of a liberated humankind provides a point of departure for the modern attempt to achieve an eternal perspective on our humanity. For secular existentialism, a philosophy of human nature compatible with modern humanism, the free individual is unique and isolated in this hostile, possibly indifferent, certainly gargantuan, immensity of the universe. Existentialism has no philosophy of external nature, let alone a comforting one, while its philosophy of human nature is fixated on one doctrine: we are gratuitously free although we must self-consciously bear full responsibility for the choices we make. Why? Actions have no meaning but they still have consequences. We are responsible for what we do even if we feel no moral guilt. Even 'the absurd man' must suffer the consequences of his gratuitous choices.[3]

If God is no longer the measure of all things, why should we think of humankind as the measure? What about external nature? Contemporary pagans would claim that our ancient ancestors practised religions that were based on celebrations of the seasonal cycles of nature, the eternally valid measure of all things. The Quran, as we saw in Chapter 8, spiritualizes the periodicities and soothing rhythms of nature and dignifies them as 'signs of God': the sun must rise in the East and set in the West (Q:2:258) just as the moon has to move through its phases until it becomes like 'a withered old end of a date-stalk' *('urjūn al-qadīm*; Q:36:39). And, to take an example from outside the Quran, the tides surge and ebb, their periodic rise and fall governed by the attraction of the moon and sun. But none of these rhythms are eternal, necessary or self-directing. They are regularities, not necessities – persistent recurrences, not causally determined sequences. We, however, are free to think, make distinctions, defy natural laws, imagine otherwise, and ponder our existential situation. It is the privilege of humankind. The Quran readily admits it while rejecting our modern conclusion that we are radically free and self-sufficient (Q:96:6–7).

6

Modern humankind need not be the measure but we moderns are the measurers and therefore the beginning of all things. Let us agree to begin with the contemporary human condition, a concession more strategic than substantive: wherever we may begin, as secular humanists know, we religious thinkers arrive finally at God. The theist insists that a full understanding of human beings implies a fundamental if implicit reference to God and his will since our awareness and acknowledgment of the divine can alone make us genuinely human. Even a partial understanding of the will of God – which is all we can expect for a *deus arcanus* (the arcane God) – amounts to providing a sound if incomplete anthropology. That is the narrow certainty of faith. Can it be translated into a broader rationally justified certainty?

With an enduring deadlock between incompatible metaphysical outlooks, the only point of entry for fruitful exchange is the human setting where we are equipped with reason as our only uncontroversial technique and resource. In the theist's dialogue with the adherents of non-theistic faiths and of atheistic humanism, faith in God cannot be the starting-point. The human point of entry in inter-faith engagement implies that humankind is, to the delight of Protagoras, the measure of all faiths.[4]

Consider the volatile issue of Christian–Muslim dialogue. If this is theologically valuable – and does not collapse into the merely diplomatic enterprise of maintaining good relations between rival religious super-powers – then the Muslim and Christian protagonists must begin inside the parameters set by the secularized matrix of modern life. They may then explore further to ascertain which faith gives the more satisfying characterization of the human condition and, derivatively, of the divine will for humankind. The conflicting portraits of the will and essence of the deity may share something in common – but what is in common need not unite rivals. The secular condition of godless humanity therefore becomes, by default, the only starting-point for assessing traditional faiths as well as all faiths in their mutuality. To begin with humankind, however, does not imply that we should end there. But to seek God as a terminus must be the calculated intellectual ambition of a valid epistemology of Islamic doctrine, not the presumption of a pre-rational dogmatic temper claiming revealed warrant.

7

In Chapter 7, we explored one strategy for dealing with a subversive secularism that threatened the authority of revelation: we identified the essential religious core of a faith by removing secular accoutrements and then defended only that residue. We now explore an opposed strategy where instead of stripping away the inessentials to find a core, we make a faith absorb or assimilate the surrounding secular knowledge without that faith losing its religious authenticity. It is a modern strategy for dealing with a secularism which renders obsolete and irrelevant religious content and authority. This strategic theme is connected to two larger concerns already explored in this essay: first, the regrettable fact that the analogical and exegetical intellects, active in classical Islamic civilization, created little new knowledge, merely extracting valid judgements from existing bodies of ideas. Second, as we saw in Chapter 1, the tradition-directed meta-religion of Islam contains strict limits on innovation (*bid'ah*), a pressing concern in the encounter between Islam and modern secularism.

An unprecedented amount of secular knowledge, provided by the special sciences, needs to be integrated into a viable religious world-view. Can Islam and the other historical religions absorb the knowledge supplied by the positive sciences, without compromising the integrity or diluting the strength of their religious doctrines? Most Islamic intellectuals are suspicious of the secular social sciences whose methods and contents pose a threat to the authority of 'revealed knowledge'. Muslim thinkers, alarmed by the rapid secularization of western Christianity as it failed to absorb the overwhelming amount of secular knowledge, strengthened their commitment to Islamic intellectual self-sufficiency.

Some Muslim thinkers proposed the abolition of the division between religious and secular knowledge – and aimed to render all knowledge religious (Islamic). If successful, this would be the most radical strategy for subverting secularism. All knowledge claims would be Islamized: expressed in Islamic vocabulary and nomenclature and thus appropriated by Muslims. The most prominent advocate of this view was Ismail al-Faruqi (1921–1986), a Palestinian–American activist–thinker and scholar of comparative religion, who taught at Temple University until he was, mysteriously, murdered.[5] The very record of his activities is exhausting: he wrote and taught and preached with the zeal of a political activist. He never stopped to assess the fundamental philosophical foundations of his project. Is knowledge intrinsically religious or secular?

I canvass this area here; elsewhere I explore it at length.[6] First, the al-Faruqi project, which collapsed in the late 1990s, is easy to mock: we can equally Indianize or 'Sinologize' knowledge. A Christian could plausibly argue for a

Christianization of knowledge as the Holy Spirit underwrites the truth of every true proposition no matter who discovers it. Moreover, one civilization sends out the space probes while another consults its scriptures on earth. If the secular West produces new knowledge while Muslims merely Islamize it, then that is an unfair division of labour.

In Chapter 6, I questioned the appealing claim that the Islamic scripture had attained prescience of modern science some 14 centuries ago. We explored the apologetic impulse behind the Muslim tendency to scour the scripture in the hope of finding in its enigmatic verses some confirmation of recent scientific discoveries. Al-Faruqi's project was a sophisticated and more comprehensive version of this apologetic ambition. Stray remarks in scripture become the bases of entire disciplines such as Islamic psychology or Islamic economics; a superficial veneer of Islamic terms concealed the labours and findings of wholly secular social scientists. It was reminiscent of the simplistic way that Muslims in the 1980s wanted to benefit from western technology and science while wanting to remain insulated from western cultural and moral ideals that favoured secularism and, in Muslim eyes, decadent hedonism. One could isolate what one needed and dispose of the rest – much like one gets rid of the seeds in one's mouth while eating a pomegranate.

Second, Al-Faruqi, like Al-Ghazālī before him, effectively insists on Islam as the sole source of significant truth. Other more modern thinker-activists, including Sayyid Qutb and the influential Pakistani ideologue, the late Abū al-'Alā Maudūdī, do the same. They dismiss secular notions of independent reason and democratic political organization on the sole ground that these were secular novelties alien to scripture. We could retort that knowledge is multi-cultural and multi-civilizational. This cosmopolitan view was, as we saw in Chapter 2, advocated by the Arab thinker Al-Kindī. If one needed a prophetic sanction for it, there is the famous remark attributed to Muhammad, possibly a later fabrication to justify the study of 'the alien sciences': 'Seek knowledge even as far as China'. But we do not need this warrant: common sense needs no religious sanction.

If we claim that knowledge cannot be compartmentalized into secular and religious, how do we reconcile religious awareness with secular knowledge? While the methods and conclusions of the sciences cannot be ignored, a Muslim thinker may impose a religious interpretation on the facts discovered by the empirical scientist or the social theorist. In this way, we can assimilate novelty. Knowledge in itself is neither religious nor secular. Only its uses can be assessed as religious or secular, moral or immoral.

Let us consider some examples. A Muslim thinker must assign an Islamic significance to claims made by secular historians and psychologists. There is a precedent for this in the way that, for example, a Christian thinker appropriates the Marxist claim that the treatment of workers as mere commodities amounts to exploitation. The Christian argues that such treatment is contrary to the Christian law of love which demands that we treat individuals as ends, not merely as means. In his encyclical *Rerum Novarum* (Concerning New Things) issued on 15 May 1891, Pope Leo XIII (Pope from 1878) addressed the moral problems created by the Industrial Revolution. He endorsed the workers' movement and formulated a doctrine of work, minimum wage, profit, and industrial relationships. He did so in the context of social justice interpreted in the light of absolute New Testament commandments which were easier to obey in a socialist rather than a capitalist economy. The encyclical was nicknamed 'On the Condition of the Working Classes', a Catholic equivalent to the Marxist concern with the same theme.

Take another example. Think of the recent tsunami in southern Asia in which countless thousands of people were swept away indifferently or displaced by what seems like a blind cataclysm. How should we interpret it in the light of the Quranic consciousness of the world? A fatality on such a scale threatens our confidence in the transcendent immortality of the entire human race – even though only some individuals perished. What if all humankind dies? Destruction not only of individuals but of whole populations threatens our sense of anything outliving us. We normally suppose that though we may perish, the community of our birth, culture and language will certainly outlive us. 'Though lovers be lost, love shall not', as Dylan Thomas wrote in a famous poetic refrain. But if all the lovers are lost, what is the object or subject of the love that allegedly survives? Calamity could be grand enough to undermine the foundations of our collective existence – as the Quran relentlessly preaches (Q:16:26).

Such global threats occur in the Quran though today we rightly hesitate to attribute sin as a cause of natural disasters. The Quran does warn us, however, as we saw in Chapter 9, that history is severely judgemental against societies which patronize injustice (Q:19:98). A secular reader might see nothing remarkable or religious in this scriptural warning of total calamity. The myths of all societies include warnings of total extinction. The empirical study of the way in which societies die is, however, a new field of research: the comparative examination of the causes of the death and extinction of societies would require us to compile life expectancy tables for the comparative longevity of civilizations. The autopsies, partial and moreover archaeological, are inconclusive about the cause of death of entire cultures. The religious significance of this branch of empirical knowledge, like the religious significance of atheism, interests the modern theologian and believing philosopher of religion. They must supplement secular theories of geographic determinism with insights into free human choices which are part of the moral and spiritual causes of the decline of civilizations.[7]

8

We turn now to natural theology. To an atheist, the three religions of Near Eastern origin are mistaken and, for all their sectarian differences, alike mistaken. The philosophical defence of core transcendent elements of Islam, therefore, would be no different from a philosophical defence of core metaphysical components of Judaism and Christianity. For this part of the journey, the trio can, despite their irresolvable sectarian differences, erect a united front – a united affront – to secularism.

Unlike their Christian rivals, Muslims have not produced a philosophical defence of the rationality of Islamic theism in the modern world. Christianity has developed continuous and distinguished philosophical and apologetic traditions; Christians have always responded to the rational pressures of secularism in order to reconcile traditional faith with hostile sceptical secularism. Modern Christian thinkers developed three types of defensive theo-philosophical positions: a neo-orthodox fideistic dismissal of the claims of secular reason, a reductionism born of a total capitulation to secular critique, and a half-way house that I dub 'theological revisionism' where Christians defend what is defensible rather than the entire received tradition.[8] The three positions were adopted in that order.

Only the first type of defence corresponds to anything in Islam. The conditions for the emergence of the more compromising positions would require a robust respect for agnosticism, if not total capitulation to the prerogatives of an aggressively secular reason. Many observations in this chapter, particularly on natural theology, are therefore, unavoidably, inspired by Christianity's encounter with secularism. Christianity has the longest continuous intellectual tradition of any faith encountering secular humanism. Christians have continued to produce philosophically cogent self-justification when challenged by the alien convictions of any and every age.

9

At the beginning of his short disquisition *Kashf* mentioned in Chapter 2, Ibn Rushd distinguished three Islamic approaches to the question of God's existence. The first perspective informed the outlook of orthodox theologians who believed that the existence of God is known only on the authority of revelation; they dismissed reason as futile for such a purpose. The second group, the Ash'arites and Mu'tazilites, concurred that there was a rational proof of the existence of the maximally great being of monotheism and based their arguments on the concepts of temporality (*ḥuduth*) and contingency or possibility (*jawāz* or *imkān*). They differed, as we saw in Chapter 3, about the moral and religious implications of such knowledge: the Mu'tazilites saw reward and punishment as independent of revealed law while the Ash'arites insisted that they are conditional on the advent of revealed legislation. Third, Ibn Rushd mentions the mystics who claim to experience God directly but adds dismissively that their method is not rational. Thus only the second group would be interested in natural theology. The traditionalists and the mystics reject the enterprise as unnecessary, even blasphemous.[9]

The Quran has nothing that can be construed as the a priori ontological contention for the existence of God but it hints at the two empirical arguments, the cosmological and teleological. (In Chapter 8, we discussed the teleological argument which finds considerable Quranic support.) An embryonic form of the cosmological argument is found in the scripture as it appeals to the fact that the existence of the world could not be self-explanatory. To say that the world is more than it appears to be is effectively to appeal to the principle of sufficient reason: there is an explanation for everything since to deny this would entail that some things might happen for no reason. The Quran appeals to this controversial premise when it asks the pagans if they were self-created out of nothing and thus their existence needs no explanation (Q:19:66–7; 52:35–6). The Quran elsewhere assumes a first uncaused cause. It repeatedly claims that God is the originator of the universe and that he initiates creation and repeats it (Q:30:27). He merely says to a thing that he intends to create: '"Be!" And it is' (Q:16:40).

The cosmological argument never appealed to Muslim philosophers or theologians. Natural causality had little integrity given the scripture's overwhelming emphasis on God as the only true agent. Furthermore, Al-Ghāzalī destroyed the appeal of this argument when he insisted that the alleged necessity in the principle of causality was an illusion based on observation of mere correlation of events. Observation shows that the correlation is not logically necessary since the alleged effect accompanies the cause rather than happens through or because of it: *'inda-hū la bi-hī* (with it, not because of it). An identical notion is expressed in Latin scholasticism as *cum se non per se*, an observation associated, in modern philosophy, with Hume's theory of causality.

10

Natural theology, in an ambitious form, aims to provide proofs of the central tenets of theism. It claims that God's existence is decided by universal rational criteria; it seeks to offer proofs comprehensible to all rational beings. Traditional rational theology aims to isolate those neutrally describable facts, presupposed or implied by the experience of believers and sceptics alike, which provide incontestable premises for a valid argument whose soundness entails the existence of God. Such a successful natural theology would imply that disbelief is positively and demonstrably irrational.

Classical natural theologians were ambitious. Aquinas, for example, tired to demonstrate Christian truths not only to Christian heretics but also to Jews and Muslims who rejected the authority of the Christian revelation and tradition. Similarly, the First Vatican Council (1869–70), convened by Pope Pius IX, pontificated that the existence of God can 'certainly (*certo*) be known by the natural light of human reason from the things which are created'.[10]

The aims of such a natural theology may be untenable. Contemporary philosophers of religion concur that there are no deductively valid arguments from premises evident to most or all rational human beings to the existence or to the non-existence of God. Perhaps enough inductive force resides in those arguments (from such premises) which can be formulated as inductive arguments, taken together, to make the conclusion that there is a God far more probable than the opposite contention. At best we have probability, never certainty. Some philosophers of religion, such as the late D.Z. Phillips and other disciples of Ludwig Wittgenstein, would dismiss this modest attempt as well – dismissing as laughable such scientific-sounding assessments of religious claims. They would remind us that we are talking about God, not probabilities and predictions about tomorrow's weather.

Even if natural theology fails to provide impregnable rational proofs for God's existence, a modest version of it is still valuable. Even if it shows that God's existence is merely plausible and probable, it would at least confirm a faith in which people already participated. Historically natural theology was developed long after the faithful had established their traditions of worship and devotion. Rational theology provided an internal justification for an existing religious practice by crystallizing and sharpening the believers' amorphous pre-philosophical intuitions about God into a systematic world-picture. Even simple believers and worshippers entertaining intellectually feeble or confused intuitive notions of God felt that their beliefs were vindicated once natural theology delivered its supporting arguments.

While rational arguments in favour of theism offer retrospective justification for an enduring form of life, they rarely propel anyone across the threshold into the sanctuary from an initial position of disbelief or indifferentism. A conclusive argument such as the ontological proof may, if successful, lead rational atheists to intellectually assent to God's existence and, in time, to worship him. A modest natural theology cannot effectively convince staunch atheists and agnostics but it can dissuade the ordinary reasonable person from becoming an atheist in the first place and also encourage the prudent agnostic who sits on the fence to come over to the side of faith. Moreover, natural theology can reinforce the individual believer's personal religious experiences and intuitions which, taken alone, have little evidential value or objective standing.

11

Traditional natural theologians intended to make the case for theism coercive and compelling, not merely persuasive and plausible. The evidence for God's existence is now seen, however, as at best persuasive and permissive, not decisive or compelling. A discipline originally inspired by the wish to prove the irrationality of atheism has been gradually reduced into one inspired by defensive motives grounded in the desire to shield faith against the secularist's charge of irrationality.

Apart from some professed analytical and neo-scholastic Thomists, few writers today argue that natural theology offers us a proof of God's existence. Few natural theologians now accept 'the five ways' of Aquinas who argued that the existence of God is *per se notum* (self-evident), since it is known in and of itself.

Can the existence of God be proved today? Many modern philosophers of religion think that there is no argument, deductively valid with true premises, for establishing the existence of the maximally great being of orthodox monotheism. Others contend that no one has even produced an argument, sound and conforming to the requirements of strict probability, in support of theism. The classical arguments have been convicted of being logically unsound (ontological argument) or as implying false empirical presuppositions (all others); there is therefore neither a logical nor an empirical ladder from the world of human thought and experience to a transcendent creator. To make things worse for believers, there are many sources of universally acknowledged hostile evidence, including the existence of natural and moral evil, the radical inaccessibility of God, the prevalence of religious conflict, and the chronic ambiguity of nature. Accordingly, radical critics of religion, such as Kai Nielsen and J.L. Mackie, dismiss natural theology as an incoherent ambition: the concept of God in mature monotheism, as opposed to the crude anthropomorphisms of the Roman and Greek religions, is senseless to begin with.[11]

There are many views about natural theology and its aims among modern Christian philosophers of religion. At one extreme are some Catholic theologians and analytical Thomists, such as Hugo Meynell, who believe in the project of classical natural theology and have contributed to a modern version of it.[12] Richard Swinburne argues that the concept of God is coherent and that the existence of God can be shown to be highly probable.[13]

Terence Penelhum, a Protestant, joins Sir Anthony Kenny, a lapsed agnostic Catholic, in thinking that religion needs natural theology; both thinkers are uncommitted on the question of its possibility.[14] The Calvinist Alvin Plantinga and John Hick (who is an agnostic Christian) join Christian philosophers (such as Basil Mitchell) in holding the bold and provocative view that religion does not need natural theology although having one is an advantage.[15] Mitchell substitutes for natural theology a painstakingly argued theological and moral 'cumulative case' for Christian theism. Plantinga defends classical arguments for the existence of God using some unnecessarily technical logical techniques.[16] Islamic thinkers would entertain a range of opinions on the possibility of natural theology but they would begin with an ambitious view that would then be tempered by hostile critique. Muslims would not see rational theology as crucial to their faith since Islam is still a young, virile and passionately practised faith.

If the enterprise of natural theology fails, the theistic metaphysic would become merely consistent with natural knowledge, not a logical or empirically possible consequence of it. This would then imply that there is, conceptually, no irrationality or impropriety in contemporary atheism and agnosticism. Theism and atheism would both be epistemically permissible and equally defensible stances – implying a deadlock between faith and rejection which, in a secularized age, would be asymmetrically damaging to religious faith.

12

It is virtually a dogma among modern philosophers of religion that Kant, a German Pietist, and Hume, perhaps a deist, together destroyed the philosophical credentials of natural theology. They are supposed to have exposed some conceptual impropriety embedded in the inference from observed features of the natural world (or of our experience) to the existence of a transcendent author of nature. One cannot legitimately proceed from a general analysis of the contingency of finite being, or from an analysis of the presuppositions of order and regularity in human experience, or from an analysis of our experience of value or finally from a consideration of the logical presuppositions of our thought about God, to deduce or make probable his existence.

Let us examine the philosophical critique of classical natural theology. For Kant, there is 'no knowledge outside the realm of sense-experience'. The 'knowledge' of God, argues Kant, is not a particular theoretical understanding of the world or of the transcendent realm; rather, it is a presupposition of the autonomous moral life of human beings. It is one of the imperatives of the practical reason that there is a God. It is only in and through our apprehension of the moral law that we are assured of the existence of God. This view is, for obvious reasons, a poor argument for the existence of God whatever one might say about Kant's demolition of some arguments of classical natural theology.[17]

For Hume, all genuine or acceptable reasoning conforms to either deduction or induction. Whatever does not fit this model is bogus and fit for the furnace.[18] Theistic conclusions, Hume argued, cannot be established by the use of the criteria and presuppositions of secular history. Miracles cannot form a reliable part of history. Hume offers a priori reasons for rejecting as unreliable the historical records of miracles.[19] In the *Dialogues Concerning Natural Religion*, he contends (through his dramatic mouthpiece) that theistic conclusions cannot be established by appealing to the criteria employed in natural science: theology is therefore not an experimental discipline. It follows, for Hume, that theistic conclusions cannot be established in any way since 'no matter of fact can be a priori'. And the only third way of establishing the foundations of religious knowledge would be revelation, an option criticized and rejected by the Scottish sceptic.

Hume accepts as legitimate those beliefs that arise naturally and spontaneously in the human mind, beliefs such as, to use his example, the belief in the existence of our own bodies. Such a belief, Hume claims, is neither justified by evidence nor held on the basis of evidence. Fortunately, nature has caused us to believe instinctively in such a reality because 'it is an affair of too great importance to be trusted to our uncertain reasonings and speculations'.[20] Inconsistently, however, Hume rejects religious beliefs on the sole ground that they are not adequately evidenced. In other words, the commitments of secular common sense are groundless but not necessarily arbitrary and we may therefore reasonably believe what we are naturally led to believe. But Hume extends no such courtesy to religious convictions which some religious instinct might also wisely prompt in human hearts and minds. He is therefore guilty of philosophical double standards.[21]

13

Both Hume and Kant attempted to undermine the possibility of natural theology by appealing to reasons deriving from their theories of knowledge. Their rejection of religious knowledge was motivated by their adoption of a particular philosophical position. Both thinkers, despite their differences, assess theological and metaphysical theses in accordance with alien criteria derived from secular common sense, natural science and mathematics. Their philosophical outlook presupposes that there is a logical contrast between our epistemological situation in science and mathematics, on the one hand, and theology and metaphysics, on the other. Scepticism about metaphysics and theology is supported by exploiting the possibility of a logical contrast between two epistemological situations: between our alleged epistemological insecurity in theology and metaphysics and our supposed epistemological security in science and logic. The Humean–Kantian epistemologies are rooted in special pleading and are a disguised form of mitigated sceptical doctrine.

They impart substance to some intuitions about the nature of logical and scientific knowledge and then use the resulting criterion to erect a logical contrast between different areas of inquiry, namely those which satisfy the criterion (and hence qualify as cognitive) and those which do not.

More precisely, Hume endorsed a revised version of Cartesian methodological doubt but supplemented it with another type of scepticism which moves beyond being provisional and methodological to being permanent and substantive. Indeed the divorce between philosophy and religion dates to Hume who pushed empiricism to the point of atheism. He even doubted the causal presuppositions of secular science.[22]

Why should we, however, accept such restrictive positivist epistemologies? Humean positivism provides too restrictive and dogmatic a philosophical method to do justice to our pre-philosophical intuitions about the range and extent of even humanly accessible knowledge, let alone our intuitions about knowledge beyond that scope. Admittedly, we cannot uncritically accept all intuitions; we need some theory to decide which areas of human speculation provide reliable intuitions and which do not. But to pontificate that genuine knowledge is co-extensive with empirical science and the formal logico-mathematical disciplines is to beg the question about the nature and extent of knowledge. Ironically, Hume's rigid empiricism is held on a priori grounds: it violates the very intuition of experimental inquiry on which it is founded since it is unempirical to decide by a priori argument in which areas of research genuine knowledge is or is not possible.

We see this if we examine the development of Hume's empiricism by the logical positivists of the early twentieth century. It is a standing reproof to positivist critics of theology and metaphysics that they failed to formulate a criterion of meaning which was a death-warrant solely for those allegedly suspect disciplines and not also, inadvertently, for areas of insight or inquiry the positivists wanted to retain as legitimate. One must not exaggerate the significance of such a failure but, equally, one cannot dismiss it as entirely inconsequential or fortuitous. Unduly restrictive epistemologies are self-defeating just as excessively liberal ones are useless.

Offered as knowledge-claims, a self-defeating assumption lies at the root of these sceptical epistemological doctrines. Philosophical assertions and doctrines, philosophical techniques and methods used to solve particular problems, philosophical claims about the status and capacities of reason and the possible scope of our knowledge, and self-reflexive meta-philosophical propositions about the discipline of philosophy itself, are no part of the subject-matter of any of the special descriptive sciences or of mathematics or of common sense. If we strictly and consistently adhere to the empiricist positivist conception of knowledge, derived from the writings of Hume and Kant, we destroy not merely the possibility of religious and metaphysical knowledge but also the possibility of philosophical knowledge. For the strict empiricist who endorses the Kantian slogan about the impossibility of knowledge outside the realm of sense-experience, philosophy itself can only be, in the words of one philosopher of religion, 'either a hermeneutic device for clarifying what other people say or a neutral liaison between branches of inquiry which do have cognitive status'.[23] Thus the Humean and Kantian philosophical schemes cannot coherently offer us knowledge-claims about the limits of knowledge in general unless they permit the possibility of philosophical knowledge in particular. And if they allow that, it is arbitrary to deny the possibility of religious knowledge.

14

We have examined some secular grounds for rejecting classical natural theology. Religious thinkers, such as Al-Ghazālī and the Ash'arites in the Islamic tradition, no less than Pascal and Kierkegaard in the Christian tradition, offered religious grounds for undermining the enterprise of establishing God's existence by unaided human reason. Among Christian thinkers, natural theology was often seen as incompatible with the possibility of genuine faith. Why? Faith could not co-exist with the possibility of coercive rational argument for God's existence since that would imply an intellectually compelling case for theism. This in turn would prevent believers from experiencing the uncertainty that true faith presupposes. In Chapter 2, during a discussion of the Islamic model of faith, we refuted the main assumption behind this critique of natural theology.

Many devout religious thinkers have argued that even if natural theology were possible, it would be religiously profitless to develop it since it could not inspire zealous faith in God. It might not even help us to reach a valid concept of the deity. Pascal spoke for all devout believers when he lamented that the God of the philosophers is not the God of Abraham, Isaac and Jacob. Such fideists believe that natural theology misidentifies the problem. The cause of religious doubt is not an intellectual deficiency in our understanding, a deficit of the kind a successful natural theology might remove. Rather it is sinful perversity which is an incurable condition. The cause of doubt is not reason but sin; the cure for doubt is not natural theology but faith. Without faith, natural theology is useless for the sinful heart and mind will cloud the understanding; with faith, natural theology is unnecessary. We have already questioned, in Chapter 2, the anti-intellectualism behind this superficially clever-sounding dismissal of natural theology and other theorizing about God.

15

The history of modern western philosophy, especially the development of methods rooted in scepticism about revelation, is part of the story of the rise of western secularism. We traced the broader history of the triumph of western secularity in Chapter 1 but we deferred a discussion of the philosophical component. I consider that here in the context of my proposal for a revival of philosophy among Muslims – especially western Muslims, a vanguard of intellectual reform for the rest of Islamic civilization. I will give a light sketch of a vast philosophical terrain and locate our concerns within it.

In the pursuit of knowledge, the extremes of dogmatism and scepticism characterize western thought, ancient and modern. The dynamic shift from one end of the continuum to the other dominates that endless curiosity about the world, a feature of the modern western intellectual heritage. Dogmatism is, however, harmful while extreme scepticism is irrelevant. A temptation to absolutize what is relative is inevitably followed by a total retreat into doubt until doubt becomes orthodoxy. The Quran prohibits *shakk* (intellectual doubt) as we saw in Chapters 2 and 7. Islamic civilization has not shifted from one extreme to another. Instead it has, for about a millennium, been fixated at the faith (certainty) end. The revival of philosophy would redress that ancient imbalance.

The triumph of doubt in modern philosophy has relevant consequences for us since we are proposing the rebirth of philosophy among Muslim believers. The chief consequence is that modern philosophy contains no positive doctrine; it is fixated on method. Until the middle of the twentieth century, many thinkers identified philosophy with the process or method of empirical science, a view called logical positivism by its admirers and dismissed by its detractors as 'scientism', a kind of scientific fanaticism. If logical positivism (or empiricism) had any doctrinal content, it was eliminated under its own critical scrutiny, until the school subsided into linguistic analysis, and, fortunately, died a natural death.

Scientism was later accompanied also by its sidekick, a prevalent and euphoric technicism dependent on an instrumentalist and pragmatist philosophy of science. By the time logical positivism (or empiricism) was eventually recognized as philosophical polemics masquerading as an impartial method, philosophers had permanently lost the traditional metaphysical focus of philosophy. Positivism dismissed the substantive problems as ridiculous and relegated the rest to technicalities for specialists who enjoy interminable exchanges in the footnotes of obscure academic journals. In particular, in the aftermath of logical positivism, many dismissed philosophy of religion as a soft area in favour of logic and the allegedly hard-core duo of metaphysics and epistemology.

Western philosophy of the past hundred years – logical positivism and its even more anti-metaphysical American version called pragmatism[24] – is effectively an attempt to assimilate the dramatic impact of science and secular doubt on all departments of life. Other important philosophical movements, such as the philosophy of the later Wittgenstein, are largely a reaction to the excesses and exaggerations of logical positivism and its scientistic proclivities. Wittgenstein's thought influenced movements outside philosophy – in the social sciences and humanities. Among political philosophies, Marxist materialism is methodologically a form of rational utilitarianism synthesized with a fanatical form of logical positivism.

Existentialism qualifies as a school of philosophy although it has no distinctively philosophical method. It contains a philosophical anthropology, a synthesis of empirical and conceptual claims. Pragmatism and logical positivism are epistemological methods disguised as philosophies: they have no accompanying philosophical doctrine. Existentialism, by contrast, has a doctrine but no essential or distinctive method. One could say that its method is phenomenological since we are asked to examine carefully all phenomena immediately present to our consciousness.

Apart from systems associated with Hume, Nietzsche and a few others, modern western philosophies are laicized versions of Christian theology. Kant argued that metaphysics is valid only as regulative of all experience but not as constitutive of any supernatural reality. This amounts to a laicization of the metaphysical tradition of western Christian scholasticism. Those modern thinkers who retained God in their philosophies did so solely as a human necessity. As we explored in Chapter 3, Kant needed God but only as a postulate, not for the sake of the content of any substantive doctrine about him. God was reduced to being a precondition of a human moral sense whose demands, according to Kant, we cannot conscientiously deny. Descartes needed God in order to secure the foundations of human knowledge against the machinations of an evil demon. No wonder, Pascal, a Christian fanatic, craved for the God of the three patriarchs in preference to the anaemic God of the philosophers.[25]

Muslims would see a God of the gaps as artificial since God is no senile presence in the Quran. In the Hebrew Bible, the young and virile God of the Torah subsides into a background senile presence by the time we reach the end of the canon (*Ketub'im*; writings). In the Quran, by contrast, revealed over a short period of time, God remains uniformly youthful and powerful throughout the canon and is indeed, as we saw in Chapter 11, the only truly free and active agent.

The sceptical tradition triumphs in the West as substantive philosophies perish. Modern westerners inherit the sceptical rather than the metaphysical Christian tradition in philosophy. The sceptical and rather modest view of human reason's capacity to attain knowledge and certainty is not the monopoly of religious thinkers: Hume's estimate of unaided reason is less generous than that of other modern thinkers. He shares with Al-Ghazālī this distrust of reason although Al-Ghazālī was, unlike Hume, a staunch believer.

Disastrously, for religious thinking, all modern western systems of philosophical reflection are forms of unqualified empiricism. Rationalism has collapsed; the philosophical problem of reason has been replaced by the sociological concern with rationality. Logical positivism inherited an older and broader logical empiricism. Both narrow the region of genuine knowledge to an isthmus that constricts the intuitively grasped breadth of human interests and concerns by arbitrarily selecting one type of experience as epistemologically privileged and fundamental. Empiricism is more natural to secularism than to faith while rationalism is a more congenial setting for theological speculation. Our current situation is especially bad for an irreducibly transcendent faith such as Islam.

Western philosophy has survived and flourishes. Regrettably, however, epistemology has, owing to Descartes' influence, virtually hijacked the subject. Contemporary philosophy has no doctrine or metaphysics, only method and a few logical techniques. Descartes' legacy is doubt, not doctrine, caution, not conviction.[26] With Christian belief currently in abeyance in much of the West, there is something terminal about morality. This explains the popularity of moral philosophy although many of its practitioners are preoccupied with sterile meta-ethical debates that yield disappointingly meagre results. Only a revived theo-philosophical tradition would appeal to Muslim intellectuals – and that tradition is virtually moribund in the West.

Western philosophy, like God, might die in the near future in the company of the university, the natural home of philosophy (and the humanities) and now the last surviving western medieval feudal institution. Several modern thinkers, inspired by Richard Rorty, have debunked the myth of philosophy as supervisor of other disciplines. Rorty is heir to a Wittgensteinian radical scepticism about the very enterprise of philosophy but he combines it with an American sense of pragmatic urgency. This fundamental attack on philosophy's ancient self-image is likely to continue.[27]

16

Modern western philosophy does not run the risk, present in religion, of misleading people about matters of moment by actually teaching them something substantive. One occupational privilege of working as a philosopher today is that no one of any influence is likely to be misled by the irrelevant musings of the thinker. We noted in the Introduction that issues in the real world are now the province of writers, artists, poets, journalists and social critics. Philosophers, even moral philosophers, have opted for the security and isolation of the academic office. Apart from a few public intellectuals, the only exceptions have been some politically active continental existentialist thinkers – and these have recently died.

Continental philosophy would appeal to Muslims. In the past, it was dismissed as metaphysical nonsense dressed up as wisdom. This might be unfair – though admittedly the flamboyant and aphoristic style of some thinkers in that tradition, particularly Nietzsche, makes their claims less susceptible to philosophical analysis. The Catholic universities in America have taken continental philosophy seriously. Fortunately, there is now a dialogue between the analytic (Anglo–German, American–Scandinavian) and the continental European styles of philosophizing. This line of distinction is fluctuating and dubious; many thinkers, especially Gottlob Frege, a German logician of genius, have influenced both schools. The attempt to integrate these two philosophical methods, though not doctrines, is plausible and fruitful. One excellent journal has professed this aim in its editorial.[28]

Some political philosophies might be appealing to Muslims at a time of upheaval. Marxism appealed to some secularized Muslims but it has, since its universal and sudden collapse, lost its glamour. Marx, a historian and economist, gave us no distinctively philosophical method or doctrine. His metaphysical and methodological ingredients are both present in the philosophies of Hegel and Feuerbach. Machiavelli is more relevant to modern political life than Marx. Indeed, Freud, the metaphysician who dared to replace the transcendent and the conscious with the local and the subconscious, has outlived Marx who replaced the transcendent with the material and the historical – arguing that humankind is not an abstract being 'squatting' outside the world.

Liberalism as a political philosophy and ideology is often a defence of the personal biases of a privileged western academic class whose professed self-identity is liberal. Muslims see nothing 'liberal' in a creed whose hallmarks, at its extreme, are an idolatry of art allied to an obsession with extending the arena of obscenity. The grand issues – tackling racism, maintaining single standards of justice, securing freedom and liberty for all humanity as opposed to western humanity – are hardly addressed. Establishment liberals mistake their own affluence for a universal condition.[29]

There is no philosophical movement among modern Muslims resembling the work of the Mu'tazilite theologians or the Muslim philosophers of the past: no philosophical theology, no philosophy of religion, no natural theology, no theodicy, and no conscientious atheism. Revivalist and activist movements and a haphazard attempt to update Islamic legal provisions currently exhaust the genius of this once fecund civilization. A few Arab thinkers and poets, particularly Palestinian and Lebanese, saddened at their political impotence in the Arab Middle East, are attracted to existentialism (*al-wujūdiyyah*). Some Arab Christians, influenced by British and French intellectual movements, have even tried to stimulate a liberal renaissance. But its impulses are exclusively foreign – and therefore unlikely to influence Muslims.[30]

Does perennial moral reform require philosophy? In its most ambitious form, philosophy, like mature monotheism, harmonizes the varied interests of humankind and tests their validity. The Bible, along with the rational Graeco-Roman heritage, bequeathed to westerners the legacy of perennial moral reform. For Muslims, the Quran must now play a similar role. But it can do so only if it is treated as revelatory rather than as a closed moral and legislative system. I have argued in this essay that if we wish to extract new insights about our modern condition, then reason must be used not merely analogically but also critically and philosophically.

Liberal and sceptical influences on a religion, at some stages in its development, can deepen the life of faith and thus make believers rediscover their spiritual character so that prayer amounts to worship and not merely a socially prudent habit. Without the spiritual introspection that philosophical insight brings, religion is no more than ritual. Muslim civilization would be enriched by the revival of a certain type of philosophy which could supplement the Quran's ancient religious and spiritual confidences. Perhaps, wisdom will find an alternative, an Islamic, soil to grow in. Such wisdom, suitably rigorous, as it was among the Greeks, could one day soon supplement the Islamic revelation as a source of reform and enlightenment.

Notes

1 Locating Islam in the modern world

1 Unfortunately, neither the European Community nor the United Nations wishes to see a Muslim state even in the backwaters of eastern Europe because that would officially associate Islam, once again, with the white Christian continent of Europe. Some white nations in Europe and Asia, such as Albania and a few former Soviet republics, are Muslim nations but none are officially Islamic in their constitution.

2 References to the Quran are given in parentheses in the text. The number of the chapter (*sūrah,* lit. grade or step on a ladder) is followed by the number of the verse (*āyah*). Thus, Q:22:78 refers to the 78th verse of the 22nd chapter of the scripture in its current arrangement. Chronologically, the earliest revelation is at Q:96:1–5. Like Paul's letters in the New Testament, Quranic chapters are arranged in decreasing order of length. Muslims usually quote the Quran by citing the name of the chapter only, for example *al-sūrat al-baqarah,* the title of the longest chapter ('the chapter of the cow'). The chapters are not named by warrant of major theme but rather, as in most Semitic writing, either by the first few words of the opening verse or by some strange word or incident that amazed the original audience. The place of revelation is given as either Mecca or Medina though many chapters are composite. The earliest revelations are Meccan. The first chapter was, uniquely, revealed twice, once in each city. It consists of 'the seven oft-repeated verses' (*sab 'an min al-mathānī*) used in all daily prayers. Some commentators regard it as an exordium to the Quran proper (based on Q:15:87). The Muslim scripture is, phonetically, rendered as *al-Qur'ān,* meaning 'the lecture' or 'the recital'. The noun *qur'ān* means a piece of revelation and is indefinite; it can occur in nominative, accusative or genitive construction. Al-Quran refers to the whole revelation. (In direct quotations, all nouns are given in the case ending used in the Quran). In this book, translations of the Quran and Muhammad's traditions are my own. If I interpret these texts in an original or idiosyncratic way, I alert the reader. See the note on transliteration and abbreviations at the beginning of this book.

3 H.A.R. Gibb, *Mohammedanism: An Historical Survey,* London: Oxford University Press, 1969, p. 2.

4 It is high time we move beyond the platitudinous pieties that provide the public face of western foreign policy. In western parlance, Muslim moderates are those believers who are happiest when governed from London and Washington. Muslims, of all political leanings, are increasingly convinced that the West is incapable of maintaining a balanced and just view of the Muslim world. Sadly, therefore, the conflict between Islam and the West, 'that war with the longest truce', will be resolved only in the sphere of physical power in deference to the maxim 'Might makes Right'.

5 Oil has invited foreign intervention and suffering for the Arabs. It has also enabled the Muslim Middle East to go from camels to computers in a few decades.

6 Mount Sinai, however, is alluded to often and twice named, once as *ṭūr saynai* in genitive construction (Q:23:20) and once as *ṭūr sīnīn* in rhetorical poetic plural (Q:95:2).

7 This is the *ḥadīth* literature recording the *sunnah* (the known path) of Muhammad's conduct. The word *ḥadīth* literally means something new, hence a narrative or incident. It was compiled and fully codified by the fourth Islamic (tenth Christian) century. (For more on the Islamic calendar, see next note.) The science of *ḥadīth* criticism was originally part of jurisprudence, Islam's master discipline. The traditions are classified as strong, good, weak (including fabricated or forged), and strange (or rare). The criteria for authentic (strong) traditions are prohibitively rigorous. The materials were collected and sifted out by pious and conscientious scholars. Six compilations are considered authoritative. For details of *ḥadīth* and of the special category of *ḥadīth nabawi* (or *ḥadīth qudsī*), the divine utterance distinct from the Quran, see Mahmoud Ayoub, *Islam: Faith and History*, Oxford: Oneworld, 2004, pp. 113–17, 121–2.

8 The Byzantine Empire lasted from 330 to 1453 when Constantinople was captured by Muslims. All dates and comparisons given in this chapter are approximate. Islam recognizes a lunar, not solar astronomical, year (see Q:2:189). The Quran abolished the extra intercalary month (Q:9:36–7) whose addition synchronized the lunar year with the solar year. This intercalary device is found in the Jewish luni-solar calendar, enabling rabbis to split a given month, usually Adar, into two months (Adar I and II) if required.

9 The *Negus* (Amharic for king) refers to the pious Christian ruler of Abyssinia who showed exemplary tolerance at a critical point in Islamic history when a party of exiled Muslims took refuge from Meccan persecution in Abyssinia, in 'the first' or 'lesser' emigration in roughly 615 CE. The refugees were granted asylum despite an aggressive Meccan embassy sent to bring them back. The Christian ruler heard the early verses of Chapter 19 (probably vv. 16–36) and respected the competing Quranic account of Jesus and his mother while remaining a Christian.

10 I have omitted mystical and supernatural events in Muhammad's life. The Sufis focus on events such as the Prophet's night journey to paradise, the *mi'rāj* (ascent). He departed for heaven from the platform of Jerusalem in the year before the migration to Medina, an incident vaguely mentioned in the Quran (Q:17:1). Muhammad's western biographers often dismiss the internal (Muslim) tradition about the Prophet's life as apocryphal but gratuitously elevate to canonical truth much vague external speculation about the man and his activities. See, for example, F.E. Peters' pointlessly lengthy anthology and essay *Mecca: A Literary History of the Muslim Holy Land*, Princeton, NJ: Princeton University Press, 1994. I review it in 'Pilgrim's Regress', *The Times Higher Education Supplement*, June 1995.

11 Shi'ites bitterly dismiss the first three caliphs and the dynasty of the Umayyads as usurpers; Sunnis reject Shi'ite theology as an elaborate revenge fantasy. The Shi'ite–Sunni split originally occurred over the theology of political leadership but gradually became a complete doctrinal schism. Shi'ites claim that the *imāmah* (imamate) is the institution of divinely guided imams, varying in number, who inherit the prophetic charisma of Muhammad, a post-Quranic view rejected as heretical by orthodoxy. *Shī'ah*, the noun, means partisan group. *Shī'ī* is the derived adjective.

12 To appoint a man, even a saint, as God's deputy (*khalīfah*) is to invite him to become a megalomaniac. Intelligent citizens demand accountability, not perfect virtue, of their rulers while good rulers know that private virtue becomes socially prevalent only if enough individuals are already virtuous. One cannot enforce virtue without inviting hypocrisy. These political themes are beyond the scope of this philosophical essay.

13 See *passim* Abu 'Abd Allah Muhammad Ibn Sa'd, *Kitāb Al-Ṭabāqat Al-Kabīr*, S. Moinul Haq (trans. and ed.) Karachi: Pakistan Historical Society Publications, 1976, 2 vols, and Abu Ja'far Muhammad Ibn Jarīr Al-Tabari, *Tarīkh Al-Umam wa Al-Mulūk*, Beirut: Mu'assasah Al-Alam li Al-Matbu'at, 1989. The uncouthness of pre-Islamic

paganism might be exaggerated by Muslim chroniclers in order to emphasize the contrasting glory of the new faith. Think here, for comparison, of those whom western historians call 'the barbarians' who attacked and conquered Rome. Their behaviour is no more barbaric than that of other fighters of the time. In any case, if they were backward barbarians, it is difficult to account for their military strategy which defeated the allegedly glorious Roman empire.

14 The Quran warns the Prophet's wives and Muslim women generally not to imitate the sexual mores of the days of ignorance, in particular, to abjure the sin of *tabarruj*, wanton display of female beauty (Q:33:33; 24:60).

15 This is the pre-Islamic practice of female infanticide (*wa'd*; Q:81:8–9; see also 17:31; 16:58–9). Cf. 'The birth of any daughter is a loss' (*Ecclesiasticus*: 22:3) in the Old Testament Apocrypha. The Quran also prohibits offering children as a pagan sacrifice (Q:6:137, 140) and condemns killing them out of fear of poverty and famine (Q:17:31).

16 The Egyptian martyr–activist Sayyid Qutb popularized this view. More recently, it re-surfaces in the Egyptian martyr Abdul Salām Al-Faraj's banned pamphlet, 'The Hidden Obligation' (*Al-Fardah Al-Ghayyibah*), referring to jihad as a disputed sixth canonical pillar of faith that must be used to fight 'the near enemy', the regimes imposed on the Islamic world by western powers. I explore the ideas of both activists in my *The Final Imperative*, London: Bellew, 1991, pp. 1–2, 86–94.

17 *Al-hanifiyyah*, in honour of Abraham the *hanīf*, is virtually an alternative name for Islam. The word *hanīf* is effectively a Quranic neologism since the Quran spiritualizes it. *Ummah muslimah* refers to the community of Islam descended from Abraham and Ishmael (Q:2:128). The expression *ummah al-muhammadiyyah* does not occur in the Quran. Those who accept Muhammad as the messenger of God are Muslims. In scholarly convention, *islām* is the act of surrender of will to God while *Islām* designates the faith, historically established by Muhammad, a faith structured around a confession of belief in God and his final messenger, and the formal performance of duties that flow from this confession. The duties are the five pillars: confession of faith and then formal prayer, annual pilgrimage, limited legal charity and fasting in the month of Ramadan. Anyone who submits his or her will to God at any time prior to the appearance of Muhammad, is called a Muslim (or muslim), a submitter to the divine will as revealed at that stage of history. The option to remain a Muslim in this generic sense is not available in a post-Muhammadan age. Those who hear of Muhammadan Islam and reject it are culpable even if they submit, privately or informally, to the will of God.

18 Allah (God) does not possess gender or sexual orientation. In using the third person singular masculine pronoun to refer to God, I follow the dominant linguistic convention.

19 The names of God do not define or limit him; they describe aspects of his nature as this relates to humankind. They do not describe his essential nature. A comment such as 'God is Love' is, according to Muslims, *ultra vires*: it goes beyond the sanction of revelation.

20 The word *samad* is used uniquely in this short chapter, entitled 'Sincerity', a chapter said to be as weighty as a third of the whole Quran. The word *ikhlās*, meaning sincerity, literally means pure and solid, not hollow or affected. It does not occur in this *sūrah* although its root is used elsewhere in expressions such as *mukhlisīn la hū al-dīn* (sincere ones towards him in the faith; Q:40:65) and in *al-dīn al-khālis* (the sincere faith; Q:39:3). This short chapter (Q:112), popular among worshippers, is also called *al-tauhīd* which means unifying or unification, that is, monotheism.

21 The early Israelites were probably henotheists who recognized Yahweh as their tribal god while acknowledging that other gods, such as Baal and Dagon, were the deities of their enemies, especially the Philistines. The Hebrew God became increasingly ethical and international though never quite the only universal God of mature monotheism.

22 *Fa-yakūnu* is present tense instead of the expected past tense as *fa-kāna* (and he was) to indicate that God's creation continues to happen in this remarkable way.

23 *Iblīs* is probably derived from the Greek *diabolos*, meaning slanderer; it occurs often in the New Testament (*diabolou*; gen. case; Matthew 4:1).

24 The angels temporarily doubt the wisdom of the divine intention; only Iblīs (or *Al-Shayṭān*) insists on its foolishness. Like Lucifer, the fallen angel of light in Milton's *Paradise Lost*, the Quranic Satan confronts God despite knowing that he must ultimately lose.

25 For representative selections translated from classical sources, including the Quran, Muhammad's traditions and early biographies, Sufis writings, sectarian polemics, and the legal codes of the first jurists, see the comprehensive anthology by John Alden Williams (ed.), *The Word of Islam*, Austin, TX: University of Texas Press, 1994.

26 The Reconstructionist movement, an offshoot of Conservative Judaism, rejects the elitist self-image of Jews as distinguished by some genetic trait which makes them exclusively godly. The best exponent of this view is Mordecai Menachem Kaplan (1881–1983), the founder of this movement. The classical argument for Jewish elitism as a genetic endowment is made by Judah Halevi (*c.* 1075–1141) in his *Sefer ha-Kuzari* 1:88–95, 98–9, discussed in Barry Freundel, *Contemporary Orthodox Judaism's Response to Modernity*, Jersey City, NJ: KTAV, 2004, *passim*.

27 Two classical comparative religious studies scholars are Abū Rayḥān Al-Birūnī (973–1049) and Muhammad Ibn 'Abd Al-Karīm Shahrastānī (1076–1153). Al-Birūnī was the first Muslim to write a work of comparative religion. His work on Indian religions (*Kitāb Al-Hind*) was sponsored by a caliph eager to know whether the Hindus and Buddhists, as subject peoples, could be classified as 'people of the book', a Quranic expression that is *de facto* limited to Jews and Christians but could mean any society that received, at some stage, a divine revelation. If they were a scriptured people, they would pay the tribute (*al-jizyah*; Q:9:29) as a token of their status as a protected and privileged minority. There would be no need to engage them in battle. There were admittedly political motives for Al-Birūnī's work – but as much can also be said about most comparative religious studies today. A later scholar, Shahrastānī, compiled 'the doctrinal opinions of all the world's peoples' in his *Kitāb Al-Milāl wa Al-Niḥāl* (The Book of Religions and Systems) written in 1128. Shahrastānī writes about Islamic sects, Jews, Christians, Manichaeans, Mazdaeans, hermetic Sabians, ancient Arab cults and Hindu groups.

28 Matthew 15:24. Henceforth, biblical references, if given without comment, are given in the text. The Quran confirms that Jesus's mission was restricted to the Israelites (Q:3:49).

29 The Catholic dogma of the Immaculate Conception – the view that Mary was free from original sin – is compatible with the Quran; it is implied by its rejection of *peccatum originale* (original sin) as unjust and morally unworthy of God.

30 The Quran would reject the Christian view that Jesus was the anointed one whose advent was promised by the Hebrew prophets since the Quranic notion of messiah, like the Hebrew one, is of a human, not divine figure. Nor would the Quran endorse a Christian interpretation of the Hebrew Bible (*Tanakh*) according to which the advent of Jesus, as the Messiah from the House of David, is encoded in it. (The expression, *āl Dāwūd*, the House of David, occurs uniquely in Q:34:13 in a divine address to the members of that family.) There is a further complication. The concept of the Messiah is absent from the Torah; and the Quran would reject the remaining two portions of the *Tanakh*, the *Nebi'īm* (Prophets) and *Ketub'īm* (Writings) as humanly produced work. (Indeed Jews themselves treat these second two portions as less sacred than the Torah.) The Quran would endorse the authenticity of only parts of the Torah, the books of Moses, since the grammar and history contained in the Torah (*Ḥummash*) are evidently posterior to the time of the historical Moses, a view not disputed by competent critical scholars.

31 Muslim apologists argue that John 14:26 is foretelling the advent of Muhammad, not the Holy Spirit, since Muhammad brought a comprehensive scripture and hence taught

all humankind 'all things'. Indeed the Quran suggests that the Quran, as scripture, has also been foretold (Q:26:192–7). This type of theological controversy is fruitless since all scriptures contain cryptic remarks that are elastic enough to cover the aspirations of many contenders. In such religious quarrels, everyone is right since there are many relevant texts and each is partly plastic to our wishes.

32 Jacob is renamed *Yisra'ēl*, the one who struggled with God (Genesis 35:10). The Hebrew etymologies of theophoric or otherwise significant biblical names, such as *Jabr'ēl* (strength of God; Gabriel), *Ab-raham* (renaming of Abram at Genesis 17:5 to mean father of nations, lit., father of the womb) and *Yōsēf* (one who increases; Joseph), are lost when the words are transliterated into Arabic.

33 The view that speech, like wine, intoxicates, was popular with some Sufis. 'He who keeps silent shall be saved' was a popular tradition among the mystics. This Prophetic tradition, like others popular with Sufis, is probably a fabrication.

34 Thomas Paine (1737–1809), the activist who inspired the American Revolution, pioneered the historical critical study of the Bible. In his *The Age Of Reason*, he locates numerous contradictions, improbabilities, anachronisms, historical and scientific falsehoods, and morally unworthy claims in the Hebrew Bible and the New Testament. He counsels Christians to reject the authority of scripture and to embrace deism as the only rational alternative. The divine media of revelation are nature and the human constitution. Institutional religion with its ubiquitous appeal to revealed authority and human hierarchy is the product of the avarice and mendacity of priests eager to profit from the gullibility and ignorance of believers. See his *The Age Of Reason*, Secaucus: Citadel Press, 1948, 1974, especially pp. 83, 186. Paine's motto, 'My nation is the world, and my religion is to do good', is the creed of secular humanism.

35 It has been argued that Europeans never converted to Christianity and retained their ambivalence towards the classical paganism which Christianity formally displaced. Graeco-Roman traditions of art, philosophy and culture have periodically erupted in the Enlightenment and the Romantic movement, not to mention the birth of empirical science which in Europe was conceived in opposition to religion. A version of this point has been made by Camille Paglia. Among Muslims, it has been made repeatedly by many writers including Maryam Jameelah, a Jewish convert to Islam. See her *Islam and Modernism*, Lahore: Mohammed Yusuf Khan, 1968 and *Islam versus the West*, Lahore: Mohammed Yusuf Khan, 1968. Westerners are reluctant to accept even valid opinions and criticisms if these happen to come from Muslim quarters.

36 Serious interest in the politics of radical Islam dates from precisely Christmas 1978 when the pro-American Pahlavi dynasty in Iran was overthrown. The date marked Ayatollah Khomeini's imminent triumphant return, from exile in France, to Teheran and revolutionary success at the beginning of 1979. For details, see Anoushiravan Ehteshami, *After Khomeini: The Iranian Second Republic*, London: Routledge, 1995.

37 No ruler with the exception of the late Enver Hoxha, the Albanian communist leader, has tried to ban the obligatory Friday prayer assembly. There have been a few eccentric modernist religious thinkers in Tunisia and Egypt who have given verdicts prohibiting fasting in Ramadan but they have not been taken seriously.

38 The *salaf* is the primitive and original community, the paragons of virtue. The word is Quranic (*salafan;* acc.; Q:43:56). It can have a negative meaning: a community or custom of the past, 'something discarded or obsolete' (*mā qad salaf;* Q:4:23). Any subsequent Muslim generation is the *khalf* (Q:7:169), the successor, and therefore corrupt and compromised, a description thought to apply particularly to modern Muslims.

39 This is the argument of the exiled Iranian intellectual Daryush Shayegan in his *Cultural Schizophrenia: Islamic Societies Confronting the West*, John Howe (trans.), London: Saqi Books, 1992. I have assessed such critiques of the alleged limitations of Islamic aesthetics in my review essay on his book in *Muslim World Book Review*, vol. 13, no. 3, 1993, pp. 25–7. I argue that there is, among Muslims, no ambivalence towards art,

an alleged ambivalence which Shayegan calls schizophrenia. The dogmas of Islam do, however, prevent artists from imposing on others a dictatorship of vulgarity under the pretext of 'modern art'. For more, see my 'Islam and Art', *The Independent*, January 1994.

40 The five axiological categories (*al-aḥkām al-khamsa*) of the holy law are: obligatory (mandatory), recommended (commendable), morally neutral (permissible), reprehensible (detestable but allowed), and absolutely forbidden. The *Sharīʿah* covers areas considered private morals and etiquette in western thought. Conversely, it privatizes one transgression that is public in western law: in case of murder, parties may settle out of court and accept blood money as compensation (*diyah*) and forgive the perpetrator (Q:4:92). Some Islamic legislation must appear idiosyncratic to westerners – for example, the ban on adoption (Q:33:4). Judged by western criteria, Islamic procedure seems unfair since there is no due process, no jury, prosecution or defence. Judges investigate, call witnesses from both sides, interpret the law, and determine the verdict – all *in camera*.

41 George Abernethy and Thomas Langford (eds), *Introduction to Western Philosophy: Pre-Socratics to Mill*, Belmont, CA: Dickenson, 1970, p. 5. Heraclitus is nicknamed 'the obscure'; his 130 extant fragments are enigmatic and prophetic.

42 The last Ottoman sultan-caliph, Abd Al-Majid II, was deposed in 1924 (1342 AH). King Fuad I (Fu'ād Al-Awwal) of Egypt (d. 1936) coveted the title but failed to attain it.

43 *Al-muhaymin* is a divine name (Q:59:23). In the indefinite accusative case (*muhayminan*), it describes the Quran's status as a guardian of earlier revelation (Q:5:48).

44 The Muslim confession of faith is a double testimony: affirmation of the existence of one God and an endorsement of Muhammad as his envoy. The office of prophetic revelation is abolished after the advent of the Arabian Prophet who is sent to all humankind (Q:4:79; 21:107; 34:28). The belief in Muhammad as the seal of the prophets (*khātam al-nabiyyīn*, Q:33:40) is a defining, not optional, feature of Islam. For Jews, there are no prophets after Haggai, Zechariah, and Malachi, the three 'minor' prophets whose oracles close the Prophetic (second) division of the tripartite Tanakh (Hebrew Bible).

45 There are many movements towards climax and finality in Islamic civilization. For example, the honorific title of the seal of the poets (*al-shuʿarāʾ*) is awarded to the Persian Sufi poet Nūr Al-Dīn Jamī (1414–92). There are seals of the saints (*al-auliyāʾ*), theologians (*al-mutakallimūn*) and martyrs (*al-shuhadāʾ*). Such an attitude has paradoxical potentiality: it can either inhibit future endeavours or act as a spur to ambition (if the ambition is legitimate). No one has been awarded the title of the seal of the philosophers, a title not coveted by Muslims. It should go to Ibn Rushd.

46 This insight has been developed by the Bosnian Muslim scholar and Quran translator Enes Karic who argues that the modern secular globalization enterprise must acknowledge an ancient religious analogue in historical Islam viewed as a project of spiritual globalization. See his 'The Process of Globalization from an Islamic Perspective' in *Philosophy Bridging the World Religions*, Peter Koslowski (ed.), Dordrecht, Boston: Kluwer Academic, 2003, pp. 161–78, especially p. 167. For a relevant critical exchange between Karic and the present author, see pp. 179–82 of the same volume.

47 Some atheist (free-thinking) publishing houses, such as Prometheus, increasingly reserve their wrath for Islam. Prometheus still publishes predictable tracts by Marxians such as Paul Kurtz and Kai Nielsen who attack all theisms as absurd and dangerous. Nielsen's latest manifesto appears in *Atheism and Philosophy*, Amherst, NY: Prometheus, 2005. Prometheus now supplements its titles on polemical atheism with books on Islam and terrorism. It publishes someone called Ibn Warraq, a prudentially anonymous author who singles out Islam for bitter anti-religious diatribes. See his imbalanced attack in *Why I am not a Muslim* (1995), aping Bertrand Russell's analogous title. Ibn Warraq edited four more volumes for Prometheus: *The Origins of the Koran* (1998),

The Quest for the Historical Muhammad (2000), *What the Koran Really Says* (2002), and *Leaving Islam* (2003). The last volume explored Islamic laws of apostasy. The Islamophobia and prejudicial rigour in these tracts prevents objective assessment of some genuinely conscientious reservations about Islam. Instead, Islam is crucified on behalf of all supernatural faiths. Judging by the anger and frustration in his works, Ibn Warraq is probably an evangelical missionary Christian hiding behind a Muslim name.

48 Legal theorists standardly distinguished between types of legitimate innovation using these five axiological categories.

49 A religion is original if it can absorb any number of external influences and still remain distinctive just as thinkers of genius can absorb an indefinite number of alien influences without losing their own special or unique qualities.

50 Although Jews and Muslims continue to have religious and political differences, the greatest Jewish philosopher–halakhist Maimonides (Moses Ben Maimon) (1135–1204) classed Islam as a monotheistic faith since it abjured idolatry. See his *Mishneh Torah*, Hilkhot Ma'akhalōt Asurōt 11:7, quoted by Barry Freundel in Freundel, op. cit., p. 77, p. 80.

51 Buber's maxim is quoted and discussed in Peter Ochs' *Pierce, Pragmatism and the Logic of Scripture*, Cambridge: Cambridge University Press, 1998, 2006, pp. 290, 293–6, 353, 354–5. I review this book in 'Prophet Warning', *The Times Higher Education Supplement*, January 1999.

52 Theology has no idiomatic equivalent in Arabic but its sense is artificially captured by *'ilm al-lāhūt*, knowledge of God. Theology is subsumed under *'ilm al-tawḥīd*, knowledge of (divine) unity.

53 Muhammad promised his followers that in every century, God would raise someone to revive Islam. This tradition, supported by a fairly strong chain, is accepted on the authority of the traditionist Abū Dāwūd Al-Sijistānī. The theologian Abū Ḥāmid Al-Ghazālī is regarded as the reformer (*mujaddid*) for the sixth Islamic century.

54 Admittedly, it could be argued that western philosophy before, say, Hobbes, is useless; nothing is gained by studying the errors of ancient thinkers. I argue thus in my review of Ted Honderich (ed.), *The Philosophers: Introducing Great Western Thinkers*, Oxford: Oxford University Press, 1999, in *The Times Higher Education Supplement*, October 1999.

55 The Shi'ite clerical hierarchy is an innovation with no Quranic or traditional Prophetic support. The status of *ḥujjat al-Islām* (the argument of Islam) is lower than *ayatollah* (sign of God). All ranks are reached through popular acclamation and a reputation for charisma, piety and scholarship. The *marja-e-taqlīd* (Persianized Arabic; centre of blind imitation) is a senior figure; ayatollahs coalesce around him.

56 The word *madrasah* (place of learning) is not Quranic but its verbal root *da/ra/sa* (to study earnestly) and the associated noun *dirāsah* (assiduous study) occur often (Q:3:79; 6:105, 156; 7:169; 34:44; 68:37). The reference at Q:7:169 is to the intensive study of the Torah. The word *midrash* (interpretation) is from a corresponding Hebrew root.

57 Literalism in scriptural interpretation is possible in Islam and in Judaism because the scriptures have been preserved in their original languages, and these languages are still available and widely used. Since the scripture of Christianity is in translation, Christian literalism is incoherent – except as an attenuated literalism of divine intention.

58 In 1962, Jalal Al-i Ahmad, a former member of the Tudeh (Communist) party, used this influential term. He borrowed it from the Iranian Ahmad Fardid, an oral scholar who was influenced by Martin Heidegger's views of western technology and its dangerously universal reach. Through the Islamic revolution of 1979, Ayatollah Khomeini succeeded in halting the process of westoxication in Iran.

59 Richard Khuri, an Arab Christian, advocates a Christianization of Islam's political project. See his *Freedom, Modernity and Islam*, Syracuse, NY: Syracuse University Press, 1998. I review it in 'A Third Way for Islam' in *The Times Higher Education*

Supplement, October 1998. The Tunisian writer Habib Boulares has also argued for an apolitical Islam in his *The Fear and the Hope*, Lewis Ware (trans.), London: Zed Books, 1990.

60 The British tampered with Islamic family and personal law during their stay in India. Anglo-Muhammadan law was a mixture of Islamic law (on endowments and inheritance) and western secular rulings. This hybrid legal code survives as the basis of modern Indian legislation on Muslim affairs. Rabbinic Judaism resisted changes only to personal status law when Jews lived under varied rulers; rabbis accepted the principle of *dīna de-malkhūta dīna* (the law of the land is law), a conciliatory and politically judicious maxim traceable to Mar Samuel who headed the academy at Nehardea (second to third century BCE). The phrase occurs often in the Babylonian Talmud (Nedar'im 28a, Gittin 10b, Baba Kamma 113a three times, 113b, Baba Bathra 54b, 55a). It is not found in the Jerusalem Talmud.

61 The *Sharī'ah* privatizes crimes such as murder by allowing the family of a murdered victim to forgive the murderer 'for God's sake'. It makes an ostensibly private act such as apostasy, however, into a public crime against the state by treating it as treason.

62 The tradition has two versions: 'God will not allow Muhammad's community (or: my community) to agree on an error (*La yajmā' Allāh ummata Muhammadin (ummati) 'alā dalālah.*) It is related by the traditionist Muhammad Ibn 'Isā Al-Tirmidhī in his collection (*Jami'*) with a fair (*hasan*) chain of authenticity.

2 Human reason and divine revelation

1 *The Nature and Destiny of Man*, New York: Charles Scribner's Sons, 1949, vol. 1, pp. 165–6.

2 Karl Barth opts for faith alone. For details, see Chapter 7. St Anselm (1033–1109) prioritized the two opponents in his slogan about faith seeking understanding. See S.M. Deane (trans.), *St Anselm: Basic Writings*, LaSalle, IL: Open Court, 1974, 2nd edition, Part 1. St Thomas Aquinas synthesized faith and reason.

3 For more on consensus (*ijmā'*), see David Waines, *An Introduction to Islam*, Cambridge: Cambridge University Press, 2003, 2nd edition, pp. 82–3.

4 Thomas Aquinas, *Summa Contra Gentiles*, Book 1, Chapter 6. Aquinas gloats that the miracles Muhammad performed – namely, according to him, the promise of silken sensuality in this and another life and the power of the sword – are worthless since 'such signs are not lacking even in bandits and tyrants' (*quae signa etiam latronibus et tyrannis non desunt*). A religion, established by such worldly means, would appeal only to carnal human beings, 'bestial men residing in the desert, totally ignorant of divine truths' (*homines bestiales in desertis morantes, omnis doctrinae divinae prorsus ignari*).

5 I discuss the pagan rejection of the resurrection in the context of idolatry in Chapter 9.

6 Muhammad Abū Zakrah discusses Quranic *jadal* in his *I'jāz Al-Qurān*, Egypt: Dār Al-Fikr Al Arabiyy, 1970, Introduction, Part II, pp. 364–88.

7 In 1984, hundreds of unarmed Iranian pilgrims, demonstrating during the Hajj, were shot dead by Saudi police near the Mosque of the Jinn. The Saudi authorities quoted this passage about the ban on argument (*jidāl*). The real motives were connected to Shi'ite–Sunni rivalry and tensions associated with an ancient Arab–Persian racial divide.

8 Such pragmatic arguments (which include Pascal's wager) succeed by banning third possibilities. Pascal's threat was contained in the duality of 'salvation or extinction' or 'damnation or extinction'. These are not the only options for the believer's bet.

9 The Quran never directly addresses disbelievers. The two apparently direct addresses (at Q:66:7, 36:59) are, as the context supplied by the previous verse in each case shows, anticipated divine reproaches to rejectors on the day of judgement. In this life, however, Muhammad mediates between the divine judgement and the rejectors (e.g. at Q:109:1–6).

10 Kierkegaard argued that academic and rationalist approaches to Christian faith soften the existentialist impact of its dramatic truth. No one earns the right to eternal life merely by understanding the nature of immortality. For a critique of Kierkegaard's views of subjectivity and detachment in the religious life, see my *The Light in the Enlightenment*, London: Grey Seal, 1990, Chapter 2.

11 G.K. Chesterton, *Orthodoxy*, Garden City, New York: Image Books/Doubleday, 1959), p. 83, first published in 1908.

12 Terence Penelhum, *God and Skepticism*, Boston: Reidel, 1983, pp. 169–82 and his *Reason and Religious Faith*, Boulder, Col: Westview Press, 1995, *passim*.

13 Compare the version in Genesis 37:31–5 where Jacob is deceived by his sons' lies.

14 For further discussion of the Quranic view of faith, see Chapter 9.

15 His spiritual autobiography was translated by Montgomery Watt as *The Faith and Practice of Al-Ghazālī*, London: Allen & Unwin, 1953. Recent translations of Al-Ghazālī's works are Michael Marmura (trans.), *The Incoherence of the Philosophers*, Provo, UT: Brigham Young University Press, 2000, and Richard McCarthy (trans.), *Deliverance from Error*, Louisville: KY: Fons Vitae, 2000, 2nd edition.

16 Arthur Schopenhauer, who influenced the young Nietzsche, observed that religions do not reward excellence of mind – the intellectual virtues – but only the virtuous restraint demonstrated in the submission of our wills to the divine will.

17 Paul fulminates against Greek philosophy in 1 Corinthians 1:20–5. The less specific condemnation in Colossians 2:8, not written by Paul, is compatible with the apostle's general distrust of human wisdom where it conflicts with the truths found in Christ.

18 The Murji'ah recommended that we postpone judgement until God decides, a view that became Sunni orthodoxy. It is based on Q:9:106 and on the maxim 'All judgment [command] belongs to God' (Q:6:57; 12: 40; see also Q:6:62).

19 A.J. Wensinck, *The Muslim Creed: Its Genesis and Historical Development*, London: Frank Cass, 1965, p. 190.

20 The sociologist Boaventura dos Santos coined it to refer to the death of some forms of knowledge. He argued that powerful people preserve and privilege the kinds of knowledge that benefits them. Epistemicide has been called the mother and the brother of genocide by writers who sense an imposed western colonial epistemology underpinning cultural imperialism with its accompanying linguacide and devaluation of indigenous cultures.

21 For details, see Stephen Gaukroger, *Descartes: An Intellectual Biography*, Oxford: Oxford University Press, 1995. In my review, 'Evader of Wives and Hemlock' in *The Times Higher Education Supplement*, February 1996, I discuss Descartes' fear of persecution and speculate about Ibn Rushd's possible influence on the so-called father of modern philosophy.

22 Al-Kindī was a pioneering Muslim, not merely Arab, philosopher.

23 See A.L. Ivry, *Al-Kindī's Metaphysics: A Translation of Ya'qūb Ibn Isḥāq Al-Kindī's Treatise 'On First Philosophy'*, Albany: NY: State University of New York Press, 1974.

24 This division includes the revealed branches of knowledge: the Quran, Prophet's traditions (*ḥadīth*), and jurisprudence. Sub-branches of *ḥadīth* studies include '*ilm al-rijāl* (knowledge of the men) which assesses the moral character of transmitters of traditions, a genre that is the forerunner of modern biography. Ancillaries include Arabic grammar and the biography (*sīrah*) of Muhammad.

25 Although systematic Arabo-Islamic philosophy ends for Sunni Islam with the death of Ibn Rushd, the Tunisian 'Abd Al-Raḥmān Ibn Khaldūn (d. 1406) is the first Muslim theoretician to examine the world wholly from an empirical perspective. The empiricist tradition of Islamic philosophy begins with his *The Prolegomena*, the world's first social philosophy of history. See Franz Rosenthal (trans.), *The Muqaddimah: An Introduction to History*, New York: Bollingen Foundation, 1958.

26 Ibn Rushd is the greatest commentator on Aristotle in the history of philosophy, a fact which would be conceded today if only there were less fundamental hostility to Islam.

27 Like Ibn Rushd, Leibniz synthesized many disciplines. Leibniz was trained in scholastic philosophy; his juristic training reached the level of doctor of law.

28 This should not be confused with *istiḥsān*, a method of legal reasoning typically used with *qiyās* (analogy). We practise *istiḥsān* when we prefer those principles of the law which promote the general purposes of the law. It is the Hanafi equivalent of *istiṣlāh*.

29 Ibn Rushd was not only a philosopher but also a medical expert and a judge.

30 He wrote a commentary on Plato too. See Erwin Rosenthal (trans.), *Averroës' Commentary on Plato's Republic*, Cambridge: Cambridge University Press, 1956.

31 Aristotle's *Physics, Rhetoric* and *Poetics*.

32 For example, *Talkhīṣ Kitāb Al-Jadal* (Middle Commentary on Aristotle's 'Logic').

33 Prometheus published conference proceedings to honour Ibn Rushd for the then forthcoming 800th anniversary of his death. See Mourad Wahba and Mona Abousenna (eds), *Averroës and the Enlightenment*, Amherst, NY: Prometheus, 1996. The choice of an atheist publisher is significant.

34 George Hourani (trans.), *Kitāb Faṣl Al-Maqāl with its Appendix (Damina)*, Leiden: E.J. Brill, 1959. The philosophical material is in the Introduction to this short treatise. The rest contains discussions of five theological problems including free will, the status of miracles, and the bodily resurrection.

35 This is an example of 'normative ambiguity'. The question 'Are there classes?' is normatively ambiguous. It could be asking whether there are, sociologically, such entities or, alternatively, whether there should be, politically, any classes.

36 For a summary of Al-Ghazālī's critique of philosophy, see Watt, op. cit., pp. 25 ff. and pp. 37–8.

37 Al-Rāzī dismissed religion as a source of interminable and violent conflict. There is no moral or religious purpose in the cosmos; salvation is through unaided human wisdom and the contemplation of eternal and celestial realities. In the end, all shall be saved. Al-Rāzī's philosophical works were not preserved except unintentionally through extensive quotations in the works of his critics, both orthodox theologians and Muslim philosophers.

38 Oxford University's Nolloth chair is named for this sub-branch of philosophy of religion. Martin Buber (1878–1965) was 'Professor of the Philosophy of the Jewish Religion and Ethics' at Frankfurt University from 1924 to 1933. I have not found any post or endowed chair named for the philosophy of the Islamic religion.

39 Orthodox Muslims do not entertain the possibility that the presence of evil (and the associated suffering) in the world might be a persuasive argument against the existence of a powerful but morally good God. By contrast, this disquiet has been an enduring source of the rejection of a just and loving deity in formerly Christian nations. Indeed, it is as important as reservations based on the alleged scientific refutation of religious belief.

40 The desire to see religious belief autonomous is not unique to religious believers. Some followers of Wittgenstein also deny that religious claims are answerable to external rational assessment. Religion, they argue, is one among scores of language-games each expressive of a distinctive form of life. In effect, this position, while upholding the autonomy of religious faith, fatally undermines the possibility of philosophy of religion as a critical discipline that judges truth-claims. For an exchange on this tendentious topic, see Kai Nielsen and D.Z. Phillips, *Wittgensteinian Fideism?* London: SCM Press, 2005.

41 The Hellenic Jewish rationalist Philo Judaeus interpreted the Hebrew Bible as a collection of allegories. He argued that Moses had anticipated Plato's thought. See Harry Wolfson, *Philo: Foundations of Religious Philosophy*, Cambridge: Cambridge University Press, 1948, vol. 1, pp. 164 ff.

42 Tertullian, 'The Prescriptions against the Heretics' in E.L. Miller (ed.), *Classical Statements on Faith and Reason*, New York: Random House, 1970, p. 3.

3 The moral challenge of secular humanism

1 Most western atheists and agnostics study the Bible and know the findings of biblical criticism better than most Christians do. By contrast, few atheists and agnostics of Muslim background know the Quran. They have learnt, from hostile western sources, a few platitudes about it.

2 Atheism is ably explained by Ernest Nagel, 'A Defense of Atheism', in Steven Cahn (ed.), *Reason at Work*, New York: Harcourt Brace & Co., 1996, pp. 597–609.

3 The Peace of Augsburg recognized Lutheranism in a Holy Roman Empire dominated by Catholicism. The treaty did not permit tolerance of Calvinism or other Protestant groups but it facilitated the establishment of national churches, still a feature of European Christianity. The treaty proved a death-warrant for the imperial Latin notion of *corpus Christianum* (the Christian body politic).

4 See David Berman, *A History of Atheism in Britain: From Hobbes to Russell*, London, New York: Croom Helm, 1988; Routledge, 1990. See my review in *International Studies in Philosophy*, vol. 23, no. 1, 1991, pp. 100–1. Berman does not cover Nietzschean humanism.

5 Don Cupitt, the English 'atheist priest', contends that there is no objectively existing God to comfort us. I criticize Cupitt's views in 'Bliss in the Drab House of Life', *The Times Higher Education Supplement*, October 1997. Cupitt sums up his position in *After God: The Future of Religion*, London: Weidenfeld and Nicolson, 1997.

6 Less famously, Nietzsche also said that 'God, as Paul created him, is a denial of God'. (*Deus, qualem Paulus creavit, dei negatio*). See *The Anti-Christ*, R.J. Hollingdale (trans.), Harmondsworth: Penguin, 1968, p. 163, published in one volume with *The Twilight of the Idols*. Nietzsche here rejects Christian morality but praises Islamic morals as heroic and manly (sections 59–60); he eulogized Buddhism as a form of 'spiritual hygiene' superior to a mere religion (sections 20–3). The quotation about God being only man's mistake is from *The Twilight of the Idols*, op. cit, p. 23.

7 *De Augmentis Scientiarum* (1623), Books 7–8.

8 Al-Ash'arī's major disquisitions are *Al-Ibānah 'an Uṣūl Al-Diyānah* (Discourse on the Foundations of Religion) and *Maqālāt Al-Islamiyyīn* (The Treatises of the Islamic Schools). The latter work is descriptive and shows intimate knowledge of the Mu'tazilite school. For Al-Ash'arī's ideas, see Montgomery Watt, *The Formative Period of Islamic Thought*, Edinburgh: Edinburgh University Press, 1973.

9 For arguments against the secularists' use of the Euthyphro dilemma to establish the autonomy of morality, see H.O. Mounce, 'Morality and Religion' in Brian Davies (ed.) *Philosophy of Religion*, Washington: Georgetown University Press, 1998, pp. 253–85. The 'Euthyphro' dilemma is misleadingly named since it is formulated by Plato's Socrates.

10 *A Treatise of Human Nature* (1739–40), 2nd revised edition of L.A. Selby-Bigge (first published in 1896) with text revised and notes by P.H. Nidditch, New York: Oxford University Press, 1978, p. 478. See also Book 3, Part 2, Section 1, pp. 477–84.

11 Ibid., p. 479.

12 Ibid., p. 478.

13 Ibid., pp. 478–9.

14 Ibid., pp. 478–9.

15 Righteous pagans are found in the third part of the Hebrew Bible, the *Ketub'īm* division, which contains insufficiently holy material. A good person could here be identified with the prudent person whose secular prudence was analogous to religious piety. There is no religious basis to many of the insights in the five books of wisdom in the Hebrew Bible: Job, Proverbs, Ecclesiastes, Ecclesiasticus and Wisdom, the last two being apocryphal.

Later redactors probably added a religious veneer, especially to Ecclesiastes, to justify their canonization. The secular humanist character of the wisdom literature of the ancient East derives from its international and cosmopolitan scope: Israelite sages borrowed from secular Egyptian and Mesopotamian sources. The material was 'sceptical wisdom' about the practical science of living a good life and knowing where to place one's trust. Sane counsels of common and good sense alternate with acute insights into character so that the young would be able to negotiate their way through a wicked world.

16 A subtle classical discussion of this issue is in the work of the Persian Ash'arite theologian 'Abd Al-Karīm Shahrastānī (d. 1153), a thinker suspected of Isma'ili (Shi'ite) sympathies. He noted the limitations of orthodox *kalām* in his *Nihāyat Al-Aqdām fī 'ilm Al-Kalām* (The Furthest Steps Taken in Theology) but was equally sceptical of the ambitions of philosophers. His approval of Al-Ash'arī's moral views is discussed in Majid Fakhry, 'The Classical Arguments for the Existence of God', *The Muslim World*, vol. 47, 1957, pp. 133–4. For Shahrastānī's work on comparative religion, see Chapter 1, note 27.

17 Logical independence is a technical matter. To say that morality is logically independent of religious belief means that the proposition 'Janet is a religious woman' does not entail the proposition 'Janet is a morally good woman' since 'religious' does not (literally) mean 'morally good'.

18 Margaret Smith, *Muslim Women Mystics: The Life and Works of Rābi'a and other Woman Mystics in Islam*, Oxford: Oneworld, 1994, p. 50.

19 It is impossible to rehabilitate the concept of piety in modern secular culture. For a heroic attempt to rehabilitate another offender, the concept of manliness, see Harvey Mansfield, *Manliness*, New Haven: Yale University Press, 2006. In the aftermath of feminism, manliness sounds absurd, at least in civilian life, and especially in academia.

20 This is part of the larger point that European Christian societies, unlike Islamic ones, produced philosophical systems with claims as controversial and peculiar as the dogmatic complexities of Judaeo-Christian theism. The speculative schemes of thinkers such as Descartes, Berkeley and Locke are as incredible as the Trinity or the Incarnation. Islamic culture has no metaphysics or ethics other than those of Islam although some Shi'ite and Sufi claims contain controversial metaphysical content not found in Islamic orthodoxy.

21 Kant espoused Pietism, a form of German Protestant fundamentalism emphasizing good works and a holy life more than confession of dogma.

22 Marxists sometimes dismiss ethics itself, like law, as an irrational bourgeois relic, a code designed to deviously serve the interests of the ruling class.

23 Islamic ethics, despite being religious, is works-based; its chief category is merit rather than grace. Two Muslim thinkers, Abū Naṣr Al-Fārābī (d. 950) and Abū Ali Miskawayh (d. 1030) wrote on Islamic ethics; both merely modified Greek ethics by seeking Islamic equivalents for Greek virtues.

24 The genocidal instinct surfaces with predictable frequency in Europe and in the lands that Europeans subjugated and managed. Genocide is an ancient European tradition rather than an aberrant occurrence. See my 'Bosnia: Palestine within Europe?' in *The Runnymede Bulletin*, October 1992.

25 Matthew 19:13–15, Mark 10:13–16. Luke 18:15–17.

26 William Golding's novel *Lord of the Flies*, published in 1954, makes this point.

27 I am paraphrasing and clarifying an insight of the late Gillian Rose whose sudden death meant that her ideas were left obscurely expressed. They were published posthumously in her *Mourning Becomes the Law: Philosophy and Representation*, Cambridge: Cambridge University Press, 1996.

28 Betty Friedan (1921–2006), the late American feminist, once described the suburban American household in this disparaging but convincing way. She wrote the feminist manifesto, *The Feminine Mystique* (1963).

4 The book sent down

1 Allah is God's essential name (*al-ism al-dhāt*). God's 99 other names denote his attributes (*al-asmā al-ṣifāt*), a few of which are discussed in Chapter 11.

2 The Quran as the book (*al-kitāb*) is the revelation on earth or heaven. It is also an earthly manuscript (*muṣ-ḥaf*) and, liturgically, an oral recitation (*al-qur'ān*). All three formats contain the words of God. *Qur'ān* is a verbal noun of the form *fu'lān* (based on the verb *fa/'a/la* as a template) which implies continuous action, hence an eternal reading. The oral revelations appearing on earth as *Al-Qur'ān* (the recital) are celestial speech preserved in 'a guarded tablet' (*lauḥ maḥfūz*; Q:85:22). The Quran is kept 'in a guarded book' (*fī kitābin maknūnin*; Q:56:78) inaccessible to the touch of sinners (Q:56:79). This supernatural diction descends to earth as 'a glorious recital' (*qurānan majīdun*; Q:85:21) and as 'the glorious recital' (*al-qurān al-majīd*; Q:50:1). The night of the Quran's initial descent is the night of power (*laylat al-qadr*; Q:97:1–3), extolled as a blessed night (*laylat mubārakah*; Q:44:3), better than a thousand months of devotion (Q:97:3), a period of time which is, in the Prophet's commentary on the verse, considered roughly an average human life-time.

3 Orthodoxy has inflexibly maintained that the illiterate Muhammad dutifully conveyed to his amanuensis the words that came to him from Gabriel, extolled as 'the holy spirit' and 'the faithful spirit' (Q:16:102; 26:193). The Prophet distinguished the inspired utterances in exalted Arabic from his own speech in the Qurayshi dialect and from the occasional 'divine saying' (*ḥadīth qudsī*) where Muhammad is divinely inspired to voice a revelation which, he is told, is not part of the Quran. There is a concession to the Qurayshi dialect in the spelling of some Quranic words: the standard and the dialectal spelling, differing in respect of one consonant, are both given with one consonant superimposed on the other. See *basṭatan* (abundantly) at Q:2:247 and compare its spelling at Q:7:69 where the sibilant *sīn* is superimposed on the sibilant *ṣād*. See also Q:52:37 and Q:88:22. Muhammad, the unlettered messenger (*al-rasūl al-nabī al-ummiyy*; Q:7:157; 62:2), could not transcribe the book with his 'right hand'(Q:29:48). While not an established writer, he could perhaps read and write as much as any ordinary merchant handling ledgers and business deals. The Quran demands that business transactions be written down (Q:2:282) which implies that such writing was not common before its revelation. Muhammad's ability to write or sign a business contract does not, however, explain how after his fortieth year, he could have produced the world's most widely read masterpiece in its original language.

4 It is a blunder to call the Quran 'the Christ of Islam'. Muslims do not worship their scripture. Christ, unlike the Quran, reveals the moral life of God and invites a human participation in it. The comparison of Christ with the Quran is wholly misguided despite its popularity among participants in inter-faith conferences.

5 We have a document prepared by Alexander's secretary, Eumenes, dictated to him by Alexander (356–23 BCE) as he lay ill in the summer heat in Babylon where he died in his fever. The first item on his list is the conquest of Arabia. Another desideratum is the forced deportation of the Iranian aristocracy to Europe. Both plans, if successful, would have critically affected the rise and spread of Islam. See Michael Wood, *In the Footsteps of Alexander the Great: A Journey from Greece to Asia*, Berkeley, CA: University of California Press, 1997, p. 234.

6 No parallel dramatic tradition developed alongside poetry in pre-Islamic Arabia. By contrast, the Greeks were obsessed with drama, especially tragedy. The tragic motif, as a religious theme, is foreign to orthodox Islam.

7 The first two portions are *nasīb* (remembrance of the lost beloved) and the *raḥīl* (quest for the beloved). For more on the Islamic ode (*qaṣīda*), see Michael Sells, 'Towards a Multidimensional Understanding of Islam: The Poetic Key', *Journal of the American Academy of Religion,* vol. 64, no. 1, 1996, pp. 145–66.

8 Gorgias of Leontini (*c.* 480–380 BCE) was an orator-sophist and a famed peripatetic teacher of rhetoric.

9 Muhsin Khan (trans.), *Summarized Ṣaḥīḥ Al-Bukhārī*, Riyadh: Maktaba Dār Al-Salām, 1994, Part 69, The Book of Medicine, Ch. 18, *ḥadīth* no. 1980, p. 944. (This is a dual Arabic–English text. I have used my own translations). The quoted tradition is well-attested with an authoritative chain of transmission.

10 The revelation of the Quran marks the beginning of the end of secular Arabic poetry. A few genres such as the *khamriyyāt* style, extolling the pleasures of alcohol, survived and even flourished, ironically, in the Islamic world precisely because the Quran had eventually, after equivocal comments (Q:2:219; 4:43; 5:90) firmly prohibited the consumption of strong drink (Q:5:91), deferring its pleasures to another world (Q:56:18–19; 76:21). The best *khamriyyāt* poets lived sober lives! Again, the poetry of the vagabond-poets (*al-ṣu'lūk*), expelled from society on account of their dissipation, was admired by some in urban centres. (Sufi poets were allowed to use erotic and alcohol-related imagery.) Finally, the genre of *ṭardiyyāt*, dealing with hunting themes, appealed to Islamic nobility in the court environment.

11 'Abd Allah Ibn Muslim Ibn Qutaybah (d. 889), *Ta'wīl Mushkil Al-Qurān*, Cairo: no publisher, 1954, p.10. The title translates as: A Commentary on the Complexities of the Quran. Ibn Qutaybah's scholarship on Quranic incapacitation *(I'jāz)* is indispensable since his work is transitional between the earlier and the later approaches to that theme. For publication details of classical scholarship on the inimitability of the Quran, see Chapter 5.

12 Q:54:1–2 hints at the miracle of the moon being split by Muhammad. Incidentally, Muslims take books and literary criticism much more seriously than westerners suppose. The contemporary Muslim reputation for literary philistinism is undeserved.

13 The New Testament is not, in its origins, a scripture but rather an inspired commentary on a previous scripture, the Hebrew Bible. Unlike the Quran, the Bible is nowhere self-described as literally true or inerrant revelation. At most, the Greek New Testament describes the Hebrew Bible, probably the Law (Torah) and the Prophets (*Nebi'īm*) as 'God-inspired' (*theopneustōs*; 2 Timothy 3:16).

14 Lower biblical criticism is mainly textual studies; higher criticism includes historical, literary, source, form, and redaction. Form criticism was originally developed for the Hebrew Bible. In its later application to the New Testament, its aim was to identify authentic Jesus traditions by isolating them from the evangelists' redaction. It was applied to the Gospels principally by Karl Ludwig Schmidt, Martin Dibelius, and Rudolf Bultmann. See Stephen Harris, *The New Testament*, Mountain View, CA: Mayfield, 1995, 2nd edition, pp. 70–6.

15 Variant codices were destroyed but at least seven variant readings (*ḥarf*, sing; pl. *aḥrūf*), were recognized as equally legitimate. These permitted minor variations in vocalization and pronunciation of individual words; barring a few exceptions (such as Q:27:82), this had virtually no effect on meaning or legal import of passages.

16 The various areas of critical biblical scholarship are irrelevant to Quranic studies although some correspond to methodological categories in *ḥadīth* criticism which seeks to sift through oral traditions in order to establish the words, works, and silences of the historical Muhammad. There is much misguided orientalist 'scholarship' about the 'canonization' of the Quran. Some western scholars favour the Islamic view of the amalgamation of the scripture. See for example, John Burton, *The Collection of the Qur'an*, Cambridge: Cambridge University Press, 1977. For a sympathetic survey of hostile orientalist claims, see Farid Esack, *The Quran: A Short Introduction*, Oxford: Oneworld, 2002, pp. 78–99.

17 Jeremiah 1:9 and Ezekiel 2:8–3:3 refer to a similar model of revelation. Indeed Ezekiel 'eats' the word of God. Moses received a revelation that had been written by God himself!

18 John Milton, like other classical authors, conventionally attributes his works (such as *Paradise Lost*) to the Muse while at the same time claiming authorship.

19 An attempt to explain the origins of the Quran occurs in the context of the pagan accusation that Muhammad forged the text as shown by the abrogation of one revelation by another (Q:16:101). In their search for a human author, the rejectors identified a Persian convert, possibly a Christian slave. The Quran mocks the desperate suggestion that a Persian slave could write a Quran in 'clear Arabic speech' (Q:16:103).

20 The only original source for this controversial tradition is the voluminously descriptive work of the Baghdadi historian-exegete Abu Ja'far Muhammad Ibn Jarir Al-Tabari (d. 923). See his *Tarīkh Al-Umam wa Al-Mulūk*, Beirut: Mu'assasah Al-Alam li Al-Matbu'at, 1989, pp. 75–6. Some volumes of his universal history are available in English. See Montgomery Watt and M.V. McDonald (trans.), *The History of Al-Tabarī*, *vol. 9, Muhammad at Mecca*, Albany, NY: State University of New York Press, 1988. Al-Tabarī tends to uncritically record all anecdotes and traditions in currency. His account, however, rightly suggests that Muhammad ardently desired to unite his people and was therefore tempted to compromise the revelation's content in order to appease the pagan Quraysh, a view corroborated by the Quran (Q:17:73–4).

21 The towns are the city-sanctuary of Mecca and the nearby southern fertile town of Tā'if where Muhammad, at the lowest ebb of his career, had unsuccessfully tried to establish Islam. The Prophet's biographers have named the two candidates for self-confessed greatness; neither is known to subsequent history. The standard source for the Prophet's life is Alfred Guillaume (trans.), *The Life of Muhammad: A Translation of (Ibn) Is'hāq's Sīrat Rasūl Allāh*, Karachi: Oxford University Press, 1995.

22 Satanic inspiration is described as *wiswas* (insinuation or whisper; conjugated at Q:20:120; 114:4–5) *nazgh* (lit., wanton suggestion, hence incitement to discord; Q:7:200; 41:36), and *ṭā'if* (a visitation; Q:7:201); the word *humazah* (pl. *humazāt*) refers to any scandalous or slanderous suggestion made by humans or the Devil (Q:104:1).

23 See Chapter 6 for the rationalist (Mu'tazilite) view of the Quran's status.

24 Kenneth Cragg, *Muhammad and the Christian*, London: Darton, Longman and Todd, 1984, p. 83, reprinted by Oneworld, Oxford, 1999. Page references are to the 1984 edition. I review Cragg's book in 'Rivals for the Hand of Grace', *Studies in Contemporary Islam*, vol. 1, no. 1, 1999, pp. 86–90. Cragg's interpretation of Islam is a mixture of insight and oversight.

25 Cragg, op. cit., p. 87.

26 R.J. Hollingdale (trans.), *Ecce Homo*, Harmondsworth: Penguin Books, 1979, pp. 102–3.

27 Cragg, op. cit., p. 81.

28 Ibid., p. 6.

29 Ibid., 81–3.

30 Ibid., p. 84.

31 Ibid., p. 86.

32 One of the Prophet's cousins, 'Abd Allah Ibn 'Abbās (d. 690) is considered the first exegete. The Ahbash, a Lebanese sect, supported by Syrian Alawites, an offshoot of Shi'ism, hold the heretical view that the archangel Gabriel was the first interpreter. The Ahbash regard orthodox Muslims as disbelievers. See Tariq Ramadan, *Western Muslims and the Future of Islam*, Oxford: Oxford University Press, 2004, pp. 29–30, n. 43 and n. 44 on p. 234.

33 Cragg, op. cit., pp. 85 ff.

34 Ibid., p. 86.

35 Ibid., p. 147.

36 Fazlur Rahman, *Islam and Modernity*, Chicago: University of Chicago Press, 1984.

37 The grammarian-exegete Abū Al-Ḥasan Al-Waḥīdī (d. 1075) wrote a commentary on the history and primary reasoning of the revelation: see Adnan Salloum (trans.), *Asbāb Al-Nuzūl*, Beirut: Dār Al-Kutub Al-Ilmiyyah, 1991.

38 What is wrong with a scripture containing a human component in its genesis if it is a wholly true component? A scripture with a human element may be wholly true but the possibility of that component being false cannot be excluded absolutely. To make the appeal to scriptural authority fully secure, we must exclude a priori the possibility of error in the genesis of the scripture.

39 The question of the precise mechanics of *tanzīl* is an idle worry that gets us nowhere. It is neither easy nor necessary to answer this psychological question in theology. However *tanzil* works, Muhammad has, as the Quran testifies, no active role which could compromise or attenuate the divine initiative in revelation, let alone seek to induce or influence such an initiative in order to fabricate a revelation (Q:7:203; 28:86). If we can show that any Quranic claims are false, then the scripture's provenance cannot be divine.

5 The book as 'the frustrater'

1 This reductionist view of the Quran informed the racist determinism entertained by nineteenth-century historians who shaped the colonialist ideologies of orientalist synthesizers studying the Muslim Orient with the intention of subduing it. Ernest Renan popularized the view of the desert as originator of Semitic revelation. The Quran refers to the desert and its dwellers: *badw* (noun) and verbal forms meaning 'to live in deserts' occur (Q:12:100; 33:20). Two more (and different) words are also used (Q:24:39; 56:73). There are numerous allusions to the seas and oceans though the Arabs were not then a maritime nation. The Quran does not mention forests but trees and vegetation are mentioned.

2 Margot Adler quotes pagans who hold this view. See her compendium of American paganism, *Drawing Down the Moon*, New York, NY: Penguin, 1979, 1986.

3 The verb *'a/ja/za*, meaning to frustrate, is conjugated often; God warns 'those who strive to frustrate' (*sa'aw mu'ājizīna*) the divine purposes in the earth and in the heavens (e.g. at Q:34:5, 38; see also Q:29:22).

4 The word *karāmah* is not Quranic but its root *ka/ra/ma* occurs often as in *rizqun karīmun* (a generous provision; Q:33:31; 34:4) and *ajrun karīmun* (a generous reward; Q:57:11, 18) both promised to believers. A *karāmah* (pl. *karāmāt*) is a small bounty or gift. For Catholic criteria of canonization, see note 23 to Chapter 7.

5 Aquinas argued that God alone can work miracles and that he does so immediately, without the intervention of an intermediate cause or agency. The Quran's position implies that while God's permission is a necessary condition for any miracle to transpire, it is both necessary and sufficient only in the case of the *mu'jizah*. In other cases, it is only necessary but not sufficient since prophetic (human) agency is involved. However, on both accounts, God is involved in every miracle. See *Summa Theologiae*, 1a110.4, 1a2ae.5.6. For convenient access to Thomas' thought, see Brian Davies, *The Thought of Thomas Aquinas*, Oxford: Oxford University Press, 1992, in which the quoted selections are found.

6 The two biblical testaments are translated by committees of Christian and sometimes Jewish scholars. The Quran, a work of daunting linguistic complexity, is, foolishly, tackled by single individuals.

7 The Quran cannot be sold. A charitable donation (*hadiyyah*, lit. gift; Q:27:35, 36; also *hady* at Q:48:25) can be made in lieu of payment.

8 Sayyid Quṭb's voluminous commentary is now partly available in English. Several volumes have been translated and edited by Adil Salahi and published by The Islamic Foundation, Leicester, England. The latest is volume 12 (2006), a commentary on

chapters 21–5. Volume 8 (2003) is a commentary on Chapter 9, one of the two Quranic chapters whose main theme is jihad.

9　The pronoun *hū* ('he' or 'it') is ambiguous since Arabic lacks the neuter gender. 'Nor would poetry suit it' is therefore also possible if the pronoun refers to the Quran.

10　The Quran and the Prophet's sayings approve of poetry unless its chief themes are wine, a jingoistic love of the fatherland, self-indulgent obsession with private sexual confessions, and an unhealthy interest in the beauty of imaginary women. See my *The Muslim Poetic Imagination*, London: Scorpion, 1982, Preface.

11　Walter Kaufmann and R.J. Hollingdale (trans.), *The Will to Power*, New York: Vintage Books, 1968, Section 822 (dated 1888), p. 435, emphasis in original. These remarks are found in Nietzsche's posthumously published notebooks.

12　Thomas Hardy was a poet and a novelist. His poetry explores our tragic and futile struggle against the forces of an indifferent and malevolent universe. See his *Wessex Poems and Other Verses*, New York: Harper, 1898, now available on the internet.

13　W.B. Yeats, 'The Scholars' (1915), in *The Collected Poems of W.B. Yeats*, New York: Scribner, 1996, 2nd edition.

14　Alford Welch (trans.), *The Quran and its Exegesis*, London: Routledge & Kegan Paul, 1976, p. 60. This is a translation of the work of the German Islamicist Helmut Gatje. Al-Zamakhsharī's Quran commentary is mentioned in note 23 below.

15　Al-Baqillānī, *I'jāz al-Qurān*, Cairo: Al-Matba'ah Al-Salafiyyah, 1930, p. 13.

16　Al-Juwaynī, *Al-'Aqīdah Al-Nizāmiyya*, M. Kawthari (ed.), Cairo: Dār Al-Kutub, 1948, pp. 54–5.

17　They committed the crime of *shatm* (lit., harsh speech), the extra-Quranic crime of insulting any messenger of God. It merits capital punishment. Unlike other crimes, the penalty cannot be commuted or averted even if the accused formally repents; the sentence and punishment are irrevocable.

18　Instead of turning within to understand ourselves, we scatter our attention by filling our lives with activities and distractions. When we moderns run from idea to idea, we fail to encounter the crucial ideas that enable authentic poetry: our own naked self, self-realization, communication with other selves, and the freedom to transcend the self.

19　Compare Luther's German translation of the Bible which established German as a language fit for scholarship. Radically, Luther chose a vernacular in preference to Latin, the lingua franca of European scholarship.

20　For example, 'Certainly the mercy of God is near to those who do good' (*inna raḥmata Allāh qarībun min al-muḥsinīn*; Q:7:56) seems incorrect. The adjective should be feminine (*qarībatun*) to agree with the feminine noun (*raḥmah*) it qualifies. Cf. Q:61:13 where *fatḥun qarībun* (a near victory) is correctly declined to suit the masculine subject (*fatḥun*). Again, the standard expression meaning 'upon him/it' (*'alaihī*) appears as *'alaihū* only at Q:48:10. Critics call it an error but Muslim apologists defend it as an archaic form. The standard (correct) expression is used in the rest of the Quran.

21　Michael Sells has explored Quranic recitation in *Approaching the Quran: The Early Revelations*, Ashland, Oregon: White Cloud Press, 2000, with an attached audio CD of recitation. Sells was accused of excessive sympathy for Islam and of brainwashing Christian students.

22　Persians perhaps wondered why God had chosen to reveal his will in Arabic, the language of a competing and despised culture. See note 4 to Chapter 6.

23　The Persian Quran commentator Abū Al-Qāsim Maḥmūd Ibn 'Umar Al-Zamakhsharī (d. 1144) belonged to the tradition of rationalist scholastic interpretation. His commentary *Al-Kashshāf 'an Ḥaqā'iq Ghawāmid Al-Tanzīl* (The Unveiler of the Truths of the Sciences of Revelation), sympathetic to Mu'tazilite views, was edited and condensed by the Persian Shafi'ite judge–commentator Abdallah Ibn 'Umar Al-Bayḍāwi (d. *c.* 1286) who excised the heretical Mu'tazilite doctrines but deferred to Al-Zamakhshari's expertise in rhetoric.

24 There are alleged grammatical infelicities including sudden changes in the person and number of the pronoun. This makes the text ambiguous. Pronouns are sometimes unattached and, for rhetorical effect, the number of the pronoun changes in the same verse (e.g. the switch from the aloofness of 'he' to the intimacy of 'we' at Q:41:12). In Arabic rhetoric, this last feature is called *iltifāt*. See M.A.S. Abdel Haleem, 'Grammatical Shift for the Rhetorical Purposes: *Iltifāt* and Related Features in the Quran' in *Bulletin of the School of Oriental and African Studies*, vol. LV, Part 3, 1992.

25 The Quran has many neologisms, including names for hell and heaven: *saqar* (Q:54:48; 74:42), *al-ḥuṭamah* (the great crusher; Q:104:4–6), *hāwiyah* (a bottomless pit; Q:101:9, 11). Paradise has many levels and curious features. The Quran and the Prophetic traditions name its highest part as *Firdaws* (Q:18:107; 23:11); a river running through it is *Al-Kawthur* (lit. abundance; Q:108:1) and a fountain is *Salsabīl* (lit. ask for the way; Q:76:18). The tree of *Zaqqūm* grows in hell to supply food for sinners (Q:44:43–6). The records of the deeds of sinners and of the righteous are kept in separate sealed records called *Sijjīn* and *'Illiyyūn* respectively (Q:83:7–8, 18–19). Quranic neologisms are not restricted to eschatology.

26 For example, the term *kalālah* refers to a person who leaves as heirs neither descendants nor ascendants (Q:4:12, 176). It has excited speculation in the context of laws of collateral inheritance. For more on such minutiae, see Cilardo Agostino, *The Quranic Term Kalala*, Edinburgh: Edinburgh University Press, 2005.

27 Is it an *Arabic* Quran if it contains foreign loan words? This question distressed early commentators. Quranic commentaries contain a section called '*Ajā'ib Al-Qurān* listing foreign words and their origins. Purists denied that the Quran contained foreign words arguing glibly that it was the speech of God – for whom no language is foreign! The philologist-exegete Jalāl Al-Dīn Al-Suyūti (d. 911) claimed that foreign words entered Arabic as Arabs traded with and travelled to foreign lands – but added that such words were 'Arabicized' by the time of the Quran's descent. Most of the foreign words were Persian (e.g. *sijjīl*, baked clay; Q:15:74, *ramzan*, by signals; Q:3:41, *barzakh*, barrier; Q:25:53). (The Hebrew Bible also contains words of Persian origin.) Hebrew belongs to the same subdivision of the Semitic family as Arabic and many Hebraic words are related but they occur in the Quran in Arabic transliteration. An exception is *ḥiṭṭah* (repentance; Q:7:161). An objective and exhaustive discussion of Quranic philology is in Al-Suyūti's *Al-Itqān fī 'Ulūm Al-Qurān*, Beirut: Maktab Al-Thaqafiyyah, 1973, in 2 volumes. See volume 1, pp. 135–41.

28 The Quran uses several forms of emphasis including the 'energetic mode'. This mode is restricted to the present indicative, normally active voice (e.g. *la-tarawunna*; you shall most certainly see; Q:102:7). It occurs occasionally in the passive (*la-tus'alunna*; you shall most certainly be called to account; Q:16:56; 102:8). (The context requires these translations to be in the future tense.) The mode is created by adding *l* at the beginning of a verb and a doubled *n* (*nn*) to the last syllable. Reciters dwell on the nasal sound; the Quran is alert to the aural dimension of rhetoric.

29 Many accounts of the Moses' narrative and the single longest continuous narrative, the tale of Joseph, contain dialogue exchanges but little or no narrative as background or explanation, as if it were unnecessary or unworthy of the divine author to go into detail. The audience is expected to know the background. Commentary is especially required to make sense of Quranic allusion or honorary mention (*dhikr*, Q:19:2; also at Q:19:16, 41, 51, 54, 56), a glimpse that says little and implies much.

30 The mystery of the *al-ḥurūf al-muqaṭṭa'āt* (the disjointed letters) remains unsolved. The opening verses of some chapters consist of small random selections from individual letters of the Arabic alphabet, as if the author were to say: 'Here is the raw material of natural language. Now watch the emergence of supernatural speech!' The letters

are part of the revelation: reciters cannot omit them even though they have no agreed meaning. Translation disguises such charming idiosyncrasies of the original. The hostile explanation for the disjointed letters was the orientalist conjecture that Muhammad stuttered these letters before the text began to flow smoothly. This view, like the absurd accusation of epilepsy, is the unworthy residue of Christian fanaticism. Some Muslims have, based on a Quranic clue (Q:74:30–1), tried to interpret these random letters in terms of a mathematical theory involving the number 19. Orthodox Muslims believe that the letters cannot be interpreted or understood, their presence being evidence of the mystery of the book. This sacred matter should not be reduced to a discursive matter that amuses experts.

31 Examples include the two biblical testaments and the later writings of Ludwig Wittgenstein. The most influential books were not written as books, let alone carefully edited and copy-edited for publication. Indeed men such as Socrates, Alexander and Jesus wrote nothing. So much for the proverb, 'the pen is mightier than the sword'.

32 The enneads are 54 essays, six divisions of nine each. Each division is an ennead, composed between 254–76 and later arranged by subject by Plotinus' student Porphyry (*c.* 232–304). Ibn Sīnā (980–1037) was influenced by his predecessor Al-Fārābī (*c.* 870–950), both of whom were neo-Platonists.

33 'As tedious a piece of reading as I ever undertook, a wearisome confused jumble … Nothing but a sense of duty could carry any European through the Koran.' This was Carlyle's initial reaction. See his six lectures *On Heroes, Hero-worship and the Heroic in History*, published in 1841. The third lecture ('The Hero as Prophet') is a tribute to Muhammad. Carlyle's negative verdict on the Quran as literary achievement was partly due to his reliance on George Sale's prejudiced and incompetent translation which masked cynicism and hostility to Islam. Published in 1734, Sale avows in his preface his loathing for Islam and Muhammad.

34 The melodiously recited Quran, conveyed by radio and television, has an electrifying effect on audiences. Listeners are elated as the reciter builds up the tension to a climax and artfully releases it. In Islamic lands, the Quran is experienced as a descent (*tanzīl*): the divine word falls on human ears but paradoxically also rises above the din and cacophony of cities such as Cairo where it is powerfully recited. The Egyptians savour a self-congratulatory proverb: 'The Quran was revealed in Mecca but recited in Cairo'. The aniconic art of Quran recitation gives some reciters a reputation comparable to that of opera or Gospel singers in the West. The recited Quran has continued to have a dramatic impact from the earliest days starting with 'Umar who converted after listening to the first few verses of Chapter 20. (The Bible in Arabic has been chanted to no appreciable effect on the audience.) For details, see Kristina Nelson, *The Art of Reciting the Quran*, Austin: University of Texas Press, 1985.

35 The Englishman (Muhammad) Marmaduke Pickthall (1875–1936) converted to Islam and became the Quran's first *Muslim* translator whose native tongue was English. He was also the first westerner to note the majesty of the Quranic recital: 'that inimitable symphony the very sounds of which move men to tears and ecstasy'. See the Preface to his *The Glorious Quran*, published by many publishers and translated into most languages.

36 This remark is attributed to Aquinas. It was probably inspired by the case of Muhammad since Aquinas lived in an age when Islam was a threatening presence on European frontiers.

37 The feminist Camille Paglia has argued for this position. See note 35 to Chapter 1.

38 *Henry V*, Act IV, scene 1, lines 149, 151.

6 The scope of the book

1 The word 'imām' means register here. Its standard meaning, as a passive participle, is 'one placed in front', hence a leader of prayer. It has other unrelated meanings, including

an open highway (Q:15:79). The Quran takes considerable liberties with words; Arabic dictionaries record its idiosyncratic usages.

2 The Comforter (*paraklētos*), the Holy Spirit, mentioned in the New Testament is a teacher of all truths but his teachings are not in the form of a written revelation (John 14:26). The Quran claims that the Torah, in the original form of tablets given to Moses, was an explanation of all things (Q:6:154; 7:145). The Quran frequently links itself to the Torah (Q:28:48–9) calling it the criterion (*al-furqān*; Q:2:53), a title it shares with the Quran (Q:3:3–4; 25:1). It eulogizes the Torah's contents as a guide and a mercy (Q:46:12), as a light, as comprehensive guidance (Q:6:91, 154). Indeed the Quran is an Arabic confirmation of the Torah (Q:46:12). The Gospel is also mentioned but praised much less often (Q:3:3; 5:46).

3 Some works of Plato and St. Augustine were added to this list.

4 Since the early sixteenth century, Iranians are committed to Shi'ism. Twelver Shi'ism (named for its dozen imams) is a Persianized version of an earlier Arab sectarian tradition. It has dominated Iran since the Sāfavid dynasty (1501–1732). Iranians, an Aryan nation, are a people with a proud past that even Islam has failed to erase. The first Shah of Iran's Pahlavi dynasty, Reza Khan Shah (r. 1925–41), made Zoroastrianism the state religion alongside Shi'ism. His son, Muhammad Reza Shah (r. 1941–79), the ruler deposed by Khomeini, was so proud of Iran's glorious pagan past that he tried to introduce a calendar going back to King Cyrus. Iranians date their history by their defeat at the hands of Arabs, givers of the true faith since the time of 'Umar, the second caliph. We owe most of the classical scholarship of Islam in all fields, especially philosophy and mysticism, to Arabicized Persians who wrote in Arabic. Most Iranians are ambivalent towards Arabs and probably never forgave God for preferring Arabs for the gift of the Arabic Quran!

5 For more on the *mawālī* arrangement and full conversions, see Frederick Denny, *An Introduction to Islam*, Upper Saddle River, NJ: Pearson Prentice Hall, 2006, pp. 76 ff. This is a substantial introduction to Islam whose only weakness is the perfunctory treatment of Islamic philosophy.

6 Paul and Constantine in Christianity, like Ashoka (nicknamed the Buddhist Constantine) were religious and political co-founders of Christianity and Buddhism respectively. Moreover, with most so-called founders of religions, we have only the fact of the legend. Muhammad is exceptional since he mattered to his contemporaries – and they took note of his life and work.

7 Shi'ism and sectarian groups in its marginalia (such as the Isma'ilis) represent a parochial version of Quranic Islam with its universal vision of human religious destiny. Only Sunni Islam has, in principle if not in practice, preserved this ecumenical scope.

8 There are two important exceptions. First, Bilāl Ibn Rabah (d. *c*. 641), a slave of African origin, living in Mecca, was freed by Abu Bakr. Bilāl became a symbol of African liberation struggles against colonialism. Secondly, Salmān Al-Fārsi (d. 657), as his second name indicates, was Persian. Born in Persia (in the same year as Muhammad), and named Rouzbeh, he was a zealous Zoroastrian who converted to Christianity before he met Muhammad and embraced Islam. Muhammad, unduly fond of this convert, named him Salman (lit., one who is safe) and called him 'my family'. After ascertaining that the Quran was silent on military tactics for a battle fought in Medina in the fifth year after Muhammad moved there, Salman suggested an innovative strategy to deal with the siege of the city by the Meccans. The battle is accordingly called 'the battle of the trench' (*khandaq*). Salman might have translated the Quran into Persian which, if true, would make him its first translator into any language.

9 Ismail Al-Faruqi, *'Urubah and Religion*, Amsterdam: Djambatan, 1962, in 2 volumes. The first volume is on Arabism.

10 I criticize the Arab imperialistic undertones of his work in my review of Kate Zebiri's *Muslims and Christians Face to Face*, Oxford: Oneworld, 1997, a pro-Christian study of Islamic–Christian relationships. See *The Times Higher Education Supplement*, December 1997.

11 Paul's Corinthian correspondence is as relevant to a modern audience in a large city (such as New York or Los Angeles) in the twenty-first century as it was in first century Corinth. The ancient world is ancient only in some ways. In terms of sexual licence, it is not outdated. Even in permissive modern cultures, few people are committing incest with their step-mothers (see 1 Corinthians 5:1).

12 See A.S. Tritton, 'The Speech of God', *Studia Islamica*, vol. 33, 1971, pp. 5–22.

13 Friedrich Nietzsche, *Beyond Good and Evil*, Marianne Cowan (trans.), Chicago: Henry Regnery, 1955, section 121, p. 81. I have slightly modified the translation. Nietzsche, a classical scholar, contrasts the colloquial (demotic) Greek of St Paul and others to the high classical Greek of Aristophanes, Sophocles, Thucydides and Plato. Luke's Greek, in his Gospel and the book of Acts, is virtually classical.

14 The Quran uses *al-dīn* only in the singular and with the definite article since there is only one true religion. The plural *adyān* never occurs. Early Muslims interpreted this verse to be a divine mandate for taking the unified enterprise of Muslim faith and secular power into lands, East and West. The new faith destroyed the two powerful empires of its day although the Roman empire was by this time only a shell of its former glory.

15 In the pre-scientific Quranic outlook, angels travel from a world beyond our framework of time and space to visit the lower empirical realm. Gabriel visited Muhammad at Mount Ḥirā' and brought down the Quran; angels fought on the Muslim side ensuring victory for Islam in the decisive battle of Badr (in Ramadan 2 AH) and in other military engagements (Q:3:123; 8:9, 12; 9:25–6). The Prophet and his companions cured demoniacs by using Quranic verses, since considered apotropaic; they conducted exorcisms to cast out demons and misbehaved spirits.

16 S.A. Wadud, *Phenomena of Nature and the Qur'an*, Lahore: Sayed Khalid Wadud, 1971.

17 Maurice Bucaille, a French convert, has argued for the scientific potential of the Quran in two books that are bestsellers in the Muslim world: *The Bible, the Qur'an and Science*, A.D. Pannell and Maurice Bucaille (trans.), Paris: Seghers, 1983, 10th edition. In 1984, Seghers published the popular third edition of a sequel, *What is the Origin of Man?* Harun Yahya, the prolific Turkish writer, has inherited the mantle of Bucaille. Yahya has numerous books on the subject and actively maintains a website. Among Sufis, 'Aisha 'Abd Al-Rahman Al-Tarjumana has argued that the Quran is abreast of the best of modern science in her booklets and pamphlets published by the now defunct Diwan Press once based in Norwich, England. The female Egyptian Quranic commentator Bint Al-Shati' has rejected all such exegesis as being motivated by a pseudo-scientific reconciliation of faith and empirical science. See her piece in *Al-Ahram*, 7 January 1972.

18 Quranic references to geography are also inexplicit. The expression 'Iram of the Pillars' (*Iram dhāt al-'Imād*; Q:89:7) may refer to Damascus, Alexandria, or 'Ād. Such vagueness is also found in the Quran's descriptions of the holy land (*al-arḍ al muqaddasah*; Q:5:21) which could refer to Canaan or Palestine (Q:5:21; 7:137) or even Arabia, possibly Mecca (Q:27:91; 28:57, 85; 90:1–2; 95:1–3). Places in the itinerary of the traveller called *dhū al-qarnayn* (Q:18:83–98) are referred to in a nebulous way. Again, even more obscurely, Mary withdrew to 'an eastern place' (*makānan sharqiyyan*; Q:19:16); the place of her labour is described as 'a remote place' (*makānan qaṣiyyan*; Q:19:22). The comparative form of the same adjective is used to describe the mosque in Jerusalem as *al-aqṣā* (the most remote; Q:17:1). Arabic, like Hebrew, has no separate superlative degree on the level of lexicography though it exists syntactically. One must manipulate the context or employ a circumlocution to express it.

19 Muhammad's father-in-law, Abu Bakr, is called by this sobriquet which means 'father of the virgin', the virgin being 'Aisha, the only wife of the Prophet who was not a widow or divorced. Most of Muhammad's companions were given affectionate nicknames. Calling people by epithet is part of Arab culture; the Quran condemns only the use of abusive or vulgar epithets (Q:49:11). Muhammad's uncle, Abd Al-'Uzzā, named in honour of a female idol, is referred to by the derogatory epithet Abu Lahab, 'father of flame [of hell]' (Q:111:1). He died, a disbeliever, after the battle of Badr. Zaid Ibn Ḥārithah, Muhammad's freed slave and adopted son, is the only Muslim named in the Quran (Q:33:37). Other examples of indefinite Quranic descriptions include Moses' teacher who taught him esoteric knowledge beyond prophecy (Q:18:60–82). He is described as 'one of our servants … whom we had taught knowledge from us' (Q:18:65), identified by some with the wandering mystic Al-Khiḍr (lit., 'the evergreen man').

20 The Quran takes countless liberties with the Arabic language. For example, *fitnah* has many meanings including trial, its standard meaning, but also subterfuge (Q:6:23), punishment (Q:51:14) and so on. The word *ummah*, meaning community or religion (Q:43:22, 23), has an idiosyncratic sense in two passages (Q:11:8; 12:45) where it means a long or indefinite period of time. The title of Chapter 8 is *Al-Anfāl* (Q:8:1), an unusual plural of *nafl* (voluntary thing or action) which has the normal plural *nawāfil*. Some suggest it is a plural of a plural. The word is incorrectly translated as war booty; the correct translation is 'windfall'. Again, the word for years is *sinīn* (Q:7:130, 12:47; 30:4); the singular is *sana* (Q:5:26) and *'ām* (Q:9:28; 12:49). In Q:28:27, however, *thamāniya ḥijaj* (lit., eight pilgrimages) means eight years. Such a use is poetic licence as in 'a boy of eight winters'. The Quran uses poetic descriptions – for example, 'in the stomach of Mecca' (*bi baṭni Makkata*; Q:48:24) where the prosaic intention is the valley of Mecca.

21 The Quran protests against our search for knowledge beyond the bounds of religiously legitimate interest. It does so dramatically during its account of the controversy over the number of sleepers who slept in the cave (*al-kahf*; Q:18:22), a Quranic story reminiscent of one apparently legendary account of the persecution of Christians in Ephesus during the time of Decius (reigned 249–51 CE).

22 A share of the inheritance left to a widow (Q:4:12), which varies from a quarter to an eighth, depending on whether heirs include children, might explain the two different periods of waiting. The reduced period (four months and ten days) could correspond to a larger share of the inheritance. Jurists still differ on whether the maintenance is chargeable to the late husband's estate for one year or for only four months and ten days.

23 'Critical commonsensism' is associated with the American pragmatist Charles Pierce. He argued that common sense is philosophically sound if it is the starting-point rather than the terminus of inquiry.

24 Q:17:60 refers to a tree cursed in the Quran; the verse requires commentary.

25 Friedrich Engels, Marx's collaborator, claimed that cannibalism was the universal primitive form of dealing with vanquished enemies, which implies the universality of the practice at least among warring tribes. See selections from his *Anti-Duhring: Herr Eugen Duhring's Revolution in Science*, reprinted in Eleanor Kuykendall (ed.), *Philosophy in the Age of Crisis*, New York: Harper & Row, 1970, pp. 185–9. See p. 188.

26 The Noachide laws are not scripture but *midrash* (commentary) on Genesis (including Genesis 2:16) and consist of six prohibitions (on idolatry, blasphemy, sexual sins, murder, theft, and eating from a living animal) and one injunction, namely, to formulate a legal system. While Jews must keep the whole Torah, a Gentile who follows these seven rules qualifies, according to Maimonides, as a righteous person (*ḥasid*) with a share in the next life. This view is different from the Quranic view of messengers sent to all peoples – to guide them and make them culpable in the event of rejection. The notion that following the Noachic covenant constitutes an inchoate form of universal

guidance is, in any case, part of Jewish theology inspired by the Torah, not the Torah itself.

27 Muslim commentators claim that 'Imrān is Moses' grandfather (see Q:3:33). The Torah does not mention the name of Moses' father (or grandfather). Amram the Levite is identified as his father in 1 Chronicles 6:3 (in the third division of the Hebrew Bible). This has led some scholars to suspect that Moses was an illegitimate child.

28 The Quran names as Al-Jūdiyy (Q:11:44) the mountain on which the ark eventually alighted, a possible reference to Mount Ararat in Turkey.

7 The authority of the book

1 These are the five (scrolls), the Hebrew name for the Torah, the equivalent of the Latinized Greek designation 'Pentateuch' which also means five scrolls.

2 The *lex talionis* (law of equals) is called *al-qiṣāṣ* (Q:2:178–9) and applies only to murder (Q:17:33). Just retaliation replaces the pre-Islamic tribal vendetta. The Quran improves morally on the Mosaic law of retaliation: 'If any one remits the retaliation by way of charity, it is an act of atonement (*kaffārah*) for himself' (Q:5:45). For extreme offences – theft, false witness, highway robbery, and sexual immorality – the Quranic punishments are deliberately brutal and exemplary (*nakal*; Q:5:38). Amputation of hands and feet, flogging, execution, and exile are stipulated (Q:5:33, 38; 24:2). Stoning to death (for adultery) is found only in the Prophet's traditions although some Muslim and non-Muslim scholars speculate about a lost 'stoning verse' (*āyat al-rajm*) about that transgression. Substantial evidence is required for conviction in all *ḥudūd* (extreme) offences. Where evidence was inadequate, wise jurists followed the maxim, 'It is better to be mistaken in forgiveness than in punishment'.

3 Ironically, the final duo of apotropaic chapters of the Quran provide protection and deliverance from the toxic effects of magic (Q:113:4; Q:113; Q:114).

4 The Mosaic law did not require fire from heaven to consume an offering as proof of prophetic credentials. The Quranic point is *ad hominem*. In Leviticus 9:24 a fire from heaven consumes an offering prepared by Moses and Aaron but the community still rebels against Yahweh. Again, Elijah prepares a crucial experiment in his contest with the 400 false prophets of Baal in which 'the God who answers with fire is God indeed' (1 Kings: 18:20–40). Compare Q:37:123–6 where the false god Baal (*Ba'al*) is mentioned. There is no mention of false prophets, a notion the Quran even linguistically rejects.

5 It would be strategically absurd to send a female prophet to warn a patriarchal culture where even male prophets had a rough time.

6 Compare the view of Maimonides, the Jewish philosopher and exegete–halakhist: prophecy emerges naturally in persons who have perfected themselves morally, intellectually and spiritually. God may prevent its emergence; if he does not, it is inevitable. See Maimonides, *Guide for the Perplexed* 2:32, 36, *Mishneh Torah, Hilkhot Yesodei ha-Torah* 7:7; Mishnah commentary, introduction. Quoted by Barry Freundel, *Contemporary Orthodox Judaism's Response to Modernity*, Jersey City, NJ: KTAV, 2004, pp. 40–1, 45.

7 Moses uses the address 'My people!' and presumably speaks in Hebrew although the Arabic for 'Hebrew' never occurs in the Quran. Muhammad is described as an Arab as opposed to *A'jamiyy* (Persian) messenger sent to warn, naturally enough, fellow Arabs, at least in the first instance (Q:41:44). Jesus is portrayed as aloof and distant from his people whom he invariably addresses as 'Children of Israel!'

8 A *nabī* is a prophet who warns verbally. His mission is limited and purely religious. A *rasūl* is an apostle-prophet, such as Moses or Muhammad, sent to warn with the aid of a law that is binding until God annuls it through another *rasūl*. The passive participle *mursal* (one sent; Q:13:43) is an alternative for the active form *rasūl*.

9 In the Jewish tradition, mainly in Maimonides' writings, a prophet can acknowledge (or confirm) another prophet as Jacob confirmed his son Joseph, a view corroborated in

the Quran (Q:12:6). The prophet's message must not promote idolatry or undermine or alter the word of God. A prophet must predict a series of good events which must come true. Prophecies for evil may be rescinded by God but prophecies for good must come to pass, a compulsion based partly on a controversial interpretation of Jeremiah 28:8–9. A prophet must defend the Jewish people before God, as Moses did, even in the face of legitimate divine anger (Numbers 14:13–19 partly corroborated at Q:7:155).

10 This verse was revealed shortly after Muhammad's brush with death at the battle of Uhud and affirms the absolute mortality of all prophets. Abu Bakr commented on the verse immediately after the Prophet's death in 10 AH (632 CE) as his body awaited burial and many grief-stricken and shocked believers, such as 'Umar Ibn Al-Khaṭṭāb, refused to believe that the Prophet was only mortal. Abu Bakr contrasted Muhammad's mortality with God's eternity.

11 The Quran condemns bitheism (Q:16:51). Jesus is interrogated by God: 'Jesus, Mary's son! Did you say to humankind: "Take me and my mother as two gods (*ilāhayn*) in derogation of the only true God (*Allāh*)?"'(Q:5:118). A version of the Trinity (or possibly tri-theism) is also declared anathema (Q:5:75).

12 See Deuteronomy 18:21–2 for the major criterion for distinguishing a true from a false prophet. A false prophet must be executed (Deuteronomy 18:20). Disobedience of a true prophet will incur the wrath of God (Deuteronomy 18:19).

13 The *ḥerem* (lit. ban or curse of destruction) refers to a barbaric regulation in Israel's holy war which required the destruction of captives and war booty as a purgative that proved one's sincerity of commitment to God who alone gives victory. It now refers to excommunication from the congregation of Israel. The word *ḥerem* occurs at *Wa elleh HaDavār'īm* (Deuteronomy) 7:2.

14 In the Quran, the expression 'false prophet' never occurs even as the disbelievers' description of the Prophet. The Quran uses the circumlocution 'they rejected him' (*kadhdhabū-hū*; Q:91:14). The *sīrah* (biography) materials mention the rivalry between Muhammad and a false messenger, Musaylimah, from the enemy tribe of Banu Ḥanīfah. He was engaged in battle at Al-Aqraba in 633 CE, a year after the Prophet's demise. It is among the bloodiest battles of early Islamic history. The false prophet was killed by an army sent by the first caliph, Abu Bakr, and led by the brilliant general Khalid Bin Al-Walīd, itself an indication of the strategic importance of the confrontation.

15 Muhammad interpreted the revelation of one very late Medinan chapter to mean his death was imminent (Q:103:1–3). This is the last complete chapter to be revealed. The last verse is thought to be Q:5:3.

16 The Gospels contain some uneasy exchanges between John the Baptist and Jesus. The New Testament writers and editors seem concerned to downplay the Baptist's importance. The spiritual rivalry between the two men is palpable, especially in Luke 7:18–35.

17 'I do not seek in order that I may believe, but I believe in order that I may understand' is associated with St Anselm of Canterbury (1033–1109). This is misguided priorities but it is at least an improvement on Tertullian who said faith was certain because it was impossible! Thomas Aquinas has, owing probably to the influence of Muslim thinkers, the correct ranking of loyalties: he accepts on faith revealed truths which go beyond reason but rejects those that contradict it.

18 This is the gist of Anthony Storr's psychological critique of prophetic self-assurance in his *Feet of Clay: A Study of Gurus*, London: HarperCollins, 1996. I assess Storr's thesis in my review of his book in *The Times Higher Education Supplement*, January 1997. Storr includes secular thinkers such as Freud in his list of gurus.

19 Many western critics accuse Muhammad of religious self-aggrandizement in appropriating the title of 'seal of the prophets' (Q:33:40) and in demanding excessive loyalty from believers since they must place him above their families (Q:33:6).

Furthermore, the Quran prohibits anyone from marrying Muhammad's widows (Q:33:53) and discourages any potential suitors who might be waiting for Muhammad to die (Q:33:32) – all of which is evidence, it is argued, of Muhammad's sexual insecurity. The Quran gives the Prophet's widows the title of 'the mothers of the believers' to further discourage their re-marriage. Muhammad had more than the quota of (full) wives allowed to others (Q:33:50) in addition to an unlimited number of concubines acquired in war. The Quran itself prohibits him from taking any more wives 'even if their beauty attracts you' (Q:33:52). Critics accuse Muhammad of changing the laws of incest in order to marry an attractive woman who happened to be the wife of his adopted son, an incident recorded in the Quran (Q:33:37). This marriage was literally arranged in heaven (Q:33:37). Ostensibly, all these arrangements, favourable to Muhammad, were made by God, via revelation. His young wife 'Aisha confronted him and noted acidly that 'Your Lord is quick to please you'. Non-Muslim critics routinely accuse Muhammad of being a debauched sensualist who used God's word to justify his secret desires. There is interminable debate about these polemical accusations.

20 The Quran relates this incident with significant differences (Q:37:100–7). Cf. Genesis 22:1–14. The Quranic narrative portrays the intended victim as knowing and concurring in his fate. The Quran does not name the son but Muslim tradition holds it to be Ishmael, the first-born, rather than Isaac.

21 I question the assumption that all epistemologies rest on faith in my 'Is There an Epistemic Parity Between Faith and Rejection?' in *The Southern Journal of Philosophy*, vol. XXVI, no. 3, 1988, pp. 293–305.

22 Richard Swinburne argues for this view in his *Faith and Reason*, Oxford: Clarendon Press, 1981, pp. 181–3. He has re-iterated his position in his 'Christianity and the Discourse of the World Religions', Peter Koslowski (ed.), *Philosophy Bridging the World's Religions*, Boston: Kluwer Academic, 2003, pp. 7–20.

23 Q:30:2–6 contains a prediction. In a rare notice of external history, the Quran notes with sadness the defeat of the Christian Byzantines at the hands of the Persian Sassanids and predicts victory for the Christians 'within a few years' (*fī biḍ'i sinīn*; Q:30:4; cf. Q:12:42 where *biḍ'a sinīn* describes Joseph's extended stay in prison). These three criteria are a modified version of criteria found in Swinburne, op. cit., pp. 181–3; see note 22 above. One criterion of sainthood in Catholicism overlaps with these criteria of prophethood. Saints had, like prophets, the ability to predict the future. For canonization, the Church added four more requirements: wrestling successfully with the Devil, miraculous cures of diseases (for which witnesses were required), defying the law of space by appearing in more than one place at the same time, and the emission of a floral or fragrant odour (from the corpse or some bodily relic of the saint).

24 I criticize Swinburne's thesis in my 'Religious Messages and Cultural Myths', *Sophia*, vol. 25, no. 3, 1986, pp. 32–40 and from another angle in my 'The Virtues of Fundamentalism', *Scottish Journal of Religious Studies*, vol. 9, no. 2, 1988, pp. 41–9.

25 See Karl Barth, *Dogmatics in Outline*, Colin Gunton (trans.), London: SCM Press, 2001, *passim*.

26 James Usher (1581–1656) was a Calvinist theologian. By his reckoning, the earth is now 6,000 years old. We find mistakes about geology and biology in the works of most thinkers of the past. Usher's error is no more absurd than the scientific blunders in the works of Aristotle.

27 It is a subtly amusing and refined irony that modern Christian writers, such as Swinburne cited in note 22 above, are condescending towards both the Christian apologists and their secular critics of the nineteenth century: the apologists had misdirected their hostility while the secularists had failed to keep the target in focus. One army had missed the mark while the other was fighting in the wrong battlefield. With the benefit of hindsight, however, we realize that the Christian apologists took the right side in the right battle. But they lost; and they knew it and we know it.

28 The encyclical was posted on 30 September 1943. I have translated and paraphrased paragraph 45. In note 33, the Pontiff refers to Augustine's relevant works and biblical commentaries in Latin. Like the Islamic fatwa, the papal encyclical letter lacks the authority of an *ex cathedra* statement.

29 An instance of studied ambiguity is temporal vagueness. The Arabic word *yaum* (like the Hebrew *yōm*) can denote various periods of time, even years and centuries. It occurs in the singular (Q:7:53) and plural (Q:10:3). One day (*yaum*) can equal a thousand (Q:22:47; 32:5) or even fifty thousand years of human reckoning (Q:70:4). In Q:41:9, the world is said to be created *fī yaumayn* (in two days). Another example of deliberate vagueness is the claim that Joseph was sold for 'a few dirhams' (*darāhim ma'dūdah*; Q:12:20) rather than for the exact sum of twenty shekels of silver (Genesis:37:28).

30 Two verses on the maintenance of widows out of the estate of a dead husband (Q:2:234, 240) contradict each other, a contradiction removed by appeal to a doctrine of abrogation or of gradual progressive revelation.

31 For more on this, see my 'The Limits of Internal Hermeneutics' and Johan Vos' 'The New Testament Interpretation of Scripture' both in Hendrik Vroom and Jerald Gort (eds), *Holy Scriptures in Judaism, Christianity and Islam*, Amsterdam, Atlanta, GA: Editions Rodopi, 1997, pp. 107–12 and 98–106 respectively.

32 Friedrich Schleiermacher (1768–1834) suggested that Gefühl or taste for the infinite, 'the feeling of absolute dependence' (*das Gefühl der schlechthinigen Abhangigkeit*) was the essence of Christianity. See his *On Religion: Addresses in Response to its Cultured Critics*, Terence Tice (trans.), Richmond: John Knox, Press, 1969, originally published in 1798. See especially the second address.

33 It is alleged that the Quran misidentifies Mary, the mother of Jesus, with the sister of Moses and Aaron (Q:3:32; 34; 19:38). Muslims answer that Mary, the mother of Jesus, is called 'the sister of Aaron' in Q:19:28 to indicate her priestly lineage, not to indicate direct blood relationship to Aaron. Descriptions such as 'Sons of Adam' or 'Children of Israel' need not and often cannot, without absurdity, presuppose direct physical consanguinity.

34 For an example of such an attitude, see Akbar Ahmed, *Post-Modernism and Islam*, London: Routledge, 1992. I critique his work in 'The Graham Greene Fallacy', *The Observer*, June 1992. Another example is furnished by the work of the South African activist Farid Esack, discussed in Chapter 11.

8 A sign is enough – for the wise

1 Although Islam is a religion centred on legal regulation of conduct, only some 500 or so Quranic verses, out of a total of 6,236, have nomothetic or directly prescriptive content.

2 For more on Quranic parables, see Chapter 2.

3 The word *'ajīb* as an adjective is used in the Quran (at Q:50:2 as *shayun 'ajīb*, a strange thing; cf. *shay'un 'ujāb* at Q:38:5). It occurs as *quranān 'ajaban* (a marvelous recital; Q:72:1). The word is used with *āyah* in the expression *āyātinā 'ajaban* (a wonder among our signs; Q:18:9). Ibn Baṭṭūtah (1304–77), the traveller–jurist, uses *'ajībah* to describe the marvels he saw during his extensive adventures. See H.A.R. Gibb (trans.), *Travels of Ibn Baṭṭūtah, A.D. 1325–1354*, Cambridge: Cambridge University Press, 1958.

4 Paul in Romans 1:18–23 emphasizes this point to the philosophically literate audience. Psalms 19:1–2 concur.

5 Compare the ancient scheme of the four elements of air, water, fire and earth, of which two (water and fire) coincide with the Quran's list.

6 Many realities are endowed with religious meaning: a grandchild, referring to Jacob as Abraham's grandson, is a divine favour, a sign (Q:21:72); a neologism calls it a 'bonus' (*nāfilatan*; acc.; as a bonus; Q:17:79; 21:72), hence a special grace from God. The word for grandchildren, *ḥafadah* (pl., descendants) is also used (Q:16:72).

A person may reasonably expect a child but living to see another generation calls for special gratitude because, fortunately, generations, unlike centuries, occasionally overlap. Again, the mummified relics of the Pharaoh are a sign of God, a didactic reminder for later generations (Q:10:91). His body was saved on account of his near-death repentance.

7 The Quran never calls Muhammad a sign of God (*āyatu Allāh*) but commends his conduct as 'a beautiful pattern' (*uswatun ḥasanatun*; Q:33:21). Jesus and his mother are jointly described 'as a sign' (*āyatan*; Q:23:50) The deportment of evil persons can furnish 'signs for the seekers', a reference to Joseph's cruel but eventually repentant brothers (Q:12:7).

8 This distinction is explored in John Stuart Mill's posthumously published trio of essays. See his 'Nature', in *Nature, the Utility of Religion and Theism*, London: Longmans, Green, Reader, and Dyer, 1874, pp. 5–6.

9 *Imā'ah* (also *imā'*) is modern Arabic for sign or gesture. It is not used in the Quran.

10 The Greek *sumbolon* was more literal than ours. It referred to a mark or token that ratified treaties between states. A pair of symbola, as tallies used by parties to an agreement, could be two pieces of a bone or coin. A symbol can be understood as the union of two parts as complements; one attests or testifies to the other. In mature monotheism, we do not see the reality that the symbol purports to represent, hence the indispensability of the symbol. Nature and human community attest only symbolically to God's presence and wisdom.

11 Paul Tillich tried, unsuccessfully, to distinguish between symbols and signs. Symbols point beyond themselves to something else. But, surely, signs do so too although their significance is fixed by convention. Again, a symbol such as a crescent may function as a conventional sign (as it does when it merely indicates a mosque). Tillich obscurely claimed that symbols, unlike conventional signs, participate in the reality to which they point. He cites the case of a nation's flag as a symbolic reality. But a flag is more or less arbitrary and can be altered to reflect a new national self-image. Some symbols are purely conventional while others are not. Both signs and symbols can be misunderstood and can mislead. See Paul Tillich, *Dynamics of Faith*, New York: Harper & Row, 1957, pp. 41ff.

12 The range is already vast but we should also note related notions such as relics and the conventional use of certain colours and emblems. A lock of hair can signify the person who is loved just as a flag symbolizes a nation. The colour white is a symbol of purity.

13 A more fundamental discovery, namely, the priority of form (or function) over matter is more ancient, dating to Pythagoras. It allowed the birth of geometry.

14 Christine Overall argued for this view in her 'Miracles as Evidence against the Existence of God', *Southern Journal of Philosophy*, vol. 23, 1985, pp. 347–53. I criticize her position in my article listed in note 25 below.

15 The secular version of this principle is the law of nature's consistency. This is an unproven but not unjustified heuristic principle for scientific endeavour.

16 The American philosopher of science, Edward Grant contends rightly that while Muslim civilization gave birth to modern empirical science, the *institutionalization* of that enterprise was a European achievement. See his 'When did Modern Science begin?' in *The American Scholar*, Winter 97.

17 For example, in the case of a manufactured object such as a building: material cause (building materials); formal cause (the idea of the building in the mind of the architect); efficient cause (the builder); and final cause (a place to live in, to make money as a builder, and so on). For a natural object, the efficient and the final cause coalesce in the formal cause since all natural objects begin as ideas in the mind of God.

18 The theory of relativity was a crisis of methodological reform in physics. It showed how absolute Newtonian space–time was superseded by a relativizing of the perception of duration and length but it did not question the shared realist epistemology and

metaphysics of both paradigms; it accepted the objectivity of natural laws. The word 'relativity' is misleading since it does not correspond to the kind of relativism in areas such as morals where relativism implies that there is no objective moral standard or reality. Modern physics acknowledges an unexplained practical limitation on physical measurement but there is no fundamental shift in the meaning of physical reality as understood on the classical model. The classical view is compatible with the scriptural view of physical reality as objective.

19 Francis Bacon, *The New Organon and Related Writings*, Fulton Anderson (ed.), Indianapolis, IN: The Library of Liberal Arts, 1960, pp. 47–60, 114, 282. *Novum Organon* was published in Latin in 1620.

20 Fire is an ambiguous sign: it is a blessing indicating human society and warmth (Q:20:10; 27:7) especially in the desert (Q:56:71–3) but it is also the paradigm of divine punishment. The Prophetic traditions restrict punishment by fire to God; the Islamic penal code still prohibits the use of fire in punishing criminals since it is a divine prerogative.

21 For more on Islamic natural theology, see Majid Fakhry, 'The Classical Arguments for the Existence of God', *The Muslim World*, vol. 47, 1957, pp. 133–45.

22 William Lane Craig vs. Walter Sinnott-Armstrong, *God?: A Debate between a Christian and an Atheist*, New York: Oxford University Press, 2004, p. 64.

23 David Hume, *Dialogues Concerning Natural Religion*, Indianapolis, IN: Hackett, 1980, p. 37. See also p. 36. The *Dialogues* were published posthumously in 1779 but written earlier.

24 The word *qaṣd* occurs in the Quran (Q:16:9) and means showing or exhibiting something. The notion of displaying has a tenuous link to the concept of purpose (*maqṣid*). A branch of Islamic learning is called *maqāṣid al-sharī'ah,* the 'purposes' of the holy law.

25 This is valid by *modus ponens*. I explore the concept of divine purpose, in the context of divine causation and determination (and over-determination) of natural and supernatural events, in 'Miracles as Evidence for the Existence of God', *Scottish Journal of Religious Studies*, vol. XI, No.1, 1990, pp.18–23.

26 Bacon, op. cit., p. 25.

27 Orthodox Islam has no theodicy to explain either moral or natural evil. The Mu'tazilite rationalists tried to develop one but orthodoxy nipped it in the bud.

28 See also *mutashābihan* (allegorically; Q:2:25) and *mutashābihin* (in similitude; Q:6:99, 141).

9 Faith and the varieties of rejection

1 *A'jamiyy* and *fārsī* both mean Persian. Any non-Arab is called *a'jamiyy* in pejorative opposition to *'arabiyy* (Arab); *a'jamiyy* literally means any foreigner or person incapable of articulate or eloquent speech. (Prophetic traditions refer to Salmān Al-Fārsī, a Persian companion of the Prophet.) The reference in Q:30:2 is to the Persian capture of Jerusalem from the Byzantine Greek Christians in 614 AD. Al-Majūs, worshippers of the sacred fire, are probably Persian Zoroastrians. The Sabians are the Mandaeans, star worshippers who combined their creed with Gnostic and Judaeo-Christian ideas. Other groups include 'the companions of the wood' (*aṣ-ḥāb al-aykah*; Q:15:78; 26:176; 38:13; 50:14) who rejected Shu'ayb (Q:26:176-7). The people of Tubba'(Q:44:37; 50:14) refers to a royal Yemeni dynasty; 'the overthrown cities' (Q:53:53; 69:9) might refer to Sodom and Gomorrah and other rebellious cities of the plain. The identity and location of the Al-Rass tribe (Q:25:38; 50:12) is perhaps connected to shallow wells (the root meaning of *rass*) found in the centre of the Arab peninsula. The people of the elephant (Q:105:1) are identified with a military expedition, headed by elephants, to destroy the Meccan sanctuary in the year of Muhammad's birth. The Abyssinian Christian king of Yemen ordered the attack. It was unsuccessful; the Quran gives the credit to God (Q:105:1–5). Other communities include *aṣ-ḥāb*

al-ḥijr (people of the rocky tract; Q:15:80), a place north of Medina; and the *aṣ-ḥāb al-ukhdūd* (owners of the ditch; Q:85:4), an allusion to the last Himyarite king of Yemen, a Jew who persecuted Christians by burning them and throwing them into a ditch (Q:85:4–8).

2 Muhsin Khan (trans.), *Summarized Ṣaḥīḥ Al-Bukhārī*, Riyadh: Maktaba Dār Al-Salām, 1994, Part 23, The Book of Funerals, *ḥadīth* no. 680, p. 338. The tradition has a strong chain of transmission. The Prophet compares the new-born child to a wholesome animal born without mutilation. This dogma of humankind's original nature as perfectly submissive to God is a corollary of Islam's rejection of original sin. There is a Christian analogue to this claim in Paul's view that all human beings possess a rudimentary knowledge of God's existence, power and wisdom, a knowledge they wickedly seek to suppress (Romans 1:18–20).

3 The trilateral root *ka/fa/ra* occurs in different ways. Doubling the middle radical generates the intensive form *kaffārah* (Q:5:45, 89), a concealment of sin, an expiation or atonement for evil. (It is related to the Hebrew *kippūr*). *Kaffār* is the intensive form of *kāfir* (Q:14:34; 39:3). There are three plurals. The commonest (nominative) plural is *kafirūn* while *kuffār* is less often used. The third plural, *kawāfir* (gen. case) is used uniquely at Q:60:10. The frequent Quranic phase 'those who deny faith and reject our signs' (*allazina kafarū wa kazzabū bi āyātinā*; Q:2:39; 5:86; 84:22) uses *ka/fa/ra* and *ka/za/za/ba* in juxtaposition to capture two shades of meaning. The verb *la/ḥa/da* is also used with the preposition *fī* to mean distorting or perverting as in 'those who pervert our signs' (*yulḥidūna fī āyātinā*; Q:41:40). The associated sin of *ilḥād* (profanity) occurs in the context of pilgrimage to Mecca (Q:22:25).

4 'Master of immense grace' (*dhū faḍl al-ʿazīm*) is not listed among the 99 names of God although it is a Quranic name (Q:2:105; 8:29; 57:21, 29).

5 Much of the Quran's literary power is concentrated in these punishment narratives. For example, the 'Ad people were annihilated by a violent wind. 'God made it rage against them consecutively for seven nights and eight days; you could see people lying overwhelmed in its path, as if they were roots of hollow palm-trees, tumbled down' (Q:69:7). Another disobedient community is destroyed by a noisy thunderstorm (Q:69:4–5). This cycle of warning followed by dramatic punishment is repeated indefinitely as God continually apprises complacent human beings that the fruits of nemesis are bitter and rotten. For more on the Quran's punishment narratives and of the way they mirror Muhammad's struggles with his community, see David Marshall, *God, Muhammad and the Unbelievers*, London: Curzon, 1999.

6 'If ten Jews had believed in me, all the Jews would have believed in me.' Muhammad reportedly said this when he arrived in Medina. See Muhsin Khan, op. cit., Part 56, Book of the Merits of the Prophet's Companions, Chapter 47, *ḥadīth* number 1598, p. 754. The Prophet is referring to the quorum (*minyan*; Hebrew for number) necessary for public Jewish services. The Talmud claims that if ten Jewish men pray together, the divine presence graces the occasion.

7 The Hebrew Bible, however, in the *Nebi'īm* (Prophets) division, portrays God grieving over Israelite rejection.

8 Paul also uses the expression 'was darkened' (*eskotisthē*) in Romans 1:21 to describe the perverse rejection of God.

9 The biblical version (Exodus 4:21) suggests a divine arbitrium: the active hardening of the Pharaoh's heart is God's own rather wanton idea.

10 Q:60:10 uses *'iṣam al-kawāfir* (lit. the bond of infidelities) to refer simultaneously to the tie of marital and religious infidelity. The biblical link between religious and sexual infidelity is found in the *Nebi'īm* (Prophets), especially in the book of Hosea.

11 The treaty appeared to be detrimental to Muslim interests but was in fact, as time proved, to their final advantage. Compromise is here nourished by political necessity, not theological conviction.

378 Notes

12 Quranic recitation begins with a plea for immunity from diabolic influence. The formulaic expression used to do this derives from Q:3:36. Seeking this safeguard from the Devil precedes the mention of the name and mercy of God contained in the Invocation (Q:1:1).

13 Hebrews 11:6 reads (literally): 'It befits any-one who approaches God to believe that he is, and that, for those who are seeking him, he becomes a reward-giver.' And, as James writes with refined sarcasm in the context of a debate on faith and works: 'You believe that there is one God. Well done! Even the demons believe that – and tremble!' (James 2:19).

14 For further details, see Section 15 of Chapter 6.

15 The temptations of Jesus in the desert, especially the second temptation, implicitly condemn the experimental approach to supernatural faith. Ironically, in ages of revelation, belief in God was experimental. Elijah set up a crucial experiment to expose the false prophets (1 Kings 18:20–40). As for 'primitive' religion, it was unashamedly prudential and prescribed utilitarian acts of obeisance to placate the gods and ask for favours such as rain. Even today, it is not irreligious, I would argue, in the aftermath of the failure of classical natural theology, to pray for a grand miracle to disambiguate our ambivalent situation.

16 The ex-Jesuit Jack Miles traces the evolution in the character of Yahweh from a tribal deity to a universal God in his *God: A Biography*, New York: Alfred A Knopf, 1995. I review his effort in *The Times Higher Education Supplement*, December 1995. The Hebrew Bible's portrait of God is more developmental and gradualist than the one found in the Quran.

17 Pascal is a precursor of Kierkegaard in craving and thirsting for certainty in religion, a kind of religious analogue of Descartes' thirst for secular certitudes.

18 R.J. Hollingdale (trans.), *Ecce Homo*, Harmondsworth: Penguin, 1979, p. 51.

19 Simone de Beauvoir, *Adieux: A Farewell to Sartre*, Patrick O'Brien (trans.), London: Deutsch, Weidenfeld and Nicolson, 1984, p. 434.

20 In modern Arabic, *wasaniyy* means a person devoted to idols. It is not used in the Quran but a related word for idols (*awsan*; pl; Q:22:30; 29:17, 25) occurs. The word *ṣanam*, used always in plural (*aṣnām*; Q:7:138; 14:35; 21:57) occurs often. Modern Arabic uses *wasaniyyah* to denote idolatry. The translation of the Greek *idolatreia* in the Arabic translation of the Bible used by Christian and Jewish Arabs is not *shirk* but *wasaniyyah* which is not a Quranic neologism and conceals no theological depth.

21 There are several Quranic words for share or allotted portion: *naṣīb* (Q:4:7; 6:136; 28:77) and *qismah* (Q:4:8; 53:22) are the most widely used. The portion of inheritance or any good fortune is called *ḥazz* (Q:4:11; 28:79). The word *kifl* (*kiflayn*; acc. dual; 57:28) is rare and forms part of the name of *dhū al-kifl* (the man with a portion), referring arguably to Ezekiel (Q:21:85; 38: 48). A portion of sin is called *dhanb* (pl. *dhunūb*; Q:51:59). The Quran tends to restrict *shirk* to religious contexts.

22 If the passage refers to Ezra, it does not seem to correspond to any extant Jewish tradition. Admittedly Jewish literature is extensive: the Hebrew canon, apocryphal and pseudepigraphical works, the paraphrastic–exegetical materials of the Targum (amplified translations of the Hebrew Bible into Aramaic), and the Mishnaic and Talmudic (rabbinic) texts. The name 'Uzair, a diminutive in Arabic, makes one question whether the reference is to Ezra, the post-exilic priest and legislator, 'the second Moses', to whom we owe the existence of Judaism. If it is a reference to him, then it is odd because the Babylonian Exile or Captivity (586 B.C.E. – 38 BCE) had cured the Israelites of their inveterate idolatry. By Ezra's time, the worship of Yahweh is still tainted by hypocrisy and opportunism, vices among the failings of our common humanity, but there is none of the crude idolatry which angered Jeremiah and later Ezekiel, the prophet of the exile, and also infuriated Malachi, the last prophet in Judaism. The Quranic passage accusing Jews of committing idolatry in this particular way is isolated but Jews are often

accused elsewhere of being no better than idolaters and disbelievers (Q:2:87–103; 4:46; 5:41–3).

23 In the conflict between Moses and the Egyptian sorcerers (Q:7:103–26; 10:75–81; 20: 56–76; 26:10–51), the techniques of magic are exposed as fraudulent in the face of the miraculous serviceability of nature at the hands of Moses, God's spokesman. The magician–idolater Al-Samiriyy (Q:20:85–97) exemplifies the irreverent relationship to the supernatural world. See Chapter 8 for an exploration of the relationship between Islam's opposition to magic and the emergence of modern science.

24 Ninian Smart offered a polythetic characterization of religion in terms of seven dimensions of the sacred: the ritual, doctrinal, mythic, experiential, ethical, organizational and artistic. Smart defined religious studies as a descriptive science of all ultimate human commitments; he included traditional religions along with the secular ideologies of political nationalism and applied Marxism. See his comprehensive survey in *Dimensions of the Sacred*, London: HarperCollins, 1996.

25 *Romeo and Juliet*, Act II, scene ii, lines 100ff.

26 A moving discussion of this aspect of Raleigh's thought is in Jonathan Dollimore, *Death, Desire and Loss in Western Culture*, Harmondsworth: Penguin, 1998.

27 *Shirk al-ʿibādah* is contrasted with a lesser deviation such as *shirk al-mʿārifah*, attributing knowledge of the unseen to a human being. This is derived from Q:31:34 which lists five areas of knowledge as being forbidden to human beings: the time of the hour of judgement, the decision to send down rain, the contents of the wombs, future (human) actions, and the land in which one is destined to die.

28 Arab Christians use *al-badaliyyah* to refer to vicarious atonement by sinless substitution.

29 A secular analogue but not equivalent to modern idolatry is reification, a Marxist concept, associated with Georg Lukacs: we must avoid reducing a living and independently dignified being into a mere thing or commodity. Such reification leads to alienation. Alienation or self-alienation (*Selbstverfremdung*) is a related notion developed by Marx and his followers. Marx saw the religious life as a symptom of a self-estranged and unfulfilled human existence. He extended the Feuerbachian claim that God is a projection of our alienated human nature into a theory of social and political alienation.

30 Idolatry sounds anachronistic to us. Indifference to religious convictions and imperatives, however, characterizes our secular age just as enthusiasm and heresy marked the ages of religious passion. Indifference agitates Christian missionaries preaching the Gospel to westerners who believe in less and less every decade: the loss of faith in Christianity has been followed by a cynical rejection of the family, community, and even friendship and marriage. Inevitably, indifference is inarticulate. Indifferentists may refuse to tell us about the things that agitate them in their thoughtful moods. How can we deal with those who show no interest in the matter? How does one argue for the necessity of religion to someone who barely cares about the religious offer? Many westerners have abandoned the idea that religion can offer solutions to life's problems, especially, the universal complications of identity, love, and belonging. Some would, however, reject only established religion rather than the private individual's religious or spiritual search for transcendent meaning. They would argue that they are indifferent to the offers of religious officialdom, not to God. And these two would coincide only in the case of highly institutionalized faiths such as Roman Catholicism and Shi'ism.

31 Realism is the philosophical doctrine that there is an objectively correct way of seeing the world since there exists a world independent of human thought and language. Anti-realism would emphasize the language-dependence of reality and the primacy of personal subjectivity. Anti-realism resembles idealism - the view that the familiar material world is dependent for its existence on minds. Anti-realism also shares some features with pragmatism.

32 David Swenson (trans.), *Concluding Unscientific Postscript*, Princeton, NJ: Princeton University Press, 1941, pp. 179–80. (The introduction, notes and completion of translation are by Walter Lowrie.)

33 Ibid., p. 178.

10 Human nature and the Quran

1 Only in human beings does existence precede essence.

2 Jean-Paul Sartre, *Existentialism and Humanism*, Philip Mairet (trans.), London: Eyre Methuen, 1948, 1973, p. 56. Anna Boschetti has called him the Pope of his movement in her *The Intellectual Enterprise: Sartre and 'Les Temps Modernes'*, Richard McCleary (trans.), Evanston, IL: Northwestern University Press, 1988, p. 18.

3 Cf. Psalms 8:4. The Quran never quotes from the Bible except for a verse (in Arabic translation) from the Psalms at Q:21:105. The quotation resembles Psalm 23:13 and Psalm 37:11, 29. Psalm 37:11 is quoted in Matthew 5:5 as one of the beatitudes: 'The meek (*praeis*) shall inherit the earth'. The Quran uses *ṣāliḥūn* (the righteous) instead of meek.

4 Muslim art is aniconic. The Quran opposes the worship of idols, not necessarily the manufacture of images (Q:34:13). For commentary on *imago Dei*, see Claus Westermann, *Creation*, John Scullion, SJ (trans.), Philadelphia: Fortress Press, 1974.

5 The Jewish philosopher–exegete Maimonides holds a similar view: one is only entitled to discuss negative, not positive, attributes of God. See his *Guide for the Perplexed*, 1:51, 54, 60. For discussion, see Barry Freundel, *Contemporary Orthodox Judaism's Response to Modernity*, Jersey City, NJ: KTAV, 2004. Maimonides was probably influenced by Ash'arite theology.

6 This high regard for humankind is no incidental emphasis. In Q:17:70, the verbs *karramnā* (we conferred special favours) and *faḍḍalnā* (we preferred above others) are both intensive in meaning as indicated by the doubled middle radicals. The only contrary assertion is in Q:76:1 which asks cryptically and rhetorically: 'Has there not been over man a long period of time (*al-dahr*) when he was nothing – [not worthy of being] mentioned?' This might refer to the late appearance of our species in the history of the universe.

7 Quoted in A.J. Arberry, *Sufism*, New York: Harper Torchbooks, 1970, p. 28. Such a saying is called a *ḥadīth qudsī* (holy narrative). It was revealed to Muhammad but he was instructed not to include it in the Quran.

8 It corresponds to conscience although the Quranic term is more active in connotation.

9 Compare the Platonic view about the tripartite division of the soul: the spirit and the appetites were like two wild untamed horses that needed to be controlled by reason, the third part. This control was to be exercised individually and socially, hence Plato's preference for authoritarian rule.

10 The Invocation is the phrase, 'In the name of God, the Merciful (*Al-Raḥmān*), the compassionate (*Al-Raḥīm*).' It does not open Chapter 9 but occurs once inside a chapter in a letter by Solomon addressed to Sheba (Q:27:30). Except in the opening chapter (Q:1:1), the Invocation is not numbered as a separate verse.

11 Metaphorically it refers to heaven (*jannah*, sing., Q:2:35; *jannāt*; pl. at Q:2:25). The root *ja/na/na* supplies words indicating a thing that is dense or hidden from view – for example, by foliage (as in a garden). It also refers to an embryo (*janīn,* sing.) hidden in the womb (*ajinnah*; pl.; Q:53:32). The jinn (pl; *jinnī,* sg.) are so-called since they are invisible denizens of our world. This simultaneous branching out into the literal, metaphorical and transcendent is characteristic of Arabic and indicates that Arab metaphysics assumed the commerce between the sensible and the supra-sensible worlds.

12 In the Quran, as in the Bible, the Devil is called by pejorative titles. He is the arch-deceiver (Q:31:33) who makes human evil appear beautiful. Iblīs resembles the

Greek *diabolos*; the Arabic *Al-Shayṭān* resembles the Hebrew *Satan* meaning advocate. Satan is not an important figure in the Hebrew Bible. In the New Testament and the Quran, however, he is an active and malicious historical agent.

13 A form of this simple verb appears in the augmented form of *istaqāma*, meaning 'to straighten out': a hint of struggle and recalcitrance reside in its formation and meaning. The active voice describes the behaviour of believers as those who 'remain straightened out' (*istaqāmū*) after acknowledging that God is their Lord (Q:41:6, 30; 46:13).

14 The law has other sources including analogical reasoning (*qiyās*), consensus (*ijmā'*), and personal intellectual effort (*ijtihād*). All actions – moral, legal, and spiritual – are on a continuum. Between the extremes of absolutely obligatory and absolutely forbidden are the intermediate categories of commendable, neutral, and reprehensible (but permitted). For more on Islamic law and its differences from western law, see my 'Relationships Between Muslim Parents and Children in a Non-Muslim Country', Michael King (ed.), *God's Law versus State Law*, London: Grey Seal, 1995, pp. 31–43. I explore the issues in a simpler way in 'Do not Mock the *Sharī'ah* as Barbaric!' in *The Independent*, September 1997.

15 This verse echoes the Prophet's inaugural call at Mt Ḥirā' by using the same masculine singular imperative *iqra'* (Q:96:1).

16 Theology is not the study of God but a study about God. Indeed 'thealogy' as the study of the goddess is popular with pagan and feminist 'thealogians'. Aquinas defines theology as the discipline which speaks of all things in terms of their relation to God. In Islam, theology collapses into hermeneutics and law since the classical Muslim mind is largely exegetical and analogical: it deals with legal practicality, not theological speculation.

17 Do not confuse this maxim with the related Quranic motto 'God does not burden a soul with more than it can bear', discussed in Section 13 of this chapter.

18 Only Adam is appointed. The noun *khalīfah* has no feminine form although lexically it appears to be feminine.

19 John Calvin would have denied the first part of Locke's estimate of humankind. Notwithstanding that, Calvin tried to establish a theocracy!

20 *Iblīs* is not a fallen angel but rather one of the elemental beings made of fire. Like humankind, these beings, the jinn, are free to accept or reject God (Q:15:26; 37:71). Satan was a jinn (Q:18:50) and could therefore disobey God. Angels are not free to disobey God and hence cannot fall from grace through disobedience.

21 The Quran does not identify the members of this sub-group but commentators speculate that the prophets of resolve are Noah, Abraham, Moses, Jesus and Muhammad. All except Noah received scriptures. Abraham's scripture, simply called 'scrolls' (*ṣuhuf*; Q:53:36–7; 87:18–19), is no longer extant even in fragmentary form.

22 No one can understand the military success of Islam without studying these two Quranic chapters. Salaḥ Al-Dīn Ayyūbī (1138–94 CE), the chivalrous Saladin of western fame, required all his soldiers to memorize these two chapters as a condition of enlisting in his army. The two Quranic chapters demand military discipline and zeal. Towards the end of his life, Ayyūbī fasted constantly to make up for the many fasts he missed as a result of being at war and is said to have taken a vow never to smile until he had re-conquered Jerusalem from the Crusaders. He died of physical exhaustion. His reputation for chivalry is deserved but he was not the playful and fun-loving knight of western romance.

23 The caliph 'Uthman refers to this army of Tabuk and of his role in equipping it. See Muhsin Khan (trans.), *Summarized Ṣaḥīḥ Al-Bukhari*, Riyadh: Maktaba Dār Al-Salām, 1994, Part 52, Book of Wills and Testaments, Chapter 7, *ḥadīth* number 1202, p. 578. Here we ignore the moral question of the type of zeal appropriate to faith: the question of the moral legitimacy as opposed to political or strategic necessity of ancient Islamic militancy in the pursuit of empire or (in the modern world) resistance to western

encroachment on Muslim lands and natural resources. We deal only with the psychology and rationality of enthusiastic religious motivation.

24 See also Q:3:168. 'The sitting ones' also refers to those Israelites who refused to fight their way into the promised land (Q:5:24). *Al-qā'ida* is from this root and implies stability and firmness, the positive sense of sitting secure in one place. The word literally means foundations (or pillars). The same root also yields *al-qawā'id* (pl.), the Quranic euphemism for older women past the prospect of marriage (Q:24:60). These women need not conceal what little may be left of their beauty. The word is related to the Hebrew *Akeidah* which refers to the 'binding' of Isaac by Abraham (Genesis 22).

25 Descartes has this honour. William Barrett has correctly questioned this dogma: 'Kant can justly be called the father of modern philosophy, for out of him stem nearly all the still current and contending schools of philosophy: Positivism, Pragmatism and Existentialism.' See Barrett's *Irrational Man*, Garden City, NY: Doubleday, Anchor Books, 1962, p. 162.

26 Commenting on the reward of eternal life, Aquinas argues that 'by such a reward the will is moved to assent to what is proposed, although the mind is not moved by anything understood' (*De Veritate*, 14.1). For Thomas's views, see Brian Davies (ed.), *The Thought of Thomas Aquinas*, Oxford: Oxford University Press, 1992, which contains this quotation.

27 The morality of this motivation is a different matter. This Quranic doctrine has been abusively criticized by secularists alarmed at the violent enthusiasm of Islamic resistance to western colonial designs. Prudish Christian critics mock it: a person lives a life of self-restraint until death only to be resurrected to a life of sensual self-indulgence for all eternity! Undeniably, the Quran contains superb poetry about the delights of paradise, including sexual pleasure, but adds that attaining the pleasure of God is the highest prize in the hereafter (Q:9:72), a caveat ignored by Christian, secular, and even Muslim readers!

28 This book, known as *Qohelet* (the gatherer) in Hebrew, is in the least holy (third) portion of the Hebrew Bible. Its canonization is unjustified since its message is blatantly sceptical and bitter, its central moral observations subversive of Hebrew ethics. Biblical critics detect traces of a pious redactor adding a religious veneer to what was originally a nihilistic pericope. This suspicion is confirmed as we note contradictions such as the rejection of an after-life at 3:18–22 followed by its acceptance much later at 12:7. The book is attributed to Solomon, the sage who is said to have written it in his old age. This is a standard literary fiction since Solomon is the father of all wisdom in Israel.

29 Most Jews believe in an after-life. 'All Israel has a share in the after-life.' See Mishnah Sanhedrin 10:1, Sanhedrin 90a, quoted by Freundel, op. cit., p. 175. The Sadducees denied the resurrection, the after-life, and the Messiah since these concepts are not mentioned explicitly in the Torah, the earliest and holiest part of the Hebrew Bible.

30 The word for life is used in the indefinite singular (*hayātin*, a life) to indicate contempt: Jews would opt for any kind of life, even one of disgrace and misery, if only they could avoid death.

31 *Islām* is here declined as *silm*. The usage is unique to this passage.

32 Traditionally, Semitic cultures began the new day at evening, just after the evening (*maghrib*) prayer in Muslim lands. Industrialized and urbanized cultures prefer the convention of the midnight hour which has no basis in nature.

33 Legal majority is attained at about age 12 or 13 in most law codes.

34 Calvin's *Commentary on Psalms* 73:6. Psalm 73 is a hymn to the triumph of divine justice. The translation from the Latin is mine.

35 This is not a Quranic term but it derives from *hisāb* (reckoning) which is a frequent Quranic term (Q:13:40; 88:26). The derived neologism *husbān* (plural) refers to thunderbolts sent from heaven as divine punishment (Q:18:40).

36 The enthusiasm of past ages is foreign to us; we would call it fanaticism. The word for zeal is *ḥamās*, an acronym of the Islamic movement active in modern Palestine. The adjective is *mutaḥammis* (zealous). The word does not occur in the Quran.

37 For more on asceticism in the world's religions, see Vincent Wimbush and Richard Valantasis (eds), *Asceticism*, New York: Oxford University Press, 1995.

38 These include poverty and the renunciation of property, the vows of celibacy and complete obedience to superiors, which together form the basis of the monastic life. Islam rejects monasticism as unnatural and unscriptural. Incidentally, the treasury of merits earned by such works of supererogation, inspired by counsels of perfection, supplied the indulgences sold by the Catholic Church. Indirectly, this corrupt practice laid the foundations of the Reformation.

39 '… [I]t is the mark of an educated man to look for precision in each class of things just so far as the nature of the subject admits.' David Ross (trans.), *The Nicomachean Ethics*, Oxford: Oxford University Press, 1980, Book 1, Chapter 3, 1094^b24, p. 3.

40 After Noah's son drowns in the deluge, Noah complains to God that the divine promise was to save his family and that his son was part of his family. God replies that a rebellious or sinful son forfeits membership of a righteous family. The exchange is marked by a divine brevity which shocks us (Q:11:45–7). This tradition is not found in the Bible.

41 This tradition is reported in the traditionist Muhammad Ibn 'Isā Al-Tirmidhī's *The Collection (Jami')*. It has strong support.

11 'Greater is God!'

1 The neologism *ḥayawān*, used uniquely here, replaces the normal word for life (*ḥāyah*) which occurs often as 'the life of the world' (*al-ḥayāt al-dunyā*; Q:6:130; 14:27). *Al-ḥayāt al-ṭayyiba* is used in Islamic ethics (*al-akhlāq*) to refer to the good life, a notion borrowed from Greek ethics – although the Quran has 'a good life' (*ḥayātan ṭayyibatan*; Q:16:97). Summaries of Islamic morals occur at: Q:2:177, 17:22–39, 23:1–11; 25: 63–76, 31:12–19, 70:23–35. Islamic morals are mainly original but some elements are negative, based on a repudiation of pagan morality (see Q:17:26–7, 31). Abū Naṣr Al-Fārābi (d. 950) and Abū Ali Miskawayh (d. 1030) both wrote treatises on Islamic ethics.

2 The city of Cairo is eulogized as *Al-Qāhirah*, the conqueror.

3 Like Islam, Judaism has few credal doctrines. The cardinal teachings of the catechism for children are: *kabbalat ol malkhūt shamay'im* (acceptance of the yoke of heaven) and *torah tzivah lanū mosheh* (the Torah was given to us by Moses).

4 Jews find that fidelity to law (*halakhah*) and Jewish values serve as a check against mystical kabbalistic excesses, especially false claims to being the Messiah.

5 Abū Qasim Al-Junayd of Baghdad (d. 910) represented sober devotional Sufism.

6 Al-Ghazāli (d. 1111) laboured to make orthodox law-centred Islam compatible with a potentially antinomian Sufi mysticism. Sufi pantheism, however, especially the monist variety associated with the thirteenth-century Spanish mystic Muḥyi Al-Din Ibn Al-'Arabi (d. 1240), inevitably estranged orthodoxy. (The mainstream suspicion of Sufism persists to this day, abetted by the fact that most western converts opt for Sufism rather than mainstream Islam.) While the Quran was not ontologically monist, it rejected the moral dualism of Persian Zoroastrianism which saw light and darkness as independent powers. The Quran sees darkness and light as equally God's creation (Q:6:1; 113:1–3) but subordinates Satan to God (Q:7:11–18; 38:78–83).

7 The tenth-century mystic–saint Manṣūr Al-Ḥallāj (d. 922) had ecstatically exclaimed 'Ana Al-Ḥaqq!' (I am the truth), identifying himself with God. He was brutally executed, ostensibly for offences against the dignity of the holy law (*Sharī'ah*). Many historians suspect sectarian politics in Abbasid Baghdad. Al-Ḥallāj was a secret sympathizer of the Qarmatians, an extremist Isma'ili sect that threatened the Baghdad government.

Al-Ḥallāj was also suspected of Christian sympathies since he apparently believed in *ḥulūl* (divine indwelling or incarnation).

8 He may be identified with Jonah, one of the Minor Prophets, but the Quranic Jonah would repudiate the ethnic conservatism of this part of the Hebrew Bible. (The book of Ruth is an internal corrective to the racist outlook of Jonah.) Reform Jews treat the Jonah narrative as a fable. The Quran treats it as literal history. Prophets do not question the divine will although God allows a fugitive expression of specific grievances from these men whom he befriends and loves. Those who enjoyed close relationships with God could, naturally, occasionally question the ways of the Almighty. Hence, the case of Noah who complains about the drowning of his son in the deluge after God promised deliverance for Noah's whole household (Q:11:42–7).

9 The Quran contains countless powerful passages about hell (e.g. Q:4:55–6; Q: 22:19–22; 47:15; 69:30–7; 51:42–56).

10 This lack of sentimentality distinguishes it temperamentally from the second and third divisions of the Hebrew Bible (*Tanakh*) and from much of the New Testament.

11 God rewarded the God-fearing Joseph by plotting on his behalf so that he could lawfully detain his brother under the royal Egyptian law code (Q:12:76).

12 God is the only owner. All land is an endowment or trust (*waqf*; pl. *awqāf*). The holy land (*al-arḍ al-muqaddasah*; Q:5:22) is a divine trust and belongs solely to God. Its human owners merely administer the trust of property.

13 For Muslim female perspectives, see Leila Ahmed, *Women and Gender in Islam*, New Haven: Yale University Press, 1992, and Amina Wadud, *Qur'an and Woman: Reading the Sacred Text from a Woman's Perspective*, New York: Oxford University Press, 1999. For a sociological and historical survey, see Nikki Keddie and Beth Baron (eds), *Women in Middle Eastern History*, New Haven: Yale University Press, 1991. The Norwegian scholar Tove Stang Dahl offers a Christian critique of Muslim family values among the urban poor in her case-study, *The Muslim Family: A Study of Women's Rights in Islam*, Ronald Walford (trans.), Oslo, Boston: Scandinavian University Press, 1997.

14 Donald Schon, 'The Loss of the Stable State', in Herbert Richardson and Donald Cutler (eds), *Transcendence*, Boston: Beacon Press, 1969, p. 64.

15 Sufis use the term *fanā'* to refer to the annihilation of the mortal self in God, the only true and immortal agent.

16 The annual pilgrimage, including its shorter version (*'umra*), is the only duty ordained in relatively precise detail in the Quran (Q:2:158, 196–200; 22:26–37).

17 In pre-Islamic Arabia, *muru'ah* (virility) was linked to virtue. Our word 'virtue' is also linked to strength and manliness through the Latin *vir* (man). The expression 'in virtue of' meaning 'by the authority or power invested in' preserves the link to the original sense.

18 Defensive jihad in defence of Islamic territory is an individual duty (*farḍ al-'ayn*) incumbent on all Muslims. Offensive jihad, in pursuit of empire, is a collective duty (*farḍ al-kifāyah*, lit. duty of the sufficiency), a vicarious obligation performed by a select group in order to render blameless the rest of society. It derives from Q:9:122 by *ijtihād* (exercise of personal reasoning). The whole (able-bodied) community must not go to war; a contingent of scholars should remain at home so that they can advise the fighters about the Islamic life-style once they return to civilian life. (Only a caliph can authorize or declare the jihad.)

19 'Even a smile is charity' is a Prophetic tradition.

20 Islamic tradition, based on the Prophet's sayings, cites 21 ways of attaining martyrdom, among which a popular one is death caused by the rigours of the Meccan pilgrimage. The Prophet told his followers that, in preparation for burial, the angels themselves wash the bodies of martyrs who fall on the battlefield. Muhammad was not a martyr.

21 A benefit of having no philosophical culture is that Muslims have not been tempted by the reductionism rampant among Christians updating their faith to suit the post-positivist, post-Christian world. Islam has not produced the equivalent of a Rudolf Bultmann or a Don Cupitt. Some Muslim apologists, under western pressure, do, however, try to attenuate modern Islam's *political* ambitions by claiming, what is patently untrue, that even the classical jihad was a defensive undertaking rather than an aggressive military outreach for universal conquest.

22 Mosques in Muhammad's day were simple places of worship, functional and fragile, reflecting the transient futility of this life. The Prophet's mosque in Medina was orig-inally a humble, dust-coloured and frail structure. Along with the Holy Mosque in Mecca, it was frequently extended by rulers paying homage to Islam.

23 Sidney Brichto and Richard Harries (eds), *Two Cheers for Secularism*, Yelvertoft Manor: Pilkington Press, 1998. Rabbi Brichto and Bishop Harries seem, at times, to be giving three cheers.

24 Reductionism is found in the work of the South African progressive writer Farid Esack whose reading of the Quran is seen by orthodox Muslims as an abject capitulation to secular criteria. Predictably he has been accused of trying to Christianize Islam in an attempt to impress Anglo-American audiences. See his *On Being a Muslim*, Oxford: Oneworld, 1999. The book is titled after Hans Kung's tome *On Being a Christian*, a summa of modern Catholic anguish. Esack's slim volume, however, is written in a flippantly joyful style reminiscent of a teenage magazine. I reviewed it in *The Times Higher Education Supplement*, December 1999. Esack is in good company: the careers of 'Muslim' scholars who write on Islam, in western academia, is increasingly a tri-umph of image management. Authentic Muslims do not recognize themselves in their pages.

12 Preface to a philosophy of Islam

1 J.L. Mackie, *The Miracle of Theism*, Oxford: Clarendon Press, 1982. The title alludes to a Humean witticism that nothing short of a miracle could produce religious belief.

2 Richard Howard (trans.), *Diary of a Genius*, London: Pan Books, Picador edition, 1976, p. 52.

3 Albert Camus, 'The Absurd Man', in Justin O'Brien (trans.), *The Myth of Sisyphus and Other Essays*, New York: Vintage Books, 1991, p. 67.

4 Protagoras of Abdera (c. 490–20 BCE), mentioned by Plato in the Meno (*Men.*, 91E), wrote: 'Of all things (*chrēmata*), the measure is man, of the things that are that they are, and of the things that are not that they are not' (Fragment # 1). The meaning of this, as with all pre-Socratic writings, is unclear.

5 Ismail Al-Faruqi, *Islamization of Knowledge*, Herndon, VA: IIIT, 1982.

6 I have discussed al-Faruqi's Islamization project in my review of John Esposito (ed.), *The Oxford Encyclopedia of the Modern Islamic World*, New York: Oxford University Press, 1995, four volumes. My review is in *The Times Higher Education Supplement*, September 1995.

7 See Jared Diamond, *Collapse: How Societies Choose to Fail or Succeed*, New York: Viking Penguin, 2005. Diamond is a bio-geographer who examines eco-collapse and lists some dozen geographic factors that explain the debacle of entire societies.

8 Shabbir Akhtar, *The Light in the Enlightenment*, London: Grey Seal, 1990, Chapter 5.

9 For more on classical Islamic scholasticism, see Majid Fakhry, 'The Classical Arguments for the Existence of God', *The Muslim World,* vol. 47, 1957, pp. 133–45.

10 Vatican I, *Constitutio de Fide Catholica*, caput 2. The dogma of papal infallibility for *ex cathedra* pronouncements was promulgated by this council whose proceedings were suspended when Italian troops occupied Rome in October 1870.

11 Kai Nielsen, *Atheism and Philosophy*, Amherst, NY: Prometheus, 2005, Chapters 3, 5, and 11.

12 Hugo Meynell, *The Intelligible Universe*, London: Macmillan, 1982, pp. 1–6.

13 Richard Swinburne, *The Coherence of Theism*, Oxford: Clarendon Press, 1977.

14 See Terence Penelhum, *Reason and Religious Faith*, Boulder, Col: Westview Press, 1995; Anthony Kenny, *Faith and Reason*, New York: Columbia University Press, 1983.

15 See Alvin Plantinga, *God and Other Minds*, Ithaca, NY: Cornell University Press, 1967; John Hick, *Arguments for the Existence of God*, London: Macmillan, 1971, and his *Faith and Knowledge*, Ithaca, NY: Cornell University Press, 1966; Basil Mitchell, *The Justification of Religious Belief*, New York: Seabury Press, 1973.

16 For recent work on natural theology, see William Lane Craig's debate with the atheist Walter Sinnott-Armstrong in their *God?: A Debate Between a Christian and an Atheist*, New York: Oxford University Press, 2004, and Yeager Hudson, *The Philosophy of Religion*, Mountain View, CA: Mayfield, 1991, pp. 73–116.

17 For an appraisal of Kant's views, see Richard Schacht, *Classical Modern Philosophers: Descartes to Kant*, London: Routledge & Kegan Paul, 1984, pp. 221–58, especially pp. 249–58 on the possibility of theology and rational theology.

18 Richard Schacht discusses Hume's dismissive comments at the end of his *The Inquiry Concerning Human Understanding* in Schacht, op. cit., p. 183. See also pp. 175–220.

19 'Of Miracles' in Hume's *Enquiry Concerning Human Understanding*, Section 10. For arguments that challenge the a priori Humean judgement that miracles cannot form a reliable part of history, see Gary Colwell, 'Miracles and History', *Sophia*, vol. 22, no. 2, 1983, pp. 9–14 and J.C. Thornton, 'Miracles and God's Existence', *Philosophy*, vol. 59, 1984, pp. 219–29.

20 David Hume, *A Treatise of Human Nature*, 2nd revised edition of L.A. Selby-Bigge with text revised and notes by P.H. Nidditch, New York: Oxford University Press, 1978, Book 1, Part IV, Section 2, p. 187.

21 Hume's admirers tend to be be overly impressed by his attacks on Christianity and never note these double standards in his thought.

22 Hume's sceptical views on causality are anticipated by Al-Ghazālī. Both philosophers' views are anticipated by the Buddha who questioned our untutored intuitions of causality and our firm but rationally unjustified belief in the persistence of the self over time.

23 John Smith, 'Faith, Belief, and the Problem of Rationality in Religion', in C.F. Delaney (ed.), *Rationality and Religious Belief*, Notre Dame, IN: University of Notre Dame Press, 1979, p. 58.

24 See Richard Rorty, *Philosophy and the Mirror of Nature*, Princeton, NJ: Princeton University Press, 1979.

25 Most western philosophers required a God of the gaps to complete their systems: Plato, Aristotle, Augustine, Anselm, Aquinas, of course, but also Descartes, Spinoza, Leibniz, Locke, Berkeley, Kant, Hegel, Schopenhauer, Peirce, James, Bergson, and Whitehead. Most of these philosophers – the exceptions are the three medieval saint–thinkers – needed God as a hypothesis rather than as a being worthy of unconditional worship.

26 This is Anthony Kenny's motto in his *A Brief History of Western Philosophy*, Oxford: Blackwell, 1998. This successfully replaces Bertrand Russell's *History of Western Philosophy*.

27 Rorty set out his stall in two tracts; the first is mentioned in note 24 above. He strengthened and refined his thesis in *Consequences of Pragmatism*, Minneapolis: University of Minnesota Press, 1982. See also Cornel West, *The American Evasion of Philosophy: A Genealogy of Pragmatism*, Madison: University of Wisconsin Press, 1989.

28 *The International Journal of Philosophical Studies* (IJPS) was a re-launch of *Philosophical Studies*, a journal founded in Ireland in 1953. Under the editorship of Dermot Moran, it was re-launched in 1998 by Routledge.

29 I am thinking of Michal Ignatieff and John Gray, both widely seen as establishment liberals. Gray's apologia for universal western military hegemony is wrapped in a liberal cloth. See his *Enlightenment's Wake: Politics and Culture at the Close of the Modern*

Age, London: Routledge, 1995. I have reviewed it in *The Times Higher Education Supplement*, December 1995.

30 See Kenneth Cragg, *The Arab Christian: A History in the Middle East*, London: Mowbray, 1992. Cragg discusses the Coptic Christian influences on Nagib Mahfouz, an Egyptian writer suspected of being an apostate. I have reviewed Cragg's book in *Muslim World Book Review*, Vol. 13, No. 1, 1992, pp. 49–50. Albert Hourani's *Arabic Thought in the Liberal Age 1798–1939*, Cambridge: Cambridge University Press, 1983, originally published in 1962, examines the emergence of secular nationalism in the Arab Middle East as it confronted colonial European influence. In the background are two partly indigenous trends: restating ancient Islamic social principles in suitably modern forms and separating religion from politics. Both trends continue to characterize the contemporary Middle East. Hourani discusses mainly Egypt and Lebanon.

Bibliography

There are no philosophical works on the Quran's engagement with secularism. The Al-Bukhari collection listed here contains all of Muhammad's canonical traditions quoted or paraphrased in this book. Precise references are given only in the case of lesser known traditions.

Abū Zakrah, Muhammad, *I'jāz al-Qurān*, Egypt: Dār Al-Fikr Al-Arabiyy, 1970.

Adler, Margot, *Drawing Down the Moon*, New York, NY: Penguin, 1979, 1986.

Agostino, Cilardo, *The Quranic Term Kalala*, Edinburgh: Edinburgh University Press, 2005.

Ahmed, Akbar, *Post-Modernism and Islam*, London: Routledge, 1992.

Ahmed, Leila, *Women and Gender in Islam*, New Haven: Yale University Press, 1992.

Akhtar, Shabbir, *The Muslim Poetic Imagination*, London: Scorpion, 1992.

Arberry, A.J., *Sufism*, New York: Harper Torchbooks, 1970.

Ayoub, Mahmoud, *Islam: Faith and History*, Oxford: Oneworld, 2004.

Bacon, Francis, *The New Organon and Related Writings*, Fulton Anderson (ed.), Indianapolis, IN: The Library of Liberal Arts, 1960.

Baqillānī, Al-, *I'jāz Al-Qurān*, Cairo: Al-Matba'ah Al-Salafiyyah, 1930.

Barth, Karl, *Dogmatics in Outline*, Colin Gunton (trans.), London: SCM Press, 2001.

Barrett, William, *Irrational Man*, Garden City, NY: Doubleday, 1962.

Berman, David, *A History of Atheism in Britain: From Hobbes to Russell*, London, New York: Croom Helm, 1988; Routledge, 1990.

Boulares, Habib, *The Fear and the Hope*, Lewis Ware (trans.), London: Zed Books, 1990.

Braaten, Carl and Philip Clayton (eds), *The Theology of Wolfhart Pannenberg*, Minneapolis, MN: Augsburg Publishing House, 1988.

Brichto, Sidney and Richard Harries (eds), *Two Cheers for Secularism*, Yelvertoft Manor: Pilkington Press, 1998.

Bucaille, Maurice, *The Bible, the Qur'an and Science*, A.D. Pannell and Maurice Bucaille (trans.), Paris: Seghers, 1983), 10th edition.

Bukhari, Al-, *Summarized Ṣaḥīḥ Al-Bukhārī*, Muhsin Khan (trans.), Riyadh: Maktaba Dār Al-Salām, 1994.

Burton, John, *The Collection of the Qur'an*, Cambridge: Cambridge University Press, 1977.

Cahn, Steven (ed.), *Reason at Work*, New York: Harcourt Brace & Co., 1996.

Camus, Albert, *The Myth of Sisyphus and Other Essays*, Justin O'Brien (trans.), New York: Vintage Books, 1991.

Chesterton, G.K., *Orthodoxy*, Garden City, NY: Doubleday, 1959.

Cragg, Kenneth, *Muhammad and the Christian*, London: Darton, Longman and Todd, 1984, reprinted by Oneworld, 1999.

Craig, William Lane vs. Walter Sinnott-Armstrong, *God?: A Debate Between a Christian and an Atheist*, New York: Oxford University Press, 2004.

Cupitt, Don, *After God: The Future of Religion*, London: Weidenfeld and Nicolson, 1997.

Dahl, Tove Stang, *The Muslim Family: A Study of Women's Rights in Islam*, Ronald Walford (trans.), Oslo, Boston: Scandinavian University Press, 1997.

Davies, Brian (ed.), *Philosophy of Religion*, Washington: Georgetown University Press, 1998.

—— *The Thought of Thomas Aquinas*, Oxford: Oxford University Press, 1992.

Delaney, C.F. (ed.), *Rationality and Religious Belief*, Notre Dame, IN: University of Notre Dame Press, 1979.

Denny, Frederick, *An Introduction to Islam*, Upper Saddle River, NJ: Pearson Prentice Hall, 2006.

Diamond, Jared, *Collapse: How Societies Choose to Fail or Succeed*, New York: Viking Penguin, 2005.

Dollimore, Jonathan, *Death, Desire and Loss in Western Culture*, Harmondsworth: Penguin, 1998.

Donohue, John and John Esposito (eds), *Islam in Transition*, New York: Oxford University Press, 2007.

Ehteshami, Anoushiravan, *After Khomeini: The Iranian Second Republic*, London: Routledge, 1995.

Engels, Friedrich, *Anti-Duhring: Herr Eugen Duhring's Revolution in Science*, reprinted in Eleanor Kuykendall (ed.), *Philosophy in the Age of Crisis*, New York: Harper & Row, 1970.

Esack, Farid, *On Being a Muslim*, Oxford: Oneworld, 1999.

—— *The Quran: A Short Introduction*, Oxford: Oneworld, 2002.

Esposito, John (ed.) *The Oxford Encyclopedia of the Modern Islamic World*, New York: Oxford University Press, 1995.

Fakhry, Majid, 'The Classical Arguments for the Existence of God', *The Muslim World*, vol. 47, 1957, pp. 133–45.

Faruqi, Ismail Al-, *Islamization of Knowledge*, Herndon, VA: IIIT, 1982.

—— *'Urubah and Religion*, Amsterdam: Djambatan, 1962, 2 volumes.

Freundel, Barry, *Contemporary Orthodox Judaism's Response to Modernity*, Jersey City, NJ: KTAV, 2004.

Gaukroger, Stephen, *Descartes: An Intellectual Biography*, Oxford: Oxford University Press, 1995.

Ghazālī, Abu Ḥāmid, Al-, *Deliverance from Error*, Richard McCarthy (trans.), Louisville: KY: Fons Vitae, 2000.

—— *The Incoherence of the Philosophers*, Michael Marmura (trans.), Provo, UT: Brigham Young University Press, 2000.

Gibb, H.A.R., *Mohammedanism: An Historical Survey*, London: Oxford University Press, 1969.

Grant, Edward, 'When did Modern Science begin?' in *The American Scholar*, Winter 97.

Gray, John, *Enlightenment's Wake: Politics and Culture at the Close of the Modern Age*, London: Routledge, 1995.

Haleem, M.A.S. Abdel, 'Grammatical Shift for the Rhetorical Purposes: *Iltifāt* and Related Features in the Quran' in *Bulletin of the School of Oriental and African Studies*, vol. LV, Part 3, 1992.

Hardy, Thomas *Wessex Poems and Other Verses*, New York: Harper, 1898.

Harris, Stephen, *The New Testament*, Mountain View, CA: Mayfield Publishing Co., 1995.

Honderich, Ted (ed.), *The Philosophers: Introducing Great Western Thinkers,* Oxford: Oxford University Press, 1999.

Hourani, Albert, *Arabic Thought in the Liberal Age 1798–1939*, Cambridge: Cambridge University Press, 1983.

Hudson, Yeager, *The Philosophy of Religion*, Mountain View, CA: Mayfield, 1991.

Hume, David, *A Treatise of Human Nature*, 2nd revised edition of L.A. Selby-Bigge with text revised and notes by P.H. Nidditch, New York: Oxford University Press, 1978.

Ibn Isʼḥāq, *Sīrat Rasūl Allāh*, Alfred Guillaume (trans.), Karachi: Oxford University Press, 1995.

Ibn Khaldūn, Abd Al-Raḥmān, *The Muqaddimah: An Introduction to History*, Franz Rosenthal (trans.), New York: Bollingen Foundation, 1958.

Ibn Qutaybah, Abd Allah Ibn Muslim, *Taʼwīl Mushkil al-Quran*, Cairo: no publisher, 1954.

Ibn Rushd, *Kitāb Faṣl Al-Maqāl with its Appendix (Damina)*, George Hourani (trans.), Leiden: E.J. Brill, 1959.

Ibn Saʻd, Abu Abd Allah Muhammad, *Kitāb Al-Tabāqat Al-Kabīr*, S. Moinul Haq (trans. and ed.), Karachi: Pakistan Historical Society Publications, 1976, 2 volumes.

Ibn Warraq, *Why I am not a Muslim*, Amherst, NY: Prometheus, 1995.

Jameelah, Maryam, *Islam and Modernism*, Lahore: Mohammed Yusuf Khan, 1968.

—— *Islam versus the West*, Lahore: Mohammed Yusuf Khan, 1968.

Juwayni, Al-, *Al-ʻAqīdah Al-Nizāmiyya*, M. Kawthari (ed.), Cairo: Dār Al-Kutub: 1948.

Keddie, Nikki and Beth Baron (eds), *Women in Middle Eastern History*, New Haven: Yale University Press, 1991.

Kenny, Anthony, *Faith and Reason*, New York: Columbia University Press, 1983.

—— *A Brief History of Western Philosophy*, Oxford: Blackwell, 1998.

Khuri, Richard, *Freedom, Modernity and Islam*, Syracuse, NY: Syracuse University Press, 1998.

Kierkegaard, Søren, *Concluding Unscientific Postscript*, David Swenson (trans.), Princeton: Princeton University Press, 1941.

Kindī, Al-, *Al-Kindī's Metaphysics: A Translation of Yaʼqūb Ibn Isḥāq Al-Kindī's Treatise 'On First Philosophy'*, A.L. Ivry (trans.), Albany, NY: State University of New York, 1974.

King, Michael (ed.), *God's law versus State law*, London: Grey Seal, 1995.

Koslowski, Peter (ed.), *Philosophy Bridging the World Religions*, Dordrecht, Boston: Kluwer Academic, 2003.

Mackie, J.L. *The Miracle of Theism*, Oxford: Clarendon Press, 1982.

Mansfield, Harvey, *Manliness*, New Haven: Yale University Press, 2006.

Marmura, Michael (trans.), *The Incoherence of the Philosophers*, Provo, UT: Brigham Young University Press, 2000.

Marshall, David, *God, Muhammad and the Unbelievers*, London: Curzon, 1999.

Meynell, Hugo, *The Intelligible Universe*, London: Macmillan, 1982.

Miles, Jack, *God: A Biography*, New York: Alfred A. Knopf, 1995.

Mill, John Stuart, *Nature, the Utility of Religion and Theism*, London: Longmans, Green, Reader, and Dyer, 1874.

Miller, E.L. (ed.), *Classical Statements on Faith and Reason*, New York: Random House, 1970.

Nelson, Kristina, *The Art of Reciting the Quran*, Austin: University of Texas Press, 1985.

Niebuhr, Reinhold, *The Nature and Destiny of Man*, New York: Charles Scribner's Sons, 1949.

Nielsen, Kai, *Atheism and Philosophy*, Amherst, NY: Prometheus, 1985; reprinted 2005.

Nielsen, Kai and D.Z. Phillips, *Wittgensteinian Fideism?* London: SCM Press, 2005.

Nietzsche, Friedrich, *The Anti-Christ*, R.J. Hollingdale (trans.), Harmondsworth: Penguin, 1968, published in one volume with *Twilight of the Idols*.

—— *Ecce Homo*, R.J. Hollingdale (trans.), Harmondsworth: Penguin Books, 1979.

—— *The Will to Power*, Walter Kaufmann and R.J. Hollingdale (trans.), New York: Vintage Books, 1968.

Ochs, Peter, *Pierce, Pragmatism and the Logic of Scripture*, Cambridge: Cambridge University Press, 1998, 2006.

Overall, Christine, 'Miracles as Evidence against the Existence of God', *Southern Journal of Philosophy*, vol. 23, 1985, pp. 347–53.

Paine, Thomas, *The Age Of Reason*, Secaucus: Citadel Press, 1948, 1974.

Penelhum, Terence, *God and Skepticism*, Boston: Reidel, 1983.

—— *Reason and Religious Faith*, Boulder, CO: Westview Press, 1995.

Peters, F.E., *Mecca: A Literary History of the Muslim Holy Land*, Princeton, NJ: Princeton University Press, 1994.

Peterson, Michael, William Hasker *et al.* (eds), *Reason and Religious Belief: An Introduction to the Philosophy of Religion*, New York: Oxford University Press, 1991.

Rahman, Fazlur, *Islam and Modernity*, Chicago: University of Chicago Press, 1984.

Ramadan, Tariq, *Western Muslims and the Future of Islam*, Oxford: Oxford University Press, 2004.

Richardson, Herbert and Donald Cutler (eds), *Transcendence*, Boston: Beacon Press, 1969.

Rorty, Richard, *Philosophy and the Mirror of Nature*, Princeton, NJ: Princeton University Press, 1979.

—— *Consequences of Pragmatism*, Minneapolis: University of Minnesota Press, 1982.

Rose, Gillian, *Mourning Becomes the Law: Philosophy and Representation*, Cambridge: Cambridge University Press, 1996.

Rosenthal, Erwin (trans.), *Averroës' Commentary on Plato's Republic*, Cambridge: Cambridge University Press, 1956.

Ross, David (trans.), *The Nicomachean Ethics*, Oxford: Oxford University Press, 1980.

Sartre, Jean-Paul, *Existentialism and Humanism*, Philip Mairet (trans.), London: Eyre Methuen, 1948, 1973.

Schacht, Richard, *Classical Modern Philosophers: Descartes to Kant*, London: Routledge & Kegan Paul, 1984.

Sells, Michael, 'Towards a Multidimensional Understanding of Islam: The Poetic Key', *Journal of the American Academy of Religion*, vol. 64, no. 1, 1996, pp. 145–66.

Shati', Bint Al-, *Al-Ahram*, 7 January, 1972.

Shayegan, Daryush, *Cultural Schizophrenia: Islamic Societies Confronting the West*, John Howe (trans.), London: Saqi Books, 1992.

Schleiermacher, Friedrich, *On Religion: Addresses in Response to its Cultured Critics,* Terence Tice (trans.), Richmond: John Knox, Press, 1969.

Smart, Ninian, *Dimensions of the Sacred*, London: HarperCollins, 1996.

Smith, Margaret, *Muslim Women Mystics: The Life and Works of Rābi'a and other Woman Mystics in Islam*, Oxford: Oneworld, 1994.

Storr, Anthony, *Feet of Clay: A Study of Gurus*, London: HarperCollins, 1996.

Suyūtī, Al-, *Al-Itqān fī 'Ulūm Al-Qur'ān*, Beirut: Maktab Al-Thaqafiyyah, 1973, 2 volumes.

Swinburne, Richard, *The Coherence of Theism*, Oxford: Clarendon Press, 1977.

—— *Faith and Reason,* Oxford: Clarendon Press, 1981.

Tabarī, Abū Ja'far Muhammad Ibn Jarīr Al-, *Tarīkh al-Umam wa al-Mulūk,* Beirut: Mu'assasah al-Alam li al-Matbu'at, 1989.

Tillich, Paul, *Dynamics of Faith,* New York: Harper & Row, 1957.

Tritton, A.S., 'The Speech of God', *Studia Islamica,* vol. 33, 1971, pp. 5–22.

Vroom, Hendrik and Jerald Gort (eds) *Holy Scriptures in Judaism, Christianity and Islam,* Amsterdam, Atlanta, GA: Editions Rodopi, 1997.

Wadud, Amina, *Qur'an and Woman: Reading the Sacred Text from a Woman's Perspective,* New York: Oxford University Press, 1999.

Wadud, S.A., *Phenomena of Nature and the Qur'an,* Lahore: Sayed Khalid Wadud, 1971.

Wahba, Mourad and Mona Abousenna (eds) *Averroës and the Enlightenment,* Amherst, NY: Prometheus, 1996.

Wahīdī, Abū Al-Ḥasan Ali Bin Aḥmad, Al-, *Asbāb Al-Nuzūl,* Adnan Salloum (trans.), Beirut: Dār al-Kutub al-Ilmiyyah, 1991.

Waines, David, *An Introduction to Islam,* Cambridge: Cambridge University Press, 2003.

Watt, W. Montgomery, *The Faith and Practice of Al-Ghāzalī,* London: Allen & Unwin, 1953.

—— *The Formative Period of Islamic Thought,* Edinburgh: Edinburgh University Press, 1973.

Wensinck, A.J. *The Muslim Creed: Its Genesis and Historical Development,* London: Frank Cass, 1965.

Westermann, Claus, *Creation,* John J. Scullion, SJ (trans.), Philadelphia: Fortress Press, 1974.

Williams, John Alden (ed.), *The Word of Islam,* Austin, TX: University of Texas Press, 1994.

Wimbush, Vincent and Richard Valantasis (eds), *Asceticism,* New York: Oxford University Press, 1995.

Wolfson, Harry, *Philo: Foundations of Religious Philosophy,* Cambridge: Cambridge University Press, 1948, vol. 1.

Wood, Michael, *In the Footsteps of Alexander the Great: A Journey from Greece to Asia,* Berkeley, CA: University of California Press, 1997.

Yeats, W.B., *The Collected Poems of W.B. Yeats,* New York: Scribner, 1996, 2nd edition.

Zebiri, Kate, *Muslims and Christians Face to Face,* Oxford: Oneworld, 1997.

Index